Hooked on Horror III

Genreflecting Advisory Series

Diana Tixier Herald, Series Editor

Historical Fiction: A Guide to the Genre
Sarah L. Johnson

Canadian Fiction: A Guide to Reading Interests
Sharron Smith and Maureen O'Connor

Genreflecting: A Guide to Popular Reading Interests, 6th Edition
Diana Tixier Herald, Edited by Wayne A. Wiegand

The Real Story: A Guide to Nonfiction Reading Interests
Sarah Statz Cords, Edited by Robert Burgin

Read the High Country: A Guide to Western Books and Films
John Mort

Graphic Novels: A Genre Guide to Comic Books, Manga, and More
Michael Pawuk

Genrefied Classics: A Guide to Reading Interests in Classic Literature
Tina Frolund

Encountering Enchantment: A Guide to Speculative Fiction for Teens
Susan Fichtelberg

Fluent in Fantasy: The Next Generation
Diana Tixier Herald and Bonnie Kunzel

Gay, Lesbian, Bisexual, and Transgendered Literature: A Genre Guide
Ellen Bosman and John Bradford; Edited by Robert B. Ridinger

Reality Rules!: A Guide to Teen Nonfiction Reading Interests
Elizabeth Fraser

Historical Fiction II: A Guide to the Genre
Sarah L. Johnson

Hooked on Horror III

A Guide to Reading Interests

Anthony J. Fonseca and
June Michele Pulliam

Genreflecting Advisory Series
Diana Tixier Herald, Series Editor

LIBRARIES
U N L I M I T E D
A Member of the Greenwood Publishing Group

Westport, Connecticut • London

Library of Congress Cataloging-in-Publication Data

Fonseca, Anthony J.
  Hooked on horror III : a guide to reading interests / Anthony J. Fonseca and June Michele Pulliam.
      p. cm. -- (Genreflecting advisory series)
  Includes bibliographical references and indexes.
  ISBN 978-1-59158-540-4 (alk. paper)
  1. Horror tales--Bibliography. 2. Horror films--Catalogs. I. Pulliam, June Michele. II. Title.
Z5917.H65F66 2009
  [PN3435]
  016.80883'8738--dc22   2008045518

British Library Cataloguing in Publication Data is available.

Library of Congress Catalog Card Number: 2008045518
ISBN: 978-1-59158-540-4

First published in 2009

Libraries Unlimited, 88 Post Road West, Westport, CT 06881
A Member of the Greenwood Publishing Group, Inc.
www.lu.com

Printed in the United States of America

The paper used in this book complies with the
Permanent Paper Standard issued by the National
Information Standards Organization (Z39.48–1984).

10   9   8   7   6   5   4   3   2   1

*For Zanibar (1986–2006), Tasha (1991–2007),
Moosie Moe (2006–2007), and Minerva (2006–2008),
who slept on my hands while I worked on this manuscript.*
—June Pulliam

Contents

Preface: The Appeal of Horror and the Genre's Popularity

Do you really *read* that stuff? If you are a horror fan, you may have heard that question more than once in your life, and if you are not, you may even have found yourself asking it. The answer in either case is a resounding "yes." From ancient oral narratives and retellings of dark and fantastic tales of supernatural, sometimes evil beings, to the inception of "the Gothic" as a literary style in the late eighteenth century, to the more recent blockbuster sales of novels by Stephen King, Anne Rice, and Dean Koontz, it is obvious that tales of terror captivate audiences of diverse ages and ethnicities. Even today, nearly a decade into the new millennium, horror fiction is alive and well. Consider the following sampling of statistics from various sources over the past fifteen years.

1. The following sales rankings are taken from the *Bowker Annual Library* and *Book Trade Almanac*, one of the best sources for sales information. These figures for the year 2006 best sellers are from its fifty-second edition, published in 2007:

   - *Hannibal Rising*, by Thomas Harris, ranked fifth, with 1.2 million hardcover copies sold.

   - *Lisey's Story*, by Stephen King, also sold 1.2 million hardcover copies. King's *Cell* was also in the top ten, selling 1 million copies. *Cell* also sold almost 1.5 million mass market copies.

   - *Brother Odd*, by Dean Koontz, rounded out the top fifteen, selling 650,000 copies. *The Husband*, also by Koontz, sold over 400,000. Koontz sold over 2 million mass market copies as well (*Velocity* and *Forever Odd*).

   - Novels by Laurell K. Hamilton, Robin Cook, and the writing team of Douglas Preston and Lincoln Child each sold over 200,000 hardcover copies. Lincoln and Child also sold over 500,000 mass market copies.

   - Alice Siebold's *The Lovely Bones*, a sensitive portrayal of a family torn apart by the murder of a child, sold 785,719 mass market copies.

2. *Publishers Weekly* (July 9, 2001) noted that Neil Gaiman's *American Gods* sold 83,000 copies after three printings. The August 31, 2002 issue of *PW* stated that *Black House*, by Stephen King and Peter Straub, published by Random, totaled 1.5 million copies in the first printing. Meanwhile, *Blood and Gold*, by Anne Rice, published by Knopf, totaled 750,000 copies in its first printing, and Dean Koontz's *One Door Away from Heaven*, published by Bantam, totaled 525,000 copies in its first printing.

3. *Publishers Weekly* (April 2, 2001) chronicled the release of Stephen King's novel *Dreamcatcher*. The novel was launched by Scribner with a 1.25 million copy printing, and it debuted in the number one slot after a week or less in the stores. King's first week's sales at just the three national book chains totaled about 46,000 copies.

4. According to *American Demographics Magazine* (July 1989), in 1987 there were approximately 1.2 million buyers of books about the supernatural and occult fiction. *American Demographics* predicted approximately the same number of buyers for the year 2010.

5. In *Publishers Weekly* (September 20, 1993), Robert K. J. Killheffer, in "Rising from the Grave," noted that a 1988 Gallup organization study showed that there were at least two dominant segments in the horror audience: young males and older educated people, mostly females. Earlier, in *The New York Review of Science Fiction* (November 1991), David G. Hartwell, in "Notes on the Evolution of Horror Literature," wrote that this aforementioned Gallup poll indicated that the teenaged readership for horror is almost exclusively male, but that much of the most popular horror is read by women. He noted that 60 percent of the adult audience is female, namely women in their thirties and forties. *Note*: this information also appears in Hartwell's introduction to the anthology *Foundations of Fear*, published by Tor in 1992; the Gallup poll referred to can be found in the *Gallup Annual Report on Book Buying* (Princeton, NJ: Gallup).

These statistics may surprise readers who are unfamiliar with the genre or who simply eschew its authors, as they wonder, what makes people enjoy being scared? One easy answer to that question is that life is scary and uncertain, and horror fiction allows us to experience the emotions of fear in a controlled setting and to defeat our fears by facing them vicariously. Although the world of horror fiction is peopled with various monsters—the ranks of the undead, serial killers, ghosts, and mad scientists—the real world is populated by its own horrors, which are no less terrifying and unsettling. Daily we hear and read about militant followers of terrorist organizations who think nothing of abruptly ending the lives of civilians who are just going about their everyday business; overly nationalistic citizens attacking innocent bystanders because of their appearance, out of a misplaced and misguided sense of justice; angry loners randomly poisoning people to protest government policy; drunk drivers who carelessly take away the lives of our loved ones; child molesters who cruelly ruin young lives; and unscrupulous CEOs who, without compassion or any sense of fairness, downsize labor forces and release toxins on communities to increase the profits of billion-dollar corporations. The list of real-life horrors could go on indefinitely.

In horror fiction, such evildoers are made into fictional monsters and, unlike their real-life counterparts listed in the previous paragraph, they can usually be killed, or at least contained. There will always be more terrorists to take the place of those who die or are killed by military action. Overly zealous nationalism rears its ugly head again and again whenever economies falter or entire groups of people are held responsible for the actions of a few. There seems to be no end to the number of drunk drivers and child molesters who escape through the cracks in our justice system, only to ruin more lives. Our belief in free enterprise at all costs will always make it possible for large corporations to "right size" as they call it, devastating the lives of loyal employees to increase their share prices. But in horror fiction, it is not only possible, but probable, that innocent people *will* triumph over evil. Even though Freddy Kreuger or Michael Myers may live to see another sequel, the pure hearted can ultimately stop them from wreaking havoc in the world. More important, the fans of horror fiction can walk away from the narrative safe in the knowledge that they are beyond the pursuit of invincible creatures capable of invading dreams and inclined to murder indiscriminately. In this sense, horror fiction allows us to face, fight, and defeat our fears vicariously.

So what types of people enjoy horror fiction? Do only people with fears they'd rather not face directly become fans of the genre? Do only people with a taste for blood read Peter Straub, Poppy Z. Brite, Brandon Massey, or Gary A. Braunbeck? We were not entirely sure of this answer until, in 1995, we met our students in our first-ever team taught horror class at Louisiana State University. More than anything else, we found ourselves pleasantly surprised by the diversity of the students who were attracted to the opportunity to study vampires, werewolves, serial killers, ghosts, and indescribable masses of alien cells. Given the nature of the genre and its fans, we had expected a homogenous sea of black-clad, pierced, and tattooed "children of the night," eager to begin discussing the latest best-selling Koontz maniac, King monster, Rice bloodsucker, or Straub über-entity. We expected a group of mostly males who read horror and watched horror films because they enjoyed "the scare" or took perverse pleasure in reading about the dismemberment of bodies. After all, this was the kind of reaction we always got after telling friends that we enjoyed the genre, and we had apparently bought into their rhetoric despite ourselves.

What we found was a class composed of honor students, athletes, older nontraditional students, black-clad Goths, buzz-cut boys in baseball caps, body builders, girls with long wavy hair and blue finger nails, film buffs, Pagans, Catholics, Southern Baptists, a few miscellaneous weird people who sat in the back—and one quiet student who looked a lot like Stephen King. The most remarkable feature to us was that the class was mostly female. All were eager to read writers we had at that time heard little of, and many were pleasantly surprised that they enjoyed Bram Stoker's *Dracula*, Mary Shelley's *Frankenstein*, and Kim Newman's *Anno Dracula*. Not one of these students had ever committed a murder, tortured an animal, possessed an insatiable desire to drink blood, or (at least as far as we know) harbored thoughts of torturing his or her professors and classmates. These students were simply an eclectic collection of average people who had one thing in common: they all enjoyed reading and studying horror. Some liked the adrenaline rush associated with the production of fear; others emphasized the thematic concerns that could be read between the lines, taking a more intellectual approach; still others simply thought horror fiction was fun and exciting, suspenseful and entertaining. The point we are making here is that horror appeals to people in all walks of life and for various reasons, not always associated with a desire to be scared.

Of course we are not the first to grapple with this question, as many cultural and literary critics have already attempted to describe the appeal of horror. William Patrick Day argues that people are simultaneously repulsed and attracted to horror, that it is a sort of fantastical manifestation of negative wish fulfillment (*In the Circles of Fear and Desire: A Study of Gothic Fantasy*, University of Chicago Press, 1985). In other words, a horror novel or film is like the accident that causes us to rubberneck, even though we know in our hearts that we really don't want to see other humans broken and bloodied. Terry Heller takes a more physiological approach to the question of why we enjoy horror. He feels that horror gives people a safe adrenaline rush, like skydiving with a parachute they know will always open, or riding a roller coaster (*The Delights of Terror: An Aesthetics of the Tale of Terror*, University of Illinois Press, 1987). People engage in these thrill-seeking activities because these death-defying acts allow them the chance to transcend the drudgery of daily life and, in a sense, to come face to face with mortality and walk away. One could say that according to this theory, horror allows us to face our fears and master them. Literary critic Carol J. Clover, on the other hand, examines horror from a psychoanalytic perspective. She notes that in slasher films, audience members are at various times encouraged to view the world from the perspective of the monster and the victim (*Men, Women, and Chainsaws: Gender in the Modern Horror Film*, Princeton University Press, 1992). This gives the horror fan a chance to vicariously experience fear from multiple points of view and to emerge unscathed from the theater.

We feel that horror does all of these things and also entertains and educates. For example, Stephen King's modern classic, *Carrie*, gives a candid-camera view of a dysfunctional family who would be the quintessential guests on *Dr. Phil* in an episode entitled "My Mommy Is a Fundamentalist Freak Who Locks Me in the Closet" or an episode of *Jerry Springer* entitled "My Daughter Is the Spawn of Satan." Carrie White's home life is painful, yet the reader cannot turn away from Margaret White's savage abuse of her child in the name of religion. The reader, like Susan Snell—the only major character to survive Carrie's rampage on the night of the Black Prom—is able to walk among the exploding gas stations of Chamberlain, Maine, and watch people doing St. Vitus dances of pain while stepping on downed power lines. Yet the reader finishes the book having vicariously faced down the monster, no worse for wear. Simultaneously, the reader is invited to see the world through Carrie's eyes, and any of us who have been picked on child in school can sympathize with Carrie's corrosive anger and know the literal meaning of the phrase "if looks could kill." Above all, the reader of *Carrie* experiences a good story told from multiple points of view by a talented writer, and he or she perhaps learns a bit of a lesson at the end about how, if it takes a village to raise a child, it also takes a community to create a monster. This is a lesson learned all too well from the past decade's gun-toting children at Columbine, Virginia Tech, and the University of Illinois, who have performed their own version of Carrie's destruction of Chamberlain.

The important thing for readers' advisors to remember when dealing with patrons who are horror fans is that they are not a monolith, and therefore they do not read horror for the same reason, which means that they will not all enjoy the same writers. Those who are Goths and Emos (black-clad, pale-skinned followers of bands such as Bauhaus, Nick Cave, Nine Inch Nails, TKK, and Evanescence, as well as authors such as Poppy Z. Brite, Christa Faust, and Caitlin R. Kiernan) may prefer the decadence of John Shirley and Kathe Koja, whereas those who enjoy action adventure will certainly want books by Dean Koontz or Steve Alten. And the more sophisticated horror fans (those who have read almost everything in the genre) will probably wish to find alternative literary works by the likes of Kim Newman, Bentley Little, Tananarive Due, or Ramsey Campbell. Fans of the old *Twilight Zone* series may prefer more philosophical, disquieting horror, of the type seen in our chapters on psychological horror and everyday horror, and they'll want to read Glen Hirshberg or Christopher Fahy. These readers are not disturbed individuals who need counseling. They are simply people who enjoy curling up with a scary or thought-provoking book. School librarians in particular should attempt to understand the reading tastes of their younger horror patrons, for it is in the school libraries that horror works are often challenged and sometimes singled out for censorship. The bottom line is that no child has ever murdered in the name of R. L. Stine or Christopher Pike.

Rule number one of readers' advisory is one of Ranganathan's Five Laws: every reader his or her book. Horror appeals to more than simply the baser human emotions, and every horror fan who happens to be a library patron deserves his or her book of choice. No one individual or group has the right, especially given our constitutional freedom of expression, to prevent the match of that reader with that book, even if the book is the latest by Joe R. Lansdale or Jack Ketchum, authors known for their "splatterpunk" fiction, a type of visceral literature that crosses any and every line it approaches. In short, horror fans are not second-class readers simply because they are genre readers and enjoy scary books. They are potential library patrons with the same rights and privileges as the patron who seeks novels by Jane Austen, Zora Neale Hurston, William Faulkner, Amy Tan, or Gabriel Garcìa Márquez. *Hooked on Horror* is just one of many tools that can aid librarians in granting horror patrons those rights.

Introduction: The Goals of This Book

General Information

Hooked on Horror seeks to provide users with an in-depth guide to the horror genre, which has often been overlooked by literary critics, readers, and librarians. The consensus among literary authorities seems to be that "scary stories" are best left for children, to be told around campfires and published by presses that would cater to young adults, and that adults who enjoy horror are at best, childish, and at worst, ghouls who secretly admire the likes of Jeffrey Dahmer. Cutting our teeth in the academic world of English departments, we grew accustomed to the ivory tower view that Stephen King, Ramsey Campbell, and Anne Rice were simply not acceptable reading material; that the fiction of these writers was somehow inferior to that of authors who published Literature (with a capital L). Imagine our shared surprise when we discovered that some library directors and librarians also viewed horror fans as nothing more than a subclass of "genre" readers (and a disturbed ones at that), and therefore as less serious than patrons who read classics or works by Joyce Carol Oates or Toni Morrison, or even the latest Oprah selection.

It is perhaps because of this attitude that very few readers' advisory tools exist for the horror genre. In fact, horror almost always gets grouped with other ghettoized genres, science fiction and fantasy, which robs readers of even the possibility of comprehensive bibliographies and readers' advisory tools devoted solely to that genre. In other words, horror fiction is mistakenly treated as a subgenre of what, for want of a better term, would be called fantastical literature or speculative fiction, and therefore usually gets less than one-third of the length of a book-length bibliography—when it gets any recognition whatsoever. It is the need for an in-depth, book-length source on horror fiction that this text addresses.

Hooked on Horror differs from dark fantasy bibliographies in that it is primarily intended as a readers' advisory resource and therefore reflects popular reading interests. It is not a critical or historical guide and review source, or a list of "the best of the genre," although the best can certainly be found here. For this reason, annotations are usually descriptive rather than evaluative. And unlike other readers' guides, *Hooked on Horror*, as its title suggests, deals only with horror fiction, without treating it as the red-headed stepchild of the fantastic. Because it deals solely with the horror genre, it provides the reader with a more complete list of annotated novels, collections by single authors, and anthologies by diverse hands than currently exists anywhere. In addition we, the authors, are both professional reviewers and devoted fans, which means we understand the genre and its appeal to readers.

Of course, the main function of a readers' advisory tool is to enable librarians to be conversant in an area of literature with which they may have little or no experience and to help them recommend titles to readers that they will enjoy. This book attempts to fill that need by grouping titles according to popular reading interests and by suggesting similar titles for reader favorites. Users of this text can also find similar titles by identifying important subject headings based, not on LOC or Sears headings, but on standardized terminology indicative of themes and issues central to the genre itself, and then by matching—using these subject keywords—fictional texts with similar reads. In this way, they can identify reads that may not be completely similar but that contain the same thematic concerns as the original book under consideration. Going beyond the generalizations used in previous genre guides, which group titles under broad, umbrella-term headings such as *monsters*, we have attempted to identify and reflect readers' tastes as specifically as possible, tagging items with specific terms such as *Frankenstein's Monster (character)*, *Subterranean Horror*, *Serial Killers*, *Werewolves*, and *Zombies*. In other words, what we hope to accomplish with this text is to fill the need for a readers' advisory guide geared specifically toward horror fans, keeping in mind their preferences and using the terminology they use.

One of the most daunting problems in selecting or recommending genre fiction of any type, horror fiction included, is that generally it is not thoroughly reviewed in mainstream review sources. *The New York Times Book Review* may condescend to review the latest best sellers by Koontz or Rice or King, but it does so only because readers would demand the blood of the reviewers if they failed to acknowledge these popular works. Library trade journals such as *Kirkus Reviews*, *Booklist*, and *Library Journal* consistently provide brief annotations with some evaluative content, but these summaries may prove inadequate for readers' advisory purposes because these journals typically evaluate based on the literary merit or circulation potential of a work, not on its appeal to fans of the genre. *Booklist* reviews only "recommended" titles, which imposes a literary standard on the genre that may not match the preferences of fans. Although there is an obvious need for such review sources, a readers' advisory guide cannot, by its very nature, serve as a critical guide or source of reviews. Instead of sticking solely to literary review sources, we recommend that librarians and readers examine genre-oriented periodicals such *Cemetery Dance* (briefly annotated in chapter 19). These are the best sources of horror reviews readily available. Other excellent sources for horror reviews can be found on the World Wide Web, including sites such as *Dark Echo's Page* (www.darkecho.com), *HorrorNet* (www.horrronet.com), and *Necropsy: The Review of Horror Fiction* (www.lsu.edu/necrofile). In addition, fans of the genre can use Web directories, such as the horror area of about.com (http://horror.about.com). The publishing mega-site Amazon.com also often provides substantive guest reviews, sometimes by published reviewers or dedicated fans.

Scope of This Guide

Writing a selective bibliography of genre fiction is a daunting task. Many of the novels, short story collections, and anthologies published in any given year are cursed with an ephemeral existence. Often first editions of horror texts are released in paperback, and sometimes second printings are not forthcoming. Only works by best-selling writers tend to enjoy what would be the publishing world's version of immortality. For this reason, while attempting to demonstrate the broad spectrum of titles available to readers of the horror genre, we have been selective in what we chose to include and annotate in this guide, keeping in mind availability and access.

Novels, Anthologies, and Collections

As we did the first and second editions of *Hooked on Horror*, we consider this readers' guide to be a "thorough" bibliography of horror currently in print and available. The first edition of *Hooked on Horror* included horror in print (either released or reissued) up to 1998. The second edition, a continuation of the first, focused on titles published or reissued between 1998 and January 2002. This edition extends the coverage to titles released or reissued between 2003 and May 2008. This was not an arbitrary decision, but rather a practical one. To inform readers and librarians of titles they can readily get their hands on, we have attempted to thoroughly cover the most recent titles.

We began with a list of books in print in the years 2003–2008 and used one main selection criterion—availability. To that end, we consulted the OCLC database WorldCat to find titles, limiting our lists to only those titles that are owned by fifty or more libraries worldwide. Our reasoning was that a fictional text's being owned by at least fifty libraries would make it readily available to readers, via interlibrary loan if in no other way. We used this criterion with novels, anthologies, and collections by single authors. With reference works and books of criticism we were also selective, choosing mainly those books that would appeal to our primary target audience of horror fans, with secondary concern for what we consider to be a secondary audience, horror scholars. In the case of these texts, we ignored the ownership rule we used for fiction, since by definition these nonfiction books are not intended for popular readers and would likely be owned by only a handful of libraries. Although we attempted to be as inclusive as possible, we found that some works published since 2003 were largely unavailable, even through the publisher, forcing us to eliminate those titles.

Included in our list are titles in horror series, such as Anne Rice's <u>Vampire Chronicles</u> or Laurell K. Hamilton's <u>Anita Blake Series</u>, as long as the most recent work in that series was published in 2003 or later. The reason for this is that it is possible, perhaps even likely, that the author will once again take up the series; and readers may likely begin requesting older titles in that series. Also included are titles and series that are considered classics and titles that were major award winners (we include all Bram Stoker Award and International Horror Guild award titles in this edition). Where a series had no official or designated name (located in either the Library of Congress cataloging information on the title page of the book or in OCLC), we consulted *Fantastic Fiction* (http://www.fantasticfiction.co.uk/), the premiere Web site dedicated to, among other listings, horror bibliography, and more recently, readers' advisory. We adopted that site's designation of series title, or if the site had no such designation for a series, we simply created a series name, typically based on the first novel or the name of the protagonist of the series.

In addition, individual works that have achieved the status of "classic," and *all* works by those writers considered benchmark authors, are covered in this guide. For the sake of inclusion, we identified and included *all* classics of the genre, such as Bram Stoker's *Dracula*, Mary Shelley's *Frankenstein*, and Richard Matheson's *I Am Legend*, even when some of these classics were currently out of print or temporarily between editions. Most libraries own these classics, and readers are often acquainted with the tales, so their placement in this work serves as an entry point for users, helping them identify specific subgenres and themes that readers of classics enjoy.

Finally, we identified eight of the most popular authors in the genre—Robert Bloch, Ramsey Campbell, Stephen King, Dean Koontz, Graham Masterton, Richard Matheson, Anne Rice, and Peter Straub—and included all of their work. Readers often request texts by those particular authors because of their popularity and reputation. As more university curricula include horror classics, which is a trend seemingly sweeping the nation's universities., these works will likely be reissued by publishers. We calculated which texts would eventually be designated "modern classics," either because they were award winners or because they received consistent rave reviews, and we included all of those in this edition.

Users of this guide will find a full range of horror fiction—everything from atmospheric, gothic texts, such as those by Ramsey Campbell and Thomas Tessier and character-driven novels like those of Tananarive Due, to erotic horror such as works by Anne Rice—with no exclusions being made based on a work's subtlety, its level of sensuality, its inclusion of overt sexuality, or its reliance on graphic violence. We did, however, exclude works of Christian fiction, science fiction, fantasy, and much paranormal romance if those works did not exhibit what we consider the main characteristic of horror: an emphasis on some type of monster or threatening entity that had the potential, and realized the potential, of causing great harm to humanity. In other words, the inclusion of an angel, an alien, a dragon, or even a vampire or werewolf in a text did not on its own merit its inclusion in this guide. That angel, alien, dragon, vampire, or werewolf had to be menacing rather than helpful; it had to show its ability to bring death and destruction to innocent human beings. In Christian fiction, science fiction, fantasy, and much paranormal romance, these types of supernatural beings are often not monstrous. *The Lord of the Rings* contains many a threatening mutant, troll, and dragon, but these monsters are not the raison d'être of the text. They simply exist in the world inhabited by the characters. By contrast, in dark fantasy–based horror, fairies and angels or demons are the central antagonists, and they are extremely menacing and destructive. In short, for a text including one of these beings to be labeled horror, that being must be monstrous, perhaps even evil, and must be the emphasis of the dread in the text.

History, Criticism, and Reference

Horror's most prominent reference and critical works, as well as some of its more informative periodicals, are listed at the end of this guide. With these titles, more selectivity was exercised in terms of their usefulness to readers and readers' advisors, because there are not the focus on the work. However, more flexibility was applied regarding publication dates, because many of these works are published by academic presses and therefore have a short publication run but are nevertheless readily available through university interlibrary loan departments. These critical and biographical works are still consulted by fans and scholars for their groundbreaking ideas, so users of this guide will find "classics" by such scholars as Montague Summers, Mike Ashley, Julia Briggs, William Patrick Day, David Punter, and Carol Clover, among others.

Young Adult Titles

Young adult horror (YA titles) are generally not covered in this guide because the inclusion of writers such as R. L. Stine and Christopher Pike would triple the number of titles, making it unwieldy for users. Instead, we leave the compilation of a YA readers' advisory guide to horror to other bibliographers; it would take a book-length study, rather than the inadequate chapter listing that we could at best manage, to do justice to YA horror. The only YA titles found in this guide are crossover works that also appeal to adults, such as William Sleator's *The Boy Who Couldn't Die* or Libba Bray's <u>The Gemma Doyle Trilogy</u>, the first book of which spent a good deal of time on *The New York Times Review of Books'* best-seller list in 2005.

The Role of Film in Horror

Horror fiction has been greatly influenced by the film industry. What would have become of Mary Shelley's *Frankenstein,* had not Boris Karloff popularized the creature and the work with his movie performance? Would Bram Stoker's Count have become a pop culture icon had not Bela Lugosi, and later Frank Langella and Gary Oldman, brought him to life on the big screen? And although the figure of the zombie was first introduced to Western consciousness in William Seabrook's 1929 travelogue *The Magic Island*, it was the medium of film that solidified the creature, first in *White Zombie* (1932), and later in George A. Romero's 1968 *Night of the Living Dead*. Because of this interplay between film and literature, and because an increasing number of libraries include DVDs in their collections, we offer information about horror films in this guide. However, because the sheer number of horror films still available for purchase is immense, and because of space limitations, only a sampling is included. After all, this guide is primarily a bibliography, not a filmography. Therefore, only horror films available on VHS or DVD that we consider important in forming the genre, films that no public library with a large horror fan base should be without, were chosen for inclusion.

Of course, virtually all horror fans and most librarians are familiar with the horror classics of film, beginning with Fritz Marnau's *Nosferatu* (1922), Tod Browning's *Dracula* (1931), James Whale's *Frankenstein* (1932), Karl Freund's *The Mummy* (1932), and George Waggner's *The Wolf Man* (1941). These are titles that all libraries with a large horror fan patronage should include in their collections, not only for the quality of the filmmaking that each represents, but also for the important role each has played in changing the very landscape of the genre itself, by completely reinterpreting Bram Stoker's and Mary Shelley's works in the first three instances, and bringing to the screen for the first time stories about Howard Carter's demise after opening King Tut's tomb in 1922 and monsters previously only known from folklore in the latter two films.

Bela Lugosi's portrayal of the suave, sophisticated, Eastern European noble in Browning's *Dracula* was instrumental in the Count's evolution into the sympathetic creature he became in 1973, when Jack Palance presented audiences with a Dracula who was more a victim of love (and later in 1992 when Gary Oldman portrayed the Count as both a victim of love and of the Church he fought for). These films have in turn influenced literature, resulting in the sophisticated vampires of Anne Rice, Chelsea Quinn Yarbro, and P. N. Elrod, as well as vampires who react to and defy this new suave, sympathetic type, such as the heartless monsters of *Thirty Days of Nights* (both the film and literary vampires) or the corpulent and swaggering Jules Duchon of Andrew Fox's *Fat White Vampire Blues*.

Horror films often take the pulse of a society at a given moment in its cultural history, and the films we have included from the 1950s through the 1980s capture the prevalent fears of those eras. Pop culture icons such as Jack Arnold's *The Incredible Shrinking Man* (1957), Dan Siegel's *Invasion of the Body Snatchers* (1956), Alfred Hitchcock's *Psycho* (1960) and *The Birds* (1963), Brian De Palma's *Carrie* (1976), and Ridley Scott's *Alien* (1979) can be found in this guide. In addition, some of the B-movie counterparts of these classics, such as Nathan Juran's *Attack of the 50-Foot Woman* (1958), Herk Harvey's *Carnival of Souls* (1962), and George Romero's *Night of the Living Dead* (1968) are annotated because, in part, they bring to light our anxieties about changing gender roles, female sexuality, and second wave feminism, as well as McCarthyism, communism, the Cold War and its resulting nuclear build-up, the civil rights movement, space exploration, and nature.

When choosing contemporary films, we selected mainly those works that received critical acclaim and that tested the boundaries of the horror movie—sometimes qualifying them as "art." Therefore, users of this guide will find films such as Jonathan Demme's Oscar-winning *The Silence of the Lambs* (1992), Guillermo Del Toro's Cannes Film Festival Winner *Cronos* (1992), M. Night Shyamalan's Hitchcock-esque *The Sixth Sense* (1999), Alejandro Amenabar's shocker *The Others* (2001), E. Elias Merhing's metatextual *Shadow of the Vampire* (2001), Gore Verbinski's original and disturbing film *The Ring* (2002), Edgar Wright's clever zombie film parody *Shaun of the Dead* (2004), and Matt Reeves's original (and in many ways brilliant) but underappreciated sleeper *Cloverfield* (2008).

New to This Edition

Space constraints make it impossible for us to list most of the titles that we included in the first and second editions. Therefore, we recommend that users of this guide supplement it with previous editions, rather than consult it as a stand-alone product. Although some titles are repeated for various reasons, librarians and readers will need to consult the first edition for writers such as Clive Barker, Suzy McKee Charnas, Robin Cook, Jeanne Kalogridis, Bentley Little, Brian Lumley, Michael Palmer, Fred Saberhagen, John Saul, Dan Simmons, and Chelsea Quinn Yarbro.

The first two editions of *Hooked on Horror* received many reviews, both positive and negative. Before beginning this edition, we carefully considered the criticism and comments. In light of the feedback we received from reviewers, as well as input from practicing readers' advisors, we made various changes to this edition, while increasing our efforts to preserve other features, as follows:

1. We continued our "book connections" for the films that conclude each chapter. By adding this feature, we hoped to encourage horror movie buffs to pick up a novel or a collection of stories that had thematic similarities to a favorite film. The ultimate goal here is to increase library circulation by adding new readers to horor's patronage.

2. Whereas the first edition of *Hooked on Horror* had a similar titles listing at the end of only some of the annotated texts, the second edition and this edition have a "similar titles" listing at the end of every annotated entry. Our hope here is to facilitate the ease with which users will locate "read-alikes." Although there is a measure of subjectivity in identifying similar titles, we relied on our combined experience and expertise to identify the most likely candidates for readers.

3. In this edition, we added more classic texts by writers such as Clara Reeve, H. P. Lovecraft, E. F. Benson, Joseph Sheridan Le Fanu, and Bram Stoker. We also added more classic films.

4. We omitted the list of benchmark authors and their bibliographies that was included in our first edition. (Readers who wish to consult such a list should refer to either the lists in chapter introductions or the first edition of this book).

Final Note

From the outset, we understood the impossibility of creating a comprehensive bibliography of this rich and varied genre, so we instead set out to create what we considered a thorough and useful guide for librarians and readers. Therefore, when considering content, we included all novels that are generally classified as horror, as well as some that straddle genres but obviously fit the definitions we set forth for each subgenre. We hope that as readers' advisors or horror fans, you find this volume helpful. We are always seeking ways to make our work more useful, and to that end, we invite your comments and suggestions, which can be sent to us via our publisher, Libraries Unlimited, at lu-books@lu.com.

Part 1

Introduction to Horror Fiction

Chapter 1

A Definition of Horror

The Definition of Horror as Used in This Book

> Horror is not a genre, like the mystery of science fiction or the western. It is not a kind of fiction meant to be confined to the ghetto of a special shelf in the ghetto of libraries or bookstores . . . horror is an emotion.
>
> —Douglas E. Winter in the introduction to *Prime Evil* (New York: New American Library, 1988)

> Tragedy is when I cut my finger. Comedy is when you fall down the sewer and die. Horror is when you return from the dead and haunt me for laughing at your nasty trip down the sewer.
>
> —June Pulliam's embellishment on an old saw

On the most basic level, horror fiction features a monster, which can be supernatural, human, metaphorical, or a combination of these three. This monster can take on various shapes. It can be a zombie, one of the walking dead, the living impaired who (in some fiction) stumble around aimlessly chanting "Brains! Brains!" and snacking on anyone in high heels who has the misfortune to trip on the terrain while trying to flee. The monster can also be the vengeful ghost of a child molester, horribly disfigured through the vigilante justice of outraged parents and fully equipped with twelve-inch razors for fingernails and the ability to invade victims' dreams, cracking jokes as it slaughters the innocent. It can be the hideous and therefore unlovable creation of a mad scientist who fancies himself greater than God but is nothing more than a deadbeat dad who has spawned illegitimate offspring that he refuses to parent. Or the monster can be a preternaturally beautiful immortal, who is physically, emotionally, and intellectually superior to the humans who envy her every move, but who must nevertheless drink the blood of her admirers for survival.

Simply put, horror is a work of fiction that contains a monster of some type, one that often has the effect of scaring the reader. Yet a work of horror fiction does not necessarily have to have as its raison d'être the intention of producing fear in the reader. Of course most works in the genre do, and readers' advisors will find that this type of horror fiction predominates in the listings in this guide. However, there are many excellent and well-respected works in the genre that do not intend to produce fear. Anne

Rice's <u>Vampire Chronicles</u>, for example, emphasize the philosophical dilemma of out-living friends and family while never growing old; and the popular series ponders the possibility of an amoral universe. Although these speculations about the nature of life, humanity, and divinity may be horrific to some, *The Vampire Lestat* or *Interview with the Vampire* has little in common with a novel like *'Salem's Lot*, which achieves the loftiest of all horror fiction goals: to scare readers (in this case into remembering to keep their feet covered with the blankets at night). Despite the obvious differences in authorial in-tent, all three of these novels are considered horror works by publishers, booksellers, bookstores, libraries, fans, professors who teach horror literature, and the authors themselves. By the same token, Laurell K. Hamilton's <u>Anita Blake, Vampire Hunter Series</u> and P. N. Elrod's <u>Vampire Files</u> share more with the hard-boiled detective novels of Raymond Chandler than they do with the latest vampire series by L. A. Banks, Jemiah Jefferson, Kim Newman, or Andrew Fox, yet each of these works is about vampires, werewolves, and/or vampire hunters, thus placing each solidly in the genre.

But our simple definition has limitations. What of novels like Gary A. Braunbeck's *Keepers*, which smacks of magical realism and mythology as much as it does of horror; or Joe R. Lansdale's Southern gothic collection *Mad Dog Summer and Other Stories*, which has a wonderful tale of the hurricane that hit Galveston at the dawn of the twen-tieth century? Although stories of the grotesque and tales of psychological horror are for the most part devoid of both supernatural monsters like vampires and ghosts and bloodthirsty psychopaths and vengeful strippers, they are no less frightening. They ex-plore, either literally or figuratively through poetic description, the inner torment stemming from mental illness, child abuse, guilt, or countless other types of human suffering and emotional instability. These fictional works are indeed disquieting be-cause these are the novels that question the very nature of our world, taking that in-quiry one step further. They challenge both the reader's reality and the fictional reality created by the author.

Psychological horror can perhaps best be understood through examining exam-ples of the subgenre, Tananarive Due's *The Between* and Ramsey Campbell's *Obsession*. In *The Between*, Hilton has built a secure middle-class life for himself thirty years after nearly drowning as a teen. But when Hilton's wife, the first African American judge in Dade County, receives racist death threats, he starts having disturbing nightmares that are so vivid that they become alternative life experiences, causing him to wonder if he is schizophrenic or if he didn't really survive a brush with the ocean three decades pre-viously when he nearly drowned. Campbell's novel about being haunted by our child-hoods suggests that the characters' obsession with their own guilt due to youthful indiscretions, to which they attribute their adult fears, are more horrific than any ghost or phantom from a supernatural realm. In the gothic world of Campbell, adults suffer not only because they are unable to break away from a harmful situation, but because they are unwilling to challenge cultural expectations that created the harmful situa-tion, and thus they are willing participants in their own victimization. This behavioral pattern is evident in one of the classic works of the subgenre, Daphne DuMaurier's *Rebecca*. The nameless, cringing second Mrs. Maxim de Winter will forever be com-manded by her husband, and the far more interesting but dead Rebecca, Maxim's first wife, will eternally cast a shadow over her.

Our simple, monster-based definition helped determine how we categorized the world of horror literature into subgenres. In the past, horror genre guides have used style-based categories (i.e., gothic horror, comic horror, splatterpunk, gentle reads, etc.). In contrast, our categorization for the most part emphasizes a type of monster or horror that predominates. Our reasoning is simple: most horror readers who like a vampire novel like it because it has vampires, and those who enjoy a psychological thriller starring a maniacal sociopath enjoy slasher narratives with human monsters. Therefore, when these readers seek a similar read, in most cases they are literally looking for another work with the same type of monster.

In four instances, however, we veered from this classification schema: comic horror, splatterpunk, psychological horror, and everyday horror. Because the first two subgenres are defined mainly by their approach to telling the story, not individual elements in the story itself, we felt obliged to treat them differently. So although comic horror and splatterpunk are not, according to our definition and overall categorization, actual subgenres, they are treated as such for the purpose of practicality, to enhance the usefulness of this guide. As for psychological and everyday horror, we simply felt that we would be remiss of we excluded those texts that seemed to argue either "we have met the monsters, and they are us" or "same scare, different day," because these make up a reasonably large portion of the texts in the genre.

Defining horror fiction is undoubtedly difficult, especially since it is not all of one type. It would be easy if we could state that horror is solely fiction that contains threatening monsters, but that definition would preclude works by some of the masters of horror and gothicism, such as Edgar Allan Poe, Nathaniel Hawthorne, Ambrose Bierce, and their descendants, Rod Serling, Christopher Fahy, and Glen Hirshberg, where the threat of evil is only perceived but is no less real than had it been tangible. It would also be easy if we could state that horror is fiction that intends to horrify, or that it has the intention of scaring the reader, but this would not account for comic horror or the philosophically challenging Vampire Chronicles of Anne Rice, which definitely belong to the genre. In addition, we could point out that horror fiction is the story of monsters, and that the word *monster* stems from the Latin word *monstere*, which means portent or omen, often a divine warning; therefore, horror fiction is arguably fiction that attempts to warn its readers of a certain danger or an action or belief that can have negative results. Yet not all fiction that attempts to instruct, even metaphorically, is horror fiction, not even that which uses the supernatural as metaphor, as do fantasy and magical realism. Perhaps the best way to describe horror as a genre is through its various subgenres, which allows the reader to put the horror puzzle together, supplying the pieces and giving a general framework for their interrelationships or assembling the limbs to create an entire body of knowledge. Of course, these subgenres are often insufficient in and of themselves to accurately describe a work of horror, but when put together, they allow us to see the whole.

Ghosts and Haunted Houses: Dealing with Presences and Absences

Ghost and haunted house stories are tales of guilt thought to be long buried in the unconscious mind. The ghost or the haunted house serves as a portent to the person guilty of repressing knowledge of wrongdoing, as well as to others who know nothing of his or her sin. The haunted house can also be likened to an abused child, a victim of events that either happened in the house itself or on the site of the house.

Golem, Mummies, and Zombies: Wake the Dead and They'll Be Cranky

The dead can be purposefully reanimated, as in the case of zombies created by black magic, or by accident. Or the dead can be raised by the living who simply cannot accept the finality of death, as in Stephen King's *Pet Sematary*. The golem, another form of reanimated dead, can be seen in Mary Shelley's *Frankenstein*. Strictly speaking, they are not reanimated bodies, but rather crazy quilts of body parts, genes, and souls.

Vampires and Werewolves: Children of the Night

Vampires are creatures of the night who must often enter into parasitic relationships with others. Thus vampirism has frequently been used as a metaphor for love, the parent/child bond, sexual relationships, and power structures in general. Vampires are easily the most identifiable and often the most sympathetic—in short, the most appealing—of all monsters, mainly because vampires must, in some way, resemble the humans on which they prey. Werewolves are related to vampires and hence are included in this subgenre. The werewolf derives from vampire folklore that specified the undead could usually turn into bats and wolves.

Demonic Possession, Satanism, Black Magic, and Witches and Warlocks: The Devil Made Me Do It

Tales of black magic and demonic possession involve innocents possessed by demons or by the devil himself. Tales of satanism and black magic can also be about witches, warlocks (note that not all witches and warlocks practice black magic), and others who willingly become involved with dark forces.

Mythological Monsters and "The Old Ones": Invoking the Dark Gods

Every mythology has its monsters. From Kali the Destroyer in India, to the destructive one-eyed giant Cyclops in ancient Greece, to the Anglo-Saxon man-eater Grendel, to Lucifer in Christianity, all cultures incorporate some being into their belief systems that, although humanlike, is nonetheless monstrous and destructive, often threatening entire populations.

Telekinesis and Hypnosis: Chaos from Control

In the nineteenth century, Dr. Anton Mesmer popularized the idea of mesmerism (later known as hypnotism), whereby an individual could get others to do his or her biding through mind control. This pseudo-science, compounded with the reality that some charismatic individuals are able to exert an almost superhuman influence over others, gave rise to stories about evil individuals using the powers of their minds to control others. Telekinesis is another form of mind power. The individual with telekinetic powers can move objects with his or her mind.

Small Town Horror: Villages of the Damned

Small town horror is the dark side of *The Andy Griffith Show*. Mayberry is an appealing place because its diminutive size permits a sort of neighborly intimacy just not possible in the big city. But small size makes small towns equally dangerous. Their remote location removes them from the laws governing civilization as a whole. These villages outside of the mainstream may be governed by customs different from our own, such as laws requiring human sacrifices to pagan gods or demons. This type of horror, often referred to as small town horror, scares the reader with the realization that once he or she is away from the sanctity and security of a civilization that plays by a known set of rules, anything is possible.

Maniacs and Sociopaths, or the Nuclear Family Explodes: Monstrous Malcontents Bury the Hatchet

Father doesn't always know best, Mom isn't always content to stay home and clean the house while wearing pearls and her Sunday best, and there's no one to turn to in this supposedly self-sufficient family when the stress of everyday life becomes too much. Seriously disturbed children, and sometimes parents, are often the result. Works in this subgenre play on the all-too-American fear that every family unit has a dark side that surfaces only behind closed doors, and that children from these types of families will grow up to turn order into chaos.

Technohorror: Evil Hospitals, Military Screw-Ups, Mad Scientists, and Alien Invasions

With experiments in genetic cloning and anthrax scares and germ warfare, technohorror once again takes its place among the most popular subgenres of horror fiction. People are naturally afraid of the unknown. Technohorror exploits that fear, especially when it results from scientific experimentation gone awry or knowledge being misused. More than any horror subgenre, technohorror taps into Americans' (and others') fears when faced with the modern age's realization that any seemingly benevolent discovery, such as Einstein's Theory of Relativity, can easily find itself being transformed, Jekyll-and-Hyde fashion, into an element of destruction.

Ecological Horror: Mother Nature Has Her Revenge

The Judeo-Christian Bible says, "And man shall have dominion over all Earth's creatures." But what happens when those creatures, or even nature itself, strikes back? Horror fiction in this category shows the frightening result of humanity's tinkering with the forces of nature. Sometimes natural monstrosities aren't even the fault of humans, because nature itself can be completely unpredictable and chaotic, and thus scary. Or if humans are to blame, it is because of their androcentric view of the universe, which makes them heedless in dealing with a world that doesn't necessarily put them at the top of the food chain.

Psychological Horror: It's All in Your Head

Narratives in this subgenre expand upon the proposition that what happens in someone's mind can be just as real, and often just as terrifying, as being menaced by a vampire or hunted by Hannibal Lecter. The source of terror can be guilt over one's actions, living in proximity to one's tormentor, or just having to deal with events so extraordinarily awful that we have no previous frame of reference for guidance. The lack of a supernatural element in this type of horror often makes it seem more erudite than its more fantastical counterparts, and thus it is more likely to be accepted as mainstream literature, rather than being dismissed as trite genre fiction.

Splatterpunk: The Gross Out

Emerging sometime in the late 1980s, splatterpunk is a style of writing rather than a theme with any particular type of monster. It is also known by the name "extreme horror." In the typical splatterpunk story, graphic sex and violence abound as a result of the decadent indulgences of bored mortals and immortals, rather than as shocking excesses of monsters that must be stopped. Punk, alternative, and heavy metal music are often part of the backdrop of a splatterpunk story. There are no reluctant vampires or antiheroes here: splatterpunk monsters revel in their monstrosity.

Comic Horror: Laughing at Our Fears

Although Freddy Kreuger may have been the first monster to crack jokes before disposing of his victims, lines such as "she has a nice neck" in *Nosferatu* can be seen as comic threats that predate Freddy's by more than fifty years. Humor and horror also go hand in hand in the reactions of both the characters in horror texts and their readers and viewers. Despite this relationship between fear and laughter, true comic horror is a relatively new subgenre.

Everyday Horror: When the Mundane Becomes Monstrous

Everyday horror is the newest mode of horror. It is a writing style more than a subgenre dependant on a specific type of monster. In everyday horror, familiar tropes of the horror genre are grafted on to the bizarre complexity of modern life: a world full of rapidly mutating viruses, strange new technology, and corporations that can manipulate us into buying things so skillfully that we do not know our minds have been hacked by their marketing departments. In such a universe, vampires, zombies, and ghosts seem to be quite at home.

Chapter 2

How to Use This Book

Most librarians would agree that the purpose of a good readers' advisory program is to encourage reading and improve circulation by matching patrons with books that they will love. The job of the readers' advisor often involves interviewing patrons to determine their reading tastes based on limited information that draws connections between the types of books they usually read, the topics and thematic concerns they are drawn to, the writing styles they enjoy and those they don't particularly like, the settings (geographic locations, historical periods) they find most appealing, and the individual writers they like or hate. Based on this interview, a readers' advisor creates a list of books that the patron will possibly enjoy. This task is daunting enough for general fiction, but it can become nearly impossible when that particular patron is one like those identified in our preface, a reader whose reading preferences are limited almost exclusively to a single genre (in this case horror)—and that genre is one that the librarian is unfamiliar with. If the librarian who is serving as a readers' advisor also happens to be a horror fan and happens to have read nearly everything written in the genre in the past five years, or at least reviews of all books in print and available through ILL, then perhaps that librarian will be able to identify five to ten books the patron might enjoy.

However, it is unrealistic to expect any librarian to keep abreast of so many published works. For this reason, several publications exist for the sole purpose of aiding readers' advisors in their efforts to identify similar titles and authors to suit any given patron's reading tastes. These text-based and online publications alert librarians to the existence of readily available genre fiction that may be of interest to the reader at hand. By using Libraries Unlimited's <u>Genreflecting</u> series or its *Readers' Advisor Online* database, Gale's <u>What Do I Read Next</u> series, *Novelist,* and other tools, a librarian can match a popular title, such as the latest best seller by Stephen King, with other titles that possess the same general appeal and will therefore more than likely appeal to the reader. Before 1999 there was only one <u>Genreflecting</u> guide, and it covered all genres—horror, fantasy, romance, Western, science fiction, adventure, and crime fiction—in a single print volume; it was therefore unable to extensively cover works in any particular genre. Of course, this limited its usefulness for hard-core fans of a single genre.

Hooked on Horror III focuses solely on the horror genre. It lists, annotates briefly, and matches with similar titles virtually every readily available horror title, thereby giving users an in-depth look at the possibilities of the genre. Although it treats each of the subgenres of horror (such as vampires and werewolves, technohorror, and small town horror) separately, identifying similar titles by grouping them under one umbrella term, it also links titles within one subgenre with similar ones in other subgenres.

The entries also indicate when a book has received an award and when it is available in other formats. The awards appear at the beginning of the entry and are indicated as follows:

B Bram Stoker Award Winner

P Pulitzer Prize Winner

I International Horror Guild Winner

Hooked on Horror III identifies and matches many features that readers enjoy. The most obvious is the subgenre designation itself. In other words, all works that deal mainly with vampires are grouped in the vampires and werewolves chapter; all novels and collections of stories about serial murderers, stalkers, and maniacs can be found in the maniacs chapter; and all works dealing with technology or scientific experimentation are grouped together in the technohorror chapter. This makes it easy for fans of "Vampire's Point of View" narratives, Hannibal Lecter–type villains, and medical thrillers to find similar titles at a glance. The reader, or the readers' advisor, need only turn to the annotated lists in the chapters and skim the descriptions to create a bibliography of similar reads.

The second layer of matching can be found at the end of virtually all annotations in this guide, where a few titles that are similar to the work under consideration are identified. For the purpose of matching similar titles this way, we asked ourselves, "What title does this most read like?" We based our answers—the brief lists of similar titles—on thematic concerns, plot structures, or writing style. Of course, these matches are subjective. Also, because some books are entirely too unusual for accurate matching, we were unable to assign obviously similar titles to all texts, and in some cases, we simply had to use our own best judgment.

Finally, we assigned subject headings to each entry. These headings serve as keyword identifiers that are indexed, so that the entries that are assigned the same subject heading (keyword) end up being grouped together in the index, under that subject/keyword term. In this respect, *Hooked on Horror III* acts as a database, in print form, linking similar items based on specific literary elements such as setting, character types, or thematic issues. For example, a fan of *Rosemary's Baby* may realize that the aspect of the novel that he or she most enjoyed or identified with was its setting, New York City, or that one of the main characters was an actor, or that the main thrust of the story concerns demons and impregnation. Each of these themes is standardized in a subject term, which is then assigned to the novel. Once indexed, these subject terms act as additional access points. All users need do is find *Actor as Character*, *New York City*, *Demons*, or *Pregnancy* in the subject index, and they will find not only a reference to Levin's novel of demonic possession, but also a list of all works that were assigned one of those subject terms, as indicated by the page numbers listed after the term. Readers then need only turn to one of those pages, and they will find other titles that were assigned the subject term in question, which denotes that these titles are reasonably similar reads in that they are concerned with at least one of the major themes of the original fictional text under consideration.

We attempted to handle standardization with either scaffolding—for example, New Orleans is standardized as *Louisiana—New Orleans*, which allows for all texts set in Louisiana to be grouped together—or extensive *See* and *See Also* listings. These subject headings, aside from being match points for finding similar titles, also serve as access points when users need to find a work based on limited information. For example, a reader who has heard about the "Anita Blake" novels but knows nothing besides the recurring character's name will find in the subject index that *Blake, Anita (character)* is a subject keyword that refers back to various Laurell K. Hamilton books, each of which is indicated by a list of relevant page numbers. Those conducting scholarly research may find this useful as well. A researcher desiring to analyze horror novels that deal with cursed objects need only consult the index, where the term *Cursed Objects* serves as an access point. Our hope is that we have put enough care and hard work into the making of this bibliographic reference tool that all users will be saved valuable time, whether searching for horror titles they will likely enjoy or creating scholarly bibliographies of similarly themed titles.

1

2

3

4

5

6

7

8

9

10

Chapter 3

A Brief History of the Horror Genre and Its Current Trends

The first horror novel was published in 1764, when Horace Walpole penned the tale of a family curse, a damsel in distress, and a giant helmet that crushes humans, *The Castle of Otranto*. In England the popularity of this novel encouraged the publication of other Gothic novels, such as Anne Radcliffe's *The Mysteries of Udolpho*, Clara Reeve's *The Old English Baron*, and M. G. Lewis's *The Monk*, the latter becoming the prototype for the erotic horror novel. At about the same time, the first Gothic satire, Jane Austen's *Northanger Abbey*, became popular. On this side of the Atlantic, there were some early American Gothic texts as well, such as those by Charles Brockden Brown and Washington Irving, but generally speaking, these precursors to the modern horror novel bear little resemblance to what we now recognize as the horror tale. Brown's *Wieland* bordered on being what we now recognize to be psychological horror, and Washington Irving came very close to writing comic horror in *The Legend of Sleepy Hollow*, but neither writer seems to have captured the atmosphere, the gothic sensibilities, or the emotion of horror as the modern fan of the genre would know it. It wasn't until the mid-1800s that two American writers, Edgar Allan Poe and Nathaniel Hawthorne, began publishing short fiction that for all practical purposes could be considered the literary ancestor of what we now call horror. Poe wrote often through the eyes and consciousness of a maniacal killer or a madman (see chapter 11, "Maniacs and Sociopaths, or the Nuclear Family Explodes: Monstrous Malcontents Bury the Hatchet"), and Hawthorne examined, in a more reasoned and detached prose the darkest recesses of the disturbed mind (see chapter 14, "Psychological Horror: It's All in Your Head"). Another American, Ambrose Bierce, known more for his fanciful, weird fiction than for his horror fiction, later added the themes of aliens, demons, shape-shifters, and indescribable monsters in his explorations of what would later be called *cosmic horror* (a term coined to describe H. P. Lovecraft's fiction).

Although a few canonical authors (namely Edith Wharton and Henry James) dabbled in the horror genre near the turn of the century, monsters basically lay dormant until the 1930s, when Americans saw the resurgence of horror fiction in the weird tales of *Blackwood's*. Masters like Lovecraft and Arthur Machen introduced generations of Americans to the fear of the Old Ones, darker gods who reigned before humans inhabited the Earth and who, after their millennia-long slumbers, desired to regain their stronghold on the planet by bringing about either the subjugation of humanity or the apocalypse. The benchmark texts of this decade were Lovecraft's Cthulhu Mythos tales (for example, *The Dreams in the Witch House and Other Weird Stories*, *The Lurker at the*

Threshold, The Shadow Out of Time) and Machen's novella of subterranean gods, *The White People.*

The 1950s saw some resurgence in the genre; however, the benchmark texts of that era were those adapted for the screen, such as Richard Matheson's *The Incredible Shrinking Man* (1957). The most recent wave of popular horror began in 1968, when Ira Levin published *Rosemary's Baby*, and thanks to the perennial best sellers of Levin, Stephen King, Anne Rice, Dean Koontz, and Peter Straub, the 1970s and 1980s saw no break in the popularity of horror. Benchmark texts of this period include King's *Carrie* and *The Shining*, Straub's *Shadowland* and *Ghost Story*, Rice's *Interview with the Vampire*, Levin's *The Stepford Wives*, Koontz's *Demon Seed*, and various titles on the Manitou legend by Graham Masterton.

Today's up and coming writers promise to keep the genre viable and exciting. After a decline in the 1990s, the first years of the twenty-first century have witnessed growth in the number of horror titles published (see the preface). Aside from best-selling authors like King, Koontz, and Rice, who re-create the traditional horror tale, newcomers like Bentley Little, Glen Hirshberg, and Peter Crowther have been reintroducing the weird tale in a way that deals with the horrors of everyday life. Brandon Massey, Tananarive Due, and Jemiah Jefferson, as well as Owl Goingback and Koji Suzuki, have been giving horror a multicultural voice. Elizabeth Hand writes dark fantasy steeped in several mythologies. Charlee Jacob, Jack Ketchum, and Gary A. Braunbeck have been proving that even gory stories can be intelligent forays into psychology, sociology, and philosophy. And Ramsey Campbell continues to show the world that works of horror can be erudite as well as entertaining. Concurrently, horror films continue to be a big draw at the box office, with the success of the <u>Saw</u> series, *Hannibal Rising*, *28 Days Later*, *Diary of the Dead* (the fifth film in George Romero's <u>Night of the Living Dead</u> oeuvre), *The Descent*, and *High Tension*, just to name a few. Classic horror films are also being remade: John Carpenter's 1978 film *Halloween* was remade by Rob Zombie in 2007; Tobe Hooper's 1974 film *The Texas Chainsaw Massacre* was remade by Marcus Nispel in 2003; and in 2006 Wes Craven's 1971 film *The Hills Have Eyes* was remade by Alexandre Aja. And perhaps the most refreshing recent voice in horror cinema of recent date, Rob Zombie, got his authorial and directorial starts in horror film, with *House of 1000 Corpses* and *The Devil's Rejects*, two original movies that are a pastiche of popular horror from the 1960s and 1970s. Horror films based on the works of Japanese writers have also surged in popularity, thanks in part to the success of Gore Verbinski's 2002 film *The Ring*, based on Koji Suzuki's manga *Ringu* and the popular Japanese made-for-television film based on it. *The Ring's* success led to production of another film for American audiences based on the work of a Japanese writer, *The Grudge* (2004), as well as another film of Suzuki's work, *Dark Water* (2005). And there is the new wave in horror, the use of hand-held cameras that give the film a sense of verisimilitude, as in *The Blair Witch Project* (1999) and *Cloverfield* (2008), both of which are presented as being "documentaries."

Trends

Following are some of the current trends that we have noticed in our readings for this edition:

- **Alternative literature.** The literary term "alternative literature" refers, on one level, to the rewriting or retelling of classic works in the genre, which involves shifting the point of view so that a different character tells the story, adding details omitted by the earlier work, or changing the story completely. This trend can be seen in the various rewritings of Bram Stoker's *Dracula*, such as Kim Newman's <u>Anno Dracula Series</u>, which examines the world that would have been had the Count defeated Van Helsing's party of vampire hunters. Other retellings of *Dracula* are done from the point of view of other characters, such as Barbara Hambly's *Renfield: Slave of Dracula*, Tim Lucas's *The Book of Renfield: The Gospel According to Dracula*, Allan C. Kupfer's *The Journal of Professor Abraham Van Helsing*, and Jeanne Cavealos's edited collection of short stories *The Many Faces of Van Helsing*. Other examples include Christopher Golden's and James A. Moore's *Bloodstained Oz*, a dark fantasy retelling of Frank Baum's *The Wizard of Oz*.

- **Comic horror.** As horror entrenches itself as an established genre with its own rules, it has become easier to manipulate those rules for comic effect. The past decade has seen a surge in the number of comic horror titles. An example is Andrew Fox's <u>Fat White Vampire Series</u>, in which Fox's title character, morbidly obese and poorly educated New Orleans cabbie Jules Duchon, is the antithesis of Anne Rice's handsome and erudite immortal Lestat, and Max Brooks has created *The Zombie Survival Guide*, a step-by-step manual that will save us all from the undead—well, about as well as duct tape will save us from a terrorist attack. Dean Koontz's <u>Odd Thomas Novels</u> are about a fry cook with psychic powers who is called upon repeatedly to use his paranormal abilities to solve crimes, while Julie Kenner's *California Demon* is about the adventures of a demon-hunting soccer mom. And Christopher Moore, the undisputed king of comic horror, continues to publish novels about the problems of dealing with demons that have been accidentally summoned, or really stupid angels who lack the intellect to use their supernatural abilities wisely. The past decade has also seen a proliferation in the number of comic horror films (most of them far wittier than the Wayans Brothers' *Scary Movie* franchise). These films include the well-known and critically acclaimed zombie parody *Shaun of the Dead*, as well as the zombie films *Bubba Ho-tep* and *Fido*. Kevin Smith's *Dogma* questions the nature of God when he or she is out of the office, while two fallen angels plot to end time. And *Gacy: The Crawl Space* is a biopic in which the killer's neighbors are constantly commenting about that strange smell coming from his property.

- **The horrors of everyday life.** Life itself, in its everyday ugliness and frightening lack of order and justice, is sufficiently terrifying. This type of horror is most often seen in psychological horror, a subgenre devoid of supernatural elements. However, some familiar phenomena, such as the workings of cell phones or insane insurance policies, are so unfamiliar and even eccentric that they have nearly supernatural qualities. This type of horror has proliferated so much since the second edition of *Hooked on Horror* that we've put these works in a separate chapter, "Everyday Horror: When the Mundane Becomes Monstrous" (chapter 17). Examples of this type of horror include Bentley Little's *The Policy*, which is as much about our desire to believe that with enough money we can be indemnified against any misfortune as it is about insurance companies; and Stephen King's *Cell*, in which a frequency broadcast through people's wireless devices turns them into violent zombies. Other examples are Ramsey Cambpell's *The Overnight*, Christopher Fowler's *Breathe: Everyone's Got to Do It*, and Glen Hirshberg's *American Morons* and *The Two Sams*.

- **Genre-crossing** (also known as genreblending). Horror crosses over into other well-established genres such as action adventure, detective fiction, and romance. For titles associated with this trend, see the list of cross-genre horror in the appendix.

- **Historical horror**. Historical figures can be represented as monsters or monster-killers, adding a new dimension to their actions and often to the myths that surround them. In some cases, these historical figures are simply used as characters that inform the tale. Examples include fictionalized accounts of actual events, such as Robert Bloch's *American Gothic*, about the early twentieth-century serial killer Herman Mudgett (who took his victims in the shadow of the 1900 Chicago World's Fair); John Boyne's *Crippen*, about the infamous nineteenth-century murder case; and T. K. Welsh's *Resurrection Men*, about those who procured cadavers for medical students in the days before there was a systemized way of doing so. Other texts are similar to Tananarive Due's *Joplin's Ghost*, which weaves the story of the musician into the contemporary life of an unsuspecting singer. Robert Olen Butler's *Severance* is a collection of short stories told by historical and literary figures who died by beheading.

- **Paranormal romance**. The past decade has seen an explosion in paranormal romance, a genre of fiction that is a true cross between horror and romance in that a couple pursues a relationship in a world where supernatural creatures are part of their everyday reality, as in Laurell K. Hamilton's Anita Blake, Vampire Hunter Series, Kelley Armstrong's Women of the Otherworld Series, or P. N. Elrod's edited collections *My Big Fat Supernatural Wedding* and *My Big Fat Supernatural Honeymoon*, whose contributors include authors who are well-known names in either the romance or horror genres or both. Because *Hooked on Horror III* is a guide to reading interests in the *horror*, rather than the *romance*, genre, we have included only titles of this sort that contain both a substantial horror element (i.e., one of the types of monsters identified in this text) and a sustainable sense of horror (i.e., an atmosphere of dread or terror, or a comic examination thereof).

Part 2

An Annotated Bibliography of
Horror Novels and Films

Chapter 4

Ghosts and Haunted Houses: Dealing with Presences and Absences

Ambrose Bierce, in *The Devil's Dictionary*, defines the word *ghost* as "the outward manifestation of an inward fear." Though humorous, Bierce's commentary on spirits implies what writers of traditional ghost tales have known for a long time: most sightings are more a result of an individual's overactive imagination fed by guilt, remorse, grief, or paranoia, than they are actual visitations of otherworldly beings. On one level, ghost and haunted house stories can be understood as the reemergence of the repressed. In his essay "The Uncanny," Sigmund Freud said of the repressed that "the uncanny is that species of the frightening that goes back to what was once well-known and had long been familiar" but that the individual was compelled to repress (124). When this material returns, it is no longer in its old familiar form, but surfaces as "uncanny," something that is familiar to us in a way that is not immediately recognizable to the conscious mind, yet resonates in the unconscious mind, which still retains this repressed material—since it would view this information as being far too threatening and dangerous to be dealt with directly.

Both the ghost and the haunted house are literary tropes that represent the uncanny. The ghost or the haunted house serves as a portent, or warning, to the haunted person, who usually doesn't fully appreciate the danger lurking there. This is the case in Richard Matheson's *Stir of Echoes*, in which an ethereal presence in Tom Wallace's rental house compels him to investigate his landlord's past. In the film *What Lies Beneath*, the ghost that haunts Claire Spencer's summer cottage reveals her husband's violent nature. Ghosts can also help the repressed knowledge of the haunted protagonist to resurface, so that he or she can thwart those who would do harm. In Nina Kiriki Hoffman's *Stir of Bones*, Susan, the novel's teenage protagonist, is protected by the ghost of Nathan when he helps her articulate repressed knowledge about her own strengths, which will ultimately permit her to escape her abusive father. The ghosts of servants in the film *The Others* haunt their former abode to help end the painful confusion of more recent ghosts—by attempting to help them realize that they are indeed dead and in spirit form as well.

The poltergeist-infested abode can also signal the living, who know nothing of the past sin. Haunted houses of this type are often those built on Native American burial grounds, an action that shows disrespect for the religious customs of a minority culture (the houses thus remind Europeans that they are responsible for these Native American dead), or those built on sites where great social wrongs have occurred. In Stephen King's *Bag of Bones*, a racially motivated rape and murder is the cause not only of a house's being haunted (indirectly), but of an entire town's being supernaturally besieged. The uncanny, then, can represent what is repressed not merely by an individual only, but also by an entire community or culture, unknown to the hapless descendants, who are then left to deal with this inexplicable, uncanny phenomenon.

But the ghost is not always helpful, not always concerned with warning the living (or aiding other ghosts). Sometimes the ghost is a selfish creature who craves justice that was denied in life, or even just really wants attention. Some, like Eva Gali in Peter Straub's *Ghost Story* (which combines both the vengeful ghost and the angered Native American god narratives), require that those who wronged her in life pay for what they have done. This is particularly true in the film adaptation, which emphasizes the ghost aspect of the tale over its mythological aspect. The ghost of Beloved in Toni Morrison's novel of the same name wants the life that was denied to her by her mother, who killed her as an infant in order to spare her the horrors of slavery.

Ghosts and haunted houses often go hand in hand, and in this chapter we include works that include either of those elements. However, contrary to popular belief, ghosts don't necessarily reside in haunted houses, and haunted houses do not necessarily have individuated ghosts in them. A metaphorical comparison may better help explain the difference between the two. Haunted houses are a sort of architectural version of abused children who lash out at the world, as in Shirley Jackson's 1949 novel *The Haunting of Hill House*. Hill House is not haunted by any particular ghost; it is simply "evil" because of the way it was built by the twisted, puritanical man who erected it. In essence, it was born bad. This is not to say that old houses are the only ones that are haunted. The brand new, prefabricated suburban homes in the 1980s film *Poltergeist* are haunted because the builder located his development on top of an old cemetery without bothering to remove the bodies. Unlike ghosts, haunted houses don't try to educate later occupants about the wages of sin or repressed guilt. They lash out and frighten anyone unfortunate enough to come under their roofs, sometimes with fatal consequences. This is the case in Tananarive Due's *The Good House*, in which a voodoo priestess had once unleashed a vengeful spirit to protect her family; however, the spirit did not die with her. It continues to haunt the house generations later and offers violence to all who enter. Sometimes haunted houses are in need of love themselves. Hill House repeatedly urges Eleanor Vance to "come home," presumably to care for the decaying and awkwardly framed manse.

Finally, more than any other subgenre, ghost and haunted house tales lend themselves to the short story format. Many entries referenced in this chapter include entire anthologies and single-author collections of ghost and haunted house stories. Perhaps this is because the conventions of this genre are so ingrained in our consciousness that not much is needed to establish the details of a given tale. Thus, it is quite easy to write a ghost or haunted house story in such an abbreviated format.

This chapter includes works that trace the ghost story from its literary beginnings to its development, by late nineteenth- and early twentieth-century writers like Henry James, M. R. James, and Oliver Onions, into the form we recognize today, in the works of Shirley Jackson, Stephen King, and Peter Straub (as well as in several films by various directors). Representative titles in this chapter include not only scary, but also emotive, tragic tales, such as Morrison's *Beloved*, Graham Masterton's *Spirit*, and Anne

Rice's *Violin*. In addition, we cover works that trace the beginnings of the literary haunted house in Britain, with the prototypes being *Wuthering Heights*, *The Old English Baron*, *The Castle of Otranto* (annotated in chapter 7), and *Northanger Abbey* (annotated in chapter 16). We also describe novels that demonstrate how the Americanization of the haunted house led to the development of the haunted forest or haunted landscape, which is the analogy for the haunted colonial American mind, as seen in the fiction of Nathaniel Hawthorne.

Benchmark titles in this chapter include *Ghost Story*, *The Haunting of Hill House*, *Beloved*, Clara Reeve's *The Old English Baron*, Richard Matheson's *Stir of Echoes* and *Hell House*, Oliver Onion's *The Beckoning Fair One*, Emily Brontë's *Wuthering Heights*, and three films: *The Sixth Sense*, *The Others*, and *The Ring*.

The appeals of the ghost and haunted house tale are varied, stemming from both psychological and sociological concerns. Most humans have a fear of the dead returning, typically due to guilt. It is not unusual to find folklore in which the murdered dead return as revenging revenants, seeking to avenge themselves from beyond the grave. Most Americans grew up with similar stories of revenging revenants, usually told around the campfire or with flashlights being used for dramatic effect; these universal stories of "things that go bump in the night" come back to haunt us as adults, particularly when we are falling asleep in our beds—and suddenly we hear creaking noises when there is no physical evidence of a cause. Then there are ghosts that echo social concerns. For example, the Japanese fear of the ghastly return of a suicide by drowning, which may stem from the fear that water supplies will become contaminated, fuels many ghost stories from that culture. On the more positive side, tales of ghosts and other spirits feed a basic psychological need to affirm the human belief that there is some kind of life after death. In general, for these reasons ghost stories tend to be more psychological than other tales of the supernatural, relying less on action and gore, and more on atmosphere and suggestion.

Note: Many collections and anthologies of ghost stories can be found in chapter 18. Individual titles can be accessed through the subject/keyword index under *Afterlife, The*; *Haunted Houses*; or *Revenging Revenant*. In addition, users are advised to check chapter 7, "Demonic Possession, Satanism, Black Magic, and Witches and Warlocks: The Devil Made Me Do It," which contains many titles of interest to readers who enjoy ghost stories.

Ghosts

Austin, Sherry.

Mariah of the Spirits and Other Southern Ghost Stories. *Johnson City, TN: The Overmountain Press, 2002. 181p. ISBN 1570722315.*
    (See chapter 18, "Collections and Anthologies.")

Baldwin, Barbara J., Jerri Garreston, Linda Maul, and Sheri L. McGathy.

Trespassing Time: Ghost Stories from the Prairie. *Manhattan, KS: Ravenstone Press, 2005. 239p. ISBN 0965971260.*
(See chapter 18, "Collections and Anthologies.")

Barker, Clive.

Coldheart Canyon. *New York: HarperCollins, 2001. 676p. ISBN 0060182970.*
In 1920, a glamorous movie vamp and her manager go shopping in Romania, where they purchase the panorama on the walls of a subterranean monastery room. The tiles, which are cursed, are remounted in the star's mansion in Coldheart Canyon, a Hollywood residential area. As a result, the many ghosts who haunt the canyon are now imprisoned in the mansion. **Similar titles:** *Spirit*, Graham Masterton; *The Picture of Dorian Gray*, Oscar Wilde; *Steel Ghosts*, John Michael Curlovich.

Actor as Character • California—Hollywood • Cursed Objects • Haunted Houses • Immortality • Sado-Masochism

Bear, Greg.

Dead Lines. *New York: Ballantine, 2004. 256p. ISBN 0345448375.*
Deeply grieving Peter Russell longs to connect with his murdered daughter and his dead best friend. He thinks his prayers are answered when someone presents him with the Trans, a sleek, handheld broadband interpersonal communication device capable of flawless operation anywhere in the world. But he soon finds that the Trans is very different from other technological devices of its ilk, and now the unsolicited calls from the dead just won't stop. **Similar titles:** *Cell*, Stephen King; *The Harrowing*, Alexandra Sokoloff; *Violin*, Anne Rice; *The Sixth Sense* (film); *Poltergeist* (film).

Cell Phones • Death—Grieving • Internet, The • Writer as Character

Berman, Steve.

Vintage: A Ghost Story. *New York: Haworth Positronic-Harrington Park Press, 2007. 149p. ISBN 1560236310.*
In Weird, New Jersey, a gay teen Goth who has been kicked out of his parents' house teams up with a black-clad female friend to embark on a ghostly adventure. Intent on making contact with the spirit of a high school football star who had been killed in a hit-and-run, the boy manages to successfully commune with the ghost and immediately finds himself becoming enamored of the handsome spirit. He also inadvertently awakens a graveyard full of ghosts. **Similar titles:** *The Harrowing*, Alexandra Sokoloff; *Dead Lines*, Greg Bear; *Violin*, Anne Rice.

Adolescence • Eroticism • Gay/Lesbian/Bisexual Characters • High School • Homoeroticism • New Jersey • Parapsychology • Popular Culture

Bleys, Olivier.

The Ghost in the Eiffel Tower. *New York: Marion Boyars Publishers, Ltd., 2003. 356p. ISBN 0714530948.*

> In 1888 in France, two apprentice architects, Armand and Odilon, are working with Gustave Eiffel to build the Eiffel Tower. For them, the tower is the symbol of an age of scientific marvels, but in the gas-lit streets of Paris, strange beliefs, dark desires, and mysterious forces still persist. The two become involved with spiritualists and hold meetings in the morgue, while an American draftsman works to destroy the project. **Similar titles:** *Come Fygures, Come Shadowes,* Richard Matheson; *What Rough Beast,* H. R. Knight; *Move Under Ground,* Nick Mamatas.
>
> *Eiffel Tower • France—Paris • Parapsychology • Popular Culture • Psychics*

Bonansinga, Jay.

Oblivion. *Baltimore, MD: Cemetery Dance Publications, 2004. 339p. ISBN 1587670585.*

> Defrocked after botching an unauthorized exorcism, Martin Delaney has since sunk into alcoholism and despair. Then he is contacted by his former student, Jimmy Dodd, who brings him to the White House to deal with a malignant presence that has been there since the edifice's erection. Delaney's attempts to exorcise the presence from the building dredge up a long-forgotten moment in history. **Similar titles:** *The Exorcist,* William Peter Blatty; *White House Horrors,* Martin H. Greenberg (editor); *Perfect Circle,* Sean Stewart.
>
> *Clergy as Character • Exorcisms • Washington, D.C. • White House, The*

Boyd, Donna.

The Awakening. *New York: Ballantine, 2003. 208p. ISBN 0345462351.*

> Mary wakes up in a sanitarium, barely remembering an accident that killed her husband and daughter. Her therapist convinces her to return to what he says is her family home. The catch is that the people who live there are not new tenants; they are supposedly her nearest and dearest—and they are far from deceased—or so it seems. But why can't they see her, and what of her nightly torment of a blood-spattered kitchen in her dreams? **Similar titles:** *Stir of Echoes,* Richard Matheson; *The Hidden,* Sarah Pinborough; *The Others* (film); *The Sixth Sense* (film).
>
> *Afterlife, The • Amnesia • Families • North Carolina—Chapel Hill*

Brontë, Emily.

Wuthering Heights. *New York: Penguin, 2003, ©1847. 292p. ISBN 0141439556.*

> Caroline Earnshaw has loved Heathcliff ever since her father brought him home as a stray waif. But when Catherine's father passes away, her brother becomes the new head of household and refuses to countenance her relationship with the gypsy foundling, instead encouraging her to

marry the gently bred Edgar Linton. Heathcliff is driven mad by his thwarted love, and after Catherine's death he seeks to destroy both the Linton and Earnshaw families. **Similar titles:** *The Phantom of the Opera*, Gaston LeRoux; *Northanger Abbey*, Jane Austen; *Frankenstein*, Mary Shelley; *Wieland*, Charles Brockden Brown.

England • Families • Gothicism • Racism • Revenge

Cady, Jack.

Ghosts of Yesterday. *San Francisco, CA: Night Shade Books. 2003. 239p. ISBN 1892389487.*
 (See chapter 18, "Collections and Anthologies.")

Campbell, Ramsey.

The Darkest Part of the Woods. *New York: Tor, 2004, ©2002. 368p. ISBN 0765346826.*
 (See chapter 10, "Small Town Horror: Villages of the Damned.")

Ghosts and Grisly Things. *New York: Tor, 2001, ©1998. 300p. ISBN 0312867573.*
 (See chapter 18, "Collections and Anthologies.")

The Influence. *London: Headline, 1996, ©1988. 312p. ISBN 0747250758.*
 (See chapter 7, "Demonic Possession: Satanism, Black Magic, and Witches and Warlocks: The Devil Made Me Do It.")

Carey, Mike.

The Devil You Know. *New York: Warner, 2007. 416p. ISBN 0446580309.*
 (See chapter 16, "Comic Horror: Laughing at Our Fears.")

Chetwynd-Haynes, R., and Stephen Jones, eds.

Great Ghost Stories. *Carroll & Graf, 2004. 327p. ISBN 0786713631.*
 (See chapter 18, "Collections and Anthologies.")

Curlovich, John Michael (pseudonym of Michael Paine).

Steel Ghosts. *New York: Berkley, 2005. 312p. ISBN 0425200701.*
 Tom Kruvener, now a New York City film executive, had to deal with a lot of baggage before he could bring himself to return to his hometown. But he is back in Pennsylvania to convert the abandoned steel mill where his father was killed into a movie studio. However, he is not prepared for what he finds in the mill—ghosts. But since his plans are to make a horror B-flick, this seems appropriate, that is, until more gruesome accidents begin to occur. **Similar titles:** *Coldheart Canyon*, Clive Barker; *Scream Queen*, Edo Van Belkom; *Ancient Images*, Ramsey Campbell.

Death—Grieving • Families • Horror Movie Industry • Pennsylvania—Pittsburgh • Precognition

Datlow, Ellen.

The Dark: New Ghost Stories. *New York: Tor, 2003. 378p. ISBN 0765304449.*
(See chapter 18, "Collections and Anthologies.")

1

de Lint, Charles (writing as Samuel M. Key).

From a Whisper to a Scream. *New York: Orb, 2003, ©1992. 320p. ISBN 0765304341.*
(See chapter 11, "Maniacs and Sociopaths, or the Nuclear Family Explodes: Monstrous Malcontents Bury the Hatchet.")

2

Due, Tananarive.

3

Joplin's Ghost. *New York: Washington Square Press, 2006, ©2005. 496p. ISBN 0743449037.*
At the age of ten, Phoenix Smalls is nearly killed by a falling piano. Weeks after her recovery, she sleepwalks to a piano bench and flawlessly plays Scott Joplin's "Weeping Willow," even though she has not had the musical training to perform such a difficult piece. Flash forward to her twenties, trying to make it as a rhythm and blues singer, when she finds herself haunted by Joplin. **Similar titles:** *The Good House*, Tananarive Due; *Nightmare House*, Douglas Clegg; *Bag of Bones* and *The Shining*, Stephen King; *The Year of Things Past*, M. A. Harper.

4

African American Characters • Florida • Joplin, Scott (character) • Music—Ragtime • Music—Rhythm and Blues

Egan, Jennifer.

5

6

The Keep. *New York: Alfred A. Knopf, 2006. 239p. ISBN 1400043921.*
Danny desperately needs to escape some mobsters, when an invitation from his cousin Howie to join him in his newly acquired castle in Austria arrives, complete with plane tickets. It's a godsend—or is it? Howie plans to turn the isolated tower into a spiritual retreat. However, the tower is "spiritual" in more than one sense of the word—Danny soon spots a lovely blonde apparition lurking in the keep, the tower fortress that was the last stand of its previous occupants. **Similar titles:** *Earthbound*, Richard Matheson; *Within the Shadows*, Brandon Massey; *The House Next Door*, Anne River Siddons.

7

Austria • Frame Tale • Germany • Organized Crime • Prisons

Farris, John.

8

9

You Don't Scare Me. *New York: Forge, 2007. 302p. ISBN 0312850646.*
A young woman who suffered a terrifying childhood abduction by her drug abusing, gambling stepfather finds herself constantly fending off attacks from him, even after his death. Studying math and probability in college and suffering fits of blepharospasm—dangerous, post-traumatic episodes that leave her unable to open her eyes for minutes—Chase is almost killed when she steps in front of an oncoming bus during an episode.

10

In such states, the long-dead stepfather is able to haunt her. Her only hope is to end his evil game by finding her way into the Netherworld to fight him. **Similar titles:** *The Home*, Scott Nicholson; *Stir of Bones*, Nina Kiriki Hoffman; *The Servants*, Michael Marshall Smith.

Academia • Afterlife, The • Domestic Violence • Families • Parallel Universe • Police Officer as Character • Revenging Revenant

Finch, Paul.

Cape Wrath. *Tolworth, Surrey, UK: Telos Publishing, 2002. 123p. ISBN 190388960X.*
Archeology students investigate the lonely island of Craeghatir, in search of the tomb of Ivar, the ninth-century Viking who made quite a reputation for himself by raping and pillaging his way through the British Isles. Unfortunately, they find what they've come looking for. One by one they are killed, in a variety of sacrificial methods normally reserved for warriors or kings. This novel combines subtle nuance with gory details. **Similar titles:** *The Tower*, Simon Clark; *Shadow Coast*, Philip Haldeman; *Candyman* (film).

Academia • Archeology • England • Revenging Revenant • Vikings

Garton, Ray.

The Loveliest Dead. *New York: Leisure, 2006. 372p. ISBN 0843956488.*
After the inexplicable death of their four-year-old son Josh, Jenna and David Kellar hope to make a new start in the home they just inherited outside of Eureka, California. But the house is haunted by the ghosts of children who play on swings, then disappear, and one of them resembles their deceased son. Then Jenna begins to have visions that her son is alive once again, and David starts suffering from blackouts. **Similar titles:** *Spirit*, Graham Masterton; *Stir of Echoes*, Richard Matheson; *The Manor*, Scott Nicholson.

California—Eureka • Death—Grieving • Parapsychology • Poltergeists • Precognition • Psychics

Gorey, Edward, ed.

The Haunted Looking Glass: Ghost Stories Chosen by Edward Gorey. *New York: New York Review of Books, 2001, ©1959. 251p. ISBN 0940322684.*
(See chapter 18, "Collections and Anthologies.")

Haining, Peter, ed.

The Mammoth Book of Modern Ghost Stories: Great Supernatural Tales of the Twentieth Century. *New York: Carroll and Graf, 2007. 582p. ISBN 0786719605.*
(See chapter 18, "Collections and Anthologies.")

Haldeman, Philip.

Shadow Coast. *New York: Hippocampus Press. 2007. 255p. ISBN 097717347X.*
Three men find themselves in a maritime predicament and end up crashing on a massive rock wall off the Olympic Peninsula of Washington. Mark, who has come to see his troubled wife, an archeologist, washes up along a beach, where he is

saved by a local reverend, a Native American scout, and the wife of a man who had disappeared earlier. Now Mark's wife has mysteriously disappeared, and the two spouses left behind realize that they are up against a deadly Native American trickster god. **Similar titles:** *The Manitou*, Graham Masterton; *Dead in the Water*, Nancy Holder; *The Resort*, Bentley Little; *Bag of Bones*, Stephen King.

Archeology • Clergy as Character • Cursed Objects • Maritime Horror • Marriage • Native American Characters • Secret Sin • Washington—Olympia • Weather • Wilderness

Hand, Stephen, Damian Shannon, and Mark Swift.

Freddy vs. Jason. *New York: Simon & Schuster, 2004. 254p. ISBN 1844160599.*
In this novelization of the film of the same name, Freddy Krueger, now in Hell, becomes restless when the townspeople of Springwood learn to control their dreams enough to keep him from living through them. So he manages to release Jason Voorhies to Elm Street, to remind its citizens what fear is. Jason, however, gets a little too carried away, so Freddy is left with the task of stopping Jason's rampage. **Similar titles:** <u>Buffy the Vampire Slayer Series</u>, various authors; <u>Final Destination Series</u>, Nancy A. Collins; *Nightmare on Elm Street* (film).

Dreams • Krueger, Freddy (character) • Revenging Revenant • Voohries, Jason (character)

Harper, M. A.

The Year of Past Things. *Harvest Books, 2004. 256p. ISBN 0151011168.*
Phil Randazzo is haunted by his new wife's ex-husband, legendary Cajun musician A. P. Savoie, who appears at will and inhabits everyday objects in their New Orleans home. The couple tries various remedies to rid themselves of Savoie's annoying presence—exorcists, psychics, even a well-known novelist—but to no avail. **Similar titles:** *A House Divided*, Deborah LeBlanc; *Joplin's Ghost*, Tananarive Due; *The Manor*, Scott Nicholson; *Heart-Shaped Box*, Joe Hill; *What Lies Beneath* (film).

Cajuns • Louisiana—New Orleans • Marriage • Music—Cajun • Revenging Revenant

Herbert, James.

Nobody True. *New York: Tor, 2006, ©2003. 373p. ISBN 0765350610.*
In this first-person narrative, James True, who is capable of having out–of–body experiences, is brutally murdered during one of these episodes. The police believe that James is yet another victim of a serial killer. However James, now unfettered by a physical body, can investigate his murder in ways the police cannot, and what he discovers is far more shocking. **Similar titles:** <u>The Talisman Series</u>, Stephen King and Peter Straub; *Valley of Lights*, Stephen Gallagher; *The Laughing Man*, T. M. Wright; *The Others* (film); *The Sixth Sense* (film); *Ghost Story* (film).

Doppelgangers • Parapsychology • Revenging Revenant • Serial Killers

Hill, Joe.

20th Century Ghosts. *New York: William Morrow, 2007. 316p. ISBN 0061147974.*
(See chapter 18, "Collections and Anthologies.")

🅑 **Heart-Shaped Box.** *New York: William Morrow, 2007. 376p. ISBN 0061147931.*
An aging heavy metal rock star makes a devil of a deal online: he purchases a dead man's suit, complete with the ghost, included at no extra charge. But this seemingly whimsical sale is no joke. In no time the rock star has a new complaint. He discovers that he was set up, and the ghost is in no way helpful. In fact, it wants to see the last of its human owner, since he is a man with baggage created while carelessly rambling through life. **Similar titles:** *The Year of Past Things*, M. A. Harper; *Violin*, Anne Rice; *Kiss the Goat*, Brian Stableford.

Cursed Objects • Families • Internet, The • Music—Rock Music • Revenging Revenant

Hoffman, Nina Kiriki.

A Stir of Bones. *New York: Viking, 2003. 211p. ISBN 0670035513.*
Wealthy teenager Susan appears to have everything, but she is tightly controlled by her abusive father, who punishes his daughter's transgressions by beating her mother. Then Susan meets Nathan, the ghost of a boy who committed suicide after World War I. Now, more than anything, Susan wants to join her ethereal friend in death—if only to escape her father's tyranny. Hoffman's thoughtful style mimics the confusion of her adolescent protagonist. **Similar titles:** *You Don't Scare Me*, John Farris; *The Boy Who Couldn't Die*, William Sleator; *Coraline*, Neil Gaiman; *Paperhouse* (film).

Adolescence • Domestic Violence • Haunted Houses • Suicide

Jackson, Thomas Graham.

Six Ghost Stories. *Ashcroft, BC: Ash-Tree Press, 1999, ©1919. 145p. ISBN 1899562680.*
(See chapter 18, "Collections and Anthologies.")

James, M. R.

Ghost Stories of an Antiquary. *New York: Dover, 1971, ©1911. 152p. ISBN 0486227588.*
(See chapter 18, "Collections and Anthologies.")

Koontz, Dean.

The House of Thunder. *Thorndike, ME: Thorndike Press, 2000, ©1982. 504p. ISBN 0786228652.*
(See chapter 14, "Psychological Horror: It's All in Your Head.")

Shadow Fires. *Thorndike, ME: Thorndike Press, 2001, ©1987. 775p. ISBN 0786228644.*
(See chapter 12, "Technohorror: Evil Hospitals, Military Screw-Ups, Mad Scientists, and Alien Invasions.")

LeBlanc, Deborah.

Grave Intent. *New York: Leisure, 2005. 374p. ISBN 0843955538.*
(See chapter 10, "Small Town Horror: Villages of the Damned.")

Little, Bentley.

The Burning. *New York: Signet, 2006. 391p. ISBN 0451219147.*
(See chapter 17, "Everyday Horror: When the Mundane Becomes Monstrous.")

Maberry, Jonathan.

Ghost Road Blues Trilogy.

(See chapter 10, "Small Town Horror: Villages of the Damned.")

Mantel, Hilary.

Beyond Black. *New York: Henry Holt, 2005. 365p. ISBN 0805073566.*
A clairvoyant who is in daily contact with the dead and the soon to be dead travels England's modern spiritualism circuit. During her travels she meets Colette, a down-on-her-luck divorcee who needs a new life. Colette becomes the psychic's personal assistant, running interference between her new employer and the living and dead who seek her out. Mantel's writing is subtle and witty. **Similar titles:** *Come Fygures, Come Shadowes*, Richard Matheson; *In Shadows*, Chandler McGrew; *Kindred Spirit*, John Passarella.

England • Precognition • Psychics • Religion—Spiritualism

Massey, Brandon.

Within the Shadows. *New York: Kensington, 2005. 357p. ISBN 0758210698.*
A novelist who writes occult adventure stories is visited by otherworldly spirits, and after he enters a strange mansion he finds himself in a tug-of-war between two supernatural presences. The problems begin when he meets a gorgeous but possessive woman who has decided that he is her soul mate, and she becomes his personal stalker. Add to the mix three crazed cats and the spirit of a young boy named Sammy, who likes to communicate via Microsoft Word files and Scrabble boards. **Similar titles:** *Bag of Bones*, Stephen King; *Earthbound*, Richard Matheson; *Joplin's Ghost*, Tananarive Due; *Face*, Tim Lebbon.

African American Characters • Haunted Houses • Psychosexual Horror • Stalkers • Suburbia • Writer as Character

Masterton, Graham.

Prey. *New York: Leisure, 2000, ©1992. 352p. ISBN 0843946334.*
(See chapter 8, "Mythological Monsters and 'The Old Ones': Invoking the Dark Gods.")

Spirit. *New York: Leisure, 2001, ©1995. 424p. ISBN 084394935X.*

Five-year- old Peggy Buchanan was very close to her sisters Laura and Elizabeth, so close, in fact, that even after she dies from a fall into the family swimming pool one winter, she returns again and again, at various ages, often to avenge a wrong-doing committed against one of her sisters. But Peggy's spirit becomes too over-protective and overzealous, and people begin to mysteriously die agonizing deaths caused by severe frostbite and its complications. **Similar titles:** *Coldheart Canyon*, Clive Barker; *Lasher*, Anne Rice; *Beloved*, Toni Morrison; *The Loveliest Dead*, Ray Garton.

Actor as Character • California • Childhood • Child Molesters • Death—Grieving • Families • New England • Parenting • Revenging Revenant

Matheson, Richard.

Come Fygures, Come Shadowes. *Colorado Springs: Gauntlet Press, 2003. 144p. ISBN 1887368604.*

As a spiritualist medium, Morna has the gift of contacting the dead, and she wishes to bring her eighteen-year-old daughter Claire into the family business as well. Unfortunately, Claire has no desire to be a clairvoyant, and when she's forced to sit for séances and be the conduit for ectoplasmic manifestations, she becomes violently ill and feels as if she's been sexually violated. **Similar titles:** *Beyond Black*, Hilary Mantel; *The Parasite*, Ramsey Campbell; *What Rough Beast*, H. R. Knight.

New York City—Brooklyn • Parapsychology • Psychics • Religion—Spiritualism

Earthbound. *New York: Tor, 2005, ©1982. 223p. ISBN 0765311712.*

Part ghost story, part erotica, part psychological drama, this novel showcases Matheson's ability to marry elements of suspense with the usual tropes of horror. A television scriptwriter and his wife revisit the cottage in which they spent their honeymoon, in hopes of rekindling their almost dead love. During their first night there, he receives a visitation from a mysterious, drop-dead gorgeous young woman. Locals inform him that the woman is a ghost and that he must leave the cottage in order to escape her control. **Similar titles:** *Within the Shadows*, Brandon Massey; *Woman*, Richard Matheson; *Scared Stiff*, Ramsey Campbell.

Haunted Houses • Marriage • New York—Long Island • Psychosexual Horror • Writer as Character

Stir of Echoes. *New York: Tor, 2004, ©1958. 223p. ISBN 0765308711.*

After being hypnotized at a party, the doors of perception are permanently opened for Tom Wallace. Now he can read minds, see into the future, and even communicate with the dead. He also can no longer have the privacy he craves. Instead, he is held captive by a sort of perverse idea of 1950s family and neighbor-hood togetherness, in which he is privy to the neighbors' most intimate secrets. And now a revenant insists he dig into his landlord's past. **Similar titles:** *Don't Dream*, Donald Wandrei; *Candles Burning*, Michael McDonald and Tabitha King; *The Sixth Sense* (film).

California • Dreams • Haunted Houses • Marriage • Mind Control • Secret Sin

Matthews, A. J. (pseudonym used by Rick Hautala).

Looking Glass. *New York: Penguin-Berkley, 2004. 342p. ISBN 0425190994.*

When the Ireland family moves to the country for peace and quiet, they discover that their new abode has its drawbacks: a hideously scarred woman begins appearing in all the house's mirrors. Now they must discover the meaning behind her presence or continue suffering the frightful appearances. **Similar titles:** *The House on Orchid Street*, T. M. Wright; *The Manor*, Scott Nicholson; *Black Creek Crossing*, John Saul; *What Lies Beneath* (film); *Dark Water* (film).

Haunted Houses • *Mirrors* • *Revenging Revenant*

McDowell, Michael, and Tabitha King.

Candles Burning. *New York: Berkley, 2006. 423p. ISBN 0425210286.*

Seven-year-old Callie can hear the dead speak, so when her father is murdered in a botched kidnapping attempt, she can hear the spirits warning her that she's in danger, too. Tabitha King completed this Southern gothic novel, which was begun by McDowell, who passed away in 1999. **Similar titles:** *The Shining*, Stephen King; *Stir of Echoes*, Richard Matheson; *In Shadows*, Chandler McGrew; *The Sixth Sense* (film).

Alabama • *Florida—Pensacola* • *Gothicism* • *Psychics*

McGrew, Chandler.

In Shadows. *New York: Dell, 2005. 399p. ISBN 0553586041.*

After police officer Jake Crowley kills a suspect during a shoot-out, he finds himself hearing ghostly whispers, which cause him to pack up and leave Galveston to return to his home in Maine. There he reunites with his old girlfriend and her blind and deaf son Pierce, who also hears the same ghostly whispers. Crowley comes to realize that the whispers come from an entity that is stalking and killing those he loves. Now Jake must embrace his special gift if he wishes to protect his loved ones. **Similar titles:** *Candles Burning*, Michael McDowell and Tabitha King; *Stir of Echoes*, Richard Matheson; <u>The Greywalker Series</u>, Kat Richardson; *Beyond Black*, Hilary McGrew.

Families • *Maine* • *Police Officer as Character* • *Psychics*

Mitchell, Mary Ann.

The Witch. *New York: Medallion Press, 2007. 463p. ISBN 1932815813.*

(See chapter 7, "Demonic Possession: Satanism, Black Magic, and Witches and Warlocks: The Devil Made Me Do It.)

Morrell, David.

🅱 **Creepers.** *New York: CDS Books, 2006. 354p. ISBN 159315237X.*

Creepers are "urban archeologists," people who illegally enter abandoned structures to gather information about the past. But when one such group happens upon the now abandoned Paragon Hotel, built in Asbury

Park's heyday, they find more than they bargained for: they discover the structure is haunted. **Similar titles:** *In This Skin*, Simon Clark; *The House That Jack Built*, Graham Masterton; *Shadow Coast*, Philip Haldeman; *The House on Orchid Street*, T. M. Wright.

Archeology • Haunted Houses • New Jersey—Asbury Park

Morrison, Toni.

 Beloved. *New York: Knopf, 2006, ©1987. 316p. ISBN 0307264882.*
Sethe and her children cross the Ohio River to freedom in the 1840s but are soon tracked down by a bounty hunter. Determined that she and her children will never be slaves again, Sethe does the unthinkable: she attempts to help her entire family escape slavery through death. She succeeds in freeing her infant daughter in this manner, but ultimately she cannot free the rest of her children from the curse of slavery or from the infant's ghost, who returns to destroy her entire family. **Similar titles:** *Bag of Bones*, Stephen King; *Nazareth Hill*, Ramsey Campbell; *Spirit*, Graham Masterton; *Beloved* (film).

African American Characters • Death—Grieving • Haunted Houses • Ohio • Parenting • Revenging Revenant • Slavery

Nicholson, Scott.

The Home. *New York: Pinnacle, 2005. 352p. ISBN 0786017112.*
At the tender age of twelve, Freeman Mills, a victim of child abuse, is sufficiently damaged enough to warrant safeguarding in a mental institution. He is incarcerated in the Wendover Home, a place where mental patients were also used as subjects of various inhumane experiments before World War II. The ghosts of these patients still linger, and Freeman has the ability to see them, an ability augmented through the facility's use of electroshock treatment. **Similar titles:** *Desolation*, Tim Lebbon; *Nazareth Hill*, Ramsey Campbell; *In the Dark of Night*, John Saul; *You Don't Scare Me*, John Farris.

Adolescence • Mental Illness • North Carolina • Parallel Universes • Parapsychology • Precognition • Psychologist/Psychiatrist as Character • Weird Science

The Manor. *New York: Kensington-Pinnacle, 2004. 320p. ISBN 0786015802.*
A group of artists, along with a clairvoyant, are invited to enjoy the rustic charm of Korban Manor under the light of the October blue moon, and everyone's artistic talent flourishes under the house's influence. But as the moon rises, guests begin to have horrible nightmares, and the border between the living and the dead becomes thin. Soon the guests realize that the manor's original owner is neither dead nor alive, but lives in the walls and the glass of the home he loved so much. This is a traditional ghost story by one of the best up-and-coming writers in the genre. **Similar titles:** *The Haunting of Hill House*, Shirley Jackson; *The Tower*, Simon Clark; *The Abandoned*, Douglas Clegg.

Artist as Character • Haunted Houses • Precognition • Psychics

Paine, Michael.

The Night School. *New York: Berkley, 2006. 325p. ISBN 0425209164.*
(See chapter 15, "Splatterpunk: The Gross Out.")

Steel Ghosts. *New York: Berkley, 2005. 312p. ISBN 0425200701.*
(See Curlovich, John Michael, in this chapter.)

Pampellonne, Terese.

The Unwelcome Child. *New York: Pinnacle Books, 2005. 318p. ISBN 0786017260.*
(See chapter 7, "Demonic Possession: Satanism, Black Magic, and Witches and Warlocks: The Devil Made Me Do It.")

Passarella, John.

Kindred Spirit. *New York: Pocket Star, 2006. 387p. ISBN 0743484800.*
On the anniversary of her twin sister's murder, television journalist Hallie Moore is filming an investigative special on her death when suddenly she experiences the killing from her sibling's point of view. Hallie's desire to uncover the truth leads her to consult with paranormal investigators and psychics—until ultimately, she becomes consumed by her work. **Similar titles:** *Ringu*, Koji Suzuki; *Beyond Black*, Hilary Mantel; *The Face of Fear*, Dean Koontz.

Families • Journalist as Character • Parapsychology • Psychics • Twins

Priest, Cherie.

The Eden Moore Trilogy.

Eden Moore's investigation into her family's origins leads her on a journey throughout the South. An orphan, she must eventually journey back in time to understand her family's supernatural origins and the source of her ability to see ghosts. **Similar titles:** *The Good House* and *Joplin's Ghost*, Tananarive Due; <u>The Greywalker Series</u>, Kat Richardson.

Biracial Characters • Families • Gothicism • Moore, Eden (character) • Precognition • Psychics

Four and Twenty Blackbirds. *New York: Tor, 2005. 288p. ISBN 0765313081.*
Eden discovers many skeletons in her family closet in this gothic thriller that introduces the series.

South, The

Wings to the Kingdom. *New York: Tor, 2006. 399p. ISBN 076531309X.*
Eden, who sees ghosts lately, is able to see quite a lot of them in her hometown on the Chickamauga battlefield, and they are all pointing at something. She stays uninvolved—until her mentally ill cousin calls from the institution where he resides after seeing Old Green

Eyes, the local supernatural manifestation. Meanwhile, tourists are being shot at on the battlefield.

Georgia—Chickamauga • *War—American Civil War*

Not Flesh Nor Feathers. *New York: Tor, 2007. 368p. ISBN 0765313103.*

(See chapter 5, "Golem, Mummies, and Zombies: Wake the Dead and They'll Be Cranky.")

Rice, Anne.

Violin. *Alfred A. Knopf, 1997. 289p. ISBN 0679433023.*

Following the death of her current lover Karl, Triana Becker seems to be losing her mind. A mysterious violinist on the streets of New Orleans forces her back into her painful past through his music, and his playing is relentless. The violinist, Stefan Stefanovsky, is in fact a ghost, damned by his hatred and guilt to wander aimlessly. Now he wants Triana. Rice, one of the masters of the gothic and horror tale, weaves a new version of the classic ghost story that is subtle in its approach. **Similar titles:** *Bag of Bones*, Stephen King; *Magic Terror*, Peter Straub; *The Beckoning Fair One*, Oliver Onions; *Heart-Shaped Box*, Joe Hill.

Death—Grieving • *Families* • *Louisiana—New Orleans* • *Marriage* • *Music—Classical*

Richardson, Kat.

The Greywalker Series.

P.I. Blaine Harper has the power to see spirits and to attract all manner of supernatural creatures. Blaine is a greywalker, one of those extraordinary individuals able to walk between this world and the next. **Similar titles:** The Anita Blake, Vampire Hunter Series, Laurell K. Hamilton; In Shadows, Chandler McGrew; The Violet Series, Stephen Woodworth; The Eden Moore Trilogy, Cherie Priest.

Harper, Blaine (character) • *Psychics* • *Washington—Seattle*

Greywalker. *New York: Roc, 2006. 341p. ISBN 045146107X.*

After being brutally beaten by an angry perp, P.I. Blaine Harper is dead for two minute before being revived. After learning that she is now a greywalker, she discovers that she is able to use her paranormal abilities to assist her new, supernatural clientele.

Afterlife, The

Poltergeist. *New York: Roc, 2007. 352p. ISBN 0451461509.*

Blaine is hired to use her paranormal powers to get to the bottom of fake data that have shown up in a university investigation into the existence of poltergeists. To make matters worse, one of the principal investigators ends up dead.

Academia • *Poltergeists*

Rickman, Phil.

The Remains of an Altar. *London: Quercus, 2006. 439p. ISBN 1905204523.*
(See chapter 17, "Everyday Horror: When the Mundane Becomes Monstrous.")

Saul, John.

Black Creek Crossing. *New York, Ballantine, 2004. 358p. ISBN 0345433327.*
(See chapter 7, "Demonic Possession: Satanism, Black Magic, and Witches and Warlocks: The Devil Made Me Do It.")

Smith, Michael Marshall.

The Servants. *Northborough, MA: Earthling Publications, 2007. 207p. ISBN 0979505402.*

An eleven-year-old boy finds himself transplanted to the fading resort town of Brighton. His dying mother plans to live out her life there with her new husband, whom the boy hates. After being taken to see the old servants' quarters of the house, the child begins to see the ghosts of servants frantically trying to right their secret world, which seems to be pulling apart at the seams. **Similar titles:** *More Tomorrow*, Michael Marshall Smith; *Coraline*, Neil Gaimon; *You Don't Scare Me*, John Farris; *The Others* (film); *The Sixth Sense* (film).

Childhood • England—Brighton • Families • Haunted Houses • Parallel Universes • Victorian Era

Sokoloff, Alexandra.

The Harrowing. *New York: St. Martin's, 2006. 239 pp. ISBN 0312357486.*

During Thanksgiving break, five college students who are not going home for the holiday remain in the dorm and find themselves bored. To relieve the tedium one of them breaks out a Ouija board, and everyone eagerly plays with it to pass the time. After the five play with the board, however, supernatural occurrences cause them to discover that other students in this dorm in 1920 were in the same predicament they are in now, and that they are even using the same Ouija board their predecessors used. **Similar titles:** *Vintage: A Ghost Story*, Steve Berman; The Harrow Academy Novels, Douglas Clegg; *Darkness, Tell Us*; Richard Laymon.

Academia • Parapsychology • Popular Culture • Revenging Revenant

Stableford, Brian.

Kiss the Goat: A Twenty-first Century Ghost Story. *Holicong, PA: Prime, 2005. 194p. ISBN 0809544849.*

Kit, a Yorkshire bus driver, realizes that her tactile hallucinations are more than just musical madness when she hears, from a rider's Discman, the very song that haunts her during her blackout episodes. She comes to realize that the song connects her to a suicide, a woman named Rose Selavy, who once worked in the same room that Kit occupies in a boarding house.

Stableford's novel is filled with historical and popular culture references. **Similar titles:** *Heart-Shaped Box*, Joe Hill; *The House on Orchid Street*, T. M. Wright; *The Dark: New Ghost Stories*, Ellen Datlow (editor); *Dark Water* (film).

Bus Driver as Character • Haunted Houses • Music • Psychics • Religion—Satanism • Suicide

Stewart, Sean.

Perfect Circle. *Northampton, MA: Small Beer, 2004. 243p. ISBN 1931520070.*
Having the ability to see ghosts is not all it's cracked up to be, if you ask DK "Dead" Kennedy, who cannot drive at night because the revenants he sees look so much like the living that he has wrecked cars trying to avoid them. And then people are always clamoring to "borrow" his unique abilities, such as a distant cousin hiring him to exorcise the ghost of a girl he just killed. Too bad these skills don't lead to financial success or to making him more beloved, as he is becoming little more than a ghost in the lives of his family. **Similar titles:** *Stir of Echoes*, Richard Matheson; *Oblivion*, Jay Bonansinga; *Within the Shadows*, Brandon Massey; *The Sixth Sense* (film).

Exorcisms • Marriage • Psychics • Texas

Straub, Peter.

Ghost Story. *New York: Pocket, 1980, ©1979. 567p. ISBN 0671826859.*
Five septuagenarians in New England share a terrible secret, one that has them all consumed by guilt. When satanic slayings of animals begin to occur, and the old men begin dying of mysterious causes, the survivors suspect an evil presence is haunting them. Can a young Hawthorne scholar save them? Can anything save the town from an evil older than humanity itself? **Similar titles:** *Phantoms*, Dean Koontz; *The Manitou*, Graham Masterton; *The Keeper*, Sarah Langan; *Nobody True*, James Herbert; *Ghost Story* (film).

New England • Reincarnation • Religion—Native American • Revenging Revenant • Secret Sin • Septuagenarians • Shape-shifters

Suzuki, Koji.

Dark Water. *New York: Vertical Press, 2004. 279p. ISBN 1932234101.*
(See chapter 18, "Collections and Anthologies.")

Ring. *Translated by Robert B. Rohmer and Glynne Walley. New York: Vertical, 2003. 286p. ISBN 1932234004. (Originally published in Japanese as Ringu [1991]).*
A newspaper reporter, Asagawa, investigates why four apparently unrelated deaths occurred in Tokyo at exactly the same time. Using his resources as a journalist, he learns that all four young victims shared the same rental cabin and watched the same videotape. Asagawa finds the cabin, locates the tape, and watches what seems to be a really bad art film, with an odd mixture of apparently random scenes. At the end of the tape is the curse, and now Asagawa has seven days to live. **Similar titles:** *Kindred Spirit*, John Passarella; *Casting the Runes*, M. R. James; *Scared Stiff: Tales of Sex and Death*, Ramsey Campbell; *Parasite Eve*, Sena Hideaki; *Ringu* (film); *The Ring* (film).

Cursed Objects • Japan • Journalist as Character • Multimedia—Videotape • Revenging Revenant

Walpole, Horace.

The Castle of Otranto: A Gothic Story, and the Mysterious Mother: A Tragedy. *Edited by Frederick S. Frank. Peterborough, ON: Broadview Press, 2003, ©1764. 357p. ISBN 155111304X.*

> (See chapter 7, "Demonic Possession: Satanism, Black Magic, and Witches and Warlocks: The Devil Made Me Do It.")

Wilde, Oscar.

The Canterville Ghost. *Cambridge, MA: Candlewick Press, 1997, ©1891. 126p. ISBN 0763601322.*

> (See chapter 16, "Comic Horror: Laughing at Our Fears.")

Woodworth, Stephen.

The Violet Series.

> In a parallel present, a small percentage of people who are born with violet eyes can communicate with the dead. The government realizes that such people are invaluable in murder investigations and steps in to regulate Violets and make use of their special gifts. **Similar titles:** The Anita Blake, Vampire Hunter Series, Laurell K. Hamilton; The Greywalker Series, Kat Richardson; The Eden Moore Trilogy, Cherie Priest.
>
> *Lindstrom, Natalie (character) • Parapsychology • Psychics*

> **Through Violet Eyes.** *New York: Dell, 2004. 333p. ISBN 0553803379.*
>
> > Natalie Lindstrom works with FBI agent Dan Atwater to find a serial killer who is targeting Violets.
> >
> > *Federal Bureau of Investigation • Serial Killers*

> **With Red Hands.** *New York: Dell, 2004. 333p. ISBN 0553586459.*
>
> > Natalie Lindstrom has retired from her job of being an expert witness who has the ability to contact murder victims and learn about their last memories. Now mother to a five-year-old daughter, who is also a Violet, she does not want the girl to follow in her footsteps as a crime-fighting clairvoyant. But an old friend wants Natalie's help with a case. Complicating her life further, Natalie's mother claims to be in contact with a serial killer who was executed long ago. **Similar titles:** The Anita Blake, Vampire Hunter series, Laurell K. Hamilton; The Greywalker Series, Kat Richardson; The Eden Moore Trilogy, Cherie Priest.
> >
> > *Federal Bureau of Investigation • Parenting • Serial Killers*

> **In Golden Blood.** *New York: Dell, 2005. 303p. ISBN 0440242525.*
>
> > Wishing to get away from those who would drain her by using her as a crime-solving tool, Natalie Lindstrom agrees to go to Peru with an archeologist to help him unearth artifacts—using her unique abilities to communicate with the dead at the dig site. But she only opens herself up to channeling 500-year-old horrors.
> >
> > *Archeology • Corporate Horror • Peru*

From Black Rooms. *New York: Bantam, 2006. 334p. ISBN 0440242533.*

After her last experience with archeology, Natalie has decided to embark on yet another career, this time channeling the spirits of famous dead painters. But Natalie's past comes back to haunt her. The Violet-killing serial killer she captured in the first novel in this series, *Through Violet Eyes,* has escaped from prison and is now working with a group who are trying to contact Dr. Bartholomew Wax, a geneticist who specializes in Violets.

Artist as Character • Serial Killers

Haunted Houses

Amis, Kingsley.

The Green Man. *London: Vintage, 2004, ©1969. 175p. ISBN 0099461072.*
(See chapter 16, "Comic Horror: Laughing at Our Fears.")

Bailey, Dale.

House of Bones. *New York: Penguin-Signet, 2003. 384p. ISBN 0451210794.*
Eccentric billionaire Ramsey Lomax bribes the city to halt the demolition of the notorious Dreamland housing project so he can reside there for two weeks and investigate alleged ghostly activity. He advertises for people to accompany him, and four respond, including a medium, a journalist who was a former resident, a doctor about to lose her career, and a veteran with a shady past. Almost immediately the foursome senses the presence of malignant forces. **Similar titles:** *The Haunting of Hill House,* Shirley Jackson; *The Infinite,* Douglas Clegg; *The House on Orchid Street,* T. M. Wright; *The Haunting* (film).

Haunted Houses • Housing Projects • Journalist as Character • Physician as Character • Psychics

Benson, Amber.

The Ghosts of Albion Series.
(See chapter 7, "Demonic Possession: Satanism, Black Magic, and Witches and Warlocks: The Devil Made Me Do It.")

Blaine, Chris (various authors using pseudonym).

The Abbadon Inn Series.
The Abbadon Inn sits on a quiet street in the charming Victorian town of Cape May, New Jersey. Abandoned and vacant for years, it's ready for renovation—that is, if the spirits that reside within like the new owner. **Similar titles:** *Nazareth Hill,* Ramsey Campbell; *In This Skin,* Simon Clark; The Harrow Academy Novels, Douglas Clegg.

Haunted Houses • New Jersey

Blaine, Chris (pseudonym for Elizabeth Massie).

Twisted Branch. *New York: Berkley, 2005. 324p. ISBN 042520524X.*

> The Abbadon Inn's new owner, a retired police officer, discovers that those sounds she hears at night are more than just the natural noises made by an old house when it settles. It seems that ghosts inhabit nearly every room of this cursed abode.

> *Family Curse • Police Officer as Character • Revenging Revenant*

Blaine, Chris (actual author unknown).

Dark Whispers. *New York: Berkley, 2005. 292p. ISBN 0425206297.*

> Karen and John Dalton are the newest proprietors of the inn. While restoring one of the rooms, Karen discovers an old box, filled with love letters written by a gangster who died in the 1950s. Her curiosity gets the better of her and she begins reading, only to find that events in the letters begin to play themselves out in the present.

> *Cursed Objects • Epistolary Format • Marriage • Organized Crime*

Blaine, Chris (pseudonym for Matthew J. Costello).

Drowned Night: A Novel of the Abbadon Inn. *New York: Berkley, 2005. 324p. ISBN 0425206769.*

> (See chapter 7, "Demonic Possession: Satanism, Black Magic, and Witches and Warlocks: The Devil Made Me Do It.")

Campbell, Ramsey.

Nazareth Hill. *New York: Forge, 1997, ©2006. 383p. ISBN 0312863446.*

> When eight-year-old Amy is held up by her father so she can see inside one of the windows of Nazarill, a decrepit building in Partington, England, she spies something spidery and ghostlike. Eight years later, her father becomes the caretaker of Nazarill, now a renovated hostelry. When one of Nazarill's tenants dies of heart failure, Amy suspects the ghost she saw as a child is seeking revenge. **Similar titles:** *The Shining* and *Bag of Bones*, Stephen King; *The Mammoth Book of Modern Ghost Stories*, Peter Haining (editor); *Beloved*, Toni Morrison; The Abbadon Inn Series, Chris Blaine.

> *Adolescence • Haunted Houses • Parenting • Photographer as Character*

Clark, Simon.

In This Skin. *New York: Dorchester, 2004. 384p. ISBN 0843951575.*

> The condemned, decaying building of Chicago's Luxor dance hall, which resembles an Egyptian temple, possesses a strange magnetism. An unmarried, pregnant couple with nowhere else to go decide to set up housekeeping in the small manager's apartment at the top. But the spirits there are not just found in a bottle; mysterious forces from another dimension lurk beneath its once-shiny floors and want to keep these hapless humans

for eternity. **Similar titles:** *The Hidden World* and *The Doorkeepers*, Graham Masterton; *Creepers*, David Morrell; The Abbadon Inn Series, Chris Blaine.

Haunted Houses • Illinois—Chicago • Parallel Universes

The Tower. *New York: Leisure, 2005. 353p. ISBN 0843954922.*

An up-and-coming band is thrilled to be able to stay for free at the Tower, an ancient house that has currently changed hands and needs a caretaker until the new owner can begin renovations. The house's remote location is an added attraction, because the band will have plenty of uninterrupted time to practice before they head for the recording studio. But of course there's a catch: the Tower is inhabited by an evil presence. **Similar titles:** *Cape Wrath*, Paul Finch; *The Abandoned* and *The Infinite,* Douglas Clegg; *The Manor*, Scott Nicholson.

England • Haunted House • Music—Rock Music • Revenging Revenant

Clegg, Douglas.

Harrow Academy Novels.

Harrow House, a mediocre prep school for boys, is distinguished by dissonant architecture and a legacy of recent student suicides, but Harrow House is also the site of a malefic psychic energy that is capable of exploiting the personal demons of all who enter. **Similar titles:** The Beast House Chronicles, Richard Laymon; *Finding Satan*, Andrew Neiderman; *The Night School*, Michael Paine; The Abaddon Inn Series, Chris Blaine.

Harrow House • Haunted Houses • New York

Mischief. *New York: Leisure, 2000. 359p. ISBN 0843947667.*

Jim Hook learns of Harrow House's history firsthand when he is abducted by a hooded gang of his fellow students who are members of the Cadaver Society. Here he discovers, among other things, that Harrow House is the alma mater of a number of celebrity satanists.

Adolescence • High School • Religion—Satanism

The Infinite. *New York: Leisure, 2002, ©2001. 377p. ISBN 0843949279.*

Harrow House is visited by Chet Dillinger, Cali Nytbird, and Frost Crane, three psychics hired on behalf of the PSI Vista Foundation. Their unique talents make it possible to investigate a recent spate of grisly deaths in the mansion.

Parapsychology • Precognition

Nightmare House. *New York: Leisure, 2004, ©2002. 340p. ISBN 084395177X.*

This is the prequel to *The Infinite, Mischief* and *The Abandoned.* In 1926 Ethan Gravesend inherits Harrow House from his grandfather, who supposedly built the mansion on cursed land. When Ethan explores his new property, he discovers a literal skeleton in the closet, which turns out to be the source of all the malefic influence that will emanate from Harrow House through the decades.

Family Curse

The Necromancer: Being the Diary of Justin Gravesend on the Year of His Rebirth, and His Forced Initiation into the Chymera Magick, Including His Early Visionaries. *Forest Hill, MD: Cemetery Dance Publications, 2003. 134p. ISBN 1587670712.*

> This novella, written in diary format, tells about the early life of Justin Gravesend, the man who would go on to build Harrow House. Raised by a fire-and-brimstone preaching father, Justin leaves his country home in Wales to attend university and immerse himself in the decadence of London. In a brothel he meets the necromancer who introduces him to chimera magick and ultimately leads him to construct Harrow House.

> *Diary Format • England—London • Magic • Victorian Era • Wales*

The Abandoned. *New York: Leisure, 2005. 370p. ISBN 0843954108.*

> Harrow House, once a mansion and then a school, is now boarded up and abandoned. But some people cannot leave well enough alone. This is the case when someone new arrives in Watch Point and begins fixing up the old house, releasing the evil influence that is pent up inside. Soon after Harrow House is the site of a wild party, where the teenaged guests get out of hand. Ultimately a boy is found hanging in the cemetery.

> *Dreams • Human Sacrifice*

Desmond, Sean.

Adam's Fall. *New York: Thomas Dunne Books, 2000. 245p. ISBN 031226254X.*

> The unnamed occupant of B-46 in Adam's House is a Harvard senior, working on his English honors thesis so he can obtain a fellowship to study in England. But things change when his roommate catches him with his girlfriend and then commits suicide. The occupant begins to hear strange noises that on one could be causing. Then a shadow man emerges from the fog and begins to communicate with him, demonstrating knowledge of his deepest, darkest desires. **Similar titles:** *Needful Things*, Stephen King; *Stir of Echoes*, Richard Matheson; *Keepers*, Gary A. Braunbeck.

> *Academia • Massachusetts—Cambridge • Secret Sin • Suicide*

Due, Tananarive.

The Good House: A Novel. *New York: Atria, 2003. 482p. ISBN 0743449002.*

> Angela, a busy professional, brings her son Corey to her grandmother's rural home so they can spend the summer together and have a normal family life. But Corey inexplicably kills himself, and Angela doesn't return to her grandmother's house for three years. When she finally does come back, strange things begin to happen to her loved ones, making Angela realize the house harbors a terrible secret that she must decipher in order to live. **Similar titles:** *Tropic of Night*, Michael Gruber; *Nightmare House*,

1

2

3

4

5

6

7

8

9

10

Douglas Clegg; *Bag of Bones* and *The Shining*, Stephen King; *The Manor*; Scott Nicholson.

African American Characters • Family Curse • Religion—Voodoo • Revenging Revenant • Washington State

Gates, R. Patrick.

The Prison. *New York: Kensington-Pinnacle, 2004. 384p. ISBN 0786016396.*

Even the "big house" can be haunted. Tim Stage, fresh from the correctional officers' training facility, feels he is ready to walk the walls of The Hill. But he's been there before in disturbing dreams in which he wandered through the building's eerie hallways, dealing with the increasing madness of the inmates and the desires of deceased prisoners. **Similar titles:** *The Green Mile*, Stephen King; *Nazareth Hill*, Ramsey Campbell; *The Hidden*, Sarah Pinborough.

Dreams • Haunted Houses • Mental Illness • Prisons

Gresham, Stephen.

Haunted Ground. *New York: Pinnacle, 2003. 350p. ISBN 0786015373.*

(See chapter 14, "Psychological Horror: It's All in Your Head.")

Hawthorne, Nathaniel.

The House of Seven Gables. *New York: Oxford University Press, 1998, ©1851. 328p. ISBN 0192836455.*

(See chapter 14, "Psychological Horror: It's All in Your Head.")

Jackson, Shirley.

The Haunting of Hill House. *New York: Penguin, 2006, ©1949. 182p. ISBN 0143039989.*

Four people spend a weekend at Hill House to study the paranormal and find themselves haunted by a sinister spirit. To make matters worse, one of the guests, Eleanor, a shy young woman in her thirties, seems to be singled out by the "house." Jackson shows her mastery of storytelling and characterization in this classic of the genre, and *Hill House* is written in Jackson's characteristic effective third-person objective style. **Similar titles:** *Hell House*, Richard Matheson; *The Manor*, Scott Nicholson; *The Lottery and Other Stories*, Shirley Jackson; *The Haunting* (film).

Academia • Haunted Houses • New England • Parapsychology • Religion—Christianity—Protestantism • Suicide

King, Stephen.

Bag of Bones. *New York: Scribner, 1998. 529p. ISBN 0684853507.*

A thriller writer returns to his lake home in Maine to investigate his wife's death. In the process, he leaves himself open to visitations from various ghosts, one of which desires to destroy him and the entire town for a past evil committed by their ancestors. This vintage King is truly remarkable in its ability to frighten with subtlety. **Similar titles:** *Violin*, Anne Rice; *Beloved*, Toni Morrison; *The Good House* and *Joplin's Ghost*, Tananarive Due.

Haunted Houses • Maine • Racism • Rape • Secret Sin • Writer as Character

The Shining. *New York: Pocket Books, 2002, ©1977. ISBN 0743437497. 505p.*
(See chapter 7, "Demonic Possession: Satanism, Black Magic, and Witches and Warlocks: The Devil Made Me Do It.")

Laws, Stephen.

Darkfall. *New York: Dorchester, 2003, ©1992. 358p. ISBN 0843952180.*
A Christmas Eve party in a high-rise is marred when an impending storm causes all the residents in Fernley House, with the exception of the superintendent, to suddenly vanish. Could it be that the walls, doors, and floors have absorbed human beings? A secret government researcher may have the answers to this paranormal puzzle, if only he can prevent his team's being snatched up one by one. **Similar titles:** *The Overnight*, Ramsey Campbell; *Breathe*, Christopher Fowler; *The Resort*, Bentley Little.

Corporate Horror • England • Haunted Houses • Parallel Universes • Parapsychology • Weather • Weird Science

Laymon, Richard.

Friday Night in the Beast House. *London: Headline, 2007, ©1979. 154p. ISBN 9780755337644.*
(See chapter 11, "Maniacs and Sociopaths, or the Nuclear Family Explodes: Monstrous Malcontents Bury the Hatchet.")

The Midnight Tour. *New York: Leisure, 2007, ©1994. 596p. ISBN 0843957530.*
(See chapter 14, "Psychological Horror: It's All in Your Head.")

LeBlanc, Deborah.

A House Divided. *New York: Leisure, 2006. 326p. ISBN 0843957301.*
(See chapter 10, "Small Town Horror: Villages of the Damned.")

Masterton, Graham.

The House That Jack Built. *New York: Leisure, 2000, ©1996. 383p. ISBN 0843947462.*
(See chapter 7, "Demonic Possession: Satanism, Black Magic, and Witches and Warlocks: The Devil Made Me Do It.")

Matheson, Richard.

Hell House. *Sutton: Severn House, 2004, ©1971. 301p. ISBN 0727860992.*
A scholar and his students come to study the Belasco House, also known as Hell House, the most haunted place on Earth. Hell House, site of unimaginable decadence and cruelty during its original owner's lifetime, has

driven its inhabitants to madness, suicide, and murder. Can the professor and his helpers survive their stay in a dwelling no one has attempted to inhabit in twenty years? **Similar titles:** *The Haunting of Hill House*, Shirley Jackson; *Stir of Echoes*, Richard Matheson; *The Manor*, Scott Nicholson; *The Haunting* (film).

Academia • Haunted Houses • Parapsychology • Revenging Revenant • Secret Sin

Mittelmark, Howard.

Age of Consent. *New York: Signet, 2007. 307p. ISBN 0451220579.*

It looks like the perfect house in small town America, but its inhabitants are vindictive spirits that want nothing more than to coax a normal family, the Coulters, inside, and then encourage its members to experiment with sex, drugs, and self-mutilation. As his father frantically researches the house's past, Peter Coulter begins having sex and using hard drugs. His sister becomes depressed and begins hearing voices telling her to cut herself. **Similar titles:** *Nazareth Hill*, Ramsey Campbell; *Darkness Wakes*, Tim Waggoner; *The Exorcist*, William Peter Blatty.

Addictions—Drugs • Adolescence • Body Modification—Self-Mutilation • Haunted Houses • High School • Parenting • War—Vietnam War

Oliphant, Margaret.

The Library Window. *Edited by Elizabeth Winston. Tampa: University of Tampa Press, 2006, ©1896. 74p. ISBN 1597320129.*

The first volume in the <u>Insistent Visions</u> critical edition series of classic horror tales, this is the story of a young woman who becomes obsessed with a mysterious window while staying at her aunt's house in Scotland. Finally gathering enough courage to peer inside, she discovers a ghostly figure, which seems to be writing a manuscript. As her infatuation with the ghost grows, her health becomes more and more fragile. **Similar titles:** *Ghost Stories*, Henry James; *The Beckoning Fair One*, Oliver Onions; *Green Tea and Other Stories*, Joseph Sheridan Le Fanu.

Doppelgangers • Haunted Houses • Scotland • Victorian Era

Onions, Oliver.

The Beckoning Fair One. *Mineola, NY: Dover Publications, 2004, ©1911. 96p. ISBN 0486436470.*

In one of the most famous horror novellas of all time, a writer who moves into a haunted house finds himself becoming the target of the affections of a female ghost. At first the presence is subtle, but as it becomes more and more insistent, he loses contact with the outside world and is in danger of losing his grip on reality. **Similar titles:** *Carmilla*, Joseph Sheridan Le Fanu; *Earthbound*, Richard Matheson; *Within the Shadows*, Brandon Massey; *A Stir of Bones*, Nina Kiriki Hoffman.

England—London • Haunted Houses • Mental Illness • Victorian Era • Writer as Character

Pinborough, Sarah.

The Reckoning. *New York: Leisure, 2005. 338p. ISBN 0843955503.*

After Gina's mother murdered her father, the house on the family estate has stood empty. Now, twenty-five years later, Gina returns with two of her friends after another of their number suddenly commits suicide, only to discover how violently the house affects people. Told through flashbacks and foreshadowing, this novel has many subplots. **Similar titles:** *The Haunting of Hill House*, Shirley Jackson; *The Abandoned*, Douglas Clegg; *The House Next Door*, Anne River Siddons.

England • Family Curse • Haunted Houses • Suicide

Reeve, Clara.

The Old English Barron. *New York: Oxford, 2003, ©1805. 144p. ISBN 0192803271.*

This thoughtful and eerie adaptation of Walpole's *The Castle of Otranto* transfers the story to medieval England. Sir Philip Harclay returns home, only to discover that his old friends, Lord Lovel and his pregnant wife, are dead. Since then the estate has twice changed hands, and there is now a mysterious set of rooms that no one dare enter, except for a fearless peasant youth whom Harclay has taken under his wing. **Similar titles:** *The Castle of Otranto*, Horace Walpole; *Wieland*, Charles Brockden Brown; *Northanger Abbey*, Jane Austen; *The Monk*, Matthew Lewis.

Castles • England • Gothicism • Medieval Era • Revenging Revenant

Siddons, Anne Rivers.

The House Next Door. *New York: Pocket Star, 2007, ©1978. 336p. ISBN 1416544925.*

An upper-middle-class husband and wife living in the suburbs of Atlanta take turns narrating this tale of a house with a mind of its own. Colquitt and Walter Kennedy live in a charming, peaceful suburb where construction starts on the vacant lot next door. It seems an ambitious young architect endeavors to build the perfect modern home. But within just a few years, three different families that have inhabited the house meet with strange accidents and inexplicable mysteries. **Similar titles:** *The Keep*, Jennifer Egan; *The Reckoning*, Sarah Pinborough; *The Haunting of Hill House*, Shirley Jackson.

Frame Tale • Georgia—Atlanta • Haunted Houses • Marriage • Suburbia

Smith, Bryan.

Queen of Blood. *New York: Leisure, 2008. ISBN 0843960612.*
(See chapter 15, "Splatterpunk: The Gross Out.")

Straub, Peter.

Lost Boy, Lost Girl. *New York: Random, 2003. 281p. ISBN 1400060923.*
After his sister-in-law's inexplicable suicide, Tim Underhill returns to his hometown of Millhaven, Wisconsin, to help his brother and his nephew Mark. A few weeks later Mark disappears, and he is feared to have become the victim of a serial killer who has been snatching local teens from a park. But after his mother's suicide, Mark and his best friend Jimbo had

become obsessed with a local abandoned house, which unknown to him at the time, is connected to the Underhill family and is also the gateway of Millhaven's evil. **Similar titles:** *In the Night Room*, Peter Straub; *Black Creek Crossing*, John Saul; *The Beast House*; Richard Laymon; *Toybox*, Al Sarrantonio.

Haunted Houses • Underhill, Tim (character) • Wisconsin • Writer as Character

Wright, T. M.

The House on Orchid Street. *New York: Leisure, 2003. 322p. ISBN 0843950900.*

After looking at a Victorian mansion in the country, a young woman decides to purchase the house, not realizing that it once anchored a poor urban neighborhood and was the only house to survive a fire. As it turns out, this neighborhood was home to some rather strange characters: a morbidly obese nudist; a young boy who suffered a head injury; a teenaged boy who was periodically locked in a shed by an abusive mother; a young Latina mother who worked more than one job to support two children; and a large, mentally disabled man who accidentally killed people by hugging them too hard. **Similar titles:** *Looking Glass*, Rick Hautala; *The Two Sams*, Glen Hirshberg; *Dark Water*, Koji Suzuki; *Dark Water* (film).

Artist as Character • Haunted Houses • Marriage • Parapsychology • Police Officer as Character • Psychics

Film

Beloved. *Jonathan Demme, dir. 1998. 172 minutes.*

In Demme's eerie and atmospheric interpretation of Morrison's Pulitzer Prize–winning novel of the same name, escaped slave Sethe (Oprah Winfrey) does the unthinkable to keep her children from being put back into bondage: she tries to kill them all. She succeeds in freeing only her infant daughter Beloved in this manner, but Beloved will not lie quietly and instead returns twenty years later to destroy her entire family. Danny Glover also stars. **Similar titles:** *Beloved*, Toni Morrison; *Bag of Bones*, Stephen King; *Joplin's Ghost*, Tananarive Due.

African American Characters • Death—Grieving • Haunted Houses • Parenting • Revenging Revenant • Slavery

Bones. *Ernest R. Dickerson, dir. 2001. 96 minutes.*

Jimmy Bones, a benevolent gangsta who makes his living running numbers in his small black urban neighborhood, refuses to increase his income by becoming one of the first crack dealers of the 1970s. After Jimmy refuses on the grounds that he doesn't want to hurt the residents of his neighborhood, he is murdered by Lupovitch and a couple of his confederates. Twenty years later, Bones's boarded up house is turned into a night club, and the presence of Jeremiah's sons summons Bones's spirit—and he is angry. **Similar titles:** The Vampire Huntress Legend, L. A. Banks; *Mojo: Conjure Stories*, Nalo Hopkison (editor).

Addictions—Drugs • African American Characters • Organized Crime • Police Officer as Character • Revenging Revenant

Candyman. *Bernard Rose, dir. 1992. 99 minutes.*

Candyman is the embodiment of the urban legend about the Hook, an escaped lunatic with a hook for a hand who menaces young lovers in compromising positions. And when two graduate students attempt to unearth the legend of Candyman, they find the real revenant, a black man who was lynched in the 1890s for miscegenation and now exacts revenge on those who would doubt his existence. This artistic movie is based on "The Forbidden" by Clive Barker and stars Virginia Madsen and Tony Todd, with a soundtrack scored by Philip Glass. **Similar titles:** *One Rainy Night*, Richard Laymon; *Havoc Swims Jaded*, David J. Schow.

African American Characters • Housing Projects • Illinois—Chicago • Popular Culture—Urban Legends • Racism • Reincarnation • Revenging Revenant

Dark Water. *Walter Salles, dir. 2005. 105 minutes.*

Newly divorced mother Dahlia reenters the workforce to find affordable and reasonably safe housing for herself and her daughter. This is how she ends up in a hideous apartment complex on Rikers Island. Through a hall that could lead to the darkest dungeon ever imagined is a ninth-floor apartment with tiny rooms and ugly paint. But when a stain that looks like an oozing sore appears in Ceci's bedroom and pieces of black hair come out of the faucet, Dahlia realizes that there is something wrong with the building—something far worse than poor maintenance. **Similar titles:** *Dark Water* and *The Ring*, Koji Suzuki.

Child Molesters • New York—New York City • Parenting • Revenging Revenant

Ghost Story. *John Irvin, dir. 1981. 110 minutes.*

Fred Astaire, Melvyn Douglas, Douglas Fairbanks Jr., and John Houseman star in this adaptation of Peter Straub's novel about a vengeful ghost. The four elderly men harbor a secret from their youth: their involvement in the accidental death of Eva Galli, a beautiful young secretary. Now their pasts have come back to haunt them, as Galli's ghost is out for revenge. Although subtle in its entirety, Irvin's film includes some truly scary moments. Patricia Neal and a young Alice Krige also star. **Similar titles:** *Ghost Story*, Peter Straub; *Bag of Bones*, Stephen King; *Spirit*, Graham Masterton.

New England • Revenging Revenant • Secret Sin • Septuagenarians

The Haunting. *Richard Wise, dir. 1963. (black and white). 112 minutes.*

This eerie and faithful version of Shirley Jackson's *The Haunting of Hill House* is considered a classic among horror film lovers. Although the film lacks the special effects found in most of today's blockbusters, fine acting and good direction make it very chilling and atmospheric. Julie Harris and Claire Bloom star. **Similar titles:** *The Haunting of Hill House*, Shirley Jackson; *Hell House*, Richard Matheson.

Haunted Houses • New England • Parapsychology • Religion—Christianity—Protestantism • Suicide

J. D.'s Revenge. *Arthur Marks, dir. 1976. 95 minutes.*

(See chapter 7, "Demonic Possession: Satanism, Black Magic, and Witches and Warlocks: The Devil Made Me Do It.")

1 2 3 4 5 6 7 8 9 10

Nightmare on Elm Street. *Wes Craven, dir. 1984. 91 minutes.*

Freddy Krueger, a school janitor who molested children, eludes conviction due to a technicality; so a posse of enraged parents burn him to death. But the ghost of Freddy returns, entering their children's dreams and causing them to die hideous deaths. Robert Englund and a very young Johnny Depp star. **Similar titles:** *Freddy vs. Jason*, Stephen Hand et al.; *Feral*, Brian Knight.

Child Molester • Dreams • Krueger, Freddy (character) • Revenging Revenant • Secret Sin • Vigilantism

The Others. *Alejandro Amenebar, dir. 2001. 101 minutes.*

At the close of World War II, Grace (Nicole Kidman) and her photo-allergic children live in an isolated and sprawling mansion on the isle of Jersey, waiting for her husband to return from battle. Cut off from civilization and even from electricity, the small family lives with only the help of three mysterious servants, who serendipitously appeared a week after the previous help departed in the middle of the night with no explanation. Soon after the children claim to see strange people in the house, and Grace herself finds furniture disturbed and locked doors left open. This fine film is gothic and atmospheric. **Similar titles:** *The Haunting of Hill House*, Shirley Jackson; *The Servants*, Michael Marshall Smith.

Afterlife, The • Death—Grieving • England • Gothicism • Haunted Houses • Parapsychology • War—World War II

Poltergeist. *Tobe Hooper, dir. 1982. 114 minutes.*

A developer and his wife discover that their brand-new suburban home is haunted when their daughter is snatched by one of the poltergeists she communicates with through the television. But it's not enough to hire a medium to journey to the spirit world to retrieve their daughter; the family must also discover the reason for the haunting in the first place. **Similar titles:** *The House That Jack Built*, Graham Masterton; *Dead Lines*, Greg Bear.

California • Haunted Houses • Multimedia—Television • Parenting • Poltergeists • Psychics • Revenging Revenant • Suburbia

The Ring. *Gore Verbinski, dir. 2002. 115 minutes.*

Several teenagers watch a strange tape they find in a VCR instead of the football game they thought they had recorded. Each dies horribly within a week of having watched the recording. One of those teens is the niece of reporter Rachel Keller, who puts herself in harm's way when she investigates the source of the tape. *The Ring* is a disturbing and original ghost story, and you will want to sleep with the lights on after you watch it. **Similar titles:** *Ring* and *Dark Water*, Koji Suzuki.

Journalist as Character • Multimedia—Videotape • Parenting • Revenging Revenant • Washington—Seattle

Ringu. *Hideo Nakata, dir. 1998. 96 minutes.*

A group of teenagers watch a videotape that seems like a bad art house film but has a curse at the end. They all die horribly a week later, seemingly frightened to death. The tape becomes an urban myth, and a reporter investigates. *Ringu* was made for Japanese television from Koji Suzuki's enormously popular novel of the same name (*Ring* in English). **Similar titles:** *Ring* and *Dark Water*, Koji Suzuki.

Japan • Journalist as Character • Multimedia—Videotape • Revenging Revenant

The Shining. *Stanley Kubrick, dir. 1980. 146 minutes.*
(See chapter 7, "Demonic Possession: Satanism, Black Magic, and Witches and Warlocks: The Devil Made Me Do It.")

The Sixth Sense. *M. Night Shyamalan, dir, 1999. 107 minutes.*
Bruce Willis stars as a child psychologist who must help a little boy come to terms with his special gift: he sees dead people. During the course of the child's therapy, Willis's character learns the truth about himself. The fine film is chilling and original. **Similar titles:** *The Awakening*, Donna Boyd; *Dead Lines*, Greg Bear; *The Servants*, Michael Marshall Smith.

Afterlife, The • Childhood • Gothicism • Haunted Houses • Parallel Universes • Pennsylvania— Philadelphia • Psychologist/Psychiatrist as Character

Two Thousand Maniacs! *Herschell Gordon Lewis, dir. 1964. 87 minutes.*
(See chapter 10, "Small Town Horror: Villages of the Damned.")

What Lies Beneath. *Robert Zemeckis, dir. 2000. 130 minutes.*
When Claire Spenser begins hearing voices and seeing strange faces in her lakeside home, she believes at first that the house is haunted by the ghost of her neighbor. But her neighbor isn't dead; she is just absent after a blow-up with her spouse. Now Claire's husband believes that she's suffering a mental breakdown brought about by their only daughter's leaving for college or her going through "the change." But Claire continues to investigate, and with the help of the ghost, discovers the truth about her husband. **Similar titles:** *Bag of Bones*, Stephen King; *Looking Glass*, A. J. Matthews; *The Year of Things Past*, M. A. Harper.

Haunted Houses • Marriage • Music • Revenging Revenant • Secret Sin • Vermont

June's Picks

Books: Tananarive Due, *The Good House* (Atria); Nina Kiriki Hoffman, *A Stir of Bones* (Viking); Shirley Jackson, *The Haunting of Hill House* (Penguin); Graham Masterton, *Spirit* (Leisure); Richard Matheson, *Stir of Echoes* (Tor)

Films: *Bones, Candyman, The Haunting, Nightmare on Elm Street, The Ring*

Tony's Picks

Books: Ramsey Campbell, *Nazareth Hill* (Forge); Shirley Jackson, *The Haunting of Hill House* (Penguin); Stephen King, *Bag of Bones* (Scribner); Toni Morrison, *Beloved* (Knopf)

Films: *Bones, Candyman, Dark Water, The Ring*

Chapter 5

Golem, Mummies, and Zombies: Wake the Dead and They'll Be Cranky

Common to all cultures are burial customs that are more than just accepted methods of sanitary body disposal; according to some folklore, these customs are supposed to ensure that the dead stay that way, to prevent them from walking, in body and in spirit, among the living. As a matter of fact, burial customs have historically been important throughout the world. Ancient Egyptians took great care in making sure that their dead rulers, who were thought to be divine, could successfully make the journey from this world to the next. Not only were the bodies carefully preserved through mummification, but the tomb was also stocked with everything the dead would need in the next world, such as food and slaves. Furthermore, precautions were taken against invaders who might derail this journey. The various curses to protect the gravesites of the pharaohs became so well known and ingrained in popular culture that they inform most of the stories surrounding Howard Carter's discovery of King Tut's tomb in 1922. Carter's death from lymphoma in 1924, soon after he opened Tut's tomb, was rumored to have been caused by the curse protecting the boy pharaoh's resting place.

Modern stories concerned with Egyptian mummies create monsters from the dead for whom all precautions weren't taken, and who, when unearthed by naive archeologists centuries later, are cursed to roam the earth in search of what they need to rest. This is the case with three works entitled *The Mummy*: the 1932 Universal Studios film starring Boris Karloff, the 1999 comic action adventure film (annotated in chapter 16 but referenced here), and Anne Rice's novel *The Mummy, or Ramses the Damned*. In each instance, the mummy of the title was denied the proper rites of burial to ensure a peaceful passage into the next world, so when he is unearthed, he is doomed to a living death—until he can either find a specified item that he needs to rest eternally or enact revenge on the person who dared disturb his resting place. Similarly, the modern burial rite, as depicted in horror fiction, must ensure these same types of precautions. When they are not taken, the results can be even more disastrous. The dead can literally rise, either as ghosts to haunt the living, or worse still, in disgusting corporeal form, altered by maggots and decay. Both ghosts and zombies usually seek revenge on the living who disappointed or angered them.

Furthermore, it isn't just the royal dead who can be roused from their eternal slumbers. Even the average Joe or Jane Doe may become a reanimated corpse, if circumstances are favorable for the creation of zombies. Whether the dead are purposefully reanimated, as is the case in H. P. Lovecraft's novella *Herbert West: Re-Animator*, or reanimated by accident, as in George Romero's <u>Night of the Living Dead Series</u>, in which the newly deceased rise from their graves possibly due to radiation released by a recent space probe, they are always dangerous to the living. In Lovecraft's novella, the reanimated dead are far from happy that Herbert West has given them a second chance at "life," and they eventually take their revenge on the author of their misery. In *Night of the Living Dead*, the newly deceased return to life imbued with an insatiable desire for human flesh. Throughout Romero's <u>Night of the Living Dead Series</u>, we never learn the precise cause of the zombie apocalypse. However, various theories are bandied about, including everything from a radiation leak from a recent space probe to the arrival of the Rapture. In Stephen King's *Pet Sematary*, if the bereaved are unable to accept the death of a loved one, the latter can be interred in the Micmac burying ground, a place once hallowed by the Micmac tribe, but which has since been profaned by white people. Buried here, the dead return bodily. But just as in W. W. Jacob's famous short story "The Monkey's Paw," the dead are in no physical condition to resume their lives among the living. In "The Monkey's Paw," an inconsolable couple rashly wish on the cursed object of the title, asking that their recently departed son, killed in a factory accident, be allowed to live again. But once the father realizes that the son's visage will be mangled, he must use his remaining wish to return the son to his final resting place. The protagonist of *Pet Sematary* lacks this sagacity and learns the hard way that it's a very bad idea to raise the dead since, similar to George R. Romero's zombies, the reanimated are bent on the destruction of their loved ones.

But what about the resuscitated dead themselves? How do they feel about this whole ordeal? A few writers have tackled that question. Edgar Allan Poe's story "The Facts in the Case of M. Valdemar" and H. P. Lovecraft's *Herbert West: Re-animator* explore the physical pain caused when the dead are returned to life. The nameless narrator of Poe's tale hypnotizes a man on his death bed and manages to communicate with his greatly distressed spirit for several months, keeping the body intact. The conversations he has with M. Valdemar indicate that a living death is in no way desirable. The narrator must eventually break contact, and the body putrefies in a matter of moments, right before his eyes. It is similarly clear that mad scientist Herbert West causes great pain to his subjects through his experiments with mortality.

The golem, or human made out of clay, is another manifestation of the reanimated dead. But unlike mummies or zombies, the golem was never a human being with a soul. Instead, its creator bypassed the natural process of reproduction and artificially created something monstrous that will ultimately attempt to destroy its maker. You might say that, in biblical terms, Adam was the first golem, but because he was created by God, his creation was not considered unnatural. The original man-made golem comes from a sixteenth-century Jewish folktale in which Rabbi Judah Loew, the Maharal, creates a large man of clay to protect residents of the Prague ghetto of Josefov from anti-Semitic attacks. The problem with the original golem was that it had no soul and, like many children, it became insolent and demanding, ultimately turning on the congregation and its creator; so it had to be disabled and entombed. The story of the golem first appeared in print in 1847 in a collection of Jewish tales entitled *Galerie der Sippurim*, and in 1909 a fictional account was published by Yudl Rosenberg. Of course, the most famous literary and folkloric golem is found in Mary Shelley's classic novel *Frankenstein*, in which Victor Frankenstein's creature is assembled from parts stolen from the local charnel house. Instead of making a god among men as he intended, Dr. Frankenstein forms a creature so hideous that all run from it, and even its creator cannot love it. The subsequently tormented and lonely creature finally seeks to destroy his maker out of desperation. Contemporary golem stories range from murderous fictional characters brought to life by authors (ultimately taking corporeal form), as in Stephen King's *The Dark Half*, to an assassin cloned from stolen DNA who is drawn to his genetic "twin," believing the original human had appropriated his life, as is the case in Dean Koontz's *Mr. Murder*. In the 1956 film *Invasion of the Body Snatchers* (annotated in chapter 12), the living are replaced not by men (or women) of clay, but by golem formed from alien plant matter.

If the reanimated dead are cranky, they are also a powerful metaphor for a second universal human fear—being controlled by others. The zombie is a particularly apt representation of this fear. The zombie was not born in Romero's 1968 *Night of the Living Dead*, but in Haitian lore. Bokurs, "witch doctors" who practice a sinister form of voodoo, are reputed to drug the living in order to put them in a coma that resembles death, only to revive them after they have been buried and use them for manual labor and criminal activity. The drug attacks the central nervous system in such a way that after the victim is revived, he or she has no free will and can only be directed to do the simplest of tasks. It has yet to be determined whether the creation of zombies through these means is folklore, as chronicled in William Seabrook's 1929 travelogue *The Magic Island*, or has some basis in scientific fact, as claimed by ethno-botanist Wade Davis in his 1985 book *The Serpent and the Rainbow*. Soon after the publication of Seabrook's travelogue, the figure of the zombie regained its toehold in the American popular consciousness. The first zombie film, Victor Halpern's *White Zombie* (1931), represents the "living dead" as created through a combination of toxic compounds and black magic. The film owes a good deal to Seabrook's account of the practice. In *White Zombie*, Creole Haitian zombie master Murder Legendre uses his mostly black living dead to toil in the sugar mills. But when Legendre uses his powers to deprive a virginal white woman of her free will and presumably her ability to preserve her virtue, he has gone too far for the white people on the island, and he must be stopped. *Invasion of the Body Snatchers* explores Cold War anxieties about communism, which is represented as an ideological system under which people are transformed via "thought control" into mindless automatons whose identity is completely subordinated to that of the state. Danny Boyle's film *28 Days Later* (annotated in chapter 13 but also listed here) recontextualizes and combines two horror types, the werewolf and the zombie, to create mindless undead creatures not as reanimated corpses, but as quick-moving, living human beings whose minds have been horribly altered by a virus that wipes away all conscious thought and makes its hosts subject to primal anger, leaving them compelled to tear asunder all uninfected humans.

Ultimately, narratives about golem, mummies, and reanimated stalkers touch upon contemporary questions about life itself. Should people who are in persistent vegetative states, such as Terri Shaivo, be permitted to die? Are people like Jack Kevorkian angels of mercy or murderers when they help the terminally ill to end their lives before they lose the ability to control their bodies or think rationally? If life begins at conception, can a twenty-year-old be prosecuted for underage drinking, since he could be considered nine months older than the age represented on his birth certificate? The answers to all of these questions reside in our own personal beliefs about life itself, which is usually defined as more than simply possessing vital signs. Don Coscarelli's 2002 film *Bubba Ho-Tep* (annotated in chapter 16 but referenced here) explores the eternal existential question—what is the purpose of life? *Bubba Ho-Tep* juxtaposes the reanimated mummy of the title with the elderly and infirm inhabitants of a nursing home. In life, Bubba Ho-Tep was cursed to eternal torment when he was buried without his names, which prevented him from passing into the afterlife and compelled him to prolong his liminal existence by stealing the souls of the living. Bubba Ho-Tep has found the proverbial nest on the ground in an East Texas nursing home, where the forgotten inhabitants have been stripped of their legal ability to determine their fates and are warehoused, to await death without bothering their loved ones overmuch. The residents' lack of agency and the maintenance of their deteriorating bodies through medical science for no greater reason than to prolong life demonstrates the zombie narrative's preoccupation with questions about the definition of life. The comic zombie film *Shaun of the Dead* (annotated in chapter 16 but referenced here) likewise focuses on the meaning of life: when the living lead a bland and monotonous existence, the sudden appearance of the walking dead among them is merely redundant. Finally, David Wellington's Monster Nation Trilogy, set in a post-apocalyptic world, is also concerned with existential questions. When the dead return to life, the complex workings of civilization, such as government and capitalist networks of supplies, rapidly collapse, simplifying existence for the remaining living, who are now more preoccupied with getting enough to eat while not becoming dinner for a zombie, rather than with what's on television or whether their smiles are as white as they can be.

The appeals of the golem or mummy/zombie story are very similar to those of the ghost and haunted house story, as both types of monsters are metaphoric representations of the universal fear of the dead returning to haunt the living, whether justified in their return (because of some crime or insult committed against them while they were alive) or unjustified. Perhaps this stems from the visceral fear of dead bodies themselves, which may be the impetus behind the fear of cemeteries that can be found in most cultures. Where the zombie is concerned, there may be a fear of the loss of autonomy; no one wants to have his or her will completed controlled by another person, and this would be especially true of Americans, who pride themselves on individualism and free will. Finally, certain golem tales appeal to that part of the human psyche that aggrandizes the idea of creation for its own sake. Most human beings would enjoy "playing God" if they were given the chance, which would include the ability to animate and reanimate humans and humanoid creatures.

Note: Readers who enjoy titles in this chapter can find other stories about golem, mummies, and zombies in Chapter 18, "Collections and Anthologies." The subject/keyword index contains references to specific titles under the keywords *Mummies* and *Zombies*.

Bailey, Hilary, and Mary Shelley.

Frankenstein's Bride and Frankenstein. *Naperville, IL: Landmark, 2007,* *©1995 and 1818. 236p. + 253p. ISBN 1402208707.*

This sequel to Mary Shelley's *Frankenstein*, which also includes the text of that novel, is set in 1825 London. Victor Frankenstein has befriended a wealthy young Englishman and has taken an interest in Maria Clementi, a music hall singer who is mysteriously mute when she is not on stage. Victor, ever the mad scientist, plots to cure her muteness. Meanwhile, an unknown assailant launches serial attacks on him and his family, killing Frankenstein's wife and child. **Similar titles:** *The Secret Life of Laszlo, Count Dracula*, Roderick Anscombe; *Resurrection Men*, T. K. Welsh; *Dracula* and *The Jewel of Seven Stars*, Bram Stoker.

Alternative Literature • England—London • Frankenstein, Victor (character) • Frankenstein's Monster • Revenge • Weird Science

Braunbeck, Gary A.

Mr. Hands. *New York: Leisure, 2007. 269p. ISBN 0843956100.*
(See chapter 8, "Mythological Monsters and 'The Old Ones': Invoking the Dark Gods.")

Brooks, Max.

World War Z: An Oral History of the Zombie War. *New York: Three Rivers Press, 2007. 352p. ISBN 0307346617.*

The son of comedian Mel Brooks recounts how in the near future, civilization is destroyed by zombies. The novel recounts humanity's last stand by piecing together the accounts of the remaining survivors, including a Chinese scientist who explains how his government suppressed accounts of the outbreak soon after he encountered one of the first known zombies. **Similar titles:** <u>The Monster Nation Trilogy</u>, David Wellington; <u>The Rising Series</u>, Brian Keene; *The Zombie Survival Guide: Complete Protection from the Living Dead*, Max Brooks; *Fido* (film).

Apocalypse • Documentary Techniques • Futurism • Zombies

The Zombie Survival Guide: Complete Protection from the Living Dead. *New York: Three Rivers Press, 2003. 254p. ISBN 1400049628.*
(See chapter 16, "Comic Horror: Laughing at Our Fears.")

Cave, Hugh B.

The Mountains of Madness. *Baltimore, MD: Cemetery Dance Publications, 2004. 157p. ISBN 1587670690.*

The lives of two Americans, writer Janice Hall and businessman Dan Colby, intersect on the Caribbean island of St. Joseph after Dan wakes up disoriented in a graveyard near the coffee plantation he has just leased. Janice has come to the island in search of her family's roots before a slave revolt. Soon unsettling signs of voodoo begin appearing all over the plantation, scaring Dan's workers and giving him and Janice nightmares. An engaging read from a master of pulp writing. **Similar titles:** *The Restless Dead*, Hugh B. Cave; *Darkfall*, Dean Koontz; *From a Whisper to a Scream*, Charles De Lint.

African American Characters • Dreams • Religion—Voodoo • Slavery

Cheiro (Count Louis Hamon).

A Study of Destiny. *Edited by Sean Donnelly. Tampa: University of Tampa Press, 2006, ©1898. 92p. ISBN 1597320145.*

In this novella an Englishman teams with an elderly German archeologist to explore Egyptian tombs. While on an excavation, the two spot a mysterious stranger hanging around one of the tombs, and against their better judgment, they decide to investigate. This is the second volume in the <u>Insistent Visions</u> critical edition series of classic horror tales. **Similar titles:** *The Jewel of Seven Stars*, Bram Stoker; *The Complete John Silence Stories*, Algernon Blackwood; *Ghost Stories of an Antiquary*, M. R. James.

Archeology • Egypt • Mummies • Victorian Era

Clark, Simon.

Death's Dominion. *New York: Leisure, 2006. 342p. ISBN 0843954930.*

(See chapter 12 "Technohorror: Evil Hospitals, Military Screw-Ups, Mad Scientists, and Alien Invasions.")

Frank, Gary.

Forever You Will Suffer. *Palm Beach, FL: Medallion Press, 2006. 418p. ISBN 1932815694.*

Rich Summers takes a cab to visit the graves of his mother and sister. Upon returning to the cab, he finds that his driver has been replaced by a zombie, who kidnaps him and deposits him at the home of his ex-girlfriend Katrina. But Katrina is missing, and as soon as Rich learns this, her house becomes another dimension where past events and alternate realities take over. **Similar titles:** *Matinee at the Flame*, Christopher Fahy; <u>The Love Story Series</u>, Christopher Moore; *Beloved*, J. F. Gonzales.

Demons • Parallel Universes • Reincarnation • Zombies

Greatshell, Walter.

Xombies. *New York: Berkley, 2004. 346p. ISBN 0425197441.*

(See chapter 12, "Technohorror: Evil Hospitals, Military Screw-Ups, Mad Scientists, and Alien Invasions.")

Irvine, Alexander C.

The Narrows. *New York: Del Rey, 2005. 341p. ISBN 0345466985.*

A childhood injury prevents Jared Cleaves from serving in the military during World War II, so he finds himself helping Uncle Sam by working in a factory instead. Jared becomes involved in the Ford golem production line, better known as the "Frankenline." Eventually Jared finds himself trying to discover the supernatural force that lurks beneath the city itself. **Similar titles:** *Necropolis*, Tim

Waggoner; *World War Z: An Oral History of the Zombie War*, Max Brooks; The Monster Nation Trilogy, David Wellington; *Fido* (film).

Automotive Industry • Michigan—Detroit • Subterranean Horror • War—World War II

1

Keene, Brian.

Dead Sea. *New York: Leisure, 2007. 337p. ISBN 084395860X.*

A virus infects the rat population of New York City, but rather than kill off the vermin, it thrives within them and then begins spreading, ultimately to the human population. After one bite, or one quick exchange of even the minutest drop of blood or saliva, a human instantly dies, and just as instantly resuscitates as a mindless, flesh-eating zombie. Lamar Reed, a young gay man, must make a harrowing journey through the carnage that Baltimore has become. **Similar titles:** *Peeps*, Scott Westerfield; *I Am Legend*, Richard Matheson; *Manitou Blood*, Graham Masterton; *28 Days Later* (film).

Apocalypse • Epidemics • Futurism • Gay/Lesbian/Bisexual Characters • New England • Zombies

2

3

4

Ghoul. *New York: Leisure, 2007. 341p. ISBN 0843956445.*

Three teenaged boys, Timmy, Barry, and Doug, are looking forward to the summer of 1984. After all, what could be better than summer vacation? What the three don't know is that something will begin digging up bodies in the local cemetery located near their clubhouse, and that ghoul also wants live women to breed with. The boys' summer plans will have to be put on hold because it turns out that one of their fathers is supplying the creature with females. **Similar titles:** *The Traveling Vampire Show*, Richard Laymon; *Possessions* and *Rabid Growth*, James A. Moore; The Beast House Chronicles, Richard Laymon.

Adolescence • Cemeteries • Families • High School

5

6

🎗 **The Rising Series.**

The dead are returning to life, and civilization comes to a grinding halt as all remaining humans devote most of their time to not being eaten. This task is more difficult than it seems, because the reanimated dead are highly intelligent. **Similar titles:** The Monster Nation Trilogy, David Wellington; *Necropolis*, Tim Waggoner; The Night of the Living Dead Series (film).

Apocalypse • Zombies

7

8

The Rising. *New York: Leisure, 2003. 321p. ISBN 0843952016.*

Jim Thurmond, a construction worker in West Virginia, is one of the few who has survived the zombie attack; he's been holed up in a shelter constructed some years earlier for the predicted failure of the world due to Y2K.

Appalachia • Weird Science • West Virginia

9

City of the Dead. *New York: Leisure, 2005. 357p. ISBN 0843954159.*

The reanimated dead are now possessed by demons that are angry at God for attempting to banish them to The Void. Meanwhile, resurrection is not confined to humans: dogs, cats, and other animals

10

are also reanimated—and are also hungry. In the midst of this chaos, a band of survivors attempts to live to see another day while barricaded in a Manhattan skyscraper.

Animals Run Rampant • Demons • New York—New York City

King, Stephen.

The Dark Half. *New York: Viking, 1989. 431p. ISBN 067082982X.*
Thad Beaumont, best-selling author of slasher novels, would like to say he has nothing to do with the series of monstrous murders that keep coming closer to his home. But how can he disown the ultimate embodiment of evil that goes by the name of one of his characters and signs its crimes with Thad's bloody fingerprints? **Similar titles:** *Mr. Murder*, Dean Koontz; *Dr. Jekyll and Mr. Hyde*, Robert Louis Stevenson; *Mr. X*, Peter Straub; *Fight Club* (film).

Maine—Castle Rock • Police Officer as Character • Serial Killers • Writer as Character

Pet Sematary. *London: Hodder & Stoughton, 1984. 417p. ISBN 0340341483.*
When his son's cat is hit by a car, Louis Creed doesn't want to expose his child to the grim realities of death at his tender age. Over a few beers, a helpful neighbor tells Louis about the Micmac burying ground, which has the power to reanimate the dead. Then his son is killed by a speeding truck, and since he can't accept the boy's death either, he puts him in the Micmac burying ground as well. As a result, the boy becomes a dangerous zombie. **Similar titles:** *Herbert West: Re-animator*, H. P. Lovecraft; *Magic Terror*, Peter Straub; *Re-animator* (film).

Death—Grieving • Maine • Physician as Character • Religion—Native American • Zombies

Knight, J.

Risen. *New York: Kensington, 2004. 407p. ISBN 0786016124.*
A battered woman kills her husband, only to have him return from the dead and forgive her. A deputy is accidentally shot, and he also resurrects. In a small town, the dead are rising from their graves—and promptly going back to their old lives, as better people. A reporter, his love interest, and her son suspect that the risen all become devoted to the god Seth. But what exactly is this ancient god's plan for humankind? **Similar titles:** *The Mummy, or Ramses the Damned*, Anne Rice; *The Harvest*, Scott Nicholson; *The Stupidest Angel*, Christopher Moore.

Journalist as Character • Religion—Ancient Egyptian • Zombies

Koontz, Dean.

Mr. Murder. *New York: Berkley Books, 1993. 376p. ISBN 0399138749.*
Marty Stillwater, well-known writer of murder mysteries, is being stalked by Alfie, his double, a genetically engineered hit man who, unknown to Marty, was cloned from his DNA. Alfie is psychically drawn to Stillwater, believing that the original from which he was cloned has stolen his life and memories. Alfie aims to get them back. **Similar titles:** *The Dark Half*, Stephen King; *Frankenstein*, Mary Shelley; *Dr. Jekyll and Mr. Hyde*, Robert Louis Stevenson.

California • Cloning • Organized Crime • Serial Killers • Writer as Character

Koontz, Dean, and Edward Gorman.

Dean Koontz's Frankenstein (series).

Victor Frankenstein is alive and well in the twenty-first century, only now he is known as Victor Helios, a biotech multimillionaire. Finding humanity terribly flawed, he seeks to replace human beings with preprogrammed personalities that only he can control. **Similar titles:** *Frankenstein's Bride*, Hilary Bailey; *Frankenstein*, Mary Shelley; *Mr. Murder*, Dean Koontz; *The Dark Half*, Stephen King.

Alternative Literature • Frankenstein, Victor (character) • Futurism • Louisiana—New Orleans • Police Officer as Character • Replicants

Prodigal Son. *London: HarperCollins, 2005. 400p. ISBN 0007203136.*

In Book I of Dean Koontz's Frankenstein trilogy, one of Frankenstein's creations decides it wants the perfect bride, so the creature figures the best way to accomplish this goal is to take various parts of different women—who aren't quite dead yet.

Serial Killers

City of Night. *London: HarperCollins, 2005. 474p. ISBN 0007203128.*

In this second book of the trilogy, Victor Frankenstein is in New Orleans, since there is no better place than the voodoo capitol to create not one, but an entire race of manufactured humans. One such creature, Victor's bodyguard Deucalion, now both ethically and morally humanized, realizes that the race is prone to mutations that cause them to become killers of humans.

Marriage

Langan, Sarah.

The Keeper. *New York: HarperTorch, 2006. 382p. ISBN 006087290X.*
(See chapter 10, "Small Town Horror: Villages of the Damned.")

The Missing. *New York: Harper, 2007. 400p. ISBN 0060872918.*
(See chapter 13, "Ecological Horror: Mother Nature Has Her Revenge.")

Laymon, Richard.

To Wake the Dead. *New York: Leisure, 2003. 386p. ISBN 0843951044.*

Amara, once a princess of Egypt, has her eternal slumber disturbed 4,000 years later by a band of archeologists. Brought to California to be displayed in a museum, Amara goes on a murderous rampage. *To Wake the Dead* was originally published as *Amara* in the UK, where Richard Laymon was immensely popular during the 1990s. **Similar titles:** *Queen of the Damned* and *The Mummy, or Ramses the Damned*, Anne Rice; *The Jewel of Seven Stars*, Bram Stoker; *The Mummy* (film, 1932); *The Mummy* (film, 1999).

California • Mummies • Religion—Ancient Egyptian • Revenging Revenant

Little, Bentley.

The Burning. *New York: Signet, 2006. 391p. ISBN 0451219147.*
(See chapter 17, "Everyday Horror: When the Mundane Becomes Monstrous.")

Lovecraft, H[oward]. P[ierce].

Herbert West, Reanimator and Other Stories. *Whitefish, MT: Kessinger, 2004. 250p. ISBN 1419123475.*

Ever since his student days at Miskatonic University, Herbert West has been consumed by the drive to reanimate the dead. In this novella, his nameless assistant chronicles the progress of his friend's gruesome experiments, which ultimately result in West's demise. The tale has been widely anthologized, and Stewart Gordon's 1985 film *Re-animator* is a comic interpretation. **Similar titles:** *Pet Sematary*, Stephen King; *Frankenstein*, Mary Shelley; Dean Koontz's Frankenstein, Dean Koontz and Edward Gorman; *Re-animator* (film).

African American Characters • Afterlife, The • Massachusetts—Arkham • Miskatonic University • Physician as Character • Weird Science • West, Herbert (character) • Zombies

McKinney, Joe.

Dead City. *New York: Pinnacle, 2006. 288p. ISBN 0786017813.*

A series of brutal hurricanes that devastate the Gulf Coast send a flood of refugees to San Antonio. But nature's fury has done something far worse than displace a large human population—it has also caused them to be infected with a virus that turns them into zombies. Soon all signs of civilization, such as electricity and a working communications system, disappear, and the living find themselves outnumbered. **Similar titles:** The Monster Nation Trilogy, David Wellington; *City of the Dead* and *Dead Sea*, Brian Keene; *28 Days Later* (film); *28 Weeks Later* (film).

Epidemics • Louisiana—New Orleans • Police Officer as Character • Popular Culture • Texas—San Antonio • Epidemics—Viruses • Weather

Nicholson, Scott.

The Harvest. *New York: Pinnacle-Kensington, 2003. 383p. ISBN 0786015799.*
(See chapter 12, "Technohorror: Evil Hospitals, Military Screw-Ups, Mad Scientists, and Alien Invasions.)

Paffenroth, Kim.

Dying to Live: A Novel of Life among the Undead. *Mena, AZ: Permuted Press, 2006. 192p. ISBN 097897073X.*

In a functional, post-zombie society, Jonah Caine happens upon an enclave barricaded in a museum. The inhabitants eagerly help him escape the pursuing zombies and welcome him to the safety of their compound, where he is told that even if he is infected, he will be treated humanely. Jonah and his fellow survivors discover something worse than zombies—another post-zombie society that is barricaded in a prison and run by the most viscous of inmates. **Similar titles:** The

<u>Monster Nation Trilogy</u>, David Wellington; *Dead Sea*, Brian Keene; *World War Z*, Max Brooks; *Land of the Dead* (film), *Fido* (film).

Apocalypse • Futurism • Prisons • Zombies

Paine, Michael.

The Mummy: Dark Resurrection. *Milwaukie, OR: Dark Horse Books, 2006. 297p. ISBN 1595820523.*

Josh Brandt is self-absorbed, foolhardy, and at times stupid. His grandfather and father were both Egyptologists who died at the hands of Imhotep, the legendary mummy who walks cursed, and Brandt attempts to follow in the footsteps of his ancestors by financing a dig in search of a long-lost tomb of a princess named Ankh-es-en-Amun, the heart's desire of Imhotep, thus unleashing the ultimate curse—painful and horrifying death—on many in his party. **Similar titles:** *Queen of the Damned* and *The Mummy, or Ramses the Damned*, Anne Rice; *The Jewel of Seven Stars*, Bram Stoker; *To Wake the Dead*, Richard Laymon; *The Mummy* (film, 1932); *The Mummy* (film, 1999).

Archeology • Cursed Objects • Imhotep (character) • Mummies • Universal Studios

Priest, Cherie.

The Eden Moore Trilogy.

Eden Moore's investigation into her family's origins leads her on a journey throughout the South. An orphan, she must eventually journey back in time to understand her family's supernatural origins and the source of her ability to see ghosts. **Similar titles:** *The Good House* and *Joplin's Ghost*, Tananarive Due; <u>The Greywalker Series</u>, Kat Richardson.

Biracial Characters • Families • Gothicism • Moore, Eden (character) • Precognition • Psychics

Four and Twenty Blackbirds. *New York: Tor, 2005. 288p. ISBN 0765313081.*

(See chapter 4, "Ghosts and Haunted Houses: Dealing with Presences and Absences.")

Wings to the Kingdom. *New York: Tor, 2006. 399p. ISBN 076531309X.*

(See chapter 4, "Ghosts and Haunted Houses: Dealing with Presences and Absences.")

Not Flesh nor Feathers. *New York: Tor, 2007. 368p. ISBN 0765313103.*

In this third novel in the <u>Eden Moore Trilogy</u>, a flood brings to the surface century-old corpses from Chattanooga's cemeteries. The dead are reanimated by a force that compels them to converge on the Read House, haunted by the ghost of Caroline Read, to resolve an atrocity that occurred over a hundred years ago. **Similar titles:** *Dead City*, Joe McKinney; <u>The Vampire Huntress Legend</u>, L. A. Banks; *Bag of Bones*, Stephen King; *City of the Dead*, Brian Keene.

Haunted Houses • Tennessee—Chattanooga • Zombies

Rice, Anne.

The Mummy, or Ramses the Damned. *New York: Ballantine Books, 1989. 436p. ISBN 0345360001.*

As a mortal, King Ramses sought the elixir of life to bring eternal prosperity to his people. But because humans aren't meant to be immortal, his experiment failed, and Ramses himself was "doomed forever to wander the earth, desperate to quell hungers that can never be satisfied." Ramses is reawakened in Edwardian London, where he becomes Dr. Ramsey, expert in Egyptology. **Similar titles:** *The Vampire Lestat* and *Servant of the Bones*, Anne Rice; *The Jewel of Seven Stars*, Bram Stoker, *Cronos* (film).

Egypt • England—London • Mummies • Religion—Ancient Egyptian

Shelley, Mary.

Frankenstein. *Oxford: Oxford University Press, 2001, ©1818. 192p. ISBN 0195149017.*

Dr. Victor Frankenstein thirsts for knowledge that humans aren't meant to know, and he builds a creature out of spare parts from charnel houses. The result is a hideous being whose appearance terrifies humans, dooming him to loneliness. The creature's painful solitary condition causes him to destroy his maker and his family. This is a classic that has inspired various films and alternative retellings. **Similar titles:** *Dracula*, Bram Stoker; *Herbert West: Re-animator*, H. P. Lovecraft; *Donovan's Brain*, Curt Siodmak; *The Invisible Man*, H. G. Wells.

Diary Format • Frankenstein, Victor (character) • Frankenstein's Monster (character) • Revenge • Switzerland • Weird Science

Skipp, John, ed.

Mondo Zombie. *Baltimore, MD: Cemetery Dance, 2006. 497p. ISBN 1587670402.*

(See chapter 18, "Collections and Anthologies.")

Sleator, William.

The Boy Who Couldn't Die. *New York: Amulet Books, 2004. 162.p. ISBN 0810948249.*

Until recently, sixteen-year-old Ken's wealthy parents have been able to protect him from the harsh realities of mortality. But that changes when his best friend is killed in a plane crash. This experience leads Ken to Cheri Beaumont, who promises protection from death for $50. Cheri delivers what she promises—Ken discovers that nothing can hurt him. But immortality comes with a catch—namely, the realistic "dreams" of killing people that now plague Ken. **Similar titles:** *Mondo Zombie*, John Skipp (editor); *Doppelganger*, David Stahler Jr.; *The Dust of Eden*, Thomas Sullivan.

Adolescence • Death—Grieving • Doppelgangers • Immortality • New York—New York City • Parapsychology • Religion—Voodoo • Zombies

Smith, Bryan.

Deathbringer. *New York: Leisure, 2006, 342p. ISBN 0843956771.*

(See chapter 10, "Small Town Horror: Villages of the Damned.")

Stoker, Bram.

The Jewel of Seven Stars. *Oxford: Oxford University Press, 1996, ©1903. 214p. ISBN 0192832190.*

An Egyptologist accidentally awakens the soul of the mummy, which then possesses his daughter. He can save her only by bringing the body of the mummy back to life. **Similar titles:** *The Mummy, or Ramses the Damned*, Anne Rice; *To Wake the Dead*, Richard Laymon; *Frankenstein*, Mary Shelley; *The Mummy* (film, 1932).

Archeology • Cursed Objects • Lawyer as Character • Mummies • Police Officer as Character • Religion—Ancient Egyptian

Stone, Del, Jr.

Dead Heat. *Austin, TX: Mojo Press, 1996. 186p. ISBN 1885418108.*
(See chapter 16, "Comic Horror: Laughing at Our Fears.")

Sullivan, Thomas.

Dust of Eden. *New York: Onyx, 2004. 355p. ISBN 0451411382.*

Since time out of mind, men have guarded the red dust in a crater in the Middle East, because legend has it that this is the very stuff out of which the first humans were created. But some of the dust is purloined and smuggled into the United States in a funeral urn, and a widow accidentally discovers the dust can raise the dead. Now that the secret is out, someone else gets possession of the dust and uses it for far darker purposes. **Similar titles:** *Pet Sematary*, Stephen King; *The Boy Who Couldn't Die*, William Sleator.

Cursed Objects • Death—Grieving • Popular Culture • Religion—Christianity • Resurrection

Waggoner, Tim.

Necropolis. *Farmington Hills, MI: Gale Group-Five Star, 2004. 248p. ISBN 1410402150.*

Detective Matt Adrian accidentally follows a killer into another dimension, where he discovers the city of Necropolis, which is inhabited by vampires, werewolves, witches, ghosts, and zombies. But when Adrian is killed while in Necropolis, he becomes a zombie and has only two days to find an antidote for his condition before he quite literally goes to pieces. **Similar titles:** The Anita Blake, Vampire Hunter Series, Laurell K. Hamilton; The Fat White Vampire Series, Andrew Fox; The Talisman Series, Stephen King and Peter Straub.

Parallel Universes • Serial Killers • Vampire Hunters • Werewolves • Witchcraft • Zombies

Wellington, David.

The Monster Nation Trilogy (aka Zombie Series).

In cities across the United States, the dead are returning to life and eating the living. Most are mindless things, but one woman, who died while barricading herself in an oxygen bar, is reasonably sentient. **Similar titles:** <u>The Rising Series</u>, Brian Keene; *World War Z*, Max Brooks; <u>The Night of the Living Dead Series</u> (films); *28 Days Later* (film).

Apocalypse • Cannibalism • Futurism • Religion—Paganism • Soldier as Character • Zombies

Monster Nation. *New York: Thunder's Mouth Press, 2004. 285p. ISBN 1560258667.*

Nilla cannot remember her own name or much about her past existence, but does retain a basic sense of humanity—despite having been turned into a zombie. She struggles to contain her urge to feast on the living, and also tries to protect them from other zombies.

Monster Island. *New York: Thunder's Mouth Press, 2006. 282p. ISBN 1560258500.*

As Manhattan is destroyed by plague, the last few bastions of humanity are in the Middle East, Afghanistan, and Somalia. Dekalb, an American UN relief official, is desperate to protect his daughter. Mama Halima, the beloved leader of the new Free Women's Republic, has promised to keep Dekalb's daughter safe on the condition that he use his connections in the first world to get her the drugs that will keep her HIV at bay. So Dekalb travels to Manhattan. **Similar titles:** <u>The Rising Series</u>, Brian Keene; *The Stand*, Stephen King; *Dead Heat*, Del Stone Jr.; <u>The Night of the Living Dead Series</u> (films).

Mummies • New York—New York City • Physician as Character • Religion—Islam

Monster Planet. *New York: Thunder's Mouth Press, 2007. 302p. ISBN 9781560258674.*

Dekalb's now teenaged daughter Sarah sets off to find Aayan, one of the members of the Freewomen's Army of Somiland who journeyed with her now-deceased father to zombie-infested Manhattan to obtain drugs to protect Mama Halima. But she must first battle Mael Mag Och, an ancient and sentient zombie who is still very much alive in spite of having his head consumed by another of his kind.

Egypt • Mummies • New York—New York City • Physician as Character • Religion—Islam

Film

28 Days Later. *Danny Bolye, dir. 2002. 113 minutes.*
(See chapter 13, "Ecological Horror: Mother Nature Has Her Revenge.")

28 Weeks Later. *Juan Carlos Fresnadillo, dir. 2007. 99 minutes.*
(See chapter 13, "Ecological Horror: Mother Nature Has Her Revenge.")

Bride of Frankenstein. *James Whale, dir. 1935. (black and white). 75 minutes.*
Boris Karloff reprises his role as Frankenstein's monster in this rendition of the second half of Mary Shelley's novel. The lonely and somewhat inarticulate creature that evaded destruction in *Frankenstein* now demands that his creator make him a mate. This classic also stars Elsa Lancaster and Colin Clive. **Similar titles:** *Frankenstein*, Mary Shelley; *Donovan's Brain*, Kurt Sidomak; *The Invisible Man*, H. G. Wells.

Frankenstein, Victor (character) • Frankenstein's Monster (character) • Germany • Weird Science

Bubba Ho-Tep. *Don Coscarelli, dir. 2002. 92 minutes.*
(See chapter 16, "Comic Horror: Laughing at Our Fears.")

Dawn of the Dead. *George A. Romero, dir. 1978. 126 minutes.*
(See The Night of the Living Dead Series in this chapter.)

Day of the Dead. *George A. Romero, dir. 1985. 102 minutes.*
(See The Night of the Living Dead Series in this chapter.)

Dead Alive (Brain Dead). *Peter Jackson, dir. 1992. 104 minutes.*
(See chapter 16, "Comic Horror: Laughing at Our Fears.")

Diary of the Dead. *George A. Romero, dir. 2007. 95 minutes.*
(See The Night of the Living Dead Series in this chapter.)

Fido. *Andrew Currie, dir. 2006. 91 minutes.*
(See chapter 16, "Comic Horror: Laughing at Our Fears.")

Frankenstein. *James Whale, dir. 1931. (black and white). 71 minutes.*
James Whale's rendition of the first half of Mary Shelley's novel is set in the twentieth century. But in this film, Dr. Frankenstein's creation isn't a monster due to his creator's hubris in usurping the powers of God or because of the intolerance of society at large. Instead, it is monstrous because it is made with inferior parts. If Dr. Frankenstein's bumbling assistant hadn't procured an abnormal brain, then presumably the creature would have truly been the new Adam. This classic stars Boris Karloff as the monster. **Similar titles:** *Frankenstein*, Mary Shelley; *Donovan's Brain*, Kurt Sidomak; *The Invisible Man*, H. G. Wells.

Frankenstein, Victor (character) • Frankenstein's Monster (character) • Germany • Weird Science

I Walked with a Zombie. *Jacques Tourner, dir. 1943. (black and white). 69 minutes.*
Wishing to escape the cold Canadian winters, Betsy takes a job as a private nurse in Haiti for Paul Holland's catatonic wife, Jessica. While the local physician believes that Jessica's condition was caused by a brain fever, Paul's half-brother Wesley thinks that his sibling deliberately drove his wife mad to prevent her from leaving him. And Paul and Wesley's mother believes that she is to blame for Jessica's malady, since she participated in the voodoo rites of the natives. Tourner's film is very loosely connected to Charlotte Brontë's 1847 novel *Jane Eyre*. **Similar titles:** *Wuthering Heights*, Emily Brontë; *The Jewel of Seven Stars*, Bram Stoker.

Families • Haiti • Nurse as Character • Religion—Voodoo • Zombies

Invasion of the Body Snatchers. *Don Siegel, dir. 1956. 80 minutes.*
(See chapter 12, "Technohorror: Evil Hospitals, Military Screw-Ups, Mad Scientists, and Alien Invasions.")

Land of the Dead. *George A. Romero, dir. 2005. 93 minutes.*
(See The Night of the Living Dead Series in this chapter.)

The Mummy. *Karl Freund, dir. 1932. (black and white). 72 minutes.*

When the mummy's tomb is desecrated by archeologists, he is reanimated and kills those responsible for disturbing his rest. He then discovers that the reincarnation of his mate is among the band of archeologists. Boris Karloff stars as the mummy. Be sure to look for the zipper in the back of the mummy costume. **Similar titles:** *The Mummy,* Anne Rice; *The Jewel of Seven Stars,* Bram Stoker; *To Wake the Dead,* Richard Laymon.

Archeology • Egypt • Imhotep (character) • Immortality • Mummies • Reincarnation • Revenging Revenant • Witchcraft

The Mummy. *Stephen Sommers, dir. 1999. 124 minutes.*

(See chapter 16, "Comic Horror: Laughing at Our Fears.")

The Night of the Living Dead Series.

The newly dead inexplicably reanimate, and they hunger for human flesh. And once the dead bite the living, the living too will die and be reborn as zombies. **Similar titles:** <u>The Monster Island Series</u>, David Wellington; <u>The Rising Series</u>, Brian Keene.

Apocalypse • Cannibalism • Zombies

Night of the Living Dead. *George A. Romero, dir. 1968. (black and white). 96 minutes.*

Seven strangers are thrown together in a remote farmhouse next to the cemetery and work to keep zombies at bay while fighting among themselves due to their ethnic and generational differences. This first film in Romero's series is a watershed text, which definitively transformed the figure of the zombie from the walking dead reanimated by voodoo and subject to the will of the zombie master into ravenous and unstoppable creatures returned to life perhaps due to radiation or even the Rapture, but always hungry for human flesh.

African American Characters • Pennsylvania

Dawn of the Dead. *George A. Romero, dir. 1978. 126 minutes.*

A pregnant broadcast journalist, her helicopter pilot boyfriend, and two others realize that law enforcement officers can't keep at bay much longer the ensuing chaos caused by the dead returning to life. Thus, they take a helicopter to escape Pittsburgh for somewhere safer. Eventually they find a mall, which is stocked with everything they'll need to exist comfortably for quite a while—including zombies.

African American Characters • Consumerism • Journalist as Character • Pennsylvania • Police Officer as Character

Day of the Dead. *George A. Romero, dir. 1985. 102 minutes.*

Sometime after events depicted in *Night of the Living Dead* changed the world forever, the government realizes that exterminating the zombies is a losing battle, as they now outnumber humans approximately 40,000 to one. Thus, a group of scientists are housed in an underground missile silo and protected by a skeleton crew of military personnel in the hopes that a technological solution to the zombie problem can be found. Dr. Logan conducts bloody vivisections of the living dead to learn how to condition them to not eat the living.

Florida • Hispanic American Characters • Soldier as Character • Weird Science

Land of the Dead. *George A. Romero, dir. 2005. 93 minutes.*

An outpost of survivors inhabit an allegedly safe island (formerly the city of Pittsburgh). However, this island is no utopia, but the same old class warfare bankrolled by the wealthy Mr. Kaufmann. Kaufmann and his WASP friends live high above it all in Fiddler's Green, an exclusive condominium tower with restaurants and world-class shopping, while the others outside live in squalor and serve those in the Green as servants, sex workers, and soldiers who keep the zombies at bay. But one of these people has had enough.

Hispanic American Characters • Pennsylvania—Pittsburgh

Diary of the Dead. *George A. Romero, dir. 2007. 95 minutes.*

On the day that the newly dead first come to life, a group of film students are making a low budget flick about a mummy who returns to life. When they discover that they are now trapped by the zombies, the crew decides to use their filmmaking abilities to document this momentous event for posterity.

Documentary Techniques • Horror Movie Industry

Night of the Living Dead. *Tom Savini, dir. 1990. 92 minutes.*

This remake of Romero's classic film of the same name stars Tony Todd, who in the same year played the title character in Bernard Rose's film *Candyman*, as Ben. Savini's interpretation of Romero's original retains the same racial and generational tensions exhibited by the seven thrown together in the farmhouse where they hide from the zombies. However, the character of Barbara is transformed utterly. She trades her skirt and heels for a pair of pants and work boots and learns to shoot a rifle. **Similar titles:** The Monster Island Series, David Wellington; The Rising Series, Brian Keene.

African American Characters • Apocalypse • Cannibalism • Pennsylvania • Zombies

The Plague of the Zombies. *John Gilling, dir. 1966. 91 minutes.*

Sir James Forbes is summoned to a Cornish village by his former star pupil, Dr. Peter Tompson, who is at a loss to understand the spate of mysterious sudden deaths that plague his patients. Sir James arrives with his daughter Sylvia, best friend of Peter's wife Alice. Not much later, Alice wanders from her home while in a trance and is found dead. Desperate to understand the nature of the recent deaths, Sir James and Peter exhume his late wife, only to discover that she has become a zombie. This Hammer studios zombie film is loosely based on Bram Stoker's 1897 novel *Dracula*. **Similar titles:** *Dracula*, Bram Stoker; The Anno Dracula Series, Kim Newman.

Alternative Literature • England • Physician as Character • Religion—Voodoo • Victorian Era • Zombies

Re-Animator. *Stuart Gordon, dir. 1985. 86 minutes.*

(See chapter 16, "Comic Horror: Laughing at Our Fears.")

The Return of the Living Dead. *Dan O'Bannon, dir. 1985. 91 minutes.*

(See chapter 16, "Comic Horror: Laughing at Our Fears.")

Shaun of the Dead. *Edgar Wright, dir. 2004. 99 minutes.*

(See chapter 16, "Comic Horror: Laughing at Our Fears.")

Son of Frankenstein. *Rowland V. Lee, dir. 1939. (black and white). 99 minutes.*

The son of Dr. Frankenstein, played by Basil Rathbone, returns to his ancestral castle approximately twenty-five years after the monster's presumed death. But the creature isn't dead—he's only disabled, and he's guarded by Igor (Bela Lugosi), the last of his father's misshapen attendants. The doctor's scientific curiosity gets the better of him, and he reanimates the creature. **Similar titles:** *Herbert West: Re-animator*, H. P. Lovecraft; *Frankenstein*, Mary Shelley.

Frankenstein's Monster (character) • Germany • Immortality • Revenge • Weird Science

White Zombie. *Victor Halperin, dir. 1932. (black and white). 69 minutes.*

This first-ever zombie film stars Bela Lugosi, fresh from his role as the blood-sucking count in Tod Browning's *Dracula*. Beaumont, a white Haitian planter, falls in love with Madeline, an American traveling to his country to marry Neil, her fiancé who is stationed in a bank there. Beaumont persuades the couple to wed at his remote plantation in the hope that he can persuade Madeline to be his bride instead before the ceremony. Desperate, Beaumont consults with Murder Legendre, the local voodoo master, and with Legendre's help, poisons Madeline. **Similar titles:** *The Beetle*, Richard Marsh; *The Mountains of Madness* and *The Restless Dead*, Hugh B. Cave.

Haiti • Religion—Voodoo • Zombies

Young Frankenstein. *Mel Brooks, dir. 1974. 106 minutes.*

(See chapter 16, "Comic Horror: Laughing at Our Fears.")

Zombie (Zombi 2). *Lucio Fulci, dir. 1979. 91 minutes.*

An unpiloted ship makes its way into the harbor in New York City. When two coast guardsmen investigate, they are attacked by a zombie lurking on board. Meanwhile, the deceased boat owner's daughter and a reporter searching for answers journey to a Caribbean island, the last place her father had traveled before his ship mysteriously returned. There they discover that both the newly dead and even the conquistadores who came to the island 400 years ago are returning to life to consume the living. **Similar titles:** <u>The Rising Series</u>, Brian Keene; <u>The Monster Nation Trilogy</u>, David Wellington.

Cannibalism • Journalist as Character • New York—New York City • Physician as Character • Zombies

June's Picks

Books: Max Brooks, *World War Z: An Oral History of the Zombie War* (Three Rivers Press); Kim Paffenroth, *Dying to Live* (Permuted Press); Mary Shelley, *Frankenstein* (Oxford University Press); William Sleator, *The Boy Who Couldn't Die* (Amulet Books); David Wellington, <u>The Monster Nation Trilogy</u> (Three Rivers Press)

Films: *Frankenstein*, <u>The Night of the Living Dead Series</u>, *White Zombie*

Tony's Picks

Books: Anne Rice, *The Mummy, or Ramses the Damned* (Ballantine Books); Tim Waggoner, *Necropolis* (Gale Group-Five Star)

Films: *Frankenstein, Night of the Living Dead* (1968)

1

2

3

4

5

6

7

8

9

10

Chapter 6

Vampires and Werewolves: Children of the Night

The most popular of all monsters, vampires have evolved considerably since their introduction into literature and popular culture with the nineteenth-century publication of the serial adventure *Varney the Vampyre* and Bram Stoker's *Dracula*. Count Dracula, prototype of virtually all vampires as we know them today, was originally a monstrous, megalomaniacal foreigner who represented British xenophobia and the Western European fear of the Other (vampires are derived from an Irishman's interpretation of the mythology of Transylvania, or what is today known as Romania). This saber-toothed, bloodsucking creature, originally cousin to the werewolf, evolved into a suave, sophisticated, intelligent superhuman—and then de-evolved into a bloodthirsty superpunk who, like the werewolf, rips victims to shreds. There are only a few famous werewolves in fiction, but notable vampires are plentiful, ranging from the monstrous nosferatu of *Varney* and of Stoker's *Dracula* to the sophisticated aristocrat of Anne Rice's <u>Vampire Chronicles</u>. Vampires have since evolved into other forms, including the mind-controlling, war-mongering mutant humans in Dan Simmons's *Carrion Comfort* and the parasite-positive creatures suffering from a viral infection in Scott Westerfield's *Peeps* (annotated in chapter 13). Despite these differences, all vampires and werewolves qualify as full-fledged monsters because they must somehow feed on their victims' vital essences: flesh, blood, emotion, love, even tendencies toward violence.

At its most fundamental level, vampirism involves a creature of the night and his or her parasitical relationship with another. This relationship has been used as a metaphor for love, the parent–child bond, sexual relationships, the relationship between parasite and host, and power structures in general. Yet vampires have become easily the most identifiable and often the most sympathetic, the most appealing, of all the genre's monsters, mainly because vampires must, in some way, resemble the humans on which they prey. Moreover, vampirism is often represented as a sort of dark godhood, as a variant of immortality, with a little bloodlust thrown in for a good scare. The classical vampire is generally an "undead" human being—like the mummy, ghost, or werewolf—but generally only the vampire can retain, and sometimes eclipse, human beauty. Also, vampires often possess extraordinary powers: super strength, hypersexuality, and the abilities to hypnotize victims, control the weather, shape-shift, or compel animals to do their bidding; they also often possess the ability to fly. In general, vampires range from superhuman predators to subhuman beasts, states appealing to both sides of the human experience, ranging from when we need to feel strong and invulnerable to those times when we feel powerless and seek to deal vicariously with this shortcoming. Finally, vampires are almost always erotic or sensual in some way, which is one of their greatest appeals to readers.

Some vampires embrace their undead existences as a superior form of being. In Jemiah Jefferson's' Voice of the Blood Series and Whitley Strieber's The Hunger Series, the children of the night are forever young and can spend their existence nightclubbing and indulging in the pleasures of the flesh. In *Blade* and the Anno Dracula Series, vampires are more animalistic, and see humans as nothing more than cattle. Other vampires experience their undeath as a curse rather than a blessing, and some would like to be human again. Count Ragoczy de Saint-Germain of Chelsea Quinn Yarbro's Saint-Germaine Series is a beautiful immortal, but immortality has its price: although he is noble and genteel, he must conceal his undead nature from ignorant humans, lest they harm those he loves and protects. Anne Rice's Vampire Chronicles is populated with nosferatu, who are unable to lose their aversion to shedding human blood. In Rice's *Interview with the Vampire*, a bitter Louis loathes his maker, who has transformed him into a creature that must do what he finds morally repugnant to survive. And while Rice's Lestat de Lioncourt revels in his undead state, he also often pities and envies the mortals who must slake his thirst. In *Tale of the Body Thief*, Lestat is granted his wish to be human once again, only to find that he has been tricked into switching bodies with a human who, among other things, has the flu at the time of the change. Andrew Fox's Fat White Vampire Blues Series (annotated in chapter 16) gives us Jules Duchon, a working-class vampire with little formal education who has not become wealthy or good looking throughout his decades of immortality. Instead, he has become morbidly obese, has bad knees, and must drive a cab to support himself.

Of all vampire texts, Bram Stoker's *Dracula* is the most widely known and arguably the most influential in the genre. *Dracula* is most frequently the basis of alternative literature that rewrites the story or adds deeper knowledge to previously established characters. Some recent examples include Allen C. Kupfer's *The Journal of Professor Abraham Van Helsing*, Tim Lucas's *The Book of Renfield: The Gospel of Dracula*, and Barbara Hambly's *Renfield, Slave of Dracula*. Novels such as these rewrite the Dracula story from the point of view of characters who received little attention in Stoker's original tale. Kupfer's tale speculates on the life of Van Helsing, the enigmatic leader of the vampire hunters in Stoker's novel, paying particular attention to how the metaphysician came to know of the vampire in the first place. Lucas similarly follows the early development of Renfield, Dr. Seward's zoophagous patient, whereas Hambly's interpretation of Renfield shows him allying himself with Dracula's three vampire wives to defy the master. At any rate, all later vampire narratives must pay some sort of homage to *Dracula*, with its skillful combination of traditional Eastern European vampire folklore and nineteenth-century British xenophobia. Later vampire narratives sometimes add to the Dracula mythology established by Stoker, sometimes refute it, and often do a little of both. Kim Newman's Anno Dracula Series returns the legend to its beginnings, as an alternative history speculating on what the Victorian era would have been like if Dracula had defeated Van Helsing and his party of vampire hunters. Newman incorporates facts about the "real" Dracula (according to scholars Raymond McNally and Radu Florescu), Romanian Prince Vlad Tepes, into his representation of Dracula. Newman's series also incorporates into the narrative every well-known literary and folkloric vampire from every culture. Vampires have indeed come a long way, and writers in the subgenre are constantly rewriting the vampire myth anew, with the possibilities being endless.

And then there are werewolves, cousins to the vampires. The werewolf comes from traditional vampire folklore, in which the undead frequently assume the form of a wolf to facilitate their nocturnal feedings. The werewolf is the alter ego of the suave, sophisticated vampire: if the vampire is a sort of monstrous superego, the werewolf is the raging id. The werewolf represents our most essential desires—for food, sex, comfort, even violence—in their most bestial form. Famous werewolves include Lawrence Talbot of Universal Studios fame, as well as the very sympathetic lycanthrope portrayed by Oliver Reed in the Hammer Studios film *The Curse of the Werewolf*. Also, the film *Ginger Snaps* as well as the novel *Blood and Chocolate* ruminate on the difficulties of being a female werewolf, because the creature is such an exaggeration of masculinity, while the "wolf girl" in the film *Blood Moon* who really suffers from hirsutism and earns her keep as part of a traveling freak show exposes the true natures of beasts and humans.

In the past decade werewolves, vampires, and other children of the night have flourished outside of the horror genre and have become the staple of paranormal romance, a subgenre of romance that features vampiric and lycanthropic lovers. The underpinnings of paranormal romance can be found in Yarbro's <u>Saint-Germain Chronicles</u> and in Kelley Armstrong's <u>Women of the Otherworld Series</u>, in Laurell K. Hamilton's comic <u>Anita Blake, Vampire Hunter Series</u> (annotated in chapter 16), as well as in works by Mary Janice Davidson.

Note: Stories about vampires and werewolves can also be found in the collections and anthologies described in chapter 18. Refer to the subject/keyword index for specific titles under the various keywords that include terms such as *Vampire Clans, Vampire Hunters, Vampire's Point of View,* and *Werewolves.*

Vampire Series

The Angel Investigations Series (various authors).

Buffy the Vampire Slayer spin-off character Angel heads up a detective agency that specializes in occult and supernatural cases. But how many times can you save the world from demons and still keep your hair and physique perfect? **Similar titles:** <u>The Buffy the Vampire Slayer Series</u>, various authors; <u>The Wicked Willow Series</u>, various authors.

Angel Investigations • Buffy the Vampire Slayer (character) • Demons • Vampire Hunters

Gardner, Craig Shaw.

Dark Mirror. *New York: Simon & Schuster, 2004. 261p. ISBN 0689867018.*

Angel meets his double—in fact, a parade of doubles—who want to replace him and others on the team, which means they need to be dead. To figure out where the clones originate, the team must pit their brains against killers who know their every move—even before they make them. Clues lead back to the Seven Sinners, a demonic cult that employs demons capable of shape-shifting into any human or vampire.

Apocalypse • Doppelgangers • Shape-shifters

Holder, Nancy, Joss Whedon, and David Greenwalt.

Heat. *New York: Simon Spotlight, 2004. 456p. ISBN 0689869061.*

Jhiera the seductress returns, and she may be the key to freeing China's terra-cotta samurai army. The escaped demonic form of an ancient Chinese emperor is in L.A. searching for her, hoping to persuade her to thaw his soldiers, which are strategically located around the globe. In Sunnydale Buffy Summers, now working as a school counselor, will have to put her new career aside and work with Angel and Gunn to stop the apocalypse.

Apocalypse • California—Sunnydale • Samurai • Statues

Mariotte, Jeff.

Solitary Man. *New York: Pocket, 2003. 293p. ISBN 0689860153.*

A seventy-one-year-old widow contacts Angel Investigations to offer her services as an amateur detective, which works out well because a recent robbery of antiquities has left Angel and company a little shorthanded. When an elderly killer looking for the items surfaces, the widow/sidekick becomes a hindrance. Can the team members, who are barely talking to one another, put their differences aside in time to save her and each other?

California—Los Angeles • Cursed Objects • Religion—Christianity—Catholicism • Septuagenarians

Sanctuary. *New York: Simon Pulse, 2003. 307p. ISBN 0689856644.*

A night of karaoke turns sour when it is interrupted by a drive-by shooting and kidnapping. Now Angel and company are forced to interview human and demon witnesses. But each tells a different story. The team scour Los Angeles, and it becomes clear that this is a complex crime, not a simple kidnapping for money.

California—Los Angeles • Kidnapping

Mariotte, Jeff, Joss Whedon, and David Greenwalt.

Angel: Love and Death. *New York: Simon Spotlight, 2004. 295p. ISBN 068987085X.*

A radio talk show host decides it's time to exterminate all the "monsters" in our midst, so throngs of angry Americans head for Los Angeles, intent on hunting down every demon and vampire. Meanwhile, Angel Investigations attempts to solve a haunted house murder. In the middle of all this emotional turmoil, Valentine's Day looms large. But will it bring another massacre of historical proportions?

Haunted Houses • Holidays—Valentine's Day • Vampire's Point of View • Vigilantism

McConnell, Ashley.

Book of the Dead. *New York: Simon Spotlight, 2004. 297p. ISBN 0689870841.*

An obscure volume of spells, *The Red Compendium*, is found at an occult store in Los Angeles. This legendary book contains the magic of history's most noted mages, and an alienated high school student who steals several books suddenly tries to become a master wizard. Angel Investigations is on the case.

California—Los Angeles • Cursed Objects • Magic • Vampire's Point of View • Witchcraft

Passarella, J. G.

Monolith. *New York: Simon Spotlight, 2004. 323p. ISBN 0689870221.*

As demons leave Los Angeles in droves, a giant monolith suddenly appears in the middle of Hollywood Boulevard, so Angel Investigations decides to deal with their family issues another time (the strife between Angel and his son, Connor) to get to the bottom of the mystery. Meanwhile, a trapped demon tricks a failing actress into carrying out an ancient ritual.

Apocalypse • California—Los Angeles

Vornholt, John.

Seven Crows. *New York: Simon Pulse, 2003. 278p. ISBN 0689860145.*

In a sleepy Arizona town, a federal agent has tracked down a smuggling ring involving vampires, but he is removed from the case when a local sheriff makes a call to Washington. Buffy Summers and Angel are hired, and decide to investigate, because bodies are turning up in the surrounding desert, some drained of blood, some missing body parts. Meanwhile, more crows seem to be flocking to the area, and there is talk of a skinwalker.

Arizona • Federal Bureau of Investigation • Immigration • Religion—Native American • Shape-shifters • Witchcraft

---

Armitrout, Jennifer.

The Carrie Ames Novels.

Dr. Carrie Ames is attacked and left for dead, but not by a maniacal killer. She has been bitten by a vampire and is now beginning to exhibit signs of vampirism herself. **Similar titles:** <u>The Crimson Series</u>, Trisha Baker; <u>The Wereling Trilogy</u>, Stephen Cole; *Ivy Cole and the Moon*, Gina Farrago.

Ames, Carrie (character) • Eroticism • Physician as Character • Vampire Hunters • Vampire's Point of View

The Turning. *Don Mills, ON: Mira Books, 2006. 379p. ISBN 077832298X.*

A fellow member of the undead saves Carrie from extinction at the hands of her maker's lover, but at a price—she must pledge allegiance to a group of humanitarian vampires dedicated to the extermination of vampires everywhere.

Possession. *Don Mills, ON: Mira Books, 2007. 384p. ISBN 0778324184.*

Carrie has been a vampire for two months and has exchanged lords, after killing her maker, Cyrus, in favor of the humane vampire, Nathan. But now Nathan has become possessed by The Soul Eater—and he has begun to slaughter innocent human beings. Carrie has to find Nathan before his own Extinction Movement does.

Baker, Trisha.

The Crimson Series.

In the 1940s, the vampire Simon Baldevar seduces Meghann O'Neill and turns her into a creature of the night so that she can better be his consort. But this is only the beginning of his manipulation of Meghann. **Similar titles:** The Wereling Trilogy, Stephen Cole; *Red Death*, P. N. Elrod; *The Turning*, Jennifer Armitrout; *Interview with the Vampire*, Anne Rice.

Domestic Violence • Eroticism • Magic • O'Neill, Meghann (character) • Vampire's Point of View

Crimson Kiss. *New York: Pinnacle, 2001. 432p. ISBN 0786014164.*

After thirteen years of Simon's abusive and controlling behavior, Meghann has had enough and kills her maker. But of course the undead cannot be killed.

Crimson Night. *New York: Pinnacle, 2002. 448p. ISBN 0786014172.*

Meghann is pregnant by her maker Simon, and though she will die without his help in childbirth, she is willing to take that chance rather than have anything to do with him. But Simon eventually persuades Meghann to accept his help by threatening the lives of her friends if she refuses.

Pregnancy

Crimson Shadows. *New York: Pinnacle, 2003. 411p. ISBN 078601556X.*

The third book of the trilogy ties up many loose ends, while leaving enough mystery to keep reader interest from waning. The author reintroduces the main players of the earlier two novels: the evil, twisted Mikal; the misunderstood and brooding, but ultimately dignified Simon; and the protagonist of the series, Meghann, who balances her obligation toward and love for her maker against his condescension and abuse, while keeping in mind the two children they have sired.

Parenting • Twins

Banks, L. A. (pseudonym for Leslie Esdaile).

The Vampire Huntress Legend.

Meet Damali Richards, a rising star of Warriors of Light Records. She also just happens to have discovered another talent—she is destined to be the vampire huntress. **Similar titles:** The Joe Pitt Novels, Charlie Huston; The Voice of the Blood Series, Jemiah Jefferson; *Expired*, Evie Rhodes.

African American Characters • Demons • Music Industry • Richards, Damali (character) • Vampire Clans • Vampire Hunters

Minion. *New York: St. Martin's Griffin, 2003. 296p. ISBN 0312316801.*

Being new to the vampire huntress game, Damali makes her first mistake: she gives away her secret identity to the vampires and demons that would have her destroyed. An age-old war escalates as dark forces strive to slay Damali before she gains her full powers.

The Forbidden. *New York: St. Martin's Griffin, 2005. 466p. ISBN 0312336225.*

A pregnant Damali meets her arch-nemesis, Lilith, who is as sexy as she is evil and dangerous. Worse yet, Lilith has been given carte blanche to open the gates of hell if need be. When Damali's unborn is taken from her by an induced miscarriage, she and her lover, the newly rehumanized ex-vampire Carlos, along with the ragtag remnants of an overtaxed team of guardians, set off to destroy Lilith and her minions.

Lilith (character)

The Damned. *New York: St. Martin's Griffin, 2006. 487p. ISBN 0312336241.*

The battle with Lilith has loosed the lost souls from hell into the world, and now they threaten to infect humanity with their dark desires, ushering in Armageddon. Meanwhile, Damali Richards deals with the problems that are part and parcel of her relationship with a former vampire, Carlos. Fortunately for both of them, he is sent away to retrieve *The Book of the Damned* while Damali prepares her forces for the final showdown with hell's escaped demons.

Arizona • Eroticism • Lilith (character)

The Forsaken. *New York: St. Martin's Griffin, 2006. 432p. ISBN 0312352352.*

Damali has called it quits with Carlos, the ex-vampire. So who is this mysterious stranger who has piqued her interest? Lilith has been given permission to seek revenge on the forces of light, the Guardian Team, and to do so she has resurrected a powerful being, the second male Netura, currently exiled in the Sea of Agony. The Guardians have relocated to the West Coast, where Damali's new music takes on a strange twist.

California • Eroticism • Lilith (character)

The Cursed. *New York: St. Martin's Griffin, 2007. 491p. ISBN 0312352379.*

Armageddon begins. Lilith, awaits the birth of her heir. Now installed as Vampire Council chairwoman, replacing Cain, she uses her new power to create an army of vampires, witches, and warlocks to combat the guardians. The battle expands exponentially, to involve characters once thought dead, Valkyries, the Ark of the Covenant, and illegal downloads.

Apocalypse • Lilith (character) • Religion—Christianity

The Buffy the Vampire Slayer Series (various authors).

She may not look it, but Buffy Summers is humanity's best hope for preventing plagues of the undead from threatening all we know and love.

Too bad she has that final in history to study for. **Similar titles:** <u>The Wicked Willow Series</u>, various authors; <u>The Angel Investigations Series</u>, various authors.

Buffy the Vampire Slayer (character) • California—Sunnydale • Demons • High School • Vampire Hunters

Burns, Laura J., and Melinda Metz.

Colony. *New York : Simon Spotlight Entertainment, 2005. 245p. ISBN 1416900578.*

In this interactive <u>Buffy the Vampire Slayer</u> novelization, readers control the action, leading to more than a dozen possible endings. Because of the high incidence of death and violence, the mayor of Sunnydale has invited a woman called Belakane to speak at Sunnydale High School, where Buffy Summers and the Scoobies attend. Her program builds self-esteem in teenagers. But it turns out Belakane is a demon, and part of her plot is to enlist workers to build her colony.

Ciencin, Scott.

Mortal Fear. *New York: Simon Pulse, 2003. 479p. ISBN 0743427718.*

While most teens her age scavenger hunt and play games, Buffy Summers chases down different pieces of a soul sword before it can be reassembled and used for evil. Little does she know that she may be a pawn for evil. Meanwhile, Xander and Willow are sickened by a strange virus that is becoming epidemic, causing the local population to engage in vicious attacks against each other—and against Buffy.

Epidemics • Magic • Violence, Theories of • Rosenberg, Willow (character)

DeCandido, Keith R. A.

Blackout. *New York: Simon Spotlight, 2006. 232p. ISBN 1416919171.*

In this pseudo-historical Buffy adventure, readers are transported back to New York City in 1977. It seems that the vampire population is ecstatic about the Son of Sam serial killings—because they allow them to get away with bleeding the local population without suspicion. In addition, a citywide blackout gives them free rein, and Spike and Drusilla are there to take advantage of the situation.

New York—New York City • Serial Killers • Son of Sam Killings • Spike (character)

DeCandido, Keith R. A., and Joss Whedon.

The Deathless. *New York: Simon Spotlight, 2006. 209p. ISBN 1416936300.*

The recession hits Sunnydale. Ring Day reminds Buffy Summers that she is strapped for cash, since she can't afford even the least expensive silver band, and she is perplexed by the fact that an average split-level house has all the vampires spooked. Her research reveals that an attempt to resurrect a long-dead sorcerer is imminent. Within a day, half the senior class goes missing.

Magic • Parapsychology

Gallagher, Diana G.

Bad Bargain. *New York: Simon Spotlight, 2006. 192p. ISBN 1416919198.*

When your school is built over a place called the Hellmouth, you come to expect a few demons and other ghouls now and then. Such is the case at Sunnydale High, although most there have forgotten about the problem because the Hellmouth has been sealed for years—that is, until the first annual band fund-raising rummage sale leads to items being kept in storage in the school basement. Suddenly, people who buy items at the sale become weird.

Cursed Objects

Gallagher, Diana G., Joss Whedon, and David Greenwalt.

Spark and Burn. *New York: Simon Spotlight, 2005. 239p. ISBN 141690056X.*

Readers are introduced to Spike's past in this novelization: A nineteenth-century lad named William meets a woman called Drusilla and finds himself fundamentally changed. In fact, you could say his life was turned around—or at least he was turned—by her. Now named Spike, he travels Europe with a band of vagabond vampires and learns about their true enemies—the skilled ones chosen to fight them, the ones known as the Slayers.

Europe • Spike (character)

Moore, James A., and Joss Whedon.

Chaos Bleeds. *New York: Simon Pulse, 2003. 324p. ISBN 074342767X.*

An old nemesis, Ethan Rayne, visits Sunnydale, and says he needs Buffy's help dealing with a wager made against an ancient evil entity. In fact, he needs the entire gang, which he has offered to battle against foes from other dimensions, including some long-dead villains. Only the weapon Hope's Dagger can help Buffy and company to survive, if she can find it in time.

Computers

Odom, Mel.

Cursed. *New York: Simon Pulse, 2003. 440p. ISBN 068986437X.*

Someone has placed a price on Spike's head, and he knows that the only way he'll be safe is to seek and destroy the demon that put a hit out on him. He arrives in Los Angeles, where he has to form an uneasy alliance with Angel, who has found himself in the middle of a demon clan war. At stake is the fate of the world.

Angel Investigations • California—Los Angeles • Spike (character) • Vampire Clans • Vampire's Point of View

Ostow, Micol, and Steven Brezenoff.

The Quotable Slayer. *New York: Simon Pulse, 2003. 202p. ISBN 0743410173.*

(See chapter 19, "Reference.")

Clegg, Douglas.

The Vampyricon Trilogy.

Aleric Atheffelde is a low-born Breton with a knack for training birds. His skills lead him to a new life at the baron's castle, where he is shanghaied into the Crusades by a seductive female vampire—and later turned into a vampire himself. **Similar titles:** <u>The Wereling Trilogy</u>, Stephen Cole; *The Turning*, Jennifer Armitrout.

Atheffelde, Aleric (character) • England • Europe • Frame Tale • Medieval Era • Vampire Clans • Vampire's Point of View

> **The Priest of Blood.** *New York: Ace, 2005. 310p. ISBN 0441013279.*
>
> Aleric departs from England, along with others in his clan, to visit the legendary vampire city, Alkemara.
>
> **The Lady of Serpents.** *New York: Ace, 2006. 304p. ISBN 0441014380.*
>
> Aleric returns to claim the vampire throne after having breached the veil between the everyday world and the world of the vampire myth stream. As a result of this transgression, the world Aleric returns to is sadly altered. He soon finds himself imprisoned and forced to fight gladiatorial battles with humans. The only way to return things to normal is to destroy the sorceress Enora.
>
> **The Queen of the Wolves.** *New York: Ace, 2007. 320p. ISBN 0441015239.*
>
> Aleric is involved in a bloody civil war among vampires to determine whether vampires will peacefully coexist with humans, and even protect them, or if they will completely dominate humankind and use them as cattle.

Elrod, P. N.

The Jonathan Barrett, Gentleman Vampire Series.

Set during the American Revolution, this series tells of a seventeen-year-old country gentleman who is sent to Cambridge and makes the acquaintance of a seductive beauty, who turns out to be otherworldly. Barrett offers a unique point of view of the times, for he is a loyal British supporter. **Similar titles:** <u>The Saint-Germain Chronicles</u>, Chelsea Quinn Yarbro; <u>The Vampire Files</u>, P. N. Elrod.

Barrett, Jonathan (character) • England • Families • Vampire's Point of View • War—American Revolutionary War

> **Red Death.** *Dallas, TX: BenBella, 2004, ©1993. 284p. ISBN 1932100199.*
>
> The first novel in the <u>Gentleman Vampire</u> series describes the tumult of Revolutionary War America. A student, Jonathan Barrett, is sent to England, where he meets and falls for a beautiful woman. But then he discovers that she truly is out of this world, when he is felled by a musket shot and with her help, rises as undead.
>
> **Death and the Maiden.** *Dallas, TX: BenBella, 2004, ©1994. 274p. ISBN 1932100202.*
>
> Now that Jonathan is a vampire, he must struggle to control his desire for blood while in the presence of his family. But although Jonathan may be a

vampire, his family members are the real bloodsuckers: He must watch his back around them, particularly his cousin, who is always scheming to get hold of the family fortune.

Families

Death Masque. *Dallas, TX: BenBella, 2004, ©1996. 285p. ISBN 1932100210.*

Jonathan returns to England to find Nora Jones, the woman who made him a vampire, so that he can learn more about his newly acquired condition. But Nora is missing. In the course of his search, Jonathan learns many secrets about his family and also uncovers a plot against them.

Families

Dance of Death. *Dallas: BenBella, 2004, ©1996. 264p. ISBN 1932100229.*

Jonathan learns that he has a four-year-old son, which is unfortunate, because his enemies now have a hostage that they can use against him. The only hope for Jonathan's, and his son's, survival lies in Nora's return.

Families • Parenting

The Vampire Files.

Jack Fleming, a former newspaper reporter turned private detective in 1930s Chicago, wants to be a novelist. But fate has other plans for him: A mysterious stranger saves his life after a mob hit. But to do so, she makes him into a vampire. Not only must he deal with being an undead P.I., he also has a lot of explaining to do to his girlfriend. **Similar titles:** The Anita Blake, Vampire Hunter Series, Laurell K. Hamilton; The Smoke Trilogy, Tanya Huff; *Sunglasses After Dark*, Nancy A. Collins.

Fleming, Jack (character) • Illinois—Chicago • Journalist as Character • Organized Crime • Vampire Hunters • Vampire's Point of View

Bloodlist. *New York: Ace Books, 1990. 200p. ISBN 0441067956.*

Jack Fleming's suspicions that he may have become a vampire are confirmed. Now an immortal, he is out for revenge against both the gangsters who "killed" him—and whoever turned him into a vampire.

Lifeblood. *New York: Ace Books, 1990. 208p. ISBN 0441847765.*

Jack Fleming, journalist vampire, continues to search for his maker while trying to evade a pair of deadly vampire hunters.

Bloodcircle. *New York: Ace Books, 1991. 208p. ISBN 0441067174.*

Jack Fleming discovers his maker as well as the person who originally turned the latter into a vampire.

Art in the Blood. *New York: Ace Books, 1991. 208p. ISBN 0441859453.*

This book follows the exploits of vampire private investigator Jack Fleming in a case where he must help find the killer of an artist. This novel is typical of the entire series in that it is fun and easy to read.

Artist as Character

Fire in the Blood. *New York: Ace Books, 1991. 198p. ISBN 0441859461.*

Jack Fleming and his partner, private investigator Charles Escott, are hired by a wealthy Chicago man to find his daughter's expensive bracelet, which might have been stolen by her boyfriend. Naturally the investigation leads Jack and Charles into murder and intrigue with Chicago's organized crime element.

Blood on the Water. *New York: Ace Books, 1992. 199p. ISBN 044185947X.*

Jack Fleming runs afoul of the Chicago mob due to his continuing investigation of a missing expensive bracelet. Also, because his lover and best friend are threatened by these people, Jack must wrestle with killing someone to keep those he cares about safe.

Chill in the Blood. *New York: Ace Books, 1998. 327p. ISBN 0441005012.*

It's 1937, and now that Prohibition has been repealed, Chicago's warring organized crime families have stepped up their battle for turf. Once again, Jack is in the middle of it all.

The Dark Sleep. *New York: Ace Books, 1999. 359p. ISBN 0441005918.*

Jack and his partner Charles are hired by an heiress to get some papers back from an old flame so that she can't be blackmailed with them. But the case turns violent, putting the mortal Charles in danger. And worse still, Jack's girlfriend is being perused by a radio producer who is interested in more than her singing talents.

Lady Crymsyn. *New York: Ace, 2000. 410p. ISBN 0441007244.*

Jack Fleming has scrounged up enough money to open the Lady Crymsyn, a nightclub that will give his chanteuse girlfriend a venue for her vocal talents. But when the renovations begin, a dead woman in red, handcuffed to a wall, is discovered.

Cold Streets. *New York: Ace, 2003. 384p. ISBN 0441010091.*

Jack and his human partner Charles save a kidnapped girl before her captors can kill her, but the resolution of this job is only the beginning of Jack's troubles. One of the kidnappers realizes that Jack is a vampire and tried to blackmail him to prevent him from testifying in court.

Song in the Dark. *New York: Ace, 2005. 384p. ISBN 0441013236.*

When he agrees to help out his friend Gordy Weems, a crime boss who is currently too injured to take care of business, Jack finds himself on the other side of the law. As a result, he nearly ends up tortured to death at the hands of Hog Bristow, a rival gangster. When Jack kills Bristow in self-defense, he makes some very dangerous enemies.

Farren, Mick.

The Renquist Quartet.

A mercenary twelfth-century swordsman is mortally wounded. To save his life, Lamia the Great Vampire gives him the dark gift, but he has not seen her since then. Now Victor Renquist survives by accepting jobs for various political and intelligence agencies. He currently controls a small colony of nosferatu in the United States. Good thing he is on our side. **Similar titles:** The Red Moon Series, Billie Sue Mosiman; The Lawson Vampire Novels, Jon F. Merz; The Vampire Huntress Legend, L. A. Banks; *Blade* (film).

Renquist, Victor (character) • *Vampire Clans* • *Vampire's Point of View*

The Time of Feasting. *New York: Tor, 1996. 384p. ISBN 031286213X.*

In this action-oriented tale, vampire clan leader Victor Renquist has a few problems: his clan is getting restless during "the time of feasting," which occurs every seven years, and a young upstart vampire named Kurt wants to oust him as leader. When bodies start turning up all over New York City, Renquist realizes that Kurt and his followers threaten to expose the clan.

Gay/Lesbian/Bisexual Characters • *New York—New York City*

Darklost. *New York: Tor, 2000. 480p. ISBN 0312869797.*

Victor Renquist and his vampire clan leave New York for Los Angeles, where they discover an ex-clan member who wants to challenge Renquist's power, as well as "The Nine," a group of Cthulhu worshippers who threaten to lure the old gods back into modern society. Renquist must meet both the threat to his power and the threat of annihilation of the human race.

California—Los Angeles • *Cthulhian Monsters* • *Gay/Lesbian/Bisexual Characters* • *Police Officer as Character* • *Religion—Satanism*

More Than Mortal. *New York: Tor, 2001. 416p. ISBN 0312879016.*

Renquist is struggling to rebuild his American-based vampire colony when he receives a summons from three females of his species. Knowing this is not a friendly visit between old friends, Victor drops everything to go to England, where he learns that archeologists have disturbed the gravesite of Taliesin, better known as Merlin.

Archeology • *Arthurian Legend* • *England* • *Magic* • *Merlin (character)*

Underland. *New York: Tor, 2004, ©2002. 448p. ISBN 0765342162.*

Victor Renquist has been recruited by the National Security Agency to investigate an underworld culture created by Nazi survivors in a place where Cthulhian aliens thrive beneath the earth's mantle.

Aliens • *Antarctica* • *Cthulhian Monsters* • *Nazism*

Fox, Andrew.

The Fat White Vampire Series.

(See chapter 16, "Comic Horror: Laughing at Our Fears.")

Garton, Ray.

The Live Girls Series.

Walter Benedek is a newspaper reporter whose sister and niece are killed by his brother-in-law, a mild mannered man who became a bloodthirsty vampire after frequenting Live Girls, a strip club in Times Square. **Similar titles:** *Sips of Blood*, Mary Ann Mitchell; *The Long Last Call*, John Skipp.

Journalist as Character • New York—New York City • Vampire's Point of View • Writer as Character

Live Girls. *New York: Leisure, 2006, ©1987. 337p. ISBN 0843956747.*

Davey Owens has a dead end job as an editor for a publication house, so when he gets a chance to get into Live Girls, he takes it. After receiving fellatio from a dancer named Anya, he finds himself bleeding from his penis, becoming lethargic, and transforming into a fledgling vampire. Then he meets Benedek, and the two decide to take Live Girls down.

Psychosexual Horror • Publishing Industry • Stripper as Character

Night Life. *New York: Leisure, 2007, ©2005. 338p. ISBN 0843956755.*

The proprietors of the 42nd Street peep show have relocated after the City has cleaned up Times Square by purging it of adult businesses. Now they live a tame life in the suburbs, drinking bottled blood. But when two reporters begin to investigate the now defunct strip club, they unwittingly draw the attention of the vampires who were forced to flee New York when their hangout was shut down, and they become the targets of retribution.

New York—New York City • Suburbia

Hamilton, Laurell K.

The Anita Blake, Vampire Hunter Series.

(See chapter 16, "Comic Horror: Laughing at Our Fears.")

Harris, Charlaine.

The Sookie Stackhouse series (aka The Southern Vampire Mysteries).

(See chapter 16, "Comic Horror: Laughing at Our Fears.")

Hart, Raven.

The Savannah Vampire Series.

William Cuyler Thorne, a model citizen of Savannah, is also a vampire, and he must now deal with the elder vampire Reedrek's European followers. To fight them, William must form his own clan. **Similar titles:** The Red Moon Series, Billie Sue Mosiman; The Lawson Vampire Novels, Jon F. Merz; The Vampire Huntress Legend, L. A. Banks; The Renquist Quartet, Mick Farren; *Blade* (film).

Georgia—Savannah • Thorne, William Cuyler (character) • Vampire Clans • Vampire's Point of View • Witchcraft

1

The Vampire's Secret. *New York: Ballantine, 2007. 390p. ISBN 0345479777.*

Thorne chooses a handsome young newbie named Jack McShane, as well as the seductress Eleanor, for his clan, but the only hope for survival lies in the secret of a vial of voodoo blood.

Police Officer as Character • Religion—Voodoo

2

3

The Vampire's Kiss. *New York: Ballantine, 2007. 328p. ISBN 0345498569.*

Thorne, desperately searching throughout Europe for his wife and son, seeks to save the daughter of the strongest voodoo priestess in the New World, for her blood may make him stronger than even elder vampires. Back at home in Savannah, a werewolf clan is attempting to pump drugs into the local economy, drawing the attention of Seth, an alpha werewolf.

Addictions—Drugs • Europe • Kidnapping • Werewolves • Zombies

4

5

Hendee, Barb, and J. C. Hendee.

The Noble Dead Series.

Half-vampire Magiere would like to retire after she ends the vampire reign of terror in Miiska, but a prominent Bela councilman's daughter is found dead—and it looks as though she was bitten by one of the undead. So much for retirement. **Similar titles:** The Vampyricon Trilogy, Douglas Clegg; *King Rat*, China Miâville; The Vampire Earth Series, E. E. Knight.

Fairies • Leesil (character) • Magiere (character) • Vampire Hunters • Vampire's Point of View

6

7

Dhampir. *New York: Roc, 2003. 375p. ISBN 0451459067.*

Former con artist Magiere, who is half-vampire, and her elf partner, Leesil, are tired of village life, ready to move on to greener pastures. Then a trio of ancient vampires learn of Magiere's talents—and want her exterminated.

8

Thief of Lives. *New York: Roc, 2004. 410p. ISBN 0451459539.*

Magiere and her elf partner are being pressured to once more hunt down and kill vampires. But her investigations lead Magiere to believe that the killer might be a different kind of evil.

9

Traitor to the Blood. *New York: Roc, 2006. 355p. ISBN 0451460669.*

Leesil confronts the sins of his past, and Magiere follows him into the Warlands, prepared to slaughter any who intervene. But her own past may spell the end for the duo.

10

Rebel Fay. *New York: Roc, 2007. 372p. ISBN 0451461215.*

Magiere and half-elf Leesil find themselves in the Elven Territories. Leesil is looking for his mother, who has been kidnapped. Chap, the canine protector, is naturally along for the journey to battle the Most Aged Father. Meanwhile, Magiere's half-brother continues his quest for the orb, among the ongoing clash among elves, humans, and the undead.

Cursed Objects • Magic

Sister of the Dead. *New York: Roc, 2005. 405p. ISBN 045146009X.*

Magiere and Leesil make the transition from friendship to relationship, so they journey to find Magiere's parentage and Leesil's mother. Elfin scholar Wynn and her dog Chap go along for the ride, none of them realizing that they are being tracked. To their surprise, Magiere finds her village hostile to the inquiries about the vampire that fathered her with an unwilling mother.

Child of a Dead God. *New York: Roc, 2008. 407p. ISBN 0451461878.*

Magiere and Leesil still seek a long-forgotten orb that would prove disastrous if it fell into the hands of Magiere's half-brother. Dreams of an icy castle cause her to take a journey through elf territory to stop a force of vampire minions. The Most Ancient Father aids her on the quest, but he has a hidden agenda. This novel is full of supernatural espionage, dangerous secrets, and greed for power.

Cursed Objects • Families

Huff, Tanya.

The Smoke Trilogy.

Henry Fitzroy and his ex-lover, Tony Foster, move to Vancouver. Here Tony studies film and becomes a production assistant on the set of the television show *Darkest Night*, the most popular vampire detective series in North America. **Similar titles:** *Midnight Mass*, F. Paul Wilson; The Vampire Earth Series, E. E. Knight; The Angel Investigations Series, various authors; *The Cursed*, L. A. Banks.

Canada—British Columbia—Vancouver • Fitzroy, Henry (character) • Foster, Tony (character) • Gay/Lesbian/Bisexual Characters • Popular Culture • Television Industry

Smoke and Shadows. *New York: Daw, 2005. 416p. ISBN 0756401836.*

Trouble begins when special effects wizard Arra Pelindrake demonstrates that she has more than mere technological prowess. She opens a "gate," and one of the minions of the Shadowlord is able to come into our dimension. Can Fitzroy and Foster stop it?

Magic • Parallel Universes • Witchcraft

Smoke and Mirrors. *New York: DAW, 2006. 416p. ISBN 075640262X.*

Foster, a lowly production assistant on the set of *Darkest Night*, helps shoot haunted house scenes—in a house that is actually inhabited by spirits. When Tony gets locked in the house, he must endure the ghosts constantly reenacting their deaths. Huff's series is full of wisecracking characters and plot twists.

Haunted Houses

Smoke and Ashes. *New York: Daw, 2007. 416p. ISBN 0756403472.*

Now a director in training on the set of *Darkest Night*, Foster is fortunately also a wizard in training. The set of *Darkest Night* is also the set of a pending demonic convergence.

Demons • Haunted Houses

Huston, Charlie.

The Joe Pitt Novels (aka Joe Pitt Casebooks).

Private Investigator Joe Pitt has a hard life, or should we say "unlife." An unaffiliated vampire, he struggles in the underground of vampire clans of New York, living as a mercenary. The trouble is, with so much vampire warring going on, he is kept very busy. **Similar titles:** The Vampire Files, P. N. Elrod; *Expired*, Evie Rhodes; *London Under Midnight*, Simon Clark.

African American Characters • New York—New York City • Pitt, Joe (character) • Vampire Clans

Already Dead. *New York: Del Rey, 2005. ISBN 034547824X.*

Manhattan is inhabited by warring vampire clans, and the most powerful of them, the Coalition, works to protect its members from public scrutiny and prosecution. Vampirism spreads via a virus, and one of the Coalition's number is afflicted with a rogue variation, which causes his victims to turn into zombies, resulting in unwanted public attention for the undead. The Coalition hires vampire private investigator Joe Pitt to find this carrier.

Epidemics—Viruses • Zombies

No Dominion. *New York: Del Rey, 2006. 251p. ISBN 0345478258.*

Joe Pitt investigates the appearance of a new drug that has just hit the street, which causes vampire users to do unpredictable things and has the potential to expose the existence of the undead to the rest of the world. Meanwhile, Joe's HIV positive girlfriend, Evie, is becoming suspicious of his secrecy and disappearances.

Addictions—Drugs • Epidemics—AIDS

Half the Blood of Brooklyn. *New York: Del Rey, 2007. 240p. ISBN 034549587X.*

Pitt is drawn into the midst of a war among several rival vampire clans in Manhattan and Brooklyn. To further complicate matters, a rogue vampire killer stalks the undead community. And then Joe's HIV-infected girlfriend Evie takes a turn for the worse, and he's faced with the dilemma of curing her by giving her some of his blood but also turning her into one of the undead.

Addictions—Drugs • Epidemics—AIDS • Vampire Hunters

Jefferson, Jemiah.

The Voice of the Blood Series.

Ariane Dempsey, a budding biochemist, encounters a vampire and finds herself drawn to a world of darkness and power. Enter Daniel Blum, a vampire known worldwide for his taste for violence and decadence. **Similar titles:** The Hunger Series, Whitley Strieber; The Vampire Chronicles, Anne Rice; *Fledgling*, Octavia Butler.

African American Characters • Blum, Daniel (character) • Dempsey, Ariane (character) • Eroticism • Immortality • Ricari, Orfeo (character) • Vampire's Point of View

Voice of the Blood. *New York: Leisure, 2001. 283p. ISBN 0843948302.*

A graduate student in biology accidentally confronts a vampire who, out of hunger, has trashed her laboratory and killed her mice. Jefferson's emphasis is on characterization in this well-written novel that is as highly erotic and philosophical as the early novels of Anne Rice.

Academia • California—Los Angeles • California—San Francisco

Wounds. *New York: Leisure, 2001. 361p. ISBN 0843949988.*

Jaded, bored, and depressed, the vampire Daniel spends most of his time seeking new distractions. Then he encounters an erotic dancer unique in her psychic abilities. Such is Daniel's infatuation that he consistently does her bidding, even when it endangers his life.

Stripper as Character

Fiend. *New York: Leisure, 2005. 326p. ISBN 0843953640.*

Vampire Orfeo Ricari, a devout Catholic, is the subject of this vampiric bildungsroman. Ricari, both likeable and pitiable, often acts with the innocence of a child. Will he be able to survive an encounter with the evil Daniel?

Homoeroticism

A Drop of Scarlet. *New York: Leisure, 2007. 368p. ISBN 0843957247.*

Following the death of Daniel, the vampire Ariane Dempsey is living in Portland with a new lover, a brilliant, recently turned physicist. Ariane attracts the attention of vampires worldwide when she synthesizes a drug to help stabilize vampiric mood swings.

Oregon—Portland

Kith, Trystam (pseudonym used by Chelsea Quinn Yarbro).

The Trouble in the Forest Series.

This series combines vampires with the folkloric/mythological character Robin Hood. None of the king's men dare go into Sherwood Forest, for those that are brave or foolish enough to do so are found dead—if they are ever found at all. **Similar titles:** *Smoke and Mirrors: Short Fictions and Illusions*, Neil Gaiman; *Hot*

Blooded, Christine Feehan, Maggie Shane, Emma Holly, and Angela Knight; *More Than Mortal*, Mick Farren.

Alternative Literature • DeSteny, Hugh (character) • England • Medieval Era • Popular Culture • Robin Hood (character) • Sheriff of Nottingham (character) • Vampire Clans • Vampire Hunters

A Cold Summer Night. *Waterville, ME: Five Star, 2004. 332p. ISBN 1594142246.*

People disappear when they enter Sherwood Forest. Former Crusader Hugh DeSteny has seen this kind of thing before, when he fought vampires while on the crusades. Robin Hood, the master vampire, kidnaps a maiden intended for one of the sheriff's men, so DeSteny is called into action.

A Bright Winter Sun. *Waterville, ME: Five Star, 2005. 333p. ISBN 1594142246.*

As the battle between good and evil in Sherwood Forest continues, Hugh DeSteny plans to destroy Robin Hood and his Merry Vampires during the Fair of the Eve of All Saints. But the undead who stalk the woods have plans as well. And little do the sheriff's men know that Maid Marion is no longer the meager maiden she was when she was kidnapped.

Knight, E. E.

The Vampire Earth Series.

David Valentine fights against traitorous humans, genetically created monsters, vampires, and aliens. Chosen to become a protector of humans, or a "wolf," he joins a resistance group to defeat the alien race that has enslaved Earth in order to perform experiments on humans and use them for food. **Similar titles:** The Angel Investigations Series, various authors; The Smoke Trilogy, Tanya Huff; *The Cursed*, L. A. Banks.

Aliens • Futurism • Valentine, David (character) • Vampire Hunters

The Way of the Wolf. *New York: New American Library, 2003. 391p. ISBN 0451459393.*

In the first novel of this futuristic series, readers are introduced to Valentine. With his canine superpowers, he becomes an elite warrior, but can even he manage to lead an insurgency against such a superior invading force?

Eugenics

Choice of the Cat. *New York: Roc, 2004. 343p. ISBN 0451459733.*

David Valentine becomes a commanding officer and oversees a retreat by his outnumbered men, which results in his finding himself being court-martialed. But then the Cat spy he met in battle offers him a chance to join their resistance group. He accepts the demanding training and tough initiation, which exponentially increases his abilities. His first mission as a Cat involves dangerous intelligence gathering. **Similar titles:** <u>The Angel Investigations Series</u>, various authors; <u>The Smoke Trilogy</u>, Tanya Huff; *The Cursed*, L. A. Banks.

Apocalypse • Soldier as Character • Vampire's Point of View

Merz, Jon F.

The Lawson Vampire Novels.

Shiva, a deadly assassin, half vampire and half werewolf, is assigned to take out the head of the Vampire Council. Of course, this will be anything but a cakewalk. **Similar titles:** <u>The Vampire Earth Series</u>, E. E. Knight; <u>The Vampire Huntress Legend</u>, L. A. Banks; <u>The Noble Dead Series</u>, Barb Hendee and J. C. Hendee.

Police Officer as Character • Vampire Hunters • Vampire's Point of View

The Destructor. *New York: Kensington, 2003. 348p. ISBN 0786015357.*

Vampire rogue hunter/protector Lawson will have the help of another "Fixer," the mysterious Jarvis. Can the two protectors, working together, stop the most evil woman alive?

Espionage • Werewolves

The Syndicate. *New York: Kensington, 2003. 348p. ISBN 0786015365.*

Lawson, protector of the Balance, which keeps the existence of vampires hidden from humans, is told that his cousin Marilyn is missing. Traveling to New York, he discovers that whoever has taken her has hidden her well, so he turns to a psychic friend and finds himself being led into violent confrontations with hit men toting machine guns and assault weapons.

Kidnapping • Psychics

Mitchell, Mary Ann.

Marquis de Sade Series.

The Marquis de Sade is alive and well as a member of the undead, and now he's introducing fourteen-year-old girls to his vices. Mitchell's emphasis is on action in this series. **Similar titles:** <u>The Vampire Chronicles</u>, Anne Rice; *Live Girls*, Ray Garton; *The Long Last Call*, John Skipp; *Darkness Wakes*, Tim Waggoner.

Marquis de Sade (character) • Sado-Masochism • Vampire's Point of View

Sips of Blood. *New York: Leisure, 1999. 358p. ISBN 0843945559.*

The Marquis de Sade's tastes are decadent and insatiable. And as if that weren't bad enough, he and his dominatrix mother-in-law are members of the undead; they accidentally turn others into vampires while indulging their carnal desires.

Eroticism

Quenched. *New York: Leisure, 2000. 363p. ISBN 0843947179.*

Will and his bitter, crippled father Keith are adjusting to their new lives as vampires after the Marquis de Sade and his mother-in-law accidentally turn them. With no money and no one to tutor them in the ways of the undead, they must learn how to obtain victims without attracting too much attention. Turns out, their only hope for survival is to find their maker.

California—San Francisco • Eroticism • Reincarnation

Cathedral of Vampires. *New York: Leisure, 2002. 355p. ISBN 0843950234.*

Cecilia, a vampire, seeks vengeance for Sade's role in the death of her child. The count himself, ensconced in his French chateau while debauching and eating villagers, has adapted the local cathedral so that he can lock up vampires. There he incarcerates Cecilia.

France • Prisons

Tainted Blood. *New York: Leisure, 2003. 334p. ISBN 0843950919.*

The battle between de Sade and the woman who turned him and made his life into a living hell finally comes to a head. De Sade decides to hunt down Marie, which leads him to a suburban American home—a fairly normal abode except for the fact that its inhabitants are undead.

Gay/Lesbian/Bisexual Characters • Homoeroticism • Incest • Suburbia

The Vampire de Sade. *New York: Leisure, 2004. 337p. ISBN 0843954175.*

The Marquis is a vampire living in present-day Paris. He begins to dream of his niece, Liliana—which creates a problem for him since vampires should lack the ability to dream. It seems magic is being used against him. The Marquis soon learns that it comes from his former lover, Marie Laveau.

Dreams • Eroticism • Laveau, Marie (character) • Magic • Religion—Voodoo

Mosiman, Billie Sue.

The Red Moon Series.

Dell is a normal teenage girl who worries about dating and grades until the day she develops lesions on her body. Then she discovers that she too, like her parents and her brother, is a vampire. **Similar titles:** *Ivy Cole and the Moon*, Gina Farrago; *The Turning*, Jennifer Armitrout; *Blood and Chocolate*, Annette Curtis Klause; <u>The Buffy the Vampire Slayer Series</u>, various authors.

Adolescence • Immortality • Vampire Clans • Vampire's Point of View

Red Moon Rising. *New York: DAW, 2001. 320p. ISBN 0886779553.*

Dell, with the help of Mentor, the creature who has helped her species for generations, must discover what sort of vampire she'll be: a Predator, who kills without remorse; a Craven, who is utterly incapable of taking blood and so must depend on the kindness of Predators to survive; or a Normal, something in between a Craven and a Predator.

Physician as Character • Porphyria • Psychics • Shape-shifters • Texas—Dallas

Malachi's Moon. *New York: Daw, 2002. 352p. ISBN 0756400481.*

Malachi, the child of a vampire and a human, possesses many of the powers of vampires. In fact, he may well be a threat to the most dangerous kind of vampires, the Predators. One of them begins stalking Malachi through his dreams, and eventually sends assassins his way. Meanwhile, in Thailand, imprisoned vampire Charles Upton plans to escape and wreak havoc on the vampire world by gathering the Predators together to destroy the other two kinds of vampires.

Dreams • Malachi (character) • Upton, Charles (character)

Craven Moon. *New York: Daw, 2003. 320p. ISBN 0756401208.*

Malachi, a dhampir feared to be the slayer foretold in ancient vampire prophecy, enjoys his new life with his wife and son. Too bad his nemesis, Charles Upton, is busy creating an army of predators, and a human with a dark soul, to defeat Malachi. When Malachi's wife is killed, he must choose between remaining docile and accepting a violent mission.

Apocalypse • Families • Malachi (character) • Upton, Charles (character)

Moore, Christopher.

The Love Story Series.

(See chapter 16, "Comic Horror: Laughing at Our Fears.")

Newman, Kim.

The Anno Dracula Series.

Kim Newman rewrites Stoker's narrative using historical, literary, and popular cultural figures to create an intricate reworking of the *Dracula* story, while including every known vampire myth. **Similar titles:** *Renfield, Slave of Dracula*, Barbara Hambly; *The Man from the Diogenes Club*, Kim Newman; <u>The Vampire Chronicles</u>, Anne Rice; *From Hell* (film).

Alternative History • Alternative Literature • Beauregard, Charles (character) • Diogenes Club • Dracula (novel) • England—London • Holmwood, Arthur (character) • Jack the Ripper (character) • Seward, John (character) • Tepes, Vlad (character) • Vampire's Point of View • Victorian Era

 Anno Dracula. *New York: Avon, 1994, ©1992. 409p. ISBN 038072345X.*

What would've happened if Dracula had actually defeated Van Helsing? Knowlegable about history, Newman writes highly literate prose in this astounding work.

Jack the Ripper (character) • Seward, John (character) • Victorian Era

Bloody Red Baron. *New York: Avon, 1995. 370p. ISBN 0786702524.*

This novel picks up twenty years after *Anno Dracula* ends. Previously, the evil Prince Vlad was chased from England, and all thought he had been defeated. However, Vlad Tepes has been regrouping his forces in Germany and has gotten one of his own vampires to assassinate Archduke Ferdinand to start World War I.

War—World War I

Judgment of Tears: Anno Dracula, 1959. *New York: Carroll & Graf, 1998. 240p. ISBN 0786705582.*

> Vlad Tepes sets out to marry yet again for political gain, this time in Rome, the Eternal City. But someone is murdering vampire elders, some who were born to darkness as long ago as the Middle Ages. Featured in this novel are John and Morticia Adams, James Bond, Father Merrin from *The Exorcist*, an enormous Orson Wells, and a gloomy Edgar Allan Poe.

Italy—Rome

Rice, Anne.

The New Tales of the Vampire Series.

In this vampire series, Rice's emphasis is on historical accuracy rather than vampirism per se, featuring main characters such as one of the few strong Rice-created females, and a 500-year-old vampire elder. **Similar titles:** The Saint-Germain Chronicles, Chelsea Quinn Yarbro; *The Vampire Armand* and *Blood and Gold*, Anne Rice.

Homoeroticism • Italy • Religion—Christianity • Vampire's Point of View

Pandora: New Tales of the Vampire. *New York: Alfred A. Knopf, 1998. 288p. ISBN 0375401598.*

> This pseudo-historical romp through the Rome of Augustus Caesar and modern-day Paris, stars Pandora, an innocent Roman girl made into a vampire by Marius.

Akasha and Enkil (characters) • Italy—Rome • Marius (character) • Pandora (character)

Vittorio, the Vampire. *New York: Alfred A. Knopf, 1999. 292p. ISBN 0375401601.*

> Set in Renaissance Italy, this is a first-person narrative by the 500-year-old vampire who was educated in the Medici court. The story chronicles his transformation from human to immortal at the hands of Ursula, the vampire who haunts his family.

Artist as Character • Clergy as Character • deRanari, Vittorio (character) • Italy—Florence

The Vampire Chronicles.

This series of novels made household names of Lestat de Lioncourt and his protégé Louis. Lestat, a French nobleman, is turned into a vampire during the eighteenth century. The series follows his adventures in modern-day New Orleans. The chronicles have gained a large fan base since the publication of the first volume in 1976 and are considered the yardstick against which all vampire series are judged. **Similar titles:** The Saint-Germain Chronicles, Chelsea Quinn Yarbro; The Voice of the Blood Series, Jemiah Jefferson; The Crimson Series, Trisha Baker.

Europe • Homoeroticism • Lestat de Lioncourt (character) • Louisiana—New Orleans • Vampire's Point of View

Interview with the Vampire. *New York: Ballantine, 2004, ©1976. 352p. ISBN 0345476875.*

This first novel in Rice's Vampire Chronicles series is structured around the confessions of reluctant vampire Louis, who during a time of overwhelming grief was seduced into undeath by Lestat de Lioncourt. Rice transports readers into the world of the undead in nineteenth-century New Orleans. An immensely popular best seller that led to Rice's own "immortality" on the best-seller list, this novel was made into a film in 1995.

Armand (character) • Claudia (character) • Louis (character)

The Vampire Lestat. *New York: Ballantine, 1985. 481p. ISBN 0394534433.*

Lestat responds in the first person to what he views as slander from his former lover Louis in his tell-all book *Interview with the Vampire*. Specifically, we learn of his lengthy undead and pre-undead existence and subsequent search for the meaning of life.

Akasha and Enkil (characters) • Armand (character) • Claudia (character) • Marius (character) • Music—Rock Music

The Queen of the Damned. *New York: Ballantine, 1989. 491p. ISBN 0394558235.*

The mother of all vampire-kind, Akasha has freed herself from Enkil, her husband and jailer for the past 2,000 years, and has taken Lestat as an unwilling personal assistant to help execute her plan to kill nine out of every ten men on Earth.

Akasha and Enkil (characters) • Babylon • Lightner, Aaron (character) • Maharet and Mekare (characters) • Marius (character) • Religion—Ancient Egyptian • Talamasca, The

The Tale of the Body Thief. *New York: Ballantine, 1992. 435p. ISBN 0679405283.*

Lestat has a chance to become mortal once again. Bored with the undead life, Lestat longs to experience human pleasures such as eating and making love once more, but he also rediscovers the mortification of being encased in mortal flesh when his new body is laid low by the flu.

New York—New York City • Talamasca, The • Talbot, David (character)

Memnoch the Devil. *New York: Alfred A. Knopf, 1995. 354p. ISBN 0679441018.*

Lestat has a spiritual awakening. For centuries Lestat has doubted the existence of God and Satan, until the devil appears to him personally. Satan shows Lestat the world of the living and the dead and asks him to be his second in command. *Memnoch the Devil* was originally supposed to be the last book of Rice's Vampire Chronicles, but her fans persuaded her to add more titles.

Armand (character) • Claudia (character) • Maharet and Mekare (characters) • New York—New York City • Religion—Christianity • Satan (character)

The Vampire Armand. *New York: Alfred A. Knopf, 1998. 387p. ISBN 0679454470.*

After his encounter with Satan, Lestat lies unconscious on the floor of a cathedral, and all the vampires of the world have gathered at his side. On this occasion David Talbot bids Armand to take the opportunity to tell about his human life with Marius in Renaissance Italy, and later as leader of a coven of vampires in Paris.

Armand (character) • Frame Tale • Italy—Venice • Marius (character) • Religion—Christianity • Renaissance Era • Santino (character) • Talbot, David (character)

Blood and Gold: The Story of Marius. *New York: Alfred A. Knopf, 2001. 470p. ISBN 0679454497.*

Rice follows the lonely life of Marius, caretaker of Akasha and Enkil, Those Who Must be Kept. Plucked from his life as a Roman patrician 2,000 years ago, Marius finds immortality to be both a blessing and a curse, allowing the scholar and artist sufficient time to achieve all of his life's goals, yet preventing him from engaging in relationships with others for fear of revealing his burden.

Akasha and Enkil (characters) • Immortality • Italy—Rome • Marius (character) • Religion— Druidism

Blackwood Farm. *New York: Ballantine, 2003. 527p. ISBN 0375411992.*

Tarquin Blackwood, a young vampire, seeks Lestat's help. Lestat takes Tarquin as a mentee but notices a strange creature attach itself to the youngster. Goblin, an invisible doppelganger who has been with Tarquin his whole life, is the cause of the frame tale that ensues. Quinn recounts his life to Lestat.

Blackwood, Quinn (character) • Doppelgangers • Mayfair, Mona (character)

Blood Canticle. *New York: Alfred A. Knopf, 2003. 320p. ISBN 037541200X.*

After centuries of disillusionment, Lestat de Lioncourt is led back to the Catholic church in this episode of <u>The Vampire Chronicles</u>.

Blackwood, Quinn (character) • Doppelgangers • Religion—Christianity—Catholicism

Simmons, Wm. Mark.

The Chris Csejthe Series.

(See chapter 16, "Comic Horror: Laughing at Our Fears.")

Stein, Jeanne C.

The Anna Strong Chronicles.

Bounty hunter Anna Strong is very good at catching criminals. She's gotten even better at it since one of her targets turned her into a vampire. Soon she discovers that there is an entire vampire network, headed by a group called The Watchers, vampires who broker peace with humans and attempt to keep the more volatile of the undead at bay. **Similar titles:** *Sunglasses After Dark*, Nancy A. Collins; The Anita Blake, Vampire Hunter Series, Laurel K. Hamilton; *Blood Will Tell*, Jean Lorrah.

Bounty Hunter as Character • Shape-shifters • Strong, Anna (character) • Vampire Hunters • Vampire's Point of View

The Watcher. *New York: Ace, 2007. 291p. ISBN 0441015468.*

After Anna shows her fangs to two humans, she is ordered to take a "vacation," lest a sect of vampire hunters called The Revengers finds and destroys her.

California—San Diego • Mexico • Police Officer as Character • Religion—Wicca

Blood Drive. *New York: Ace, 2007, ©2006. 297p. ISBN 0441015093.*

Anna's brother has been dead for fourteen years. His last girlfriend appears out of the blue and says he has a daughter, but the thirteen-year-old has gone missing. Anna's search for her niece leads her to a shape-shifting teacher, who agrees to help her. But the two end up someplace neither expected—in the world of child pornography.

Child Molesters • Families

Strieber, Whitley.

The Hunger Series.

For thousands of years, Miriam has been forever young and has enjoyed the love of numerous companions in darkness. **Similar titles:** *Carmilla*, Joseph Sheridan Le Fanu; *Tale of the Body Thief*, Anne Rice; *The Hunger* (film); *Dracula's Daughter* (film); *Nadja* (film).

Blaylock, Miriam (character) • New York—New York City • Roberts, Sarah (character) • Vampire's Point of View

The Hunger. *New York: Morrow, 1981. 320p. ISBN 0688037577.*

Although Miriam is forever young, her magic cannot deliver the same for her lovers; for them she can merely bestow eternal life trapped in a rotting husk of a body. **Similar titles:** *Carmilla*, Joseph Sheridan Le Fanu; *Tale of the Body Thief*, Anne Rice; *The Hunger* (film); *Dracula's Daughter* (film); *Nadja* (film).

Aging • Gay/Lesbian/Bisexual Characters • Homoeroticism • Religion—Ancient Egyptian

The Last Vampire. *New York: Pocket, 2001. 303p. ISBN 0743417208.*

In the long-awaited sequel to *The Hunger*, Interpol agent Paul Ward travels throughout the world, exterminating those vampires known as the Keepers as he finds them. After one of his assassinations, he discovers the book that lists the names and locations of all the Keepers throughout the world. In no time, he and his accomplices have eliminated all but one vampire, Miriam Blaylock, and now Paul has traced her to New York City.

France—Paris • Vampire Hunters • Ward, Paul (character)

Lilith's Dream: A Tale of the Vampire Life. *New York: Simon & Schuster, 2002. 400p. ISBN 074345152X.*

Lilith (Adam's first wife from the Bible and creator of all vampires and humans) faces off in Manhattan against CIA-based vampire hunter Paul Ward. After fleeing her cave in Egypt upon learning of the destruction of virtually all the world's vampires, Lilith, with the aid of rock star Leo Patterson, kidnaps Ward's child and takes possession of the body of Miriam Blaylock.

Lilith (character) • Vampire Hunters • Ward, Paul (character)

Wellington, David.

The 99 Coffins Series.

An archeological dig uncovers something disturbing—a series of 100 Civil War–era coffins, each containing a corpse that has had its heart cut out. Special F.B.I. deputy Jameson Arkeley recognizes the remains. They are those of a forgotten Union vampire corps. **Similar titles:** The Anna Strong Chronicles, Jeanne C. Stein; The Vampire Files, P. N. Elrod; *Blood Will Tell*, Jean Lorrah.

Arkeley, Jamison (character) • Federal Bureau of Investigation • Malvern, Justina (character) • Pennsylvania • Police Officer as Character • Vampire Hunters • War—American Civil War

99 Coffins: A Historical Vampire Tale. *New York: Three Rivers Press, 2007. 292p. ISBN 0307381714.*

Arkeley contacts expert Laura Caxton, who had vowed never to face the vampires again, but before they can act, one of the vampires is re-animated, setting the stage for the full vampire army to come to life—all he needs is 100 hearts.

13 Bullets: A Vampire Tale. *New York: Three Rivers Press, 2007. 323p. ISBN 0307381439.*

Special F.B.I. deputy Jameson Arkeley, known for having stopped vampires in his past, made a mistake. When he whittled down the living dead to a single survivor, he did not finish the job of eradicating the bloodsuckers. Justinia Malvern has been kept alive in rural Pennsylvania, where a series of vampire killings suggests that she may be feeding her needs again. Arkeley, believing that Malvern has a contingent of minions, commandeers state trooper Laura Caxton to help him find the lair and wipe them out.

Yarbro, Chelsea Quinn.

The Saint-Germain Chronicles.

He's seen it all. He's done it all. But then again, that is par for the course when you've been "alive" for hundreds of years. This series is unique in that it takes readers on trips through various historical eras, with events being glimpsed through the lens of a centuries-old vampire. **Similar titles:** <u>The Vampire Chronicles</u> and <u>The New Tales of the Vampire Series</u>, Anne Rice; <u>The Jonathan Barrett, Gentleman Vampire Series</u>, P. N. Elrod.

Saint-Germain, Count Ragoczy de (character) • Vampire's Point of View

Hotel Transylvania. *Grand Central Publishing, 2002, ©1978. 384p. ISBN 0312392486.*

> Saint-Germain must save Madeleine de Montalia, an independent young woman with whom he has fallen in love, from the clutches of an evil cult. This novel is set in eighteenth-century France.

France—Paris • Gothicism • Religion—Cults • Religion—Satanism

The Palace. *New York: Warner Books, 2002, ©1978. 519p. ISBN 0312594747.*

> In fifteenth-century Florence, Francero Ragoczy da San Germano builds himself a home that rivals the most sumptuous in the city, and people suspect many things. The stranger never eats in public, has no mirrors in his home, and even his manner of lovemaking is strange.

Epistolary Format • Italy—Florence • Spanish Inquisition

Blood Games: A Novel of Historical Horror. *New York: Warner, 2004, ©1979. 613p. ISBN 0446613797.*

> Saint-Germain shows up in ancient Rome, where he must come to terms with the cruelties and casual disregard of human life he encounters among his new countrymen.

Italy—Rome

Path of the Eclipse. *New York: Tom Doherty, 1989, ©1981. 467p. ISBN 0812528107.*

> The fourth in Yarbro's Count Saint-Germain novels finds the alchemist vampire in medieval China with Buddhists, Muslims, and Hindus, all attempting to flee the wrath of the Monguls. Yarbro's gentle vampire protagonist is more human than superhuman; he eschews violence and can only receive sexual gratification through completely satisfying his partner.

China • Epistolary Format • Religion—Buddhism • Religion—Christianity • Religion—Hinduism • Religion—Islam

Tempting Fate. *Lancaster, PA: Stealth Press, 2001, ©1982. 662p. ISBN 1588810259.*

> In a series of letters intermixed with narration, Yarbro places Saint-Germain in the Bolshevik Revolution, where he must help a Russian countess escape, as well as assist a young war orphan.

Epistolary Format • War—Russian Revolution

The Saint-Germain Chronicles. *New York: Pocket Books, 1983. 206p. ISBN 0671459031.*

> (See chapter 18, "Collections and Anthologies.")

Darker Jewels: A Novel of the Count Saint-Germain. *New York: Orb, 1995, ©1993. 398p. ISBN 0312890311.*

> Saint-Germain is assigned to help Istaven Bathory, Transylvanian king of Poland, ward off the Ottoman Turks. En route, he runs into problems with sus-

picious clergymen, arranged marriages, and feuding nobles. This book is dense with period and place description.

Clergy as Character • Espionage • Gothicism • Poland • Religion—Christianity—Catholicism

Better in the Dark: An Historical Novel. *New York: Tor, 1993. 412p. ISBN 0312855044.*

Captured and taken to Saxony during the Dark Ages, Saint-Germain begins a romance with a beautiful lady of King Otto's court. But once more he is doomed to be hunted, this time as a witch.

Epistolary Format • Gothicism

Mansions of Darkness: A Novel of Saint-Germain. *New York: Tor, 1996. 430p. ISBN 0312857594.*

Saint-Germain travels to seventeenth-century Spanish America, where he runs into the forces of the Spanish Inquisition, as well as the usual vampire hunters. Yarbro weaves a tapestry of historical romance, vampire fiction, and anthropology.

Native American Characters • Peru • Spanish Inquisition

Writ in Blood: A Novel of Saint-Germain. *New York: Tor, 1997. 543p. ISBN 0312863187.*

Czar Nicholas sends Saint-Germain, who resides in St. Petersburg, to deliver a top-secret peace proposal to Edward VI of England and Germany's Kaiser Wilhelm. Saint-Germain must contend with the political ambitions of the Czar's kinsmen, as well as the machinations of an ambitious arms manufacturer, Von Wolgast.

England—London • Epistolary Format • Espionage • War—World War I

Blood Roses: A Novel of Saint-Germain. *New York: Tor, 1998. 382p. ISBN 0312865295.*

Saint-Germain settles in a small French town in the fourteenth century, during the time of the Black Death. Can he use his knowledge of healing without arousing suspicion about his true nature?

Epidemics • France

Come Twilight: A Novel of Saint-Germain. *New York: Tor, 2000. 479p. ISBN 0312873301.*

Saint-Germain and Rogerian, his servant, flee to the seventh-century village of Mont Calcius, where the sole inhabitant is a young pregnant woman. Forced to save her life by giving her immortality, Yarbro's vampiric hero unwittingly creates the leader of a rival group of vampires who threaten to disturb the peaceful coexistence between vampires and humans.

Epistolary Format • Religion—Christianity • Spain • Vampire Clans • Vampire Hunters

A Feast in Exile. *New York: Tor, 2001. 496p. ISBN 0312878435.*

In this Saint-Germain romance, the vampire-hero, alias Sanat Ji Manik, lives in Delhi at the end of the fourteenth century. With him are his faithful servant Rojire and Avasa Dani, a young Indian woman abandoned by her husband. Enemies surround them, namely the relatives of the corrupt sultan who is constantly demanding more in taxes. And the brutal warlord Timur-i is approaching Delhi, intent on sacking the city.

India • Torture

Borne in Blood: A Novel of the Count Saint-Germain. *New York Tom Doherty, 2007. 367p. ISBN 0765317133.*

In the twentieth novel of this long-running series, the 4,000-year-old vampire finds himself in Switzerland in the early 1800s, helping with the recovery from the Napoleonic wars and severe winters. He also is dealing with the emotional baggage of the family problems suffered by his lover—who has had to send her children away to be raised by their hard-hearted grandfather—as well as the advances of the beautiful ward of a local nobleman.

Epistolary Format • Families

Vampire Stand-Alone Novels

Acevedo, Mario.

The Nymphos of Rocky Flats. *New York: Eos, 2007. 354p. ISBN 006143888X.*
(See chapter 16, "Comic Horror: Laughing at Our Fears.")

Anscombe, Roderick.

The Secret Life of Lazslo, Count Dracula. *New York: St. Martins, 2006, ©1994. 416p. ISBN 0312357664.*
(See chapter 14, "Psychological Horror: It's All in Your Head.")

Butler, Octavia.

Fledgling. *New York: Seven Stories Press, 2005. 317p. ISBN 1583226907.*
Butler confronts racism in a supernatural universe. Fledgling vampire Shori Matthews has survived a horrific attack, in which her would-be assassins burned down her house and left her for dead. Although Shori's body knits itself back together in a matter of a few days, her memory of her former life disappears. Now she struggles to learn what it is to be a vampire and to discover why someone wants her dead. **Similar titles:** The Living Blood Series and *The Between*, Tananarive Due; *Dark Corner*, Brandon Massey; *Blade* (film).

African American Characters • Families • Racism • Vampire Clans • Vampire's Point of View

Cisco, Michael.

The Tyrant. *Canton, OH: Prime, 2004. 250p. ISBN 1894815858.*
Having "done" Europe, hoards of vampires decide to invade New York City, and eventually to conquer the New World. Father Joe Cahill, a whisky-drinking priest

who decides to redeem himself by fighting the undead, joins forces with his activist niece and Carol Hanarty, a nun who makes explosives. **Similar titles:** *The Exorcist*, William Peter Blatty; *London Under Midnight*, Simon Clark; *I Am Legend*, Richard Matheson; *Midnight Mass*, F. Paul Wilson.

Clergy as Character • New York—New York City • Vampire Hunters

Clark, Simon.

London Under Midnight. *Sutton, UK: Severn House Publishing, 2006. 214p. ISBN 0727863983.*

Journalist Ben Ashton is investigating the appearance of the proliferation of the phrase "Vampire Sharkz: They're coming to get you," which has suddenly been graffitied throughout London. His search unearths an old girlfriend, who has recently joined the ranks of the undead. And she is not alone—over the past year, an increasing number of Londoners have been made into vampires due to the machinations of the African trickster god Edshu. **Similar titles:** *'Salem's Lot*, Stephen King; *Manitou Blood*, Graham Masterton; The Joe Pitt Novels, Charlie Huston.

Journalist as Character • England—London • Religion—African

Collins, Nancy A.

Ⓑ 🎖 **Sunglasses After Dark.** *Clarkston, GA: White Wolf, 2000, ©1989. 192p. ISBN 1565048490.*

Denise Thorne, heiress, is raped by a vampire. After nine months in a coma, she is reborn as Sonja Blue, a vampire who can inhabit dream worlds, and who violently kills both cruel humans and the unruly undead. Considered by critics and vampire fans to be one of the finest original vampire tales of the past decade, this novel is unique and erudite. **Similar titles:** The Anna Strong Chronicles, Jeanne C. Stein; The Buffy the Vampire Slayer Series, various authors; The Anita Blake, Vampire Hunter Series, Laurel K. Hamilton.

Blue, Sonja (character) • Dreams • Psychics • Rape • Vampire Hunters • Vampire's Point of View

Fingerman, B. H.

Bottomfeeder. *Berkley, CA: M. Press, 2006. 268p. ISBN 1595820973.*
(See chapter 16, "Comic Horror: Laughing at Our Fears.")

Golden, Christopher.

The Gathering Dark. *New York: Berkley, 2003. 373p. ISBN 0441010814.*
Peter Octavian, an elder vampire turned human, is now a powerful mage. Father Jack Devlin realizes that Octavian may be the best defense against the whispers, demons that have been attacking villagers around the world and transporting entire towns into a hellish dimension. With the addition of a witch and one of Octavian's old flames, the demon hunters set off to

face the evil. **Similar titles:** <u>The Lawson Vampire Novels</u>, Jon F. Merz; <u>The Renquist Quartet</u>, Mick Farren; <u>The Vampire Earth Series</u>, E. E. Knight.

Clergy as Character • Demons • England • Kidnapping • Parallel Universes • Religion —Christianity—Catholicism • Spain • Vampire's Point of View • Witchcraft

Golden, Christopher, and James A. Moore.

Bloodstained Oz. *Northborough, MA: Earthling Publications, 2006. 116p. ISBN 0976633965.*
Golden and Moore's dark fantasy version of Frank L. Baum's *The Wizard of Oz* is set in a bleak Depression-era Kansas. From here Dorothy ventures to an Oz populated by vampiric versions of the Tin Man, the Cowardly Lion, and the Scarecrow. **Similar titles:** <u>The Vampyricon Trilogy</u>, Douglas Clegg; *King Rat*, China Miâville; *Neverwhere*, Neil Gaiman; *Tideland* (film).

Alternative Literature • Oz (fictional setting) • Wizard of Oz (film)

Hambly, Barbara.

Renfield, Slave of Dracula. *New York. Berkley, 2006. 306p. ISBN 0425211681.*
In this rewriting of *Dracula,* told from Renfield's point of view, we learn, via his more lucid moments in diaries and letters, that he is mentally ill, but that eventually the Count's strength becomes his own, enabling him to fight his master. Hambly's alternative retelling of *Dracula* uses a style similar to the original: much of the narrative unfolds through journals and notes. **Similar titles:** *The Book of Renfield*, Tim Lucas; *The Journal of Professor Abraham Van Helsing*, Allen C. Kupfer; *The Many Faces of Van Helsing*, Jeanne Cavelos (editor).

Alternative Literature • Diary Format • Dracula (character) • Dracula (novel) • England—London • Epistolary Format • Harker, Jonathan (character) • Harker, Mina Murray (character) • Holmwood, Arthur (character) • Mental Illness • Renfield (character) • Seward, John (character) • Transylvania • Van Helsing, Abraham (character) • Westerna, Lucy (character)

Hayter, Sparkle.

Naked Brunch. *New York: Three Rivers Press, 2003. 322p. ISBN 1400047439.*
(See chapter 16, "Comic Horror: Laughing at Our Fears.")

Hinton, S. E.

Hawkes Harbor. *New York: Tor, 2004. 256p. ISBN 0765305631.*
(See chapter 8, "Mythological Monsters and 'The Old Ones': Invoking the Dark Gods.")

Hubbard, Susan.

The Society of S. *New York: Simon & Schuster, 2007. 304p. ISBN 1416534571.*
Ariella Montero has never met her mother; she was abandoned at birth. Her father, a scientist who homeschools her, allows her little contact with the world outside the home. The pieces of the puzzle of her life come together when her father tells her that he was vampirized shortly before marriage, and that Ari is a hybrid—and has a choice to make. **Similar titles:** <u>The Crimson Series</u>, Trisha Baker;

Ivy Cole and the Moon, Gina Farrago; *The Turning*, Jennifer Armitrout; *Blood and Chocolate*, Annette Curtis Klause.

Adolescence • Family Curse • High School • Parenting • Road Trips • South, The • Vampire's Point of View

Jacob, Charlee.

This Symbiotic Fascination. *New York: Leisure, 2002. 394p. ISBN 084394966X.* (See chapter 15, "Splatterpunk: The Gross Out.")

King, Stephen.

'Salem's Lot. *Garden City: NJ: Doubleday, 1975. 439p. ISBN 0385007515.*
Jerusalem's Lot is a town well acquainted with darkness and evil. After all, the sins of the town legend, Hubie Marsten, were kept alive in rumor and gossip. But there is a new evil in the Marsten house, in the form of Richard Throckett Straker, an antique furniture dealer who is also a vampire. King's book works well on scares and suspense. **Similar titles:** *Needful Things*, Stephen King; *London Under Midnight*, Simon Clark; *Midnight Mass*, F. Paul Wilson; <u>The Vampire Earth Series</u>, E. E. Knight.

Clergy as Character • Haunted Houses • Maine • Physician as Character • Secret Sin • Teacher as Character • Vampire Hunters • Writer as Character

Kostova, Elizabeth.

The Historian: A Novel. *New York: Little, Brown, 2005. 656p. ISBN 0316011770.*
A graduate student in history once found a mysterious, old book—and that legacy still haunts his daughter, a brilliant scholar in her own right. The story is told initially through dialogue and later supplemented by letters. On the trail to finding the elusive Prince Dracul, the main characters weave in and out of exotic European locations and through numerous libraries and archives, from the better known largesse of Oxford University to small one-room archives in Istanbul, and finally the oldest monasteries in Europe. **Similar titles:** *Renfield, Slave of Dracula*, Barbara Hambly; <u>The Vampire Chronicles</u>, Anne Rice; *The Ghost Writer*, John Harwood; *The Open Curtain*, Brian Evenson.

Antiquarianism • Dracula (character) • England—London • Europe • Librarian as Character • Road Trips

Kupfer, Allen C.

The Journal of Professor Abraham Van Helsing. *New York: Doherty, 2004. 204p. ISBN 0765310112.*
Professor Abraham Van Helsing, the sagacious physician and metaphysician who guides the band of vampire hunters in Bram Stoker's *Dracula*, was once a young man who was incredulous about the reality of the vampire until he saw with his own eyes evidence of the fiend's existence. This novel, written in diary format, is a window into Van Helsing's early years

and includes the marginal notes of his good friend, Dr. Daniel Kupfer, and Van Helsing's grandson, which provide additional insight into the famous vampire hunter's character. **Similar titles:** *The Many Faces of Van Helsing*, Jeanne Cavelos (editor); *The Book of Renfield*, Tim Lucas; *Renfield, Slave of Dracula*, Barbara Hambly; *Van Helsing*, Kevin Ryan.

Alternative Literature • Diary Format • Romania • Vampire Hunters • Van Helsing, Abraham (character)

Laws, Stephen.

Fear Me. *New York: Leisure, 2005. 435p. ISBN 0843954868.*
(*Originally published as* Gideon *in 1993*). Gideon, a supernatural sexual predator, has been slowly draining the life from Bernice, Yvonne, and Jacqueline. Believing that there is strength in numbers, the three lure him to an underground parking garage and shoot him many times, enough times to kill any mortal, and leave him for dead. But of course, Gideon is not dead. He recovers and plots his revenge. **Similar titles:** *Drawn to the Grave*, Mary Ann Mitchell; *Live Girls*, Ray Garton; The Voice of the Blood Series, Jemiah Jefferson.

Psychosexual Horror • Revenging Revenant • Vampire's Point of View

Laymon, Richard.

Bite. *New York: Leisure, 1999, ©1996. 378p. ISBN 0843945508.*
(See chapter 16, "Comic Horror: Laughing at Our Fears.")

The Traveling Vampire Show. *New York: Leisure, 2001. 391p. ISBN 0843948507.*
(See chapter 14, "Psychological Horror: It's All in Your Head.")

Lebbon, Tim, and Steve Niles.

30 Days of Night: A Novelization. *New York: Pocket Star Books, 2007. 325p. ISBN 1416544976.*
(See chapter 10, "Small Town Horror: Villages of the Damned.")

Le Fanu, Joseph Sheridan.

"Carmilla." In *In a Glass Darkly. Aegypan, 2006, ©1872. 276p. ISBN 1598188356.*
A young girl, Laura, befriends the temptress Carmilla, a young aristocratic girl who is really a vampire. This influential nineteenth-century novella is characterized by its highly descriptive prose and indirect style, as well as by its use of first-person narration in journal form, included in the frame tale format of the collection in which it appears, *In a Glass Darkly*. **Similar titles:** The Crimson Series, Trisha Baker; *Ivy Cole and the Moon*, Gina Farrago; *Blood and Chocolate*, Annette Curtis Klause; *Dracula's Daughter* (film); *Nadja* (film).

Diary Format • Homoeroticism • Karenstein, Carmilla (character) • Vampire Hunters

Lorrah, Jean.

Blood Will Tell. *Dallas, TX: BenBella, 2003, ©2001. 277p. ISBN 1932100032.*

An ex-Olympic marksman turned small town detective in Kentucky is called in to investigate the death of a mid-forties professor, found dead due to advanced old age—with a mysterious smile on his face. As more similar bodies are found, the case gets even stranger, especially when the detective begins to suspect that her current love interest possesses a supernatural secret that can solve the case. **Similar titles:** <u>The Anna Strong Chronicles</u>, Jeanne C. Stein; <u>The Anita Blake, Vampire Hunter Series</u>, Laurel K. Hamilton; <u>The Vampire Files</u>, P. N. Elrod.

Academia • Incest • Kentucky • Police Officer as Character • Secret Sin • Vampire's Point of View

Lucas, Tim.

The Book of Renfield: The Gospel of Dracula. *New York: Simon & Schuster, 2005. 403p. ISBN 0743243544.*

This retelling of Bram Stoker's *Dracula* from the point of view of the zoophagous patient in Dr. Seward's lunatic asylum explains how Renfield evolved from being an eccentric orphan, tormented by his peers and his guardians, into madness in adulthood. And though it is Renfield's tale, it is related through Seward's journals, which have been kept on wax cylinders and transcribed by Mina Harker. **Similar titles:** *Renfield, Slave of Dracula*, Barbara Hambly; *The Journal of Professor Abraham Van Helsing*, Allen C. Kupfer, *The Many Faces of Van Helsing*, Jeanne Cavalos (editor).

Alternative Literature • Diary Format • Dracula (character) • Dracula (novel) • England • Harker, Mina Murray (character) • Holmwood, Arthur (character) • Mental Illness • Renfield (character) • Seward, John (character) • Van Helsing, Abraham (character)

Lumley, Brian.

Harry Keogh: Necroscope and Other Weird Heroes! *New York: Tor. 2005, ©2003. 319p. ISBN 0765310600.*

(See chapter 18, "Collections and Anthologies.")

Martinez, A. Lee.

Gil's All Fright Diner. *New York: Tor, 2005. 268p. ISBN 0765311437.*

(See chapter 16, "Comic Horror: Laughing at Our Fears.")

Massey, Brandon.

Dark Corner. *New York: Dafina, 2004. 449p. ISBN 0758202490.*

Mason Corner, Mississippi, is a small town where in which 90 percent of the residents are the African American descendants of plantation owner Edward Mason. Mason's nickname for the place, "Dark Corner," was his cruel joke. When David's estranged father dies unexpectedly, he inherits the family fortune and business, so he hops the next plane to Dark Corner, hoping among other things to learn more about the parent he knew so little about. Soon after David's arrival, Kyle Coirait, a 168-year-old vampire of French African descent, settles into Mason's plantation, Jubilee, which is said to be haunted. **Similar titles:** *'Salem's Lot*, Stephen King; The Eden Moore Series, Cherie Priest; The Joe Pitt Novels, Charlie Huston; *Fledgling*, Octavia Butler.

African American Characters • Family Curse • Haunted Houses • Mississippi • Slavery • Vampire Hunters

Masterton, Graham.

Descendant. *Sutton, UK: Severn House, 2006. 216p. ISBN 0727891715.*

During World War II, American James Falcon worked for the Allies hunting vampires, who were supplying the Nazis with the names of members of the European resistance. In 1957, the British recruit him to hunt down one of the worst of the vampires, Dorin Duca, who now works with the Soviets. In the midst of this espionage, Falcon must contend with the indignities of warm beer and British food. **Similar titles:** *Bloody Red Baron*, Kim Newman; *The Nymphos of Rocky Flats*, Mario Acevedo; *Bottomfeeder*, B. H. Fingerman.

England • Espionage • Russia • Vampire Hunters • War—Cold War • War—World War II

Manitou Blood. *New York: Leisure, 2005. 256p. ISBN 0843954256.*

(See chapter 7, "Demonic Possession: Satanism, Black Magic, and Witches and Warlocks: The Devil Made Me Do It.")

Matheson, Richard.

"I Am Legend." In *I Am Legend*. *New York: Tor, 1995, ©1954. 312p. ISBN 0765357151.*

A virus transmitted worldwide by a nuclear war has turned all but one man into a vampire, and he is determined to survive rather than join the ranks of undead ghouls, who wait for him outside his door on a nightly basis. Matheson's frightening and original novella was the basis for the movies *The Last Man on Earth*, starring Vincent Price, and *The Omega Man*, starring Charlton Heston. **Similar titles:** *Bloodlines* and *The Incredible Shrinking Man*, Richard Matheson; *Blade* (film); *Invasion of the Body Snatchers* (film).

Epidemics • New York—New York City • Radiation • Vampire Hunters • Weird Science

Mignola, Michael, and Christopher Golden.

Baltimore, or, The Steadfast Tin Soldier and the Vampire. *New York: Bantam, 2007. 284p. ISBN 0553804715.*

While fighting in the Ardennes during World War I, Lord Henry Baltimore is bitten and infected by a vampire bat. Years later, he summons three friends who have had experiences with the occult—a merchant sea captain who was with him when Baltimore found his family had been killed and his wife infected, a nobleman, and a surgeon. Together they attempt to track down The Red King, a vampire responsible for the 1919 influenza epidemic. **Similar titles:** *The Turning*,

Jennifer Armitrout; *Interview with the Vampire* and *The Vampire Lestat*, Anne Rice.

Epidemics • Physician as Character • Soldier as Character • Vampire Hunters • War—World War I

Moore, James A.

Blood Red. *Northborough, MA: Earthling Publications, 2005. 336p. ISBN 0976633914.*
(See chapter 10, "Small Town Horror: Villages of the Damned.")

Polidori, John.

"The Vampyre." In *The Vampyre and Other Writings.* *Edited by Franklin Charles Bishop. Manchester, UK: Carcanet, 2005. 249p. ISBN 185754787X.*
John Polidori, traveling companion to Lord Byron, wrote this story during his stay at Lake Geneva with Mary Shelley and Percy B. Shelley during their contest to write a chilling tale: Lord Ruthven preys on men and women of good fortune, gleefully seeking their ruin. Aubrey, his traveling companion, is eventually appalled by the lord's behavior and quits his company, only to discover that Ruthven may be more than mortal. **Similar titles:** *Frankenstein*, Mary Shelley; *Dracula*, Bram Stoker.

England • Greece • Lord Ruthven (character)

Rhodes, Evie.

Expired. *New York: Dafina Books. 2005. 292p. ISBN 0758208707.*
Tracie Burlingame is a tough woman, having gone from living in the projects as a child to being a successful owner of several New York City hair salons. This strength permits Tracie to endure losing one son to drug addiction. But when her youngest child is found thrown off the roof with the blood drained from her body, Tracie has difficulty mustering the strength to confront the unimaginable—that a supernatural creature has taken her child from her. **Similar titles:** The Joe Pitt Novels, Charlie Huston; The Demon Hunter Series, D. L. Gardner.

African American Characters • New York—New York City • Parenting

Rice, Anne.

Merrick. *New York: Alfred A. Knopf, 2000. 307p. ISBN 0679454489.*
(See chapter 7, "Demonic Possession: Satanism, Black Magic, and Witches and Warlocks: The Devil Made Me Do It.")

Romkey, Michael.

American Gothic. *New York: Del Ray, 2004. 304p. ISBN 0345452100.*
The carnage of the American Civil war leads Nathanial Peregrine to despair, and to accept the embrace of the vampire. But immortality isn't all it's cracked up to be, and at the dawn of the twentieth century, Nathanial

travels to Haiti, where he meets a woman who makes him long to be mortal again. Can Dr. Laville, an expert on diseases of the blood, help him redeem his soul? **Similar titles:** *Tale of the Body Thief*, Anne Rice; *The Turning*, Jennifer Armitrout; *Blood and Chocolate*, Annette Curtis Klause.

Haiti • Immortality • Physician as Character • War—American Civil War

Rook, Sebastian.

London, 1850. *New York: Scholastic, 2005. 237p. ISBN 0439633923.*

A twelve-year-old street urchin intent on boarding a newly arrived ship in search of food or money encounters a bunch of flying bats and a boy his own age, who regales him with the tale of a vampire plague that has killed the entire crew. The two boys vow to stop the horrors and begin a dangerous adventure from London to Mexico, to confront the Mayan bat god at the root of the infestation. **Similar titles:** The Jonathan Barrett, Gentleman Vampire Series, P. N. Elrod; The Saint-Germain Chronicles, Chelsea Quinn Yarbro.

England—London • France—Paris • Mexico • Religion—Mayan • Vampire Hunters

Ryan, Kevin.

Van Helsing. *New York: Pocket Star, 2004. 272p. ISBN 0743493540.*

The novelization of the Universal Pictures' blockbuster of the same name provides the story for this journey from industrialized Europe to the wild Carpathian Mountains, where Dracula, the Wolf Man, and Frankenstein's monster threaten to topple civilization. A secret society charges one man, Van Helsing, with defeating these monstrosities. **Similar titles:** *The Many Faces of Van Helsing*, Jeanne Cavalos (editor); *The Journal of Professor Abraham Van Helsing*, Allen C. Kupfer.

Frankenstein's Monster (character) • Transylvania • Vampire Hunters • Van Helsing, Abraham (character) • Werewolves

Saberhagen, Fred.

A Coldness in the Blood. *New York: Tor, 2003. 383p. ISBN 0765340119.*

When fellow vampire Dickon and his human partner show up frightened on his doorstep carrying a small Egyptian statue, elder vampire Matthew Maule offers them protection for the day. Maule awakens to discover that the statue has been smashed, the human has been murdered, and Dickon is missing. And Maule has now run afoul of a vampire even more powerful than himself. **Similar titles:** The Red Moon Series, Billie Sue Mosiman; The Renquist Quartet, Mick Farren; The Noble Dead Series, Barb Hendee and J. C. Hendee.

Cursed Objects • Magic • Religion—Ancient Egyptian • Vampire Clans • Vampire's Point of View

Shepard, Lucius.

The Golden. *Urbana, IL: Golden Gryphon Press, 2006, ©1993. 203p. ISBN 193084638X.*

The branches of the "Family" gather for a grand affair at Castle Banat, for centuries a sanctuary for the vampires of Europe. A project 300 years in the making, the creation of a mortal called the Golden, bred to produce the most perfect blood, has finally come to fruition. The vampires assemble to experience a decanting, which promises to be unlike any other in the past. But then Golden is viciously murdered before the event, and only a hybrid vampire uneasy with his own nature can solve the case. **Similar titles:** *Expired*, Evie Rhodes; *Fledgling*, Octavia Butler; The Renquist Quartet, Mick Farren; *Blade* (film).

Castles • France—Paris • Police Officer as Character • Vampire Clans • Vampire's Point of View

Simmons, Dan.

Carrion Comfort. *New York: Warner, 1990, ©1989. 884p. ISBN 0446359203.*

In this extremely complex and lengthy narrative, mind-controlling vampires dictate human history by feeding off of and magnifying the violence inherent in humans. Through Simmons's multilayered, suspense-oriented, and erudite prose, the plot takes unexpected twists and turns at every juncture. This story features believable, multidimensional characters, and is told through multiple points of view. **Similar titles:** *Midnight Mass*, F. Paul Wilson; *The Cursed*, L. A. Banks; *The Tyrant*, Michael Cisco.

Holocaust, The • Mind Control • Nazism • Pennsylvania—Philadelphia • South Carolina— Charleston • Vampire Hunters • Vampire's Point of View • Violence—Theories of

Stoker, Bram.

Dracula. *New York: Penguin, 2007, ©1897. 448p. ISBN 014062063X.*

The mother of all vampire texts, Stoker's classic tale is one of the few horror novels that has stood the test of time. Count Dracula, who plans to take over England, arrives to feed from and subsequently infect with vampirism the wives and girlfriends of his enemies. The story unfolds through journal entries written in shorthand, phonograph recordings, and personal correspondence among the vampire hunters, as well as the occasional newspaper article. **Similar titles:** *Carmilla*, Joseph Sheridan Le Fanu; *Midnight Tales* and *The Jewel of Seven Stars*, Bram Stoker; The Anno Dracula Series, Kim Newman; *Bram Stoker's Dracula* (film).

Diary Format • Documentary Techniques • Dracula (character) • England—London • Eroticism • Harker, Jonathan (character) • Harker, Mina Murray (character) • Holmwood, Arthur (character) • Renfield (character) • Seward, John (character) • Transylvania • Vampire Hunters • Van Helsing, Abraham (character) • Victorian Era • Westerna, Lucy (character)

Van Belkom, Edo.

Blood Road. *New York: Kensington, 2004. 317p. ISBN 0786015632.*

(See chapter 11, "Maniacs and Sociopaths, or the Nuclear Family Explodes: Monstrous Malcontents Bury the Hatchet.")

Wilson, F. Paul.

Midnight Mass. *New York: Tor, 2004. 332p. ISBN 0765307057.*

This rewriting and expansion of the 1990 novella of the same name features vampire armies that clash with humans in the night. After vampires have colonized Europe and decimated its natural resources, they travel to New York to try American fare. New Yorkers then organize an insurgency under the leadership of ex-alcoholic priest Joe Cahill. Headquartered in New Jersey, Cahill, with the help of family and a nun with a gift for making explosives, fights the good fight—that is, until he is bitten. Now time is of the essence for humanity, which has two weeks to win the revolution, before Cahill turns. **Similar titles:** <u>The Vampire Earth Series</u>, E. E. Knight; *Craven Moon*, Billie Sue Mosiman; <u>The Angel Investigations Series</u>, various authors; *The Cursed*, L. A. Banks.

Addictions—Alcoholism • Apocalypse • Clergy as Character • Futurism • Vampire Hunters • Vampire's Point of View

Vampire Short Stories

Allen, Angela C., ed.

Dark Thirst. *New York: Pocket Books, 2004. 304p. ISBN 0743496663.*
(See chapter 18, "Collections and Anthologies.")

Cavelos, Jeanne, ed.

The Many Faces of Van Helsing. *New York: Penguin-Ace, 2004. 382p. ISBN 0441011705.*
(See chapter 18, "Collections and Anthologies.")

Feehan, Christine, Maggie Shane, Emma Holly, and Angela Knight.

Hot Blooded. *New York: Jove, 2004. 392p. ISBN 0515136964.*
(See chapter 18, "Collections and Anthologies.")

Ford, Michael Thomas, ed.

Midnight Thirsts: Erotic Tales of the Vampire. *New York: Kensington, 2004. 325p. ISBN 0758206631.*
(See chapter 18, "Collections and Anthologies.")

Hamilton, Laurell K., Mary-Janice Davidson, Eileen Wilks, and Rebecca York.

Cravings. *New York: Berkley, 2004. 358p. ISBN 0515138150.*
(See chapter 18, "Collections and Anthologies.")

Harris, Charlaine, and Toni L. P. Kelner, eds.

Many Bloody Returns. *New York: Ace, 2007. 355p. ISBN 0441015220.*
   (See chapter 18, "Collections and Anthologies.")

1

Jackson, Monica, ed.

Creepin'. *Washington, DC: Kimani, 2007. 392p. ISBN 0373830602.*
   (See chapter 18, "Collections and Anthologies.")

2

Jones, Stephen, ed.

The Mammoth Book of Vampires. *New York: Carroll & Graf, 2004, ©1992. 621p. ISBN 0786713720.*
   (See chapter 18, "Collections and Anthologies.")

3

Matheson, Richard.

4

Bloodlines: Richard Matheson's Dracula, I Am Legend and Other Vampire Stories. *Colorado Springs, CO: Gauntlet Press, 2006. 520p. ISBN 1887368884.*
   (See chapter 18, "Collections and Anthologies.")

I Am Legend. *New York: Tor, 2007, ©1954. 312p. ISBN 0765357151.*
   (See chapter 18, "Collections and Anthologies.")

5

Newman, Kim.

The Man from the Diogenes Club. *Austin, TX: Monkey Brain, 2006. 389p. ISBN 1932265171.*
   (See chapter 18, "Collections and Anthologies.")

6

Thomsen, Brian, and Martin H. Greenberg, eds.

7

Repentant. *New York: Daw, 2003. 313p. ISBN 0756401631.*
   (See chapter 18, "Collections and Anthologies.")

8

Werewolves

Armstrong, Kelley.

9

The Women of the Otherworld Series.

Meet Elena Michaels, the only female of her kind. A she-werewolf who left her pack in upstate New York to live among humans in Toronto, she now has a career as a journalist and various relationships—with humans and witches alike. The series emphasis switches as it progresses, from werewolves to witches. **Similar titles:** The Buffy the Vampire Slayer Series,

10

various authors; <u>The Charmed Series</u>, various authors; <u>The Wendy Ward Series</u>, J. G. Passarella.

Adams, Hope (character) • Levine, Eve (character) • Michaels, Elena (character) • Winterbourne, Paige (character)

Bitten. *New York: Plume, 2003. 372p. ISBN 0452283485.*

Elena has a tough choice to make: her pack needs her help to run off a few loose cannons who are jeopardizing the secrecy and safety of the werewolf community.

Canada—Ontario—Toronto • Families • New York • Werewolves

Stolen. *New York: Viking, 2003. 399p. ISBN 0670031372.*

Elena Michaels investigates a suspicious Web notice that offers to sell vampire and werewolf paraphernalia, as well as information about lycanthropy. This leads to her meeting with the two Winterbourne witches and a team of commandos who abduct "supernaturals" and take them to a remote bunker in Maine, where a billionaire is collecting and hunting supernatural species.

Kidnapping • Maine • Weird Science • Werewolves • Wilderness

Broken. *New York: Bantam Spectra, 2006. 444p. ISBN 0553588184.*

Since female werewolves are supposedly impossible, lycanthropes are baffled when Elena is pregnant, and no one is sure of the outcome. But when time portals, necromancy, Jack the Ripper, and zombies find their way into this story, readers will turn page after page to see what happens when supernatural worlds collide.

Jack the Ripper (character) • Pregnancy • Time Travel • Werewolves

Cole, Stephen.

The Wereling Trilogy.

Tom, a teenager, sneaks away from his family on vacation and is almost killed in a tragic accident. He awakens in a cabin to find that he has been rescued by a family of werewolves. **Similar titles:** *Blood and Chocolate*, Annette Curtis Klause; <u>The Crimson Series</u>, Trisha Baker; *Interview with the Vampire* and *The Vampire Lestat*, Anne Rice.

Anderson, Tom (character) • Folan, Kate (character) • Idaho • Religion—Native American • Werewolves

Wounded. *New York: Razorbill, 2005. 264p. ISBN 1595140417.*

During a family vacation in the woods, Tom sneaks away to take a dip in a river. Swept away by the current and dashed on the rocks, he almost dies. Fortunately, he is rescued by strangers. Unfortunately, they are a family of werewolves, and the matriarch has bitten him, turning him into a lupine bridegroom.

Louisiana—New Orleans

Prey. *New York: Razorbill, 2004. 261p. ISBN 1595140425.*

Tom and Kate, on the run from Kate's mother and all of werewolf kind, hope to find a cure for Tom's lycanthropy. They make it to New York City and search for a safe place to stay where they cannot be detected. But then they discover that there is someone just as relentless as Kate's mother: Takapa, an albino werewolf with visions of building up a lupine army able to cow humans into submission.

Disabilities—Xeroderma Pigmentation • New York—New York City • Physician as Character • Weird Science

Resurrection. *New York: Razorbill, 2005, ©2003. 264p. ISBN 1595140433.*

Takapa continues his quest for world dominance by resurrecting Peter Stubbe, better known to wolfkind as Konig Man, a sort of Lucy figure for all lycanthropes. Meanwhile, Kate and Tom continue to search for the shaman Jacque so that he can cure Tom's lycanthropy. The pair journey to New Orleans for a showdown with both Takapa and Kate's mother.

Disabilities—Xeroderma Pigmentation • Louisiana—New Orleans • Physician as Character • Weird Science

---

Cox, Greg, Danny McBride, Kevin Grevioux, and Len Wiseman.

The Underworld Series.

In this novelization of the film *Underworld*, itself based on a Nancy A. Collins's short story, vampires and werewolves are at war with one another in the secret underworld. **Similar titles:** The Vampyricon Trilogy, Douglas Clegg; The Wereling Trilogy, Stephen Cole; *Blood and Chocolate*, Annette Curtis Klause.

Shape-shifters • Soldier as Character • Vampire Clans • Vampire's Point of View • War • Werewolves

Underworld. *New York: Pocket, 2003. 372p. ISBN 0743480716.*

Once werewolves were the vampires' faithful servants, but now they have grown tired of this role, so they revolt.

Underworld: Blood Enemy. *New York: Pocket, 2004. 310p. ISBN 0743480724.*

As a child, the werewolf Lucian was enslaved by Vicktor, a vampire elder. But Lucian felt himself to be above others of his kind, and when he impregnates Vicktor's daughter Sonja, she is burned alive as punishment. This second novel in The Underworld Trilogy explores the history of the blood feud between werewolves and vampires.

Underworld: Evolution. *London: Pocket, 2006. 288p. ISBN 0743480732.*

If you're a werewolf, the last "person" you probably want to meet is Selene. A Death Dealer, or vampire warrior, for 600 years, she lives to eradicate lycanthropes, considered the sworn enemy of her race. But even the best soldiers, when confronted with the truth about their enemies, as well as their commanders, can begin to have second thoughts.

Egolf, Tristan.

Kornwolf. *New York: Black Cat Books, 2006. 378p. ISBN 080211816X.*
(See chapter 16, "Comic Horror: Laughing at Our Fears.")

Farago, Gina.

Ivy Cole and the Moon. *New York: Berkley Books, 2006, ©2005. 376p. ISBN 0425212564.*
Ivy Cole, turned into a werewolf as a child, has learned the usefulness of her affliction. For one, she has no compunction about "thinning the human herd" by culling undesirables. Meanwhile, law enforcement officials hunt for "the Devil of Doe Springs," a creature that seems to want Ivy dead. This fan favorite makes good use of lycanthrope lore, accurate descriptions of Appalachia, as well as biting dialogue and excellent characterization. **Similar titles:** The Wereling Trilogy, Stephen Cole; *Blood and Chocolate*, Annette Curtis Klause; *Wolf Pack*, Edo Van Belkom; *Benighted*, Kit Whitfield.

Appalachia • Police Officer as Character • Werewolves

Gagliani, W. D.

Wolf's Trap. *New York: Dorchester, 2006. 373p. ISBN 0843957026.*
With a name like Nick Lupo, you have to suspect that this detective is good at getting into—and out of—hairy situations. You may also suspect he is a werewolf. The only problem is, so does serial killer Martin Stewart, a man Lupo is investigating, since Lupo killed Stewart's sister while a werewolf. **Similar titles:** The Anna Strong Chronicles, Jeanne C. Stein; *Sunglasses After Dark*, Nancy A. Collins; The Vampire Files, P. N. Elrod.

Child Molesters • Families • Kidnapping • Police Officer as Character • Revenge • Serial Killers • Werewolves

King, Stephen.

Cycle of the Werewolf. *Illustrated by Berni Wrightson. New York: Signet, 1985. 128p. ISBN 0451821114.*
In this graphic novel, Stephen King traces the effects of the moon's monthly phases on the small town of Tarker's Mills, where a werewolf victimizes townsfolk on a regular basis. Only a wheelchair-bound boy knows the identity of the monster and can stop it before it claims another victim. King's graphic novel is good for fans of traditional horror and young adult readers as well, and was the basis of the film *Silver Bullet*. **Similar titles:** *Blood and Chocolate*, Annette Curtis Klause; *Wolf Pack*, Edo Van Belkom; *Benighted*, Kit Whitfield; *Wolf's Trap*, W. D. Gagliani.

Clergy as Character • Disabilities—Paraplegia • New England • Werewolves

Klause, Annette Curtis.

Blood and Chocolate. *New York: Delacourt, 2007, ©1997. 288p. ISBN 0385734212.*

Vivian Gandollin, a teenage werewolf, just wants to be a normal high school girl who goes on dates and has a boyfriend. Unlike so many teenage girls, she is also at peace with her body and her sexuality, and wishes to share her most intimate self with her boyfriend. But unfortunately for Vivian, he is incapable of appreciating her. In fact, he's deathly frightened and repulsed by her lycanthropy. **Similar titles:** *Carrie*, Stephen King; The Wereling Trilogy, Stephen Cole; *Benighted*, Kit Whitfield; *Ginger Snaps* (film).

Adolescence • Animals Run Rampant • High School • Virginia • Werewolves

Van Belkom, Edo.

Wolf Pack. *Toronto: Tundra Books, 2004. 184p. ISBN 0887766692.*

After a devastating forest fire, a ranger discovers a litter of wolf cubs, but these cubs are both animal and human. Although the young ones try to fit into the human world, their true nature makes the challenges of being teenagers all the more difficult. When one of the pack is kidnapped, the others must find the cunning, strength, and courage to rescue her. **Similar titles:** *Blood and Chocolate*, Annette Curtis Klaus; *Wolf Pack*, Edo Van Belkom; *Benighted*, Kit Whitfield; *Wolf's Trap*, W. D. Gagliani; *Ginger Snaps* (film).

Animals Run Rampant • Canada • Werewolves

Whitfield, Kit.

Benighted. *New York: Del Rey, 2006. 532p. ISBN 0345491637.*

In a future world, werewolves are the majority, while "barebacks" (humans who are not lycanthropes) are a despised minority and frequently the target of discrimination and worse. One of these barebacks, Lola Galley, an attorney, works with the Department for the Ongoing Regulation of Lycanthropic Activity, a branch of the government dedicated to keeping order between the two groups. Then a friend of Lola's loses a hand to a werewolf who is out of control. **Similar titles:** The Anita Blake, Vampire Hunter Series, Laurell K. Hamilton; *Wolf Pack*, Edo Van Belkom; *Wolf's Trap*, W. D. Gagliani.

Lawyer as Character • Racism • Werewolves

Film

Blackula. *William Crain, dir. 1972. 93 minutes.*

Manuwalde, Ambassador of Ebonia, meets with Dracula to persuade him to stop supporting slave trading. Instead, Dracula makes Manuwalde one of the undead, imprisoning him in a coffin to thirst eternally. Manuwalde awakens 150 years later in 1970s Los Angeles, hungering for blood and the reincarnation of his long-deceased wife, who is now an Angelino. William Marshall stars as the first African American vampire in cinema history. **Similar titles:** *Voice of the Blood*, Jemiah Jefferson; *The Cursed*, L. A. Banks.

African American Characters • California—Los Angeles • Reincarnation • Vampire Hunters

Blade. *Stephen Norrington, dir. 1998. 120 minutes.*

Blade (Wesley Snipe) is half-human, half-vampire, cursed to crave human blood after his pregnant mother was attacked by one of the undead. Now, with the combined strengths of vampires and humans, Blade seeks to eliminate all blood-sucking fiends from the earth before they turn all humans into cattle. Gory and action-oriented with excellent special effects, this futuristic film is based on the DC Comics series of the same name. **Similar titles:** <u>The Anita Blake, Vampire Hunter Series</u>, Laurell K. Hamilton; *The Golden*, Lucius Shepherd.

African American Characters • Blade (character) • New York—New York City • Physician as Character • Revenge • Vampire Clans • Vampire Hunters

Blood Moon (Wolf Girl). *Thom Fitzgerald, dir. 2001. 97 minutes.*

Tara the Wolf Girl, the freak show's main attraction, just wants to be a normal teenager, so when fellow social outcast Ryan says he can help her, she jumps at the chance. Ryan's mother, a research chemist for a cosmetics company, is currently experimenting with a depilatory drug. However, the drug hasn't yet been tested on humans, so when Ryan injects Tara, the results are disastrous. Tara is willing to pay any price to be considered beautiful by normal standards. **Similar titles:** *Ivy Cole and the Moon*, Gina Farrago; *Blood and Chocolate*, Annette Curtis Klause.

Carnivals • Circuses • Deformity • Weird Science • Werewolves

Bram Stoker's Dracula. *Francis Ford Coppola, dir. 1992. 128 minutes.*

Coppola combines the plot of Stoker's novel with a loose interpretation of the historical fourteenth-century Romanian warlord Vlad Tepes. The result is not so much an immortal monster who must be destroyed at all costs, as a man who has defied death because his church and country have betrayed him. Gary Oldman, Winona Ryder, Anthony Hopkins, and Keanu Reeves star in this operatic film. **Similar titles:** *Dracula*, Bram Stoker; *Anno Dracula*, Kim Newman.

Dracula (character) • Dracula (novel) • England—London • Harker, Jonathan (character) • Harker, Mina Murray (character) • Holmwood, Arthur (character) • Reincarnation • Seward, Jack (character) • Vampire Hunters • Vampire's Point of View • Van Helsing, Abraham (character) • Westerna, Lucy (character)

Cronos. *Guillermo Del Toro, dir. 1992. (in Spanish, with subtitles). 94 minutes.*

In this award-winning Mexican film, an elderly antiques dealer, Jesus Gris, stumbles upon the cronos device, an invention of a fourteenth-century alchemist, which makes the bearer immortal but requires that he drink blood. In spite of several serious accidents and an attempt to embalm him, Jesus cannot die, and his discovery of the device has alerted the attention of an Anglo corporate mogul, who will stop at nothing to steal it from Gris. Ron Perlman stars. **Similar titles:** *The Cursed*, L. A. Banks; *The Turning*, Jennifer Armitrout.

Families • Immortality • Mexico • Weird Science

The Curse of the Werewolf. *Terence Fisher, dir. 1961. 91 minutes.*

This Hammer Studios production offers an unusual spin on lycanthropy—the werewolf is not a supernatural creature that merely exists and must be exterminated, but instead was created by cruelty. On his wedding night, a beggar comes to the castle of a callow marquise, who taunts him, then throws him into dungeon. Years later, when the beggar has been driven mad through his captivity, he rapes a mute peasant girl, who dies giving birth. The resulting progeny is an unsettled soul of the sort that the spirit of the werewolf can pass into, and only true love can cure him. Oliver Reed stars as the werewolf. **Similar titles:** The Wereling Trilogy, Stephen Cole; *Wolf's Trap*, W. D. Gagliani.

Animals Run Rampant • Spain • Werewolves

Dracula. *Tod Browning, dir. 1931. (black and white). 75 minutes.*

This film, an adaptation of Hamilton Deane and John Balderston's stage play of Stoker's *Dracula*, gave Bela Lugosi his first film role. As in Stoker's novel, Count Dracula comes to London via Transylvania, purchases a ruined abbey, and hopes to search for victims by night. But Lugosi's interpretation of Dracula is as a suave creature of the night first seen in Deane and Balderston's stage play. **Similar titles:** *Dracula*: Bram Stoker; The Jonathan Barrett, Gentleman Vampire Series, P. N. Elrod.

Dracula (character) • Dracula (novel) • England—London • Renfield (character) • Vampire Hunters • Van Helsing, Abraham (character)

Dracula 2000. *Patrick Lussier, dir. 2000. 99 minutes.*

Christopher Plummer stars as Abraham Van Helsing, wealthy and eccentric owner of Carfax antiques and now immortal keeper of the vanquished Dracula. When thieves attempt to steal what he has hidden in the vault, they unwittingly unleash the undead Count. Dracula flees to New Orleans to exact his vengeance on Van Helsing's daughter and create a new army of the undead. **Similar titles:** *London Under Midnight*, Simon Clark; *The Tyrant*, Michael Cisco.

Dracula (character) • England—London • Immortality • Iscariot, Judas (character) • Louisiana —New Orleans • Religion—Christianity • Van Helsing, Abraham (character) • Westerna, Lucy (character)

Dracula's Daughter. *Lambert Hillyer, dir. 1936. (black and white). 71 minutes.*

This film picks up where the 1931 version of *Dracula* leaves off, with Dr. Van Helsing having killed Count Dracula and believing he has rid the world of vampires. But Dracula's daughter, Countess Marya Zalesak, claims her father's body, and soon several people are found mysteriously killed. Otto Kruger, Gloria Holden, and Marguerite Churchill star. **Similar titles:** *Carmilla*, Joseph Sheridan Le Fanu; The Hunger Series, Whitley Strieber.

England—London • Family Curse • Homoeroticism • Psychologist/Psychiatrist as Character • Zalenska, Marya (character)

Ginger Snaps. *John Fawcett, dir. 2001. 108 minutes.*

At the ages of sixteen and fifteen, Ginger and Bridget Fitzgerald are unusual in that neither has begun to menstruate, but all of that changes for

Ginger when one night "the curse" comes cascading down her legs. Unfortunately for Ginger, a werewolf has been worrying their quiet, suburban town. Now the scent of Ginger's menses attracts the wolf, who manages to scratch her and then chases the sisters through the woods before being killed. But werewolf bites are more severe than dog bites; they have the power to transform the recipient into a lycanthrope. **Similar titles:** *Carrie*, Stephen King; *Blood and Chocolate*, Annette Curtis Klause.

Adolescence • Animals Run Rampant • Canada • High School • Menstruation • Werewolves

The Hunger. *Tony Scott, dir. 1983. 97 minutes.*

Miriam and John Blaylock are forever young and beautiful because they're vampires. When John begins to age at an accelerated pace, Miriam must seek the help of an outsider, a scientist who studies aging and who will be seduced by Miriam's promise of eternal youth. Catherine Deneuve, David Bowie, and Susan Sarandon star in this film classic. **Similar titles:** The Hunger Series, Whitley Strieber; The Vampire Chronicles, Anne Rice; The Voice of the Blood Series, Jemiah Jefferson.

Aging • Blaylock, Miriam (character) • Gay/Lesbian/Bisexual Characters • Homoeroticism • New York—New York City • Physician as Character • Roberts, Sarah (character)

Interview with the Vampire. *Neil Jordan, dir. 1987. 123 minutes.*

The film version of Anne Rice's novel of the same name sports an all-star cast, including Tom Cruise, Brad Pitt, Christian Slater, Antonio Banderas, and Kirsten Dunst. **Similar titles:** The Vampire Chronicles and The New Tales of the Vampire Series, Anne Rice.

Claudia (character) • Homoeroticism • Lestat de Lioncourt (character) • Louis (character) • Louisiana—New Orleans • Vampire's Point of View

The Lost Boys. *Joel Schumacher, dir. 1987. 97 minutes.*

A family moves to what they believe will be a peaceful town, Santa Carla, California, only to discover that they reside in the murder capital of the world, and the local gang is a pack of teenaged vampires who, like Peter Pan, never want to grow up. Kiefer Sutherland and Dianne Wiest star. **Similar titles:** *Midnight Mass*, F. Paul Wilson; *Craven Moon*, Billie Sue Mosiman; *The Cursed*, L. A. Banks.

Adolescence • California • Vampire Clans

Nadja. *Michael Almereyda, dir. 1996. (black and white). 93 minutes.*

Twin brother and sister vampires, children of Count Dracula, struggle against each other and against their own dual desires to be mortal and immortal. Set in modern-day New York City, this stylish parody of art films is also a remake of the 1936 version of *Dracula's Daughter*. It stars Peter Fonda and Elina Lowensohn. **Similar titles:** *Carmilla*, Joseph Sheridan Le Fanu; The Hunger Series, Whitley Strieber.

Gay/Lesbian/Bisexual Characters • Homoeroticism • New York—New York City • Renfield (character) • Twins • Vampire Hunters • Vampire's Point of View • Van Helsing, Abraham (character)

Nosferatu. *F. W. Murnau, dir. 1922. (black and white; silent). 94 minutes.*

This silent classic is a German adaptation of Stoker's *Dracula*. Because of the complexities of German copyright law, Murnau's film had to change the names of the principals, but Count Orlock, Murnau's version of Count Dracula, is much closer to Stoker's original idea of the vampire than the celluloid Dracula made famous by Bela Lugosi in 1931. **Similar titles:** *Dracula*, Bram Stoker; *The Vampyre*, John Polidori.

Count Orlock (character) • *Germany* • *Harker, Jonathan (character)* • *Renfield (character)*

Queen of the Damned. *Michael Rymer, dir. 2002. 101 minutes.*

In this second film based on Anne Rice's *The Vampire Lestat* and *Queen of the Damned*, Lestat (Stuart Townsend) becomes a rock star and challenges all the other vampires who hide from the human race to make themselves known. Now he has incurred the wrath of all of his kind, whose survival depends on keeping their ways secret. And he has also awakened Akasha (Aaliyah), the bloodthirsty mother of all vampires. **Similar titles:** The Vampire Chronicles, Anne Rice; *Anno Dracula*, Kim Newman.

Akasha and Enkil (character) • *California—Los Angeles* • *Immortality* • *Lestat de Lioncourt (character)* • *Maharet and Mekare (characters)* • *Marius (character)* • *Music—Rock Music* • *Vampire's Point of View*

Shadow of the Vampire. *E. Elias Merhing, dir. 2001. 92 minutes.*

In 1922, F. W. Murnau finds an actual vampire to play the role of Count Orlock and add realism to his film, *Nosferatu*. But vampires aren't as easily controlled as actors and can't be prevented from snacking on the occasional camera operator. Willem Dafoe stars as Max Schreck. **Similar titles:** *Carrion Comfort*, Dan Simmons; *The Vampyre*, John Polidori.

Actor as Character • *Alternative Literature* • *Czechoslovakia* • *Director as Character* • *Germany* • *Horror Movie Industry* • *Immortality* • *Vampire's Point of View*

The Wolf Man. *George Waggner, dir. 1941. (black and white). 70 minutes.*

This Universal Studios classic stars Lon Chaney Jr., who is bitten by a vampire in wolf form (Bela Lugosi) and therefore turned into a werewolf. Claude Rains also stars. **Similar titles:** *The Wolf Man: Hunter's Moon*, Jan Michael Friedman.

Animals Run Rampant • *Werewolves*

June's Picks

Books: Barbara Hambly, *Renfield, Slave of Dracula* (Berkley); Allen C. Kupfer, *The Journal of Professor Abraham Van Helsing* (Doherty); Tim Lucas, *The Book of Renfield: The Gospel of Dracula* (Simon and Schuster); Kim Newman, The Anno Dracula Series; Anne Rice, *The Vampire Lestat* (Ballantine); Bram Stoker, *Dracula* (Penguin)

Films: *Blacula, Blood Moon, Bram Stoker's Dracula, Dracula's Daughter, Ginger Snaps, Nadja*

Tony's Picks

Books: Nancy A. Collins, *Sunglasses After Dark* (White Wolf); Elizabeth Kostova, *The Historian: A Novel* (Little, Brown); Michael Mignola and Christopher Golden, *Baltimore, or, The Steadfast Tin Soldier and the Vampire* (Bantam); Dan Simmons, *Carrion Comfort* (Warner); Bram Stoker, *Dracula* (Penguin)

Films: *Cronos, Queen of the Damned, Shadow of the Vampire*

Chapter 7

Demonic Possession, Satanism, Black Magic, and Witches and Warlocks: The Devil Made Me Do It

Tales of black magic and demonic possession predate the Judeo-Christian Bible, so this subgenre of horror is arguably one of the oldest. Students of literature know that demons abound in the poetry of Milton and Blake, but it was not until the late 1700s that the earliest novel featuring demons was published. Matthew "Monk" Lewis's *The Monk* is a study in necrophilia, which set the stage for the "beautiful young woman as demon in disguise" theme. Nonetheless, the quintessential possession novel is a very recent development. William Peter Blatty's *The Exorcist*, the tale of a preteen girl possessed by Satan after ancient artifacts are unearthed in Iraq that later unleash the devil's power, reminds us that whether possession and demon-based stories are about misled monks or innocent-but-soon-to-be-demonic teenaged girls, what makes tales of possession particularly frightening is that more often than not, innocent humans are possessed by demons, or even by the devil himself.

Tales of satanism and black magic also take the form of stories about witches, warlocks, and other people who willingly become involved with dark forces. In Ira Levin's *Rosemary's Baby*, Guy Woodhouse sells his soul, and his wife's womb, to Satan, in exchange for worldly success as an actor. More contemporary possession/witchcraft tales include Anne Rice's The Mayfair Witches Series, which concerns itself with thirteen generations of Mayfair witches and their profitable connection to the demon Lasher.

Interestingly, most stories in this subgenre generally feature Catholics who have either lost their faith or see their brand of black magic as an extension of their faith. Indeed, satanism is often represented as the polar opposite not of Christianity, but of Roman Catholicism. This is the case in *Rosemary's Baby*. Perhaps this is because Catholicism was at one point considered the "universal" version of Christianity and is therefore a good "default" religion for horror. Or maybe this is because Catholicism is more ritual-oriented than other Christian sects, making it the perfect foil for satanism, which also values ritual. The reason could just be that the original possession narratives were produced by a culture that demonized Catholicism, and the tradition or formula was simply continued by later writers.

Despite the prevalence of Catholicism in possession stories, other Christian sects have played a role in the evolution of the subgenre. For example, many narratives feature Protestantism as the sect that ushers in evil, as is the case in the tales of Nathaniel Hawthorne, in which New England Puritans who seem to be pillars of moral rectitude in fact have relationships with the Evil One. Stephen King's *Needful Things* sets Protestants and Catholics against one another when town members give Satan a toehold as each unwittingly makes a bargain with the devil. But no matter which sect is responsible for raising the devil, the bottom line of the possession tale is that the possessed character is not responsible for his or her actions while in that state and so can be forgiven.

Works in this section are also about witches and witchcraft. Unlike narratives about possession and satanism, witches and warlocks aren't necessarily evil. In fact, many tales of witches and witchcraft are about women either practicing Wicca or adhering to an alternative spirituality. J. G. Passarella's Wendy Ward Series pursues this theme. In these novels, the protagonists choose to become witches, or become willing adherents of Wicca, practicing a religion that encourages them to experience themselves as part of the natural world. Unlike monotheistic traditions, these neo-pagan belief systems empower women by validating their ways of knowing the world and their sexuality. Not surprisingly, adherents of these beliefs are frequently persecuted. Thus, the intolerant individuals who are the witches' persecutors are the evil ones in these novels. In Libba Bray's Gemma Doyle Trilogy, the Victorian teenaged heroine discovers her supernatural abilities to travel to "the Realms" and bring back their powerful magic just at a time when she is being trained to become a model of bourgeois femininity. Witchcraft allows her to circumvent a lifestyle as constricting as the corset that became a romanticized symbol of the era. Other stories in this section include those of practitioners of another maligned belief system, voodoo. In the film *Angel Heart*, New Yorker Harold Angel is shocked by his first encounter with voodoo as practiced in the bayous of South Louisiana, in response to which one of the participants comments that "we're not all Baptists down here."

The appeals of possession and witchcraft narratives are varied. For one, most readers will find that these types of stories contain more sympathetic monsters, as they will identify with innocent but possessed characters, whose acting out is beyond their control. Such tales also play to certain Christian fears: Christian readers will be more than familiar with Satan/the devil as the ultimate monster and will have an almost visceral fear of demons. This adds a higher level of believability to these kinds of stories, which to some degree also affirm Christian beliefs—the devil will ultimately be defeated, and God's will be done. Non-Christians who enjoy the subgenre may be responding to a curiosity about matters of the occult, from alchemy, to magic, to witchcraft.

Note: Tales about demonic possession, satanism, voodoo, Wicca, black magic, witches, and warlocks can also be found in the collections described in chapter 18. Refer to the subject/keyword index for specific titles, using the keywords *Magic, Religion: Paganism, Religion: Satanism, Religion: Voodoo* and *Witchcraft*.

Demons

Armintrout, Jennifer.

Possession. *Don Mills, ON: Mira Books, 2007. 384p. ISBN 0778324184.*
(See chapter 6, "Vampires and Werewolves: Children of the Night.")

Barker, Clive.

Mister B. Gone. *New York: HarperCollins, 2007. 248p. ISBN 0060182989.*
A medieval devil pens this fictional memoir, circa 1438.

Jakabok Botch, the offspring of two demons, has a little trouble fitting in. He was born with two tails and has been made even more grotesque by a fall he took into a fire while escaping Dante's inferno, badly burning his face in the process. Jakabok finds his way to the home of Johannes Gutenberg, where he writes his diary. **Similar titles:** *Interview with the Vampire*, Anne Rice; *The Secret Life of Laszlo, Count Dracula*, Roderick Anscombe; *A Dirty Job*, Christopher Moore.

Alternative Literature • Cursed Objects • Demons • Epistolary Format • Medieval Era

Blaine, Chris (various authors using pseudonym).

The Abbadon Inn Series.

The Abbadon Inn sits on a quiet street in the charming Victorian town of Cape May, New Jersey. Abandoned and vacant for years, it's ready for renovation—that is, if the spirits that reside within like the new owner. **Similar titles:** *Nazareth Hill*, Ramsey Campbell; *In This Skin*, Simon Clark; The Harrow Academy Novels, Douglas Clegg.

Haunted Houses • New Jersey

Matthew J. Costello (writing as Blaine).

Drowned Night. *New York: Berkley, 2005. 324p. ISBN 0425206769.*
Nicholas Abaddon, whose name is associated with the Angel of the Bottomless Pit, built the cursed Abaddon Inn, known for its evil past spilling over into the lives of its inhabitants. In this tale, a mysterious entity from under the sea takes control of both people and sharks staying at the Cape May resort—resulting in grisly carnage. This is the third novel in the series.

Animals Run Rampant • Family Curse • Maritime Horror • Police Officer as Character • Psychics • Sharks

Blatty, William Peter.

The Exorcist. *New York: HarperTorch, 2004, ©1971. 385p. ISBN 0061007226.*

When twelve-year-old Regan McNeil begins acting strangely, her mother suspects she may be possessed by demons. Could Regan's possession have something to do with an elderly priest's archeological dig in Northern Iraq? And will a young priest who is questioning his own faith be able to stop the demons? This novel was made into one of the benchmark horror films of the 1970s, by director William Friedkin. **Similar titles:** *The Blood of the Lamb*, Thomas Monteleone; *Rosemary's Baby* and *Son of Rosemary*, Ira Levin; *The Manitou*, Graham Masterton; *Stigmata* (film); *The Exorcist* (film).

Clergy as Character • Demons • Exorcisms • Religion—Christianity–Catholicism

Carey, Mike.

The Devil You Know. *New York: Warner, 2007. 416p. ISBN 0446580309.*

(See chapter 16, "Comic Horror: Laughing at Our Fears.")

Clark, Francis.

Waking Brigid. *New York: Tor, 2008. 366p. ISBN 0765318105.*

The gory death of a rich Savannah gentleman is recognized as the handiwork of satanists. The worshippers of Belial suddenly find themselves being pursued by a clandestine order of priests and nuns who still practice the magic of their pagan forebears. For Brigid Rourke, a nun being initiated into the magic circle, the challenge is to help destroy the evil—and stay alive. **Similar titles:** <u>The Angel Investigations Series</u>, various authors; <u>The Anna Strong Chronicles</u>, Jeanne C. Stein; <u>The Violet Series</u>, Stephen Woodworth.

Clergy as Character • Demons • Georgia—Savannah • Magic • Parapsychology • Religion—Christianity—Catholicism • Religion—Satanism • Victorian Era

Corman, Avery.

The Boyfriend from Hell. *New York: St. Martin's, 2006. 249p. ISBN 0312349793.*

A freelance journalist's boyfriend decides to leave her for a singer and the promise of a cable show. So she sinks all of her energies into her latest assignment—an investigation of The Dark Angel Church, known for being the home of a satanic cult that follows the tenets laid forth by a writer who is handsome and charming. **Similar titles:** *Rosemary's Baby*, Ira Levin; *The Beloved*, J. F. Gonzales; *Live Girls*, Ray Garton.

Journalist as Character • New York—New York City • Religion—Christianity—Catholicism • Religion—Satanism • Writer as Character

Delaney, Matthew B. J.

 Jinn. *New York: St. Martin's Griffin, 2003. 439p. ISBN 0312276702.*

Pierre Devereaux discovers the wreck of a World War II rescue ship while directing an undersea documentary. When he and his crew bring the ship into the harbor, they discover that it wasn't empty; it contained some malignant but invisible force. Now horribly mutilated bodies are strewn throughout the streets of Boston, leading Detective Will Jefferson to believe that he is up against a supernatural being. **Similar titles:** *Riverwatch*, Joseph M. Nacisse; *The Shell Collector*, Christopher Golden; <u>The Pendergast Novels</u>, Douglas Preston and Lincoln Child; *Cloverfield* (film).

Demons • Maritime Horror • Massachusetts—Boston • Police Officer as Character

Due, Tananarive.

The Good House: A Novel. *New York: Atria, 2003. 482p. ISBN 0743449002.*

(See chapter 4, "Ghosts and Haunted Houses: Dealing with Presences and Absences.")

Gallagher, Stephen.

Valley of Lights. *Tolworth, Surrey, UK: Telos, 2005, ©1987. 298p. ISBN 0450406644.*

(See chapter 8, "Mythological Monsters and 'The Old Ones': Invoking the Dark Gods.")

Gardner, T. L.

The Demon Hunter Series.

After committing suicide, Elijah is resurrected by the Angel Gabriel, and he becomes The Protector, endowed with supernatural power to fight demonic forces on Earth. Because of the importance of his calling, Elijah is pursued by the authorities, who need his abilities to fight evil. **Similar titles:** *Expired*, Evie Rhodes; <u>The Joe Pitt Novels</u>, Charlie Huston; <u>The Living Blood Series</u>, Tananarive Due.

African American Characters • Angels • Demons • Federal Bureau of Investigation • Protector, The (character) • Racism • Satan (character)

Demon Hunter. *Jamaica, Queens, NY: Q-Boro Books, 2005. 300p. ISBN 0976954303.*

Elijah is sent to London, where he receives weapons and guidance from a priest and vanquishes a demon. He returns to the States and fights an ongoing array of demons, fiends, succubae, and other emissaries of evil.

Racism • Satan (character)

Sacrifice. *Jamaica, Queens, NY: Q-Boro Books, 2008. 299p. ISBN 1933967382.*

In Book 2 of <u>The Demon Hunter Series</u>, Elijah struggles with his decision to leave behind the woman he loves: her soul is held prisoner by a vengeful demon, currently banished on Earth. Meanwhile, Shemhazai, one of the original fallen angels, plots to free himself from the Egyptian desert. **Similar titles:** *Expired*, Evie Rhodes; <u>The Joe Pitt Novels</u>, Charlie Huston; <u>The Living Blood Series</u>, Tananarive Due.

Archeology • Demons

Golden, Christopher.

Wildwood Road. *New York: Bantam, 2005. 311p. ISBN 055338208X.*

On Halloween, Michael nearly hits a girl while driving home. Anxious to help her get to safety, he takes her to the run-down house she says is her home. He later finds himself being haunted by her image—and by a group of wraiths, who transform his wife into a harridan. When he tries to find the girl for an explanation, it's as if she, or the house, never existed. **Similar titles:** *Earthbound*, Richard Matheson; *Within the Shadows*, Brandon Massey; *The Boys Are Back in Town*, Christopher Golden.

Artist as Character • Revenging Revenant • Witchcraft

Gonzalez, J. F.

The Beloved. *New York: Leisure, 2006. 369p. ISBN 0843956941.*

(See chapter 17, "Everyday Horror: When the Mundane Becomes Monstrous.")

Gray, T. M.

Ghosts of Eden. *Waterville, ME: Five Star, 2005. 279p. ISBN 1594143048.*

In 1947, Saxon Farady returns to the Maine resort island that is her hometown after a five-year stint in a mental institution. She has killed her father in self-defense, and her mother has disowned her. But Saxon knows what her mother doesn't—that the family home is inhabited by an evil entity known as the Serpent. **Similar titles:** *Demon Theory*, Stephen Graham Jones; *The Influence*, Ramsey Campbell; *A House Divided*, Deborah LeBlanc.

Demons • Family Curse • Haunted Houses • Maine

Huggins, James Byron.

Nightbringer. *New Kensington, PA: Whitaker House, 2004. 302p. ISBN 088368876X.*

(See chapter 8, "Mythological Monsters and 'The Old Ones': Invoking the Dark Gods.")

Jackson, Monica, ed.

Creepin'. *Washington, DC: Kimani, 2007. 392p. ISBN 0373830602.*

(See chapter 18, "Collections and Anthologies.")

Jackson, Shirley.

The Haunting of Hill House. *New York: Penguin, 2006, ©1949. 182p. ISBN 0143039989.*

(See chapter 4, "Ghosts and Haunted Houses: Dealing with Presences and Absences.")

Jones, Stephen Graham.

Demon Theory. *San Francisco: MacAdam/Cage, 2006. 439p. ISBN 1596921641.*

Hale receives an unsettling phone call from his ailing mother on Hallow-een night, and when he goes home to check on her, he finds her missing from the house where his sister disappeared years earlier—and where something now waits for him, too. Written as a film treatment, *Demon Theory* is peppered with footnotes and popular culture and horror film references. **Similar titles:** *Hallows Eve*, Al Sarrantonio; *Ghosts of Eden*, T. M. Gray; The Harrow Academy Novels, Douglas Clegg; *Scream* (film); *Fade to Black* (film).

Demons • Holidays—Halloween • Horror Movie Industry • Popular Culture

Kenner, Julie.

California Demon: The Secret Life of a Demon-Hunting Soccer Mom. *New York: Berkley Books, 2006. 342p. ISBN 042521043X.*

(See chapter 16, "Comic Horror: Laughing at Our Fears.")

Kenyon, Nate.

Bloodstone. *Waterville, ME: Five Star, 2006. 360p. ISBN 1594144389.*

In White Falls, people dream that the dead claw out of the depths of their graves. Although Billy Smith is thousands of miles from the sleepy town, he has also had these nightmares. Paroled in California following a drunk driving conviction, he is drawn to a young woman whom he has never met, becomes her kidnapper, and the two travel to meet their destinies—in White Falls. **Similar titles:** *In Silent Graves* and *Prodigal Blues*, Gary A. Braunbeck; *Blood Angel*, Justine Musk; *Hallows Eve*, Al Sarrantonio.

Addictions—Drugs • Dreams • Families • Maine • New England • Secret Sin

King, Stephen.

Christine. *Thorndike, ME: Thorndike Press, 2000, ©1983. 917p. ISBN 0786226315.*

Dennis, who narrates this story in the first person, has a best friend named Arnie Cunningham, a high school loser whose only talent is his mechanical ability. Enter Christine, a vintage Plymouth possessed by an angry spirit that rivals Arnie's anger. This is one of King's more character-driven, psychological works. **Similar titles:** *Carrie*, Stephen King; *One Rainy Night*, Richard Laymon; *Shadowland*, Peter Straub.

Adolescence • Cursed Objects • High School • Maine • Revenge

Cujo. *New York: Warner, 2000, ©1981. 352p. ISBN 0751504408.*

(See chapter 13, "Ecological Horror: Mother Nature Has Her Revenge.")

Desperation. *New York: Viking, 1996. 690p. ISBN 0670868361.*

(See chapter 8, "Mythological Monsters and 'The Old Ones': Invoking the Dark Gods.")

Koontz, Dean.

Cold Fire. *New York: Berkley, 2004, ©1991. 431p. ISBN 0425199584.*

Jim Ironheart suffers from visions that allow him to see when disaster will occur, in time for him to prevent the tragedy. But can he and a young reporter who has taken a personal interest in Ironheart survive a showdown with evil? **Similar titles:** *The Dead Zone*, Stephen King; *Mist and Stone*, Diana G. Gallagher and Constance Burge; *Blood Angel*, Justine Musk.

Dreams • Journalist as Character • Precognition • Psychics

The Mask. *Oxford: Isis Press, 1999, ©1981, 384p. ISBN 0753159538.*

Paul and Carol want nothing more than to have beautiful, perfect children. Then one day an accident grants their wish—they now have Jane, a homeless teenaged girl who seems to be the perfect daughter. But Jane has a hidden agenda, which may involve murder. **Similar titles:** *Spirit*, Graham Masterton; *Secrets in the Attic*, V. C. Andrews; *The Beloved*, J. F. Gonzales; *The Omen* (film).

. Demons • Matricide/Patricide • Parenting

Laidlaw, Marc.

 The 37th Mandala. *New York: Leisure, 1999, ©1996. 352p. ISBN 084394658X.*

Derek Crowe, a hack who wants to make money off New Age philosophy, unwittingly awakens an evil force when he converts followers using a mandala historically connected to Cambodia's killing fields. The mandalas, represented by Crowe in his best-selling book *The Mandala Rites* as comforting angels who can help any human who calls them, are actually otherworldly beings who feed off human suffering. **Similar titles:** *Wither*, J. G. Passarella; *Valley of Lights*, Stephen Gallagher; *The Manitou*, Graham Masterton.

California—San Francisco • Demons • Magic • Numerology • Religion—Paganism • War—Vietnam War • Writer as Character

Laimo, Michael.

The Demonologist. *New York: Leisure, 2005. 369p. ISBN 0843955279.*

(See chapter 15, "Splatterpunk: The Gross Out.")

Lee, Edward.

Messenger. *New York: Leisure, 2004. 337p. ISBN 0843952040.*

(See chapter 15, "Splatterpunk: The Gross Out.")

Monstrosity. *New York: Leisure, 2003. 373p. ISBN 0843950757.*

(See chapter 15, "Splatterpunk: The Gross Out.")

Levin, Ira.

The Rosemary's Baby Books.

Young marrieds Guy and Rosemary Woodhouse move into their dream apartment in the Bramford, where they hope to start a family. They don't believe the Bramford's sinister reputation. Maybe they should. **Similar titles:** *The Wicker Man*, Anthony Shaffer and Robin Hardy; *The Long Lost*, Ramsey Campbell; *Demon Seed*, Dean Koontz; *Rosemary's Baby* (film).

New York—New York City • Religion—Satanism

Rosemary's Baby. *New York: Penguin, 1997, ©1967. 319p. ISBN 0451194004.*

The Woodhouses meet what seem like proper Victorian spinsters, only these elderly neighbors practice cannibalism—and one of them claims to have conjured Satan. Rosemary herself doubts that the sweet old couple next door are practicing satanists. But they are, and they have designs on her womb.

Actor as Character • Marriage • Pregnancy • Religion—Christianity—Catholicism

Son of Rosemary. *New York: Dutton, 1997. 256p. ISBN 0525943749.*

Rosemary awakens from a long coma to learn that her demonic son is now a charismatic religious leader preaching messages of peace and hope. She also notes the demonic look that he had in his eyes as an infant.

Antichrist (character) • Incest • Televangelism

Lewis, M[atthew] G.

The Monk: A Romance. *Orchard Park, NY: Broadview Press, 2004, ©1796. 479p. ISBN 1551112272.*

In this novel, one of the ancestors of erotic horror, Satan tempts a well-respected clergyman. Readers will find here a chilling character study of the degeneration of a human being and his soul. **Similar titles:** *The Exorcist*, William Peter Blatty; *The Castle of Otranto*, Horace Walpole; *Wieland, or the Transformation*, Charles Brockden Brown; *The Old English Baron*, Clara Reeve.

Clergy as Character • Gothicism • Psychosexual Horror • Satan (character) • Shape-shifters

Lovecraft, H. P.

The Case of Charles Dexter Ward. *New York: Ballantine Books, 1995, ©1943. 127p. ISBN 0345384210.*

(See chapter 8, "Mythological Monsters and 'The Old Ones': Invoking the Dark Gods.")

The Lurker at the Threshold. *New York: Carroll and Graf, 2003, ©1945. 196p. ISBN 0786711884.*

(See chapter 8, "Mythological Monsters and 'The Old Ones': Invoking the Dark Gods.")

Marano, Michael.

 Dawn Song. *New York: Tor, 2000, ©1998. 400p. ISBN 0812545478.*
(See chapter 8, "Mythological Monsters and 'The Old Ones': Invoking the Dark Gods.")

Masterton, Graham.

The Devil in Gray. *New York: Leisure, 2004. 355p. ISBN 0843953616.*
Grisly murders in Richmond, Virginia, have Detective Decker baffled. He must use supernatural means, including speaking with his deceased girlfriend and consulting a voodoo priestess, to discover what is behind the crimes—the Devil's Brigade, a band of special troops that committed atrocities using voodoo to demoralize Union soldiers during the Civil War. **Similar titles:** *A Terrible Beauty*, Graham Masterton; *Darkfall*, Dean Koontz; *The Restless Dead*, Hugh B. Cave.

Police Officer as Character • Religion—Voodoo • Virginia—Richmond • War—American Civil War

The House That Jack Built. *New York: Leisure, 2000, ©1996. 383p. ISBN 0843947462.*
High-powered attorney Craig Bellman and his wife Effie escape the harsh streets of New York City and move into Valhalla, a century-old mansion erected by a legendary gambler and womanizer. Soon after the couple moves in, ghostly voices make their supernatural presences known to Effie. **Similar titles:** *Prey*, Graham Masterton; *Nazareth Hill*, Ramsey Campbell; *Creepers*, David Morrell.

Haunted Houses • Lawyer as Character • New York • Pregnancy • Revenging Revenant

The Manitou Series.

The Manitou (ghost) of a powerful Native American medicine man is reborn in modern-day New York City. This classic is well-crafted and suspenseful, with emphasis on characterization and atmosphere. **Similar titles:** *The 37th Mandala*, Marc Laidlaw; *The Exorcist*, William Peter Blatty; *Crota*, Owl Goingback.

Demons • Erksine, Harry (character) • Native American Characters • New York—New York City • Religion—Native American

The Manitou. *Kingston, RI: Moyer Bell, 2001, ©1975. 174p. ISBN 1587541033.*
Karen Tandy goes to her doctor with what looks like a tumor on her neck, but X-rays reveal a fetus-like growth. Desperate, she turns to a well-known psychic, drawing him into the ultimate test of faith in himself and in the power of the spiritual world; Now he must save Karen and fight the Manitou.

Medical Horror • Police Officer as Character • Pregnancy • Psychics

Revenge of the Manitou. *London: Sphere, 1980. 261p. ISBN 0722159870.*
Only a year before, the Manitou had been vanquished, or so everyone thought. So no one believes little Tony when he claims that there is a man in his closet whose face seems to grow from the wood. Once again, Harry Erskine is called upon to save the world from the wrath of Misquamacus. **Similar titles:** *The 37th Mandala*, Marc Laidlaw; *The Exorcist*, William Peter Blatty; *Crota*, Owl Goingback.

Burial. *New York: Tom Doherty, 1996. 512p. ISBN 0614055202.*

Twenty years after Karen Tandy gave birth to the Manitou from what appeared to be a tumor on her neck, the Native American spirit Misquamacus is back to avenge the near extermination of his people. He teams up with the spirit of a voodoo priest, and the two manage to reduce both New York City and Chicago to rubble. Once again, Harry Erskine must do battle with Misquamacus before he manages to return the entire planet to a pre-Columbian state.

Illinois—Chicago • Psychics • Religion—Voodoo

Manitou Blood. *New York: Leisure, 2005. 256p. ISBN 0843954256.*

A plague sweeps through New York City, compelling its victims to drink the blood of others. Now phony psychic Harry Erskine must enlist the help of his former girlfriend Amelia, a genuine clairvoyant, as well as Native American shaman John Singing Rock to stop Misquamacas, who is exploiting the unwilling spirit of Vasile Lup, an infamous vampire gatherer, to wreak havoc. **Similar titles:** *London Under Midnight*, Simon Clark; *I Am Legend*, Richard Matheson; *Dead Sea*, Brian Keene.

Epidemics • Psychics

Prey. *New York: Leisure, 1999, ©1992. 352p. ISBN 0843946334.*

(See chapter 8, "Mythological Monsters and 'The Old Ones': Invoking the Dark Gods.")

Maturin, Charles Robert.

Melmoth the Wanderer. *Edited by Victor Sage. London: Penguin, 2000, ©1820. 659p. ISBN 014044761X.*

An Irish gentleman makes a deal with the devil that enables him to live for as long as he wishes. Eventually he wants to dissolve his pact, but to do so he must travel the world looking for someone who will assume his deal with the devil and volunteer for eternal life. Although cumbersome at times, Mantuin's novel provides an excellent example of early gothic literature. **Similar titles:** *The Castle of Otranto*, Horace Walpole; *The Monk*, Matthew Lewis; *Wieland, or the Transformation*, Charles Brockden Brown.

England—London • Gothicism • Immortality • Ireland • Satan (character)

Maynard, L. H., and M. P. N. Sims.

Demon Eyes. *New York: Dorchester, 2007. 338p. ISBN 084395972X.*

Emma is given what most would consider good news. She is offered a promotion—to personal assistant for the managing director of Keltner Industries. At first she and her girlfriend are happy, thinking that the only downside is that Emma will be traveling for long periods of time. But when her lover dies in a freak accident, Emma begins to suspect there may be even more problems with accepting the offer. Is it possible that the Keltners have an unnatural interest in Emma? **Similar titles:** *Rosemary's Baby*, Ira Levin; *The Parasite*, Ramsey Campbell; *Unholy Birth*, Andrew Neiderman.

Corporate Horror • Demons • Gay/Lesbian/Bisexual Characters • Psychosexual Horror

Michaels, Barbara, and Elizabeth Peters.

Prince of Darkness. *New York: HarperTorch, 2005, ©1969. 336p. ISBN 0060745096.*
(See chapter 10, "Small Town Horror: Villages of the Damned.")

Moore, James A.

The Corbin Family Novels.

Chris Corbin and his sister Brittany think they have it made after their family comes into a lot of money. But when humanoid demons start breaking into the family home in search of one of their late mother's pendants, they find out just how hard it can be for teenagers in a cruel and unpredictable world. **Similar titles:** The Buffy the Vampire Slayer Series, various authors; The Harrow Academy Novels, Douglas Clegg; *Blood Red*, James A. Moore.

Adolescence • Corbin, Brittany (character) • Corbin, Chris (character) • Families • High School

Possessions. *New York: Dorchester, 2004. 339p. ISBN 0843951710.*

Chris Corbin and his sister Brittany feel as though the world has come to an end when their mother is killed in a terrifying traffic accident. Now strange and evil-looking humanoids are trying to steal some of the jewelry that she left to her family.

Religion—Satanism • Stalkers

Rabid Growth. *Leisure, 2005. 323p. ISBN 0843951729.*

Chris Corbin cannot put his life back together because the evil entity he thought he defeated has planted its seeds in the bodies of his best friends. As their personalities change, one by one, he cannot tell whom he can trust, or whom he can save from an excruciating death.

Aliens • Religion—Satanism • Replicants

Newbies. *New York: Dorchester, 2004. 197p. ISBN 0843954744.*

In this loosely related follow-up to *Possessions*, Chris ships his sister Brittany off to Dunhaven Academy so she can receive a good education and some discipline. She has serious trouble fitting in, and her only friend there is a misfit named Casey. But students disappear or supposedly commit suicide, and of course Brittany gets blamed. To save herself, she begins to investigate, and figures out that someone may be using black magic at the school.

Suicide • Witchcraft

Powers, Tim.

 Declare. *New York: William Morrow, 2001. 517p. ISBN 0380976528.*

Andrew Hale, an Oxford lecturer who first entered Her Majesty's Secret Service as an eighteen-year-old, is called back to finish a job begun after the end of World War II. Hale must bring down the Soviet government before it can harness powerful, otherworldly forces concentrated on the summit of Mount Ararat. **Similar titles:** *Judgment of Tears: Anno Dracula 1959,* and *The Man from the Diogenes Club,* Kim Newman; The Pendergast Novels, Douglas Preston and Lincoln Child; The Repairman Jack Series, F. Paul Wilson.

England • Espionage • Middle East, The • Parapsychology • Russia—Moscow • Turkey —Mount Ararat • War—The Cold War

Spector, Craig.

Under-ground. *New York: Tor, 2005. 254p. ISBN 0765306603.*

In this dark fantasy version of *The Big Chill*, a clique of seven high school students have a wild bash at one of the group's ancestral Virginia home. At the end of the night one of their number is dead, and one is forever trapped in another dimension. Twenty years later, a survivor convinces the rest of the group to journey to the home once again to free their friend. **Similar titles:** *The Good House,* Tananarive Due; *The Boys Are Back in Town,* Christopher Golden; *Obsession,* Ramsey Campbell; *It,* Stephen King.

Haunted Houses • Human Sacrifice • Magic • Parallel Universes • Virginia

Stoker, Bram.

The Jewel of Seven Stars. *Oxford: Oxford University Press, 1996, ©1903. 214p. ISBN 0192832190.*

(See chapter 5, "Golem, Mummies, and Zombies: Wake the Dead and They'll Be Cranky.")

Straub, Peter.

If You Could See Me Now. *New York: Ballantine, 2000, ©1977. 322p. ISBN 0345438671.*

This early Straub chiller is about a pact made between two young lovers. When Miles returns to his hometown twenty years afterward, he suspects that he will not be meeting the seductive Allison of his youth, but a savage demon fueled by revenge. **Similar titles:** *Ghost Story* and *Shadowland,* Peter Straub; *The Beloved,* J. F. Gonzales; *Hellraiser* (film).

Demons • Parapsychology • Revenge

Shadowland. *London: Voyager, 2001, ©1981. 480p. ISBN 0007119577.*

Two teenaged friends, Tom Flanagan and Del Nightingale, spend a summer as apprentices to a magician to polish up their amateur act. But horrible events begin to occur at the boys' school, where they are picked on regularly. Is black magic at the core of these "accidents"? **Similar titles:** *If*

You Could See Me Now and *Mr. X*, Peter Straub, The *Traveling Vampire Show*, Richard Laymon; *The Talisman*, Peter Straub and Stephen King.

Adolescence • High School • Magic • New England • Revenge

Waggoner, Tim.

Darkness Wakes. *New York: Leisure, 2006. 321p. ISBN 0843957948.*
(See chapter 15, "Splatterpunk: The Gross Out.")

Walpole, Horace.

The Castle of Otranto: A Gothic Story, and The Mysterious Mother: A Tragedy. *Edited by Frederick S. Frank. Peterborough, ON: Broadview Press, 2003, ©1764. 357p. ISBN 155111304X.*

Considered one of the first, if not the first-ever, works of horror, *The Castle of Otranto* traces the fate of the cursed family of Manfred, Prince of Otranto, and his haunted castle. Will an important wedding be marred by giants, ghosts, and demons? **Similar titles:** *Northanger Abbey*, Jane Austen; *The Monk*, Matthew Lewis; *Wieland, or the Transformation*, Charles Brockden Brown; *The Old English Baron*, Clara Reeve.

Castles • Family Curse • Ghosts • Haunted Houses • Italy • Medieval Era

Wilson, F. Paul.

Gateways. *New York: Tor, 2006, ©2003. 435p. ISBN 0765346052.*
(See chapter 12, "Technohorror: Evil Hospitals, Military Screw-Ups, Mad Scientists, and Alien Invasions.")

Possession

Brown, Charles Brockden.

Wieland, or the Transformation. *New York: Modern Library, 2002, ©1798. 376p. ISBN 0375759034.*

In this tale of one family's slide down the slippery slope of reality, Theodore Wieland hears mysterious voices. Are these the result of delusions, ventriloquism, or divine forces? And are they related to a visiting stranger? This Gothic thriller is based on a real-life story of a man beset by religious guilt that erupts into murderous mania. **Similar titles:** *Thirty-two Stories*, Edgar Allan Poe; *The Ghost Stories of Edith Wharton*, Edith Wharton; *The Ghost Stories of Henry James*, Henry James.

Colonial Era • Epistolary Format • Family Curse • Gothicism • New England • Ventriloquism

Campbell, Ramsey.

Ancient Images. *New York: Tor, 1990, ©1989. 311p. ISBN 0812502639.*

Film editor Sandy Allan has a chance to work on a rare Lugosi/Karloff movie that one of her colleagues has just located. But when her colleague mysteriously dies, strange things begin to happen to those associated with the movie—or with the

British short story on which it was based. **Similar titles:** *The Claw*, Ramsey Campbell; *Coldheart Canyon*, Clive Barker; *Heart-Shaped Box*, Joe Hill; *The Ring*, Koji Suzuki; *The Ring* (film).

Cursed Objects • England • Horror Movie Industry

The Claw. *London: Little, Brown. 1992, ©1983. 380p. ISBN 0356091503.*

Alan Knight, a writer from Norwich, agrees to take a talisman from Nigeria back to his hometown, to present it to one of the African studies museums there. However, he is unaware of the curse passed on to him, as it is to all who have the claw in their possession. A local youth who accidentally scratched himself on the claw becomes extremely violent, and members of his own family also begin to feel its influence. **Similar titles:** *Matinee at the Flame*, Christopher Fahy; *The Beckoning Fair One*, Oliver Onions; *Ancient Images*, Ramsey Campbell.

Africa • Cursed Objects • England • Parenting • Religion—African • Writer as Character

The Influence. *London: Headline, 1996, ©1988. 312p. ISBN 0747250758.*

After Hermione's Aunt Queenie dies, she begins to suspect that her niece's new friend is somehow Queenie's ghost, and that Queenie's spirit is ultimately trying to possess the niece. To stop this, Hermione must visit her aunt's grave, which turns out to be more dangerous than she thinks. **Similar titles:** *The Return*, Walter de la Mare; *The Parasite*, Ramsey Campbell; *Gifted Trust*, John Paul Allen and Alan M. Clark; *Kiss the Goat*, Brian Stableford; *What Lies Beneath* (film).

Family Curse • Reincarnation • Revenging Revenant • Wales

The Nameless. *London: Little, Brown. 1992, ©1985. 278p. ISBN 0356207773.*

(See chapter 4, "Ghosts and Haunted Houses: Dealing with Presences and Absences.")

The Parasite. *London: Headline, 1993, ©1980. 369p. ISBN 0747240612.*

As a ten-year-old, Rose Tierney participates in a séance held in a house where murder had once occurred, unwittingly leaving herself open to the spirit of an occultist named Peter Grace, who spent his life working on methods of transferring souls into the bodies of the living after death. Now an adult, Rose suspects that the soul of Pete Grace may have been passed into her body. **Similar titles:** *The Return*, Walter de la Mare; *The Parasite*, Ramsey Campbell; *Come Fygures, Come Shadowes*, Richard Matheson; *Kiss the Goat*, Brian Stableford; *Supernatural* (film).

England—Liverpool • Nazism • Parapsychology • Pregnancy • Religion—Cults • Stalkers

De la Mare, Walter.

The Return. *Mineola, NY: Dover, 1997, ©1922. 193p. ISBN 0486296881.*

Arthur Lawford falls asleep on the grave of an eighteenth-century pirate, only to wake up and discover that his face is no longer his own. While he believes himself to be essentially unchanged psychologically, he notices that another personality is insinuating itself into his consciousness. **Simi-**

lar titles: *Dr. Jekyll and Mr. Hyde*, Robert Louis Stevenson; *Rebecca*, Daphne du Maurier; *The Parasite*, Ramsey Campbell; *Missing Monday*, Matthew J. Costello.

Doppelgangers • England • Mind Control

Earley, Pete.

The Apocalypse Stone. *New York: Forge, 2006. 366p. ISBN 0765310252.*

As a circuit court judge who seems to be on his way to a seat on the state supreme court, Evan Spencer is already a very powerful man. But when he stumbles upon an ordinary stone that turns out to be a powerful ancient relic, his ability to affect the outcome of events both in and out of his courtroom is greatly augmented. Yet Evan is plagued by disturbing visions and stigmata, and a priest is actively seeking the relic. **Similar titles:** *The Claw*, Ramsey Campbell; *Dispatch*, Bentley Little; *The Wind Caller*, P. D. Cacek.

Clergy as Character • Cursed Objects • Lawyer as Character • Religion—Christianity • Virginia

Golden, Christopher.

The Boys Are Back in Town. *New York: Bantam, 2004. 347p. ISBN 0553382071.*

Will James returns to his hometown to attend his ten-year class reunion. When he comes into contact with his old acquaintances, Will can actually feel his memories changing to much darker events than what he initially recalled, particularly concerning one of his best friends, who died in a drunk driving accident. A teenager living in Will's old house brings him a book, *Dark Magick*, which prompts him to realize that his shifting memories are due to guilt. Now he must travel back in time to right a wrong. **Similar titles:** *Wildwood Road*, Christopher Golden; *Missing Monday*, Matthew J. Costello; *Matinee at the Flame*, Christopher Fahy; *20th Century Ghosts*, Joe Hill.

Adolescence • Death—Grieving • Time Travel • Witchcraft

Harwood, John.

 The Ghost Writer. *Orlando, FL: Harcourt Trade, 2004. 369p. ISBN 0151010749.*

One day ten-year-old Gerard Freeman sneaked into his mother's room and unlocked a secret drawer, only to find a picture of a woman he has never seen before, along with a story of murder. Now an adult and working as a librarian, Gerard corresponds with an English pen pal, Alice Jessel, who lives in an institution. But her description of the grounds begins to sound eerily familiar, like something he had read as a ten-year-old. **Similar titles:** *The Historian*, Elizabeth Kostova; *Galilee*, Clive Barker; *November Mourns*, Tom Piccirilli.

Australia • England • Librarian as Character • Secret Sin

Kiernan, Caitlin R.

Alabaster. *Burton, MI: Subterranean Press, 2006. 182p. ISBN 1596060603.*

(See chapter 18, "Collections and Anthologies.")

King, Stephen.

Cujo. *New York: Warner, 2000, ©1981. 352p. ISBN 0751504408.*
(See chapter 13, "Ecological Horror: Mother Nature Has Her Revenge.")

The Shining. *New York: Pocket Books, 2002, ©1977. 505p. ISBN 0743437497.*
Alcoholic ex-teacher Jack Torrance has a second chance at life and at saving his relationship with his family. He has been hired as the caretaker for the Overlook Hotel during the off-season winter months. The hotel itself has different ideas; it wants to add the psychic power that Jack's son Danny possesses to its own powers, and it will stop at nothing, not even at supplying Jack with liquor, to achieve its goal. **Similar titles:** *Nazareth Hill*, Ramsey Campbell; *The Green Man*, Kingsley Amis; *A House Divided*, Deborah LeBlanc; *The Shining* (film).

Addictions—Alcoholism • Colorado • Haunted Houses • Psychics

The Tommyknockers. *New York: Putnam, 1987. 558p. ISBN 0399133143.*
Unknown to the residents, aliens have come to the small town of Haven, Maine, and have given the inhabitants extraordinary powers. After Bobbi Anderson stumbles across a metal object buried for millennia, the town becomes a very dangerous place for outsiders. **Similar titles:** *Dreamcatcher*, Stephen King; *The Body Snatchers*, Jack Finney; *Possessions* and *Rabid Growth*, James A. Moore; *Invasion of the Body Snatchers* (film).

Aliens • Maine • Mind Control • Police Officer as Character • Replicants

Koontz, Dean.

Hideaway. *New York: Putnam, 1992. 384p. ISBN 0399136738.*
Hatch Harrison dies from a car accident but is revived by a brilliant doctor some seventy-five minutes later. Unfortunately, when he comes back from the afterlife, Hatch brings with him a demon that is using his body as a place to hide. Suffice it to say that no one should anger Hatch Harrison, or more specifically, his inner demon. The first hundred pages are incredible. **Similar titles:** *The Dead Zone*, Stephen King; *The Exorcist*, William Peter Blatty; *The 37th Mandala*, Mark Laidlaw; *World of Hurt*, Brian Hodge.

Afterlife, The • Artist as Character • Demons • Doppelgangers

Winter Moon. *New York: Random House, 2001, ©1994. 472p. ISBN 0553582933.*
When heroic LAPD officer Jack McGarvey and his family inherited the Quartermass Ranch in Montana from someone they'd never met, they considered themselves lucky. Little did they know what had happened to its previous owner, Eduardo Fernandez, an old farmer who saw something in the moon. The writing in this novel is more subtle and traditional than Koontz's writing usually is. **Similar titles:** *The Tommyknockers*, Stephen King; *The Resort*, Bentley Little; *The House That Jack Built*, Graham Masterton.

Aliens • Hispanic American Characters • Montana • Police Officer as Character • Zombies

Laymon, Richard.

One Rainy Night. *New York: Dorchester, 1999. 410p. ISBN 0843946903.*
(See chapter 13, "Ecological Horror: Mother Nature Has Her Revenge.")

LeBlanc, Deborah.

Family Inheritance. *New York: Leisure, 2004. 358p. ISBN 0843953470.*
A traiteur (a Cajun folk healer) tries to heal a patient, but he sees a death's head with a vertical mouth, the spirit of insanity and destruction. As a result, his patient dies, and he has no choice but to leave the area. Thirty years later his daughter, also a healer, living in Memphis, is called back to her Louisiana roots when her younger brother starts to hear voices and suddenly becomes violent. **Similar titles:** *Voodoo Season: A Marie Laveau Mystery*, Jewel Parker Rhodes; *Leslie*, Omar Tyree; *Morbid Curiosity*, Deborah LeBlanc; *The Skeleton Key* (film).

Cajuns • Louisiana • Magic • Religion—Voodoo • Traiteur as Character

Lovecraft, H. P.

The Shadow Out of Time. *Edited by S. T. Joshi and David E. Schultz. New York: Hippocampus Press, 2001. 136p. ISBN 0967321530.*
(See chapter 8, "Mythological Monsters and 'The Old Ones': Invoking the Dark Gods.")

Pampellonne, Terese.

The Unwelcome Child. *New York: Pinnacle Books, 2005. 318p. ISBN 0786017260.*
The story begins in Martha's Vineyard in 1919, with a scared young woman being restrained on an abortionist's cot in a home for "good girls gone bad." Fast-forward to 1995: Annie Wojtoko, a thirty-something slasher film actress living in a dank New York City apartment, decides to take a break from her life as a "buxom victim" to visit her mysteriously pregnant best friend in Martha's Vineyard. **Similar titles:** *Rosemary's Baby*, Ira Levin; *The Parasite*, Ramsey Campbell; *Unholy Birth*, Andrew Neiderman.

Marriage • Massachusetts—Martha's Vineyard • Pregnancy • Revenging Revenant

Sullivan, Thomas.

Second Soul. *New York: Onyx, 2005. 291p. ISBN 0451412028.*
Michael Carmichael has a brush with death in a skiing accident that lands him in a frozen lake. As Michael is drowning, a bus hits a bear and crashes, and he watches as it burns with people trapped inside. Now recovering from his injuries, Michael begins noticing that reality isn't quite what he remembered it to be: food rots very quickly in his presence, animals are afraid of him, and someone has been paying his bills. **Similar titles:** *Reassuring Tales*, T. E. D. Klein; *The Collected Strange Stories*, Robert Aickman; *Ghosts of Yesterday*, Jack Cady; *The Spaces Between the Lines*, Peter Crowther.

Afterlife, The • Mental Illness • Parallel Universes • Revenging Revenant

Stableford, Brian.

Kiss the Goat: A Twenty-first Century Ghost Story. *Holicong, PA: Prime, 2005. 194p. ISBN 0809544849.*

(See chapter 4, "Ghosts and Haunted Houses: Dealing with Presences and Absences.")

Thomas, Lee.

The Dust of Wonderland. *New York: Alyson, 2007. 316p. ISBN 1593500114.*

When Ken Nicholson returns to New Orleans, it isn't to celebrate Mardi Gras or help rebuild storm-ravaged neighborhoods. Instead, a late-night call from his ex-wife breaks the tragic news that their son has been attacked and is in a coma. Nicholson then begins to see visions that an old evil that was responsible for several gory deaths at a gay club may be responsible, and that the spirit of his ex-lover, Travis Brugier, has possessed his son's girlfriend. **Similar titles:** *Lasher*, Anne Rice; *The Shining*, Stephen King; *Hideaway*, Dean Koontz.

Families • Gay/Lesbian/Bisexual Characters • Louisiana—New Orleans • Parenting • Stalkers

Wilde, Oscar.

The Picture of Dorian Gray. *New York: Tom Doherty, 1999, ©1891. 240p. ISBN 0812567110.*

When handsome young Dorian Gray sees a portrait that has been painted of him, he bitterly regrets that he must someday grow old. He wishes that the painting would age instead, and that he would eternally keep his youth. Dorian's wish comes true, and he becomes a sort of dark Peter Pan who can never grow up. **Similar titles:** *Drawn to the Grave*, Mary Ann Mitchell; *The House of Seven Gables*, Nathaniel Hawthorne; *The Hunger*, Whitley Strieber; *The Hunger* (film).

Aging • England—London • Secret Sin • Victorian Era • Wish Fulfillment

Witchcraft

Armstrong, Kelley.

The Women of the Otherworld Series.

Meet Elena Michaels, the only female of her kind. A she-werewolf who left her pack in upstate New York to live among humans in Toronto, she now has a career as a journalist and various relationships—with humans and witches alike. The series emphasis switches as it progresses, from werewolves to witches. **Similar titles:** The Buffy the Vampire Slayer Series, various authors; The Charmed Series, various authors; The Wendy Ward Series, J. G. Passarella.

Adams, Hope (character) • Levine, Eve (character) • Michaels, Elena (character) • Winterbourne, Paige (character)

Bitten. *New York: Plume, 2003. 372p. ISBN 0452283485.*

(See chapter 6, "Vampires and Werewolves: Children of the Night.")

Stolen. *New York: Viking, 2003. 399p. ISBN 0670031372.*

(See chapter 6, "Vampires and Werewolves: Children of the Night.")

Dime Store Magic. *New York: Dell, 2007, ©2004. 414p. ISBN 0553590154.*

This third book in the series picks up where *Stolen* left off. Elena, a werewolf, and Paige, a witch, rescue thirteen-year-old Savannah from a group that is kidnapping supernatural creatures, and who have already murdered Savannah's mother Eve. Now Paige is tasked with raising her friend Eve's sometimes surly and difficult teenaged daughter while protecting her from other sorcerers.

Demons • Parenting • Witchcraft

Industrial Magic. *New York: Bantam, 2007, ©2004. 528p. ISBN 0553590162.*

In a world where sorcerers and witches are bitter enemies, the witch Paige must attempt to recruit sorcerers into her alternative coven, a group meant to re-empower a new generation. Meanwhile, she must continue to protect Eve's growing daughter from those who would harm her.

Demons • Parenting • Witchcraft

Haunted. *New York: Spectra, 2005. 528p. ISBN 0553587080.*

This sequel crosses romance with horror. Eve, a witch who got herself in trouble by playing with black magic, is spending the afterlife looking in on her now teenaged daughter. Being a ghost isn't such a terrible fate, since Eve meets up with her old flame Kris, who has also passed on. Unfortunately, the angels want Eve for one of their own.

Afterlife, The • Demons • Parenting • Witchcraft

Broken. *New York: Bantam Spectra, 2006. 444p. ISBN 0553588184.*

(See chapter 6, "Vampires and Werewolves: Children of the Night.")

No Humans Involved. *New York: Bantam Books, 2007. 342p. ISBN 0553805088.*

Jaimie Vargas, celebrity medium and necromancer who can reanimate the dead, must free the souls of six murdered children. And these youthful apparitions are no ordinary ghosts, but beings who should not exist—dark forces have used magic inappropriately to trap these souls in between this world and the next.

Afterlife, The • Demons • Witchcraft

Personal Demon. *New York: Bantam, 2008. 371p. ISBN 0553806610.*

Tabloid journalist Hope Adams, fathered by a demon, has supernatural abilities along with her writing skills. Now she's been chosen by Benico Cortez to infiltrate a paranormal gang of kids who have been causing problems for Cortez's corporation.

Demons • Journalist as Character • Witchcraft

Bachman, Richard (pseudonym used by Stephen King).

Thinner. *New York: New American Library, 1984. 282p. ISBN 0453004687.*
(See King, Stephen, *Thinner*, in this section.)

Bachman, Richard, with Christopher Golden.

Accursed. *New York: Del Rey, 2005. 385p. ISBN 034547130X.*
A plague that transforms people into reptilian monsters sweeps from the slums to other areas of the city, and two wizards must take action, with the help of the spirits of Lord Byron, Queen Boadicea, and Admiral Nelson.

England—London • Epidemics

Witchery. *New York: Del Rey, 2006. 381p. ISBN 0345471318.*
The powerful protectors of Albion (England), William and Tamara Swift, discover that young women, both human and fairy, are vanishing—leaving behind no trace of their last whereabouts. As she pieces together information based on rumors and her knowledge of the solstice, Tamara comes to realize that even given their magical powers, they face a daunting task.

Demons

Benson, Amber.

The Ghosts of Albion Series.

In an alternate universe, ghosts, vampires, and wizards populate Victorian England. Originally a computer-animated Web movie series, <u>Ghosts of Albion</u> has spawned two novelizations. **Similar titles:** <u>The Anno Dracula Series</u>, Kim Newman; *The Doorkeepers*, Graham Masterton; *Bloodstained Oz*, Christopher Golden and James A. Moore.

Byron, George Gordon, Lord (character) • England • Magic • Victorian Era • Witchcraft

Bray, Libba.

The Gemma Doyle Trilogy.

Gemma Doyle is a young girl at a strict boarding school. In this stultifying atmosphere she discovers she can access The Realms, another dimension where people can have whatever they desire and are allowed to retrieve some magic to transform themselves in the real world. **Similar titles:** <u>The Talisman Series</u>, Stephen King and Peter Straub; *Newbies*, James A. Moore; <u>The Eden Moore Trilogy</u>, Cherie Priest; *Coraline*, Neil Gaiman; *Paperhouse* (film).

Adolescence • Doyle, Gemma (character) • England—London • Indian Characters • Magic • Parallel Universe • Teacher as Character • Victorian Era

A Great and Terrible Beauty. *New York: Delacorte, 2003. 403p. ISBN 0385730284.*
Gemma learns too late the fate of two girls who also dabbled in Realms-based magic. This erudite and compelling dark fantasy is written in Victorian prose.

Rebel Angels. *New York: Delacorte, 2006. 548p. ISBN 0385730292.*

> In this sequel, Gemma must venture into The Realms once again to find the Temple and bind the magic she had released, before the dark creatures who reside there are able to gain enough power leave their realm and cross over into the everyday world.

The Sweet Far Thing. *New York: Delacorte, 2007. 819p. ISBN 0385730306.*

> Gemma has successfully bound to herself the magic of The Realms. Now, on the eve of her debut, as the mysterious burned East Wing at Spence Academy is being rebuilt, her friends see the deceased Pippa, who continues to live in The Realms.

The Charmed Series (various authors).

These novelizations, based on the television series of the same name, are about the three Halliwell sisters, who happen to be the world's most powerful good witches. They are known throughout the supernatural community as "The Charmed Ones," and each sister possesses unique magical powers, which they use to battle evil forces in California. **Similar titles:** The Buffy the Vampire Slayer Series, various authors; The Wicked Willow Trilogy, various authors; The Eden Moore Trilogy, Cherie Priest.

Adolescence • California • Charmed (television series) • Magic • Witchcraft

Burns, Laura J.

Inherit the Witch: An Original Novel. *New York: Simon Spotlight, 2004. 212p. ISBN 0689867085.*

> Juliana O'Farrell's daughter Lily turns thirteen, the traditional age at which her powers should become manifest. However, she has yet to cast a single spell, or even show a propensity for magic. Juliana worries that a demon may have stripped her daughter's magic, so she calls on the Power of Three to serve as mentors, or at least to babysit.

Parenting

Ciencin, Scott.

Luck Be a Lady: An Original Novel. *New York: Simon Spotlight, 2004. 214p. ISBN 0689857934.*

> Phoebe Halliwell may be ready to change, but her ex-husband, a demon, isn't ready to let her go. He devises a plot against the Power of Three, keeping watch over Phoebe, and during a battle, he accidentally transports himself to 1940s Hollywood, bringing the three sisters with him. There they discover demons attempting to shake down local businesses. So Paige poses as a young starlet, while Phoebe contends with Cole.

California—Hollywood • Demons • Time Travel

Dokey, Cameron.

Picture Perfect. *New York: Simon Spotlight, 2005. 199p. ISBN 141690025X.*

> The Power of Three must overcome their differences to face a new foe. Phoebe invites her sisters to attend the grand reopening of a San Francisco

landmark, which is associated with a tragic love affair between its architect and a newly divorced artist. With the permission of the artist's daughter, Phoebe has been reprinting the old love letters in her column, which may precipitate a horrifying unveiling of a mural.

Artist as Character • California—San Francisco • Cursed Objects • Journalist as Character

Dokey, Cameron, and Jacklyn Wilson.

Truth and Consequences: An Original Novel. *New York: Simon Pulse, 2003. 196p. ISBN 0689857918.*

Phoebe accepts a friendly dinner date with a handsome stranger, but is caught breaking bread with him by her steady boyfriend Cole, when he returns from work early. His mistrust of her comes to the fore, and a rift is created between the two that leads them into the underworld and also threatens to destroy the Power of Three.

Demons • Hell

Gallagher, Diana G., and Constance Burge.

Mist and Stone: An Original Novel. *New York: Simon & Schuster, 2003. 210p. ISBN 0689857896.*

Social worker Paige Matthews wants to make a difference for juvenile delinquent Todd Corman, but he has been bounced from foster home to foster home for so long that he doesn't trust any authority. Despite the boy's protestations, Paige determines to break through, even after Phoebe tells her that she has read the boy's future, and it may involve the darklighters.

Parenting • Precognition • Social Worker as Character

Gallagher, Diana G., and Constance M. Burge.

Something Wiccan This Way Comes: An Original Novel. *New York: Simon Pulse, 2003. 215p. ISBN 0689855540.*

The newest member of the Power of Three, Paige Matthews, reads about a Wiccan convention near Las Vegas. She thinks the retreat could be enlightening, but Piper and Phoebe have reservations. After learning of the serial killings of practicing Wiccans, the three decide that attending may be very important.

Kidnapping • Nevada—Las Vegas • Religion—Wicca • Serial Killers

Giron, Sephera.

Borrowed Flesh. *New York: Leisure, 2004. 340p. ISBN 0843952571.*

Sometimes retin A and botox just aren't enough. This is the case for a twenty-first-century immortal witch whose eternal beauty has but one catch—she needs regular virgin sacrifices to keep her skin fresh and healthy. Everything seems to be going along fine until a friend of her latest sacrifice starts sniffing around looking for answers. Giron captures female stereotypes well. **Similar titles:** *Drawn to the Grave*, Mary Ann Mitchell; *Mortality*, Steven Ford; *The Hunger*, Whitley Strieber.

Aging • Human Sacrifice • Immortality

Harrison, M. John.

The Course of the Heart. *San Francisco: Night Shade Books, 2004. 184p. ISBN 1892389975.*

On a hot May night, three Cambridge students carry out a ritual that changes their lives. Now, years later, none of the participants can remember what happened, but each is immured in private torment. Meanwhile a creepy acquaintance from their schooldays who fancies himself a sorcerer visits each, speaking in riddles about another realm. **Similar titles:** *The Talisman Series*, Stephen King and Peter Straub; *Obsession*, Ramsey Campbell; *The Boys Are Back in Town*, Christopher Golden.

England • Magic • Witchcraft

Hearn, Julie.

The Minister's Daughter. *New York: Simon Pulse, 2005. 263p. ISBN 0689876904.*

The life of a small English village is disrupted when the new minister comes to town. A dour old Puritan with no tolerance for any sort of frolicking, he targets the outspoken Nell as an example of impiety. Later, when his eldest daughter tries to conceal an out of wedlock pregnancy, it is all too easy for her to level an accusation of witchcraft against Nell—and her poor grandmother. **Similar titles:** *Witch Child*, Celia Rees; *The Limits of Enchantment*, Graham Joyce; <u>The Wendy Ward Series</u>, J. G. Passerella.

Charles II, King of England (character) • England • Magic • Midwifery • Religion—Christianity —Puritanism • War—English Civil War • Witchcraft

King, Stephen (writing as Richard Bachman).

Thinner. *New York: Signet, 1985, ©1984. 318p. ISBN 0451161343.*

Billy Halleck, an attorney who is fifty pounds overweight and pushing a heart attack, sideswipes an old gypsy woman as she crosses the street. Rather than express remorse, he uses his professional wiles to avoid compensating the woman's family for her death. Now cursed with the word "thinner," Billy begins to lose weight uncontrollably. **Similar titles:** *Bag of Bones*, Stephen King; *Grave Intent*, Deborah LeBlanc; *Unspeakable*, Graham Masterton.

Lawyer as Character • Maine • Magic • Revenge • Witchcraft

Koontz, Dean.

Darkfall. *New York: Berkley, 2007, ©1984. 371p. ISBN 0425214591.*

Two detectives, Jack Dawson and Rebecca Chandler, are called in to investigate brutal gangland slayings. Dawson soon realizes that a practitioner of black magic is summoning creatures from the depths of hell to exact revenge, and Dawson's children will be brutally murdered if he does not back off the case. But read on, gentle reader—the final seventy pages of this novel are a masterpiece of suspense. **Similar**

titles: *The Mountains of Madness* and *The Restless Dead*, Hugh B. Cave; Carrion *Comfort*, Dan Simmons; *The Devil in Gray*, Graham Masterton; *White Zombie* (film).

Demons • New York—New York City • Organized Crime • Parenting • Police Officer as Character • Religion—Voodoo

Leiber, Fritz.

The Conjure Wife. *New York: Tor, 1991, ©1978. 184p. ISBN 0812512960.*
When sociology professor Norman Saylor rummages through his wife Tansy's closet one afternoon, he discovers that she has been using white magic to further his career. Determined to set her straight, he confronts her and then burns many of her protective charms. Suddenly, all hell breaks loose in Saylor's life, and his only hope is to try to save himself and his wife through the witchcraft he once eschewed. **Similar titles:** *The Collected Strange Stories*, Robert Aickman; *My Soul to Keep*, Tananarive Due.

Academia • Magic • New England • Witchcraft

Massey, Brandon.

Within the Shadows. *New York: Kensington, 2005. 357p. ISBN 0758210698.*
(See chapter 4, "Ghosts and Haunted Houses: Dealing with Presences and Absences.")

Masterton, Graham.

Unspeakable. *Sutton, Surrey, UK: Sutton House, 2007, ©2005 274p. ISBN 9780727864895.*
Holly, a deaf social worker with a talent for lip reading, "overhears" enough of a conversation to put away a Native American who nearly beat his wife and child to death. But the abusive father will not go quietly—instead, he puts a Native American curse on her. Soon after, Holly's life begins to fall apart. **Similar titles:** *Thinner*, Stephen King; *Grave Intent*, Deborah LeBlanc; *Crota*, Owl Goingback.

Child Abuse • Oregon—Portland • Religion—Native American • Revenge • Social Worker as Character • Witchcraft

Mitchell, Mary Ann.

Drawn to the Grave. *New York: Leisure, 1997. 313p. ISBN 0843942908.*
Carl becomes terminally ill, but unable to face his own mortality, he searches the world for a cure. In the Amazon rain forest, he finds a cure that necessitates his becoming intimately acquainted with his victim before stealing her life. However, Carl overlooks one thing—the desire of his latest victim to survive and wreak vengeance. **Similar titles:** *The Picture of Dorian Gray*, Oscar Wilde; *My Soul to Keep*, Tananarive Due; *Borrowed Flesh*, Sephera Giron.

Aging • Eroticism • Immortality • Magic • Revenge

The Witch. *Aurora, IL: Medallion, 2007. 463p. ISBN 1932815813.*

When Cathy discovers her husband's affair with their son's teenaged baby sitter, she hangs herself in the basement. But that's not the last of Cathy. Her son's grief calls her back to the world of the living, and she haunts the family home, unseen by all but her child. It turns out Cathy has some unfinished business with the living. **Similar titles:** <u>The Wendy Ward Series</u>, J. G. Passarella; <u>The Sorority Trilogy</u>, Tamara Thorne; <u>The Wicked Willow Trilogy</u>, various authors.

Childhood • Demons • Revenge • Revenging Revenant • Suicide • Witchcraft

Passarella, J[ohn]. G.

The Wendy Ward Series.

Windale, Massachusetts, is heir to a colorful colonial past, including women accused of witchcraft. Today, the town is home to many a new-age witches knowledgeable in occult lore and the use of herbs. **Similar titles:** *Bag of Bones,* Stephen King; *Shadowlands,* Peter Straub; <u>The Eden Moore Trilogy</u>, Cherie Priest; *The Blair Witch Project* (film); *Blair Witch 2: Book of Shadows* (film).

Massachusetts • Ward, Wendy (character) • Witchcraft • Wither, Elizabeth (character)

 Wither. *New York: Pocket, 1999. 304p. ISBN 0671024809.*

Every 100 years, strange things seem to happen to the residents of Windale. One of the new witches is about to learn that the history of her town is more than just a quaint legend.

Adolescence • Revenging Revenant • Secret Sin

Wither's Rain. *New York: Pocket Star Books, 2003. 428p. ISBN 0671024825.*

Wendy Ward watched the witch Elizabeth Wither be crushed beneath tons of falling stone from an old mill. So why is she still haunted by the demonic witch? Wendy, a college student and white witch, wants nothing more than to get over her battle with Wither. But it seems that Wither has taken over the body of a depressed young girl, and is plotting revenge.

Academia • Magic • Religion—Wicca • Revenge

Wither's Legacy. *New York: Pocket, 2004. 480p. ISBN 0743484797.*

In the final book of this trilogy, Elizabeth Wither makes true her vow to haunt Wendy, Kayla, Abby, and Hannah. She sends her minion, a seven-foot-tall demon that possesses an enchantment spell that makes it looks human—except for the yellow eyes and razor-sharp teeth. This demon desires human flesh and Wendy Ward, for only the young Wiccan's death can free the demon from its enslavement.

Demons • Religion—Wicca

Rees, Celia.

The Witch Child Series.

When her adoptive mother is killed by witch-hunting Puritans, Mary is forced to flee England. Friends help her escape to what they believe is safety in colonial

New England, just outside of Salem. **Similar titles:** *The Minister's Daughter*, Julie Hearn; The Eden Moore Trilogy, Cherie Priest; The Wendy Ward Series, J. G. Passarella.

Adolescence • Native American Characters • Nuttall, Mary (character) • Religion—Christianity— Puritanism • Witchcraft

Witch Child. *Cambridge, MA: Candlewick Press, 2001, ©2000. 261p. ISBN 0763614211.*

> Unfortunately for Mary, the child of a witch, she finds herself among Puritans who are suspicious of any woman with gifts of healing and second sight.
>
> *Colonial Era • Massachusetts • Precognition*

Sorceress. *Cambridge, MA: Candlewick Press, 2003. 342p. ISBN 0763618470.*

> Agnes, a Native American descendant of Mary's, has inherited her gift for second sight. Agnes is able to use her ability to help an anthropologist piece together Mary's life after her diary is found concealed in a colonial quilt. Agnes's visions are the frame through which the events in Mary's life are revealed.
>
> *Frame Tale • Psychics • Religion—Native American • War—King Phillip's War*

Reese, James.

The Book of Shadows Trilogy.

This series about the supernatural and self-discovery stars Herculine, a young orphan who witnesses her mother's death. She finds herself living in a convent where, accused of witchcraft, she awaits her death. Visited and rescued by two ghosts and a witch, she learns her true identity. The narrative takes the form of a witch's journal of spells and occult knowledge. **Similar titles:** The New Tales of the Vampire Series, Anne Rice; The Saint-Germain Chronicles, Chelsea Quinn Yarbro; The Gemma Doyle Trilgogy, Libba Bray.

d'Azur, Sebastiana (character) • Gay/Lesbian/Bisexual Characters • Gothicism • Herculine (character) • Religion—Wicca • Witchcraft

The Book of Shadows. *New York: HarperTorch, 2002. 640p. ISBN 0066210151.*

> Herculine serves as the first-person narrator of this tale. She is branded as "unnatural" after she pulls a prank in her convent school. And in nineteenth-century France, being called unnatural is no trifling accusation. Sebastiana d'Azur, a "Soror Mystica," teaches her how to use her unique gifts.
>
> *Clergy as Character • France—Brittany • Religion—Christianity—Catholicism*

The Book of Spirits. *William Morrow, 2006, ©2005. 548p. ISBN 0060561076.*

> Herculine travels to America disguised as a man. During the sea voyage she falls in love with Celia, the slave of a cruel master. The two

flee to Florida to live among the Indians before the start of the Seminole war.

African American Characters • *Florida* • *New York—New York City* • *Poe, Edgar Allan (character)* • *Slavery*

The Witchery. *New York: William Morrow, 2006. 466p. ISBN 0060561084.*

Sebastiana summons Herculine to Cuba to work with the alchemist Queverdo Brù. But Brù is a demonic and abusive man who only wishes to ill-treat Herculine as he perfects his practice of the alchemical arts.

Alchemy • *Cuba—Havana* • *Florida—Key West* • *Hispanic Characters*

Rhodes, Jewel Parker.

Voodoo Season: A Marie Laveau Mystery. *New York: Atria, 2005. 277p. ISBN 0743483278.*

Marie Levant, a first-year resident at New Orleans' Charity Hospital and a descendant of Marie Laveau, discovers that she has the gift of second sight, which she now uses to pursue the murderer of the gentle man who shared her bed for an evening. But this gift is really not a complete surprise to Marie, as she has been tormented by visions all of her life. **Similar titles:** *Merrick*, Anne Rice; *Family Inheritance*, Deborah LeBlanc; *Leslie*, Omar Tyree.

Louisiana—New Orleans • *Physician as Character* • *Precognition* • *Psychics*

Rice, Anne.

The Mayfair Witch Series.

After the death of her natural mother, Rowan Mayfair returns to New Orleans to discover her family and their legacy—the legacy of the Mayfair witches and their relationship with the spirit Lasher. **Similar titles:** The Vampire Chronicles and *Merrick*, Anne Rice; The Eden Moore Trilogy, Cherie Priest; The Wendy Ward Series, J. G. Passarella.

Curry, Michael (character) • *Epic Structure* • *Lasher (character)* • *Lightener, Aaron (character)* • *Louisiana—New Orleans* • *Mayfair, Rowan (character)* • *Religion—Christianity—Catholicism* • *Talamasca, The* • *Witchcraft*

The Witching Hour. *New York: Ballantine Books, 1993, ©1991. 1038p. ISBN 0345384466.*

For twelve generations Lasher has allowed the Mayfair family to prosper, and now Rowan, the thirteenth generation of Mayfair witches, must pay the price for that prosperity. This novel is written in Rice's usual romantic, detailed style.

Lasher. *New York: Ballantine, 1993. 628p. ISBN 0345397819.*

The Mayfair family is haunted by the spirit Lasher, who has been promised use of the womb of the first strong witch in the family in return for a favor rendered centuries earlier. Can the women of the family survive Lasher's attempts to create a child strong enough for his spirit to inhabit? **Similar titles:**

The Vampire Chronicles and *Merrick*, Anne Rice; The Wendy Ward Series, J. G. Passarella.

Incest • Mayfair, Julian (character) • Mayfair, Mona (character) • Reincarnation • Religion —Christianity—Protestantism • Religion—Paganism • Revenging Revenant • Scotland • Taltos, The • Weird Science

Taltos: Lives of the Mayfair Witches. *New York: Ballantine Books, 1996, ©1994. 556p. ISBN 0345404319.*

Ashlar, a member of a race of mythic, immortal giants, teams up with the Mayfair witches to battle an evil force. *Taltos* is a critical success as well as very popular with Rice fans, who love her ornate description and epic adventure.

Incest • Mayfair, Mona (character) • Taltos, The

Merrick. *New York: Alfred A. Knopf, 2000. 307p. ISBN 0679454489.*

David Talbot, a former member of the Talamasca, asks Merrick Mayfair, of the African American branch of the Mayfair clan, to use her powers to raise the ghost of Claudia for the benefit of his father in darkness, Louis. But before Merrick agrees to do so, she must tell the story of her own magical powers. This novel connects the stories of The Vampire Chronicles and The Mayfair Witch Series. **Similar titles:** The Mayfair Witch Series and The Vampire Chronicles, Anne Rice; *Voodoo Season: A Marie Laveau Mystery*, Jewel Parker Rhodes.

Afterlife, The • African American Characters • Claudia (character) • Dreams • Gay/Lesbian/Bisexual Characters • Guatemala • Immortality • Lestat de Lioncourt (character) • Lightner, Aaron (character) • Louis (character) • Louisiana—New Orleans • Mayfair, Merrick (character) • Religion—Mayan • Religion—Voodoo • Talamasca, The • Talbot, David (character) • Vampire's Point of View • Witchcraft

Saul, John.

Black Creek Crossing. *New York, Ballantine, 2004. 358p. ISBN 0345433327.*

Myra and Marty Sullivan are thrilled to be able to purchase a seventeenth-century house at Black Creek Crossing, especially since it's offered at a price they can afford. But soon a black cat materializes out of nowhere, smoke from a nonexistent fire fills the house, and a girl's face appears in a mirror. The Sullivan's teenaged daughter finds a book and begins to use it at school, unleashing the house's ghosts. **Similar titles:** *Morbid Curiosity*, Deborah LeBlanc; *Lost Boy, Lost Girl*, Peter Straub; *In the Dark of Night*, John Saul.

Adolescence • Haunted Houses • Massachusetts • Revenging Revenant • Salem Witch Trials • Witchcraft

In the Dark of the Night. *New York: Ballantine, 2006. 324p. ISBN 034548701X.*

In the summer before he begins twelfth grade, Eric Brewster vacations on picturesque Phantom Lake, where his family has rented a home—which is also unfortunately the former residence of Dr. Hector Darby, who had conducted secret research into the minds of serial killers before he disappeared under suspicious circumstances. **Similar titles:** *Black Creek Crossing*, John Saul; *The Abandoned*, Douglas Clegg; *The Home*, Scott Nicholson; *Deep in the Darkness*, Michael Laimo.

Adolescent Characters • Haunted House • Holidays—Independence Day • Serial Killers • Wisconsin

Thorne, Tamara.

The Sorority Trilogy.

At Greenbriar College, the elite Gamma Eta Pi sorority is a secret society, better known as the Fata Morgana. Its members belong to a centuries-old coven, and every girl who pledges becomes a member for life, whether she wants to be or not. **Similar titles:** The Wicked Willow Trilogy, various authors; The Charmed Series, various authors; *Newbies*, James A. Moore.

Academia • Arthurian Legend • Magic • Psychosexual Horror • Secret Sin • Witchcraft

Eve. *New York: Pinnacle, 2003. 254p. ISBN 078601539X.*

Eve has no idea why she's drawn to the house or the Gamma Eta Pi sorority president, Malory Thomas, nor does she understand the secret world of dark magic. But she'll soon find out.

Merilynn. *New York: Pinnacle, 2003. 222p. ISBN 0786015403.*

Merilynn has a love of herbs and potions. As a young girl, she attended the same summer camp as Eve; and now she attends Greenbrier College. As the story progresses, Merilynn's secrets, along with the evil plans of the Fata Morgana, are revealed, and more is learned about the Greenjacks and the Green Knight, a local spirit.

Samantha. *New York: Pinnacle, 2003. 286p. ISBN 0786015411.*

Mallory Thomas tries to further increase her powers by sacrificing fellow students to the Forest Knight. Suddenly the Fata Morgana sorority begins to enjoy more than its usual prosperity. Fans will appreciate the tying up of loose ends, finding out what happens to the ditzy cheerleaders, benevolent ghosts, and lecherous professor.

Tyree, Omar.

Leslie: A Novel. *New York: Simon & Schuster, 2003, ©2002. 385p. ISBN 0743228707.*

Leslie Beaudet, a Dillard University student, juggles her studies with her job as a chef and various family problems, including a brother who is involved with a local drug lord. Always one to go after what she wants, Leslie attempts to seduce one of her roommates' boyfriend. When he refuses her, she begins to practice voodoo to deal with him and with her other enemies. **Similar titles:** *Family Inheritance*, Deborah LeBlanc; *Voodoo Season: A Marie Laveau Mystery*, Jewel Parker Rhodes; The Mayfair Witch Series, Anne Rice; *The Skeleton Key* (film).

Academia • African American Characters • Families • Louisiana—New Orleans • Religion—Voodoo • Revenge

The Wicked Willow Trilogy (various authors).

Willow returns to Sunnydale, but she is reluctant to use her magical powers lest she become evil. However, if she doesn't use her powers, her friends' lives could be in jeopardy. **Similar titles:** The Buffy the Vampire Slayer Series, various authors; The Angel Investigations Series, various authors; The Charmed Series, various authors.

Buffy the Vampire Slayer (television series) • *California—Sunnydale* • *Demons* • *Rosenberg, Willow (character)* • *Vampire Hunters* • *Witchcraft*

Burns, Laura J., and Melinda Metz.

Apocalypse Memories. *New York: Simon & Schuster, 2004. 256p. ISBN 068986700X.*

Willow's friends' lives are at stake: the presence of a supernatural being who has just come to town has set off a series of bizarre events—such as a river of blood and flash floods.

Navarro, Yvonne, and Joss Whedon.

Shattered Twilight. *New York: Simon Spotlight, 2004. 258p. ISBN 0689869533.*

Willow has finally gone too far. After she saved Buffy from the evil phantom and failed to protect her coven members, they have turned against her, so she must now make amends. Willow turns to the elements for protection and uses a spirit to animate a golem, with the ultimate goal being to resurrect Tara's ghost.

Death—Grieving

Navarro, Yvonne, and Joss Whedon.

Broken Sunrise. *New York: Simon Spotlight, 2004. 261p. ISBN 0689869541.*

The trilogy ends in this volume. Buffy and company stop Tara's ghost with the magic box, and Willow's coven advises that she develop a new plan to regain Tara's spirit, which is necessary for a resurrection spell. Giles manages to keep Tara imprisoned, so Willow decides to finally deal with Spike and Oz, her captives. They are slowly being fed alive to one of her demons.

Death—Grieving

Film

Angel Heart. *Alan Parker, dir. 1987. 113 minutes.*

Private investigator Harry Angel (Mickey Rourke) is hired by Louis Cyphere (Robert De Niro) to find a missing singer, Johnny Favorite. His investigation leads him from Times Square to the French Quarter of New Orleans and the bayous of South Louisiana, where Christianity isn't the only religion practiced by the locals. Harry becomes the police's number-one suspect when everyone he contacts ends up killed in grisly ways. **Similar titles:** *Rosemary's Baby*, Ira Levin; *Second Soul*, Thomas Sullivan.

African American Characters • Doppelgangers • Dreams • Eroticism • Human Sacrifice • Incest • Louisiana—New Orleans • Psychosexual Horror • Religion—Voodoo • Satan (character) • Witchcraft

The Blair Witch Project. *Daniel Myrick and Eduardo Sanchez, dirs. 1999. 80 minutes.*

In this pseudo-documentary three students disappear while making a film about the Blair Witch legend in Burkittsville, Maryland. All that is known of their disappearance comes from their video footage, found in the woods. People particularly prone to motion sickness may be unsettled by the directors' handheld cameras, which give the film a jerky feel. **Similar titles:** <u>The Wendy Ward Series</u>, J. G. Passarella; <u>The Book of Shadows Trilogy</u>, James Reese.

Blair Witch Haunting • Documentary Technique • Haunted Houses • Maryland—Burkittsville • Popular Culture • Revenging Revenant • Wilderness • Witchcraft

Blair Witch 2: Book of Shadows. *Joe Berlinger, dir. 2000. 91 minutes.*

The small town of Burkittsville, Maryland, has been overrun with tourists. Shops now hawk Blair Witch sticks and "genuine" soil from the haunted woods, and competing groups of residents offer Blair Witch camping tours retracing the steps of the ill-fated film crew. Then one of these tour groups discovers that the Blair Witch is no mere legend but a vengeful spirit that will not be mocked. **Similar titles:** <u>The Wendy Ward Series</u>, J. G. Passarella; <u>The Book of Shadows Trilogy</u>, James Reese.

Blair Witch Haunting • Dreams • Maryland—Burkittsville • Popular Culture • Revenging Revenant • Wilderness • Witchcraft

Child's Play. *Tom Holland, dir. 1988. 87 minutes.*

With his dying breath, serial killer Charles Lee Ray, fatally wounded in a police shootout inside of a toy store, transfers his soul into a Chucky doll—which becomes the treasured plaything of little Andy Barclay. When terrible things begin to happen to people around Andy, his mother becomes worried that her young son is seriously mentally instable. Brad Dourif stars as the voice of Chucky. **Similar titles:** *It*, Stephen King; *The Parasite*, Ramsey Campbell.

Chucky (character) • Dolls • Illinois—Chicago • Parenting • Religion—Voodoo • Serial Killers

The Exorcist. *William Friedkin, dir. 1973. 122 minutes.*

Preteen Regan MacNeill becomes possessed by the devil, and her desperate lapsed Catholic mother turns to the Church for help. Before Satan can be expelled, Regan's head will spin around, and she will be seized with a fit of projectile vomiting. This benchmark horror film from the 1970s provoked great controversy when it was released in theaters, as some religious groups claimed that the film caused audience members to become demonically possessed. **Similar titles:** *The Exorcist*, William Peter Blatty; *Rosemary's Baby*, Ira Levin.

Clergy as Character • Demons • Exorcisms • Parenting • Religion—Christianity—Catholicism

Fallen. *Gregory Hoblit, dir. 1999. 123 minutes.*

(See chapter 8, "Mythological Monsters and 'The Old Ones': Invoking the Dark Gods.")

The Haunting. *Richard Wise, dir. 1963 (black and white) 112 minutes.*

(See chapter 4, "Ghosts and Haunted Houses: Dealing with Presences and Absences.")

J. D.'s Revenge. *Arthur Marks, dir. 1976. 95 minutes.*

The spirit of J. D., a murdered small-time thug, requires someone to tell his tale to bring his killers to justice, so he takes possession of a mild-mannered law student. This is one of the few horror films with African Americans as main characters. Joan Pringle and Lou Gossett star. **Similar titles:** *The Between* and *Joplin's Ghost*, Tananarive Due.

African American Characters • Louisiana—New Orleans • Revenging Revenant • Secret Sin

The Omen. *Richard Donner, dir. 1976. 111 minutes.*

When the wife of the ambassador to the United States gives birth to a stillborn child, the ambassador substitutes another baby without her knowledge. Years pass, and grisly deaths befall those in close proximity to the child. Further investigation reveals that the foundling is actually the son of Satan and can be stopped only by the seven daggers of Meggado. Lee Remick and Gregory Peck star. **Similar titles:** *The Exorcist*, William Peter Blatty; *Rosemary's Baby*, Ira Levin.

Antichrist (character) • Apocalypse • Religion—Christianity • Secret Sin

Rosemary's Baby. *Roman Polanski, dir. 1968. 134 minutes.*

This very faithful adaptation of Ira Levin's novel of the same name tells the story of a man who makes a pact with the devil. In exchange for his worldly success as an actor, his wife will bear Satan's child. Mia Farrow, John Cassavetes, and Ruth Gordon star. **Similar titles:** *Rosemary's Baby* and *Son of Rosemary*, Ira Levin.

Antichrist (character) • New York—New York City • Pregnancy • Religion—Christianity —Catholicism • Religion—Satanism • Septuagenarians • Witchcraft

The Shining. *Stanley Kubrick, dir. 1980. 142 minutes.*

Jack Nicholson stars as recovering alcoholic and abusive father and husband Jack Torrence. After losing his teaching position for assaulting one of his pupils, Jack is given a second chance as a winter caretaker of the Overlook Hotel, isolated in the Rocky Mountains. Being snowbound in the mountains with the hotel's ghosts pushes Jack over the edge. Shelly Duvall and Scatman Crothers also star. **Similar titles:** *Nazareth Hill*, Ramsey Campbell; *Dr. Jekyll and Mr. Hyde*, Robert Louis Stevenson; *The Shining*, Stephen King.

Addictions—Alcoholism • Childhood • Colorado • Haunted Houses

The Skeleton Key. *Ian Softley, dir. 2005. 104 minutes.*

Caroline Ellis, a young nursing assistant, comes to live in the remote Devereaux family plantation in the swamps of Terrebonne Parish, Louisiana, to care for Violet's husband Ben. Soon she comes to believe that Violet wishes to hasten the death of Ben, who can barely walk or speak due to a stroke. When she finds voodoo artifacts in the attic, Caroline believes that Violet is resorting to black magic to steal what is left of Ben's life and prolong her own. **Similar titles:** *Leslie*, Omar Tyree; *Family Inheritance*, Deborah LeBlanc.

Louisiana—New Orleans • Nurse as Character • Racism • Religion—Voodoo • Witchcraft

Sleepy Hollow. *Tim Burton, dir. 1999. 105 minutes.*

In this alternative retelling of Washington Irving's story "The Legend of Sleepy Hollow," Johnny Depp stars as criminal investigator Ichabod Crain, who has come to Sleepy Hollow to investigate some mysterious murders. Crain, for all his scientific methods of investigating a crime scene, is not prepared for the Headless Horseman (Christopher Walken) and the supernatural means employed to bring him to life and do the bidding of Katrina Van Tassel's (Christina Ricci) evil stepmother (Miranda Richardson). **Similar titles:** *Selected Tales*, Edgar Allan Poe; *The Savage Tales of Solomon Kane*, Robert E Howard.

Alternative Literature • Colonial Era • Crain, Ichabod (character) • Gothicism • New York • Secret Sin • Sleepy Hollow Legend, The • Witchcraft

Stigmata. *Rupert Wainwright, dir. 1999. 103 minutes.*

A Pittsburgh hairdresser who isn't particularly religious receives from her mother the rosary of a deceased South American priest who was said to have performed miracles. Now possessed by the priest, her body manifests stigmata as it struggles to tell the story of a female apostle whose words the Catholic Church silenced. Patricia Arquette and Gabriel Byrne star. **Similar titles:** *The Exorcist*, William Peter Blatty; *Prodigal Blues* and *Keepers*, Gary A. Braunbeck.

Alternative History • Clergy as Character • Dreams • Feminism • Pennsylvania—Pittsburgh • Religion—Christianity—Catholicism • Stigmata

Supernatural. *Victor Halperin, dir. 1933 (black and white). 60 minutes.*

A woman executed for murdering her lovers vows she'll return from the dead. She does just that when she possesses the body of Carole Lombard, a virginal heiress, and goes on to cause the young woman to misbehave. **Similar titles:** *The Influence* and *Parasite*, Ramsey Campbell.

Parapsychology • Reincarnation • Serial Killers

What Lies Beneath. *Robert Zemeckis, dir. 2000. 129 minutes.*

(See chapter 4, "Ghosts and Haunted Houses: Dealing with Presences and Absences.")

June's Picks

Books: Libba Bray, <u>The Gemma Doyle Trilogy</u> (Delacorte); Julie Hearn, *The Minister's Daughter* (Simon Pulse); Mark Laidlaw, *The 37th Mandala* (Leisure); Ira Levin, *Rosemary's Baby* (Penguin); Mary Ann Mitchell, *Drawn to the Grave* (Leisure)

Films: *The Blair Witch Project, J. D.'s Revenge, Rosemary's Baby, The Shining, Stigmata*

Tony's Picks

Books: Stephen King, *The Shining* (Pocket Books); Dean Koontz, *Hideaway* (Putnam); Graham Masterton, *The Manitou* (Severn House); Peter Straub, *Shadowland* (Voyager)

Films: *Angel Heart, Rosemary's Baby, The Skeleton Key*

Chapter 8

Mythological Monsters and "The Old Ones": Invoking the Dark Gods

Nearly every religion and mythology has its monsters. From Kali the Destroyer in India and the destructive Cyclops of ancient Greek legend to Lucifer in Christianity, virtually every culture incorporates some personification of chaos and anarchy into its belief system. This being, although usually humanoid, is nonetheless monstrous and destructive, threatening entire populations. In fact, these mythological destroyers are arguably the precursors of the monster in contemporary horror literature, because "monsters" from these old stories are divine warnings about the consequences of human actions (the word "monster" derives from the Latin *monstere*, to show). Primitive humans both embraced and feared these personifications of destruction, as they acknowledged their own animal passions and their connection to and dependence on the natural world. Later religions, however, emphasized the human ability to transcend mortal desire and suffering and to cope with and perhaps even control nature itself; so these later belief systems "demonized" the monster, making it totally Other, a repository of all that the religion's adherents loathed and feared about themselves. A quick study of horror titles indicates that the genre is generated primarily by Anglo-Saxon (English and Germanic) cultures. These two cultures are heavily influenced by strict forms of Protestantism that portray Satan, the manifestation of all that is bestial in humans, as the ultimate monster—lurking everywhere, always ready to seduce weak-willed souls from the path of righteousness.

Because of the raw power that they possess, mythological monsters make great fodder for horror fiction. They are ready-made symbols of all we fear. The Judeo-Christian Bible is an exhaustive source of evil portents, impish creatures, ghoulish harbingers of death, and hellish overlords. Even human biblical characters such as the murderous Cain and the treacherous Judas have made appearances in horror, for some vampire mythologies see Cain as the father of all vampires, because it was he who first slew his brother; others point to Judas as the father of all vampires because his betrayal of Christ caused him to walk the earth, forever damned.

And then there are more recent, fictional mythologies, populated with those monsters that began as the creations of horror writers and became cultural icons afterward. Authors like H. P. Lovecraft found previous mythologies to be too constraining, so they created their own mythological monsters. One of the most famous of all of these (bowing to perhaps only Godzilla, an "imported" mythological creation), Cthulhu, has become so ingrained in the American horror subconscious that later writers and Hollywood directors have based entire texts or films on the reawakening of this ancient fictional god or on the accidental reading of *The Necronomicon*, which some fans argue is only half fiction. Lovecraft's Cthulhu mythos has resurfaced at various times through the fiction of his "disciples," such as his contemporary August Derleth, and in later authors like Ramsey Campbell and Willing Browning Spencer. Whether a mythological monster is based on an existing religion and set of folk beliefs or is created by a writer, readers are reminded that "the old ones," or the old deities, are ever-present and can be summoned at any time, even accidentally. Their eagerness to invade the human world when awakened by an innocent is what makes them so frightening; they remind us of the consequences of our actions, regardless of our intentions.

Most people will have at least a passing familiarity with mythological creatures and monsters from mythological texts, and this is perhaps the greatest appeal of this subgenre. Like the ghost story, the tale featuring a monster borrowed directly from, or even loosely based on a mythological monster, requires very little background or set-up. The same goes for monsters based on religious texts, because mythological tales and religious stories are related (one culture's religion is often seen as more of a mythology by another culture, and this is especially true of older cultures' religions). In this respect, mythological horror has a great potential to appeal to people who are curious about other cultures' belief systems, as they offer a glimpse and invite more inquiry. For this reason, horror texts based on mythologies tend to be more intertextual, thought-provoking, and complex in their approach, for the monsters in these stories often are born of modernity's victimization of an older culture. Finally, these tales are potentially more believable, because the invading horror is typically based on long-standing belief.

Note: Tales about mythological and dark gods can also be found in the collections and anthologies described in chapter 18. Refer to the subject/keyword index for specific titles under the keywords *Cthulhian Monsters*, *Popular Culture*, *Religion*, and *Satan (character)*.

Folkloric and Literary Gods and Monsters

Aickman, Robert.

The Collected Strange Stories. 2nd ed. *London: Tartarus Press, 2001. 2 vols. 868p. ISBN 1872621473 (v. 1); 1872621481 (v. 2).*
(See chapter 18, "Collections and Anthologies.")

Alten, Steve.

The Loch. *Mayfield Heights, OH: Tsunami Books, 2005. 487p. ISBN 0976165902.*
(See chapter 13, "Ecological Horror: Mother Nature Has Her Revenge.")

Bachman, Richard (pseudonym used by Stephen King).

Desperation. *New York: Viking, 1996. 690p. ISBN 0670868361.*
(See King, Stephen, *Desperation*, in this section.)

Bishop, K. J.

The Etched City. *New York: Bantam-Spectra, 2004, ©2003. 382p. ISBN 0553382918.*
Two citizens of Copper County, a place in the heart of the Dustbowl, are forced to flee and make a new life in the city of Ashamoil, a place of dark miracles where artists occasionally turn into sphinxes, flowers routinely spring from the newly dead, and children are born part crocodile. A mercenary slave trader and an altruistic physician must survive this strange and dangerous land. **Similar titles:** *Veniss Underground*, Jeff VanderMeer; *The Doorkeepers*, Graham Masterton; *Bloodstained Oz*, Christopher Golden and James A. Moore.

Magic • Parallel Universes • Physician as Character • Shape-shifters • Slavery

Bradbury, Ray.

From the Dust Returned. *New York: Avon, 2002. 267p. ISBN 0380789612.*
A Victorian mansion in a small Illinois town is the site of a reunion for a family of immortals reminiscent of the Addams family or the Munsters. Grand Mere is a 4,000-year-old mummy, a pharaoh's daughter, who lives in the attic. Uncle Einars sports enormous wings and allows neighborhood children to use him as a kite. Other kin include vampires and ghosts, as well as Timothy, a mortal foundling who wishes to be special in the ways of his adoptive family. **Similar titles:** *A Graveyard for Lunatics*, Ray Bradbury; *The Pilo Family Circus*, Will Elliot; The Pine Cover Series, Christopher Moore.

Families • Illinois • Immortality • Mummies • Vampires

Braunbeck, Gary A.

Mr. Hands. *New York: Leisure, 2007. 269p. ISBN 0843956100.*
A suicide, a monument to slain youngsters, and an inebriated and inconsolable mother who has just lost her daughter to a molester lead to the creation of Mr. Hands—a truly frightening vehicle for revenge. If you read the short story of the same name and want more, here's your chance. Braunbeck adds a frame in which a mysterious, harried young man walks into a local bar and regales bartender Grant McCullers and Sheriff Ted Jackson with the story of child molester Ronald James Williamson. **Similar titles:** *The Dead Letters*, Tom Piccirilli; *The Wind Caller*, P. D. Cacek; *Prodigal Blues*, Gary A. Braunbeck.

Child Molesters • Frame Tale • Ohio—Cedar Hill • Parenting • Psychics • Revenge

Prodigal Blues. *Baltimore, MD: Cemetery Dance Publications, 2006. 304p. ISBN 1587671093.*
(See chapter 15, "Splatterpunk: The Gross Out.")

1

2

3

4

5

6

7

8

9

10

Clegg, Douglas.

Neverland. *Modesto, CA: Bloodletting Press, 2003, ©1991. 408p. ISBN 0972085912.*
(See chapter 10, "Small Town Horror: Villages of the Damned.")

De Lint, Charles.

Mulengro: A Romany Tale. *New York: Orb, 2003, ©1985. 400p. ISBN 0312873999.*
This reissue of a classic focuses on modern Ottawa gypsies who continue to live a secretive existence outside the mainstream, until a killer stalks its members. The murders become increasingly gory. The Ottawa municipal police want to bring the killer to justice, and they accuse one of the locals, but the gypsies know that the thing that is hunting them down is none other than the mysterious shape-shifter, Mulengro. **Similar titles:** *A Carnivore's Inquirí*, Sabina Murray; *Blood Road*, Edo Van Belkom; *From a Whisper to a Scream*, Charles De Lint.

Canada—Ottawa • Police Officer as Character • Serial Killers • Shape-shifters

Gallagher, Stephen.

The Myth Hunters. *New York: Bantam, 2006. 350p. ISBN 0553383264.*
Oliver Bascombe entertains doubts on the eve of his wedding, which he is spends in his family's Victorian mansion. Outside a blizzard rages, and Jack Frost, aka "the Winter Man," appears to Oliver, beseeching him to come with him through the Borderlands to save him from the Myth Hunter. Surprisingly, escaping to an alternate universe is not the answer to Oliver's doubts about marriage that he thought it would be: the Sandman has escaped the Borderland and has killed his father. **Similar titles:** *American Gods*, Neil Gaiman; *The Ferryman* and *Wildwood Road*, Christopher Golden.

Dreams • Frost, Jack (character) • Maine • Marriage • Sandman (character) • Serial Killers • Shape-shifters

Valley of Lights. *Tolworth, Surrey, UK: Telos, 2005, ©1987. 298p. ISBN 0450406644.*
In a sleazy hotel room Phoenix police sergeant Alex Volchak discovers three co-matose men. All they have in common is the person who rented the room, a thin man who rapidly sprints away, dropping a huge bag of baby food behind him. The unresponsive inmates of the hotel room are taken to the hospital, and it is discovered that turning them over on to their stomachs proves fatal. Meanwhile, the city is being terrorized by a vicious killer who savages children. **Similar titles:** *The 37th Mandala*, Mark Laidlaw; *The Hollower*, Mary SanGiovanni; *World of Hurt*, Brian Hodge; *Fallen* (film).

Arizona—Phoenix • Police Officer as Character • Shape-shifters

Kiernan, Caitlin R.

Daughter of Hounds. *New York: Roc Trade, 2007. 448p. ISBN 0451461258.*
Two converging storylines ultimately unite the forces of one of Deacon Silvey's daughters, a yellow-eyed girl who might be part faerie, with a hard-boiled, violent female demon killer named Soldier, fighting otherworldly evil in the streets of a New England town. The complex, dialogue-driven plot springs abundant surprises and unexpected betrayals. **Similar titles:** <u>The Violet Series</u>, Stephen

Woodworth; *Alabaster*, Caitlin R. Kiernan; The Eden Moore Trilogy, Cherie Priest.

Fairies • New England • Parapsychology

King, Stephen (writing as Richard Bachman)

Desperation. *New York: Viking, 1996. 690p. ISBN 0670868361.*
What chance does an eleven-year-old like David Carver have against an evil force, an ancient shape-shifter that emerges from the ground itself? Turns out David has a pretty good one when his directions come directly from God. Ordinary Americans, including Carver and an alcoholic writer, are thrown together by chance to face Tak, an entity that has taken control of the body of a Nevada highway patrolman and is forcing him to brutally murder innocent people. **Similar titles:** *American Gods*, Neil Gaiman; *Shadow Coast*, Philip Haldeman; *Ghost Story*, Peter Straub.

Nevada • Police Officer as Character • Religion—Christianity • Shape-shifters

Knight, Brian.

Feral. *Waterville, ME: Five Star. 2003. 266p. ISBN 1594140650.*
For six years Sharon and Gordon Chambers have been searching for their missing daughter Charity; and they believe that a trail of dead children might lead to an answer. Then one day they spot the girl in Feral Park, a playground that is actually a supernatural dimension where abandoned and abused children hide. Charity is there because she has successfully eluded her kidnapper, the Bogey Man. But what of the others? **Similar titles:** *Mr. Hands*, Gary A. Braunbeck; The Talisman Series, Stephen King and Peter Straub; *Lost Boy, Lost Girl*, Peter Straub; *Nightmare on Elm Street* (film)

Child Molesters • Dreams • Parenting • Popular Culture • Washington State

Knight, J.

Risen. *New York: Kensington, 2004. 407p. ISBN 0786016124.*
(See chapter 5, "Golem, Mummies, and Zombies: Wake the Dead and They'll Be Cranky.")

Lebbon, Tim.

Berserk. *New York: Leisure, 2005. 337p. ISBN 0843954302.*
Ten years after the death of his son during a military maneuver gone awry, Steve discovers that the Royal Air Force did not send him his child's remains. Instead, he buried an empty coffin. Now searching for the remains of his son on Salisbury Plain, Steve uncovers many who died that day, as well as the corpse of a girl who is able to speak to him, revealing that the RAF has been hording ancient monsters on the site. **Similar titles:** The Repairman Jack Novels, F. Paul Wilson; *Dark Rivers of the Heart*, Dean Koontz; *The Wave*, Walter Mosely.

Death—Grieving • England—Salisbury Plain • Government Officials

The Everlasting. *New York: Leisure, 2007. 325p. ISBN 0843954299.*

Scott's grandfather shared a special bond with him—that is, until he committed suicide. Thirty years later Scott receives a letter from his long-dead grandfather, and suddenly those memories come back to haunt him. So does the grandfather's ghost, which kidnaps Scott's wife and insists that the young man help find a long-lost group of books called *The Chord of Souls*. With the help of an immortal, Scott takes on the ghost, as well as disloyal friends he discovers during his journey. **Similar titles:** *You Don't Scare Me*, John Farris; *In Shadows*, Chandler McGrew; *Dead Man's Song*, Jonathan Maberry.

Afterlife, The • Cursed Objects • Families • Immortality • Parallel Universes • Parapsychology

Little, Bentley.

The Return. *New York: New American Library, 2002. 354p. ISBN 0451187482.*

The Mongollon Monster, a mythical creature used to frighten generations of children gathered around campfires, turns out to be more than an Indian legend: A scout master is found brutally murdered in a manner that couldn't have been executed by any human. The monster's bloody return is the harbinger of several other strange events. Overnight, the populations of entire desert towns disappear without a trace. **Similar titles:** *The Revelation*, Bentley Little; *Crota*, Owl Goingback; *Shadow Coast*, Philip Haldeman.

Archeology • Arizona • Native American Characters • Popular Culture—Urban Legends • Religion—Animism

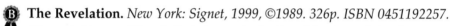 **The Revelation.** *New York: Signet, 1999, ©1989. 326p. ISBN 0451192257.*

The quiet town of Randall, Arizona, is shattered by unexplained occurrences: vandalism of public buildings, disappearing residents, and an unnaturally high miscarriage rate. Gordon just wants to protect his pregnant wife from an ancient evil that seems drawn to the couple. **Similar titles:** *The Return*, Bentley Little; *Crota*, Owl Goingback; *Rosemary's Baby*, Ira Levin.

Arizona • Clergy as Character • Demons • Pregnancy • Religion—Native American

Marano, Michael.

Dawn Song. *New York: Tor, 2000, ©1998. 400p. ISBN 0812545478.*

A succubus visits Boston and takes up residence in an apartment complex so she can learn about human emotions by taking human lovers and then killing them. However, she ends up as part of a strange army of humans and demons, readied for the battle between Belial and Leviathan. This excellent work is graphic and disturbing. **Similar titles:** *World of Hurt*, Brian Hodge; The Georgina Kincaid Series, Richelle Mead; *The Beloved*, J. F. Gonzales.

Alchemy • Demons • Gay/Lesbian/Bisexual Characters • Massachusetts—Boston • Psychosexual Horror • Shape-shifters

Masterton, Graham.

The Hidden World. *Sutton, UK: Severn House, 2003. 182p. ISBN 0727859625.*

Orphaned in an accident and bullied in school, Jessica takes comfort in reading about and drawing fairies. When a nasty fall down the stairs causes her to suffer head trauma, she begins to hear the voices of children in distress coming from the wallpaper. Jessica eventually enters this world and discovers a dimension where ordinary household objects take on a life of their own. But a great danger also lurks in this dimension. **Similar titles:** *The Door-keepers*, Graham Masterton; *Coraline*, Neil Gaiman; *The Book of Lost Things*, Michael Connolly.

Childhood • Parallel Universes • Psychics

Miâville, China.

King Rat. *New York: Tor, 1999, ©1998. 318p. ISBN 0312890737.*

Saul Garamond returns home from a journey in late evening and sneaks into his bedroom to avoid a confrontation with his estranged father. He awakens to the intrusion of police and the news that his father has been murdered. Blamed for the killing, he is forgotten in a jail cell, but is finally freed by a peculiar and impossibly strong stranger. The plot moves through subterranean and rooftop London, as Saul discovers his curious heritage and finds himself marked for death in an age-old secret war among frightful inhuman powers. **Similar titles:** *The Doorkeepers*, Graham Masterton; *Neverwhere*, Neil Gaiman; *Like Death*, Tim Waggoner; *Tideland* (film).

England—London • Pied Piper of Hamelin (character) • Rat King (character) • Subterranean Monsters

Moore, Christopher.

A Dirty Job. *New York: William Morrow, 2006. 387p. ISBN 0060590270.*

(See chapter 16, "Comic Horror: Laughing at Our Fears.")

The Pine Cove Series.

(See chapter 16, "Comic Horror: Laughing at Our Fears.")

Preston, Douglas, and Lincoln Child.

Brimstone. *New York: Warner, 2004. 752p. ISBN 044653143X.*

(See chapter 11, "Maniacs and Sociopaths, or the Nuclear Family Explodes: Monstrous Malcontents Bury the Hatchet.")

Rook, Sebastian.

The Vampire Plague Series.

London, 1850. *New York: Scholastic, 2005. 237p. ISBN 0439633923.*

(See chapter 6, "Vampires and Werewolves: Children of the Night.")

Sakers, Don.

Curse of the Zwilling. *Linthicum, MD: Speed-of-C Productions, 2003. 379p. ISBN 0971614725.*

> A small liberal arts college boasts a unique program: its Department of Comparative Religion is known for teaching ancient spells, and its students learn to practice magic. But when one of its faculty members is found dead, it gets a bad rep. Now it's up to a graduate student to discover the evil entity that has been brought onto campus in one of its artifacts. With a team of undergraduates, he squares off against an ancient terror known as the Zwilling. **Similar titles:** The Sorority Trilogy, Tamara Thorne; *Newbies*, James A. Moore; *Leslie: A Novel*, Omar Tyree.
>
> *Academia • Cursed Objects • Magic • Religion—Christianity • Witchcraft*

Sarrantonio, Al.

Halloweenland. *New York: Leisure, 2007. 293p. ISBN 0843959274.*

> Bill Grant, the hard-boiled, hard-drinking Orangefield detective is back—and so is his arch-nemesis, Samhain, the Lord of the Dead, who is attempting to usher in a new era of terror through the pregnancy of Marianne Carlin. Enter a very creepy, mysterious young girl, and the novel is a quick and deadly read. This novelization of Sarrantonio's novella entitled *The Baby!* will scare the bejesus out of readers. **Similar titles:** *Horrorween* and *Toybox*, Al Sarrantino; *The Taken*, Sarah Pinborough; *Rosemary's Baby*, Ira Levin.
>
> *Carnivals • Dreams • Pennsylvania—Orangefield • Police Officer as Character • Pregnancy • Samhain (character)*

Horrorween. *New York: Leisure, 2006. 324p. ISBN 0843956399.*

> (See chapter 18, "Collections and Anthologies.")

Toybox. *New York: Leisure Books, 2003, ©1999. 255p. ISBN 0843951745.*

> (See chapter 18, "Collections and Anthologies.")

Sedia, Ekaterina.

The Secret History of Moscow. *Rockville, MD : Prime; London: Diamond, 2007. 303p. ISBN 0809572230.*

> Galina and her sister live in suburban Moscow, which is dirty, depressing, and rife with crime and graft. When Galina's sister disappears, turning into an animal, she and police detective Yakov Richards follow her trail until it leads them to an underground city where lost souls mingle with mythological and folkloric beings in a dark, cavernous world of magic. Yet Galina and her friends find some solace, as well as a newfound appreciation for history. **Similar titles:** *Neverwhere*, Neil Gaiman; *The Hidden World*, Graham Masterton; *King Rat*, China Miâville.
>
> *Fairies • Russia—Moscow • Parallel Universes • Shape-shifters • Suburbia*

Simmons, Dan.

The Terror. *New York: Little, Brown, 2007. 784p. ISBN 0316017442.*

> How could 129 men simply disappear? The fate of Sir John Franklin's 1845 expedition still remains somewhat of a mystery today. Simmons fictionalizes what hap-

pened after Franklin died and Francis Crozier, his second in command, became captain of *The Terror*. Trapped in packed Artic ice, he and his crew begin to perish, first from disease, then hypothermia or botulism, and finally at the hands of the monstrous creature from the ice. Is it a giant polar bear? The mythological Yeti? **Similar titles:** *They Hunger*, Scott Nicholson; *At the Mountains of Madness*, H. P. Lovecraft; *Move Under Ground*, Nick Mamatas.

Arctic, The • Crozier, Francis, (character) • Folklore • Franklin, John (character)

Smith, Bryan.

Queen of Blood. *New York: Leisure, 2008. ISBN 0843960612.*
(See chapter 15, "Splatterpunk: The Gross Out.")

Sneddon, James.

The Tolltaker. *Waterville, ME: Five Star. 2004. 391p. ISBN 1594141460.*
Eight-year-old Bobby's father has been missing in action in Vietnam for the past three years, but Bobby believes he is keeping his father alive through the magic of the "safe keeper," a bracelet carved with Bobby's father name. But the Tolltaker is able to enter Bobby's dreams and it demands a steep tribute from Bobby—remove the bracelet from his wrist, and officially end his father's life. **Similar titles:** *Coraline*, Neil Gaiman; *The Hidden World*, Graham Masterton; *Bloodstained Oz*, Christopher Golden and James A. Moore.

Childhood • Dreams • War—Vietnam War

Wilson, Robert Charles.

Crooked Tree. *Ann Arbor: Univeristy of Michigan Press, 2005, ©1980. 360p. ISBN 0472115316.*
In a northern Michigan town, maimed bodies are found, but the locals are sure that no ordinary bear is responsible. Law enforcement then begins investigating the possibility that a Native American mythological figure, the shape-shifting Grizzly Woman, may have sprung to life. This viscerally appealing fan favorite is known for its use of lush description and the author's penchant for invoking pure terror verbally. It will please fans who like a gory story. **Similar titles:** *Shadow Coast*, Philip Haldeman; *Crota*, Owl Goingback; *The Manitou*, Graham Masterton.

Animals Run Rampant • Bears • Michigan • Native American Characters • Shape-shifters • Wilderness • Witchcraft

Lovecraftian Monsters (The Old Ones)

Asamatsu, Ken, ed.

Straight to Darkness: Lairs of the Hidden Gods. *Fukuoka, Japan: Kurodahan Press, 2006, ©2002. 344p. ISBN 490207513X.*
(See chapter 18, "Collections and Anthologies.")

Cannon, Peter.

The Lovecraft Chronicles. *Illustrated by Jason C. Eckhardt. Poplar Bluffs, MO: Mythos Books, 2004. 179p. ISBN 0972854533.*
(See chapter 17, "Everyday Horror: When the Mundane Becomes Monstrous.")

Jackson, Liam.

Offspring. *New York: St. Martin's/Dunne, 2006. 290p. ISBN 031235570X.*
(See chapter 10, "Small Town Horror: Villages of the Damned.")

Lovecraft, H[oward]. P[hillip].

At the Mountains of Madness. *New York: Modern Library, 2005, ©1931. 186p. ISBN 0812974417.*

A 1930s Antarctic geological exploration leads to the discovery of an ancient city. A group of scientists finds an enormous, uncharted mountain range that shows evidence of pre-*homo sapiens* sentient life. The further they investigate, the more bizarre their findings, including amphibious creatures that harken back to the *Necronomicon*. Even more disturbing are the remains of "the Old Ones." This edition of Lovecraft's classic includes the author's essay on the genre, "Supernatural Horror in Literature." **Similar titles:** *The Terror*, Dan Simmons; *Straight to Darkness: Lairs of the Hidden Gods*, Ken Asamatsu (editor); *More Annotated H. P. Lovecraft* and *The Shadow Out of Time*, H. P. Lovecraft.

Antarctica • Cthulhian Monsters • Necronomicon, The • Weird Science

The Case of Charles Dexter Ward. *New York: Ballantine Books, 1995, ©1943. 127p. ISBN 0345384210.*

Incantations of black magic unearth unspeakable horrors in a quiet town near Providence, Rhode Island. Evil spirits, resurrected from beyond the grave, wake a supernatural force so twisted that it kills without mercy. Scientist Charles Dexter Ward seeks the truth and discovers too much of it. He pays the price with his sanity. **Similar titles:** *More Annotated H. P. Lovecraft*, H. P. Lovecraft; *The Taint and Other Novellas: Best Mythos Tales, Volume One*, Brian Lumley; *Straight to Darkness: Lairs of the Hidden Gods*, Ken Asamatsu (editor).

Colonial Era • Cthulhian Monsters • Haunted Houses • Necronomicon, The • Rhode Island—Providence • Subterranean Monsters • Witchcraft

The Lurker at the Threshold. *New York: Carroll and Graf, 2003, ©1945. 196p. ISBN 0786711884.*

Ambrose Dewart returns to his ancestral home near Dunwich, Massachusetts, where he discovers that his grandfather practiced witchcraft decades earlier. His curiosity getting the better of him, Dewart pries further into his family's old manuscripts, at the risk of inviting the hideous "elder gods," beings that existed before recorded time, into the modern world. **Similar titles:** *The Shadow Out of Time*, H. P. Lovecraft; *Darker Than Night*, Owl Goingback; *Bag of Bones*, Stephen King; *The House of Seven Gables*, Nathaniel Hawthorne.

Cthulhian Monsters • Cursed Objects • Family Curse • Massachusetts—Dunwich • Miskatonic University • Native American Characters • Witchcraft

More Annotated H. P. Lovecraft. *New York: Dell, 1999. 312p. ISBN 0440508754.*
  (See chapter 18, "Collections and Anthologies.")

The Shadow Out of Time. *Edited by S. T. Joshi and David E. Schultz. New York: Hippocampus Press, 2001. 136p. ISBN 0967321530.*
  A professor of political economy experiences a nervous breakdown, after which he has neither memory of his life nor any abilities to perform day-to-day functions. After five years in this state, he finally awakens to discover, after joining an archeological expedition to Australia, that his greatest fears have been realized. This is an impressive edition of Lovecraft's final novella, with extensive notes and introductory material by two of the finest scholars of his work, Joshi and Schultz. **Similar titles:** *The Tales of H. P. Lovecraft: Major Works*, H. P. Lovecraft; *Mr. X*, Peter Straub; *The Loved Dead and Other Revisions*, August Derleth (editor).

  Academia • Amnesia • Archeology • Australia • Dreams • Miskatonic University • Time Travel

Tales of H. P. Lovecraft: Major Works. *Hopewell, NJ: Eccopress, 1997. 328p. ISBN 0880015489.*
  (See chapter 18, "Collections and Anthologies.")

Waking Up Screaming: Haunting Tales of Terror. *New York: Ballantine, 2003. 370p. ISBN 034545829X.*
  (See chapter 18, "Collections and Anthologie.")

Lovecraft, H[oward]. P[hillip], with Harlan Ellison.

Shadows of Death: Terrifying Tales. *New York: Del Rey, 2005. 324p. ISBN 0345483332.*
  (See chapter 18, "Collections and Anthologies.")

Lumley, Brian.

The House of Cthulhu. *New York: Tor, 2005, ©1984. 254p. ISBN 0765310732.*
  (See chapter 18, "Collections and Anthologies.")

The Taint and Other Novellas: Best Mythos Tales, Volume One. *Burton, MI: Subterranean Press, 2007. 279 p ISBN 1596061251.*
  (See chapter 18, "Collections and Anthologies.")

Mamatas, Nick.

Move Under Ground. *San Francisco: Night Shade Books, 2004. 185p. ISBN 1892389916.*
  Jack Kerouac, hiding from his public in Big Sur, enjoys the company of a Hindu deity and awaits word from the charismatic Neal Cassady. When Cassady sends a message babbling about the Old Ones rising out of the Pacific and sweeping across America, Jack sets out to find him. Ultimately, Kerouac, Cassady, and William S. Burroughs find themselves in a cross-country race against Lovecraftian monsters. **Similar titles:** *Shadows*

over Baker Street, John Pelan and Michael Reaves (editors); *What Rough Beast*, H. R. Knight; *The Ghost in the Eiffel Tower*, Oliver Bleys; *Everybody Scream!* Jeffrey Thomas.

Burroughs, William S. (character) • California • Cassidy, Neal (character) • Cthulhian Monsters • Kerouac, Jack (character)

McGrew, Chandler.

The Darkening. *New York: Dell, 2004. 413p. ISBN 0553586033.*

Dylan Barnes has always heard voices, but when he is suddenly stalked by two mysterious police officers, he begins to suspect that reality isn't always what it seems, especially after he is saved by a member of a secret society called Rex Deus. Hundreds of miles away, investigator Lucy Devereau wonders about the sudden electrical outages and disappearances of people across the country. Both are on a collision course with mythological gods and their human minions. **Similar titles:** *Blood Angel*, Justine Musk; The Straw Men Series, Michael Marshall; *Keepers*, Gary A. Braunbeck.

Apocalypse • Cthulhian Monsters • Parallel Universes • Police Officer as Character • Zombies

Myers, Gary, and Robert M. Price.

Dark Wisdom: New Tales of the Old Ones. *Poplar Bluff, MO: Mythos Books, 2007. 121p. ISBN 0978991133.*

(See chapter 18, "Collections and Anthologies.")

Pelan, John, and Benjamin Adams, eds.

The Children of Cthulhu. *New York: Ballantine, 2002. 469p. ISBN 0345449266.*

(See chapter 18, "Collections and Anthologies.")

Price, Robert M.

Tales out of Dunwich. *New York: Hippocampus Press, 2005. 302p. ISBN 0974878995.*

(See chapter 18, "Collections and Anthologies.")

Thomas, Jeffrey.

Everybody Scream! *Hyattsville, MD: Raw Dog Screaming Press, 2004. 290p. ISBN 0974503142.*

Punktown is filled with strange characters—the proprietor of a café claims to be one of the Roswell aliens, a former prostitute turned singer who fears that her lover yens for her conjoined twin. Now that the annual carnival is coming to town, the lives of these bizarre characters converge, and a Lovecraftian beast emerges from another dimension so slowly that his claw is actually tagged with gang graffiti. **Similar titles:** *Move Under Ground*, Nick Mamatas; *What Rough Beast*, H. R. Knight; *The Attraction*, Douglas Clegg.

Cthulhian Monsters • Punktown (fictional city)

Mythological Gods and Monsters

Campbell, Ramsey.

The Hungry Moon. *London: Headline, 1995, ©1987. 360p. ISBN 0747246270.*
   (See chapter 10, "Small Town Horror: Villages of the Damned.")

The Darkest Part of the Woods. *New York: Tor, 2002. 368p. ISBN 0765307669.*
   (See chapter 10, "Small Town Horror: Villages of the Damned.")

Connolly, John.

The Book of Lost Things. *New York: Washington Square Press, 2007, ©2006. 408p. ISBN 074329890X.*
   Everything David has ever known has been taken from him. After David's mother dies at the beginning of World War II, his father remarries, and his stepmother quickly becomes pregnant. When David takes refuge in fantasy and fairy tales with grisly realities, he eventually finds a portal to another dimension—one filled with monsters and mythological creatures. He must learn the meaning of goodness in order to find his way out. **Similar titles:** *Coraline*, Neil Gaiman; *The Hidden World*, Graham Masterton; The Gemma Doyle Trilogy, Libba Bray.

   Adolescence • Death—Grieving • England • Parallel Universes • Popular Culture—Fairy Tales

Goingback, Owl.

Ⓑ **Crota.** *New York: Pocket, 1998, ©1996. 262p. ISBN 0451197364.*
   A demonic beast with a hunger for humans and other animals terrorizes a Missouri town. Only the famed hunter Jay Little Hawk, with the aid of the town sheriff and an old shaman, can bring down the beast. This is a suspenseful, fast read. **Similar titles:** *Unspeakable* and *The Manitou*, Graham Masterton; *The Return*, Bentley Little; *Shadow Coast*, Philip Haldeman.

   Demons • Missouri • Native American Characters • Religion—Native American • Subterranean Horror

Golden, Christopher.

The Ferryman. *Baltimore, MD: Cemetery Dance Publications. 2003, ©2002. 348p. ISBN 1587670577.*
   When Jamie Hartschorn gives birth to a stillborn baby, she has a near-death experience in which Charon the Ferryman from Greek mythology comes for her. Unfortunately for Jamie, she has thrown away the silver coins he demands. Now, after returning to reality, she finds that her experience with Charon was no grief-fueled delusion. Instead, a very real mythological monster stalks her and her friends. **Similar titles:** *American*

Gods, Neil Gaiman; *The Myth Hunters*, Christopher Golden; *Family Inheritance* and *Grave Intent*, Deborah LeBlanc.

Charon (character) • Death (character) • Death—Grieving • Massachusetts—Boston • Pregnancy • Teacher as Character

Gruber, Michael.

Tropic of Night. *New York: William Morrow, 2003. 419p. ISBN 0060509546.*
A female anthropology graduate student travels to Africa with her poet husband, who turns out to be a powerful shaman. When he allows her to commune with the spirits of Yoruba sorcerers, they almost kill her. Fearing her husband will eventually use this power to destroy her, she flees to Miami and fakes her own death, but a series of murders of pregnant women and the theft of their fetuses let her know that she is still not safe. **Similar titles:** *My Soul to Keep*, Tananarive Due; *The Claw*, Ramsey Campbell; *Dead of Winter*, Don D'Ammassa.

Africa • African American Characters • Florida—Miami • Hispanic Characters • Police Officer as Character • Religion—African • Stalkers

Haldeman, Philip.

Shadow Coast. *New York: Hippocampus Press. 2007. 255p. ISBN 097717347X.*
(See chapter 4, "Ghosts and Haunted Houses: Dealing with Presences and Absences.")

Hand, Elizabeth.

Mortal Love. *New York: HarperPerennial, 2005, ©2004. 364p. ISBN 0060755342.*
Evienne Upstone was the artist's model who inspired members of the pre-Raphaelite Brotherhood and was rumored to have driven painters completely insane. Fifty years later, one of the Brotherhood's grandsons views the intensely erotic paintings that his father made of Evienne and ends up institutionalized. Over a hundred years later, an American writer in London doing research on the painters meets a mysterious woman, who he fears is a bit too familiar. **Similar titles:** *Deep Blue*, David Niall Wilson; *The Great God Pan*, Arthur Machen; *The Beloved*, J. F. Gonzales.

Academia • Artist as Character • England—London • Writer as Character

Karamesines, P. G.

The Pictograph Murders. *Salt Lake City, UT: Signature Books, 2004. 352p. ISBN 1560851821.*
Alex McKelvey longs to fit in, but the connections she feels toward the earth and to a certain eerie pictograph panel set her off from the crowd. Wanting only to enjoy the beauty of the Utah desert, she packs up her gear and her Siberian husky, Kit, and joins an archeological dig. But when the site's owner vanishes, varied forces combine to sweep up Alex and Kit in a whirlwind of pottery hunting, witchcraft, and murder. **Similar titles:** *Shadow Coast*, Philip Haldeman; *The Manitou*, Graham Masterton; *The Resort*, Bentley Little; *Bag of Bones*, Stephen King.

Archeology • Cursed Objects • Religion—Native American • Utah • Witchcraft

Keene, Brian.

Dark Hollow. *New York: Leisure, 2008. 305p. ISBN 0843958618.*

1

Adam Senft's only pleasure comes from his dog. While walking Big Steve through the local wilderness, Senft hears a mysterious sound and investigates, finding a woman sexually involved with a statue of a satyr. Soon after, the women in Lehorn's Hollow begin disappearing into the woods. Adam gathers the town's male residents to track down the statue, which has come to life—and they chance upon something evil that is collecting women so that it can reproduce itself. **Similar titles:** *Wicked Things*, Thomas Tessier; *Beasts*, Joyce Carol Oates; *She Wakes*, Jack Ketchum.

2

Marriage • Psychosexual Horror • Religion—Paganism • Satyrs • Wilderness • Writer as Character

3

Ketchum, Jack (pseudonym used by Dallas Mayr).

She Wakes. *New York: Leisure, 2004, ©1984. 355p. ISBN 084395423X.*
(See chapter 15, "Splatterpunk: The Gross Out.")

4

Knight, H. R.

What Rough Beast. *New York: Leisure, 2005. 374p. ISBN 0843954566.*

5

Harry Houdini and Sir Arthur Conan Doyle attend a séance, hoping to expose an occultist as a fraud, but the hot-headed magician accidentally frees the god Dionysus, who acts as a conduit for sexual decadence and violent tendencies. Soon one member of the séance party is accused of a grisly murder, because he is found in a locked room with the remains of his older brother, who has literally been torn limb from limb. **Similar titles:** *Come Fygures, Come Shadowes*, Richard Matheson; *The Ghost in the Eiffel Tower*, Oliver Bleys; *Move Under Ground*, Nick Mamatas; *Everybody Scream!* Jeffrey Thomas.

6

Dionysus (character) • Doyle, Sir Arthur Conan (character) • England • Houdini, Harry (character) • Religion—Paganism

7

Laimo, Michael.

Deep in the Darkness. *New York: Leisure, 2004. 369p. ISBN 0843953144.*

Dr. Michael Cayle moves his wife and daughters from the big city to a picturesque small town called Ashborough, set deep in the woods, where he will be able to practice family medicine on the residents. As luck would have it, the Cayle family has also managed to acquire the fine old house once occupied by the former town doctor before he passed away. Then Dr. Cayle discovers heavy steel doors and ancient creatures who reside in the forest. **Similar titles:** *In the Dark of Night*, John Saul; *The Darkest Part of the Woods* and *The Hungry Moon*, Ramsey Campbell; *Dark Hollow*, Brian Keene.

8

9

Families • New Hampshire • Physician as Character • Wilderness

10

Masterton, Graham.

The Manitou Series.

(See chapter 7, "Demonic Possession: Satanism, Black Magic, and Witches and Warlocks: The Devil Made Me Do It.")

Prey. *New York: Leisure, 1999, ©1992. 352p. ISBN 0843946334.*

David Williams has taken on the job of restoring Fortyfoot House, an abandoned orphanage on the Isle of Wight. He moves there with his son, but soon discovers that he may have placed both of them in terrible danger—the creature that inhabits the attic of Fortyfoot House is always hungry, and the house itself is alive with the ghosts of its past and prevent victims. Masterton is unrelenting in his use of suspense and horrific atmosphere. **Similar titles:** *The Shining*, Stephen King; *The Haunting of Hill House*, Shirley Jackson; *The House That Jack Built*, Graham Masterton.

Demons • England—Isle of Wight • Haunted Houses • Parenting • Pregnancy • Religion—Satanism • Time Travel • Witchcraft

Tuttle, Lisa.

The Mysteries. *New York: Bantam, 2005. 321p. ISBN 0553382969.*

When several people mysteriously disappear, it becomes clear that they have met a supernatural fate and have gone into the realm of the Sidhe, better known as the world of fairy folk. Some will never return, while others can be brought back but will ultimately refuse to stay in the mundane world. Tuttle draws heavily upon Celtic folklore in this dark fantasy. **Similar titles:** The Nightlife Trilogy, Rob Thruman; *Neverwhere*, Neil Gaiman; *The Secret History of Moscow*, Ekaterina Sedia; *King Rat*, China Mieville.

Fairies • Parallel Universe • Popular Culture—Urban Legends

Original Gods

Braunbeck, Gary A.

Destinations Unknown. *Baltimore, MD: Cemetery Dance, 2006. 216p. ISBN 1587670852.*
(See chapter 18, "Collections and Anthologies.")

Keepers. *New York: Leisure, 2005. 339p. ISBN 0843955775.*

Gil Stewart witnesses an accident, and the dying victim on the highway warns him that the Keepers are coming. Afterward, Gil's life is turned upside down. A dog goes to die under his house, and he receives a phone call from the institution where his nephew with Down's Syndrome resides, telling him the boy has disappeared. Gil must remember his past, as well as all the kindnesses he's done to animals and the downtrodden, before the Keepers arrive. **Similar titles:** *In Silent Graves* and *Prodigal Blues*, Gary A. Braunbeck; *The Collected Strange Stories*, Robert Aickman.

Adolescence • Afterlife, The • Families • Parallel Universes • Reincarnation • Septuagenarians

Gaiman, Neil.

American Gods. *New York: Perennial, 2003, ©2001. 608p. ISBN 0380973650.*

Shadow gets out of prison early when his wife is killed in a car accident. At a loss, he takes up with a mysterious character called Wednesday, who is actually the god Odin. Odin roams America, rounding up his forgotten fellows in preparation for an epic battle against the upstart deities of the Internet, credit cards, television, and all that is wired. **Similar titles:** *The Myth Hunter* and *The Ferryman*, Christopher Golden; *Desperation*, Stephen King.

Corporate Horror • Internet, The • Multimedia—Television • Nevada—Las Vegas • Odin (character) • Road Trips

Neverwhere: A Novel. *New York: Perennial, 2003. 370p. ISBN 0060557818.*

Businessman Richard Mayhew is enjoying an ordinary night out on the town, when witnessing a violent attack leads him away from the streets, down to London Below, a surreal, underground world. His companions are Door, the young woman he had attempted to save above; the Marquis of Carabas, a mercenary trickster; and Hunter, a mysterious huntress. Once he is Below, he realizes that to return to his world, he will have to help fight the sinister villains of this nebulous subway underworld. **Similar titles:** *Witchery*, Amber Benson; *Bloodstained Oz*, Christopher Golden and James A. Moore; *The Hidden World*, Graham Masterton.

Dreams • England—London • Shape-shifters • Subterranean Horror

The Shell Collector. *Baltimore, MD: Cemetery Dance, 2006. 128p. ISBN 158767114X.*

(See chapter 10, "Small Town Horror: Villages of the Damned.")

Kilpatrick, Nancy, and Michael Kilpatrick.

Eternal City. *Waterville, ME: Five Star, 2003. 303p. ISBN 0786249609.*

Claire Mowatt travels to Ontario to settle the inheritance of her dead Aunt Lillian, who used to be a psychic. She is forewarned of a dark force at work in the northern part of the province, aiding the CEO of an aggressive corporation to obtain her aunt's property. Claire begins to suspect that the company may have had something to do with her aunt's death, as well as the deaths of many in the area. **Similar titles:** *American Gods*, Neil Gaiman; *Breathe: Everyone Has to Do It*, Christopher Fowler; *The Resort*, Bentley Little.

Canada • Corporate Horror • Demons • Families • Parapsychology • Pollution

King, Stephen.

From a Buick 8: A Novel. *New York: Pocket Books, 2003. 487p. ISBN 0743417682.*

The appearance of a mysterious car in 1979 causes various police officers to relive past bizarre events some thirty years later. Pennsylvania State Patrol Troop D finds itself in possession of a vintage Buick, and officers discover that the doors and trunk lead to another dimension. But there are a couple of problems: both dimensions are being invaded by hideous creatures, and the son of a fallen officer, killed via vehicular homicide, is becoming obsessed with the vehicle. **Similar titles:** *Where the Woodbine Twines*, Sherry Austin; *The Boys Are Back in Town*, Christopher Golden; *Christine*, Stephen King.

Cars • Cursed Objects • Death—Grieving • Families • Obsession • Parallel Universes • Pennsylvania • Police Officer as Character • Time Travel

Koontz, Dean.

Phantoms. *New York: Berkley, 2001, ©1993. 434p. ISBN 0425181103.*

More than half of the residents of Snowfield, California, have either mysteriously disappeared or have died. Dr. Jennifer Paige, her fourteen-year-old sister Lisa, and Sheriff Bryce Hammond must get to the bottom of these strange occurrences, while they avoid being gruesomely killed by the shape-shifting creature that seems to know each person's innermost fears. One of Koontz's best. **Similar titles:** *Ghost Story*, Peter Straub; *Needful Things* and *'Salem's Lot*, Stephen King.

Computers • Police Officer as Character • Satan (character) • Shape-shifters • Subterranean Monsters

Pinborough, Sarah.

The Hidden. *New York: Leisure, 2004. 369p. ISBN 0843954809.*

When Rachel awakens in the hospital with amnesia, she maintains an optimistic outlook on life, working to make a fresh start and rebuild her memories of her old life. But when she begins to see figures in mirrors and is plagued by terrible nightmares, this task proves more daunting than she first believed it would be. Combined with the recent murders around London, her visions convince Rachel that something awful is trying to break through from another dimension. **Similar titles:** *Under-ground*, Craig Spector; *The Awakening*, Donna Boyd; *The Prison*, R. Patrick Gates; *The Looking Glass*, A. J. Matthews.

Amnesia • Dreams • England—London • Parallel Universes

The Taken. *New York: Leisure Books, 2007. 323p. ISBN 0843958960.*

The Catcher Man, an ancient Pagan figure, steals lost children, but the real horror starts when he brings them back. Mary, an aging mother, realizes that the sins of her past will return to haunt her—no longer bound by the restrictions of death. Her cherubic ten-year-old with blonde curls and a devilish grin has come back from the Catcher Man to unleash thirty years of pent-up fury, and all the inhabitants of the sleepy farming village of Watterrow will have to pay. **Similar titles:** *Pet Sematary*, Stephen King; *Toybox*, Al Sarrantonio; *Spirit*, Graham Masterton.

Clergy as Character • Parenting • Religion—Paganism • Revenging Revenant • Secret Sin

Shepard, Lucius.

A Handbook of American Prayer. *New York: Thunder's Mouth Press, 2004. 263p. ISBN 1568582811.*

While serving time for manslaughter, Wardlin Stewart accidentally develops a new religion—prayerstyle. He composes poetry and prose prayers addressed to no recognizable god, hoping to produce small results. But the result is far more spectacular than Wardlin anticipates. Whatever he asks for happens, and when he is released from prison, he becomes a national celebrity widely regarded as a shaman; but the deity he has generated through prayerstyle has taken on a life of its own. Subtle and creepy. **Similar titles:** *Dispatch*, Bentley Little; *Mojo: Conjure Stories*, Nalo Hopkison (editor); *The Prison*, R. Patrick Gates; *The Road*, Cormac McCarthy.

Arizona • Inmates • Magic • Religion • Religion—Christianity

Thurman, Rob.

The Cal Leandros Trilogy.

Elves are mean. At least that is the case when they are really *auphes*. These auphes want to bring about the utter destruction of humanity, unless a half-human, half-auphe can stop them. Thurman excels at writing witty dialogue. **Similar titles:** The Women of the Otherworld Series, Kelley Armstrong; The Anita Blake, Vampire Hunter Series, Laurell K. Hamilton; The Vampire Files, P. N. Elrod.

Alternative Literature • Fairies • Leandros, Cal (character) • New York—New York City • Shakespearean Characters • Werewolves

Nightlife. *New York: ROC- New American Library, 2006. 339p. ISBN 0451460758.*

> The auphes of New York City hold their own against vampires, were-wolves, banshees, trolls, and giant bog monsters. They also don't much like people, and they want to destroy them. A half-human, half-auphe named Cal (short for Caliban), along with a used car salesman named Robin Goodfellow and a martial arts champion, are now humanity's only hope

> *Popular Culture—Urban Legends*

Moonshine. *New York: ROC, 2007. 338p. ISBN 0451461398.*

> Cal and his brother Nick now work as private investigators, as well as "exterminators" who take on jobs such as ridding a carnival of *bodachs*, a type of Scottish evil spirit. Then they are offered a job spying on the Werewolf Mafia, which puts their friend Puck's psychic girlfriend Georgia in danger.

> *Private Investigator as Character • Psychics • Werewolves*

Madhouse. *New York: New American Library, 2008. 337p. ISBN 0451461967.*

> Legendary Scottish cannibal Sawney Beane has returned from the dead and has recruited a band of revenants to help him claim tourists as victims in New York City. It's up to Cal and Nick to stop him before he kills one of their friends.

> *Private Investigator as Character • Popular Culture—Sawney Beane Legend • Serial Killers • Werewolves*

Religion-Based Gods and Monsters

Braunbeck, Gary A.

In Silent Graves. *New York: Leisure-Dorchester, 2004. 378p. ISBN 0843953292.*
(*Originally published as* The Indifference of Heaven, *2000*). The subjects of death and deformity—not merely in their philosophical sense, but in their most raw, grotesque, physical manifestations—provide the impetus for this fairy tale for adults. An egocentric newscaster loses both his wife and unborn child on Halloween, the same night he meets "split face," a virtually indescribably deformed young man who shows him that reality is like a carnival funhouse, only more disturbing, and that life is not what it seems. **Similar titles:** *Keepers*, Gary A. Braunbeck; *American Gods*, Neil Gaiman; *The Doorkeepers*, Graham Masterton.

Angels • Death—Grieving • Deformity • Journalist as Character • Marriage • Ohio—Cedar Hill • Parallel Universes

Cavallo, Frank.

The Lucifer Messiah. *Medallion Press, 2006. 389p. ISBN 19328158.*
When Sam Mulcahey left home in the autumn of 1917 to fight the war to end all wars, he disappeared without a trace, leaving his best friend Vince a broken man who finds solace in a bottle. Thirty years later, Sam returns to Vince's doorstep in Hell's Kitchen and doesn't seem to have aged a day since the time he left. Meanwhile, in the dark alleys, even gangsters are frightened as mutilated bodies begin piling up, and rumors abound of ancient rituals being performed, heralding the coming of the Lucifer Messiah. **Similar titles:** *Rosemary's Baby* and *Son of Rosemary*, Ira Levin; *Finding Satan*, Andrew Neiderman; *The Lebo Coven*, Stephen Mark Rainey; *The Omen* (film)

Antichrist (character) • New York—New York City • Organized Crime • Satan (character) • Soldier as Character • War—World War II

Cutter, Leah R.

The Caves of Buda. *New York: Roc, 2004. 304p. ISBN 0451459725.*
Zita may be becoming senile. He has escaped from his hospital bed while screaming about demons, and is returning to his boyhood home, Budapest. Now that his granddaughter has tracked him down, she discovers that his return is not an attempt to journey down memory lane. Rather, he is aware of the imminent resurrection of a demon that will threaten the entire world. Good thing they meet up with a man well versed in magic. **Similar titles:** The Blood of the Lamb Series, Thomas F. Monteleone; *Finding Satan*, Andrew Neiderman; *The Demonologist*, Michael Laimo.

Apocalypse • Demons • Families • Hungary—Budapest • Magic • Religion—Christianity—Catholicism • Secret Sin • Septuagenarians

Due, Tananarive.

The Living Blood Series (aka The African Immortals Series).

An African American immortal must deal with human feelings of love and loyalty toward his human family. Due's emphasis is on characterization and psychology, and well-conceived plots, the use of historical fact, and a suspenseful climax make this a unique, enjoyable read. **Similar titles:** *Interview with the Vampire* and *Servant of the Bones*, Anne Rice; The Saint-Germain Chronicles, Chelsea Quinn Yarbro.

African American Characters • Immortality • Jacobs-Wolde, Jessica (character) • Religion —Christianity • Wolde, David (character)

My Soul to Keep. *New York: Eos, 2001, ©1997. 352p. ISBN 006105366X.*

Miami reporter Jessica Jacobs-Wolde thinks that her husband David is the perfect father and lover. What she does not know is that he really is Dawit, a centuries-old Abyssinian immortal, whose fellow immortals wish him to sever all human connections to protect the secret of their existence.

Florida—Miami • Journalist as Character • Marriage

The Living Blood. *New York: Pocket, 2001. 515 . ISBN 0671040839.*

Jessica Jacobs-Wolde's life was destroyed when her husband, the immortal David Wolde, disappeared after killing both their daughter Kira and Jessica herself, then reviving Jessica to immortality with his healing blood. Now she hides with her surviving daughter in rural Botswana, using her altered blood to save the incurably ill. But her daughter Fana at the age of three can raise a storm, kill with a thought, and possess her mother's mind.

Africa • Parenting

Hodge, Brian.

World of Hurt. *Northborough, MA: Earthling Publications, 2006. 151p. ISBN 0976633973.*

(See chapter 15, "Splatterpunk: The Gross Out.")

Hodgson, William Hope.

The House on the Borderland. *London: Gollancz, 2002, ©1908. 200p. ISBN 0575073721.*

A diary found in an ancient stone house in rural Ireland leads readers to subterranean horrors. This journal describes the last days of the house's owner, who sees demons in an alternative, mirror universe; he then becomes obsessed with the pit adjacent to his house, where he is attacked by half-man, half-pig creatures, and ultimately a demon that ushers in the end of the world. This atmospheric classic is sure to send chills down your spine. **Similar titles:** *The Yellow Sign and Other Stories: The Complete Weird Tales of Robert W. Chambers*, Robert W. Chambers; *Reassuring Tales*, T. E. D.

Klein; *Tales of H. P. Lovecraft: Major Works* and *Waking Up Screaming: Haunting Tales of Terror*, H. P. Lovecraft.

Cursed Objects • Demons • Diary Format • Frame Tale • Ireland • Pigs

Huggins, James Byron.

Nightbringer. *New Kengsington, PA: Whitaker House, 2004. 302p. ISBN 088368876X.*
An ancient evil has been resurrected in the hallowed halls of Saint Gregory's Abbey. The once peaceful monastery in the Italian Alps has been transformed into a house of horrors. And the entity responsible for the change can have a little more fun than usual, for the monks are currently receiving a group of visiting tourists, who have arrived at the monastery right before a snowstorm has made escape impossible. **Similar titles:** *The Mist*, Stephen King; *The Terror*, Dan Simmons; *They Hunger*, Scott Nicholson.

Clergy as Characters • Demons • Italy • Monasteries • Weather • Wilderness

Kiernan, Caitlin R.

The Silk Series.

Members of a struggling Birmingham, Alabama, underground band take up with Spyder, an former mental institution patient who was abused as a child. But there is little sympathy for the devil when the group accidentally awakens demonic forces. **Similar titles:** <u>The Gemma Doyle Trilogy</u>, Libba Bray; <u>The City Infernal Series</u>, Edward Lee; *Alabaster*, Caitlin R. Kiernan; *Queen of the Damned* (film).

Asian American Characters • Baxter, Spyder (character) • Demons • Gay/Lesbian/Bisexual Characters • Gothicism • Ky, Niki (character) • Music—Rock Music • Parallel Universes • Parker, Daria (character)

Silk. *New York: Roc, 2002, ©1998. 353p. ISBN 0451459008.*

Spyder conducts a strange ritual in her childhood home, and after she and the band awaken, they are haunted by what they believe to be demonic forces. Or is it all in their minds?

Alabama—Birmingham • Child Abuse • Drugs

Murder of Angels. *New York: ROC, 2004. 355p. ISBN 0451459962.*

After the disastrous drug-fueled experiment opened the door to an alternate universe, Spyder Baxter commits suicide, prompting Niki Ky's schizophrenia. While Daria Parker is able to channel the experience through her music, Niki begins hearing Spyder's voice, beckoning her to take her own life. Will Niki listen and jump from the Golden Gate bridge?

Afterlife, The • Mental Illness

King, Stephen.

Needful Things. *New York: Penguin, 1991. 690p. ISBN 0670839531.*
Castle Rock, Maine, is a peaceful little town. It's not exactly Mayberry, but everyone agrees to keep certain secrets and to disagree on the fine points of theol-

ogy and morality to maintain the peace. Then Leland Gaunt arrives and opens a curiosity shop in a vacant building on Main Street. Leland's store carries everyone's heart's desire, but no one can afford the prices. **Similar titles:** *'Salem's Lot*, Stephen King; *Obsession*, Ramsey Campbell; *Phantoms*, Dean Koontz.

Maine—Castle Rock • Police Officer as Character • Religion—Christianity—Catholicism • Religion—Christianity—Protestantism • Satan (character)

Kingsbury, Evan (pseudonym used by Robert Walker).

Fire and Flesh. *New York: Jove, 2003. 313p. ISBN 0515134406.*

In certain parts of the world, summer days can get so hot that people feel as though they will melt. On such a day in Calcutta, India, a young girl dies, and her father arranges for a local pier burner to incinerate the body, but he ends up being burned to ash after meeting a strange shape-shifting man. Months later, humans spontaneously combust in Miami. Two detectives realize that some creature is feeding on humans, leaving charred corpses behind. **Similar titles:** The Pendergast Novels, Douglas Preston and Lincoln Childs; *Mulengro*, Charles De Lint; *The Laughing Man*, T. M. Wright.

Clergy as Character • Florida—Miami • Police Officer as Character • Popular Culture —Spontaneous Combustion • Shape-shifters

Lackey, Mercedes.

Burning Water: A Diana Tregarde Investigation. *New York: Tor, 2005, ©1989. 330p. ISBN 0765313170.*

A Fort Worth detective has problems figuring out who is drowning and skinning victims, and often removing their hearts. He brings in Diana Tregarde, a powerful Wiccan dedicated to writing romance novels and defeating evil, to help track the serial killer. Originally billed as young adult reading, this adult favorite recounts the resurrection of the Aztec god of war, Tezcatlipoca. **Similar titles:** *Phantoms*, Dean Koontz; *What Rough Beast*, H. R. Knight; The Pendergast Novels, Douglas Preston and Lincoln Childs; The Joe Pitt Novels, Charlie Huston.

Human Sacrifice • Police Officer as Character • Psychics • Religion—Aztec • Serial Killers • Texas—Fort Worth • Writer as Character

Laws, Stephen.

The Wyrm. *New York: Leisure, 2004, ©1987. 342p. ISBN 0843952199.*

Fleeing personal demons and writer's block, an author of psychological thrillers purchases an estate in rural Scotland, hoping to cure both. Instead, he meets and falls for the daughter of the local town madman, who greets with a shotgun the bulldozers sent to raze the town's historic gallows pole to make way for new construction. But the town madman has his reasons: buried beneath the gallows is an ancient evil that will spring to life if the pole is removed. **Similar titles:** *Riverwatch*, Joseph M. Nacisse; *Bag of Bones* and *'Salem's Lot*, Stephen King; *Darkness Wakes*, Tim Waggoner.

Demons • Scotland • Secret Sin • Subterranean Horror • Writer as Character

Lee, Edward.

Messenger. *New York: Leisure, 2004. 337p. ISBN 0843952040.*
(See chapter 15, "Splatterpunk: The Gross Out.")

Monstrosity. *New York: Leisure, 2003. 373p. ISBN 0843950757.*
(See chapter 15, "Splatterpunk: The Gross Out.")

Lee, Edward, with Wrath James White.

Teratrologist. *Hiram, GA: Overlook Connection Press, 2003. 116p. ISBN 1892950820.*
(See chapter 15, "Splatterpunk: The Gross Out.")

Masello, Robert.

Vigil. *New York: Berkley, 2005. 376p. ISBN 0425203506.*
Carter Cox, a paleontologist, has two mysteries to solve. What does the legendary parchment found in the Middle Eastern desert mean; and what exactly is this creature whose fossil was found in the caves beneath an Italian lake, which carbon dating indicates is older than the earth itself? Meanwhile, a linguist smuggles the scroll out of Israel to translate it and discovers it is not parchment. It is living tissue, and the ink is actually blood. **Similar titles:** *The Wyrm*, Stephen Laws; *Finding Satan*, Andrew Neiderman; *Blood Angel*, Justine Musk.

Academia • Angels • Archeology • Cursed Objects • Demons • Religion—Christianity

Monteleone, Thomas F.

The Blood of the Lamb Series.

The Catholic Church cloned Christ in 1968. Now, just in time for the upcoming millennium, this clone, Peter Carenza, is a young priest. Father Carenza develops miraculous powers, but the potential for their abuse is frightening, as they will ultimately lead to an apocalyptic battle between good and evil. **Similar titles:** *The Exorcist*, William Peter Blatty; *Son of Rosemary*, Ira Levin; *The Lucifer Messiah*, Frank Cavello.

Apocalypse • Carenza, Father Peter (character) • Clergy as Character • Popular Culture—Cloning • Religion—Christianity—Catholicism • Windsor, Marion (character)

 The Blood of the Lamb. *New York: Tom Doherty, 1992. 419p. ISBN 031285031X.*
Father Peter Carenza travels across the United States in a Winnebago, performing miracles to ever-increasing crowds of adoring followers. This is a brilliant epic told through multiple points of view.

Journalist as Character

The Reckoning. *New York: Tor, 2001, ©1999. 419p. ISBN 0812575245.*
At the beginning of the new millennium, Father Peter Carenza is elected pope after the miracles he performed in front of large crowds. But he is no longer the gentle priest traveling the country in his Winnebago. He makes major changes to Catholic theology to win more converts. Meanwhile, abnor-

mal sunspot activity threatens to end life as we know it, as does the opening of the seven seals mentioned in the Book of Revelation.

African American Characters • Antichrist, The • Asian Characters

Moore, James A.

The Corbin Family Novels.

(See chapter 7, "Demonic Possession: Satanism, Black Magic, and Witches and Warlocks: The Devil Made Me Do It.")

Musk, Justine.

Blood Angel. *New York: Roc, 2005. 343p. ISBN 0451460529.*

People of all ages across the United States are having strange dreams and falling under the spell of a charismatic singer named Asha. Little do her fans know that her talents are linked to the ancient sorcerer summoners. The lives of three people—a young boy, a painter, and a rock musician—converge as the battle between angels and demons interrupts their daily lives. **Similar titles:** *Son of Rosemary*, Ira Levin; *The Lucifer Messiah*, Frank Cavello; The Vampire Huntress Legend, L. A. Banks; *Heart-Shaped Box*, Joe Hill.

California • Demons • Internet, The • Minnesota • Music—Rock Music • New York—New York City

Nassise, Joseph M.

Riverwatch. *New York: Pocket, 2003, ©2001. 355p. ISBN 0743470966.*

This truly terrifying novel begins when a construction worker discovers a huge underground tombstone, unleashing terror on a small town. Meanwhile, a writer named Sam befriends a man who relates tales of a long-forgotten era before the evolution of humans, when two ancient races ruled Earth. It seems that the crew has awakened an ancient evil one, a "nightshade" named Moloch, and Sam and his love interest are intricately bound to the creature. Fans of traditional monster-based, action-filled horror will enjoy this read. **Similar titles:** *The Wyrm*, Stephen Laws; *30 Days of Night: A Novelization*, Tim Lebbon and Steve Niles; *Floating Dragon*, Peter Straub.

Angels • Cursed Objects • Demons • New England • Psychics • Religion—Christianity • Subterranean Horror

Neiderman, Andrew.

Finding Satan. *New York: Pocket Star, 2006. 392p. ISBN 1416516832.*

Christopher Drew is a scientist able to track evil as it occurs via satellite as a quantifiable event that shows up on his screen as black spots. When he sees a collection of black spots on his monitor, he is able to intervene in time to prevent the disastrous results, but not before his research comes to the attention of the tabloids. The ensuing publicity brings his invention to the attention of both the Department of Homeland Security and a group of satanists, both of whom wish to use Christopher's device for their own ends. **Similar titles:** *Mischief*, Douglas Clegg; <u>The Blood of the Lamb Series</u>, Thomas F. Monteleone; *Fireworks*, James A. Moore.

Government Officials • Religion—Satanism • Terrorism • Weird Science

Unholy Birth. *New York: Pocket Star, 2007. 339p. ISBN 1416516840.*
(See chapter 14, "Psychological Horror: It's All in Your Head.")

Passarella, J. G.

The Wendy Ward Series.

(See chapter 7, "Demonic Possession: Satanism, Black Magic, and Witches and Warlocks: The Devil Made Me Do It.")

Rainey, Stephen Mark.

The Lebo Coven. *Waterville, ME: Five Star, 2004. 278p. ISBN 1594142270.*
(See chapter 10, "Small Town Horror: Villages of the Damned.")

Rice, Anne.

The Servant of the Bones. *New York: Random, 1989. 387p. ISBN 0679433015.*
In ancient Babylon, Azriel is sacrificed to become the Servant of the Bones so that his people may return to Jerusalem. But the story doesn't end for Azriel, who is condemned to an immortal existence and can only relieve some of the loneliness of his condition by telling his story to Jonathan, as well as helping his chosen scribe to foil a modern-day evangelical plot. **Similar titles:** *The Mummy: or Ramses the Damned* and *The Vampire Lestat*, Anne Rice; *My Soul to Keep*, Tananarive Due.

Angels • Babylon • Frame Tale • Immortality • Religion—Judaism

Shirley, John.

Demons. *New York: Ballantine, 2002. 372p. ISBN 034544647X.*
In this prequel to his Demon Mythos, Shirley draws seven clans of demons and sets them loose in the modern world, where they spend as much time destroying private and civic property as they do devouring and flaying the nouveau-damned. Three-legged spiders tear civilians apart and spin webs of their wasted dreams, shark-headed behemoths attack with riddles before teeth, and gambling-addicted insect-men win souls with each hand of cards. Innocents run screaming in the streets. **Similar titles:** *Neverwhere*, Neil Gaiman; *The Secret History of Moscow*, Ekaterina Sedia; *King Rat*, China Mieville.

Demons • Futurism • Torture

The Other End. *Baltimore, MD: Cemetery Dance Publications, 2007. 292p. ISBN 1587671506.*
While reporter Jim Swift covers a botched drug raid, the Rapture suddenly occurs. Left behind is half of the world's population, but those who have not mysteriously disappeared have suddenly had a change of heart. Drug lords no longer want to

kill; they turn themselves in. Child slavers, genocidal soldiers, and crooked politicians all decide to turn over a new leaf. Crackpot conspiracy theorists begin to have reasonable arguments. Swift is also left behind—to chronicle this sudden shift in values, and deal with his own problem, a teenaged daughter. **Similar titles:** *The Road*, Cormac McCarthy; *The Day After Tomorrow*, Roland Emerick, Jeffrey Nachmanoff, and Whitley Strieber; *Demons*, John Shirley; *The Stand*, Stephen King.

Apocalypse • California • Journalist as Character • Religion—Christianity

Skipp, John.

The Long Last Call. *New York: Leisure, 2007. 368p. ISBN 084395843X.*
(See chapter 15, "Splatterpunk: The Gross Out.")

Tem, Melanie.

The Deceiver. *New York: Leisure 2003. 342p. ISBN 0843950978.*
Many generations of the Harkness family have received helpful advice from a persuasive stranger at opportune moments. The stranger does not always have the same appearance, but his advice is nevertheless always helpful. Of course, the devil is in the details, and the stranger has a hidden agenda that he has had many lifetimes to bring to fruition. Tem's narrative begins in 1894 and ends in 2000, spanning five generations of the tragic, and perhaps inbred, Harkness clan. **Similar titles:** <u>The Mayfair Witches Series</u>, Anne Rice; *Needful Things*, Stephen King; *Finding Satan*, Andrew Neiderman.

Family Curse • Gothicism • Incest • Satan (character)

Thorne, Tamara.

Thunder Road. *New York: Kensington-Pinnacle, 2004, ©1995. 499p. ISBN 0786014784.*
A young man fulfills his violent destiny, and the tiny town of Madelyn in the California desert begins to experience a rash of strange phenomena: unexplained lights in the sky, people vanishing, and mutilated farm animals. Only a crazed millennialist cult leader seems to realize that the world is about to witness the Four Horsemen from the Book of Revelations. **Similar titles:** *The Road*, Cormac McCarthy; *The Day After Tomorrow*, Roland Emerick, Jeffrey Nachmanoff, and Whitley Strieber; *Demons*, John Shirley; *The Stand*, Stephen King.

Apocalypse • California • Popular Culture—Four Horsemen of the Apocalypse • Religion—Christianity • Religion—Cults

Waggoner, Tim.

Darkness Wakes. *New York: Leisure, 2006. 321p. ISBN 0843957948.*
(See chapter 15, "Splatterpunk: The Gross Out.")

Wilson, David Nial.

Deep Blue. *Waterville, ME: Five Star, 2004. 344p. ISBN 1594141428.*

Brandt, a musician whose career is rapidly going down the toilet in part thanks to his alcoholism, encounters Wally, a homeless man who agrees to teach Brandt his musical technique—only after warning him that it is necessary to feel intense personal pain. Brandt takes what Wally teaches him to his band members, but not everyone is pleased. The demonic force that feeds on the world's pain in particular wants to stop him. **Similar titles:** *Mortal Love*, Elizabeth Hand; *Heart-Shaped Box*, Joe Hill; *World of Hurt*, Brian Hodge.

Demons • Music—Rhythm and Blues

Film

Fallen. *Gregory Hoblit, dir. 1998. 123 minutes.*

Before his execution, serial killer Edgar Reese begins speaking to Detective John Hobbes (Denzel Washington) in biblical tongues and singing the Rolling Stone's "Time Is on My Side." Soon after this execution, two people are murdered in a blatant imitation of Reese's style, and the fingerprints at the scene of the crime are Hobbes's. His daughter, a theology professor, believes that behind it all is the demon Azazel, who can switch bodies with anyone he touches. John Goodman and Donald Sutherland also star. **Similar titles:** *Valley of Lights*, Stephen Gallagher; *The Parasite*, Ramsey Campbell.

African American Characters • Angels • Demons • Massachusetts—Boston • Police Officer as Character • Religion—Christianity • Serial Killers

Hellraiser. *Clive Barker, dir. 1987. 94 minutes.*

Barker directs this film version of his novel *The Hellbound Heart*. When Frank, a playboy and thrill-seeker, decides that life holds no more pleasure for him, he experiments with Lamarchand's Box, which supposedly will summon the gods of pleasure. Instead, Frank summons demons of torture, and they want more than just Frank. **Similar titles:** *Demons*, John Shirley; *The Essential Clive Barker: Selected Fictions*, Clive Barker.

Demons • Eroticism • Secret Sin • Torture

June's Picks

Books: Tananarive Due, *My Soul to Keep* (Eos), *The Living Blood* (Pocket); Neil Gaiman, *American Gods* (Perennial), *Neverwhere* (Perennial); Stephen Gallagher. *Valley of Lights.* (Telos)

Film: *Fallen*

Tony's Picks

Books: Gary A. Braunbeck, *Keepers* (Leisure), *In Silent Graves* (Leisure); Tananarive Due, *My Soul to Keep* (Eos); H. R. Knight, *What Rough Beast* (Leisure); Joseph M. Nassise, *Riverwatch* (Pocket)

Film: *Fallen*

1

2

3

4

5

6

7

8

9

10

Chapter 9

Telekinesis and Hypnosis: Chaos from Control

In the nineteenth century, Dr. Anton Mesmer popularized the idea of mesmerism (later known as hypnosis or hypnotism), whereby an adept could get others to do his or her bidding through "mind control." This pseudo-science, compounded with the reality that charismatic individuals can exert an almost superhuman influence over the minds of others, gave rise to stories about people who could use the powers of their minds to control those around them. One of the first fictional examples of this type of monster was a vampire, Count Dracula. In Bram Stoker's 1897 novel, this Transylvanian nobleman used the raw power of mesmerism on his female victims, Lucy Westerna and Mina Harker. Unlike the sophisticated Count Dracula in Tod Browning's 1931 film, who used charm and grace to control others, Stoker's Count is neither handsome nor suave. He relies solely on a superhuman ability to control the thought and physical movements of others.

In the early part of the twentieth century, it was widely accepted that hypnotism could be used to access an individual's subconscious mind and hopefully cure that person of psychological problems. However, one can argue that if hypnotism enables the mesmerist to access another's mind, then that ability has the potential for great evil. Horror authors who explore the themes of hypnotism, psychokinesis, psychic abilities, and telekinesis create situations in which misuse of this power is not only possible, but likely. After all, in the past century we have witnessed far too many examples of "charismatic" individuals who wreak havoc by controlling gullible followers. People such as Adolph Hitler, Charles Manson, Jim Jones, and David Koresh, to name a few, were living proof that it is possible for one person to psychologically and emotionally control the wills of many—with disastrous and tragic results. In one of Stephen King's fictional worlds, Johnny Smith understands this. In *The Dead Zone*, Smith emerges from a year-long coma with the ability to see the future of anyone he touches and realizes that presidential candidate Greg Stillson is the type of charismatic madman who will lead the world to the brink of doom if someone does not intervene in his fate.

Telekinesis is another type of mind control. Whereas hypnotism requires the use of a person to accomplish the hypnotist's desires, the individual with telekinetic abilities can move objects with his or her mind. What makes this power frightening is that in horror texts, typically the person with telekinetic abilities is an angry outcast who, pushed beyond the limits of endurance, goes "postal," ushering in chaos with his or her telekinetic abilities rather than with an AK-47. Stephen King's novel *Carrie* is an excellent example of the use of telekinesis to create horror. Carrie White, the butt of all jokes in high school and the recipient of extreme abuse at the hands of her fundamentalist Christian mother, explodes when her classmates play one too many pranks on her. She abuses her telekinetic abilities, in the process destroying her hometown of Chamberlain, Maine, as well as killing half of its citizens.

Average people are ill-equipped to defend themselves against an individual who can cause cars to swerve, make power lines break and fall to the ground, and stop a human heartbeat, simply by thinking about those things happening. Horror about being controlled by others or about becoming the victim of inanimate objects that have suddenly taken on a life of their own because of an outside force serves to remind readers that the loss of free will and control is always possible, sometimes with catastrophic results. This subgenre may be particularly geared toward American readers, for it threatens the loss of liberty, of the ability to control one's own actions and destiny.

The fascination with, as well as the fear of, the potential of the human brain could be one of the main appeals of this subgenre, as these texts often take on a pseudo-scientific tone. Human curiosity about psychic abilities in general, and specific abilities such as extrasensory perception (ESP), telepathic communication, mesmerism/hypnosis, and telekinesis has persisted in the face of scientific skepticism, so this type of literature has tremendous appeal to many readers. In addition, since the monsters in these texts are usually human beings, works in the subgenre are more likely to have sympathetic characters, typically societal misfits, who are pushed to the edge and develop psychic abilities in self-defense. Finally, the all-too-human desire to control others may appeal to some readers.

Note: Tales about psychics, clairvoyants, and telekinetically gifted people can also be found in the collections and anthologies described in chapter 18. Refer to the subject/keyword index for specific titles under the keywords *Mind Control, Parallel Universes, Precognition,* and *Psychics.*

Campbell, Ramsey.

Incarnate. *London: Little, Brown, 1992, ©1983. 490p. ISBN 0316904511.*
(See chapter 14, "Psychological Horror: It's All in Your Head.")

Clegg, Douglas.

Afterlife. *New York: New American Library, 2004. 261p. ISBN 0451411676.*
After the brutal murder of her husband, Julie Hutchinson begins to suffer from erotic nightmares and hideous hallucinations. She suspects that his murder may be related to his work in the 1970s on Project Daylight, in which experiments were conducted on children with ESP. Her family, the husband's mentally unstable ex-wife, and a television psychic help her to decipher the mystery, and it has to do with a secret society. **Similar titles:** *The Awakening,* Donna Boyd; *Shadow Coast,* Philip Haldeman; *Candles Burning,* Michael McDowell and Tabitha King; *The Door to December,* Dean Koontz.

Death—Grieving • Dreams • Mental Illness • Psychics • Psychosexual Horror • Revenge • Weird Science

The Hour before Dark. *New York: Leisure, 2002. 384p. ISBN 0843950447.*

As children, Nemo Raglan and his siblings played a game in which they were able to project their minds and explore unknown worlds. Years later, Nemo's father is brutally murdered in the family farmhouse in a small New England town, and the murderer leaves behind no physical evidence of his or her presence at the crime scene. But now there is an unseen presence in the house. Is it the thing that killed their father, or a message from beyond? **Similar titles:** The Fury Series, John Farris; *Firestarter*, Stephen King; *The Door to December*, Dean Koontz.

Childhood • Doppelgangers • Family Curse • Haunted Houses • Psychics

Farris, John.

The Fury Series.

Gillian Bellaver and Robin Sandza come from different worlds, but they are kindred spirits. Both possess potentially dangerous psychic abilities, and various governments and terrorist groups would do anything to exploit and control them. **Similar titles:** *The Hour before Dark*, Douglas Clegg; *Firestarter*, Stephen King; *The Door to December*, Dean Koontz.

Psychics • Terrorism

The Fury. *New York: Forge, 2000, ©1976. 334p. ISBN 0312877307.*

The daughter of one of the most politically affluent men in the world meets the son of one of the U.S. government's deadliest assassins. It's anything but a match made in heaven, since both have mastered extremely dangerous psychic abilities. But how do they keep from becoming pawns for various governments, each of which wants to use them as a weapon of mass destruction?

Espionage • Weird Science

The Fury and the Power. *New York: Forge, 2003. 348p. ISBN 0312877285.*

A young avatar named Eden Waring does battle with evil forces that desire to control her paranormal abilities. Meanwhile Mordant, also known as "The Dark Side of God," disguises himself as a Las Vegas stage magician. He has been creating unstoppable assassins by making shape-shifting imps out of unwitting audience members. Murders of several religious leaders bring Eden and her psychic detectives out of hiding.

Nevada—Las Vegas • Magic • Mind Control • Shape-shifters

Hamilton, Laurell K.

Burnt Offerings. *New York: Ace, 2007, ©1998. 376p. ISBN 0425218848.*
(See chapter 16, "Comic Horror: Laughing at Our Fears.")

Harris, Charlaine.

Definitely Dead. *New York: Ace Books, 2006. 324p. ISBN 0441014003.*
(See chapter 16, "Comic Horror: Laughing at Our Fears.")

King, Stephen.

Carrie. *London: Hodder, 2007, ©1974. 245p. ISBN 0340951419.*
Carrie White, a teen girl abused by her fanatically religions mother and by her peers at school, is the perpetual foul up and the butt of all jokes. But Carrie also has telekinetic powers that have lain dormant since she was five years old, and with the traumatic onset of her first menstruation, Carrie's telekinetic powers resurface. On the night of the Black Prom, she uses them in self-defense against her tormentors. The story is related through a combination of multiple eyewitness accounts and fictional scholarly studies. **Similar titles:** *Dragon Tears,* Dean Koontz; *Firestarter,* Stephen King; *Three Days to Never,* Tim Powers; *Carrie* (film).

Adolescence • Child Abuse • Documentary Techniques • High School • Maine—Chamberlain • Menstruation • Religion—Christianity—Protestantism • Revenge • Telekinesis

The Dead Zone. *London: Warner, 2001, ©1979. 467p. ISBN 0751504327.*
A small town schoolteacher is put into a lengthy coma after a car accident. When he emerges nearly a decade later, he has the ability to glimpse the future after touching someone. After shaking the hand of a charismatic politician, he sees that this man will ultimately destroy the world if he isn't stopped from winning office. **Similar titles:** <u>The Fury Series</u>, John Farris; *The Hour before Dark,* Douglas Clegg; *Firestarter,* Stephen King; *The Vision,* Dean Koontz; *The Dead Zone* (film).

Apocalypse • Politician as Character • Precognition • Psychics • Teacher as Character

Dreamcatcher. *New York: Scribner, 2001. 620p. ISBN 0743211383.*
(See chapter 12, "Technohorror: Evil Hospitals, Military Screw-Ups, Mad Scientists, and Alien Invasions.")

Firestarter. *New York: New American Library, 1980. 428p. ISBN 0670315419.*
An English teacher and his wife volunteer for a government experiment involving the test of a classified hallucinogen. Afterward they find they have special telepathic powers, and later that their daughter has telekinetic abilities. When the instructor begins to suspect that the government doctors are more dangerous than they look, all hell breaks loose. **Similar titles:** *The Hour before Dark;* Douglas Clegg; <u>The Fury Series</u>, John Farris; <u>The Eden Moore Trilogy</u>, Cherie Priest.

Mind Control • Parenting • Telepathy • Weird Science

The Shining. *New York: Pocket Books, 2002, ©1977. ISBN 0743437497.*
505p. (See chapter 7, "Demonic Possession: Satanism, Black Magic, and Witches and Warlocks: The Devil Made Me Do It.")

Koontz, Dean.

The Door to December. *New York: New American Library, 2002, ©1985. 518p. ISBN 0451205421.*
Laura answers her door one day to find police officers who tell her that her nine-year-old daughter, who was kidnapped by her father years before, has been

located. As it turns out, nine-year-old Melanie is nowhere to be found, but the body of her father has been located and mutilated. Laura then discovers that her daughter has been used as a guinea pig in sensory deprivation experiments, and that Melanie will be killed—unless she can find her first. **Similar titles:** *The Eyes of Darkness, Dragon Tears,* and *Mr. Murder,* Dean Koontz; *Firestarter,* Stephen King; *The Hour before Dark,* Douglas Clegg.

Kidnapping • Parenting • Weird Science

Dragon Tears. *New York: Berkley, 2006, ©1993. 412p. ISBN 0425208435.*
A young man discovers that he can use his telekinetic/telepathic powers to become "a new God," and he takes it upon himself to "thin out the herd" of humanity by ridding it of its handicapped and destitute. **Similar titles:** *The Door to December,* Dean Koontz; The Fury Series, John Farris; *Firestarter,* Stephen King.

Addictions—Drugs • Eugenics • Mind Control

The Eyes of Darkness. *New York: Berkley, 1996, ©1981. 369p. ISBN 0425153975.*
This early Koontz effort tells of a grieving mother being haunted by her son's accidental death. A year after twelve-year-old Danny was horribly mangled and killed in an accident, Tina Evans sees him in a car. When strange things begin happening in Danny's old room, Tina is faced with the possibility that her son is still alive. Koontz's writing is fast-paced and suspenseful. **Similar titles:** *Lost Boy, Lost Girl* and *In the Night Room,* Peter Straub; *The Loveliest Dead,* Ray Garton; *Dead Lines,* Greg Bear.

Afterlife, The • Death—Grieving • Nevada—Las Vegas • Parenting • Telepathy

The Mask. *Oxford: Isis Press, 1999, ©1981. 384p. ISBN 0753159538.*
(See chapter 7, "Demonic Possession: Satanism, Black Magic, and Witches and Warlocks: The Devil Made Me Do It.")

The Odd Thomas Novels.
(See chapter 16, "Comic Horror: Laughing at Our Fears.")

Lansdale, Joe R.

Lost Echoes. *New York: Vintage Crime, 2007. 341p. ISBN 0307275442.*
Getting over a childhood illness isn't easy for Harry Wilkes. Ever since he had inner ear problems, he has developed an ability to both see and hear violent events—to communicate with ghostly images. Now a college student, he has become a heavy drinker and is trying to mend his ways. But a visit from his childhood flame will challenge his chances of sobering up, as she wants him to help solve her father's death, which was dismissed as a suicide by the local sheriff. **Similar titles:** *The Dead Zone,* Stephen King; The Necroscope Series, Brian Lumley; *Come Fygures, Come Shadowes,* Richard Matheson; *The Sixth Sense* (film).

Addictions—Alcoholism • Police Officer as Character • Psychics • Texas

Lumley, Brian.

Necroscope: The Touch. *New York: Tor, 2006. 445p. ISBN 0765316099.*

A new story arc begins in this book when the now deceased Harry Keogh appears to Scott St. John, a spy for the British Secret Service, and makes him the new Necroscope. After a government official suffers evagination, a process by which his body is turned inside out, Scott must fight against the culprits, a race of psychically gifted aliens who are attempting to make God reveal himself by threatening to destroy the earth. **Similar titles:** *Halloweenland* and *Hallows Eve*, Al Sarrantonio; The Noble Dead Series, Barb Hendee and J. C. Hendee.

Aliens • England • Espionage • Keogh, Harry (character) • MI-5 • St. John, Scott (character) • Telepathy

Marsh, Richard (pseudonym used by Richard Bernard Heldman).

The Beetle. *Edited by Julian Wolfreys. Orchard Park, NY: Broadview Press, 2004, ©1897. 364p. ISBN 1551114437.*

The grandfather of modern horror icon Robert Aickman penned *The Beetle* in the same year that Dracula was written. This tale of a shape-shifting Asian stranger who stalks British politician Paul Lessingham in the streets of London is one of hypnotism and possession. The novel was initially more popular than Stoker's, and it remained in print until 1960. Narrated from the perspectives of multiple characters, this suspenseful classic is an exercise in early psychological terror. **Similar titles:** *The Collected Strange Stories*, Robert Aickman; *Green Tea and Other Ghost Stories*, Joseph Sheridan Le Fanu; *Tales from a Gas-Lit Graveyard*, Hugh Lamb (editor).

England—London • Hypnotism • Japanese Characters • Shape-shifters • Victorian Era

Matheson, Richard.

Stir of Echoes. *New York: Tor, 2004, ©1958. 223p. ISBN 0765308711.*

(See chapter 4, "Ghosts and Haunted Houses: Presences and Absences.")

Woman. *Colorado Springs, CO: Gauntlet, 2005. 125p. ISBN 1887368752.*

David, a radio psychologist, and his wife Liz, producer of a hit television show nominated for an Emmy, hold a pre-Emmy party. The tensions are high on this particular evening, as no one there is very likeable and the guests don't particularly like each other. But things come to a head when one of the guests brings Ganine, a young man who possesses a malefic energy. **Similar titles:** *Earthbound*, Richard Matheson; *Within the Shadows*, Brandon Massey; *One Rainy Night*, Richard Laymon.

California—Hollywood • Feminism • Psychologist/Psychiatrist as Character • Violence, Theories of

Nicholson, Scott.

They Hunger. *New York: Pinnacle-Kensington, 2007. 383p. ISBN 0786017139.*

An antiabortion bomber and his female accomplice flee a couple of FBI agents. They figure that they can lose the government agents by working with a troupe of whitewater rafters and moving swiftly along an Appalachian rapid. However, the river becomes the least of their worries when a mining explosion rips a hole in the mountainside, freeing a long-imprisoned colony of leather-winged, bloodthirsty creatures. **Similar titles:** The Straw Men Series, Michael Marshall; *Hunted Past Reason*, Richard Matheson; *'Salem's Lot*, Stephen King; *The Descent* (film).

Animals Run Rampant • Appalachia • Federal Bureau of Investigation • Subterranean Horror • Wilderness

Powers, Tim.

Three Days to Never. *New York: William Morrow, 2006. 420p. ISBN 0380976536.*

A twelve-year-old girl steals a videotape from the California home of her recently deceased grandmother. The tape, which is labeled as a Pee Wee Herman movie, is actually the only recording of a long-lost Charlie Chaplin film. The movie also has the ability to awaken in its viewer a latent telekinesis. Making matters worse, the family discovers that the grandmother was actually Einstein's lost daughter, and that the theft is now being investigated by the Israeli Secret Service and a special branch of the Mossad specializing in the Kabbalah. **Similar titles:** The Fury Series, John Farris; The Eden Moore Trilogy, Cherie Priest; *Come Fygures, Come Shadowes*, Richard Matheson.

Cursed Objects • Einstein, Albert (character) • Movie Industry • Multimedia—Videotape • Numerology • Parapsychology • War—World War II • Weird Science

Shayne, Maggie, Barbara Hambly, and Charlaine Harris.

Night's Edge. *Don Mills, ON: HQN, 2004. 377p. ISBN 0373770103.*
(See chapter 18, "Collections and Anthologies.")

Siodmak, Curt.

Donovan's Brain. *Mill Valley, CA: 1st Pulpless.com, 1999, ©1942. 182p. ISBN 1584450789.*
(See chapter 12, "Technohorror: Evil Hospitals, Military Screw-Ups, Mad Scientists, and Alien Invasions.")

Film

Carrie. *Brian DePalma, dir. 1976. 98 minutes.*

This faithful adaptation of Stephen King's first novel of the same name stars Sissy Spacek, Piper Laurie, John Travolta, Amy Irving, Nancy Allen, and Betty Buckley. Carrie is made into a misfit by her fanatically fundamentalist mother and spends her young life as the butt of everyone's jokes in the small town of Chamberlain, Maine. When sixteen-year-old Carrie has her first period while showering with the other girls in the locker room, her telekinetic powers are awakened, and her anger toward her tormentors culminates in their destruction. **Similar titles:** *Shadowland*, Peter Straub; *Carrie*, Stephen King.

Child Abuse • *High School* • *Maine—Chamberlain* • *Menstruation* • *Religion—Christianity —Protestantism* • *Revenge*

The Dead Zone. *David Cronenberg, dir. 1983. 103 minutes.*

A young schoolteacher, Johnny Smith (Christopher Walken), has an auto accident and loses five years of his life to a coma. When he awakens, he has gained psychic powers; he can see into other people's lives—past, present, and future—simply by touching them. At first he makes good use of his powers, helping the police, but he runs into problems when he foresees an apocalyptic future after shaking hands with an aspiring politician. **Similar titles:** *The Dead Zone*, Stephen King; <u>The Fury Series</u>, John Farris.

Politician as Character • *Precognition* • *Psychics* • *Teacher as Character*

Paperhouse. *Bernard Rose, dir. 1988. 92 minutes.*

(See chapter 17, "Everyday Horror: When the Mundane Becomes Monstrous.")

White Zombie. *Victor Halperin, dir. 1932. (black and white). 69 minutes.*

(See chapter 5, "Golem, Mummies, and Zombies: Wake the Dead and They'll Be Cranky.")

June's Picks

Books: John Farris, *The Fury* (Forge); Stephen King, *Carrie* (Hodder); Joe R. Lansdale, *Lost Echoes* (Vintage Crime)

Films: *Carrie, The Dead Zone*

Tony's Picks

Books: Stephen King, *Carrie* (Hodder); Stephen King, *The Shining* (Pocket Books); Tim Powers, *Three Days to Never* (William Morrow)

Chapter 10

Small Town Horror: Villages of the Damned

In our twenty-first-century world, chaos, ignorance, and superstition have been replaced by scientific knowledge and enlightenment. We place a higher value on human life than ever before; we have shunned cannibalism, torture, and in most first world nations, even capital punishment. We know that disease isn't an outward manifestation of sin, but something spread by viruses and bacteria, and we know that antibiotics and even virus-eating drugs can control many illnesses. At least this is the official story.

The ugly truth is that "civilized society" has not been an unqualified success. Even in first world countries, there are isolated individuals, and sometimes even isolated communities, untouched by twenty-first-century values, technology, and rationalism. Groups like the Amish and the Mennonites scorn modernity and often live without electricity, television, or cars. Much less quaint and much more dangerous are members of some religious sects, who refuse to seek medical care for their sick children, believing that God alone can cure illness, and certain small towns located off Southern interstates, places people are advised to avoid, as they are Ku Klux Klan strongholds. In towns like these, an unsuspecting traveler can fall victim to the Klan's own peculiar sense of justice.

In this chapter we describe works that explore the subgenre often referred to as small town horror. Small town horror results from the frightening realization that there are places away from home that are untouched by the accepted rules of civilized society, where any action, no matter how horrific, is possible. We have all felt this real fear at least once in our lives when we've traveled through deserted areas of highways, where the barren landscape is only sporadically punctuated by miniature hamlets. The film *I Spit on Your Grave* presents a fictional representation of one such place. A young female novelist vacations alone in a rural upstate New York resort area, only to be savagely gang raped and left for dead by young locals, who are considered fine specimens of manhood by other members of the town. She can only receive justice if she dispenses it herself, which she does in a way that is as methodical and elaborate as the crime that prompted it. In the cult classic film *Two Thousand Maniacs!*, the hapless traveling Yankees fail to feel this fear, believing that the South (at least for white people) is just a place of benign hospitality. So when these eight travelers are waved off the road by seemingly gracious locals to be the guests of honor in Pleasant Valley's annual festival, they have no idea that their hosts are actually the ghosts of Confederate civilians mowed down by the Union Army in the war's final days, that Pleasant Valley has not existed for the past century, and that they will be methodically exterminated in the festival's "games."

The relative isolation of such towns and villages makes them perfect for horrific events, which almost always occur (as slasher films teach us) when victims are separated from others. After all, the killing of wives to replace them with robots, in Ira Levin's *The Stepford Wives*, could only happen in small, insulated communities, where truly "no one can hear you scream," or more specifically, where those who hear you scream are in on the conspiracy. This is the realization that ultimately dawns on foolish Police Lieutenant Howie in Robin Hardy's *The Wicker Man*: no matter how civilized his society (the United Kingdom proper) may be, once he is on Summerisle, a pagan community in rural Scotland, he no longer makes the rules. On Summerisle, Howie is at the mercy of the locals and becomes part of their sacrificial ritual whether he agrees to be or not. In Elizabeth Massie's novel *Sineater*, members of a rural Appalachian community punish those who would abolish their quaint custom of isolating one individual living on the fringes of their society for the purpose of taking into himself the sins of the dead.

Small town horror reminds us of our own powerlessness within a larger community and of the dependence of the individual on others who make up society. This stands in stark contrast to the American myth of "rugged individualism," which implies that any one person can stand alone against the forces of conformity, no matter how outnumbered he or she might be. In addition, like antiquarian horror, small town horror reminds us that sometimes it is best not to snoop around too much, lest something unspeakable be unearthed. Newer versions of small town horror explore the conventions of the gothic, a mode of writing that is frequently set in small towns, with their stagnant environments characterized by a suffocating sense of malaise that covers everything like kudzu. Sarah Langan offers us an excellent example of this new gothicism in *The Keeper*, in which a woman who was once the beauty of a small Maine town has become the village whore. When she falls to her death, deceased residents and their pets return to life, bringing the town's long-hidden secrets with them. Other works inject the grotesque into the gothic. The characters and settings in Edward Lee's *Backwoods* and Tom Piccirilli's *Choir of Ill Children* are all exaggerated stereotypes, including snake handlers, moonshiners, and meth-addicted poor white trash.

Humans in general have a fear of being overpowered by society, for if there is any one emotion that can lead to a great sense of despair, it is a sense of helplessness, especially when placed in a new environment where it seems everyone else marches to a completely different drummer. In horror, a "you and me against the world" aesthetic is doomed to failure; this theme of relative isolation (and humans do, for the most part, share a universal fear of isolation) is the backbone of small town horror. Because the odds are so strongly weighed against the protagonist in these tales, there is a tendency to use nonformulaic endings. Because they have the decked stacked against them, the "hero(ine)s" of this subgenre do not always win.

Baldwin, Barbara J., Jerri Garreston, Linda Maul, and Sheri L. McGathy.

Trespassing Time: Ghost Stories from the Prairie. *Manhattan, KS: Ravenstone Press, 2005. 239p. ISBN 0965971260.*
>(See chapter 18, "Collections and Anthologies.")

Campbell, Ramsey.

The Darkest Part of the Woods. *New York: Tor, 2004, ©2002. 368p. ISBN 0765346826.*
>Dr. Lennox Price and his family move to the isolated locale of Goodmanswood, in England, and soon Lennox loses his mind and is committed to Mercy Hill, a local asylum. Meanwhile, his archivist daughter begins to investigate the eeriness of the place, which is haunted by the presence of something local children call the sticky man. She finds out that its history is tied to that of an alchemist who once attempted to create a direct link to the powers of the universe. **Similar titles:** *The Hungry Moon*, Ramsey Campbell; The Straw Men Series, Michael Marshall; *Wicked Things*, Thomas Tessier.
>
>*Alchemy • Archivist as Character • England • Magic • Mental Illness*

The Hungry Moon. *London: Headline, 1995, ©1986. 360p. ISBN 0747246270.*
>In a dreary Northern England town, new preacher Godwin Mann arrives one day, bringing with him an intolerant fundamentalism—which the locals swallow hook, line, and sinker. As one of his first duties, he travels into a cursed pit, which folklore has it is inhabited by an ancient pagan being. When Mann emerges from the pit, the locals believe his exorcism to be successful. Little do they know that his body is now the host of one ticked-off, evil entity. **Similar titles:** *The Darkest Part of the Woods* and *The Influence*, Ramsey Campbell; *The Exorcist*, William Peter Blatty.
>
>*Clergy as Character • Demons • England • Religion—Christianity • Religion—Paganism*

Scared Stiff: Tales of Sex and Death. *New York: Tor, 2002, ©1997. 239p. ISBN 0765300044.*
>(See chapter 18, "Collections and Anthologies.")

Clark, Simon.

Stranger. *New York: Leisure, 2003. 418p. ISBN 0843950765.*
>(See chapter 12, "Technohorror: Evil Hospitals, Military Screw-Ups, Mad Scientists, and Alien Invasions.")

Clegg, Douglas.

Neverland. *Modesto, CA: Bloodletting Press, 2003, ©1991. 408p. ISBN 0972085912.*
>Beau, along with his parents and siblings, takes a summer vacation to stay with an aunt and grandmother. There, Beau meets his cousin Sumter, who shows him an old crate containing a creature that calls itself Lucy. The

boys nickname the shack where they found the crate Neverland, but they soon find out that Neverland is a living entity that is hungry for human flesh. **Similar titles:** *The Traveling Vampire Show*, Richard Laymon; *Prey*, Graham Masterton; *Practical Demonkeeping*, Christopher Moore.

Childhood • Demons • Family Curse • Islands • Secret Sin

Curlovich, John Michael.

Steel Ghosts. *New York: Berkley, 2005. 312p. ISBN 0425200701.*
(See chapter 4, "Ghosts and Haunted Houses: Dealing with Presences and Absences.")

Farris, John.

Phantom Nights. *New York: Tor, 2005. 301p. ISBN 0765307782.*
With his dying breath, Priest Howard accuses his sleazy son Leland of being a thief. Unfortunately, Leland realizes that his father's nurse Mally overheard the accusation. Fearing that Mally has criminal evidence that could sink his budding political career, he follows Mally home, then rapes and kills her. However, there is a witness to this crime—a mute fourteen-year-old boy. **Similar titles:** *Bag of Bones*, Stephen King; *Spirit*, Graham Masterton; *Intensity*, Dean Koontz.

African American Characters • Disabilities—Muteness • Rape • Revenging Revenant • Tennessee

Gay, William.

Twilight. *San Francisco, CA: McAdam/Cage, 2006. 224p. ISBN 1596920580.*
In 1951, when the bootlegger father of teenaged siblings Corrie and Kenneth Tyler is burned to death in their small Tennessee town, they seek the services of Fenten Breece, the local undertaker. Kenneth believes that Fenten has been less than honest with them when he witnesses the undertaker removing something from their father's grave. Seeking proof of Fenten's dishonesty, they disinter their father, only to discover something much more unsettling—evidence of necrophilia. **Similar titles:** *Black Fire*, James Kidman; The *Lebo Coven*, Steven Mark Rainey; *Sineater*, Elizabeth Massie.

Extortion • Funeral Industry • Gothicism • Necrophilia • Organized Crime • Tennessee

Golden, Christopher.

The Shell Collector. *Baltimore, MD: Cemetery Dance Publications, 2006. 128p. ISBN 158767114X.*
In a small New England coastal fishing village, the dead are found disinterred, with parts missing, and a small pile of shells is always found near the disturbed graves. Suffice it to say that there is little to help the living when they attempt to stop a creature that comes ashore after a red tide. The Shell Collector is a creature covered in shells and has a humanoid shape—but the humans that it touches find that the shells begin to swarm their own flesh. **Similar titles:** *Drowned Night*, Chris Blaine; *The Terror*, Dan Simmons; *Crooked Tree*, Robert Charles Wilson.

Funeral Industry • Maritime Horror • Massachusetts

Hand, Stephen.

The Texas Chainsaw Massacre: A Novelization. *Nottingham, UK: Black Flame, 2004. 416p. ISBN 1844160602.*

> (See chapter 11, "Maniacs and Sociopaths, or the Nuclear Family Explodes: Monstrous Malcontents Bury the Hatchet.")

Hardy, Robin, and Anthony Shaffer.

The Wicker Man. *New York: Three Rivers Press, 2006, ©1978. 285p. ISBN 0307382761.*

> A devout Christian, Lieutenant Howie of the Scottish police receives an anonymous letter informing him of the disappearance of a young girl on Summerisle, a small, remote island. Howie investigates and finds that the locals will talk about anything except the missing girl, leading him to believe foul play has occurred and a conspiracy exists, led by Lord Summerisle. While avoiding what he considers heathen practices, Howie matches his wits against the locals, planning to break the case during their harvest festival. **Similar titles:** *Wicked Things*, Thomas Tessier; *The Remains of an Altar*, Phil Rickman; *Dark Hollow*, Brian Keene; *Sineater*, Elizabeth Massie.
>
> *Human Sacrifice • Islands • Police Officer as Character • Religion—Christianity—Protestantism • Religion—Paganism • Scotland*

Harvey, Kenneth J.

The Town That Forgot How to Breathe. *New York: Picador, 2005, ©2003. 471p. ISBN 0312342225.*

> (See chapter 17, "Everyday Horror: When the Mundane Becomes Monstrous.")

Hodgson, William Hope.

The House on the Borderland. *London: Gollancz, 2002, ©1908. 200p. ISBN 0575073721.*

> (See chapter 8, "Mythological Monsters and 'The Old Ones': Invoking the Dark Gods.")

Izzo, Anthony.

Evil Harvest. *New York: Pinnacle, 2007. 464p. ISBN 0786018755.*

> Some dark and malevolent but humanoid beings live in Lincoln, New York. For years they have whetted their appetites only occasionally, claiming victims at random, and usually choosing people who wouldn't be missed, like newly arrived families. But as the time of Harvest draws near, a mysterious stranger comes to town, with a tenacious determination to avenge himself on the monsters that destroyed his family. **Similar titles:** *The Harvest*, Scott Nicholson; *The Body Snatchers*, Jack Finney; *Wicked Things*, Thomas Tessier.
>
> *Replicants • Revenge • Secret Sin • Shape-shifters*

10

Jackson, Liam.

Offspring. *New York: St. Martin's/Dunne, 2006. 290p. ISBN 031235570X.*
As children go missing all over the country, four men receive individual messages bringing them to Abbotsville, Tennessee, where they discover that they are the offspring of humans and angels, and are involved in an epic battle between demons and heavenly hosts. **Similar titles:** *The King of Ice Cream*, Robert Wayne McCoy; *The Stand*, Stephen King; *Blood Angel*, Justine Musk.

Angels • Demons • Satan (character) • Tennessee

Ketchum, Jack (pseudonym used by Dallas Mayr).

The Crossings. *Baltimore, MD: Cemetery Dance, 2003. 100p. ISBN 1587670674.*
(See chapter 15, "Splatterpunk: The Gross Out.")

Offspring. *New York: Leisure, 2007, ©1999. 293p. ISBN 0843958642.*
(See chapter 15, "Splatterpunk: The Gross Out.")

Kidman, James.

Black Fire. *New York: Leisure, 2004. 339p. ISBN 0843953276.*
When Eddie Farris kills his abusive father in self-defense, his troubles have only just begun. Dark and brooding as a result, he causes his girlfriend to flee the small town of Black Hills, Pennsylvania. Soon after, the townspeople treat him as if he were the bogeyman. Seven years pass before Rachael returns, with the son he never knew in tow, claiming that his presumably deceased father has been stalking her. Is she telling the truth, or is someone setting Eddie up so that he will have a complete mental breakdown? **Similar titles:** *Twilight*, William Gay; *The Lebo Coven*, Stephen Mark Rainey; *You Don't Scare Me*, John Farris.

Child Abuse • Diary Format • Domestic Violence • Pennsylvania • Stalkers • Writer as Character

Kimball, Michael.

The Way the Family Got Away. *New York: Four Walls, Eight Windows, 2000. 143p. ISBN 1568581556.*
(See chapter 17, "Everyday Horror: When the Mundane Becomes Monstrous.")

King, Stephen.

Desperation. *New York: Viking, 1996. 690p. ISBN 0670868361.*
(See chapter 8, "Mythological Monsters and 'The Old Ones': Invoking the Dark Gods.")

The Mist. *New York: Signet, 2007, ©1985. 230p. ISBN 0451223292.*
(See chapter 12, "Technohorror: Evil Hospitals, Military Screw-Ups, Mad Scientists, and Alien Invasions.")

Skeleton Crew. *London: Warner, 2001, ©1985. 624p. ISBN 0751504386.*
(See chapter 18, "Collections and Anthologies.")

Knight, J.

Risen. *New York: Kensington, 2004. 407p. ISBN 0786016124.*
(See chapter 5, "Golem, Mummies, and Zombies: Wake the Dead and They'll Be Cranky.")

Kumar, Jay C.

Dark Woods. *New York: Berkley, 2004. 311p. ISBN 0425197077.*
(See chapter 13, "Ecological Horror: Mother Nature Has Her Revenge.")

Laws, Stephen.

Ferocity. *New York: Leisure, 2007. 342p. ISBN 084395695X.*
(See chapter 13, "Ecological Horror: Mother Nature Has Her Revenge.")

Laymon, Richard.

Blood Games. *New York: Leisure, 2003. 467p. ISBN 0843951818.*
(See chapter 11, "Maniacs and Sociopaths, or the Nuclear Family Explodes: Monstrous Malcontents Bury the Hatchet.")

Lebbon, Tim, and Steve Niles.

30 Days of Night: A Novelization. *New York: Pocket Star Books, 2007. 325p. ISBN 1416544976.*
Fans describe this novelization of the popular movie as "creepy and atmospheric." Sheriff Eben Olemaun and Deputy Stella Olemaun, a husband and wife law enforcement team in the northernmost town in the United States, are faced with a dilemma: should they stay during the thirty days of night that define the winter in that area, or head south, as many of the locals do? Complicating matters is the fact that a troupe of merciless vampires is getting ready to descend on the local citizenry, taking advantage of the dark and isolation. **Similar titles:** *The Time of Feasting*, Mick Farren; *'Salem's Lot*, Stephen King; *The Terror*, Dan Simmons; *The Shell Collector*, Christopher Golden.

Alaska • Marriage • Police Officer as Character • Vampire Hunters

LeBlanc, Deborah.

Grave Intent. *New York: Leisure, 2005. 374p. ISBN 0843955538.*
Michael Savoy ekes out a modest living running the family funeral home in Brusly, Louisiana, and with his wife, he manages to turn the business around. Then the patriarch of a traveling clan of gypsies requests burial services for his daughter and specifies that she be buried with a mysterious and valuable gold coin that is to pay her passage into the next world. But the coin is stolen, and all hell breaks loose. **Similar titles:** *Bag of Bones*

1

2

3

4

5

6

7

8

9

10

and *Thinner*, Stephen King; *Unspeakable*, Graham Masterton: <u>The Grimm Funeral Home Series</u>, R. Patrick Gates.

Afterlife, The • Cursed Objects • Funeral Industry • Gypsies • Louisiana—Brusly • Revenging Revenant

A House Divided. *New York: Leisure, 2006. 326p. ISBN 0843957301.*

A greedy developer purchases a run-down mansion in Mississippi, splits it in half, and moves it forty miles away to a small Louisiana town, where he makes the structure into two separate rental houses. But when a house is haunted, splitting it in half is not an effective form of exorcism. Instead, the spirits now plague the families who reside in both houses, and the developer also does not get off unscathed. A spider bite from the spirit-infested home causes him to slowly go insane. **Similar titles:** *Twisted Branch*, Chris Blaine; *Stir of Echoes*, Richard Matheson; *The House on Orchid Street*, T. M. Wright.

African American Characters • Contractor as Character • Families • Haunted Houses • Louisiana • Precognition • Psychics

Morbid Curiosity. *New York: Leisure, 2007. 351p. ISBN 0843958286.*

Two identical twins are sent to live with their grandparents in a small Louisiana town after the death of their father and the institutionalization of their mother. When the two don't fit in with the others at school, they eagerly accept an invitation from one of their more popular classmates—win popularity using magic. But the twins soon learn that this magic is a dangerous force, not to be trifled with. **Similar titles:** *Black Creek Crossing*, John Saul; *Haunted Ground*, Stephen Gresham; *Shadowland*, Peter Straub; *Sineater*, Elizabeth Massie.

Louisiana • Religion—Voodoo • Twins • Witchcraft

Lee, Edward.

The Backwoods. *New York: Leisure, 2005. 340p. ISBN 0843954132.*

When her sister's abusive husband is suddenly murdered, Patricia White must return to her hometown to help her sibling with the family business. But this is not an easy homecoming for Patricia, because she was raped before leaving home. On top of that, Patricia must also deal with sudden, inexplicable problems among the squatters, who have their own strange brand of religion and have always been teetotalers, but are suddenly developing an affinity for methamphetamine. **Similar titles:** <u>The Ghost Road Blues Trilogy</u>, Jonathan Maberry; *Choir of Ill Children* and *November Mourns*, Tom Piccirilli; *Sineater*, Elizabeth Massie.

Addictions—Drugs • Psychosexual Horror • Rape • Religion • Virginia

Levin, Ira.

The Stepford Wives. *New York: HarperTorch, 2004, ©1972. ISBN 0060738197.*

Joanna Eberhart and her husband relocate from New York City to the idyllic town of Stepford, home of good schools and low taxes, but Joanna notices that her female neighbors are a bit too enthusiastic about homemaking. She suspects a sinister but improbable reason for their behavior. Levin's novel leaves more up to the reader's imagination than does the film of the same name. **Similar titles:** *Rosemary's Baby*, Ira Levin; *The House That Jack Built*, Graham Masterton; *Invasion of the Body Snatchers*, Jack Finney; *The Stepford Wives* (film).

Connecticut • Feminism • Marriage • Mental Illness • Replicants • Suburbia

Lorrah, Jean.

Blood Will Tell. *Dallas, TX: BenBella, 2003, ©2001. 277p. ISBN 1932100032.*
(See chapter 6, "Vampires and Werewolves: Children of the Night.")

Maberry, Jonathan.

Ghost Road Trilogy.

The most haunted small town in America is awash with tourists. As it prepares for its annual Halloween celebration, ghosts wait in the surrounding corn fields. **Similar titles:** *Needful Things,* Stephen King; *The Backwoods,* Edward Lee; *Hallow's Eve,* Al Sarrantonio; *Blair Witch 2: Book of Shadows* (film).

Domestic Violence • Holidays—Halloween • Pennsylvania • Secret Sin • Serial Killers

 Ghost Road Blues. *New York: Pinnacle, 2006. 478p. ISBN 0786018151.*

Pine Deep, Pennsylvania, is known as the most haunted town in America because it was once stalked by a serial killer known as the Reaper. Now angry ghosts stalk its fields. Maberry revels in showing the darker side of small town life, including domestic violence and religious fanaticism.

Revenging Revenant

Dead Man's Song. *New York: Pinnacle, 2007. 480p. ISBN 078601816X.*

Pine Deep will soon be plagued by something worse than a serial killer. The murderous ghosts who beset the city on the eve of its annual Halloween celebration continue to build a cosmic evil that will only conclude when a curse is fulfilled.

Apocalypse

Massey, Brandon.

Dark Corner. *New York: Dafina, 2004. 449p. ISBN 0758202490.*
(See chapter 6, "Vampires and Werewolves: Children of the Night.")

Massie, Elizabeth.

Sineater. *New York: IBooks, 2004, ©1994. 396p. ISBN 074349783X.*

In Appalachia, the pious still depend on the sineater to cleanse the newly departed of sin so they can go to heaven. Traditionally, the sineater has led a solitary existence in the woods, only approaching humanity to partake of plates of food left on the chests of the dead. But the current sineater has broken with tradition and has a wife and family, and this change has brought about a spate of disappearances and murders in this small mountain town. **Similar titles:** *Morbid Curiosity,* Deborah LeBlanc; *The Backwoods,* Edward Lee; *The Wicker Man,* Robin Hardy and Anthony Shaffer.

Childhood • Cults • Religion—Christianity • Virginia

McCoy, Robert Wayne.

The King of Ice Cream. *Waterville, ME: Five Star, 2004. ISBN 1594141487.*
> The small town of Mill Run, Kentucky, is home to the prestigious University of Mill Run, the oldest church on the East Coast, Our Lady of Sorrows Cathedral, and a quaint ice cream parlor run by a fallen angel who is addicting the local populace to his strawberry ice cream as part of a convoluted plot to get back in God's good graces by giving hell back to Him. **Similar titles:** *Needful Things*, Stephen King; *The Stupidest Angel*, Christopher Moore; *Offspring*, Liam Jackson.
>
> *Academia • Angels • Demons • Kentucky*

Michaels, Barbara, and Elizabeth Peters.

Prince of Darkness. *New York: HarperTorch, 2005, ©1969. 336p. ISBN 0060745096.*
> Middleburg has a secret history of sorcery, and when a visitor becomes involved with the ward of noted a local author, its citizens fear their secret sin will become public. But to what ends will they go to make sure that their skeletons are kept in the closet, where they belong? This gothic romance introduces readers to the concept of a modern witches' coven based in the sordid past of colonial history. **Similar titles:** The Wendy Ward Series, J. G. Passarella; The Witch Child Series, Celia Rees; The Sorority Trilogy, Tamara Thorne.
>
> *Maryland • Secret Sin • Witchcraft • Writer as Character*

Moore, James A.

Blood Red. *Northborough, MA: Earthling Publications, 2005. 336p. ISBN 0976633914.*
> Jason Soulis, a mysterious older gentleman and the new town arrival, has plans for some of the younger ladies at the local university. He recruits them as escorts and uses them to seduce each and every member of the local clergy. But he is no ordinary pimp, and his nefarious needs are not about money: he wants to create a crisis of faith, so that his kind can move in on the residents. He may be succeeding—the town's citizenry start disappearing, replaced by golden-eyed, wraithlike versions of themselves. **Similar titles:** *Needful Things*, Stephen King; *The Body Snatchers*, Jack Finney; *The Unblemished*, Conrad Williams and Jeff VanderMeer.
>
> *Clergy as Character • Epidemics • New England • Replicants • Rhode Island • Zombies*

Fireworks. *New York: Dorchester, 2003, ©2001. 376p. ISBN 0843952474.*
> (See chapter 12, "Technohorror: Evil Hospitals, Military Screw-Ups, Mad Scientists, and Alien Invasions.")

Nassise, Joseph M.

Riverwatch. *New York: Pocket, 2003, ©2001. 355p. ISBN 0743470966.*
> (See chapter 8, "Mythological Monsters and 'The Old Ones': Invoking the Dark Gods.")

Nicholson, Scott.

They Hunger. *New York: Pinnacle-Kensington, 2007. 383p. ISBN 0786017139.*
> (See chapter 9, "Telekinesis and Hypnosis: Chaos from Control.")

Partridge, Norman.

Dark Harvest. *New York: Tor, 2007, ©2006. 169p. ISBN 9780765319111.*

Pumpkin Boy is the pumpkin-headed effigy who stands guard over the crops of a small Midwestern farming community, coming to life once a year on Halloween night to run a gauntlet of the hamlet's male youth, who must all try to cut him down before he reaches the finish line at the town church. Each year one lucky boy stops Pumpkin Boy and is rewarded for his prowess and good luck with the chance to leave the dusty little burg for good, but on this Halloween night in 1963, will the ritual end differently? **Similar titles:** *Hallows Eve, Toybox,* and *Horrorween,* Al Sarrantonio; *The Wicker Man,* Robin Hardy and Peter Anthony.

Holidays—Halloween • Midwest, The • Secret Sin

Piccirilli, Tom.

A Choir of Ill Children. *New York: Spectra, 2004, ©2003. 240p. ISBN 0553587196.*

Thomas is the wealthiest man in the small town of Kingdom Come, a swampy gothic Southern hamlet filled with a cast of Faulknerian characters. There he lives with his conjoined triplet brothers, who serve as a sort of Delphic oracle to the town; a trio of witches; and a local Bible-thumping minister who speaks in tongues and is fond of appearing in public nude. And now the carnival is coming to town, bringing with it impending menace. **Similar titles:** *November Mourns,* Tom Piccirilli; *The Backwoods,* Edward Lee; *Trespassing Time: Ghost Stories from the Prairie,* Barbara J. Baldwin, Jerri Garreston, Linda Maul, and Sheri L. McGathy.

Florida • Gothicism • South, The • Witchcraft

November Mourns. *New York: Bantam, 2005. 281p. ISBN 055358720X.*

Shad Jenkins spent two years in prison for beating up the man who tried to rape his sister Megan. Now that he's been released, he learns that Megan was found murdered without a scratch on her body. Shad must return to the backwater Appalachian community of Moon Run Hollow, home to snake handlers, moonshiners, and inbred grotesques, in order to investigate. **Similar titles:** *A Choir of Ill Children,* Tom Piccirilli; *The Backwoods,* Edward Lee; *The Way the Family Got* Away, Michael Kimball; *Bedbugs,* Rick Hautala.

Appalachia • Families • Gothicism • Rape • Revenge

Pinborough, Sarah.

Breeding Ground. *New York: Leisure, 2006. 339p. ISBN 0843957417.*

(See chapter 13, "Ecological Horror: Mother Nature Has Her Revenge.")

The Taken. *New York: Leisure Books, 2007. 323p. ISBN 0843958960.*

(See chapter 8, "Mythological Monsters and 'The Old Ones': Invoking the Dark Gods.")

Rainey, Stephen Mark.

The Lebo Coven. *Waterville, ME: Five Star, 2004. 278p. ISBN 1594142270.*

After ten years, Barry Riggs returns to his small Virginia hometown to find that his estranged brother Matt, his only living relative, has disappeared. The only clue to what happened is the word "lebo" scrawled in blood on a wall of their ransacked family home. Locals believe that Matt's disappearance is the work of Ren, a drifter and suspected satanist whom Matt allegedly rented a room to. Soon Barry discovers that his family house is the nexus of an ancient evil. **Similar titles:** *Twilight*, William Gay; *Black Fire*, James Kidman; *November Mourns*, Tom Piccirilli.

Families • Kabalism • Religion—Satanism • Virginia • Witchcraft

Sarrantonio, Al.

Hallows Eve. *Forest Hills, MD: Cemetery Dance, 2004. 270p. ISBN 1587670771.*

After his career is suddenly ruined and he loses his lover, thirty-year-old photographer Corrie Phaeder finds himself on a train to his hometown, Orangefield. He is met not with parades, but with a horrifying, surreal messenger who has the body of a scarecrow and the face of a living pumpkin. It seems that the epitome of evil, Samhain, is about to take over the town on Halloween. **Similar titles:** *Once Upon a Halloween*, Richard Laymon, *Horrorween*, Al Sarrantonio; *Deathbringer*, Bryan Smith.

Holidays—Halloween • Pennsylvania • Psychics • Samhain (character)

Shepard, Lucius.

Softspoken. *San Francisco: Night Shade Books, 2007. 179p. ISBN 1597800732.*

(See chapter 14, "Psychological Horror: It's All in Your Head.")

Simmons, William P.

By Reason of Darkness. *Canton, OH: House of Dominion, 2003. 282p. ISBN 1930997450.*

(See chapter 18, "Collections and Anthologies.")

Smith, Bryan.

Deathbringer. *New York: Leisure, 2006, 342p. ISBN 0843956771.*

A stranger arrives in the small town of Dandridge, and soon the dead are rising from their graves to hunt the living. This stranger is the Deathbringer, one of the Reapers who had a falling out with the supreme deity who created him, so he re-animates the dead into a grotesque parody of the living rather than harvest souls. It's up to Dandridge police officer Kent Gowan to stop him and restore order to his town. **Similar titles:** *'Salem's Lot* and *Needful Things*, Stephen King; *Hallows Eve*, Al Sarrantonio.

Death (character) • Immortality • Police Officer as Character • Zombies

Tessier, Thomas.

Wicked Things. *New York: Leisure, 2007. 243p. ISBN 0843955600.*
A hard-drinking P.I. narrates this story, complete with in-your-face inter-rogations, womanizing, and insurance company fraud. Sent to the idyllic town of Winship to investigate sixteen claims, he discovers that Winship is not an average small town; it is virtually impossible to locate, even with the aid of a map. Yet it has miraculously prospered economically, while its neighboring hamlets have withered; and on any given night its streets are filled with strange sounds issuing forth from the cemetery, accompanied by an eerie green glow. **Similar titles:** *The Hungry Moon*, Ramsey Camp-bell; The Straw Men Series, Michael Marshall; *The Darkest Part of the Woods*, Ramsey Campbell.

Cemeteries • Human Sacrifice • Insurance Industry • Stripper as Character

Wells, H. G.

The Croquet Player. *Lincoln: University of Nebraska Press, 2004, ©1937. 109p. ISBN 0803298420.*
(See chapter 17, "Everyday Horror: When the Mundane Becomes Mon-strous.")

Film

Hostel. *Eli Roth, dir. 2005. 94 minutes.*
(See chapter 15, "Splatterpunk: The Gross Out.")

House of 1000 Corpses. *Rob Zombie, dir. 2003. 89 minutes.*
(See chapter 15, "Splatterpunk: The Gross Out.")

I Spit on Your Grave (Day of the Woman). *Mark Zarchi, dir. 1978. 100 minutes.*
Also known as *Day of the Woman, I Hate Your Guts,* and *The Rape and Re-venge of Jennifer Hill*, this much written about film was banned in Austria, Germany, Finland, and the United Kingdom for its graphic representation of a brutal gang rape and a woman's equally brutal revenge. Jennifer Hill, a young writer from New York City, rents a cabin for the summer in up-state New York, only to be brutally gang raped and left for dead by a group of local men. But Jennifer's assailants are unwilling to take respon-sibility for their actions, and indeed, don't even understand what they've done wrong when she confronts each man, so they must pay with their lives instead. This is not a film for the faint of heart. The lack of fancy spe-cial effects or even background music makes the rape scene especially re-alistic. Buster Keaton's granddaughter Camille Keaton stars. **Similar titles:** *The One Safe Place*, Ramsey Campbell; *The Funhouse*, Dean Koontz; *Starr Bright Will Be with You Soon*, Joyce Carol Oates.

New York • Rape • Revenge • Secret Sin • Writer as Character

The Mist. *Frank Darabont, dir. 2007. 126 minutes.*

After a major storm, an unnatural mist settles over a small Maine town. A man and his son are trapped in a supermarket along with other inhabitants, as it becomes evident that there is a malignant presence lurking in the mist, and that those who venture out do so at their own risk. Then strange creatures begin to appear and start killing and eating humans. This movie is based on the Stephen King short story of the same name. **Similar titles:** *The Mist*, Stephen King; *Shadow Coast*, Philip Haldeman.

Maine • Parenting • Weather • Weird Science

Two Thousand Maniacs! *Herschell Gordon Lewis, dir. 1964. 87 minutes.*

This campy classic is a Southern version of *Brigadoon*. In the centennial month of the conclusion of the Civil War, two carloads of Northerners find themselves detoured from the main highway, heading into the small town of Pleasant Valley, where they are enthusiastically greeted by a crowd of boisterous Southerners, grinning and waving Confederate flags. Unbeknownst to the Northerners, their hosts are actually revenging revenants, ghosts of people slaughtered by Union soldiers, who will now have their vengeance. **Similar titles:** *The Backwoods*, Edward Lee; *Choir of Ill Children* and *November Mourns*, Tom Piccirilli.

Confederacy, The • Georgia • Revenging Revenant • South, The • War—American Civil War

The Wicker Man. *Robin Hardy, dir. 1973. 88 minutes.*

The people of Summerisle have returned to their ancient roots and practice pagan fertility rites to ensure the success of their crops. But lately the sacrifices made to the gods haven't been sufficient, and their crops are failing. The gods demand more. Dour and puritanical Sergeant Howie is sent to the island to investigate a missing girl who might be the next sacrifice to the gods. However, Howie soon discovers that he has been tricked into participating in the yearly ritual. Edward Woodward, Britt Ekland, and Christopher Lee star in this brilliant film, which was later novelized by Robin Hardy and Anthony Shaffer. **Similar titles:** *The Wicker Man*, Robin Hardy and Anthony Shaffer; *Sineater*, Elizabeth Massie; *Desperation*, Stephen King.

Human Sacrifice • Police Officer as Character • Religion—Christianity—Protestantism • Religion —Paganism • Scotland

June's Picks

Books: Christopher Golden, *The Shell Collector* (Cemetery Dance Publications); Robin Hardy and Anthony Shaffer, *The Wicker Man* (Three Rivers Press); Deborah LeBlanc, *Grave Intent* (Leisure); Ira Levin, *The Stepford Wives* (Harper Torch); Elizabeth Massie, *Sineater* (IBooks)

Films: *I Spit on Your Grave, Two Thousand Maniacs!, The Wicker Man*

Tony's Picks

Books: Robin Hardy and Peter Schafer, *The Wicker Man* (Three Rivers Press); Al Sarrantonio, *Hallows Eve* (Cemetery Dance)

Films: *Two Thousand Maniacs!, The Wicker Man*

Chapter 11

Maniacs and Sociopaths, or the Nuclear Family Explodes: Monstrous Malcontents Bury the Hatchet

The maniac tale is a relatively new subgenre of horror. Like a tale of psychological horror, the maniac narrative is not the story of a monstrous supernatural being. As a matter of fact, the maniac looks like you and me. Instead, the impetus of the maniac narrative is the savagery of the killer, which makes readers question whether he or she is indeed human. Thus, there is a strong correlation between the titles in this chapter and those in chapter 15, "Splatterpunk: The Gross Out."

The maniac tale has its origins in the Renaissance, when at the public execution of particularly notorious criminals, the Crown published broadsides detailing the heinous crimes of the condemned and distributed them to the crowd. These broadsides were intended to serve as cautionary tales to the sovereign's subjects, showing them that criminal behavior, which was an attack on the authority of the king himself, would be harshly dealt with. However, the crowd resisted the king's authority by manufacturing its own meaning: the broadside did not so much reinforce the power of the king as call attention to the criminal who, even briefly, defied this power. This fascination with the exploits of the criminal was eventually the basis for both true crime fiction and the modern maniac tale, which is more about crime and deviance than it is about punishment or justice.

Early examples of the subgenre, such as some of Edgar Allan Poe's excellent short stories, do not attempt to understand the maniac's behavior. Rather, their lack of explanation presumes the existence of a criminal mind. For example, Poe's "The Cask of Amontillado" merely marvels at the cruelty of the narrator, who walls up his former friend alive for some unspecified sin against him. Even the killer cannot remember exactly what his friend Fortunado did to insult him, but he "avenges" himself nonetheless. Poe's "The Tell-tale Heart" never attempts to explain why the narrator is so provoked by his victim's "vulture eye," though he does show how the killer's guilt over the crime is his own undoing.

Later tales of mania examine the mechanism that created the monster as much as they emphasize the heinous quality of his or her actions. Perhaps the relative newness of this subgenre causes writers to use another modern tool to explain the maniac's behavior: psychoanalysis. Classic psychoanalytic theory lends itself to novels that analyze the monster human, for it places the formation of the individual personality within the family, putting special emphasis on the role of the mother. Therefore, it is not surprising to see the genesis of the maniac often attributed to an overbearing mother and/or weak father. For example, in Alfred Hitchcock's film *Psycho* (based on Robert Bloch's novel of the same name), the prototype for the modern slasher film, Norman Bates is warped to psychosis by an absent father and a clinging and rejecting, critical and demanding mother. Contemporary writers of maniac fiction continue this trend, although their psychology is a bit more sophisticated: they explore the role of all family members, of the community, of trauma, and of culture in general, in the creation of sociopaths. In *Hannibal Rising*, Thomas Harris's latest installment in his The Silence of the Lambs Series, we see how Lecter's childhood experiences with starvation and violence at the close of World War II in Lithuania set him on the path to cannibalism. In the words of Hillary Rodham Clinton, these writers realize that "it takes a village" to raise a child—or, in this case, to create a monster.

The nuclear family is also a relatively new phenomenon, seeing its halcyon days in the post–World War II 1940s and in the "happy days" of the 1950s. The nuclear, nonextended family, isolated within its suburban ranch house and allegedly self-sufficient, was celebrated through the new medium of television, in fifties situation comedies such as *Leave It to Beaver* and *The Donna Reed Show*; and even touted by the "experts" as the norm to which all families should aspire. The nuclear family was the Cold War era's answer to communism. However, father doesn't always know best, and Mom isn't always content to stay home and clean while children continually tug at her skirts. When Mom and Pop burn out or find that they don't have all the answers, they often have no one to turn to for help. The result of these instances where the stress of everyday life becomes overwhelming is the production of seriously disturbed children, or perhaps maniacal parents. In Peter Straub's novella *Blue Rose*, one of the purest examples of the subgenre, the dysfunctional Beevers family produces Harry, an intelligent and charismatic child who is able to hypnotize people into killing either themselves or others. Big John, a deeply racist neighbor who shares his worldview with young Harry, is also responsible for his creation. Big John gives Harry the attention he is not getting from his parents, and so has the opportunity to share with the boy his belief that Adolph Hitler was one of the greatest men of the twentieth century. Harry's own parents' inability to actually parent adds fuel to the fire. Mr. Beevers returns from World War II suffering from post-traumatic stress disorder, and he can't hold a steady job due to his alcoholism, let alone interact with his family in a productive way. As a result, Harry's shrewish and unfulfilled mother is the family's sole breadwinner. Because she also is too self-absorbed and resentful to guide her son down a better path, he grows up to lead troops to gun down children in Vietnam.

Women are not immune to these dark forces either. In Stephen King's *Carrie* (found in chapter 9), the main character's isolation in her own nuclear family allows her anger to fester. Using her telekinetic powers, she literally causes the town to explode. The townspeople's isolation in their own nuclear families prevents them from rescuing Carrie from her abusive situation. When neighbors first hear Mrs. White's screams during childbirth and later Carrie's shouts while being beaten by her mother, they choose to "mind their own business," explaining that they thought the noise was due to "holy rolling" on the part of the family, rather than the sound of someone in genuine distress. Like Straub's and King's exemplary texts, works in this subgenre acknowledge that every family unit has a dark side that surfaces be-hind closed doors, and that children from these types of families will grow up, leave home, and turn order into chaos. In the film *High Tension*, a young woman suffering from a severe case of multiple personality disorder concocts an elaborate hallucination to explain the brutal deaths of the family of the woman she loves. And the film *Monster* fictionalizes the exploits of female se-rial killer Aileen Wurnos.

The subgenre has evolved greatly in a short period of time, with a recent trend toward the creation of the abnormal personality as an organic phenome-non. In other words, maniacs, like paranoid schizophrenics, are born, not made—although a dysfunctional family can exacerbate the situation. Here horror tackles the old nature versus nurture question. In Ramsey Campbell's novel *The One Safe Place*, it really isn't important *why* the Fancy family torments the innocent Travises. Perhaps class and circumstance have made them into vi-olent criminals, but the reason for their pathology just isn't the focus of the novel. Instead, the real issue is that the British criminal justice system is incapa-ble of protecting law-abiding citizens from dangerous deviants, in part per-haps because it makes too great an attempt to understand the criminal mind, rather than figuring out how to effectively incarcerate this type of person.

Finally, the maniac tale comes full circle with stories such as Poppy Z. Brite's *Exquisite Corpse*, Bret Easton Ellis's *American Psycho*, and the films *Ted Bundy, Gacy*, and *Dahmer*. None of these narratives attempts to rationalize the existence of the maniac. Brite's serial killers, Jay Byrne and Andrew Compton, are not the products of broken homes or victims of castrating mothers. They are merely a natural, unpleasant variation in the human species, no different from the gay men or vampires who populate Brite's other fictional worlds. The ex-cesses of Ellis's protagonist, Patrick Bateman, go unnoticed in the world of 1980s New York City, itself characterized by excesses in greed and violence. And the films *Ted Bundy, Gacy*, and *Dahmer* are only concerned with examining the crimes of these infamous serial killers, not formulating explanations for their aberrant behavior.

Fans of maniac fiction enjoy the subgenre for various reasons. Obviously the most effective appeal of this kind of literature is to inquisitiveness. Humans are naturally curious about the aberrant psychology of serial killers; this is the reason that beheadings on a Canadian bus and on a Greek vacation resort get top billing on online news sites in the midst of a presidential campaign, as they did on both CNN's and MSNBC's sites between July 30 and August 1, 2008. In part, this is due to the gore (not referring to our former vice president) appeal; in part, it seems to be due to an all-too-human delight in the abnormal. The se-rial killer as monster also has great marketing potential because of our cultural interest in psychology—in being able to explain all aspects of human behavior (so it helps that in this type of fiction, the monsters are human). Authors of these texts have kept up with modern psychology, with stories that range from explaining away violent behavior as a product of a bad home to tales that argue people can simply be born bad. But perhaps the greatest appeal of the maniac tale is that the fears on which it plays are more aligned with "real" fears, such as the fear of random violence or a murderous spouse.

Note: Stories about maniacs, sociopaths, and dysfunctional families can also be found in the collections and anthologies described in chapter 18 and in chapter 15, as well as the appendix under "Thriller," Detective Fiction," and even "Historical Fiction." Refer to the subject/keyword index for specific titles under the keywords *Rape*, *Serial Killers*, *Spree Killers*, *Stalkers*, and *Torture*.

Allen, John Paul, and Alan M. Clark.

Gifted Trust. *Duluth, GA: Biting Dog, 2003. 300p. ISBN 0972948503.*

Max Belote works as a successful publishing agent—until he begins hearing voices that tell him to abuse and kill children. Edward Paine is a beloved teacher until the voices speak to him too. A seventh-generation manifestation of a serial killer who is the pawn of evil forces is driven to kill yet again: Virago, the reincarnated maniac, is chilling and vicious. **Similar titles:** *Valley of Lights*, Stephen Gallagher; *The Parasite*, Ramsey Campbell; *The Servants of Twilight*, Dean Koontz; *Fallen* (film).

Child Abuse • Child Molesters • Publishing Industry • Reincarnation • Serial Killers • Teacher as Character

Anscombe, Roderick.

The Secret Life of Lazslo, Count Dracula. *New York: St. Martin's, 2006, ©1994. 416p. ISBN 0312357664.*

(See chapter 14, "Psychological Horror: It's All in Your Head.")

Arnzen, Michael.

Ⓑ **Grave Markings.** *New York: Dell, 1994. 451p. ISBN 0440213398.*
(See chapter 15, "Splatterpunk: The Gross Out.")

Bailey, Dale, and Jack Slay Jr.

Sleeping Policemen. *Urbana, IL: Golden Gryphon Press, 2006. 208p. ISBN 193084641X.*

(See chapter 17, "Everyday Horror: When the Mundane Becomes Monstrous.")

Bloch, Robert.

American Gothic. *New York: iBooks, 2004, ©1974. 256p. ISBN 0743479157.*

Based on historical accounts of real-life serial killer Herman Mudgett, *American Gothic* tells the story of Dr. Gordon G. Gregg, who lured his victims into his castle-like home to torture and murder them, during the Chicago World's Fair of 1892. **Similar titles:** *Psycho*, Robert Bloch; *The Devil in the White City*, Eric Larson; *Off Season*, Jack Ketchum; *Gacy: The Crawl Space* (film).

Illinois—Chicago • Popular Culture—World's Fair • Serial Killers • Torture

The Psycho Series

Norman Bates, a loner whose condition is exacerbated by a domineering mother, kills "loose" young women who arouse him. But this mama's boy is no wimp; he is impossible to stop, as even the penal system cannot curtail his violence. He returns again and again to finish the job of cleansing society. **Similar titles:** *American Gothic*, Robert Bloch; *The Face That Must Die*, Ramsey Campbell; *Psycho II* and *Psycho House*, Robert Bloch; *Ed Gein* (film); *Psycho* (film); *Peeping Tom* (film).

Bates, Norman (character) • Mental Illness • Serial Killers • Slasher

Psycho. *New York: iBooks, 2003, ©1959. 232p. 224p. ISBN 0743459075.*

Norman makes the mistake of murdering a woman who disappeared with $40,000 of her boss's money, so detectives show up at the Bates Motel to investigate. Told through several first-person narratives, Bloch's novel is based on the Ed Gein murders in the 1950s.

Bates Motel • California—Fairvale • Matricide/Patricide • Psychosexual Horror

Psycho II. *New York: iBooks, 2003, ©1982. 224p. ISBN 0743474724.*

Norman Bates, the psychotic young southwest motel manager who murdered women and dumped their bodies in a local swamp in *Psycho*, escapes from the mental institution where he was being held for observation. He makes a B-line to Hollywood to disrupt the filming of a movie about his life and his criminal insanity, turning the movie set into a reality program.

California—Hollywood • Horror Movie Industry

Psycho House. *New York: iBooks, 2004, ©1990. 224p. ISBN 0743475305.*

Ten years after Norman Bates's death, the old Bates Motel has reopened as a macabre tourist trap. A teenaged girl is found stabbed to death. Meanwhile, true crime writer Amelia Haines, who has come to Fairvale to write a book about Norman, sees the recent murder as an opportunity to make a name for herself.

Bates Motel • California—Fairvale • Journalist as Character

Boyne, John.

Crippen. *New York: St. Martin's Griffin, 2007. 368p. ISBN 0312343590.*

Boyne re-creates the celebrated Crippen murder case: in 1910, Hawley Crippen hacked to pieces his socialite wife and then tried to escape to Canada with his much younger mistress, disguised as father and son. But Scotland Yard inspector Walter Drew is on their tail in a race across the Atlantic. **Similar titles:** *The Ghost in the Eiffel Tower*, Oliver Bleys; *The Dante Club*, Matthew Pearl; *The Open Curtain*, Brian Evenson.

Crippen, Hawley (character) • Edwardian Era • England—London • Scotland Yard

Brite, Poppy Z.

Exquisite Corpse.
(See chapter 15, "Splatterpunk: The Gross Out.")

Burton, Peter, ed.

Bend Sinister: The Gay Times Book of Disturbing Stories. *London: Gay Men's Press, 2002. 390p. ISBN 1902852427.*
(See chapter 18, "Collections and Anthologies.")

Campbell, Ramsey.

The Count of Eleven. *New York: Tor, 1992. 310p. ISBN 0312853505.*
Family man Jack Orchard has a run of bad luck that threatens to tear apart his life. When he finds a discarded chain letter, he decides that it must be the cause of his bad luck, so to make amends he quickly follows the instructions on the letter—to get it out to thirteen other people without divulging the list. Whenever anyone stands between Jack and his task, however, he goes over the edge. **Similar titles:** *The Face That Must Die*, Ramsey Campbell; *The Voice of the Night*, Dean Koontz; *After Midnight*, Richard Laymon; *American Psycho* (film).

Numerology • Obsession • Serial Killers

The Doll Who Ate His Mother. *London: Headline, 1993, ©1976. 290p. ISBN 0747240604.*
A schoolteacher's brother is killed in a bizarre car accident, wherein his arm is sliced off, and then the limb mysteriously disappears. She begins to suspect that a strange-looking man she saw right before the accident took the arm, and eventually joins forces with three other people, who also claim to have had loved ones victimized by this same man. But all are unaware that he is the intended successor to a demonic cult leader. **Similar titles:** *The Nameless* and *The Parasite*, Ramsey Campbell; *The Servants of Twilight*, Dean Koontz.

Cannibalism • England—Liverpool • Parapsychology • Religion—Cults • Teacher as Character • Writer as Character

The Face That Must Die. *Lakewood, CO: Millipede Press, 2006, ©1979. 301p. ISBN 1933618027.*
Horridge is a young loner haunted by faces, by horrifying emotional experiences as a child, and by the voice of Craig, a serial killer. Sooner or later "Horridge the Horror," as he was called by cruel children in his youth, will lose his sanity. This is Campbell's subtle treatment of a psychotic killer. **Similar titles:** *Psycho*, Robert Bloch; *Blue Rose* and *Shadowland*, Peter Straub; *Zombie*, Joyce Carol Oates; *The Butcher Boy* (film).

Childhood • Gay/Lesbian/Bisexual Characters • Homoeroticism • Serial Killers

The Last Voice They Hear. *New York: Forge, 1998. 384p. ISBN 0312866119.*
Television journalist Geoff Davenport is getting mysterious phone calls from his brother, who ran away when he was eighteen. For Geoff, these calls are particularly disturbing because a serial killer has been murdering happily married couples in the area, and the brother claims to be the killer. This is a typical

atmospheric, character-driven tale by Campbell. **Similar titles:** *The One Safe Place*, Ramsey Campbell; *Mr. Murder*, Dean Koontz; *Desert Places*, Blake Crouch.

England—London • Families • Journalist as Character • Serial Killers

The Nameless. *New York: Warner, 1992, ©1985. 278p. ISBN 0708852572.*

Barbara Waugh, a literary agent in London, finds out that her daughter has been kidnapped by members of a cult in Scotland. As people who try to aid her in recovering her daughter are killed, Barbara realizes that she is quickly running of out of time—because this particular cult "initiates" its members at thirteen, and her daughter is twelve. **Similar titles:** *The Parasite*, Ramsey Campbell; *Age of Consent*, Howard Mittelmark; *Red Angel*, Andrew Harper.

England—London • Kidnapping • Parenting • Psychologist/ Psychiatrist as Character • Religion—Cults • Scotland

The One Safe Place. *New York: Tor, 1997, ©1995. 401p. ISBN 0812545559.*

The Travis family immigrates to England in search of a peaceful life, only to be stalked by the Fancys, a family of petty criminals. The Travises go to the proper authorities for help, but the police are unable to protect them in this supposedly nonviolent society that bans guns and violent films. Here, the mundane is made newly frightening. **Similar titles:** *The Last Voice They Hear*, Ramsey Campbell; *Desperation*, Stephen King; *Sleeping Policemen*, Dale Bailey and Jack Slay Jr.; *Night of the Hunter* (film).

England • Parenting • Revenge • Violence, Theories of

Secret Stories. *Hornsea, UK: PS Publishing, 2005. 419p. ISBN 1904619525.*

Dudley has his first short story published by a newly formed magazine after winning a contest, but not everyone approves of his writing, which always involves the graphic killing of women. It turns out that Dudley has followed the old saw to write what he knows—Dudley is a serial killer. This extremely convoluted character study features some dark comic moments. **Similar titles:** *The Count of Eleven*, Ramsey Campbell; *American Psycho*, Bret Easton Ellis; *Psycho*, Robert Bloch; *American Psycho* (film); *The Butcher Boy* (film).

England—Liverpool • Parenting • Serial Killers • Writer as Character

Silent Children. *New York: Forge, 2000. 352p. ISBN 0312870566.*

Hector Wollie, a contractor in the town of Jericho Close, has a taste for bringing peace to young children he feels have been abused by their parents. A pillow over the face is just fine, although a knife across the throat of a noisy kid may be called for, while Hector soothes them by singing a lullaby as he snuffs out their lives. **Similar titles:** *Seize the Night*, Dean Koontz; *Gifted Trust*, John Paul Allen and Alan M. Clark; *The Dead Letters*, Tom Piccirilli.

Child Molesters • Childhood • England • Parenting • Serial Killers • Torture

Christopher, Shane (pseudonym used by Matthew Costello).

The Kinsella/ Rodriguez Novels.

Reporter Mari Kinsella and detective David Rodriguez are the Mulder and Scully of the NYPD. They are good at getting to the truth, even when that truth involves the occult and the supernatural. **Similar titles:** *The Laughing Man*, T. M. Wright; *Incarnate*, Ramsey Campbell; <u>The Charlie Parker Mysteries</u>, John Connolly; <u>The Joe Pitt Novels</u>, Charlie Huston.

Journalist as Character • New York—New York City • Police Officer as Character • Serial Killers

In Dreams. *New York: Jove, 2006. 281p. ISBN 0515141283.*

Five apparent strangers are found together—tortured to death in the cellar of a seedy New York apartment. Kinsella realizes that the five shared one thing: they all had the same dream of dying. Meanwhile, Rodriguez is forced to follow any lead he can, including the dream angle, so they begin working together. But they work against the clock, for Kinsella has recently begun to have a death dream.

Dreams • Torture

Nowhere. *New York: Berkley, 2007. 312p. ISBN 0425215881.*

Rodriguez and Kinsella are given yet another bizarre case. A serial killer has transported himself through time, from the past to present-day New York City. All the murders have no witnesses and no clues. The investigation leads them to conclude that Jack the Ripper is behind these murders—and perhaps behind the Black Dahlia killing in 1947 in Hollywood. A fan favorite, this novel is intriguing and ingenious.

Jack the Ripper (character) • Time Travel • Weird Science

Clegg, Douglas.

Afterlife. *New York: New American Library, 2004. 261p. ISBN 0451411676.*

(See chapter 9, "Telekinesis and Hypnosis: Chaos from Control.")

Connolly, John.

 Every Dead Thing. *New York: Simon & Schuster, 1999. 395p. ISBN 0684857146.*

(See chapter 15, "Splatterpunk: The Gross Out.")

Cox, Michael.

The Meaning of Night: A Confession. *New York: Norton, 2006. 703p. ISBN 0393062031.*

(See chapter 14, "Psychological Horror: It's All in Your Head.")

Crouch, Blake.

The Andrew Thomas Novels.

Andrew Thomas, a successful crime novelist, receives a mysterious missive that ultimately reunites him with his twin brother Orson, who has been missing for over a decade. Turns out Orson knows a great deal about gory crimes, since he is a full-blown serial killer. **Similar titles:** *The Bone Parade*, Mark Nykanen; *The Last Voice They Hear*, Ramsey Campbell; *Velocity* and *Intensity*, Dean Koontz.

Doppelgangers • Mental Illness • Serial Killers • Thomas, Andrew (character) • Twins • Writer as Character

Desert Places: A Novel of Terror. *New York: Thomas Dunne Books, 2004. 280p. ISBN 0312286449.*

Thomas is led to the body of a woman who recently disappeared and is buried on his property. The note that gave him the directions is from Orson, who then kidnaps his brother, hoping to "educate" him.

Locked Doors. *New York: Thomas Dunne Books, 2005. 310p. ISBN 0312317999.*

Horror writer Andrew Thomas had a good life, until his mentally deranged twin framed him for murder. Now he has been hiding out in Alaska for seven years, writing the tale of his innocence, while a local author who recognizes him plans to pen a true crime novel. Meanwhile, the kidnapping of Andrew's former girlfriend and a mass murder make him think that his twin is out to get him again, so he travels to North Carolina, setting the stage for a confrontation.

Alaska—Yukon Territories • North Carolina

D'Ammassa, Don.

Dead of Winter. *Waterville, ME: Five Star, 2007. 303p. ISBN 1594144958.*
(See chapter 17, "Everyday Horror: When the Mundane Becomes Monstrous.")

Davis, Grubb.

The Night of the Hunter. *London: Prion, 1999, ©1953. 275p. ISBN 1853753203.*

A psychotic traveling evangelist marries the widow of a recently executed bank robber in the hopes of finding the stolen money he hid before his capture. When he can't discover the whereabouts of the money from his new bride, he kills her and tries to pry the information from her two children, who travel across the country to elude their murderous stepfather. Davis's novel was made into a stylistic and atmospheric film of the same name in 1955, starring Robert Mitchum. **Similar titles:** *Shattered*, Dean Koontz; *Sleeping Policemen*, Dale Bailey and Jack Slay Jr.; The Corbin Family Novels, James A. Moore; *The Night of the Hunter* (film); *The Stepfather* (film).

Clergy as Character • Great Depression, The • Religion—Christianity • Serial Killers • Stalkers

Delany, Samuel R.

Hogg. *Normal, IL: FC2, 2004. 268p. ISBN 1573661198.*
   (See chapter 15, "Splatterpunk: The Gross Out.")

De Lint, Charles.

Mulengro: A Romany Tale. *New York: Orb, 2003, ©1985. 400p. ISBN 0312873999.*
   (See chapter 8, "Mythological Monsters and 'The Old Ones': Invoking the Dark Gods.")

De Lint, Charles (writing as Samuel M. Key).

From a Whisper to a Scream. *New York: Orb, 2003, ©1992. 320p. ISBN 0765304341.*
   A supernatural serial killer is murdering teenaged hookers and upsetting the peaceful city of Newford, where newspaper photographer Jim McGann works. McGann believes he has a clue to the killer's identity, and he begins an investigation based on various crime scene photos he has at his disposal. But he soon finds himself investigating the possibility that an evil spirit is behind the killings. **Similar titles:** *The Mountains of Madness*, Hugh B. Cave; *A Terrible Beauty*, Graham Masterton; *Play Dead*, Anne Frasier.

   Child Molesters • Journalist as Character • Religion—Voodoo • Revenging Revenants • Serial Killers

Denton, Bradley.

Blackburn: A Novel. *New York: Picador, 2007, ©1993. 304p. ISBN 031242695X.*
   (See chapter 17, "Everyday Horror: When the Mundane Becomes Monstrous.")

Estleman, Loren D.

Dr. Jekyll and Mr. Holmes. *New York: iBooks, 2001, ©1997. 203p. ISBN 0743423925.*
   The queen herself requests Sherlock Holmes and his sidekick, Dr. Watson, to look into the strange case of Stevenson's evil twin story. Could it be that a tale that was largely taken to be fiction was actually a science experiment gone awry? Is Hyde responsible for the savage murder of a Victorian gentleman? **Similar titles:** *99 Coffins*, David Wellington; *The Dante Club*, Matthew Pearl; *Crippen*, John Boyne; *Curtains of Blood*, Robert J. Randisi.

   Alternative Literature • Holmes, Sherlock (character) • Hyde, Edward (character) • Jekyll, Henry (character) • Serial Killers • Watson, John H. (character)

Evenson, Brian.

The Open Curtain. *Minneapolis, MN: Coffee House Press, 2006. 223p. ISBN 1566891884.*
   (See chapter 14, "Psychological Horror: It's All in Your Head.")

Farris, John.

You Don't Scare Me. *New York: Forge, 2007. 302p. ISBN 0312850646.*
(See chapter 4, "Ghosts and Haunted Houses: Dealing with Presences and Absences.")

(See chapter 4, "Ghosts and Haunted Houses: Dealing with Presences and Absences.")

Fahy, Thomas.

Night Visions. *New York: Dark Alley, 2004. 292p. ISBN 0060594624.*
Haunted by memories of a brutal attack, insomniac Samatha Ranvali has not slept in months. She finds relief through an experimental study with a group called Endymion's Circle, where she is successfully treated, but it seems that with each night of newfound sleep, she has visions of attacks that are similar to the one that victimized her and killed a friend. **Similar titles:** *Insomnia*, Stephen King; *Black House*, Stephen King and Peter Straub; *The Face of Fear* and *The Vision*, Dean Koontz.

Dreams • Insomnia • Serial Killers

Fleming, Robert.

Fever in the Blood. *New York: Dafina/Kensington, 2006. ISBN 0758212399.*
Eddie was raised by drug-dealing addicts, and his abusive mother prostituted herself to further support her habit. When rival drug dealers slaughter the family, including Eddie's two sisters, he is the only survivor. He is even considered fortunate, because in the aftermath a congressman adopts him into his family. But his early childhood environment has left indelible marks on Eddie, who before the age of twenty has become a prolific serial killer, murdering women he believes to be whores. **Similar titles:** *Cris Cross*, Evie Rhodes; *Psycho*, Robert Bloch; *Starr Bright Will Be with You Soon*, Joyce Carol Oates.

Addictions—Drugs • Child Abuse • Mental Illness • Serial Killers

Fowler, Christopher.

Full Dark House. *New York: Bantam, 2003. 356p. ISBN 0553803875.*
When John May's eighty-year-old partner Arthur Bryant is killed in an explosion at the North London Peculiar Crimes Unit, he flashes back to their first case in the 1940s during the Blitz. During the Palace Theater's production of *Orpheus in the Underworld*, a dancer was found killed, her feet severed from the rest of her body, and this was just the first of many murders that decimated the cast of the production. **Similar titles:** *Curtains of Blood*, Robert J. Randisi; <u>The Charlie Parker Mysteries</u>, John Connolly; <u>The Joe Pitt Novels</u>, Charlie Huston.

England—London • Police Officer as Character • Scotland Yard • Serial Killers

11

12

13

14

15

16

17

18

19

20

Franklin, Tom.

Smonk, or Widow Town: Being the Scabrous Adventures of E. O. Smonk & the Whore of Evangeline in Clarke County, Alabama, Early in the Last Century. *New York: Morrow, 2006. 254p. ISBN 006084681X.*

In 1911, when murdering rapist E. O. Smonk is ordered to stand trial for his crimes in Old Texas, Alabama, there is hell to pay. Smonk's goons kill the men of the town and set their friend free, and lawman Will McKissick pursues Smonk through the Gulf Coast. Meanwhile Evangeline, a teenaged prostitute and skilled killer, arrives in Old Texas, pursued by a posse. Ultimately the chaos exposes the sordid past of this town, home to a one-armed preacher, a rabid dog, and a church full of dead boys dressed in their Sunday best. **Similar titles:** *Mad Dog Summer and Other Stories, The Shadows of Kith and Kin,* and *God of the Razor,* Joe R. Lansdale; *The Crossings,* Jack Ketchum.

Alabama • Clergy as Character • Gothicism • Prostitute as Character • Serial Killers • Texas • West, The

Frasier, Anne.

Play Dead. *New York: New American Library, 2004. 372p. ISBN 0451411374.*

Someone is drugging unsuspecting male escorts so that they seem dead, even as their minds remain intact and awake, and some of these victims are ending up on a table in the coroner's office. Detective Elise Sandburg and her partner David Gould, a loose cannon to say the least, follow leads to a priestess—and a college professor who did research on the drug. Eventually the officers end up in the dangerous voodoo underground. **Similar titles:** *The Mountains of Madness,* Hugh B. Cave; *A Terrible Beauty,* Graham Masterton; *From a Whisper to a Scream,* Charles De Lint.

Georgia—Savannah • Gullah Culture • Magic • Police Officer as Character • Prostitute as Character • Religion—Voodoo • Torture • Zombies

Gagliani, W. D.

Wolf's Trap. *New York: Dorchester, 2006. 373p. ISBN 0843957026.*

(See chapter 6, "Vampires and Werewolves: Children of the Night.")

Gerlach, Steve.

Rage. *New York: Leisure, 2004. 342p. ISBN 084395311X.*

Twenty-three-year-old Ben is a powder keg just waiting for someone to light the fuse. He's never had a girlfriend; his relationship with his parents is strained; and in general, he is unable to find satisfaction from anything in his life. When the woman he believes is his soul mate dumps him, his rage threatens to become out of control. **Similar titles:** *Havoc After Dark: Tales of Terror,* Robert Fleming; *The Shadows Kith and Kin,* Joe R. Lansdale; *The Count of Eleven,* Ramsey Campbell; *Fade to Black* (film).

Childhood • Families • Librarian as Character • Spree Killers

Girón, Sèphera.

Mistress of the Dark. *New York: Leisure, 2005. 325p. ISBN 0843955473.*
In this twisted fictional diary, Abigail Barnum recounts her recent reloca-
tion to New York City, where she works as a waitress in a tourist bar that
has an Adults Only back room. Most of her newfound friends are strippers and drag queens; and her private life is anything but normal. As a
side effect of her abuse of drugs and her penchant for kinky sex, Abigail
begins to hear voices and even hallucinate. But few suspect just how dangerous she is: anyone she touches has very little hope of staying alive.
Similar titles: *Starr Brite Will Be with You Soon,* Joyce Carol Oates; *The Long
Last Call,* John Skipp; *Fever in the Blood,* Robert Fleming; *Monster* (film).

*Addictions—Drugs • Dreams • Epistolary Format • New York—New York City •
Psychosexual Horror • Serial Killers • Waitress as Character*

Greenberg, Martin H., Isaac Asimov, and Joseph D. Olander, eds.

100 Malicious Little Mysteries. *New York: Sterling, 2004, ©1981. 432p. ISBN
1402711018.*
(See chapter 18, "Collections and Anthologies.")

Hand, Stephen.

The Texas Chainsaw Massacre: A Novelization. *Nottingham, UK: Black
Flame, 2004. 416p. ISBN 1844160602.*
A group of youths returning from Mexico come very close to running over
a disoriented girl who is walking in the middle of the road. The traumatized girl commits suicide in their van. But it's the aftermath of her actions
that brings about the true horror. As the group seeks help, they find only
insanity, running afoul of the Hewitts, the family that had tortured the
girl, making her delirious. **Similar titles:** *Freddy vs. Jason,* Damien Shan-
non, Mark Swift, and Stephen Hand; *King Kong,* Edgar Wallace and
Merian C. Cooper; *The Off Season,* Jack Ketchum; *The Texas Chainsaw Massacre* (film).

Cannibalism • Families • Road Trips • Secret Sin • Texas

Harper, Andrew.

Night Cage. *New York: Leisure, 2004. 310p. ISBN 0843952881.*
The Darden State Hospital contains some of the state's most dangerous
mental patients. When a nearby forest fire necessitates that they be relocated for their safety, a mother and son team of murderers manages to
"disappear" during the frenzy. Planning to escape to freedom through the
hospital's maze of underground tunnels, the two find the "night cage," a
now disused space where once brutal experiments were carried out on inmates. It is in this space that Officer Jane Laymon must hunt for the duo.
Similar titles: *Red Angel,* Andrew Harper; *Psycho II,* Robert Bloch; *Locked
Doors,* Blake Crouch.

*California • Laymon, Jane (character) • Medical Horror • Mental Illness • Police Officer
as Character*

Red Angel. *New York: Dorchester-Leisure, 2003. 358p. ISBN 084395275X.*

Trey Campbell, a corrections officer who has just returned to his job after his family was stalked and attacked by a female inmate, and Jane Laymon, a rookie police officer, team up to catch the Red Angel, an enigmatic serial murderer of children who ties duck wings to his young victims and sets them up for show. When Campbell discovers a connection between the Red Angel and a violent inmate named Scoleri, he decides to enlist his help. **Similar titles:** *The Silence of the Lambs*, Thomas Harris; *Night Cage*, Andrew Harper; *The Nameless*, Ramsey Campbell.

Child Molesters • Laymon, Jane (character) • Mental Illness • Police Officer as Character • Prisons • Psychologist/Psychiatrist as Character • Serial Killers

Harris, Thomas.

Black Sunday. *New York: New American Library, 2005, ©1975. 311p. ISBN 0451217411.*

In Harris's first novel, terrorists plot to blow up the Super Bowl, where 80,000 fans and the president of the United States are in attendance. When this novel was published thirty-eight years ago, Harris's plot was considered improbable. *Black Sunday* was made into a film of the same name in 1977. **Similar titles:** *Innocent Blood*, Graham Masterton; The Straw Men Series, Michael Marshall; *Horror: The Best of the Year*, John Betancourt (editor).

Federal Bureau of Investigation • Police Officer as Character • Popular Culture—Super Bowl • Terrorism

The Silence of the Lambs Series.

Will Graham, a former FBI agent with a talent for "seeing" into the minds of serial killers, and FBI agents Jack Crawford and Clarice Starling, pit their intellects against the likes of Hannibal "The Cannibal" Lecter, an ex-academic/psychiatrist who knows every aspect of the human mind—both the normal and aberrant ones. This is the maniac series against which all others must be judged. **Similar titles:** *Psycho*, Robert Bloch; *The Nameless*, Ramsey Campbell; The Pendergast Novels, Douglas Preston and Lincoln Child; *Black Sunday*, Thomas Harris.

Federal Bureau of Investigation • Lecter, Hannibal (character) • Police Officer as Character • Psychologist/Psychiatrist as Character • Serial Killers

Red Dragon. *New York: Dutton Adult, 2006, ©1981. 411p. ISBN 0440206154.*

Former FBI agent Will Graham, the man who captured Hannibal Lecter, is persuaded to come out of retirement to stop another serial killer, the Red Dragon. To stop the Red Dragon before he slaughters another family in his multi-state killing spree, Graham must use his extreme empathy, which allows him to actually "see" what the killer was doing at the time of the murder.

Body Modification—Tattoos • Graham, Will (character) • Police Procedural

The Silence of the Lambs. *London: Arrow, 2002, ©1988. 338p. ISBN 0099446782.*

Rookie FBI agent Clarice Starling, with the help of convicted serial killer Hannibal Lecter, must catch serial killer Buffalo Bill, who has kidnapped a senator's daughter. But to be an effective FBI agent, Starling must confront her own deepest fears as well. Readers find Harris's storytelling both literate and engaging.

Cannibalism • Crawford, Jack (character) • Gay/Lesbian/Bisexual Characters • Police Procedural • Starling, Clarice (character)

Hannibal. *New York: Random House Large Print, 2005, ©1999. 646p. ISBN 0375728341.*

This sequel to *The Silence of the Lambs* finds the good doctor Lecter alive and well. Meanwhile, Clarice Starling is being hung out to dry for the mistakes of the bureau, which is still unable to deal with women as colleagues. This novel, which focuses more on Hannibal Lecter's past crimes than on his ability to find serial killers, humanizes the enigmatic doctor by presenting us with victims who richly deserved their nasty ends.

Cannibalism • Childhood • Crawford, Jack (character) • Deformity • Epic Structure • Gay/Lesbian/Bisexual Characters • Italy • Pigs • Starling, Clarice (character)

Hannibal Rising. *New York: Delacourt, 2006. 323p. ISBN 0385339410.*

In this prequel, Harris's "Portrait of the Cannibal as a Young Man," we see the early manifestations of his preternatural intelligence. The good doctor is haunted by the fate of his baby sister Mischa during the final days of World War II in Lithuania This novel does more to humanize Lecter than any other novel in the series.

Cannibalism • Childhood • France • Lithuania • Revenge • War—World War II

Izzo, Anthony.

Cruel Winter. *New York: Kensington, 2005. 349p. ISBN 0786017325.*

Jack, Paul, and Chris welcome the new kid in school, an overweight, eccentric boy named Ronnie, and not long afterward, unseasonable cold weather sets in. But this is not the kind of snow day that the group of teen-aged boys had in mind. A serial killer begins taking people out, using a blizzard as cover, and the boys suspect the evil has something to do with the old Steadman place and Ronnie's mysterious mother. **Similar titles:** The Corbin Family Novels, James A. Moore; *Ghoul*, Brian Keene; *Desperation*, Stephen King.

Adolescence • High School • New England • Serial Killers • Weather

Jackson, Lisa.

Final Scream. *New York: Kensington, 2005. 464p. ISBN 0739456490.*

Prosperity is certainly an ironically named town, at least it would seem so to a young woman named Cassidy. Returning home, she hopes to come to grips with her past and finally lay some of her nightmares to rest, only to find that someone does not want her to delve too deeply into her childhood. A cold-blooded killer wants her dead to make sure that she does not uncover too much. **Similar titles:** *Hallows Eve*, Al Sarrantonio; *Where the Woodbine Twines: A Novel*, Sherry Austin; *The Reckoning*, Sarah Pinborough.

Childhood • Secret Sin • Serial Killers

Ketchum, Jack.

The Girl Next Door. *New York: Leisure, 2005, ©1989. 334p. ISBN 0843955430.*
(See chapter 17, "Everyday Horror: When the Mundane Becomes Monstrous.")

Off Season. *New York: Leisure, 2006, ©1980. 276p. ISBN 0843956968.*
(See chapter 15, "Splatterpunk: The Gross Out.")

Offspring. *New York: Leisure, 2007, ©1999. 293p. ISBN 0843958642.*
(See chapter 15, "Splatterpunk: The Gross Out.")

Kiernan, Caitlin R.

Low Red Moon. *New York: ROC, 2003. 337p. ISBN 0451459482.*
Parapsychologist Deacon Silvey and paleontologist Chance Matthews, married and expecting their first child, find themselves haunted by images of stigmata. Meanwhile, an unnatural and otherwordly female serial killer is looking at their unborn child as a blood offering to her gods. She abducts Chance and takes her to a sacrificial altar, where Deacon must follow, if he ever wants to see his wife and child. **Similar titles:** <u>The Women of the Otherworld Series</u>, Kelley Armstrong; *The Nameless*, Ramsey Campbell; *Age of Consent*, Howard Mittelmark.

Human Sacrifice • Parapsychology • Pregnancy • Serial Killers

King, Stephen.

 Misery. *Waterville, ME: Thorndike Large Print, 2003, ©1988. 563p. ISBN 0786250208.*
Best-selling bodice ripper novelist Paul Sheldon meets his biggest fan, a nurse tending to his body after an automobile accident. But she is also his captor, keeping him prisoner in her isolated house. Now she wants Paul to write his greatest work—just for her. This claustrophobic novel, recipient of a Bram Stoker Award, was made into a film of the same name. **Similar titles:** *Locked Doors*, Blake Crouch; *Come Out Tonight*, Richard Laymon; *The Phantom of the Opera*, Gaston LeRoux; *Misery* (film); *Fade to Black* (film).

Colorado • Kidnapping • Nurse as Character • Obsession • Stalkers • Torture • Writer as Character

Rose Madder. *New York: Viking, 1995. 420p. ISBN 0670858692.*
Rosie McClendon, an abused wife who has had enough, leaves Norman Daniels, her violent partner, and seeks a new life away from him. But Norman is not about to let Rosie go so easily, so he follows her, leaving a trail of bodies in his wake. And then he discovers that a painting that Rosie bought at a pawnshop is actually the doorway to another reality that she inhabits with her new love. **Similar titles:** *The*

Funhouse, Dean Koontz; *The Cellar*, Richard Laymon; *Creepin'*, Monica Jackson (editor).

Domestic Violence • New England • Parallel Universes • Police Officer as Character • Revenge • Stalkers

Koontz, Dean.

The Bad Place. *New York: Berkley, 2004, ©1990. 427p. ISBN 0425195481.*
Frank Pollard awakens one day to find himself on a deserted street, with no memories of how he got there. Soon his destiny will be tied to those of a computer hacker and a maniacal killer who believes he is a vampire. This suspenseful tale is related from multiple points of view. **Similar titles:** *Dark Rivers of the Heart* and *Midnight*, Dean Koontz; *Deadly Games*, Thom Racina.

Amnesia • Computer Hackers • Serial Killers

Dragon Tears. *New York: Berkley, 2006, ©1993. 412p. ISBN 0425208435.*
(See chapter 9, "Telekinesis and Hypnosis: Chaos from Control.")

The Face of Fear. *New York: Berkley, 1990, ©1985. 306p. ISBN 042511984X.*
A clairvoyant in New York has visions of the killings executed by a deranged killer called "the butcher." His latest vision, of his own death at the hands of "the butcher," may come true if he cannot overcome his own fears. This is one of Koontz's early novels; it culminates spectacularly in a high rise chase scene. **Similar titles:** *Dead Zone*, Stephen King; *The Vision*, Dean Koontz; *Night Visions*, Thomas Fahy.

New York—New York City • Parapsychology • Police Officer as Character • Precognition • Psychics • Serial Killers

The Funhouse: A Novel. *London: Headline, 1992, ©1980. 313p. ISBN 0747205604.*
In this thriller, a woman is hunted by her ex-husband, a handsome carnival barker out for revenge for her killing their son, whom she was convinced was evil. Although he had to wait twenty-five years, her ex now has his chance, so he sets out to take her children away the way she took his. **Similar titles:** *Dolores Claiborne* and *Rose Madder*, Stephen King; *The Cellar*, Richard Laymon; *The Stepfather* (film).

Domestic Violence • Revenge

Hideaway. *New York: Putnam, 1992. 384p. ISBN 0399136738.*
(See chapter 7, "Demonic Possession: Satanism, Black Magic, and Witches and Warlocks: The Devil Made Me Do It.")

Intensity. *New York: Bantam, 2000, ©1995. 436p. ISBN 0553582917.*
Chyna Shepherd witnesses the brutal murders of a friend and his entire family and decides to follow the killer to his isolated home to exact revenge. There's only one problem: the killer knows he's being followed. This suspenseful novel is a fan favorite. **Similar titles:** *Hannibal*, Thomas Harris; *The One Safe Place*, Ramsey Campbell; *Desert Places*, Blake Crouch.

Childhood • Revenge • Serial Killers

Lightning. *Detroit, MI: Thorndike Large Print, 2007, ©1989. 693p. ISBN 0786298731.*

A mysterious, tall blond man continually shows up at events of life and death in Laura Shane's life—usually to save her. Unfortunately, so does a tall dark-haired man with a facial scar, who tries to kill her. What secrets does she hold, and what is Laura Shane's destiny? A marvelous study of time travel and alternative realities. **Similar titles:** The Talisman Series, Stephen King and Peter Straub; *Mr. X*, Peter Straub.

Alternative History • Angels • Nazis • Time Travel

Seize the Night. *New York: Bantam Books, 1999. 443p. ISBN 0613223594.*

(See chapter 12, "Technohorror: Evil Hospitals, Military Screw-Ups, Mad Scientists, and Alien Invasions.")

The Servants of Twilight. *Thorndike, ME: Thorndike Large Print, 2001, ©1988. 327p. ISBN 0786228660.*

As a mother and her six-year-old son are getting in their car in a store parking lot, an old woman approaches them and insists the boy is evil and must die. Thus begins this action/suspense novel about a religious cult whose leader has marked a child for death. **Similar titles:** *The Doll Who Ate His Mother*, Ramsey Campbell; *Ghost Story*, Peter Straub; *Gifted Trust*, John Paul Allen and Alan M. Clark.

Religion—Christianity • Religion—Cults

Shattered. *New York: Berkley, 1990, ©1973. 289p. ISBN 0425099334.*

Alex Doyle and his nephew-in-law Colin travel from Philadelphia to San Francisco. Along the way, they find themselves being followed by a white Automover van whose driver has murderous intentions. **Similar titles:** *Desperation* and *The Regulators*, Stephen King; *Prodigal Blues*, Gary A. Braunbeck.

California—San Francisco • Pennsylvania—Philadelphia • Road Trips • Stalkers

Velocity. *New York: Bantam, 2005. 400p. ISBN 0553804154.*

Billy lives a quiet life as a bartender until he receives a cryptic note telling him that he has six hours to choose who is to live—a young schoolteacher or an elderly humanitarian. Initially, Billy dismisses this as a joke, until the teacher is found strangled. So when he receives the next note, he takes it seriously. Worse still, the killer leaves evidence at each crime scene that incriminates Billy. **Similar titles:** *Desert Places*, Blake Crouch; *Mr. Murder*, Dean Koontz; *Saw* (film).

Bartender as Character • California • Serial Killers

The Vision. *London: Headline, 1991, ©1977. 272p. ISBN 074720294X.*

A young woman has visions of serial killings that actually happen. Can these visions be somehow connected to her childhood, which she cannot remember, and to her fear of sex? This one is a roller coaster ride of suspense. **Similar titles:** *The Dead Zone*, Stephen King; *The Face of Fear*, Dean Koontz; *Night Visions*, Thomas Fahy.

Eugenics • Precognition • Religion—Satanism

The Voice of the Night. *Thorndike, ME: Thorndike Press, 1999, ©1980. 339p. ISBN 0786217650.*

Best friends Colin and Roy are complete opposites. Colin is introspective, compassionate, and sympathetic, while Roy is extroverted, detached—and a sociopath. When Roy begins threatening Colin, and some of their mutual acquaintances are murdered, it becomes apparent that the friendship must be severed. **Similar titles:** *Dr. Jekyll and Mr. Hyde*, Robert Louis Stevenson; *Desert Places*, Blake Crouch.

Doppelgangers • Psychosexual Horror

Watchers. *New York: Berkley, 2003, ©1987. 487p. ISBN 0425188809.*
(See chapter 12, Technohorror: Evil Hospitals, Military Screw-Ups, Mad Scientists, and Alien Invasions.")

Whispers. *New York: Berkley, 2006, ©1980. 457p. ISBN 042520992X.*
Hollywood writer Hillary Thomas returns to her home one night to find a male acquaintance hiding in her closet, prepared to rape and knife her. She manages to chase him away with a gun, but he returns, again and again—even after she stabs him to death during one of his attacks. Now her "undead" assailant not only wants to kill her; he wants to brutally mutilate her for what she did to him. Can she escape the killer who will not die? **Similar titles:** *The Bone Parade*, Mark Nykanen; *Death Instinct*, Bentley Little; *I Spit on Your Grave* (film).

California—Hollywood • Police Officer as Character • Rape • Stalkers • Twins • Writer as Character

Kunzmann, Richard.

Bloody Harvests. *New York: Thomas Dunne Books, 2006, ©2004. 454p. ISBN 0312360339.*
Are the ritual killings of several children whose organs have been harvested the work of a serial killer, or something more sinister? That is the question posed by Johannesburg police officers Harry Mason, a Christian Englishman, and Jacob Tshabalala, a Christian tribesman who understands that the practices of local tribesmen are more than just superstition. Kunzmann's debut novel is atmospheric and unsettling. **Similar titles:** *A Great and Terrible Beauty*, Graham Masterton; *The Nameless* and *The Doll Who Ate His Mother*, Ramsey Campbell.

Organized Crime • Police Officer as Character • Religion—African • Serial Killers • South Africa—Johannesburg • Witchcraft

Lackey, Mercedes.

Burning Water: A Diana Tregarde Investigation. *New York: Tor, 2005, ©1989. 330p. ISBN 0765313170.*
(See chapter 8, "Mythological Monsters and 'The Old Ones': Invoking the Dark Gods.")

Lansdale, Joe R.

God of the Razor. *Burton, MI: Subterranean Press, 2007. 295p. ISBN 9781596061156.*
(See chapter 18, "Collections and Anthologies.")

Laymon, Richard.

After Midnight. *New York: Leisure Books, 2006, ©1997. 438p. ISBN 084395180X.*
(See chapter 15, "Splatterpunk: The Gross Out.")

Among the Missing. *London: Headline, 2007, ©1999. 393p. ISBN 0755331818.*
In a small California mountain town, someone is murdering women, then behead-ing them and ravishing their corpses. Can the local police stop him before he kills again? This thriller is told from multiple points of view. **Similar titles:** *No Sanctu-ary* and *Blood Games*, Richard Laymon; *Fetish*, Tara Moss; *Severance*, Robert Olen Butler.

California • Necrophilia • Police Officer as Character • Psychosexual Horror • Rape • Serial Killers

The Beast House Chronicles.

The town of Malcasa Point has changed a lot in a few years, and so has the Beast House tour. Due to several popular books and movies about what the locals call the House of Death, the tour is bigger and better than ever. But sometimes tourists and locals alike get a bit more than they bargained for. **Similar titles:** *Hell House*, Richard Matheson; *The House That Jack Built*, Graham Masterton; The Harrow Academy Novels, Douglas Clegg.

California—Malcasa Point • Haunted Houses • Psychosexual Horror • Revenging Revenant

Friday Night in Beast House. *London: Headline, 2007, ©1979. 154p. ISBN 0755337646.*

Wishing to impress Allison enough so that she will go out with him, Mark asks her to join him on Friday night in the notorious Beast House after the day's tours are over. A bout of masculine bravado prompts Mark to hide in the infa-mous Beast Hole, the place where the creature who is rumored to incite mur-derous rampages is said to hide. Unfortunately for Mark, he learns that there is a great deal of truth behind what he believed to be merely rumors.

Adolescence • High School

The Cellar. *New York: Leisure, 2006, ©1980. 309p. ISBN 0843957484.*

When Donna Haynes's violent ex-husband Ray is released from prison, she flees with her daughter to escape his wrath. After a car accident, mother and daugh-ter end up in Malcasa Point, a small burg whose only attraction is the Beast House, a morbid tourist attraction that was once the site of some terrible atroci-ties. But the locals know what others don't—that something lurks within the cel-lar of Beast House to cause the killings, and it will provoke others to violence.

Domestic Violence • Incest

The Beast House. *New York: Leisure, 2007, ©1986. 334p. ISBN 0843957492.*

Writer Gordon Hardy and his friends come to Malcasa Point to document ev-idence of the Beast, an entity that none of them believes exists, so that hope-fully Hardy can write a best seller. But by the end of their sojourn, all have terrible evidence to the contrary.

Writer as Character

The Midnight Tour. *New York: Leisure, 2007, ©1998. 596p. ISBN 0843957530.*

The self-guided daytime tour of the Beast House is safe for the whole family, as it gives the sanitized version of the attacks and murders. If you want the real story, however, you have to get it on the Midnight Tour.

Families • Torture

Blood Games. *New York: Leisure, 2003, ©1992. 467p. ISBN 0843951818.*

Five young female alumni from Belmore University get together at a deserted Vermont lodge for their annual meeting, at the behest of Helen, the horror buff of the group. Unfortunately for them, the lodge is a place where years before guests had been ritually slaughtered by locals. Soon the girls discover that they are not alone, as a homicidal maniac resides behind the lodge. **Similar titles:** *Darkness, Tell Us* and *Among the Missing*, Richard Laymon; *Fetish*, Tara Moss.

Academia • Serial Killers • Vermont • Witchcraft

Come Out Tonight. *New York: Leisure, 2005, ©1999. 434p. ISBN 0843951834.*

As the Santa Ana winds blow fire toward L.A., teenager Toby Bones, who with his brother murdered his wealthy parents, is on the loose. Teacher Sherry Gates and her boyfriend Duane are involved in a secret rendezvous, when she is kidnapped by Toby, a student from a recent class. He beats and tries to rape her, and kills anyone who comes to her aid. **Similar titles:** *Whispers*, Dean Kootnz; *Cuts*, Richard Laymon.

California—Los Angeles • High School • Kidnapping • Rape • Serial Killers • Teacher as Character • Torture

Cuts. *New York: Leisure, 2008, ©1999. 301p. ISBN 0843951834.*
(See chapter 15, "Splatterpunk: The Gross Out.")

Darkness, Tell Us. *New York: Dorchester, 2003, ©1991. 392p. ISBN 0843950471.*

During a party at a professor's house, six college students play with a Ouija board, which encourages them to go to an isolated California mining area, Calamity Peak. With their professor tagging along to keep them safe, they travel to the spot, but on the way they are hunted by a machete-wielding serial killer. **Similar titles:** *Blood Games* and *No Sanctuary*, Richard Laymon.

Academia • California • Popular Culture—Ouija Boards • Serial Killers • Teacher as Character

Endless Night. *New York: Leisure, 2004, ©1993. 466p. ISBN 0843951842.*

A gang of sadistic cult members known as killers invades the privacy of a family home. Members of the family are tortured and murdered one by one. Finally a friend of the family, who happens to be a policeman's daughter, manages to survive and escape. But now she will be hunted by a member of the cult who has been given the assignment to "take out" potential witnesses. As he tracks her, he records his heinous and disturbing thoughts on tape. **Similar titles:** *The Servants of Twilight*, Dean Koontz; *Mad Dog Summer and Other Stories*, Joe R. Lansdale; *Offspring*, Jack Ketchum.

Adolescence • Multimedia—Audiotape • Police Officer as Character • Rape • Religion— Cults • Serial Killers • Stalkers

Into the Fire. *New York: Leisure, 2005. 374p. ISBN 0843956151.*

With the help of a big gun, Rodney kidnaps Pamela, dragging her away from her home and into the California desert to make sure it is difficult for her to escape. Miraculously, she is rescued by the mysterious Sharpie, who drives a busload of mannequins through the desert. But when Sharpie brings Pamela to the small town of Pitts, California, populated solely by the six other people he has rescued, she wonders if he can be trusted. **Similar titles:** *Desert Places*, Blake Crouch; *Cuts* and *Come Out Tonight*, Richard Laymon.

California • Kidnapping

In the Dark. *New York: Leisure, 2001, ©1994. 503p. ISBN 0843949163.*

While closing the library, Jane finds an envelope with a name on it. Inside is a $50 bill and a note, along with instructions to "look homeward angel," signed by the Master of Games. Jane soon pulls from the shelves a Thomas Wolfe novel of the same name, only to find a $100 bill and another clue. Thus begins the game that Jane willingly plays to receive amounts of cash that double with each new round. But as the money awarded increases, so do the risks. **Similar titles:** *Gerald's Game*, Stephen King; *Cuts*, Richard Laymon; *The Count of Eleven*, Ramsey Campbell; *The People Under the Stairs* (film).

Librarian as Character • Obsession • Psychosexual Horror • Stalkers • Torture

The Lake. *New York: Leisure, 2004. 352p. ISBN 0843954507.*

When she was a young, rebellious girl, Leigh longed for a summer of excitement by the lake. She met a handsome boy who was willing to row her out to an abandoned beach house, but their outing ended in horror as she watched him be mowed down by a car. Twenty years later, Leigh takes her daughter to visit the same Wisconsin lake. But now that her daughter is going through the same restless emotions, Leigh realizes that the terror she found out in that cottage is coming back to haunt her and her family. **Similar titles:** *Gerald's Game*, Stephen King; *God of the Razor*, Joe R. Lansdale; *Peaceable Kingdom*, Jack Ketchum.

Serial Killers • Wisconsin

No Sanctuary. *New York: Leisure, 2003, ©2001. 352p. ISBN 0843951036.*

Four young hikers, three of them female, go into the California woods, only to be stalked by a serial killer. Meanwhile, a bored millionaire who steals into vacated homes to "vacation" in them breaks into an isolated cabin where he finds S&M videos and clippings about missing young women. **Similar titles:** *Among the Missing* and *Darkness, Tell Us*, Richard Laymon; *Fetish*, Tara Moss.

California • Sado-Masochism • Serial Killers

One Rainy Night. *New York: Dorchester, 1999. 410p. ISBN 0843946903.*

(See chapter 13, "Ecological Horror: Mother Nature Has Her Revenge.")

Once Upon a Halloween. *Baltimore, MD: Cemetery Dance, 2000. 252p. ISBN 1587670127.*

A boy returns from a night of trick-or-treating with fear in his eyes, screaming that monsters are after him and have followed him home. However, neither his parents nor his friends will help because they do not believe him. That's unfortunate, because nude axe-wielding maniacs have visited the home of two young women doling out Halloween candy. And now they've brought the two women to the local cemetery—where they will be sacrificed. **Similar titles:** *The Traveling Vampire Show* and *Come Out Tonight*, Richard Laymon; *Hallows Eve*, Al Sarrantonio.

Holidays—Halloween • Human Sacrifice • Revenging Revenant

Savage. *(Originally published as Savage: From Whitechapel to the Wild West on the Track of Jack the Ripper). New York: Leisure, 2007, ©1994. 452p. ISBN 0843957514.*

Fifteen-year-old Trevor Bentley has more than his share of problems. His mother has been beaten, he is mugged, and he has just seen Jack the Ripper murder a prostitute. Fortunately for him, the world's most famous serial killer kidnaps and shanghais him on a boat to the New World, rather than killing him. Trevor manages to survive the journey and vows revenge. He follows Jack the Ripper across America, to the Southwest. **Similar titles:** *Nowhere*, Shane Christopher; *Curtains of Blood*, Robert J. Randisi; *Nightshadows: The Best New Horror Fiction by a Living Legend in Dark Fantasy*, William F. Nolan.

Arizona • England—London • Eroticism • Kidnapping • Jack the Ripper (character) • Road Trips • Serial Killers • Victorian Era

LeRoux, Gaston.

The Phantom of the Opera. *New York: Barnes & Noble, 1993, ©1911. 264p. ISBN 0880299053.*

The Opera Ghost in Paris, a man ill treated since childhood because of his deformed face, becomes obsessed with the beautiful singer Christine Daae. He takes her to his subterranean lair, where he tries to force her to become his bride. This is the original story that inspired four Hollywood films and Andrew Lloyd Weber's musical *Phantom*. **Similar titles:** *Wuthering Heights*, Emily Brontë; *Dracula*, Bram Stoker; *Frankenstein*, Mary Shelley; *The Phantom of the Opera* (film).

Deformity • France—Paris • Kidnapping • Music—Opera • Obsession • Stalkers

Little, Bentley (writing as Phillip Emmons).

Death Instinct. *New York: Signet, 2006, ©1992. 381p.* (See chapter 15, "Splatterpunk: The Gross Out.")

Mack, Robert L.

Sweeney Todd: The Demon Barber of Fleet Street. *New York: Oxford University Press, 2007. 300p. ISBN 0199543445.*

Mack's retelling marks the first time *Sweeney Todd* has been reprinted since the story was serialized in *The People's Periodical* in 1846 and 1847. In this lurid tale of murder and unintentional cannibalism, a barber seeks revenge on the magistrate who ruined his career and marriage. He slices members of upper class society. His accomplice dices them and then serves them in pies to her customers—to rave reviews. The text also includes explanatory notes and a chronology of publication versions. **Similar titles:** *Dr. Jekyll and Mr. Holmes*, Loren D. Estleman; *The Strange Case of Dr. Jekyll and Mr. Hyde, and Other Stories*, Robert Louis Stevenson; *The Off Season*, Jack Ketchum.

Cannibalism • England—London • Revenge • Todd, Sweeney (character) • Victorian Era

Marshall, Michael (pseudonym used by Michael Marshall Smith).

The Straw Men Series.

This is the saga of a shadowy group of men who perform rituals to honor the ancient gods and use their positions of power for influence. It chronicles the continued hunt for the murderous Upright Man. As strange events involving people who were thought dead or presumed missing occur around the country, clues lead back to Washington State—home of this mysterious cult. **Similar titles:** <u>Dean Koontz's Frankenstein</u>, Dean Koontz and Edward Gorman; *The Other End*, John Shirley; *Death's Dominion*, Simon Clark; *Keepers*, Gary A. Braunbeck.

Federal Bureau of Investigation • Religion—Paganism • Serial Killers • Washington State • Wilderness

The Straw Men. *New York: HarperCollins, 2002. 400p. ISBN 0007151861.*

A fifteen-year-old girl is abducted in Los Angeles. Her abductor is a man who is presumed dead. He is traced back to the wilderness of Eastern Washington, where he has taken up with the Straw Men.

Human Sacrifice • Kidnapping

The Upright Man. *New York: Jove, 2004. 360p. ISBN 0515136387.*

(Originally published as The Lonely Dead). A would-be suicide makes a bizarre discovery in the woods. And he knows that the creatures he has stumbled upon have seen him. Now, one of the hunted, he runs across country, leaving, one by one, dead people in his wake.

Human Sacrifice • Stalkers

Blood of Angels. *New York: Berkley, 2005. 401p. ISBN 0515140082.*

In this final book in the trilogy, ex-CIA agent Ward Hopkins and FBI agent Nina Baynam hide out in the Washington State forest, hoping to avoid the attention of the Straw Men. But Nina's supervisor shows up to tell them of a new serial killer—and of the escape of the Upright Man—who just happens to be Ward's evil twin brother. Their investigations lead to the realization that the Straw Men are planning a bloodbath.

Central Intelligence Agency • Doppelgangers • Terrorism

Massie, Elizabeth.

Ⓑ **Sineater.** *New York: IBooks, 2004, ©1994. 396p. ISBN 074349783X.*
ᛉ (See chapter 10, "Small Town Horror: Villages of the Damned.")

Masterton, Graham.

The Doorkeepers. *New York: Leisure, 2003, ©2001. 371p. ISBN 0843952407.*
Josh Winward's sister Julia is found brutally murdered, her eviscerated body thrown in the Thames. But logical police work gives Scotland Yard no substantial leads. Josh teams with his psychic girlfriend to investigate how Julia was able to live in London for ten months without leaving a trace of herself. With the help of a cryptic old nursery rhyme, Josh discovers the doors into an alternative universe. **Similar titles:** The Talisman Series, Stephen King and Peter Straub; *Mr. X*, Peter Straub; *The Secret History of Moscow*, Ekaterina Sedia.

Alternative History • England—London • Families • Parallel Universes • Psychics • Religion—Christianity—Puritanism • Veterinarian as Character

Innocent Blood. *Sutton, UK: Severn House, 2005. 288p. ISBN 0727861891.*
An exclusive Hollywood junior high school is supposedly bombed by terrorists wishing to strike what they see as the corrupt Western media. But after the bombing, one of the survivors meets with another victim of the blast, and they come to believe that this was not an act of terrorism after all. **Similar titles:** *Black Sunday*, Thomas Harris; The Straw Men Series, Michael Marshall.

California—Hollywood • Terrorism

A Terrible Beauty. *New York: Pocket Books, 2003. 369p. ISBN 0743462939.*
(See chapter 15, "Splatterpunk: The Gross Out.")

McCammon, Robert R.

Ⓑ **Mine.** *New York: Grafton, 1992, ©1989. 560p. ISBN 0586212264.*
ᛉ Mary Terror, an ex-freedom fighter from the 1960s, carries a grudge—and lots of weapons. She also steals infants and brutally murders them when they do not please her. But now she has kidnapped Laura Clayborne's child, and Laura will stop at nothing to get him back. This nonstop thriller won the Bram Stoker Award. **Similar titles:** *The Nameless* and *The Parasite*, Ramsey Campbell; *Perfect Nightmare*, John Saul.

Federal Bureau of Investigation • Journalist as Character • Kidnapping • Serial Killers

Moss, Tara.

Fetish. *New York: Leisure, 2005, ©1999. 325p. ISBN 084395633X.*
A serial killer known as the "stiletto killer" has just murdered Mac's best friend, model Catherine Gerber. Now Mac must track down the killer, who has also targeted her. **Similar titles:** *Cold Blooded*, Robert J. Randisi;

11

12

13

14

15

16

17

18

19

20

Among the Missing, Blood Games, and *No Sanctuary,* Richard Laymon; *Fever in the Blood,* Robert Fleming.

Australia • Model as Character • Serial Killers

Murray, Sabina.

A Carnivore's Inquiry. *New York: Grove, 2006, ©2004. 377p. ISBN 0141018194.*
(See chapter 14, "Psychological Horror: It's All in Your Head.")

Newman, James.

Midnight Rain. *New York: Dorchester, 2004. 354p. ISBN 0843953896.*
Twelve-year-old Kyle has a secret place, a cabin in the woods of North Carolina. But he will never be the same after he finds there a badly beaten, nude girl who is barely alive. Kyle will soon wish he never looked through the window, because when the girl dies, he becomes the only witness to her murder —and now his own life is in danger. **Similar titles:** *The Last Voice They Hear,* Ramsey Campbell; *Desperation* and *The Regulators,* Stephen King; *Sleeping Policemen,* Dale Bailey and Jack Slay Jr..

Childhood • North Carolina • Stalkers • Wilderness

Nolan, William F.

Dark Universe. *New York: Leisure, 2003. 372p. ISBN 0843951907.*
(See chapter 18, "Collections and Anthologies.")

Nykanen, Mark.

The Bone Parade. *New York: Hyperion, 2004. 324p. ISBN 1401300189.*
(See chapter 15, "Splatterpunk: The Gross Out.")

Oates, Joyce Carol (writing as Rosamund Smith).

Starr Bright Will Be with You Soon. *New York: Dutton, 1999. 264p. ISBN 0525944524.*
A thirty-seven-year-old stripper who has taken it upon herself to become "God's instrument" for cleaning up the world—by luring businessmen into secluded areas where she can slash their throats—returns home to visit her sister. Will the family be safe when Starr Brite tries to insinuate herself into a normal family unit? **Similar titles:** *Mistress of the Dark,* Sephera Giron; *Fever in the Blood,* Robert Fleming; *Mine,* Robert McCammon; *I Spit on Your Grave* (film); *Monster* (film).

Families • Nevada—Las Vegas • New York—New York City • Revenge • Serial Killer • Stripper as Character

 Zombie. *New York: Dutton, 1995. 181p. ISBN 0525940456.*
Perhaps the candidate for the most disturbing analysis of a serial killer ever written, this engrossing tale, told in journal form by the killer himself, known only as Quentin P., chronicles the meetings of killer and victim, the killer's motives, and the gory methods used. What sets Oates's novel apart from others is her ability to

allow the serial murderer to speak for himself, without the author's inter-
jecting subtle hints of condemnation or aggrandizement. **Similar titles:**
Psycho, Robert Bloch; *Exquisite Corpse*, Poppy Z. Brite; The Silence of the
Lambs Series, Thomas Harris; *Dahmer* (film).

Diary Format • Gay/Lesbian/Bisexual Characters • Necrophilia • Serial Killers • Zombies

O'Brien, Edna.

In the Forest. *London: Phoenix, 2003, ©2002. 224p. ISBN 0753816857.*

Based on the true story of an Irish kidnapping of five and triple homicide,
this tale features Michen O'Kane, a ten-year-old boy from a dysfunctional,
violent family, orphaned when his father murders his mother. Now hearing the voices of the dead, he becomes the prey of bullies and is molested
by a seemingly kind priest. Returning to his hometown as an adult, he
continues hearing voices—but these tell him to kidnap and murder a
young mother and her son, and to not stop there. **Similar titles:** *Hannibal*
and *Hannibal Rising*, Thomas Harris; *Blue Rose*, Peter Straub; *Fever in the
Blood*, Robert Fleming; *The Girl Next Door*, Jack Ketchum.

*Child Molesters • Clergy as Character • Domestic Violence • Families • Ireland • Kidnap-
ping • Serial Killers*

Pearl, Matthew.

The Dante Club. *New York: Ballantine, 2006. 464p. ISBN 0375505296.*

In 1865 a group of scholars in Boston labor to translate Dante's *Divine
Comedy* into English, so that their countrymen can read the poet's work.
When a priest is found buried alive with his feet set ablaze, and another
body is found eaten by maggots, they realize that these and other recent
bizarre deaths in the Boston area are all based on *The Divine Comedy*. **Similar titles:** The Charlie Parker Mysteries, John Connolly; The Joe Pitt Novels, Charlie Huston.

Academia • Detection • Divine Comedy, The • Massachusetts—Boston

Piccirill, Tom.

The Dead Letters. *New York: Bantam, 2006. 363p. ISBN 9780553384079.*

Understandably, Eddie Whitt wants revenge against the serial killer who
murdered his five-year-old daughter half a decade ago. But "Killjoy," as
he was called by the press, murdered twenty-one children before disappearing, leaving the police with no leads. Later, a remorseful Killjoy resurfaces as a sort of dark Robin Hood who kidnaps children from abusive
parents—to replace the children he murdered. While other parents may
accept Killjoy's twisted offering, Eddie just wants to hunt him down. **Similar titles:** *Mr. Hands* and *Prodigal Blues*, Gary Braunbeck; *Silent Children*,
Ramsey Campbell; *The People Under the Stairs* (film).

Child Abuse • Child Molesters • Death—Grieving • Parenting • Revenge • Serial Killers

Prescott, Michael.

In Dark Places. *New York: Penguin-Onyx, 2004. 384p. ISBN 0451411277.*

Psychiatrist Robin Cameron believes that any killer can be rehabilitated and is perfecting an experimental treatment to alter the brain structure of serial killers whose crimes stem from anger. She seems to be on the verge of success with Justin Gray, a killer of high school girls who didn't rape or torture his victims, and now seems nearly rehabilitated. But then Gray escapes. **Similar titles:** *Bed of Nails*, Michael Slade; *Desert Places*, Blake Crouch; *The Bone Parade*, Mark Nykannen.

Psychologist/Psychiatrist as Character • Serial Killers • Weird Science

Racina, Thom.

Deadly Games. *New York: Signet, 2003. 371p. ISBN 045121076X.*

(See chapter 12, "Technohorror: Evil Hospitals, Military Screw-Ups, Mad Scientists and Alien Invasions.")

Randisi, Robert J.

Cold Blooded. *New York: Leisure, 2005. 354p. ISBN 0843955740.*

When the local polar bear club finds a frozen body washed up on the beach at Coney Island, Detective Dennis McQueen and his new partner, Bailey Sommers, think it's just another murder in a big city. But more bodies are found with a similar MO, and McQueen knows that he's on the trail of a serial killer. **Similar titles:** *Fetish*, Tara Moss; *Among the Missing*, *Blood Games*, and *No Sanctuary*, Richard Laymon.

New York—New York City • Police Officer as Character • Serial Killers

Curtains of Blood. *New York: Leisure, 2002. 353p. ISBN 0843950684.*

To what extent did Jack the Ripper's murders inspire Bram Stoker's *Dracula*? Did the Whitechapel murders, and the blood-stained fiend responsible, ignite the bookish Stoker's questioning mind? This alternative fiction incorporates historical characters such as actor Henry Irving, dramatist Oscar Wilde, author Arthur Conan Doyle, and novelist Bram Stoker. **Similar titles:** *Crippen*, John Boyne; *American Gothic*, Robert Bloch; *Dr. Jekyll and Mr. Holmes*, Loren D. Estelman; *Full Dark House*, Christopher Fowler; *From Hell* (film).

Alternative Literature • Doyle, Sir Arthur Conan (character) • England—London • Jack the Ripper (character) • Serial Killers • Stoker, Bram (character) • Victorian Era

Rhodes, Evie.

Criss Cross. *New York: Dafina, 2006. 240p. ISBN 0758208723.*

Micah Jordan-Wells is a skilled police detective, partly due to his extraordinary ability to literally get into the minds of killers in order to track them down. However, the target of his most recent investigation, a serial killer, leaves behind evidence that indicates that Micah himself is the killer. Is this the case, or could Micah's ne'r-do-well twin brother be the culprit? **Similar titles:** *Red Dragon*, Thomas Harris, *Desert Places*, Blake Crouch; *Mr. Murder*, Dean Koontz.

African American Characters • Doppelgangers • New Jersey—Newark • Police Officer as Character • Precognition • Serial Killers • Twins

Ross, Joel S.

Eye for an Eye. *New York: Leisure, 2004. 336p. ISBN 0843953381.*

When Suzanne "Scorch" Amerce's sister is murdered by a female street gang, she goes from being a school honor student to a cold-blooded killer, slaughtering nearly everyone responsible for her sister's senseless death. The killing lands Scorch in jail, where for the next eight years she gets to know the prison psychologist. Then Scorch escapes. **Similar titles:** *The Dead Letters*, Tom Piccirilli; *Fever in the Blood*, Robert Fleming; *Mine*, Robert McCammon; *I Spit on Your Grave* (film); *Monster* (film).

New York—New York City • *Prisons* • *Psychologist/Psychiatrist as Character* • *Revenge*

Saul, John.

Perfect Nightmare. *New York: Ballantine, 2005. 339p. ISBN 034546731.*

A job opportunity in Manhattan prompts the Marshall family to put up for sale their Long Island home. However, the open house provides an opening for a madman to stalk and eventually kidnap their teenaged daughter Lindsay. Saul's novel is told alternately from the point of view of the maniac, the family he affects, and other suspects in the crime. **Similar titles:** *The Silence of the Lambs*, Thomas Harris; *The Nameless*, Ramsey Campbell; *The Bone Parade*, Mark Nykanan.

Kidnapping • *New York—New York City* • *Psychosexual Horror* • *Stalkers*

Shayne, Maggie, Barbara Hambly, and Charlaine Harris.

Night's Edge. *Don Mills, ON: HQN, 2004. 377p. ISBN 0373770103.*

(See chapter 18, "Collections and Anthologies.")

Shuman, George D.

18 Seconds. *New York: Simon & Schuster, 2006. 308p. ISBN 9780743277167.*

Sherry Moore, blind since childhood, has an unusual gift that she uses to help solve gruesome crimes: she can see the last eighteen seconds of a dead person's life. Using her paranormal ability to help the police solve the murder of a child leads her to a cold case involving a serial killer. **Similar titles:** *Criss Cross*, Evie Rhodes; *The Vision* and *The Face of Fear*, Dean Koontz; *Red Dragon*, Thomas Harris.

Disabilities—Blindness • *New Jersey* • *Precognition* • *Serial Killers*

Sigler, Scott.

Infected: A Novel. *New York: Crown, 2008. 342p. ISBN 0307406105.*

(See chapter 12, "Technohorror: Evil Hospitals, Military Screw-Ups, Mad Scientists, and Alien Invasions.")

Slade, Michael.

Bed of Nails. *New York: Penguin-Onyx, 2003. 436 p . ISBN 0451411153.*
(See chapter 15, "Splatterpunk: The Gross Out.")

Smith, Rosamund (pseudonym used by Joyce Carol Oates).
(See Oates, Joyce Carol, *Starr Bright Will Be with You Soon*, in this section.)

Stevenson, Robert Louis.

The Strange Case of Dr. Jekyll and Mr. Hyde. *New York: Viking Penguin, 2002,* ©*1886. 224p. ISBN 0670888656.*

Dr. Jekyll, a proper Victorian gentleman, creates a magic potion that transforms him into Mr. Hyde, the violent antithesis of what he is. Mr. Hyde delights in trampling children and beating to death old men. This classic novel was made into an excellent film of the same name in 1941 starring Spencer Tracey, Lana Turner, and Ingrid Bergman. **Similar titles:** *Dr. Jekyll and Mr. Holmes*, Loren D. Estleman; *Mr. Murder*, Dean Koontz; *The Return*, Walter de la Mare; *Dr. Jekyll and Mr. Hyde* (film).

Doppelgangers • England—London • Hyde, Edward (character) • Jekyll, Dr. Henry (character) • Victorian Era • Weird Science

The Strange Case of Dr. Jekyll and Mr. Hyde, and Other Stories. *New York: Barnes and Nobles, 2005. 254p. ISBN 1593083505.*

(See chapter 18, "Collections and Anthologies.")

Straub, Peter.

The Blue Rose Trilogy.

Young Harry Beevers, the fourth child in a family of five boys, is neglected by his alcoholic father and abused by his mother, a woman embittered by a spouse incapable of supporting the family. In the Beevers's household, the older boys traditionally subject their younger brothers to cruel torments while their parents turn a blind eye, and Harry is no exception. So he turns his anger outward, erupting in violence. *Note:* The Blue Rose stories continue with the detective novels *Mystery* and *The Throat* (which are not included in this book). **Similar titles:** *Carrion Comfort*, Dan Simmons; *One Rainy Night*, Richard Laymon; *Shadowland*, Peter Straub.

Beevers, Harry (character)

Koko. *London: HarperCollins, 2001,* ©*1988. 640p. ISBN 0007103670.*

Members of Harry Beevers's Vietnam platoon are being systematically murdered by a crazed killer. Is the murderer one of the platoon members? Is the killer even human? Straub readers will enjoy this detective horror follow-up to the Blue Rose stories about Beevers's childhood.

Serial Killers • Underhill, Tim (character) • War—Vietnam War

Blue Rose. *New York: Penguin, 1995, ©1990. 87p. ISBN 0146001079.*

Meet Harry's first victim—his little brother Eddie. When Harry discovers hypnosis, his daily torture of Eddie can be taken to new extremes.

Childhood • Families • Mind Control • New York • Parenting • Torture

The Throat. *New York: Dutton, 1993. 689p. ISBN 0525935037.*

Private investigator Tim Underhill enlists the aid of a reclusive genius in trying to clear a childhood friend of murder charges. This third book in <u>The Blue Rose Trilogy</u> won the Bram Stoker Award.

Blue Rose Murders • Serial Killers • Underhill, Tim (character)

Floating Dragon. *New York: Berkley Books, 2003, ©1983. 595p. ISBN 0425189643.*

A small New England town is menaced by both a poisonous gas that eats away flesh and a maniacal killer who mutilates his victims. No one is safe in this Straub tour de force of reincarnation, occultism, technohorror, and splatterpunk. **Similar titles:** <u>The Talisman Series</u>, Stephen King and Peter Straub; *Mr. X*, Peter Straub; *It*, Stephen King.

New England • Reincarnation • Serial Killers • Slasher • Weird Science

The Hellfire Club. *New York: Ballantine Books, 2004, ©1986. 526p. ISBN 0345477278.*

(See chapter 14, "Psychological Horror: It's All in Your Head.")

Mr. X. *New York: Ballantine, 2000, ©1999. 510p. ISBN 0449149900.*

Ned Dunstan has always felt an unseen presence following him, and when he comes home for his mother's funeral, he finally learns the mysterious secrets of his family and his hometown. He also discovers his own paranormal abilities. A complex and original novel of parallel realities. **Similar titles:** *The Dark Half*, Stephen King; <u>The Talisman Series</u>, Stephen King and Peter Straub; *Dr. Jekyll and Mr. Hyde*, Robert Louis Stevenson; *The Doorkeepers*, Graham Masterton.

Deformity • Doppelgangers • Families • Illinois • Lovecraft, H. P. • Mistaken Identity • Parallel Universes • Parapsychology • Secret Sin • Time Travel • Twins • Writer as Character

Stiefel, Vicki.

Body Parts. *New York: Leisure, 2004. 406p. ISBN 0843953179.*

Tally Whyte is a grief counselor who often finds herself working with attorneys and law enforcement officers, so when a serial killer nicknamed "The Harvester" begins murdering some of her friends and patients, she finds herself investigating the case. Eventually she'll find the man who harvests from his victims the very body parts he finds make them beautiful. But can Tally survive her encounter? **Similar titles:** *The Silence of the*

Lambs, Thomas Harris; *The Doll Who Ate His Mother*, Ramsey Campbell; *Red Angel*, Andrew Harper.

Massachusetts • Psychologist/ Psychiatrist as Character • Serial Killers

Tessier, Thomas.

Finishing Touches. *New York: Leisure, 2005, ©1986. 247p. ISBN 0843955597.*
(See chapter 15, "Splatterpunk: The Gross Out.")

Thomas, Lee.

The Dust of Wonderland. *New York: Alyson, 2007. 316p. ISBN 1593500114.*
(See chapter 7, "Demonic Possession: Satanism, Black Magic, and Witches and Warlocks: The Devil Made Me Do It.")

Tyree, Omar.

Leslie: A Novel. *New York: Simon & Schuster, 2003, ©2002. 385p. ISBN 0743228707.*
(See chapter 7, "Demonic Possession: Satanism, Black Magic, and Witches and Warlocks: The Devil Made Me Do It.")

Van Belkom, Edo.

Blood Road. *New York: Kensington, 2004. 317p. ISBN 0786015632.*
An Ontario waitress, sick of her dead end job and her alcoholic, ex-jock boyfriend, decides to hitch the next ride out of town. It doesn't take long before she realizes her mistake and heads back. But she gets picked up by a truck driver with a strange name and a taste for blood, and discovers that changing her mind may also cost her life. **Similar titles:** *Blood Games* and *Darkness, Tell Us*, Richard Laymon; *Bed of Nails*, Michael Slade; *From a Whisper to a Scream*, Charles De Lint.

Canada—Ontario • Kidnapping • Police Officer as Character • Road Trips • Serial Killers • Waitress as Character

Warner-Cohen, Kimberly.

Sex, Blood and Rock 'n' Roll. *Brooklyn, NY: Ig Publishing, 2006. 220p. ISBN 0977197212.*
(See chapter 15, "Splatterpunk: The Gross Out.")

Wilson, D. Harlan, and Stanley Ashenbach.

Dr. Id-entity , or, Farewell to Plaquedemia. *Hyattsville, MD: Raw Dog Screaming Press, 2007. 199p. ISBN 1933293322.*
(See chapter 15, "Splatterpunk: The Gross Out.")

Wright, T. M.

Laughing Man. *New York: Dorchester, 2003. 320p. ISBN 0843950846.*

Jack Erthmun sees dead people, and he, uh well, talks with them. This can of course be useful when you're a police detective working homicide. Earthmun finds himself chasing three different serial killers in New York City, including a gorgeous female perpetrator who prefers to make her kills in the nude. Wright's novel is populated with eccentric characters, plot twists, and surprises. **Similar titles:** *Prodigal Blues* and *In Silent Graves*, Gary A. Braunbeck; *18 Seconds*, George D. Shuman.

Cannibalism • Fairies • New York—New York City • Police Officer as Character • Psychics • Serial Killers

Film

Black Christmas. *Bob Clark, dir. 1974. 98 minutes.*

The members of a sorority prepare to say their good-byes as they leave for the Christmas holidays, but one by one the girls disappear. Could the prank phone caller who terrorizes the sorority house be the killer? And could their deaths be related to the disappearance of a local girl earlier in the week? On the surface, *Black Christmas* might seem to be another formulaic example of the slasher film. It is nevertheless artful, original, and disturbing. **Similar titles:** *Going to Pieces*, Adam Rockoff; *Darkness, Tell Us*, Richard Laymon.

Academia • Holidays—Christmas • Serial Killers • Slasher

The Butcher Boy. *Neil Jordan, dir. 1997. 109 minutes.*

Twelve-year-old Francie Brady is disturbingly angry for one so young, but he has had much to deal with at his tender age: a mother who commited suicide, an alcoholic father who drank himself to death, and a town that has nothing but scorn for the boy. Little wonder that he begins to have visions of the Virgin Mary (played by Sinead O'Connor), who understands his compulsion to kill anyone who has slighted him. **Similar titles:** *Hannibal Rising*, Thomas Harris; *Blue Rose*, Peter Straub

Addictions—Alcoholism • Childhood • Doppelgangers • Dreams • Ireland • Obsession • Pigs • Religion—Christianity—Catholicism • Revenge

Dahmer. *David Jacobson, dir. 2002. 101 minutes.*

This film spotlights the serial killer luring into his apartment his last victim, fourteen-year-old Konerak Sinthasomphone, escaped Dahmer's apartment, nude and bleeding, only to be returned to his murderer by two homophobic police officers who were convinced that the older man meant the boy no harm. During this incident Dahmer's earlier life is related in flashbacks. However, Jacobson's film does not revel in Dahmer's gory exploits. **Similar titles:** *Psycho*, Robert Bloch; *Exquisite Corpse*, Poppy Z. Brite; *Serial Killers: The Methods and Madness of Monsters*, Peter Vronsky.

Cannibalism • Dahmer, Jeffery (character) • Gay/Lesbian/Bisexual Characters • Serial Killers

The Devil's Rejects. *Rob Zombie, dir. 2005. 109 minutes.*
(See Chapter 15, "Splatterpunk: The Gross Out.")

Dr. Jekyll and Mr. Hyde. *Victor Fleming, dir. 1941. (black and white). 113 minutes.*
This faithful adaptation of Robert Louis Stevenson's story, stresses psychological horror. Excellent make-up and special effects for the time transform Spencer Tracy from the handsome Dr. Henry Jekyll into the hideous and cruel Mr. Hyde. Lana Turner and Ingrid Bergman also star. **Similar titles:** *Dr. Jekyll and Mr. Hyde*, Robert Louis Stevenson; *The Voice in the Night*, Dean Koontz.

Doppelgangers • England—London • Hyde, Edward (character) • Jekyll, Dr. Henry (character) • Victorian Era • Weird Science

Ed Gein (In the Light of the Moon). *Chuck Parello, dir. 2000. 89 minutes.*
This is a psychological portrait of the man who is often referred to as America's first serial killer. Parello's film explores both Gein's crimes and his relationship with his domineering, religious mother. Gein's crimes were the inspiration for Robert Bloch's novel *Psycho* as well as for Thomas Harris's *The Silence of the Lambs* and for the film *The Texas Chainsaw Massacre*. **Similar titles:** *Psycho*, Robert Bloch; *The Silence of the Lambs*, Thomas Harris; *Serial Killers: The Methods and Madness of Monsters*, Peter Vronsky.

Cannibalism • Gein, Ed (character) • Serial Killers • Wisconsin

Fade to Black. *Vernon Zimmerman, dir. 1980. 102 minutes.*
In this little-known but well-made film, Eric Binford is the typical shy loner who lives with his domineering mother. Harassed by peers and painfully shy, Eric lives a better existence in the movies. His particular obsession is with older films such as the Hopalong Cassidy series, Tod Browning's *Dracula*, and anything starring Marilyn Monroe or James Cagney. One day, when Eric meets a young woman who is a ringer for the late Marilyn Monroe, he is sufficiently emboldened to actually become the dark heroes he loves—and take desperate measures to win her love and dispatch his tormentors. **Similar titles:** *Psycho*, Robert Bloch; *Rage*, Steve Gerlach.

California—Hollywood • Movie Industry • Revenge • Serial Killers

Freaks. *Tod Browning, dir. 1932 (black and white). 64 minutes.*
A troupe of sideshow freaks demonstrate their camaraderie in a deadly way when one of their own is ill used by a "normal" person. Browning, who used actual sideshow freaks for this film, gives dignity to people the world often would rather not see as human. **Similar titles:** *A Graveyard for Lunatics*, Ray Bradbury; *Phantom of the Opera*, Gaston LeRoux.

Carnivals • Circuses • Deformity • Revenge

From Hell. *Albert Hughes and Allen Hughes, dirs. 2001. 122 minutes.*
In his quest to find Jack the Ripper, Inspector Frederick Abberline (Johnny Depp) is led through a vast conspiracy involving the royal family, Scotland Yard, and the Freemasons. The film does a fine job of incorporating all known theories about Jack the Ripper's identity, motivations, and victims. Heather Graham and Ian Holm also star. **Similar titles:** *Anno Dracula*, Kim Newman; *Crippen*, John Boyne.

Addictions—Drugs • England—London • Freemasons • Jack the Ripper (character) • Physician as Character • Police Officer as Character • Precognition • Prostitute as Character • Scotland Yard • Victorian Era

Gacy: The Crawl Space. *Clive Saunders, dir. 2003. 88 minutes.*
(Chapter 16, "Comic Horror: Laughing at Our Fears.")

Halloween. *John Carpenter, dir. 1978. 91 minutes.*
Young Michael Meyers murdered his sister on Halloween night, 1963, and was promptly sent to a mental institution. Now, fifteen years later, Michael has escaped and come home to kill again. This is a well-made example of the slasher film, and it has inspired several sequels, as well as the copy cat film series *Friday the 13th* and *Nightmare on Elm Street*. Jamie Lee Curtis made her debut in this influential film. **Similar titles:** *Whispers*, Dean Koontz; *Going to Pieces*, Adam Rockoff.

Holidays—Halloween • Psychologist/ Psychiatrist as Character • Serial Killers • Slasher • Stalkers

Hannibal. *Ridley Scott, dir. 2001. 131 minutes.*
This faithful adaptation of Thomas Harris's novel of the same name stars Anthony Hopkins as the infamous Dr. Hannibal Lecter, who is lured out of hiding by the evil Mason Verger (Gary Oldman), the only one of Lecter's victims to have survived. Julianne Moore does an excellent job of filling Jody Foster's shoes as FBI agent Clarice Starling in her thirties, attempting to capture America's most wanted serial killer. **Similar titles:** *Hannibal* and *Hannibal Rising*, Thomas Harris.

Cannibalism • Deformity • Federal Bureau of Investigation • Gay/Lesbian/Bisexual Characters • Italy • Lecter, Hannibal (character) • Pigs • Psychologist/Psychiatrist as Character • Revenge • Serial Killers • Starling, Clarice (character) • Washington, DC.

High Tension (Haute Tension). *Alexandre Aja, dir. 2003. 91 minutes.*
(See chapter 15, "Splatterpunk: The Gross Out.")

The Hills Have Eyes. *Wes Craven, dir, 1977. 89 minutes.*
(See chapter 15, "Splatterpunk: The Gross Out.")

Hostel. *Eli Roth, dir. 2005. 94 minutes.*
(See chapter 15, Splatterpunk: The Gross Out.")

House of 1000 Corpses. *Rob Zombie, dir. 2003. 89 minutes.*
(See chapter 15, "Splatterpunk: The Gross Out.")

I Spit on Your Grave (Day of the Woman). *Mark Zarchi, dir., 1978. 100 minutes.*
(See chapter 10, "Small Town Horror: Villages of the Damned.")

The Last House on the Left. *Wes Craven, dir. 1972. 84 minutes.*
A gang of escaped criminals kidnaps two teenaged girls who have come to New York City to attend a concert. In a great twist of irony, the group takes the girls to a location in rural New York near one of their homes, where the two are raped and murdered within sight of one of the girl's parent's homes. But what goes around comes around. The gang has car trouble and asks for assistance at the house of one of their victims. **Similar titles:** *Whispers*, Dean Koontz; *Going to Pieces*, Adam Rockoff.

Kidnapping • New York • Rape • Revenge

M. *Fritz Lang, dir. 1931. (black and white, with subtitles). 117 minutes.*

This early talkie about a psychotic child murderer who is hunted down and brought to justice by the Berlin underworld features dazzling cinematography and fine acting by Peter Lorre. **Similar titles:** *The Night of the Hunter*, Grubb Davis; *Seize the Night*, Dean Koontz.

Child Molesters • Germany—Berlin • Revenge • Serial Killers

May. *Lucky McKee, dir. 2002. 93 minutes.*

(See chapter 16, "Comic Horror: Laughing at Our Fears.")

Monster. *Patty Jenkins, dir. 2003. 109 minutes.*

Female serial killer Aileen Wuornos is somewhat humanized in Patty Jenkins's film of her bloody exploits. Wuornos, the lowest sort of prostitute who trolls for customers along the highway, makes her first kill when a john ties her up and beats her unconscious, intending to use her in a way she didn't consent to. As the film progresses, her killings look less like justifiable homicide and more like first degree murder. **Similar titles:** *Serial Killers: The Methods and Madness of Monsters*, Peter Vronsky; *Mistress of the Dark*, Sephera Giron.

Florida • Gay/Lesbian/Bisexual Characters • Prostitute as Character • Serial Killers

The Night of the Hunter. *Charles Laughton, dir. 1955. (black and white). 93 minutes.*

A psychotic traveling evangelist marries the widow of a recently executed bank robber in the hopes of finding the stolen money he hid before his capture. When he can't discover the whereabouts of the money from his new bride, he kills her and tries to pry the information from her two children, who travel across the country to elude their murderous stepfather. Robert Mitchum stars. **Similar titles:** *The Night of the Hunter*, Grubb Davis; *Shattered*, Dean Koontz.

Clergy as Character • Great Depression, The • Religion—Christianity • Serial Killers

Peeping Tom. *Michael Powell, dir. 1960. (black and white). 101 minutes.*

A photographer by day and a serial killer by night photographs his nubile female victims before he kills them. This cult classic is credited with being one of the first slasher films, the other being *Psycho*. However, unlike its more famous counterpart, *Peeping Tom* doesn't end with a pat psychological analysis of the killer. **Similar titles:** *Psycho*, Robert Bloch; *Going to Pieces*, Adam Rockoff.

England • Photographer as Character • Psychosexual Horror • Serial Killers • Slasher

The People Under the Stairs. *Wes Craven, dir. 1992. 102 minutes.*

On his thirteenth birthday, Fool and his family are being evicted from their tenement home by their money-hungry landlords, a brother and sister couple who pose as man and wife. The only way Fool can save his family is to brave the landlords' house and steal the gold that is kept there. But during his sojourn in the foreboding house, Fool discovers a secret greater than the hoard of gold kept by these people. **Similar titles:** *In the Dark*, Richard Laymon; *Dead Letters*, Tom Piccirilli.

African American Characters • Cannibalism • Child Abuse • Deformity • Incest • Racism

The Phantom of the Opera. *Rupert Julian, dir. 1925 (silent film, black and white). 93 minutes.*

Lon Chaney, "the man of 1,000 faces," stars as the deformed Eric, the masked man who haunts the opera house and falls in love with the singer Christine Daae. His obsession with Christine causes him to engineer her getting the lead in the Paris Opera's production of *Faust* by frightening away the singer who originally was cast in the role. But Christine's success as a singer is not enough to satisfy Eric, who eventually kidnaps Christine and takes her to his underground lair beneath the Opera House, where he tries to make her a prisoner of his love. **Similar titles:** *The Phantom of the Opera*, Gaston LeRoux.

Deformity • France—Paris • Music—Opera • Obsession

Psycho. *Alfred Hitchcock, dir. 1960. (black and white). 109 minutes.*

Alfred Hitchcock's classic film rendition of Robert Bloch's slasher novel of the same name hinges on the theme of a boy's love for his mother, and to what lengths he will go to prove that devotion. Based on the Ed Gein murders of the 1950s, this classic stars Anthony Perkins and Janet Leigh. Perkins went on to star in *Psycho II* and *Psycho III*, a sequel and a prequel to Hitchcock's 1960 masterpiece. **Similar titles:** *Psycho* and *Psycho II*, Robert Bloch.

Arizona—Phoenix • Bates, Norman (character) • Bates Motel, The • California—Fairvale • Matricide/Patricide • Mental Illness • Slasher

Saw. *James Wan, dir. 2004. 103 minutes.*

(See chapter 15, "Splatterpunk: The Gross Out.")

Scream. *Wes Craven, dir. 1996. 111 minutes.*

It's Halloween 1996, and exactly one year before, Sidney's mother was raped and murdered. Now a killer cognizant of the conventions of horror film is stalking Sidney. Fans of the slasher film will particularly enjoy this film, which reveals with every viewing more visual and verbal references to well-known and obscure examples of the genre. **Similar titles:** *Going to Pieces*, Adam Rockoff.

Horror Movie Industry • Journalist as Character • Police Officer as Character • Popular Culture • Revenge • Secret Sin • Serial Killers • Slasher

The Silence of the Lambs. *Jonathan Demme, dir. 1991. 118 minutes.*

Young FBI agent Clarice Starling is assigned to help find the kidnapped daughter of a senator before she becomes the next victim of Buffalo Bill, a serial killer who skins women. Clarice attempts to gain a better insight into the twisted mind of Buffalo Bill by talking to another psychopath, ex-psychiatrist Hannibal Lecter, who is now in a maximum security prison due to his cannibalistic habits. Clarice must first gain Lecter's confidence before he is to give away any information—if she can survive the ordeal emotionally intact. **Similar titles:** *The Silence of the Lambs* and *Hannibal*, Thomas Harris.

Cannibalism • Federal Bureau of Investigation • Gay/Lesbian/Bisexual Characters • Lecter, Hannibal (character) • Psychologist/Psychiatrist as Character • Serial Killers • Starling, Clarice (character)

Spider. *David Cronenberg, dir. 2003. 98 minutes.*

The rambling and incoherent Dennis Cleg, nicknamed Spider by his mother, returns to the town of his birth after his release from a mental institution to take up residence in a dreary halfway house. Through "flashbacks" we learn events of Spider's childhood, but Spider's vision of the past is disturbingly clear: young Dennis has in his memory events he couldn't have possibly been privy to. Cronenberg's interpretation of Patrick McGrath's novel of the same name is a masterful portrait of mental illness. **Similar titles:** *Desolation*, Tim Lebbon.

Childhood • England • Matricide/Patricide • Mental Illness

The Stepfather. *Joseph Ruben, dir. 1987. 89 minutes.*

Jerry Blake is a cheerleader for the traditional American family; as a matter of fact, he'd kill for it, and he has, when his past families disappointed him. Now he has assumed a new identity, has married a widow with a teenaged daughter, and is settling into his role as pater familias. The only problem is that his standards are too high, and now this family is also beginning to disappoint him. This sleeper hit stars Terry O'Quinn in one of the most masterful portrayals of a serial killer ever filmed. **Similar titles:** *The Night of the Hunter*, Grubb Davis.

Domestic Violence • Marriage • Parenting • Serial Killers

Ted Bundy. *Matthew Bright, dir. 2002. 99 minutes.*

This film is not interested in what made Ted Bundy a monster. Instead, it focuses on his career as a killer, particularly frightening in his ability to easily charm his victims into going off to secluded places with him, or to just pull them off the street and into his car in broad daylight with the swiftness of a cat snatching a bird from the air. Juxtaposed with Bundy's crimes are his last moments on Earth, when the executioner prepares him for his death. **Similar titles:** *Serial Killers: The Method and Madness of Monsters*, Peter Vronksy.

Bundy, Ted (character) • Prisons—Death Row • Serial Killers

The Texas Chainsaw Massacre. *Tobe Hooper, dir. 1974. 83 minutes.*

This drive-in theater classic tells the tale of a group of five teens who fall victim to a family of unemployed meat-packers turned cannibals. Leatherface, the film's primary monster, who is so named because he wears over his head the skin from one of his victim's faces, is loosely based on real-life serial killer Ed Gein. This campy slasher flick is historically significant in that it is the first of its kind in which the last person to survive the maniac's wrath is a female who rescues herself rather than depending on a man to save her. **Similar titles:** *Sineater*, Elizabeth Massie; *Off Season*, Jack Ketchum.

Cannibalism • Chainsaws • Serial Killers • Slashers • Texas

The Tool Box Murders. *Dennis Donnolly, dir. 1978. 93 minutes.*

This film became infamous when film critics Gene Siskel and Roger Ebert fulminated against it as a shining example of why the slasher film is misogynistic trash with no redeeming value. Yet *The Tool Box Murders* is not a slasher film per se. Handyman Vance Kingsley kills his victims with the tools of his trade in the first twenty minutes of the film in part so he can get closer to Laurie Ballard, a teenaged girl he believes is somehow his deceased daughter who has returned—and needs protecting from all that is dirty in this world. Cameron Mitchell stars in this study of dementia caused by grief. **Similar titles:** *Mr. Hands*, Gary A. Braunbeck; *Going to Pieces*, Adam Rockoff.

Death—Grieving • Families • Mental Illness • Obsession • Parenting

Two Thousand Maniacs! *Herschell Gordon Lewis, dir. 1964. 87 minutes.* (See chapter 10, "Small Town Horror: Villages of the Damned.")

June's Picks

Books: Robert Bloch, *American Gothic* (iBooks), *Psycho* (iBooks); Ramsey Campbell, *The One Safe Place* (Tor); Thomas Harris, The Silence of the Lambs Series; Graham Masterton, *The Doorkeepers* (Leisure); Peter Straub, *Blue Rose* (Penguin), *Mr. X* (Ballantine)

Films: *Dahmer, Fade to Black, Psycho, The Stepfather, Ted Bundy*

Tony's Picks

Books: Thomas Harris, *Red Dragon* (Dutton Adult); Joyce Carol Oates, *Zombie* (Dutton); Peter Straub, *Floating Dragon* (Berkley Books); T. M. Wright, *Laughing Man* (Dorchester)

Films: *Black Christmas, Dr. Jekyll and Mr. Hyde, Hannibal, The Night of the Hunter, The Tool Box Murders*

Chapter 12

Technohorror: Evil Hospitals, Military Screw-Ups, Mad Scientists, and Alien Invasions

Technohorror is the polar opposite of utopian science fiction. An optimistic view of the future sees a world in which science will, with time, cure all diseases, provide ways to feed and clothe all humanity, and allow humans to travel to the stars to meet representatives of intelligent cultures on other planets. Technohorror, on the other hand, is dystopic: it warns us that technology is not all goodness and light. Scientists can make horrible mistakes. Worse yet, scientific discoveries and new inventions can be used for the benefit of the few against the many, as is the case in medical horror, where evil HMOs put profits and science before people, or in corporate horror, in which corporations favor technology over humanity—and by extension individuality. In some cases the few who enslave the many may be our fellow (and trusted) friends and neighbors. Levin's classic novel *The Stepford Wives* depicts a fictional world in which a cadre of wealthy men who are made insecure by feminism decide to replace their wives with android replicas, for these replicants are more compliant—and more buxom—than the originals. In technohorror, the elderly can (and therefore will) be made into food for the young, organs can (and therefore will) be stolen from live patients to replenish the failing bodies of the wealthy, and clones can (and therefore will) be produced illegally, even without the consent or knowledge of the human being who is cloned.

To the optimist, the glass is half full; to the pessimist, the glass is half empty. And to the author of technohorror, the glass is likely to make ill the person drinking from it as well. In general, all horror acknowledges that things can go horribly wrong if given the chance. Technohorror very specifically incorporates this outlook, implying that *technology*, the very thing that is supposed to make our lives better and more meaningful, will be the downfall of humanity. Made more and more intelligent, computers will rebel against their designers, as in Dean Koontz's *Demon Seed* or in the extremely popular *Terminator* films. If we travel to the stars, we will attract the attention of aliens that threaten the human race, as in Stephen King's *Dreamcatcher*. What makes technohorror so compelling is that the subgenre challenges science, the "religion" of the modern world. It speculates that the medical profession, the government, the scientific community, and the military all have dark sides that should be exposed.

Mary Shelley's 1817 novel *Frankenstein* (annotated in chapter 5) is one of the first examples of the subgenre. Victor Frankenstein attempts to play god and, using the technology of the times, creates life in the form of a man, or golem (loosely defined as a man of clay). However, Victor is incapable of nurturing his "experiment." So when Victor becomes a deadbeat dad who has not the slightest idea how to care for and nurture his misshapen offspring, and is not desirous of doing anything for the creature, his "monster" evolves from being an erudite, philosophical loner into an angry young man, bent on destroying Victor's entire family. James Whale's 1931 Universal Studios version of *Frankenstein* (also annotated in chapter 5) forever changed the romantic elements in Shelley's novel, transforming her argument about the dangers of interfering with natural processes in such a fundamental way to create a final product that is an ambiguous tale of "weird science" gone wrong. H. P. Lovecraft's 1922 novella *Herbert West: Reanimator* (annotated in chapter 5) anticipates some of the elements of Whale's version of *Frankenstein*. Lovecraft's mad scientist, Herbert West, has a lengthy career that involves experimentation of the sort that aspires to bring the dead back to life. But he meets with far more ghastly results than even those experienced by Victor Frankenstein. Ultimately, what these diverse versions of the same story emphasize is moral complicity: the belief that scientists, who are only human after all, must consider *all* the implications of their experiments.

It is not just our own technology that we must fear, particularly when that of alien life forms has the potential of being so much more destructive. Hungry Martians come very close to conquering and colonizing Earth in H. G. Wells's 1898 classic *The War of the Worlds*. In Dean Koontz's *The Taking*, extraterrestrial creatures introduce new life forms to our planet via the rain, which disrupts our ability to use all technology on earth. In Jack Finney's *The Body Snatchers* (the basis for the film *Invasion of the Body Snatchers*, which has been remade twice), aliens imperceptibly take over the planet, by slowly replicating all human life on Earth, creating a life form whose difference from the original is invisible to the naked eye, unless one is extremely observant and/or paranoid. In Hideaki Sena's *Parasite Eve*, superintelligent mitochondria are a sort of alien from within, when they develop the ability to control humans through telepathy.

More than any horror subgenre, technohorror taps into Americans' everyday fears, as readers are faced with the modern age's realization that a seemingly benevolent discovery, such as Einstein's Theory of Relativity, can easily be transformed, Jekyll and Hyde fashion, into an element of destruction, such as the nuclear bombs that destroyed Hiroshima and Nagasaki. Ironically, these historical events would make Japan the birthing ground for one of the greatest film contributions to horror, Godzilla. Although there may be lulls in the technohorror publishing frenzy, the subgenre is so successful at pinpointing the insecurities of humans that, like Arnold Schwarzenegger's character in *The Terminator*, it will always be back.

The appeals of technohorror include the universal fear of technology, which gives this subgenre a pseudo-scientific appeal. Veracity or realism also plays a big role in medical horror, which is peopled with recognizable types in familiar situations, since virtually everyone has experienced the fear of doctors and needles. In general, more than other subgenres, technohorror is filled with warning texts—the tales here go to great pains to show the perils of scientific experimentation—including the fear of a technological takeover and dehumanization of the entire world.

Note: Stories about the horrors of technology can also be found in the collections and anthologies described in chapter 18. Refer to the subject/keyword index for specific titles under the keywords *Aliens, Medical Horror,* and *Weird Science*.

Aliens

Bradbury, Ray.

It Came from Outer Space. *Colorado Springs, CO: Gauntlet, 2004. 429p. ISBN 1887368663.*

> (See chapter 18, "Collections and Anthologies.")

Finney, Jack.

The Body Snatchers. *New York: Scribner Paperback Fiction, 1998. ©1955. 216p. ISBN 0684852586.*

> Originally serialized in *Collier's Magazine* before being published in 1955 in novel form, Jack Finney's novel became the basis of Don Siegel's classic 1950s film of the same name. While Siegel's film puts in doubt whether or not the human race will thwart the aliens' intentions to invade the planet, Finney's ending is more optimistic. Two other films have been made of Finney's novel, *The Invasion of the Body Snatchers* (1978) and *The Invasion* (2007). **Similar titles:** *This Rage of Echoes*, Simon Clark; *The Harvest*, Scott Nicholson; *The Stepford Wives*, Ira Levin.
>
> *Aliens • California • Doppelgangers • Replicants*

King, Stephen.

Dreamcatcher. *New York: Scribner, 2001. 620p. ISBN 0743211383.*

> Four boyhood friends on their annual hunting trip in rural Maine discover dazed people wandering around the woods in freezing weather. These mysterious strangers are all permeated by a faintly sweet smell, harbinger of the alien life force inside of them waiting to be born. Meanwhile, the U.S. military knows about this dangerous state of affairs and has quarantined the entire area, willing to sacrifice the unwanted to save the rest of the world from contamination. **Similar titles:** *The Tommyknockers*, Stephen King; *Winter Moon*, Dean Koontz; *The Body Snatchers*, Jack Finney; *28 Weeks Later* (film); *Invasion of the Body Snatchers* (film).
>
> *Addictions—Alcoholism • Aliens • Epidemics • Government Officials • Maine • Mind Control • Pregnancy • Psychologist/Psychiatrist as Character*

The Mist. *New York: Signet, 2007, ©1985. 230p. ISBN 0451223292.*

> This is the first volume devoted entirely to the classic novella *The Mist*, originally published in *Skeleton Crew*. A sudden storm damages Bridgton, Maine, so David Drayton takes his son grocery shopping to get supplies, but the two, like many of their neighbors, find themselves trapped in the store by an extremely thick fog. Worse yet, this fog seems to hide ferocious

and hungry creatures, which begin attacking the trapped humans. **Similar titles:** *The Deluge*, Mark Morris; *Shadow Coast*, Philip Haldeman; *Darkfall*, Stephen Laws; *The Mist* (film).

Maine • Parenting • Weather • Weird Science

The Taking. *New York: Bantam, 2005, ©2004. 410p. ISBN 0553584502.*

One morning, Molly and Neil Sloan awaken to a phosphorescent downpour that smells like semen. The power goes out, yet appliances come on without a clear energy source, and the hands of all clocks run backward. And in the moments before their telephone and Internet connections are gone for good, the couple learns that the strange downpour is a global phenomenon, and that Earth is under attack by aliens who are introducing horrific new flora and fauna. **Similar titles:** *Day of the Triffids*, John Wyndham; *Crawlers*, John Shirley; *The War of the Worlds*, H. G. Wells.

Aliens • Apocalypse • California • Dogs

Moore, James. A.

Fireworks. *New York: Dorchester, 2003, ©2001. 376p. ISBN 0843952474.*

During a Fourth of July fireworks display in the small town of Collier, Georgia, aliens descend upon the earth. But things go from bad to worse when citizens are taken hostage by representatives of their own government in the name of national security. **Similar titles:** *The Taking* and *Night Chills*, Dean Koontz; *Dreamcatcher*, Stephen King; *28 Weeks Later* (film).

Aliens • Georgia • Government Officials

Nicholson, Scott.

The Harvest. *New York: Pinnacle-Kensington, 2003. 383p. ISBN 0786015799.*

An alien organism lands on an Appalachian mountainside by accident, but it is starving and more than ready to feed. The buffet includes a self-righteous preacher who secretly lusts after his assistant; a moonshiner; an evil land developer; a burnt out multimillionaire who has decided that the mountains hold the answer he has looked for all his life; a trailer park wife who is ready to turn whore officially; her white trash boyfriend, who is more than willing to pimp; a psychology professor; her radio DJ husband; and an ex-librarian who has temporarily retired to take care of an ailing aunt. **Similar titles:** *The Stand*, Stephen King; *Day of the Triffids*, John Wyndham; *I Am Legend*, Richard Matheson.

Academia • Aliens • Appalachia • Clergy as Character • Librarian as Character • Zombies

Wells, H[erbert] G[eorge].

The War of the Worlds. *New York: Penguin, 2005, ©1898. 280p. ISBN 0141441038.*

A meteor falls from out of the sky, landing in a field near a small town. The citizens of the town decide to feed their curiosity by going to the landing site of the meteor. Aliens, or what are later discovered to be alien machines, emerge, incinerating everything in their path, hostile or friendly. These invaders practice colonization—using the indigenous population for its resources, which in this case turns out to be blood. Thus begins one of the greatest horror stories of all times, H. G. Wells's *The War of the Worlds*. **Similar titles:** *The Body Snatchers*, Jack Finney; *The*

Mist and *The Stand*, Stephen King; *Dawn Song*, Michael Morano; *Cloverfield* (film).

Aliens • Apocalypse • England—London • Epistolary Format • Frame Tale • Victorian Era

Williams, Conrad, and Jeff VanderMeer.

The Unblemished. *Northborough, MA: Earthling Publishers, 2006. 367p. ISBN 097663399X.*

In the near future, centuries-old reptilian creatures that had been solicited to help control the plague, but then chased underground once their purpose was fulfilled, rise again to blend in with humanity, lay eggs in some people, and eat others. Caught up in the grisly scene that London has become are people with different agendas trying to survive the infestation: a thrill-seeking photographer, a young mother and her beautiful but mentally unstable daughter, and a cannibalistic child murderer determined to mate with the invaders' new queen. **Similar titles:** *Veniss Underground*, Jeff VanderMeer; *The Etched City*, J. K. Bishop; *Necropolis*, Tim Waggoner.

Aliens • Apocalypse • Child Molesters • England—London • Futurism • Photographer as Character • Replicants • Shape-shifters

Medical Horror

Buick, Jeff.

Lethal Dose. *New York: Leisure, 2005. 357p. ISBN 0843955783.*

Gordon Buchanan's brother Billy bleeds to death after an accident, when his blood fails to coagulate properly. Yet Billy had no history of hemophilia or any other blood disorder. Soon Gordon learns that his brother had been taking Triaxcion, a new product of Veritas Pharmaceuticals, and that he has become another victim of the greed of the pharmaceutical companies and their tendency to put profit before people. **Similar titles:** *Mortality*, Steven Ford; *The Spirit Box*, Stephen Gallagher; *The Society*, Michael Palmer.

Addictions—Drugs • Consumerism • Corporate Horror • Medical Horror • Pharmaceutical Corporations

Clark, Simon.

Death's Dominion. *New York: Leisure, 2006. 342p. ISBN 0843954930.*

In the future, the valued dead can be brought back to life to serve the living; and like the Bionic Man, they are stronger and faster, and also more intelligent. These reanimated dead, referred to as "monsters," are something more than human, and the government has decided to try to wipe them out—with potentially disastrous results. **Similar titles:** *Frankenstein*, Mary Shelley; *This Rage of Echoes*, Simon Clark; *The Wave*, Walter Mosley; *Terminator* (film).

England • Eugenics • Medical Horror • Weird Science • Zombies

Costello, Matthew J.

Missing Monday. *New York: Berkley: 2004. 345p. ISBN 0425194558.*

Janna Wade has literally managed to sleep through a Monday—and still get her work done. In fact, she has lost an entire day of her life, and now her blackout results in her days becoming nightmares. Her best friend and her boyfriend suggest she see a psychiatrist, but little does she know that the psychiatrist and his wife are knee-deep in controversial experimentation. **Similar titles:** *The House of Thunder*, Dean Koontz; *Follow*, A. J. Matthews; *Doppelganger*, David Stahler Jr.; *The Machinst* (film).

Amnesia • Mental Illness • Psychologist/Psychiatrist as Character • Weird Science

Ford, Steven.

First Do No Harm. *New York: Berkley, 2004. 345p. ISBN 0425196461.*

Two medical researchers are at odds in this thriller in which a new strain of smallpox surfaces. Researcher Erin Connelly believes it will cure disease. Jacob Kohl of the CDC believes it will threaten humanity. Neither knows exactly how to isolate the virus, but both know that someone had better do so, and soon. The journey to find the virus will take both around the world—from the Congo, to the United States, to Moscow, to Nepal. **Similar titles:** *Mortality*, Steven Ford; *Lethal Dose*, Jeff Buick; *The Society*, Michael Palmer.

Centers for Disease Control • Epidemics • Medical Horror • Road Trips

Mortality. *New York: Penguin-Berkley, 2003. 437p. ISBN 0425189899.*

Dr. Paul Tobin, a cosmetic surgeon and recovering alcoholic, joins his ex brother-in-law's Florida Clinic, which possesses what it believes to be a fountain of youth cocktail. However, Paul begins to suspect there is something wrong when patients start to die of old age instead of being spared the ravages of time. **Similar titles:** *Lethal Dose*, Jeff Buick; *The Spirit Box*, Stephen Gallagher; *The Society*, Michael Palmer.

Aging • Florida • Medical Horror • Physician as Character

Gallagher, Stephen.

The Spirit Box. *Burton, MI: Subterranean Press, 2005. 276p. ISBN 1596060174.*

When several experimental drugs disappear from a North Carolina research facility, manager John Bishop has two compelling reasons to investigate the theft. First, he must preserve his facility's reputation, and second, the day before, his teenaged daughter committed suicide. Now several inexplicable influences indicate *his* involvement in the theft. **Similar titles:** *Lethal Dose*, Jeff Buick; *Mortality*, Steven Ford; *The Society*, Michael Palmer.

Addictions—Drugs • Medical Horror • North Carolina • Parenting

Matheson, Richard.

I Am Legend. *New York: Tor, 2007, ©1954. 312p. ISBN 0765357151.*

(See chapter 18, "Collections and Anthologies.")

Palmer, Michael.

The Society. *Sutton, UK: Severn House, 2006, ©2004. 351p. ISBN 0727863614.*
Several CEOs of HMOs are murdered. Dr. Will Grant, the poster boy for selfless, caring physicians, is briefly a suspect, but the police officer investigating the case, Patty Moriarty, soon clears him. Yet neither Will's nor Patty's troubles are over. Will is drugged, causing him to collapse during a delicate operation and making it appear as if he is an addict. As a result, he loses his hospital privileges and is sued for malpractice. Then Patty is shot and becomes comatose. **Similar titles:** *Mortality,* Steven Ford; *The Spirit Box,* Stephen Gallagher; *Lethal Dose,* Jeff Buick.

Corporate Horror • Massachusetts • Medical Horror • Physician as Character • Police Officer as Character

Robinson, Frank M.

The Donor. *New York: Tom Doherty, 2005, ©2004. 372p. ISBN 0765349396.*
After a minor car accident in San Francisco, Dennis Heller awakens in a hospital to discover he's just had some of his organs removed. And he recognizes the masked surgeon who comes to check on him as the same doctor in Boston who performed surgery on him during a routine physical. Now Dennis is beginning to see a connection between his millionaire father's near-death experiences and nearly miraculous recoveries. **Similar titles:** *Parasite Eve,* Hideaki Sena; *The Society,* Michael Palmer; *Lethal Dose,* Jeff Buick.

Corporate Horror • Families • Medical Horror—Organ Transplants • Physician as Character

Sena, Hideaki.

Parasite Eve. *New York: Vertical Press, 2005. 319p. ISBN 1932234195.*
Mitochondrial cells have evolved and developed a collective intelligence superior to that of our species, and they try to take over the world. The cells as a collective entity are able to "possess" humans, who then do their bidding and facilitate their parasitic growth in the bodies of particularly malleable individuals who can be manipulated by the mitochondria. The story is told in flashbacks from the cognizant mitochondria's point of view. **Similar titles:** *The Donor,* Frank Robinson; *Stranger,* Simon Clark; *Infected: A Novel,* Scott Sigler.

Epidemics • Japan • Medical Horror—Organ Transplants • Medical Horror—Parasites • Physician as Character • Popular Culture—Spontaneous Combustion • Telekinesis

Shirley, John.

Crawlers. *New York: Del Rey, 2003. 383p. ISBN 0345446526.*
The hapless residents of Quiebra, California, are victims of a secret military experiment when a capsule containing experimental bacteria falls from the sky, transforming everything into a fusion of flesh and machine that is part of a collective entity. While individuals vary in their ability to resist the bacteria or succumb to the infection, the young seem to be the

most resistant of all to the contagion. **Similar titles:** *Parasite Eve*, Hideacki Sena; *The Harvest*, Scott Nicholson; *The Taking*, Dean Koontz; *The Body Snatchers*, Jack Finney; *Invasion of the Body Snatchers* (film).

California • Epidemics • Medical Horror—Parasites • Weird Science

Sigler, Scott.

Infected: A Novel. *New York: Crown, 2008. 342p. ISBN 0307406105.*

A CIA operative and a CDC epidemiologist work together to stop the spread of a mysterious bioengineered virus that makes ordinary human beings become rampaging killers. As the epidemic works its way across the United States, the two secretly criss-cross the country, vainly looking for just one live victim who can be tested. But all they find are dead bodies. When they figure out that a former football player who has become infected may carry the cure, their lives become a race against time. **Similar titles:** *First Do No Harm*, Steven Ford; *Xombies*, Walter Greatshell; *Parasite Eve*, Hideacki Sena; *28 Days Later* (film).

Centers for Disease Control • Central Intelligence Agency • Epidemics • Medical Horror —Parasites • Spree Killers • War—Biological Warfare • Weird Science

VanderMeer, Jeff.

Veniss Underground. *New York: Bantam, 2005, ©2003. 192p. ISBN 0553383566.*

Beneath a decadent future city, subterranean "artists" create monstrous works of biology, while genetically enhanced "meerkats" decide it is time to make humanity obsolete. Nicholas, a Living Artist not quite talented enough to succeed, goes in search of the most respected mentor on the planet, but then makes the huge mistake of traveling beneath the city, where he finds terror. **Similar titles:** *The Etched City*, J. K. Bishop; *Necropolis*, Tim Waggoner; *The Unblemished*, Conrad Williams and Jeff VanderMeer.

Artist as Character • Subterranean Horror • Twins

Wells, H[erbert] G[eorge].

The Invisible Man. *New York: F. Watts, 2007, ©1897. 110p. ISBN 053116988X.*

This is Wells's classic tale of a "scientific investigator" fascinated with the properties of light, who accidentally renders himself invisible and wreaks havoc on an English village. Wells is action-oriented and has fun with science. **Similar titles:** *Frankenstein*, Mary Shelley; *Dr. Jekyll and Mr. Hyde*, Robert Louis Stevenson; *The Incredible Shrinking Man*, Richard Matheson; *Herbert West: Re-animator*, H. P. Lovecraft; *The Invisible Man* (film).

Disabilities—Xeroderma Pigmentation • England • Invisibility • Victorian Era • Weird Science

Military and Government Experimentation

Alten, Steve.

Goliath. *New York: Doherty-Forge, 2003, ©2002. 500p. ISBN 0765340240.*

Covah, a Russian-born computer fanatic intent on ridding the world of nuclear weapons once and for all, has stolen the Goliath, a U.S. nuclear-powered stealth submarine with a biochemical computer brain. He begins sinking ships and retrieving their nuclear weapons to use as leverage against nations that do not acknowledge his Declaration of Humanity; but when the sub's computer malfunctions, his mistake threatens to destroy the earth. Alten's information-laden style makes the improbable seem possible. **Similar titles:** *Dark Rivers of the Heart*, *Demon Seed*, and *Night Chills*, Dean Koontz; *The Terminator* (film).

Apocalypse • Computers • Maritime Horror • Nuclear Weapons • Sailor as Character • Terrorism

Ballard, J. G.

Kingdom Come. *London: Fourth Estate, 2006. 280p. ISBN 0007232462.*

Richard Pearson, an advertising executive, goes to London to settle affairs after his father is found dead, one of three men killed in an attack. After discovering that there is more to his father's death than anyone is telling him, Pearson decides to play detective. At the center of his sleuthing is the Metro-Centre, London's largest enclosed mall and a consumer's dream—which is also linked to racist attacks and nationalism. Is this self-enclosed façade that attempts to imitate the world also the home to games of terrorism? **Similar titles:** *The Restless Dead*, Hugh B. Cave; *Valley of Lights*, Stephen Gallagher; *Stevenson under the Palm Trees*, Alberto Manguel.

Consumerism • England—London • Futurism • Racism • Terrorism

Greatshell, Walter.

Xombies. *New York: Berkley, 2004. 346p. ISBN 0425197441.*

A new virus, Agent X, creates bloodthirsty monsters out of the human beings it infects, by first turning women, who then infect men. A young woman named Lulu is somehow immune, and to stay uninfected, she hops a submarine that is headed toward an island believed to be a safe haven. If the Xombies don't get Lulu, the stir craziness of being on a Navy sub just might. **Similar titles:** *Dead Sea*; Brian Keene; *Infected: A Novel*, Scott Sigler; *I Am Legend*, Richard Matheson; *28 Weeks Later* (film).

Apocalypse • Epidemics • Islands • Maritime Horror • Weird Science • Zombies

King, Stephen.

Firestarter. *New York: New American Library, 1981. 404p. ISBN 0451099648.*
(See chapter 9, "Telekinesis and Hypnosis: Chaos from Control.")

The Stand. *New York: Gramercy, 2001, ©1978. 1153p. ISBN 0517219018.*

A nanosecond of computer error in a Defense Department laboratory ends the world as we know it. The next day, 99 percent of the earth's population is dead, and the survivors choose to be allied with either the good Mother Abigail, a frail 108-year-old woman, or the evil Randall Flagg, a man with a lethal smile and unspeakable powers. **Similar titles:** *The Day of the Triffids*, John Wyndham; *Monster Island*, David Wellington; *The Road*, Cormack McCarthy.

Antichrist, The • Apocalypse • Computers • Magic • Nevada—Las Vegas • Road Trips • Septuagenarians • Southwest, The • War—Biological Warfare • Weird Science

Koontz, Dean.

Dark Rivers of the Heart. *New York: Ballantine, 2000, ©1994. 582p. ISBN 0553582895.*

Spencer Grant just wants to get to know the waitress named Valerie who served him on the previous night. When he follows her home, he finds himself caught up in the middle of a conspiracy that involves computers, blackmail, and murder. Do two individuals stand a chance against the strength of a government conspiracy? **Similar titles:** *Firestarter*, Stephen King; *Carrion Comfort*, Dan Simmons; *Goliath*, Steve Alten; *Demon Seed*, Dean Koontz.

Computers • Eugenics • Government Officials • Waitress as Character

Fear Nothing. *New York: Bantam Books, 2007, ©1997. 400p. ISBN 0553579754.*

A twenty-eight-year-old suspects that he is the product of military experimentation. His investigation into exactly what happened, and who is responsible, will test his limitations (he is hypersensitive to sunlight) and teach him his strengths. **Similar titles:** *Mr. Murder* and *Seize the Night*, Dean Koontz; <u>The Fury Series</u>, John Farris.

Disabilities—Xeroderma Pigmentation • Eugenics • Snow, Christopher (character) • Weird Science

Night Chills. *London: Headline, 2007, ©1976. 308p. ISBN 0747235228.*

The inhabitants of Black River are plagued by "night chills," a virus-like, scientifically engineered condition that causes them to become violent. What can save these innocent men and women who are being used as a government testing ground? **Similar titles:** *Insomnia*, Stephen King; *Floating Dragon*, Peter Straub; *First Do No Harm*, Steven Ford.

Mind Control • Rape • Violence, Theories of • War—Biological Warfare • Weird Science

Shadow Fires. *Thorndike, ME: Thorndike Press, 2001, ©1987. 775p. ISBN 0786228644.*

Rachael Leben wants nothing more than a divorce from her multimillionaire husband, Eric. Unfortunately, he is so embittered that he comes back from the dead to get even. And he isn't the only one trying to kill Rachael. This novel is suspenseful and action-oriented, with lots of plot twists. **Similar titles:** *Rose Madder*, Stephen King; *The Funhouse*, Dean Koontz; *The Parasite*, Ramsey Campbell; *The Stepfather* (film).

Domestic Violence • Government Officials • Marriage • Revenge

Twilight Eyes. *New York: Berkely, 2007, ©1987. 460p. ISBN 0425218643.*

A man sought for murder is actually humanity's best defense against the "others," demons that were genetically engineered and belong to an ancient civilization. Koontz's writing is suspenseful, and this novel is an excellent gentle read. **Similar titles:** *Phantoms* and *Midnight*, Dean Koontz; *The 37th Mandala*, Mark Laidlaw.

Demons • Eugenics • Weird Science

Matheson, Richard.

The Incredible Shrinking Man. *New York: Tor, 2001, ©1956. 351p. ISBN 0312856644.*

This collection includes the well-known novella that is the basis for the movie of the same name. It follows Scott Carey as he shrinks due to his exposure to a potent combination of insecticide and radiation. Carey's diminutive stature represents the feelings of many men after World War II that they too were shrinking in status in their homes and communities. **Similar titles:** *Richard Matheson's Off-Beat Uncollected Stories*, Richard Matheson; *Flowers from the Moon and Other Lunacies*, Robert Bloch; *The Illustrated Man*, Ray Bradbury; *The Incredible Shrinking Man* (film).

Marriage • Radiation • Weird Science

McCarthy, Cormac.

The Road. *New York: Knopf, 2006. 241p. ISBN 0307265439.*

A man shepherds his son through a post-apocalyptic world, trying to get to the Coast and presumably to safety. In this nuclear winter landscape, ash falls through the sky like grey snow, all wildlife is now extinct, and roving bands of cannibals prey on other humans to keep from starving to death. *The Road* is one of Oprah's Book Club Selections. **Similar titles:** *The Stand*, Stephen King; *The War of the Worlds*, H. G. Wells; *The Night of the Triffids*, Simon Clark; *The Day After Tomorrow*, Whitley Strieber, Roland Emerick, and Jeffrey Nachmanoff.

Apocalypse • Cannibalism • Death—Grieving • Nuclear Winter • Parenting

Mosley, Walter.

The Wave. *New York: Warner, 2006. 209p. ISBN 0446533637.*

After a series of seeming crank phone calls from a man purporting to be his long-dead father, Errol breaks into the cemetery where the father is buried to find in place of a corpse a living and younger replicant of his deceased parent. Soon after, Errol is kidnapped by government officials, who whisk him away to a secret facility and show him other regenerated dead who have miraculous powers of recuperation. **Similar titles:** *Shadow Fires*, Dean Koontz; *This Rage of Echoes* and *Death's Dominion*, Simon Clark; *The Body Snatchers*, Jack Finney.

Aliens • Government Officials • Replicants • Subterranean Monsters • Weird Science

11

12

13

14

15

16

17

18

19

20

Weird Science and Technology Gone Awry

Bakis, Kirsten.

Lives of the Monster Dogs. *New York: Farrar, Straus & Giroux, 1997. 291p. ISBN 0374189870.*

In the New York of 2009, 150 "monster" dogs arrive by helicopter and chartered plane, dressed in the clothing of nineteenth-century Prussian burghers, speaking through surgically implanted voice boxes, able to perform the tasks of humans by virtue of prosthetic hands and enhanced intelligence. The dogs come from a remote village in Canada, where German followers of mad visionary Augustus Rank have worked since 1882 to create a superior race of canine soldiers that will possess the intelligence of men but the courage and loyalty of dogs. **Similar titles:** *Neverwhere: A Novel*, Neil Gaiman; *Bloodstained Oz*, Christopher Golden and James A. Moore; *King Rat*, China Miâville.

Canada • Dogs • New York—New York City • Replicants • Weird Science

Clark, Simon.

This Rage of Echoes. *New York: Leisure, 2007. 342p. ISBN 0843954949.*
(See chapter 17, "Everyday Horror: When the Mundane Becomes Monstrous.")

Stranger. *New York: Leisure, 2003. 418p. ISBN 0843950765.*

A mysterious illness has wiped out virtually the entire world, except for the small, isolated town of Sullivan. Greg Valdiva, the town's protector, can sense if strangers are infected and is fully capable of terminating those he finds have become zombielike carriers. But xenophobia eventually turns citizens on one another, and Valdiva is forced to flee. On his journey, he finds a band of survivors, and with them, sets off to fight the ultimate threat—hives of bloblike gelatin that feed on unwary humans. **Similar titles:** *Dying to Live: A Novel of Life Among the Undead*, Kim Paffenroth; The Monster Nation Trilogy, David Wellington; The Rising Series, Brian Keene.

Apocalypse • England • Epidemics • Psychics • Zombies

Fowler, Christopher.

Breathe: Everyone Has to Do It. *Surrey, UK: Telos. 2004. 101p. ISBN 1903889677.*
(See chapter 17, "Everyday Horror: When the Mundane Becomes Monstrous.")

King, Stephen.

Cell: A Novel. *New York: Scribner, 2006. 355p. ISBN 0743292332.*
(See chapter 17, "Everyday Horror: When the Mundane Becomes Monstrous.")

Koontz, Dean.

Demon Seed. *Oxford: Compass, 2000, ©1973. 301p. ISBN 0753161699.*

Dr. Susan Harris lives a secluded but safe life, guarded round the clock by a computer that runs every aspect of her daily life. But when this artificial intelligence decides it wants to better understand the ways of the flesh, it turns against Dr. Harris and attempts to impregnate her with a cyborg-like fetus. This brilliant novel is narrated mainly by the computer, and this updated re-release adds considerably to the original 1973 novel. **Similar titles:** *Rosemary's Baby*, Ira Levin; *Goliath*, Steve Alten; *Night Chills*, Dean Koontz; *Village of the Damned* (film).

Computers • Futurism • Pregnancy • Rape

Midnight. *New York: Berkley, 2004, ©1989. 477p. ISBN 0425194515.*

A mad computer genius is terrorizing the inhabitants of Moonlight Cove. Can two of the Cove's natives and a couple of outsiders stop him before it's too late? As always, Koontz's writing is filled with action, suspense, and danger. **Similar titles:** *Demon Seed*, Dean Koontz; *Goliath*, Steve Alten; *Seven Crows*, John Vornholt.

Computers • Federal Bureau of Investigation • Religion—Native American • Replicants • Werewolves

Seize the Night. *New York: Bantam Books, 1999. 443p. ISBN 0613223594.*

Five-year-old Jimmy Wing goes missing in the quiet town of Moonlight Bay, California, and only one person, Christopher Snow, has any hope of finding him before something terrible happens. For Snow, the dark of night and of the underground passages where Wing may have been taken are not unusual, as his rare genetic disorder, xeroderma pigmentosum, forces him to live in the darkness rather than the light of day. **Similar titles:** *Fear Nothing*, Dean Koontz; *Silent Children*, Ramsey Campbell; The Fury Series, John Farris.

Animals Run Rampant • California • Child Molesters • Disabilities—Xeroderma Pigmentation • Eugenics • Snow, Christopher (character) • Subterranean Monsters • Weird Science

Watchers. *New York: Berkley, 2003, ©1987. 487p. ISBN 0425188809.*

Two altered life forms escape from a top-secret lab, and only one of them is benign. A super-intelligent dog; a murderous, grotesque beast; and a hit man who takes too much pleasure in his work populate this novel about science gone wrong. The novel is action-oriented, but characterization is solid as well. **Similar titles:** *Mr. Murder*, Dean Koontz; *Cujo*, Stephen King; *Lives of the Monster Dogs*, Kirsten Bakis.

California • Dogs • Eugenics • Serial Killers • Weird Science

Levin, Ira.

The Stepford Wives. *New York: Random House, 1972. 145p. ISBN 0394481922.*

(See chapter 10, "Small Town Horror: Villages of the Damned.")

Machen, Arthur.

The Great God Pan and The Hill of Dreams. *Mineola, NY: Dover Editions, 2006. 236p. ISBN 0486443450.*

The first of these novellas, a wonderfully gossipy story of sexual depravity and decadence in Victorian London, is populated with elitist nobility who are more than familiar with the seediest parts of London's streets. The story unfolds when these men are driven to commit suicide, and the truth comes to light via the narration of a bungled scientific experiment and the memoirs of a scholar of the paranormal. The second novella is narrated by Master Lucian Taylor, a would-be writer who is overwhelmed by the magical possibilities of the Welsh countryside—complete with ominous premonitions. **Similar titles:** *The Collected Strange Stories*, Robert Aickman; *The Beloved*, J. F. Gonzales; *Great Weird Tales: 14 Stories by Lovecraft, Blackwood, Machen and Others*, S. T. Joshi (editor); *Earthbound*, Richard Matheson.

England—London • Epistolary Format • Obsession • Psychosexual Horror • Victorian Era • Wales

Nolan, William F.

Dark Universe. *New York: Leisure, 2003. 372p. ISBN 0843951907.*
(See chapter 18, "Collections and Anthologies.")

Racina, Thom.

Deadly Games. *New York: Signet, 2003. 371p. ISBN 045121076X.*

A computer game that is captivating teenagers also seems to be turning them into homicidal killers of religious leaders. The creator of the game is a programming genius who has a dark secret: his estranged brother was imprisoned for hacking into the Pentagon. When an FBI agent who suspects the truth is murdered and his partner kidnapped, the programmer's wife, a computer company executive, races against time to stop the Easter release of a new version of the game. **Similar titles:** *Midnight*, Dean Koontz; The Fury Series, John Farris; *Blue Rose*, Peter Straub.

Computers • Espionage • Federal Bureau of Investigation • Marriage • Mind Control • Religion • Spree Killers • Violence, Theories of

Siodmak, Curt.

The Patrick Cory Novels.

Told in the form of scientific diary entries, this classic chronicles the weird experiments of Dr. Patrick Cory. This series is not for the feint of heart; Siodmak is raw and uncompromising. **Similar titles:** *Hauser's Memory*, Curt Siodmak; *Frankenstein*, Mary Shelley; *Herbert West: Re-animator*, H. P. Lovecraft.

Cory, Patrick (character) • Weird Science

Donovan's Brain. *Mill Valley, CA: 1st Pulpless.com, 1999, ©1942. 182p. ISBN 1584450789.*

Cory allows a millionaire, Warren Howard Donovan, to die, so that he can keep Donovan's brain alive in his laboratory. The only problem is that the brain develops telepathic powers.

Diary Format • Eugenics • Telepathy

Hauser's Memory. *Mill Valley, CA: 1st Pulpless.com, 1999, ©1968. 184p. ISBN 1584451173.*

> Approached by the CIA, Dr. Patrick Cory is asked to transfer the memory of a dying German scientist to another body. He succeeds, but his experiment gets out of hand when the subject escapes.

Central Intelligence Agency • Espionage

Straub, Peter.

Floating Dragon. *New York: Putnam, 1983. 515p. ISBN 0399127720.*

> (See chapter 11, "Maniacs and Sociopaths, or the Nuclear Family Explodes: Monstrous Malcontents Bury the Hatchet.")

Stevenson, Robert Louis.

The Strange Case of Dr. Jekyll and Mr. Hyde, and Other Stories. *New York: Barnes & Noble, 2005. 254p. ISBN 1593083505.*

> (See chapter 18, "Collections and Anthologies.")

Film

28 Days Later. *Danny Boyle, dir. 2002. 113 minutes.*

> (See chapter 13, "Ecological Horror: Mother Nature Has Her Revenge.")

28 Weeks Later. *Juan Carlos Fresnadillo, dir. 2007. 99 minutes.*

> (See chapter 13, "Ecological Horror: Mother Nature Has Her Revenge.")

Alien. *Ridley Scott, dir. 1979. 117 minutes.*

> A commercial exploration spacecraft unwittingly takes on an alien life form that stalks the crew in deep space, where no one can hear them scream. The monster special effects are stunning, even thirty years later. Sigourney Weaver, Tom Skeritt, John Hurt, Veronica Cartwright, and Harry Dean Stanton star. **Similar titles:** *Phantoms*, Dean Koontz; *The Harvest*, Scott Nicholson.

Aliens • Feminism • Space Exploration

Attack of the 50-Foot Woman. *Nathan Juran, dir. 1958. (black and white). 65 minutes.*

> A wealthy woman marries a gold-digging playboy, and after she discovers his perfidy, finds her only solace in drink and shrewishness. An encounter with an alien makes her literally larger than life. As her size grows proportionate to her wrath, the fifty-foot woman wreaks vengeance on her faithless spouse and his doxy before being destroyed by the military. **Similar titles:** *The Incredible Shrinking Man*, Richard Matheson; *Carrie*, Stephen King.

Aliens • Feminism • Radiation • Revenge • Weird Science

Blood Moon. Aka Wolf Girl. *Thom Fitzgerald, dir. 2001. 97 minutes.*
(See chapter 6, "Vampires and Werewolves: Children of the Night.")

Bride of Frankenstein. *James Whale, dir. 1935. (black and white). 75 minutes.*
(See chapter 5, "Golem, Mummies, and Zombies: Wake the Dead and They'll Be Cranky.")

The Cell. *Tarsem Singh, dir. 2000. 107 minutes.*
This gorgeous art film tells an extremely disturbing story about a child psychologist (Jennifer Lopez) who uses virtual reality technology to communicate with comatose, emotionally disturbed children. After a serial killer (Vincent D'Onofrio) is caught and goes into a coma, she must go into his deranged mind to find the whereabouts of his latest kidnap victim—before it is too late. The only problem is that no one is sure if it is possible to survive in the physical world after dying in virtual reality. **Similar titles:** *Fever in the Blood*, Robert Fleming; *Mr. Hands*, Gary A. Braunbeck.

Child Abuse • Dreams • Federal Bureau of Investigation • Popular Culture—Virtual Reality • Psychologist/Psychiatrist as Character • Psychosexual Horror • Serial Killers • Weird Science

Frankenstein. *James Whale, dir. 1931. (black and white). 71 minutes.*
(See chapter 5, "Golem, Mummies, and Zombies: Wake the Dead and They'll Be Cranky.")

The Incredible Shrinking Man. *Jack Arnold, dir. 1957. (black and white). 81 minutes.*
This classic movie is based on the novella by Richard Matheson, who also wrote the script. After being sprayed by radioactive mist, Scott Carey begins to shrink, until he is so small he can no longer be seen by his family and is forced to battle a spider to survive. The story is often seen as a metaphor for the feelings of insignificance of men in America after World War II. **Similar titles:** *The Incredible Shrinking Man* and *I Am Legend*, Richard Matheson.

Cats • Marriage • Radiation • Spiders • Weird Science

Invasion of the Body Snatchers. *Don Siegel, dir. 1956. (black and white). 80 minutes.*
Small town residents are being replaced by replicants devoid of emotions and hatched by pods. This is a classic science fiction/horror film with a McCarthy-era subtext. Two remakes have been made, *Invasion of the Body Snatchers* (1978) and *The Invasion* (2007), but neither holds a candle to the original cinematic interpretation of Jack Finney's novel of the same name. **Similar titles:** *Carrion Comfort*, Dan Simmons; *The Tommyknockers*, Stephen King; *The Body Snatchers*, Jack Finney.

Aliens • California • Replicants • Weird Science

The Invisible Man. *James Whale, dir. 1933. (black and white). 71 minutes.*
This movie is Whale's relatively faithful adaptation of H. G. Wells's novel of the same name. Claude Raines stars as the mad scientist who makes himself invisible and wreaks havoc on small English villages. **Similar titles:** *The Invisible Man*, H. G. Wells; *The Strange Case of Dr. Jekyll and Mr. Hyde*, Robert Louis Stevenson.

England • Invisibility • Weird Science

The Stepford Wives. *Bryan Forbes, dir. 1975. 115 minutes.*

This made-for-television movie is a faithful adaptation of Ira Levin's novel of the same name. In Stepford, every woman acts like every man's dream of the perfect wife and has no desire beyond pleasing her husband, caring for her children, and cleaning her house—and certainly has no time to help start a local feminist consciousness-raising group. One newcomer watches this dream become a nightmare, then sees this nightmare engulf her best friend. This excellent film stars Katherine Ross, Paula Prentiss, and Tina Louise, with a screenplay by William Goldman. **Similar titles:** *The Stepford Wives*, Ira Levin; *Death's Dominion*, Simon Clark.

Feminism • Replicants • Suburbia

The Terminator. *James Cameron, dir. 1984. 108 minutes.*

A cyborg is sent from the future to kill a woman pregnant with a future revolutionary leader. Arnold Schwarzenegger, Linda Hamilton, Paul Winfield, and Bill Paxton star. **Similar titles:** *Mr. X*, Peter Straub; *Lightning*, Dean Koontz.

Apocalypse • Parallel Universes • Replicants • Shape-shifters • Time Travel

Terminator 2: Judgment Day. *James Cameron, dir. 1991. 137 minutes.*

He said he'd be back. The cyborg from the future returns, this time to protect the soon-to-be savior of humanity from destruction by a rival terminator. Arnold Schwarzenegger and Linda Hamilton star. **Similar titles:** *Mr. X*, Peter Straub; *Lightning*, Dean Koontz.

Apocalypse • Parallel Universes • Police Officer as Character • Replicants • Shape-shifters • Time Travel

Village of the Damned. *Wolf Rilla, dir. 1960. (black and white). 77 minutes.*

Nine months after a bus accident, all the fertile women in an English village are suddenly pregnant. The resulting progeny are all eerily similar in appearance and can fix people with their mesmerizing stare. **Similar titles:** *Dreamcatcher*, Stephen King; *The Body Snatchers*, Jack Finney.

Aliens • England • Pregnancy

June's Picks

Books: Jack Finney, *The Body Snatchers* (Scribner Paperback Fiction); Richard Matheson, *The Incredible Shrinking Man* (Tor); H. G. Wells, *The Invisible Man* (F. Watts)

Films: *Alien, Attack of the 50-Foot Woman, The Incredible Shrinking Man, Invasion of the Body Snatchers, The Stepford Wives, The Terminator, Terminator 2*

Tony's Picks

Books: Dean Koontz, *Demon Seed* (Compass); Peter Straub, *Floating Dragon* (Putnam); H. G. Wells, *The War of the Worlds* (Penguin)

Films: *Alien, The Cell, The Incredible Shrinking Man, Invasion of the Body Snatchers*

Chapter 13

Ecological Horror: Mother Nature Has Her Revenge

Human bio-hubris has led us to believe that we are at the top of the food chain and have dominion over creation, so we can dispose of Earth and its creatures as we see fit. We chop down acres of rain forest to clear the land for cattle for the fast-food industry. We pump livestock full of antibiotics and hormones to increase production. We blind rabbits to ensure that yet another shade of eye shadow is safe for consumers. We drill holes in the earth to extract fossil fuels to run our sport utility vehicles that allow us to visit giant retail malls. On the way there we run over raccoons, squirrels, and possums that were displaced when their forest home was cleared to erect yet another strip mall or subdivision. And we wrap everything from treasures to trash in layers of plastic or Styrofoam that cannot biodegrade, that will exist for all eternity. Scientists remind us that this behavior has its consequences: several species of animals are now extinct; escalated global warming has caused increasingly stronger hurricanes, tornados, and droughts and has destroyed the polar ice caps; and overuse of antibiotics has spawned new bacteria resistant to our drugs. Horror writers too remind us that there is a price to pay when we treat the environment and Mother Nature's creatures with no regard for the consequences.

Ecological horror, a relatively recent subgenre, reflects, through metaphor and dark imagery, the frightening and very real results of humanity's thoughtless "mastery" of nature. Authors like Steve Alten (The Meg Series) argue that humans never have been and are still not at the top of the food chain. Although this novel deals with fictional creatures with prehistoric ties, it reminds us that "lions and tigers and bears" are the ultimate supreme hunters. Other horror emphasizes the revenge of the downtrodden, smaller animals in nature. Alfred Hitchcock's *The Birds* is a not-so-lighthearted view of our feathered friends. Frank Schatzing's *The Swarm* presents an intelligent life force that possesses sea animals, causing them to do its bidding—punishing the human race after a series of ecological disasters.

It should come as no surprise that various entries in this chapter cross over from the technohorror subgenre. These texts demonstrate why it is "not nice to fool with Mother Nature." Radioactivity in Japan from the bombing of Hiroshima and Nagasaki creates the fictional Godzilla, who stomps buildings as residents are enjoined to calmly exit the city. Later, when Godzilla is domesticated to become the protector of Japan, he must fight other creatures spawned by human activity, such as the Smog Monster and Mothra. In Danny Boyle's film *28 Days Later*, and the sequel *28 Weeks Later*, civilization is toppled by the rage virus, which might have originally occurred in nature or might have been crafted in a lab before it was loosed on the world by animal rights activists bent on rescuing the chimpanzees the scientists had been experimenting on.

Sometimes natural monstrosities aren't the fault of humans; nature itself is capricious and chaotic, and this too can be frightening. A loving pet like Stephen King's *Cujo* can be transformed from the family dog into a monster who rips his master limb from limb when he is infected with metaphoric rabies. In Daphne Du Maurier's short story "The Birds" (the basis for Alfred Hitchcock's film of the same name), the emblems of romantic love unleash their fury because of a blonde sexpot bent on tearing asunder the sort of love that is the basis for the traditional home. In *Cloverfield*, giant gecko-like creatures from outer space lay waste to Manhattan.

Stories as seemingly diverse as John Wyndham's *The Day of the Triffids* and the film *Willard* underscore the results of mistreating our pets. In the latter, social outcast Willard Stiles gets revenge on all who have wronged him by befriending a hoard of rats and training them to kill his enemies. But ultimately even Willard cannot stand the creatures, particularly the largest of them all, Ben. When Willard betrays the rats, they take their revenge. In *Day of the Triffids*, the ambulatory trees are not brought to earth by a meteorite shower as they are in the film version, but were kept as exotic pets before this apocalyptic event, which allowed them to proliferate. Thus, when most of the human race is blinded overnight by a meteorite shower, the Triffids are already poised to fill the void created as the planet's dominant species loses its edge.

The horrors of Mother Nature's revenge serve as reminders that we must face the repercussions of our actions when we mine the land and pollute the air and waterways or violate laws that are perceived by at least some as being "natural" ones. This sense of guilt concerning nature and a healthy universal fear of some animals and insects are two of the appeals of ecological horror. In many ways, this subgenre more than any other lends itself to works that would best be described as warning horror—the types of texts that both teach readers about ecological issues and delight them by taking them on a horrifying journey. After all, virtue is not always its own reward; even if we were considerate stewards of the earth, we could nevertheless find ourselves on the wrong end of the food chain.

Creature Features

Alten, Steve.

The Loch. *Mayfield Heights, OH: Tsunami Books, 2005. 487p. ISBN 0976165902.*
After Zach Wallace nearly drowns in the Sargasso Sea chasing a giant squid, he decides to return to his native Scotland, only to find that his father has been accused of murder after the remains of his business partner are found in Loch Ness. But the father argues that it was not a human who left a half-eaten body along the shore. **Similar titles:** <u>The Meg Series</u>, Steve Alten; *The Terror*, Dan Simmons; *Crooked Tree*, Robert Charles Wilson; *The Creature from the Black Lagoon* (film); *The Creature from the Black Lagoon* (film).
Marine Biology • Maritime Horror • Paleontology • Popular Culture—Loch Ness Monster • Prehistoric Monsters • Scotland

The Meg Series.

Paleontologist Jonas Taylor has just discovered that the fiercest predator ever to live on Earth, the giant sharklike *Carhardon megalodon*, is not extinct as was believed. Now its waters have been disturbed, and the Meg has discovered a new prey—humans. **Similar titles:** *The Loch*, Steve Alten; *Merian C. Cooper's King Kong*, Joe DeVito, Brad Strickland, and Delos Wheeler Lovelace; *Natural Selection*, Steve Freedman; *Monster*, Frank Peretti.

Marine Biology • Maritime Horror • Paleontology • Prehistoric Monsters • Sharks • Taylor, Jonas (character)

Meg. *Mayfield Heights, OH: Tsunami Books, 2005, ©1997. 438p. ISBN 0976165910.*

> Jonas Taylor's life is about to become more complicated: He has recently gone through a bitter divorce, funding for his research is getting harder to come by, and he has just accidentally unleashed the fury of a very hungry prehistoric creature. This is a fast-paced, easy read.

Asian American Characters

The Trench. *New York: Kensington, 2000, ©1999. 432p. ISBN 0786011149.*

> Taylor is forced to face his biggest fear when Angel, the baby megalodon shark he once captured, escapes from a Monterey marina. In Alten's fast-paced, plot-driven prose, Taylor battles prehistoric creatures and evil businessmen.

California

Bakis, Kirsten.

Lives of the Monster Dogs. *New York: Farrar, Straus & Giroux, 1997. 291p. ISBN 0374189870.*

> (See chapter 12, "Technohorror: Evil Hospitals, Military Screw-Ups, Mad Scientists, and Alien Invasions.")

Clark, Simon.

The Night of the Triffids. *London: New English Library, 2001. 469p. ISBN 0340766018.*

> Clark's sequel to John Wyndham's classic *The Day of the Triffids* picks up twenty-five years after the original story. Civilization was radically disrupted when the Triffids, ambulatory trees with fatally poisonous stingers, took over, leaving only pockets of survivors. Now pilot David Madsen investigates a new ecological disaster that plagues humanity—the sun's rays are no longer reaching Earth's surface, threatening humans and Triffids alike. **Similar titles:** *The Day of the Triffids*, John Wyndham; *Dead Sea* and *The Conqueror Worms*, Brian Keene; *The Road*, Cormac McCarthy.

Alternative Literature • Apocalypse • England—Isle of Wight • New York—New York City • Plants Run Rampant • Triffids (fictional creatures)

Clegg, Douglas.

Wild Things: Four Tales. Baltimore: Cemetery Dance, 2006. 97p. ISBN 1587671565.
(See chapter 18, "Collections and Anthologies.")

DeVito, Joe, Brad Strickland, and Delos Wheeler Lovelace.

Merian C. Cooper's King Kong. *New York: St. Martin's Griffin, 2005. 203p. ISBN 0312349157.*

This rewrite of the 1932 classic *King Kong* begins with Carl Denham's search for a starlet for his new project. He quickly discovers that most actresses are not eager to board a highly secretive ship filled with gas bombs. But Ann Darrow is willing, so they begin the journey to Skull Island, where the natives kidnap Ann. Denham is forced to follow—into a jungle filled with prehistoric creatures. A short foreward on the filmmaker Merrian C. Cooper is also included in this version. **Similar titles:** The Meg Series and *The Loch*, Steve Alten; *King Kong*, Edgar Wallace and Merian C. Cooper; *King Kong* (film).

Animals Run Rampant • Apes • California—Hollywood • Darrow, Ann (character) • Horror Movie Industry • King Kong (character) • New York—New York City • Prehistoric Monsters

Freedman, Dave.

Natural Selection. *New York: Hyperion, 2006. 414p. ISBN 1401302092.*

Harry Ackerman's Manta World failed when all of his captive manta rays died, but he hasn't given up hope yet of building a spectacular exhibition. So when he hears about a sighting of a manta ray–like creature called the fling ray, he dispatches a team of scientists to investigate. What they discover is a creature with big brains, big wings, and big teeth—a creature that is able to devour anything in its path, including humans. **Similar titles:** The Meg Series, Steve Alten; *Monster*, Frank Peretti; *The Conqueror Worms*, Brian Keene; *Cloverfield* (film).

Animals Run Rampant • California • Marine Biology • Maritime Horror

Golden, Christopher.

The Shell Collector. *Baltimore, MD: Cemetery Dance Publications, 2006. 128p. ISBN 158767114X.*

(See chapter 10, "Small Town Horror: Villages of the Damned.")

Jensen, Michael.

Firelands. *Los Angeles: Alyson Publications, 2004. 299p. ISBN 1555838405.*

This novel draws upon both the early American gothic novel and James Fenimore Cooper's *Leatherstocking Tales*. Set in 1799 colonial America, the story begins with Cole Seavey hunting alone in the wilderness, seeing the sky obscured by a storm cloud of the soon to be extinct passenger pigeons. The screeching birds chase Cole off the hillside to the edge of the woods, where he finds a dying woman and hears his name being called by a sinister creature. **Similar titles:** *Wieland, or the Transfor-*

mation, Charles Brockden Brown; *The Manitou*, Graham Masterton; *The Burning*, Bentley Little; *Shadow Coast*, Philip Haldeman.

Alternative Literature • *Gay/Lesbian/Bisexual Characters* • *Homoeroticism* • *Wilderness*

Kiernan, Caitlin R.

Threshold: A Novel of Deep Time. *New York: Roc, 2007, ©2001. 326p. ISBN 045146124X.*

(See chapter 17, "Everyday Horror: When the Mundane Becomes Monstrous.")

King, Stephen.

Cujo. *New York: Warner, 2000, ©1981. 352p. ISBN 0751504408.*

Murderer Frank Dodd has figured out a way to come back after death: He has managed to possess the body of Cujo, beloved family pet of the Camber family. Once Dodd's spirit and intelligence inhabit the body of the 200-pound St. Bernard, the dog goes on a rampage (attributed to rabies), dismembering and killing anyone who crosses his path. *Cujo* is another of King's masterpieces of suspense. You will never look at your pets the same way again. **Similar titles:** *Natural Selection*, Dave Freedman; The Meg Series, Steve Alten; *The Birds* (film); *Fallen* (film).

Animals Run Rampant • *Dogs* • *Maine—Castle Rock* • *Serial Killers*

Kumar, Jay C.

Dark Woods. *New York: Berkley, 2004. 311p. ISBN 0425197077.*

While on a hunting trip, a deputy sheriff witnesses his friends being injured, and when he returns to the scene of the incident, he finds the body of a local poacher and an animal that has been ripped to shreds. A science professor helps with the investigation, and they determine that the enigmatic killings seem to point in only one direction—a real live Sasquatch. **Similar titles:** *The Terror*, Dan Simmons; *Crooked Tree*, Robert Charles Wilson; *The Loch*, Steve Alten.

Academia • *Animals Run Rampant* • *Police Officer as Character* • *Popular Culture—Bigfoot* • *Washington State* • *Wilderness*

Lee, Edward.

Slither. *New York: Leisure, 2006. 357p. ISBN 0843954140.*

A team of biologists, along with a *National Geographic* photographer, venture to an island off the Florida coast to study the rare bristle worm. The island, home to a now-defunct military base, is the perfect breeding ground for a new, flesh-eating variety of this worm to mutate. Soon, one by one members of the team return to base somehow changed. **Similar titles:** *The Conqueror Worms*, Brian Keene; *Parasites Like Us*, Adam Johnson; *Peeps*, Scott Westerfield.

Academia • *Biology* • *Florida* • *Photographer as Character* • *Replicants* • *Worms*

Masello, Robert.

Bestiary. *New York: Berkley, 2006. 453p. ISBN 0425212807.*

Jurassic Park meets *The Da Vinci Code* in this thriller, in which an Iraqi billionaire hires medieval manuscript expert Beth Cox to translate and restore his family's millennium-old bestiary, an ancient text that supposedly illustrates the fantastical creatures that resided in the Garden of Eden. The book, originally created by monks, is full of hidden messages written in dead languages, but the beasts in it are not dead. **Similar titles:** *A Study of Destiny*, Cheiro. *To Wake the Dead*, Richard Laymon; *The Mummy: Dark Resurrection*, Michael Paine.

Antiquarianism • California—Los Angeles • Cursed Objects • Mummies • Paleontology

Peretti, Frank.

Monster. *Nashville, TN: WestBow, 2005. 451p. ISBN 084991180X.*

A man and wife go on a wilderness trek in Idaho; they become separated in the wilderness. Now the wife finds herself lost deep in the woods with mysterious creatures that challenge Charles Darwin's ideas of evolution. **Similar titles:** *Natural Selection*, David Freedman; <u>The Meg Series</u>, Steve Alten; *Blood Angel*, Justine Musk.

Idaho • Religion—Christianity • Wilderness

Pinborough, Sarah.

Breeding Ground. *New York: Leisure, 2006. 339p. ISBN 0843957417.*

When Chloe becomes pregnant, the joy in her relationship with her partner Matt only increases. But as the pregnancy progresses, Chloe's easygoing personality undergoes a radical change—she becomes increasingly angry and cruel. Worse still, she gains enormous amounts of weight and has lumps of fat in odd places, even after she stops eating. The reason for Chloe's horrifying transformation is revealed when she dies giving birth—to a mass of mutant spiders. **Similar titles:** *Rosemary's Baby*, Ira Levin; *The Conqueror Worms*, Brian Keene; *Natural Selection*, Dave Freedman.

Animals Run Rampant • England • Pregnancy • Spiders

Searcy, David.

 Ordinary Horror. *New York: Penguin-Viking, 2001. 230p. ISBN 0670894761.*

(See chapter 17, "Everyday Horror: When the Mundane Becomes Monstrous.")

Shirley, John.

Crawlers. *New York: Del Rey, 2003. 383p. ISBN 0345446526.*

(See chapter 12, "Technohorror: Evil Hospitals, Military Screw-Ups, Mad Scientists, and Alien Invasions.")

Van Belkom, Edo.

Wolf Pack. *Toronto: Tundra Books, 2004. 184p. ISBN 0887766692.*
(See chapter 6, "Vampires and Werewolves: Children of the Night.")

Wallace, Edgar, and Merian C. Cooper.

King Kong. *New York: Modern Library, 2005, ©1932. 192p. ISBN 081297493X.*
This reprint of the 1932 novelization of the famous film of the same name features a giant ape, ripped from his Skull Island home to be displayed to crowds in New York City only to fall hopelessly in love with the starlet Ann Darrow. **Similar titles:** *King Kong*, Joe DeVito, Brad Strickland, and Delos Wheeler Lovelace; The Meg Series and *The Loch*, Steve Alten; *King Kong*, Edgar Wallace and Merian C. Cooper; *King Kong* (film).

Animals Run Rampant • Apes • Darrow, Ann (character) • King Kong (character) • New York—New York City

Wyndham, John.

The Day of the Triffids. *New York: Modern Library, 2003, ©1951. 256p. ISBN 0812967127.*
Humans keep as pets a newly discovered species of tree, the Triffid, which is distinguished by its ability to walk about clumsily on three rootlike appendages. Soon, like kudzu and nutria, the Triffids take over entire forests and make it difficult for humans to live near their habitats. Later films such as *28 Days Later* owe a good deal to Wyndham's novel, particularly in its representation of how a rogue phenomenon can terrorize an island nation. **Similar titles:** *Night of the Triffids*, Simon Clark; *Ordinary Horror*, David Searcy; *The Stand*, Stephen King; *Black Tide*, Del Stone Jr.; *28 Days Later* (film).

Apocalypse • England—London • Islands • Plants Run Rampant • Triffids (fictional creatures)

Eerie Epidemics

Johnson, Adam.

Parasites Like Us. *New York: Viking, 2003. 368p. ISBN 0670032409.*
Anthropology professor Hank Hannah and his graduate students unleash a deadly, prehistoric contagion when they illegally exhume an ancient American burial site containing the remains of Clovis man. While Hannah is busy dealing with the resulting legal problems, two graduate students use a Clovis arrowhead to kill a pig, unwittingly unleashing a deadly, prehistoric contagion. Johnson's sardonic writing has been compared to that of the late Kurt Vonnegut. **Similar titles:** *Parasite Eve*, Hideaki Sena; *The Deluge*, Mark Morris; *Demons*, John Shirley; *28 Days Later* (film).

Academia • Apocalypse • Archeology • Epidemics • Islands

Langan, Sarah.

 The Missing. *New York: Harper, 2007. 400p. ISBN 0060872918.*

In this sequel to *The Keeper*, schoolteacher Lois Larkin takes her elementary school students on a field trip from Corpus Christi, Maine, to the neighboring town of Bedford, a town destroyed by a recent paper mill fire—which has spewed chemicals into the air that awaken a deadly, long-buried virus. Unfortunately one of the children unearths the contagious virus and turns into a flesh-eating zombie. One by one the child's friends, parents, and then neighbors become infected, insane, and inhuman. **Similar titles:** *The Keeper*, Sarah Langan; *The Deluge*, Mark Morris; The Monster Nation Trilogy, David Wellington; *28 Days Later* (film).

Epidemics • Maine • Teacher as Character • Zombies

Sena, Hideaki, and Tyran Grillo.

Parasite Eve. *New York: Vertical, 2005. 319p. ISBN 1932234195.*

(See chapter 12, "Technohorror: Evil Hospitals, Military Screw-Ups, Mad Scientists, and Alien Invasions.")

Stone, Del, Jr.

Black Tide. *Tolworth, England: Telos Publishing, 2007. 92p. ISBN 1845830490.*

A university professor and two students set out to make a study of the flora and fauna on an island off the coast of Florida in Escambia Bay before it is altered forever by a project to "revitalize" the area by dredging the bay to make it more attractive to anglers. As they set up their campsite on the island, within site of the mainland, the dredging brings from the depths toxic black microbes that become airborne and transform into bloodthirsty zombies all who breathe them. **Similar titles:** The Monster Nation Trilogy, David Wellington; *The Day of the Triffids*, John Wyndham; *Dead Heat*, Del Stone Jr.; *28 Days Later* (film); *Night of the Living Dead* (film).

Academia • Epidemics • Florida • Islands • Zombies

Westerfield, Scott.

Peeps. *New York: Razorbill, 2005. 312p. ISBN 159514031X.*

Living among us are the Peeps, or parasite positive individuals, whose malady turns them into bloodthirsty zombies and makes all they formerly loved anathema. Cal Thomas knows all about Peeps because he is a carrier; but he has never fully turned. He now works for the local Night Watch, an ancient organization that exists in every city to control the spread of the Peep contagion; and there is plenty of work for him, as the parasite is sexually transmitted. **Similar titles:** *Dead Sea*, Brian Keane; The Monster Nation Trilogy, David Wellington; *Dying to Live: A Novel of Life Among the Undead*, Kim Paffenroth.

Cats • Epidemics • Journalist as Character • New York—New York City • Rats • Zombies

Stormy Weather

Cacek, P. D.

The Wind Caller. *New York: Leisure, 2004. 355p. ISBN 0843953837.*
>   In Arizona the wind can be not only chilling, but biting, and a windy cold could appear seemingly out of nowhere, dropping the temperature by some fifteen degrees. Native American shamans understand the powers of nature and can use them to benefit others. But in the hands of outsiders, this magic might be used for ill. Gideon Berlander has learned to call the wind to do his bidding, and he is turning it into a vicious killing machine. **Similar titles:** *The Burning*, Bentley Little; *Burning Water: A Diana Tregarde Investigation*, Mercedes Lackey; *Shadow Coast*, Philip Haldeman.
>
>   *Arizona • Corporate Horror • Native American Characters • Religion—Native American • Weather*

Keene, Brian.

The Conqueror Worms. *New York: Leisure, 2006, ©2005. 326p. ISBN 0843954167.*
>   A global flood has decimated civilization and gives rise to giant, man-eating earthworms who menace a pack of survivors holed up in the mountains of West Virginia. Keene's pulp fiction style of writing is reminiscent of H. P. Lovecraft and H. G. Wells. **Similar titles:** *Slither*, Edward Lee; *The Deluge*, Mark Morris; *Night of the Triffids*, Simon Clark.
>
>   *Animals Run Rampant • Apocalypse • Weather • West Virginia • Worms*

Laymon, Richard.

One Rainy Night. *New York: Dorchester, 1999. 410p. ISBN 0843946903.*
>   An unexplainable black rain falls on the rural town of Bixby on the night that a Jamaican high school student is killed. Once the rain touches a person, that individual becomes a sociopathic murderer, brutally killing the next person he or she sees. Laymon's emphasis is on plot and graphic description. **Similar titles:** *The Burning*, Bentley Little; *Rabid Growth*, James A. Moore; *Bag of Bones*, Stephen King; *The Taking*, Dean Koontz; *Supernatural* (film); *J. D.'s Revenge* (film).
>
>   *Cursed Objects • High School • Police Officer as Character • Racism • Revenge • Weather*

Morris, Mark.

The Deluge. *New York: Leisure, 2007. 342p. ISBN 0843958936.*
>   In this post-apocalyptic novel, a flood leaves most of the earth underwater. A group of survivors bands together, but they discover that they are not alone—the flood has awakened creatures from below the earth's surface. The last of humanity suddenly finds itself in an all-out war with alien creatures. Will humans be wiped off the face of the earth? **Similar titles:**

The Missing, Sarah Langan; *The Stand*, Stephen King; *The Conqueror Worms*, Brian Keene.

Aliens • Apocalypse • Maritime Horror • Weather

Schatzing, Frank.

The Swarm. *New York: Regan Books, 2006. 881p. ISBN 0060813261.*

A team of scientists discover the Yrr, an intelligent life force that possesses sea animals to do its bidding, after several ecological disasters including toxic eyeless crabs poisoning Long Island's water supply, whales sinking ships, and the collapse of the North Sea shelf. The Yrr is angry about how the human race has treated nature, and the existence of our species hangs in the balance. Originally published in German. **Similar titles:** <u>The Meg Series</u>, Steve Alten; *The Day After Tomorrow*, Whitley Strieber, Roland Emerick, and Jeffrey Nachmanoff; *Parasites Like Us*, Adam Johnson.

Animals Run Rampant • Marine Biology • Maritime Horror

Strieber, Whitley, Roland Emerick, and Jeffrey Nachmanoff.

The Day After Tomorrow. *London: Gollancz, 2004. 256p. ISBN 0575076038.*

In the midst of an intensely hot summer, the North Pole's heat record is exceeded by fifty degrees. The rapid ice melt causes temperatures on Earth to drop radically, launching killer hurricanes and tornados and culminating in a blizzard that wipes out most life in the Northern Hemisphere. This is the novelization of the blockbuster film of the same name about global warming. **Similar titles:** *The Swarm*, Frank Schatzing; *The Deluge*, Mark Morris; *Demons*, John Shirley.

Apocalypse • New York—New York City • Popular Culture—Global Warming

Film

28 Days Later. *Danny Boyle, dir. 2002. 113 minutes.*

A group of animal rights activists break into a Cambridge laboratory to liberate the chimpanzees that are the university's research subjects. These chimps are infected with the "rage virus," which can be transmitted in seconds, rapidly transforming its victim into a type of zombie incapable of rational thought, a raving maniac compelled by the need to tear asunder all other living things. So when Jim awakes from a coma twenty-eight days after the infected chimpanzees have escaped containment, it is to an eerily abandoned London inhabited only by rage-infected humanoids. **Similar titles:** *The Day of the Triffids*, John Wyndham; *Parasites Like Us*, Adam Johnson; *The Missing*, Sarah Langan.

Apocalypse • England • Epidemics • Islands • Zombies

28 Weeks Later. *Juan Carlos Fresnadillo, dir. 2007. 110 minutes.*

Because the United Kingdom is an island nation, the rage virus has been contained. With the help of the U.S. military, all the rage infected have been destroyed and their remains properly disposed of. Now the remaining Brits, who either escaped or were out of the country during the pandemic, can return and begin to repopulate their country. But when a carrier of the virus emerges, the rage virus resurfaces with blinding speed. Now the only thing more horrifying than the virus itself is the way the military responds. **Similar titles:** *The Day of the Triffids*, John Wyndham; *Parasites Like Us*, Adam Johnson; *The Missing*, Sarah Langan.

Apocalypse • England • Epidemics • Islands • Zombies

The Birds. *Alfred Hitchcock, dir. 1963. 119 minutes.*

A promiscuous blonde bombshell pursues a staid widower to the island home he shares with his mother and daughter, and (in some interpretations) her presence in the community, and in the family unit, provokes an attack on all by the birds. The script for this film was loosely based on a Daphne du Maurier short story of the same name. Tippi Hedron, Jessica Tandy, Suzanne Pleshette, and Rod Taylor star. **Similar titles:** *Cujo*, Stephen King.

Animals Run Rampant • Birds • California • Islands

Cat People. *Jacques Tourner, dir. 1942. (black and white). 73 minutes.*

Oliver meets Irena at a zoo, where he finds her sketching a panther. Irena, who is from a small country in Eastern Europe, possesses an exotic beauty, and Oliver is so smitten with her that soon afterward her persuades her to marry him. But his new bride is terribly flawed—she is unable to consummate their marriage. Irena believes the problem is because she is from people who are descendants of panthers, and if she gives herself over to carnal passion, she will kill her lover. **Similar titles:** *Ferocity*, Stephen Laws; *Peeps*, Scott Westerfield.

Cats • Psychosexual Horror • Shape-shifters

Cloverfield. *Matt Reeves, dir. 2008. 85 minutes.*

As Hud makes a video recording of his friend Rob's party to celebrate his departure for a new job in Japan, an ear-splitting explosion is heard in the distance. Shortly afterward large chunks of debris rain on Manhattan, including the head of the Statue of Liberty. Hud keeps the camera rolling as he and his friends try to escape, and through his lens we catch glimpses of a 100-foot-high reptilian monster laying waste to the city amid the film's otherwise realistic documentary techniques. This film has been described as a post 9/11 *Godzilla* meeting *The Blair Witch Project*. **Similar titles:** *Natural Selection*, David Freedman; *The Deluge*, Mark Morris; *War of the Worlds*, H. G. Wells.

Aliens • Apocalypse • Documentary Techniques • Frame Tale • Godzilla (character) • New York—New York City

The Creature from the Black Lagoon. *Jack Arnold, dir. 1954. (black and white). 79 minutes.*

A group of scientists exploring the Amazon discover in the Black Lagoon the Gill-Man, a prehistoric, amphibious humanoid. They capture the creature, but it breaks free and kidnaps a female member of the expedition with whom it has fallen in love. This is a campy classic of 1950s horror/science fiction cinema. **Similar titles:** *The Loch*, Steve Alten; *King Kong*, Edgar Wallace and Merian C. Cooper.

South America—Amazon River Basin • Weird Science

The Descent. *Neil Marshall, dir. 2005. 99 minutes.*

A group of women set off on a caving expedition in the Appalachians. All crave the adventure that can only be had in extreme sports. But unknown to the group, their guide for this trip is taking them to a site that is not in any guidebook. The adventure soon goes bad when one of their number falls and breaks a leg and then the group discovers that they are not alone; something besides fungus lives underground. This horror film is unusual in every way, from its story to its all-female cast, who fight back rather than run screaming. **Similar titles:** *They Hunger*, Scott Nicholson; *Natural Selection*, Dave Freedman.

Cannibalism • Feminism • Spelunking • Subterranean Horror

Ginger Snaps. *John Fawcett, dir. 2000. 108 minutes.*

(See chapter 6, "Vampires and Werewolves: Children of the Night.")

Godzilla, King of the Monsters! (Godzilla). *Terry Morse, dir. 1956. (black and white). 80 minutes.*

A giant, fire-breathing lizard threatens Japan and terrifies a young reporter, played by Raymond Burr. This is the original American version of the Japanese classic (*Gojira*, Oshiro Honda, dir., 1954). It has spanned several sequels that transform Godzilla from a monster into the protector of Japan and has inspired several remakes, most notably, and most expensively, in 1998. **Similar titles:** The Meg Series, Steve Alten; *War of the Worlds*, H. G. Wells.

Godzilla (character) • Japan • Journalist as Character • Prehistoric Monsters

King Kong. *Merian C. Cooper and Ernest B. Schoesdack, dirs. 1933. (black and white). 104 minutes.*

A film crew goes to an in island in search of an exotic location for shooting their next production. There they discover King Kong, a giant ape worshipped by the locals. The crew capture the creature and bring him back to New York City, planning to make their fortune exhibiting him as a curiosity. But King Kong breaks free, lays waste to the city, and kidnaps the crew's beautiful female star, carrying her to the top of the Chrysler Building, where he uses his massive paws to swat at circling airplanes that buzz too near his head. **Similar titles:** *King Kong*, Edgar Wallace and C. Merian Cooper; *King Kong*, Joe DeVito, Brad Strickland, and Delos Wheeler Lovelace.

Animals Run Rampant • Apes • Darrow, Ann (character) • King Kong (character) • New York—New York City

Willard. *Daniel Mann, dir. 1971. 95 minutes.*

Shy loner Willard Stiles doesn't have much going for him. His life consists of going to work—where he is tormented by his coworkers and only tolerated by his boss for the sake of his late father, who founded the company—and going home at night to his shrewish mother. Dreaming of revenge, Willard befriends and trains a pack of rats who attack his enemies, but eventually the rats turn on him. Starring Elsa Lanchester and Ernest Borgnine, and featuring a famous theme song sung by Michael Jackson. **Similar titles:** *She Wakes*, Jack Ketchum.

Animals Run Rampant • Rats • Revenge

Willard. *Glen Morgan, dir. 2003. 100 minutes.*

This remake of the 1971 original, with Crispin Glover in the title role, is faithful to the original in such a way as to subtly parody it at times. In one scene, a hapless cat gets into Willard's house full of rats; scrambling for purchase on a bookshelf where it can escape the teeming mass, the cat accidentally turns on the stereo, which begins playing Michael Jackson's *Ben*, the theme song of the original film. The film's use of color and the framing of shots are especially reminiscent of graphic novels, particularly Glover's jet-black hair and nearly chalk-white face. **Similar titles:** *She Wakes*, Jack Ketchum.

Animals Run Rampant • *Rats* • *Revenge*

The Wolf Man. *George Waggner, dir, 1941. (black and white). 70 minutes.*
(See chapter 6, "Vampires and Werewolves: Children of the Night.")

June's Picks

Books: Del Stone Jr., *Black Tide* (Telos); Scott Westerfield, *Peeps* (Razorbill); John Wyndham, *The Day of the Triffids* (Modern Library)

Film: *28 Days Later, 28 Weeks Later, The Birds, Cloverfield, Willard* (2003)

Tony's Picks

Books: Steve Alten, *The Loch* (Tsunami Books); P. D. Cacek, *The Wind Caller* (Leisure)

Films: *The Birds, Cloverfield, The Descent*

11

12

13

14

15

16

17

18

19

20

Chapter 14

Psychological Horror:
It's All in Your Head

Although stories of psychological horror are for the most part devoid of supernatural monsters and bloodthirsty psychopaths, they are no less frightening. They deal with torment stemming from mental illness, child abuse, guilt, and countless other types of human suffering and emotional instability. These novels question the very nature of our world, but they take that inquiry one step further. Often they challenge the fictional reality that the writer creates. Perhaps the best way to define psychological horror is by citing one of the better examples of the subgenre, Ramsey Campbell's *Obsession*. Campbell's novel about being haunted by our childhoods suggests that the characters' obsession with their own guilt due to youthful indiscretions is more horrifying than any ghost or phantom sent from a supernatural realm to mete out justice. After all, we know that monsters are not real.

Because psychological horror is frequently characterized by more cerebral (rather than plot- or action-centered) writing, many readers who have antipathy for the horror genre as a whole will nevertheless find enjoyable works annotated in this chapter, because these authors are experimenting with style as much as they are with plot. For example, a current stylistic trend found in both horror and more mainstream literature is Victorian noir fiction, a contemporary imitation of the often introspective and meandering style of that era—infused with twenty-first-century sensibilities and observations about character. Michael Cox's *The Meaning of Night* presents a world in which a disturbed man makes a rambling confession after having murdered someone he considers responsible for every failure in his life. Roderick Anscombe's *The Secret Life of Laszlo, Count Dracula* is a nonsupernatural rewriting of *Dracula* employing the Victorian noir style.

Readers may also respond favorably to the variety of catalysts typically associated with a work of psychological horror. When she becomes lost in the woods for days, Tricia McFarland, in Stephen King's *The Girl who Loved Tom Gordon*, suffers extreme mental anguish. Maud Ruthyn, in Joseph Sheridan Le Faun's *Uncle Silas*, cracks after being bullied by an evil governess. Then there are the characters who suffer in hells of their own making. After receiving a book on demonology in the mail, the highly suggestible protagonist of Sara Gran's *Come Closer* believes herself to be possessed. In Stewart O'Nan's *A Prayer for the Dying*, a Civil War veteran questions the nature of evil after fatally infecting his wife and child with diphtheria. Still others fully inhabit parallel universes that may or may not be "real." The protagonist of Tananarive Due's *The Between* ponders whether or not he actually survived a near drowning episode in childhood, and consequently whether or not his present life as a middle-aged, middle class black man is just an illusion.

Aside from examining how we build dungeons in our own minds, psychological horror also gives voice to those darkest desires that we believe will remain eternally buried in the murky waters of the unconscious. Of course, when we repress desires in real life, they do not go away; instead, they come to life in nightmares or in other more dysfunctional ways. Similarly, when fictional characters disavow their darkest desires, those desires literally come to life in surreal fictional worlds. Sabrina Murray's unreliable narrator protagonist in *A Carnivore's Inquiry* may or may not be a cannibal who leaves a swath of dead bodies in her wake during a cross-country trek.

Our point here is not that horror is either psychological or supernatural. Although these two categories are useful in organizing horror texts, all horror contains elements of *both* psychological and supernatural elements to varying degrees. Instead, the works annotated in this chapter stand apart in that they leave the "reality" of the monster's existence up to the reader, who is left wondering what really happened. Was it all in the characters' heads all along?

The appeals of psychological horror are as varied as the plotlines that tales of this type explore. Some readers may respond positively to the more realistic fears to which this subgenre plays, while others may delight in the tendency of these works to be more thought-provoking because they are character driven, psychological texts that often avoid the pat ending. Stories of this type tend to be more open-ended, as the authors eschew explained endings. Readers may also respond to the universality of the psychologically horrifying experience, because almost all humans share in this experience. Finally, these tales tend to be more domestic. Where other subgenres stretch credulity with the introduction of supernatural creatures, psychological horror relies solely on the exploration of the darkest recesses of the human mind.

Note: Stories of psychological horror can also be found in the collections and anthologies described in chapter 18. Refer to the subject/keyword index for specific titles under keywords such as *Gothicism*, *Mental Illness*, or *Obsession*.

Aickman, Robert.

The Collected Strange Stories. 2nd ed. *London: Tartarus Press, 2001. 2 vols. 868p. ISBN 1872621473 (v. 1); 1872621481 (v. 2).*
   (See chapter 18, "Collections and Anthologies.")

Andrews, V. C.

Secrets in the Attic. *New York: Pocket, 2007. 374p. ISBN 1416530886.*
   Karen is being raised by a man she considers to be her evil stepfather, and her only escape from him is in her attic. There, she regularly meets with her friend Zippie and his brother, Jesse. In the dust and shadows, they share tales of a house with a murderous history—and eventually set into motion a scheme for getting even with the evil stepfather. But as the plan hatches, the true evil is revealed. This character study/psychological thriller contains many plot twists and atmospheric descriptions of the eerie house. **Similar titles:** *Sotfspoken*, Lucius Shepard; *Rebecca*, Daphne du Maurier; *Uncle Silas*, Joseph Sheridan Le Fanu.
   Childhood • Families • Gothicism • Parenting • Revenge

Anscombe, Roderick.

The Secret Life of Lazslo, Count Dracula. *New York: St. Martins, 2006,* ©*1994. 416p. ISBN 0312357664.*

> A young medical student, Laszlo Dracula, accidentally murders a prostitute. Twenty years later and in a new location, Laszlo again acts out his bloodlust and becomes a serial murderer. This novel, one of the few nonsupernatural versions of the *Dracula* tale, focuses on psychology and characterization. **Similar titles:** The Anno Dracula Series, Kim Newman; *Dracula*, Bram Stoker; *The Journal of Professor Abraham Van Helsing*, Allen C. Kupfer; *The Historian*, Elizabeth Kostova.
>
> *Diary Format • France—Paris • Medical Horror • Rape • Serial Killers • Weird Science*

Austen, Jane.

Northanger Abbey. *Oxford: Oxford University Press, 2000,* ©*1818. 221p. ISBN 0198337892.*

> (See chapter 16, "Comic Horror: Laughing at Our Fears.")

Austin, Sherry.

Where the Woodbine Twines: A Novel. *Johnson City, TN: Overmountain Press, 2006. 170p. ISBN 157072315X.*

> Nan Ayler must confront the baggage of her youth when her old friend Catherine Wiley returns to South Carolina, waking memories that she would prefer to forget. Transported back to her teen years, Nan makes a fateful journey to Myrtle Beach. There the two girls find a mysterious carnival, and what happens to them is unsettling. **Similar titles:** *The Between*, Tananarive Due; *The Traveling Vampire Show*, Richard Laymon; *More Tomorrow*, Michael Marshall Smith; *Carnival of Souls* (film).
>
> *Carnivals • Childhood • Obsession • Secret Sin • South Carolina—Myrtle Beach*

Bachman, Richard.

Roadwork. (See King, Stephen, *Roadwork,* in this chapter.)

Barker, Clive.

Galilee. *HarperCollins, 1998. 582p. ISBN 0060179473.*

> This novel, a departure for Barker, contains no demons or gore. Rather, it is a dark fantasy about two families, interracial sex, and the American Civil War. Galilee is the son of Sesaria, for whom Thomas Jefferson erected a mansion, and he plays the central role in bringing tensions between the Barbarossa and Geory families to a head. **Similar titles:** *Merrick*, Anne Rice; *Wuthering Heights*, Charlotte Brontë; The My Soul to Keep Series, Tananarive Due; The Eden Moore Trilogy, Cherie Priest.
>
> *African American Characters • Diary Format • Eroticism • North Carolina • Slavery • War— American Civil War*

Berliner, Janet, and George Guthridge.

The Madagascar Manifesto. *Clarkston, GA: White Wolf, 2002. 773p. ISBN 1892065584.*

Collected here are Berliner and Guthridge's three novels, *Child of the Light* (1992), *Child of the Journey* (1995), and *Children of the Dusk* (1997). *Children of the Dusk* was a Bram Stoker Award Winner. This gothic alternative history about a love triangle during a time of ethnic cleansing contemplates what would have happened if the Nazis had exiled the Jews to Madagascar, as they once planned. **Similar titles:** The Anno Dracula Series, Kim Newman; *Carrion Comfort*, Dan Simmons.

Alternative History • Gothicism • Madagascar • Nazism • Religion—Judaism • War—World War II

Bradbury, Ray.

A Graveyard for Lunatics: Another Tale of Two Cities. *New York: Perennial, 2001, ©1990. 307p. ISBN 0380812002.*

It is Halloween night, 1954, and a young film-obsessed scriptwriter has just been hired at Maximus Studios. An anonymous investigation leads him from the giant Maximus Films backlot to an eerie graveyard separated from the studio by a single wall. There he makes a terrifying discovery that thrusts him into a maelstrom of intrigue and mystery. **Similar titles:** *Whispers*, Dean Koontz; *Steel Ghosts*, Michael Paine; *Scream Queen*, Edo Van Belkom; *Fade to Black* (film).

California—Hollywood • Cemeteries • Movie Industry • Writer as Character

Braunbeck, Gary A.

Keepers. *New York: Leisure, 2005. 339p. ISBN 0843955775.*

(See chapter 8, "Mythological Monsters and 'The Old Ones': Invoking the Dark Gods.")

Brown, Charles Brockden.

Edgar Huntly, or, Memoirs of a Sleep-Walker, with Related Texts. *Indianapolis: Hackett Pub. Co., 2006, ©1799. 269p. ISBN 0872208532.*

When writing to his former fiancée Edgar Huntly, a haunted young man, recalls seeing Clithero Edny, a fellow Pennsylvanian, digging at the foot of an elm tree one night. What bothers Edgar is that this is the place where his friend Waldegrave had been murdered. Edgar confronts Clithero and learns about an accidental murder. But then Clithero disappears, and Edgar pursues him. On his journey, Edgar learns of missing letters that cause him to obsess to the point of delusion. **Similar titles:** *Wieland, or the Transformation*, Charles Brockden Brown; *The Vampyre*, John Polidori; *Melmoth the Wanderer*, Charles Robert Maturin.

Gothicism • Native American Characters • Obsession • Pennsylvania • Victorian Era • Wilderness

Burton, Peter, ed.

Bend Sinister: The Gay Times Book of Disturbing Stories. *London: Gay Men's Press, 2002. 390p. ISBN 1902852427.*

(See chapter 18, "Collections and Anthologies.")

Campbell, Ramsey.

Ghosts and Grisly Things. *New York: Tor, 2001, ©1998. 300p. ISBN 0312867573.*
(See chapter 18, "Collections and Anthologies.")

Incarnate. *London: Little, Brown, 1992, ©1983. 490p. ISBN 0316904511.*
Five individuals, each of whom has had strange experiences with dreams so realistic that they mistake them for reality, agree to undergo a scientific experiment that explores the nature of their dreams. They discover, however, that one of the individuals involved in the experiment is indeed the strange creature that has appeared to each of them in different guises, and that now seems to control their dreams and perception of reality. **Similar titles:** *Mr. X*, Peter Straub; *Strangers*, Dean Koontz; *In Dreams*, Shane Christopher.

Dreams • England • Journalist as Character • Revenging Revenant • Shape-shifters • Weird Science

The Last Voice They Hear. *New York: Forge, 1998. 384p. 0812541944.*
(See chapter 11, "Maniacs and Sociopaths, or the Nuclear Family Explodes: Monstrous Malcontents Bury the Hatchet.")

The Long Lost. *New York: Tor, 1996, ©1993. 375p. ISBN 0812550862.*
The Owains invite a long-lost relative to the family picnic, but then she begins manipulating them with her knowledge of their most closely held secrets—and her ability to deliver their darkest desires. **Similar titles:** *Needful Things*, Stephen King; *Obsession*, Ramsey Campbell; *Darkness Wakes*, Tim Waggoner.

Family Curse • Secret Sin • Wales • Wish Fulfillment • Witchcraft

Midnight Sun. *New York: Tom Doherty Associates, 1992, ©1990. 374p. ISBN 0812518039.*
As a young boy, Ben Sterling found himself being strangely attracted to the magical yet eerie powers that seem to inhabit Sterling Forest, the woods that surround his aunt's home. Twenty years later Ben, now a successful writer of children's books and a family man, inherits his aunt's house—and he is now even more attracted to the dark forces there. With the forest's shadow approaching his house, can Ben break its hypnotic hold before it takes him and his family? **Similar titles:** *The Dark Half*, Stephen King; Like *Death*, Tim Waggoner; *In the Night Room*, Peter Straub.

Family Curse • Obsession • Wilderness • Writer as Character

The Nameless. *New York: Warner, 1992, ©1985. 278p. ISBN 0708852572.*
(See chapter 11, "Maniacs and Sociopaths, or the Nuclear Family Explodes: Monstrous Malcontents Bury the Hatchet.")

Needing Ghosts. *London: Century, 1990. 80p. 0712621598.*
(See chapter 16, "Comic Horror: Laughing at Our Fears.")

11

12

13

14

15

16

17

18

19

20

Obsession. *New York: Macmillan, 1992, ©1985. 247p. ISBN 0316904538.*

Four teenagers receive an ad in the mail that says simply, "Whatever you want most, I do." When the four decide to try their luck with the ad, their wishes are fulfilled—with disastrous results. Twenty-five years later, the four suddenly find themselves under siege by a power that wants payment for granting their wishes. Subtle and erudite writing pervades this chiller. **Similar titles:** *Needful Things* and *It*, Stephen King; *The Boy Who Couldn't Die*, William Sleator: *The Long Lost*, Ramsey Campbell.

Childhood • Obsession • Wish Fulfillment

Strange Things and Stranger Places. *New York: Tor, 1993. 256p. ISBN 0312855141.*

(See chapter 18, "Collections and Anthologies.")

Chambers, Robert W.

The Yellow Sign and Other Stories: The Complete Weird Tales of Robert W. Chambers. <u>Call of Cthulhu Fiction series</u>. *Edited by S. T. Joshi. Oakland, CA Chaosium, 2000. 643p. ISBN 1568821263.*

(See chapter 18, "Collections and Anthologies.")

Christopher, Shane (pseudonym used by Matthew Costello).

In Dreams. *New York: Jove, 2006. 281p. ISBN 0515141283.*

(See chapter 11, "Maniacs and Sociopaths, or the Nuclear Family Explodes: Monstrous Malcontents Bury the Hatchet.")

Cisco, Michael.

 The Divinity Student. *Tallahassee, FL: Buzzcity Press, 1999. 149p. ISBN 096522001X.*

After being struck by lightning and brought back to life (after being filled with arcane documents during an "autopsy"), the Divinity Student is given the mission of reconstructing the *Lost Catalog of Unknown Words*. The Divinity Student, a "word finder" extraordinaire, travels through a nightmarish world of the dead to find the secret meanings of "lost words." Atmospheric and poetic, written in dreamlike, stream-of-consciousness prose. **Similar titles:** *Our Lady of Darkness*, Fritz Leiber; *The Man on the Ceiling*, Melanie Tem and Steve Rasnic Tem; *Beloved*, Toni Morrison.

Clergy as Character • Dreams • Prognostication • Religion—Christianity—Catholicism

Collins, Nancy A.

The Final Destination Series.

In this serial novelization of the movie *Final Destination*, a group of teenagers accidentally cheat death after one of them has a premonition—and now death wants what is rightfully his. So death arranges a series of freak accidents that claim the lives of the teens, one by one. **Similar titles:** <u>Charmed Series</u>, various authors; <u>The Corbin Family Novels</u>, James A. Moore; *This Rage of Echoes*, Simon Clark.

Death (character) • Parallel Universes • Precognition

Looks Could Kill. *Nottingham, UK: Black Flame, 2006. 385p. ISBN 1844163164.*

A supermodel named Sherry has a vision as she, other models, and their boyfriends board a cruise ship. Although the models listen and don't get on the ship, the head of the modeling agency ignores her warning. Before the ship leaves the harbor, it suffers a collision and begins to sink, and Sherry is disfigured by flying debris. But there is a way out for her: death visits her hospital room and tells her that she can avoid her fate, but the cost will be high—the lives of her friends.

Maritime Horror

Final Destination 2: A Novelization. *Nottingham, UK: Black Flame; New York: Simon & Schuster, 2006. 415p. ISBN 1844163180.*

Kimberly Corman is heading out on a road trip with friends, only this time the journey is anything but pleasurable. She has a vision of a horrifying car accident and just about loses her sanity when the accident actually happens. Recognizing a pattern in her history, she begins to research the phenomenon and discovers that death's natural pattern has been disturbed; to make up for the inconvenience, death intends to find ways to take the lives of people who are living on borrowed time.

High School

Costello, Matthew J.

Missing Monday. *New York: Berkley: 2004. 345p. ISBN 0425194558.*
(See chapter 12, "Technohorror: Evil Hospitals, Military Screw-Ups, Mad Scientists, and Alien Invasions.")

Cox, Michael.

The Meaning of Night: A Confession. *New York: Norton, 2006. 703p. ISBN 0393062031.*

In Victorian London, on the eve of Edward Glyver's planned assassination of an acquaintance, he confesses to a cold-blooded killing he committed in 1854, which he considered nothing more than practice for his current task: the elimination of the man he feels is ultimately responsible for every failure in his life. Cox's writing, an example of the Victorian noir, imitates the style of nineteenth-century authors such as Wilkie Collins and Charles Dickens. **Similar titles:** *Wieland, or the Transformation* and *Edgar Huntly*, Charles Brockden Brown; *Stevenson under the Palm Trees*, Alberto Manguel.

Dramatic Monologue • England—London • Obsession • Stalkers • Victorian Era

11

12

13

14

15

16

17

18

19

20

Crowther, Peter.

Spaces Between the Lines. *Burton, MI: Subterranean Press, 2007. 323p. ISBN 1596060794.*
   (See chapter 18, "Collections and Anthologies.")

De la Mare, Walter.

The Return. *Mineola, NY: Dover, 1997, ©1922. 193p. ISBN 0486296881.*
   (See chapter 7, "Demonic Possession: Satanism, Black Magic, and Witches and Warlocks: The Devil Made Me Do It.")

Desmond, Sean.

 Adam's Fall. *New York: Thomas Dunne Books, 2000. 245p. ISBN 031226254X.*
   (See chapter 4, "Ghosts and Haunted Houses: Presences and Absences.")

Du Maurier, Daphne.

Rebecca. *New York: Arrow, 1992, ©1938. 396p. 0099866005.*
   In this ghost story without a ghost, the second Mrs. De Winter is haunted by the presence of the first Mrs. De Winter, Rebecca. Rebecca is dead but not forgotten at Manderly, where the décor of the house is a monument to her taste. And while Maxim De Winter would like to forget his first wife and settle down to a nice quiet life with his second spouse, a discovery in the bay off of Manderly won't let Rebecca, or him, rest. **Similar titles:** *The Return*, Walter de la Mare; *A Bottomless Grave*, Hugh B. Lamb; *Wuthering Heights*, Emily Brontë; *Rebecca* (film).

England • Gothicism • Incest • Marriage • Obsession • Secret Sin

Due, Tananarive.

The Between. *New York: Harper Torch, 2005, ©1995. 289p. ISBN 0060819847.*
   A dedicated social worker and his wife, the first African American judge in Dade County, receive threatening letters. This incident triggers weird dreams that convince him that he may not really be alive, and that reality may not be what it seems. A disturbing and moving story, with well-developed characters. **Similar titles:** *Come Closer*, Sara Gran; *Where the Woodbine Twines*, Sherry Austin; *Looks Could Kill*, Nancy A. Collins; *J. D.'s Revenge* (film).

African American Characters • Dreams • Florida • Obsession • Parallel Universes • Racism

Ellis, Bret Easton.

Lunar Park. *New York: Knopf, 2005. 307p. ISBN 9780375412912.*
   (See chapter 17, "Everyday Horror: When the Mundane Becomes Monstrous.")

Evenson, Brian.

The Open Curtain. *Minneapolis, MN: Coffee House Press, 2006. 223p. ISBN 1566891884.*

Rudd, a teenaged loner raised by an abusive Mormon fundamentalist mother, learns about the controversial murder conviction of William Hooper Young, grandson of Church of Latter Day Saints founder Brigham Young, while doing research for a school project. The emotionally fragile Rudd becomes drawn in to the century-old crime, to the degree that he finds himself losing track of time—and ultimately believing the people he knows are involved in the murder. **Similar titles:** *Crippen,* John Boyne; *The Historian,* Elizabeth Kostova; *Stevenson Under the Palms,* Alberto Manguel.

Obsession • Religion—Mormonism • Utah—Provo • Young, William Hooper (character)

Fowler, Christopher.

Demonized. *London: Serpent's Tale, 2004, ©2003. 256p. ISBN 1852428481.*

(See chapter 18, "Collections and Anthologies.")

Gaiman, Neil.

Coraline. *New York: HarperTrophy, 2002. 162p. ISBN 0380977788.*

(See chapter 17, "Everyday Horror: When the Mundane Becomes Monstrous.")

Gifune, Greg F.

Deep Night. *North Webster, IN: Delirium Books, 2006. 517p. ISBN 192965376X.*

While Raymond is enjoying a few days of relaxation with friends in the remote woods of northern Maine, a woman staggers into camp, her clothes covered in blood. The group tries to help her, only to discover that she is carrying the ultimate in baggage—an ancient evil. Raymond recognizes the scenario all too well: as a child he suffered night terrors that were eerily similar to those of their adult visitor. **Similar titles:** *Nightbringer,* James Byron Huggins; *The Revelation,* Bentley Little; *Midnight Sun,* Ramsey Campbell.

Families • Maine • Revenge • Wilderness

Gran, Sara.

Come Closer: A Novel. *New York: Soho, 2003. 168p. ISBN 1569473285.*

Amanda leads a normal life until she begins hearing noises and finding herself in situations that can only be called bizarre. Yet whatever is haunting her is also compelling and desirable. It all begins when she receives a demonology book in the mail. Taking its quiz to determine if one has been possessed, she comes to believe that she is no longer in control of her life—and that it may already be too late to exorcise the malevolent spirit. **Similar titles:** *The Between,* Tananarive Due; *The Count of Eleven* and *Obsession,* Ramsey Campbell.

Cursed Objects • Demons • Marriage • Mental Illness • Obsession • Parapsychology

11

12

13

14

15

16

17

18

19

20

Gresham, Stephen.

Haunted Ground. *New York: Pinnacle, 2003. 350p. ISBN 0786015373.*

A typical 1950s farm boy, Ted lives with his family in Kansas. His father is a stoic farmer, his mother a woman who suffers from depression, and his brothers are always up to no good. When Cousin Judith comes to stay with the family, she brings special challenges: she is crippled, forced to wear cumbersome leg braces, and she inhabits a fascinating and somewhat dangerous fantasy world, where she has the power to raise ghosts. **Similar titles:** *Morbid Curiosity*, Deborah LeBlanc; *The Traveling Vampire Show*, Richard Laymon; *Witch*, Mary Ann Mitchell.

Disabilities—Paraplegia • Haunted Houses • Kansas • Midwest, The • Psychics

Hand, Elizabeth.

Generation Loss: A Novel. *Northampton, MA: Small Beer Press, 2007. 265p. ISBN 1931520216.*

(See chapter 17, "Everyday Horror: When the Mundane Becomes Monstrous.")

Hawthorne, Nathaniel.

The House of Seven Gables. *New York: Oxford University Press, 1998, ©1851. 328p. ISBN 0192836455.*

Young Phoebe cannot escape the family curse that is linked to a grotesque daguerreotype of the family patriarch. Hawthorne's emphasis is on atmosphere and characterization. **Similar titles:** *The Picture of Dorian Gray*, Oscar Wilde; *Poe's Lighthouse*, Christopher Conlon (editor); *Green Tea and Other Stories*, Joseph Sheridan Le Fanu.

Family Curse • Haunted Houses • New England • Obsession

Hirshberg, Glen.

The Two Sams. *New York: Carroll & Graf Publishers, 2003. 210p. ISBN 0786712554.*
(See chapter 18, "Collections and Anthologies.")

Jackson, Shirley.

The Haunting of Hill House. *New York: Penguin, 2006, ©1949. 182p. ISBN 0143039989.*

(See chapter 4, "Ghosts and Haunted Houses: Dealing with Presences and Absences.")

The Lottery and Other Stories. *New York: Farrar, Straus & Giroux, 2005, ©1949. 302p. ISBN 0374529531.*

(See chapter 18, "Collections and Anthologies.")

James, Henry.

Ghost Stories. *Hertfordshire, England: Wordsworth Editions, 2001. 344p. ISBN 1840224223.*

(See chapter 18, "Collections and Anthologies.")

Joyce, Graham.

Limits of Enchantment. *New York: Atria, 2005. 263p. ISBN 0743463447.*

Things are changing in the 1960s, even in the English countryside, where women still depend on Mammy Cullen, the local cunning woman, to deliver them in childbirth. Mammy turns her practice over to Fern, her apprentice and adoptive daughter, so Fern must use her mentor's traditional and sometimes magical ways to earn her living—in a world enamored of scientific medicine. **Similar titles:** *The Minister's Daughter*, Julie Hearn; The Merrily Watkins Mysteries, Phil Rickman.

England • Magic • Midwife as Character

Kidman, James.

Black Fire. *New York: Leisure, 2004. 339p. ISBN 0843953276.*
(See chapter 10, "Small Town Horror: Villages of the Damned.")

Kiernan, Caitlin R.

Threshold: A Novel of Deep Time. *New York: Penguin-ROC, 2007, ©2001. 326p. ISBN 045146124X.*
(See chapter 17, "Everyday Horror: When the Mundane Becomes Monstrous.")

King, Stephen.

Dolores Claiborne. *New York: Penguin, 1995, ©1992. 384p. ISBN 0451184114.*

Dolores Claiborne stands accused of murdering the wealthy old woman she has cared for over the past thirty years. Although innocent of this crime, she does confess to the 1963 killing of her husband. Dolores's confession, related in extended monologue format, reveals a plucky, capable woman, harrowed like a Gothic heroine. **Similar titles:** *Gerald's Game*, Stephen King; *The Meaning of Night*, Michael Cox; *The Secret Life of Laszlo, Count Dracula*, Roderick Anscombe.

Aging • Child Molester • Domestic Violence • Dramatic Monologue • Gothicism • Maine • Marriage • Septuagenarians

Gerald's Game. *New York: Penguin, 2004, ©1992. 448p. ISBN 0451176464.*

Jesse Burlingame and her husband Gerald vacation at a secluded cottage in the woods. When one of Gerald's "sex games" goes awry, Jesse finds herself handcuffed to a bed with no one around to save her. *Gerald's Game* offers readers an excellent study of the effects of dysfunctional families. **Similar titles:** *In the Dark*, Richard Laymon; *Scared Stiff*, Ramsey Campbell; *Dolores Claiborne*, Stephen King.

Animals Run Rampant • Families • Psychosexual Horror • Sado-Masochism

11

12

13

14

15

16

17

18

19

20

The Girl Who Loved Tom Gordon. *New York: Simon & Schuster, 2000, ©1999. 272p. ISBN 0671042858.*

> Nine-year-old Tricia McFarland wanders off the trail during a hike with her mother and older brother to escape their constant bickering, only to become lost in the woods for days. During her ordeal, as she grapples with her own mortality, her Walkman provides her only link to civilization. **Similar titles:** *The Hidden World*, Graham Masterton; *The Way the Family Got Away*, Michael Kimball; *Gerald's Game*, Stephen King; *Tideland* (film); *The Blair Witch Project* (film).
>
> *Baseball • Childhood • Maine • Wilderness*

It. *New York: Penguin, 1987, ©1986. 1104p. ISBN 0451169514.*

> Pennywise the Clown, a monstrous personification of all that is scary and evil, has returned to a small New England town to claim the souls of a handful of adults whom he terrorized as children. This novel was made into a television miniseries starring Tim Curry of *Rocky Horror Picture Show* fame. **Similar titles:** *Ghost Story* and *Floating Dragon*, Peter Straub; *American Morons*, Glen Hirshberg; *Nightmare on Elm Street* (film).
>
> *Childhood • Clowns • New England • Shape-shifters*

King, Stephen (writing as Richard Bachman).

Roadwork. *New York: Penguin, 1999, ©1981. 320p. ISBN 0451197879.*

> A lone man takes on progress: when his son dies, and then a highway project puts him out of work, Barton George Dawes has more than enough time on his hands to plot his revenge. Pushing the powers-that-be to the limit, he takes a stand against what he sees as a criminal act in progress, but in doing so he drives his wife and friends away. Will his obsession ultimately lead to chaos? **Similar titles:** *The Count of Eleven*, Ramsey Campbell; *Mr. Hands*, Gary A. Braunbeck; *The Policy*, Bentley Little; *Fight Club* (film).
>
> *Corporate Horror • Obsession • Revenge*

Klein, T. E. D.

Reassuring Tales. *Burton, MI : Subterranean Press, 2006. 167p. ISBN 1596060727.*

> (See chapter 18, "Collections and Anthologies.")

Koontz, Dean.

The Face of Fear. *New York: Berkley, 1990, ©1985. 306p. ISBN 042511984X.*

> (See chapter 11, "Maniacs and Sociopaths, or the Nuclear Family Explodes: Monstrous Malcontents Bury the Hatchet.")

The House of Thunder. *Thorndike, ME: Thorndike Press, 2000, ©1982. 504p. ISBN 0786228652.*

> In Koontz's version of "Sometimes They Come Back," Susan Thornton awakens from an accident-induced coma to find herself in the same hospital with the four men who murdered her boyfriend twelve years earlier. The only problem is that these men supposedly died violent deaths years before. Now it seems their ghosts want to finish off the witness who got away the first time, namely Susan. **Similar

titles: *The Key to Midnight* and *Whispers*, Dean Koontz; *Bag of Bones* and *The Dead Zone*, Stephen King; *Wither*, J. G. Passarella.

Amnesia • Comas • Espionage • Revenging Revenants

The Key to Midnight. *New York: Penguin, 1995, ©1979. 432p. ISBN 0425147517.*

When Alex Hunter spots Joanna Rand singing in a Kyoto nightclub, she seems vaguely familiar. After the two begin seeing one another, he realizes that she is the daughter of a famous U.S. senator. However, Joanna cannot remember her past or the reason she has a recurring nightmare about a man with metallic fingers. **Similar titles:** *The House of Thunder* and *Mr. Murder*, Dean Koontz; *Missing Monday*, Matthew J. Costello.

Amnesia • Dreams • Espionage • Japan • Mistaken Identity • Rape

Strangers. *New York: Penguin, 2002, ©1986. 688p. ISBN 0425181111.*

Across the country, a handful of people who don't know one another begin having similar nightmares and sharing a sense of paranoia. Soon their paths will cross, and they will have to face their greatest fears. Koontz is heavy on suspense. **Similar titles:** *Incarnate*, Ramsey Campbell; The Kinsella/Rodriguez Novels, Shane Christopher; *Blood Angel*, Justine Musk; *Paperhouse* (film).

Aliens • Clergy as Character • Dreams • Weird Science

Whispers. *New York: Berkley, 2006, ©1980. 457p. ISBN 042520992X.*

(See chapter 11, "Maniacs and Sociopaths, or the Nuclear Family Explodes: Monstrous Malcontents Bury the Hatchet.")

Laws, Stephen.

Darkfall. *New York: Dorchester, 2003, ©1992. 358p. ISBN 0843952180.*

(See chapter 4, "Ghosts and Haunted Houses: Dealing with Presences and Absences.")

Laymon, Richard.

The Midnight Tour. *New York: Leisure, 2007, ©1994. 596p. ISBN 0843957530.*

(See chapter 11, "Maniacs and Sociopaths, or the Nuclear Family Explodes: Monstrous Malcontents Bury the Hatchet.")

The Traveling Vampire Show. *New York: Leisure, 2001. 391p. ISBN 0843948507.*

The traveling vampire show comes to town one summer during the adolescence of three childhood friends; and when they plot to see what is forbidden to everyone under eighteen, their lives are changed forever. Events of this story unfold during the course of one day, and emphasis is on characterization. **Similar titles:** *Haunted Ground*, Stephen Gresham; *Ghoul*, Brian Keene; *It*, Stephen King.

Adolescence • Carnivals • Eroticism • Popular Culture

Lebbon, Tim.

Desolation. *New York: Leisure, 2005. 309p. ISBN 0843954280.*

Cain's father did psychological experiments on him when he was a child, which damaged him emotionally. When his father dies, Cain is free to live his own life, and he moves into a halfway house to make a new beginning. But not surprisingly, the trauma continues to haunt him. Soon Cain becomes convinced that everyone in the house is out to get him, and that his dwelling hides horrible secrets connected to his past. **Similar titles:** *The Home*, Scott Nicholson; *Boy A*, Jonathan Trigell; *Spider* (film).

Medical Horror • Psychologist/Psychiatrist as Character • Secret Sin

Le Fanu, Joseph Sheridan.

Uncle Silas: A Tale of Bartram-Haugh. *Charleston, SC: BiblioBazaar, 2007, ©1864. 482p. ISBN 143467620X.*

Maud Ruthyn, a young, naïve girl, is plagued by Madame de la Rougierre from the moment the enigmatic older woman is hired as her governess. A liar, bully, and spy, when Madame leaves the house, she takes her dark secret with her. After Maud is orphaned, she is sent to live with her Uncle Silas, her father's mysterious brother, a man with a scandalous, perhaps even a murderous, past. And once again she encounters Madame. **Similar titles:** *The House of Seven Gables*, Nathaniel Hawthorne; *Wieland*, Charles Brockden Brown; *In a Glass Darkly*, Joseph Sheridan Le Fanu.

Adolescence • England • Family Curse • Gothicism • Secret Sin • Victorian Era

Levin, Ira.

The Stepford Wives. *New York: Harper Torch, 2004, ©1972. ISBN 0060738197.*

(See chapter 10, "Small Town Horror: Villages of the Damned.")

Ligotti, Thomas.

The Shadow at the Bottom of the World. Cold Spring Harbor, NY: Cold Spring Press, 2005. 259p. ISBN 1593600585.

(See chapter 18, "Collections and Anthologies.")

Long, Jeff.

The Reckoning. *New York: Atria, 2004. 275p. ISBN 0743463013.*

Photojournalist Molly Drake accompanies a U.S. military–led team in Cambodia. They search for the bones of a pilot shot down during the war, but when Molly photographs the bones, she is promptly removed from the area by the military. She senses a cover-up not of the pilot, but of the surroundings—an ancient city shrouded in a labyrinth of fog and stone. **Similar titles:** *The 37th Mandala*, Mark Laidlaw; *Haunter*, Charlee Jacob.

Archeology • Cambodia • Journalist as Character • Popular Culture—Folklore • War—Vietnam War

Manguel, Alberto.

Stevenson under the Palm Trees. *New York: Canongate, 2004, ©2002. 105p. ISBN 1841955884.*

During the last years of his life, Robert Louis Stevenson is living in Samoa, deeply depressed and dying of tuberculosis. Then he becomes involved in the investigation of the rape and murder of a local woman, as well as an arson. When he meets Mr. Baker, a dour Scottish missionary, Stevenson begins to believe the man is somehow involved in the crimes. **Similar titles:** *The Meaning of Night*, Michael Cox; *The Dante Club*, Matthew Pearl; *The Ghost in the Eiffel Tower*; Oliver Bleys; *Crippen*, John Boyne.

Alternative History • Clergy as Character • Doppelgangers • Samoa • Stevenson, Robert Louis (character) • Writer as Character

Marsh, Richard (pseudonym used by Richard Bernard Heldman).

The Beetle. *Edited by Julian Wolfreys. Orchard Park, NY: Broadview Press, 2004, ©1897. 364p. ISBN 1551114437.*

(See chapter 9, "Telekinesis and Hypnosis: Chaos from Control.")

Massie, Elizabeth.

Ⓑ **Sineater.** *New York: IBooks, 2004, ©1994. 396p. ISBN 074349783X.*

(See chapter 10, "Small Town Horror: Villages of the Damned.")

Masterton, Graham.

Darkroom. *Sutton: Severn House, 2004. 256p. ISBN 0727860534.*

Jim Rook, a special needs teacher with the ability to see demons and spirits, is called upon by the LAPD to help solve a string of arsons and murders. Could the deaths have been the result of spontaneous combustion? **Similar titles:** *A Terrible Beauty*, Graham Masterton; *18 Seconds*, George D. Shuman; *Red Dragon*, Thomas Harris.

California—Los Angeles • Police Officer as Character • Popular Culture—Spontaneous Combustion • Rook, Jim (character) • Teacher as Character

Matheson, Richard.

Earthbound. *New York: Tor, 2005, ©1982. 223p. ISBN 0765311712.*
(See chapter 4, "Ghosts and Haunted Houses: Dealing with Presences and Absences.")

Hunted Past Reason. *New York: Forge, 2003, ©2002. 294p. ISBN 0312707398.*

Bob, an up-and-coming screen writer, needs the help of his friend Doug, an experienced outdoorsman who can show him the woods, to research a current project. But Doug is an actor whose career is on the skids, and during the trip he snaps and assaults his friend. Now, if Doug has his way, only one will leave the woods alive. **Similar titles:** *Graveyard for Lunatics,*

Ray Bradbury; *Where the Woodbine Twines: A Novel*, Sherry Austin; *Edgar Huntly*, Charles Brockden Brown.

Actor as Character • *Wilderness* • *Writer as Character*

The Incredible Shrinking Man. *New York: Tor, 2001, ©1956. 351p. ISBN 0312856644.*
(See chapter 18, "Collections and Anthologies.")

Now You See It. *New York: Tor, 2004, ©1994. 224p. ISBN 076530872X.*
A paralyzed magician must use the darkest of tricks to prevent his ungrateful son and nefarious daughter-in-law from pirating his act. Matheson's novel is filled with plot twists, wordplay, visual tricks, and suspense. **Similar titles:** *Shadowland*, Peter Straub; *Cycle of the Werewolf* and *Thinner*, Stephen King.

Disabilities—Paraplegia • *Magic* • *Mistaken Identity* • *Revenge*

Stir of Echoes. *New York: Tor, 2004, ©1958. 223p. ISBN 0765308711.*
(See chapter 4, "Ghosts and Haunted Houses: Dealing with Presences and Absences.")

Matthews, A. J. (pseudonym used by Rick Hautala).

Follow. *New York: Penguin, 2005. 312p. ISBN 0515140155.*
Pam Gardner's life is falling down around her. First she discovers her husband's infidelity; then she has a car accident that causes her to have a miscarriage, as well as to lose any memory of the wreck. And now she's either seeing ghosts or having hallucinations and is convinced that the man who attacked her also murdered her best friend. **Similar titles:** *Insomnia*, Stephen King; *Missing Monday*, Matthew J, Costello; *The Count of Eleven*, Ramsey Campbell.

Amnesia • *Obsession* • *Serial Killers*

McCauley, Kirby, ed.

Frights: Stories of Suspense and Supernatural Terror. *New York: Ibooks, 2003, ©1976. 287p. ISBN 0743458559.*
(See chapter 18, "Collections and Anthologies.")

Monteleone, Elizabeth E., and Thomas F. Monteleone, eds.

From the Borderlands: Stories of Terror and Madness. *New York: Warner, 2004, ©2003. 428p. ISBN 0446610356.*
(See chapter 18, "Collections and Anthologies.")

Murray, Sabina.

A Carnivore's Inquiry. *New York: Grove, 2006, ©2004. 377p. ISBN 0141018194.*
Twenty-three-year-old Katharine, fascinated with cannibalism, can enumerate its various literary, artistic, and historical manifestations. As she makes a cross-country journey from New York to Mexico, in her wake various bizarre murders occur. Katherine demonstrates a total lack of conscience as she relates the tale of her journey. Is she responsible? **Similar titles:** *Off Season*, Jack Ketchum; *The Dark Half*, Stephen King; *American Psycho*, Bret Easton Ellis; *Fight Club* (film).

Cannibalism • Obsession • Road Trips • Serial Killers

Neiderman, Andrew.

Unholy Birth. *New York: Pocket Star, 2007. 339p. ISBN 1416516840.*
A lesbian couple in Palm Springs decides they want to raise a child, so they look into artificial insemination. An unsolicited e-mail from a clinic that promises an ideal sperm donor and a live-in nanny leads them to Dr. Lois Matthews. Ignoring her premonitions of evil, one of the women goes through with the process, but then has regrets and, paranoid about what is growing inside her, begins to descend into insanity. **Similar titles:** *The Unwelcome Child*, Terese Pampellonne; *Rosemary's Baby*, Ira Levin; *Demon Seed*, Dean Koontz; *Rosemary's Baby* (film).

California—Palm Springs • Demons • Gay/Lesbian/Bisexual Characters • Mental Illness • Pregnancy

Oates, Joyce Carol.

Beasts. *Cambridge, MA: Perseus-Da Capo, 2002. 160p. ISBN 0786711035.*
During her first years of college, Gilian Brauer becomes obsessed with her charismatic poetry teacher, Andre Harrow, who encourages his students to write erotic prose, as well as his sculptor wife Dorcas, who carves wooden totems that express a bestial sexuality. Meanwhile, there is a disturbing rash of suicides at the college, and strange fires are breaking out all over campus. **Similar titles:** *The Collector of Hearts: New Tales of the Grotesque*, Joyce Carol Oates; *The Haunting of Hill House*, Shirley Jackson.

Academia • Addictions—Drugs • New England • Psychosexual Horror • Teacher as Character

O'Brien, Edna.

In the Forest. *London: Phoenix, 2003, ©2002. 224p. ISBN 0753816857.*
(See chapter 11, "Maniacs and Sociopaths, or the Nuclear Family Explodes: Monstrous Malcontents Bury the Hatchet.")

Oliphant, Margaret.

The Library Window. *Edited by Elizabeth Winston. Tampa: University of Tampa Press, 2006, ©1896. 74p. ISBN 1597320129.*
(See chapter 4, "Ghosts and Haunted Houses: Dealing with Presences and Absences.")

O'Nan, Stewart.

A Prayer for the Dying. *New York: Picador, 2000. 208p. ISBN 0312255012.*
Jacob Hansen, a Civil War veteran who thought his military experience had inured him to everything terrible, is stricken with guilt when a diphtheria epidemic claims the lives of many in his town. Now he must live

with the knowledge that he may have infected his wife and child, who now lay dying. The experience causes Hansen to question his faith and ponder the nature of evil. **Similar titles:** *The Girl Who Loved Tom Gordon*, Stephen King; *Matinee at the Flame*, Christopher Fahy; *I Am Legend*, Richard Matheson.

Clergy as Character • Epidemics—Diphtheria • Religion—Christianity • Secret Sin • War—American Civil War • Wisconsin

Palahniuk, Chuck.

Haunted: A Novel of Stories. *New York: Knopf, 2006, ©2005. 411p. ISBN 1400032822.*
(See chapter 15, "Splatterpunk: The Gross Out.")

Piccirilli, Tom.

The Midnight Road. *New York: Bantam Books, 2007. 317p. ISBN 0553384082.*
A tough investigator for Child Protective Services finds himself faced with the hardest case of his life when he visits a ritzy Long Island home—a commonplace event that spirals into his being plunged into a frozen harbor. He can count himself lucky to survive, at least at first. Resuscitated after being dead for some thirty minutes, he then finds himself thrown even deeper into a nightmare where anyone close to him suddenly becomes a candidate for murder. **Similar titles:** *The Dead Zone*, Stephen King; *World of Hurt*, Brian Hodge.

Afterlife, The • Child Molesters • Doppelgangers • New York—New York City • Serial Killers • Stalkers

SanGiovanni, Mary.

The Hollower. *New York: Leisure, 2007. 308p. ISBN 0843959746.*
Do we really have nothing to fear but fear itself? The Hollower forces you to go face to face with despair by mimicking the physique and voice of your closest friends and relations. The Hollower has already driven Max to suicide, and now it wants Dave Kohlar, a recovering alcoholic, as well as his clinically insane sister. **Similar titles:** *Valley of Lights*, Stephen Gallagher; *Grimm Memorials*, R. Patrick Gates; *Dead in the Water*, Nancy Holder.

Addictions—Alcoholism • Addictions—Drugs • Dreams • Mental Illness • New Jersey • Police Officer as Character • Shape-shifters

Sarrantonio, Al.

Halloweenland. *New York: Leisure, 2007. 293p. ISBN 0843959274.*
(See chapter 8, "Mythological Monsters and 'The Old Ones': Invoking the Dark Gods.")

Searcy, David.

 Ordinary Horror. *New York: Penguin-Viking, 2001. 230p. ISBN 0670894761.*
(See chapter 17, "Everyday Horror: When the Mundane Becomes Monstrous.")

Shepard, Lucius.

Softspoken. *San Francisco : Night Shade Books, 2007. 179p. ISBN 1597800732.*

A chilling and mysterious voice: that is what twenty-something writer Sanie Bullard hears after she and her husband, a law student, move into his dilapidated antebellum family mansion in South Carolina. At first she wonders if she is the victim of a practical joke perpetrated by her husband's weird, drug-addicted brother, but she discovers that something even more mysterious is responsible for the noises. **Similar titles:** *Secrets in the Attic*, V. C. Andrews; *Stir of Echoes*, Richard Matheson.

Addictions—Drugs • Families • Incest • Mental Illness • Secret Sin • South Carolina • Writer as Character

Simmons, Dan.

The Terror. *New York: Little, Brown, 2007. 784p. ISBN 0316017442.*

(See chapter 8, "Mythological Monsters and 'The Old Ones': Invoking the Dark Gods.")

Smith, James Robert, and Stephen Mark Rainey, eds.

Evermore: An Anthology. *Sauk City, WI: Arkham House, 2006. 237p. ISBN 0870541854.*

(See chapter 18, "Collections and Anthologies.")

Smith, Michael Marshall.

The Servants. *Northborough, MA: Earthling Publications, 2007. 207p. ISBN 0979505402.*

(See chapter 4, "Ghosts and Haunted Houses: Dealing with Presences and Absences.")

Straub, Peter.

The Hellfire Club. *New York: Ballantine, 2004, ©1995. 526p. ISBN 0345477278.*

This meta-fictionalized narrative traces the fall of a wealthy New England family whose male heir belongs to a club that inspires shameless self-indulgence. Straub's complex and clever narrative style weaves elements of mystery fiction into the story. **Similar titles:** *Hell House*, Richard Matheson; *Ghost Story*, Peter Straub; *From Hell* (film).

Family Curse • New England • Secret Sin • Writer as Character

In the Night Room. *New York: Ballantine, 2006, ©2004. 368p. ISBN 0345491327.*

Tim Underhill is writing a novel to cope with his sister-in-law's suicide. As a result, he has brought his creations to life in a literal sense of the word. He meets and falls in love with a character he creates, but she is engaged to a financier who has the means and the ability to come after her

14

and Tim—and he brings along his goons, one of whom is the serial killer. **Similar titles:** *The Dark Half*, Stephen King; *Lost Boy, Lost Girl* and *Mr. X*, Peter Straub; *Like Death*, Tim Waggoner.

Death—Grieving • *Underhill, Tim (character)* • *Wisconsin* • *Writer as Character*

Sullivan, Thomas.

Second Soul. *New York: Onyx, 2005. 291p. ISBN 0451412028.*
> (See chapter 7, "Demonic Possession, Satanism, Black Magic, and Witches and Warlocks: The Devil Made Me Do It.")

Tem, Steve Rasnic, and Melanie Tem.

The Man on the Ceiling. *Renton, WA: Wizards of the Coast-Discoveries, 2008. 366p. ISBN 0786948582.*
> (See chapter 17, "Everyday Horror: When the Mundane Becomes Monstrous.")

Tessier, Thomas.

Finishing Touches. *New York: Leisure, 2005, ©1986. 247p. ISBN 0843955597.*
> (See chapter 15, "Splatterpunk: The Gross Out.")

Trigell, Jonathan.

Boy A. *London: Serpent's Tale, 2008, ©2004. 256p. ISBN 1846686628.*
> At the age of nine, Boy A (Jack) commits an unspeakable murder and is dubbed "the evilest boy in Britain." Fifteen years later, Jack is released from prison because he committed the crime when he was a juvenile. To protect himself against retribution, he takes the name "Jack Burrage" and attempts to fit into society. But starting from scratch is extremely difficult. **Similar titles:** *Desolation*, Tim Lebbon; *Spider* (film).
>
> *Childhood* • *England* • *Prisons*

Waggoner, Tim.

Like Death. *New York: Leisure, 2005. 374p. ISBN 0843954981.*
> When Scott Raymond was seven, he hid under a kitchen table, watching helplessly as the rest of his family was murdered. Now an adult, Scott is working through his trauma and embarking on a career as a true crime writer. But one of the first cases he investigates leads him to a teenager who introduces him to a shadowy world that lurks beneath our own reality. **Similar titles:** *Desolation*, Tim Lebbon; *In the Night Room*, Peter Straub; *Midnight Sun*, Ramsey Campbell.
>
> *Adolescence* • *Parallel Universes* • *Writer as Character*

Wells, H. G.

The Croquet Player. *Lincoln: University of Nebraska Press, 2004, ©1937. 109p. ISBN 0803298420.*
> (See chapter 17, "Everyday Horror: When the Mundane Becomes Monstrous.")

Welsh, T. K.

Resurrection Men. *New York: Dutton-Children's Books, 2007. 214p. ISBN 0525476997.*

> This complex frame tale is loosely based on the exploits of those most infamous of resurrection men, Burke and Hare. Before about 1832, medical students had difficulty procuring enough bodies with which to study anatomy, and they employed "resurrection men," people who would unearth the bodies of the newly dead in the name of medical science, to supply their needs. Welsh's resurrection men, however, are a bit more enterprising than their fellows; not satisfied to wait around for someone to conveniently die, they turn to murder. **Similar titles:** *Savage*, Richard Laymon; *Frankenstein's Bride*, Hilary Bailey; *The Body Snatcher* (film).

> *Adolescence • Cemeteries • England—London • Frame Tale • Physician as Character*

Wilde, Oscar.

The Picture of Dorian Gray. *New York: Tom Doherty, 1999, ©1891. 240p. ISBN 0812567110.*

> (See chapter 7, "Demonic Possession: Satanism, Black Magic, and Witches and Warlocks: The Devil Made Me Do It.")

Film

The Blair Witch Project. *Daniel Myrick an Eduardo Sanchez, dir. 1999. 86 minutes.*

> (See chapter 7, "Demonic Possession: Satanism, Black Magic, and Witches and Warlocks: The Devil Made Me Do It.")

The Body Snatcher. *Robert Wise, dir. 1945. 77 minutes.*

> Until the twentieth century, medical schools had a great deal of difficulty obtaining cadavers for teaching, and they often obtained specimens through means worse than robbing the graves of the newly dead. Three years after the trial of the infamous William Burke for murdering sixteen people to supply their bodies to medical schools, Dr. MacFarland becomes involved with John Gray (Boris Karloff), a similar nefarious character who procures cadavers. **Similar titles:** *Resurrection Men*, T. K. Welsh.

> *Grave Robbing • Physician as Character • Scotland—Edinburgh*

Carnival of Souls. *Herk Harvey, dir. 1962. 78 minutes.*

> A young church organist has a near-death experience when her car veers off a bridge and she nearly drowns. Months later she leaves home to pursue her musical career in another city, but is inexplicably drawn to a now-defunct carnival haunted by beings only she can see. This low budget film, shot mostly on location in Kansas, has rightfully developed quite a cult following. What *Carnival of Souls* lacks in plot it makes up for with its eerie atmosphere. **Similar titles:** *Like Death*, Tim Waggoner; *The Between*, Tananarive Due.

> *Carnivals • Gothicism • Kansas • Music—Organ • Parallel Universes*

Fight Club. *David Fincher, dir. 1999. 139 minutes.*

A darkly comic rendition of Chuck Palahniuk's novel of the same name, in which an average, run-of-the-mill claims investigator for an automobile manufacturer becomes friends with an antisocial monomaniac. When things get out of hand and Project Mayhem is born, the unnamed narrator has to try to stop his new friend from committing acts of terrorism, including blowing up buildings to obliterate consumer capitalism. **Similar titles:** *A Carnivore's Inquiry*, Sabina Murray; The Straw Men Series, Michael Marshall.

Consumerism • Doppelgangers • Insomnia • New York—New York City • Terrorism

The Machinist (El Machinista). *Brad Anderson, dir. 2004. 102 minutes.*

Machinist Trevor Reznik quite literally requires that someone supply him with essential information: he has no idea who he actually is. He does, however, suspect that someone is stalking him. For one thing, he keeps discovering Post-it notes on his refrigerator that challenge him to a game of hangman. And he just might be seeing things—including a deformed coworker who helps others have accidents. **Similar titles:** *The Key to Midnight* and *House of Thunder*, Dean Koontz.

Amnesia • Doppelgangers • Insomnia • Secret Sin

The Others. *Alejandro Amenabar, dir. 2001. 101 minutes.*

(See chapter 4, "Ghosts and Haunted Houses: Dealing with Presences and Absences.")

Rebecca. *Alfred Hitchcock, dir. 1940. (black and white). 130 minutes.*

Hitchcock's first American film is a faithful adaptation of Daphne du Maurier's novel of the same name about a young woman who marries a widowed nobleman. Both fight the "ghost" of his deceased wife. Joan Fontaine and Lawrence Olivier star. This film was the winner of Academy Awards for Best Picture and Cinematography. **Similar titles:** *Rebecca*, Daphne du Maurier; *Wuthering Heights*, Emily Brontë.

England • Gothicism • Incest • Marriage • Obsession • Secret Sin

The Sixth Sense. *M. Night Shyamalan, dir. 1999. 107 minutes.*

(See chapter 4, "Ghosts and Haunted Houses: Dealing with Presences and Absences.")

Tideland. *Terry Gilliam, dir. 2006. 120 minutes.*

Jeliza-Rose, a poor eleven-year-old girl, is taken by her father to his family's now abandoned home in rural Texas. When her father dies soon after of a drug overdose, Jeliza-Rose, desperately hungry, ventures outside and finds strange and reclusive residents at a nearby farm. This strange and disturbing film is a subversive version of *Alice in Wonderland*. **Similar titles:** *Coraline*, Neil Gaiman; The *Way the Family Got Away*, Michael Kimball.

Addictions—Drugs • Childhood • Disabilities—Mental Retardation • Texas • Trains

The Village. *M. Night Shyamalan, dir. 2004. 108 minutes.*

The elders of the village of Coventry talk about an uneasy truce with the creatures who live in the woods surrounding their hamlet: As long as no one strays from the village into the forest, they will be safe. But when the village doctor runs out of medicine and needs to treat a mortally wounded young man, the elders decide that a blind girl should go for help. Similar to Shyamalan's other films, *The Village* features a surprising twist at the end. Brice Dallas Howard, Joaquin Phoenix, and Adrien Brody star. **Similar titles:** *Matinee at the Flame*, Christopher Fahy; *The Two Sams*, Glen Hirshberg.

Disabilities—Blindness • Obsession • Parenting • Pennsylvania

June's Picks

Books: Tananarive Due, *The Between* (Harper Torch); Daphne du Maurier, *Rebecca* (Avon); Graham Joyce, *Limits of Enchantment* (Atria); Stephen King, *Dolores Claiborne* (London Hodder Paperbacks); T. K. Welsh, *Resurrection Men* (Dutton-Children's Books)

Films: *The Body Snatcher, Carnival of Souls, Fight Club, Rebecca, The Village*

Tony's Picks

Books: Ramsey Campbell, *Midnight Sun* (Tom Doherty); Graham Masterton, *Darkroom* (Severn House); Stewart O'Nan, *A Prayer for the Dying* (Picador); Lucius Shepard, *Softspoken* (Night Shade Books)

Films: *Fight Club, The Machinist, Tideland, The Village*

11

12

13

14

15

16

17

18

19

20

Chapter 15

Splatterpunk: The Gross Out

Splatterpunk, a subgenre that emerged sometime in the late 1980s, refers more to a style of writing than a theme or the use of any specific type of monster. What separates the monster in this subgenre from any run-of-the-mill maniac, vampire, werewolf, or alien is that it revels in torturing and mutilating ordinary humans: characters relate their depravity in loving, almost sensuous detail, without apology. This is certainly the case in Poppy Z. Brite's *Exquisite Corpse,* where serial killers Jay Byrne and Andrew Compton become lovers brought together by their desire to torture, dismember, and consume beautiful young men. Patrick Bateman, in Brett Easton Ellis's novel *American Psycho,* similarly enjoys torturing and dismembering women. Patrick Bateman is perhaps a more controversial protagonist than are Brite's Jay Byrne and Andrew Compton, because he is completely contemptuous of all women (and of all poor people and minorities, for that matter). In fact, *American Psycho's* extreme gore, combined with its completely unsympathetic protagonist, made the novel and its author a flashpoint for controversy. When *American Psycho* was published in 1991, both book and author were excoriated by Gloria Steinem for their perceived misogyny, and she and other prominent feminists called for a boycott of Ellis's publisher, Vintage Books. Ellis also received many death threats after the publication of *American Psycho.* In an interesting twist of irony, Steinem is the stepmother of Christian Bale, the actor who portrays Patrick Bateman in the 2000 film of the novel.

Splatterpunk, also known as "extreme horror," is characterized by a grotesque decadence. These tales do not chronicle the shocking excesses of monsters that kill only because they must to survive, or because they have been made psychologically defective by bad parenting; these monsters kill because they are born to thoroughly enjoy their depravity in much the same way that a cat is born to delight in toying with mice. Thus, graphic sex and violence abound for their own sake, and heinous acts of torture are routinely perpetrated by bored mortals and immortals alike. For example, Brian Hodge's serial killer in *World of Hurt* has a divine mandate to torture and kill his victims, and he is portrayed as a part of the natural world just as are those whose natures make them inherently gentle. Or consider Edward Lee's <u>City Infernal Series</u>, which depicts the depraved decadence of Satan's own capital city, Mephistopolis. In the splatterpunk tale, you'll find no reluctant vampires or antiheroes, à la Anne Rice; instead, these monsters revel in their monstrosity. In addition, there are no taboos in splatterpunk. Children and pets can die horrible deaths along with anyone else. Brite's *Exquisite Corpse,* for example, depicts a world in which S & M sex is the most normal thing to occur in a banquet of excesses.

So why do some fans of horror gravitate toward this extreme version of the genre? Fans who enjoy splatterpunk are generally people who are quite literate within the genre itself and seek a type of fiction that will shock as well as challenge their ideas about horror. Splatterpunk's excesses often explore the nature of violence itself. For example, why, in a world full of technology and knowledge of the human psyche, do we have people who will harm others? Past explanations offered by earlier texts are deemed insufficient. According to Robert Bloch's *Psycho*, Norman Bates is a serial killer because his mother was a nagging shrew. But many of us are badly parented, and we do not become serial killers. Splatterpunk in general scorns such neat psychological diagnoses and perhaps hearkens back to an earlier era of horror, when monsters were monsters because they were wicked, or because they simply enjoyed doing bad things. According to the splatterpunk ethos, violence and deviant behavior aren't phenomena we can easily explain, let alone control. Unlike other subgenres of horror, splatterpunk deals with material that is truly horrifying to readers who have read and seen it all.

Stories with splatterpunk elements can also be found in the collections and anthologies described in chapter 18.

Arnzen, Michael.

 Grave Markings. *New York: Dell, 1994. 383p. ISBN 0440213398.*

An insane, egomaniacal tattoo artist is obsessed with the mad images in his mind and the need for recognition. So he seeks new flesh to fulfill his ambition. Nothing, not even death, will stop him in his art. Arnzen's clever novel features vivid, grotesque violence. **Similar titles:** *Play Dead*, Michael Arnzen; *The Bone Parade*, Mark Nykanen; *Exquisite Corpse*, Poppy Z. Brite.

Body Modification Tattoos • Mental Illness • Obsession • Serial Killers

Play Dead. *Hyattsville, MD: Raw Dog Screaming Press, 2005. 271p. ISBN 9781933293042.*

A group of down-on-their-luck gamblers who have lost nearly everything play a high-stakes card game run by a casino owner. Each must craft a suit of cards by "artfully extinguishing life" and photographing the victims. The winner gets a million-dollar jackpot, while anyone quitting the game dies, causing participants to wonder what is in this game for the person running it, the casino owner. Written in fifty-two chapters. **Similar titles:** *Grave Markings*, Michael Arnzen; *Needful Things*, Stephen King; *American Gods*, Neil Gaiman.

Gambler as Character • Nevada—Las Vegas

Bailey, Dale, and Jack Slay Jr.

Sleeping Policemen. *Urbana, IL: Golden Gryphon Press, 2006. 208p. ISBN 193084641X.*

(See chapter 17, "Everyday Horror: When the Mundane Becomes Monstrous.")

Braunbeck, Gary A.

Prodigal Blues. *Baltimore, MD: Cemetery Dance Publications, 2006. 304p. ISBN 1587671093.*

> Mark Sieber tells the story of his run-of-the-mill road trip to Topeka, which becomes a nightmare when his car breaks down near a truck stop in Missouri. There he meets a child from one of the "Have You Seen Me?" posters, and he is soon kidnapped by her cohorts—a ragtag group of four teens. In great detail, they tell Mark how they have escaped from an Internet pornographer who specializes in supplying children for rape, humiliation, and torture. **Similar titles:** *The Dead Letters*, Tom Piccirilli; *Destinations Unknown, Mr. Hands,* and *In Silent Graves*, Gary A. Braunbeck.
>
> *Child Molesters • Frame Tale • Ohio—Cedar Hill • Road Trips • Torture*

Brite, Poppy Z.

Exquisite Corpse. *London: Phoenix, 1997, ©1996. 244p. ISBN 185799437X.*

> For serial killer Andrew Compton, murder is a high art. Compton escapes from an English prison and comes to New Orleans, where he meets Jay Byrne, a dissolute playboy, serial killer, and fellow necrophile. Together they use a young Vietnamese American runaway to further the expression of their "art." This graphic and disturbing novel is a benchmark of the splatterpunk genre. **Similar titles:** *American Psycho*, Brett Easton Ellis; *Zombie*, Joyce Carol Oates; *The Off Season*, Jack Ketchum; *A Carnivore's Inquiry*, Sabina Murray.
>
> *Asian American Characters • Cannibalism • Epidemics—AIDS • Gay/Lesbian/Bisexual Characters • Homoeroticism • Louisiana—New Orleans • Necrophilia • Serial Killers*

Lost Souls. *London: Penguin, 1994, ©1992. 359p. ISBN 0140173927.*

> A disturbed teenager named Nothing discovers that his father is a blood-thirsty vampire who travels with a duo of vampire goons. On his journey to self-discovery, Nothing befriends Steve and Ghost, band members of Lost Souls. Using multiple narrators, Brite creates intensely homoerotic scenes, with careful character development interspersed with passages of extreme violence. **Similar titles:** *Exquisite Corpse* and *The Devil You Know*, Poppy Z. Brite; *Voice of the Blood*, Jemiah Jefferson.
>
> *Gay/Lesbian/Bisexual Characters • Homoeroticism • Louisiana—New Orleans • Music—Rock Music • North Carolina—Missing Mile • Vampire's Point of View*

Clegg, Douglas.

The Nightmare Chronicles. *New York: Leisure, 1999. 360p. ISBN 084394580X.*

> (See chapter 18, "Collections and Anthologies.")

11

12

13

14

15

16

17

18

19

20

Connolly, John.

The Charlie Parker Mysteries.

NYPD Detective Charlie "Bird" Parker was busy boozing at Tom's Oak Tavern when his wife Susan and young daughter Jennifer were mutilated by a killer called the Traveling Man. Consumed by guilt and his alcoholism, Charlie soon loses his job, and nearly his sanity. This series includes titles that do not fit into the splatterpunk category. **Similar titles:** <u>The Andrew Thomas Novels</u>, Blake Crouch; <u>The Pendergast Novels</u>, Douglas Preston and Lincoln Childs; *Incarnate*, Ramsey Campbell.

Addictions—Alcoholism • Parker, Charlie (character) • Police Officer as Character • Serial Killers

 Every Dead Thing. *New York: Simon & Schuster, 1999. 395p. ISBN 0684857146.*

Several months after the death of his family, Parker takes up private investigating, and one of his first cases gives him a gut feeling that the slayer is pulling the strings.

Stalkers

The Black Angel. *New York: Pocket Star, 2006, ©2005. 579p. ISBN 0743487877.*

Parker is drawn into the murder of his business partner's cousin, a New York City prostitute. He journeys to New York, only to be led to clues about the Black Angel, a statue originally from a Czech ossuary sought for centuries by various bloodthirsty spirits.

Angels • Cursed Objects • Czechoslovakia

Crouch, Blake.

The Andrew Thomas Novels.

(See chapter 11, "Maniacs and Sociopaths, or the Nuclear Family Explodes: Monstrous Malcontents Bury the Hatchet.")

Delany, Samuel R.

Hogg. *Normal, IL: FC2, 2004. 268p. ISBN 1573661198.*

An eleven-year-old boy who is sold into slavery to a pedophile eventually joins forces with the rapist/serial killer. Traumatized, he becomes like his captors and goes on a spree in which he mutilates and murders. Not for the weak of stomach, this novel contains detailed gang-rape attacks and orgies, and characters possess very little remorse or potential for redemption. **Similar titles:** *Prodigal Blues*, Gary A. Braunbeck; *Offspring*, Jack Ketchum; *Madman Stan and Other Stories* and *Endless Night*, Richard Laymon.

Child Molesters • Kidnapping • Rape • Serial Killers • Spree Killers

Ellis, Bret Easton.

American Psycho. *London: Picador Thrifty, 2002, ©1991. 384p. ISBN 033049189X.*

Twenty-something yuppie investment banker Patrick Bateman tortures, murders, and dismembers prostitutes and wealthy female acquaintances alike, sometimes keeping their body parts afterward. His violent excesses are contrasted with the economic violence perpetrated on the world by himself and his Wall Street cronies, who sneer at the poor and minorities. Ellis's controversial novel is a biting satire of the 1980s "greed is good" mentality as much as it is a portrait of a serial killer. **Similar titles:** *Exquisite Corpse*, Poppy Z. Brite; *A Carnivore's Inquiry*, Sabina Murray; *Zombie*, Joyce Carol Oates; *Lunar Park*, Bret Easton Ellis; *American Psycho* (film).

Classism • New York—New York City • Serial Killers • Torture

Gates, R. Patrick.

The Grimm Funeral Home series.

Eleanor Grimm is rumored to be a descendant of the Grimm brothers, and she's a gifted storyteller. She is also a funeral home director who seeks immortality—through whatever means necessary. **Similar titles:** *Grave Intent*, Deborah LeBlanc; *Incarnate*, Ramsey Campbell; *The Hollower*, Mary SanGiovanni; *Dead in the Water*, Nancy Holder; *Nightmare on Elm Street* (film).

Family Curse • Frame Tale • Funeral Home Industry

Grimm Memorials. *New York: Kensington, 2005, ©1990. 429p. ISBN 0786016981.*

Eleanor Grimm begins her quest for the preservation of her soul by entering the minds of her victims and forcing them to dream of themselves in distorted, disturbing fairy tales, including cannibalism and painful torture.

Cannibalism • Dreams • Magic • Popular Culture—Fairy Tales • Torture

Grimm Reapings. *New York: Kensington, 2006. 382p. ISBN 078601640X.*

Jackie attends college, while his sister Eleanor converts the funeral home into a bed and breakfast. Meanwhile, thirteen-year-old Steve Nailer learns about the family history, but little does he—or anyone for that matter—suspect that Eleanor Grimm is capable of coming back from the dead. Considered even better than the original novel of the series, this tale is truly disquieting, gory, and disturbing.

Childhood • Incest • Psychosexual Horror • Revenging Revenant

11
12
13
14
15
16
17
18
19
20

Gustainis, Justin.

The Hades Project. *Sidney, NY: Brighid's Fire Books, 2003. 433p. ISBN 0971327866.*

A special operative has been called in to investigate a grisly spree killing of twelve scientists who were working on a top secret project. Many of the scientists, both male and female, have been raped, and most of them have been mutilated. For operative Michael Pacillio, the killings call to mind the handiwork of a psychopath he had once been called on to exterminate, but that psychopath was no mere human. **Similar titles:** *World of Hurt*, Brian Hodge; *Demons*, John Shirley; *Haunter* and *This Symbiotic Fascination*, Charlee Jacob.

Clergy as Character • Demons • Espionage • Soldier as Character • Torture • War—Vietnam War

Hodge, Brian.

World of Hurt. *Northborough, MA: Earthling Publications, 2006. 151p. ISBN 0976633973.*

As a teenager, a drunken car accident leaves Andrei clinically dead for thirty-eight minutes when he is plunged into the icy depths of the Allegheny River before being revived by paramedics. At first, Andrei's recollections mimic the stereotypical near-death experience, with a tunnel of light and a vague sense of loved ones on the other side. But eight years later Andrei begins to *really* remember what happened. Hodge's pensive yet gory novella is highly original. **Similar titles:** *American Psycho*, Bret Easton Ellis; *The Midnight Road*, Tom Piccirilli; *Valley of Lights*, Stephen Gallagher; *Offspring*, Jack Ketchum; *The Butcher Boy* (film).

Afterlife, The • Joan of Arc (character) • Pennsylvania—Pittsburgh • Serial Killers • Torture

Holder, Nancy.

 Dead in the Water. *New York: Dell, 1994. 413p. ISBN 0440214815.*

The cruise begins aboard the Pandora with a message from the ship's captain: "This is how it will be when you drown." The situation only gets eerier and more frightening, as crew members and passengers alike fall into and out of nightmarish, violent alternate realities. If only they can stop Captain Reade, the demonic puppeteer of their nightmares, they may survive. But no one before, in any of Reade's previous lives, has stopped him. **Similar titles:** *The Hollower*, Mary SanGiovanni; *Grimm Memorials*, R. Patrick Gates; *Shadow Coast*, Philip Haldeman.

Demons • Dreams • Hispanic American Characters • Maritime Horror • Psychosexual Horror

Houarner, Gerard.

Road to Hell. *New York: Dorchester, 2003. 342p. ISBN 084395065X.*

Angel is the son of Max, a bestial assassin for hire who specializes in cases that involve the supernatural. After an unnatural growth spurt causes Angel to become an adult in one day, he is led through the worlds of both the living and the dead and must make his way back to his father, from whom he has been separated. Unfortunately for him, the ghosts of Max's victims work to forever trap Angel in their world, where they bombard him with the atrocities of his father. **Similar titles:**

The City Infernal Series, Edward Lee; The Repairman Jack Novels, F. Paul Wilson; The Anita Blake, Vampire Hunter Series, Laurell K. Hamilton.

Assassins • Demons • Parapsychology • Parenting • Revenging Revenant

11

Jacob, Charlee.

This Symbiotic Fascination. *New York: Leisure, 2002. 394p. ISBN 084394966X.*

Two immortals, an overweight, overly tall, plain-looking young woman and a werewolf-like shape-shifter, work in clothing retail, and as fellow misfits, they strike up a protective friendship. One becomes a serial rapist and torturer, while a Nosferatu turns the other into a murderous sexual predator. Like most vampire narratives, this becomes a study of how the human adapts to her new condition, especially to the bloodlust that means killing. **Similar titles:** *Destinations Unknown*, Gary A. Braunbeck; *The Longest Single Note* and *Spaces Between the Lines*, Peter Crowther; *Peaceable Kingdom*, Jack Ketchum.

Cursed Objects • Multimedia—Videotape • Police Officer as Character • Psychosexual Horror • Revenge • Vampire's Point of View • Werewolves

12

13

14

Haunter. *New York: Dorchester, 2003. 374p. ISBN 084395096X.*

When street people in Bangkok begin to sit in a stupor, a beatific glow on their faces and haloes around their heads, Mr. Tak, a local drug dealer, is determined to discover whatchemical is behind this change, so that he can make a profit from it. **Similar titles:** *The 37th Mandala*, Mark Laidlaw; *The Reckoning*, Jeff Long; *This Symbiotic Fascination*, Charlee Jacob.

Addictions—Drugs • Asian Characters • Cambodia • Torture • War—Vietnam War

15

Ketchum, Jack.

The Crossings. *Baltimore, MD: Cemetery Dance, 2003. 100p. ISBN 1587670674.*

Three men, reporter and veteran Marion T. Bell, renowned scout John Charles Hart, and Hart's best friend "Mother" Knuckles rescue Celine, a teenager who had been enslaved when she was kidnapped with her sister, Elena. The four of them, guns at the ready, attempt to free Elena from a slave-trading camp, resulting in a gory shootout. Set in 1848, this novel about the cruelty of human beings presents readers with a brutal, dark, and surrealistic nightmare. **Similar titles:** *Smonk, or Widow Town: Being the Scabrous Adventures of E. O. Smonk & the Whore of Evangeline in Clarke County, Alabama, Early in the Last Century*, Tom Franklin; *Mad Dog Summer and Other Stories* and *God of the Razor*, Joe R. Lansdale.

Journalist as Character • Kidnapping • Slavery • Violence, Theories of

16

17

18

Off Season. *New York: Leisure, 2006, ©1981. 308p. ISBN 0843956968.*

This retelling of the Sawney Beane story, which involves an actual robber turned cannibal who lived with his family in a cave in Scotland, offers an unflinching account of modern cannibalism. Ketchum places his cannibal clan in the America of the 1980s. A houseful of Manhattan residents vacationing in rural Maine begins to meet an early demise. What happens to

19

20

the couples is disturbing, and the author hones in on each atrocity in detail. **Similar titles:** *Exquisite Corpse*, Poppy Z. Brite; *Offspring*, Jack Ketchum; *A Carnivore's Inquiry*, Sabina Murray; *The Hills Have Eyes* (film).

Cannibalism • Families • New England • Popular Culture—Sawney Beane Legend • Serial Killers • Torture

Offspring. *New York: Leisure, 2007, ©1999. 293p. ISBN 0843958642.*

This sequel to *Off Season* takes the theme of cannibalism and makes it even more horrifying. Cannibals terrorize a small community in Maine, as the Sawney Beane blood-line continues. A new set of potential victims includes a couple and their infant child, the wife's best friend and her son, and a retired chief of police. A captivating read, this sequel unfolds at breakneck speed, fueled by Ketchum's typical uncompromising, visceral, no-nonsense prose and plotting. **Similar titles:** *Exquisite Corpse*, Poppy Z. Brite; *The Off Season*, Jack Ketchum; *A Carnivore's Inquiry*, Sabina Murray; *The Hills Have Eyes* (film).

Cannibalism • Maine • Parenting • Police Officer as Character • Popular Culture—Sawney Beane Legend • Torture

She Wakes. *New York: Leisure, 2004, ©1984. 355p. ISBN 084395423X.*

In this revised version of the first and rarest of all Ketchum's supernatural novels, a seductive evil stalks the Greek islands, hunting and feeding on the living, who are so easy and so pleasurable to kill. Her awakening summons Jordon Thayer Chase, a man who hears the voices of ancient gods and feels the power of sacred places, and who knows he must fulfill his destiny, even if it means his death. **Similar titles:** *Crota*, Owl Goingback; *Haunter*, Charlee Jacob; *The Female of the Species*, Joyce Carol Oates.

Animals Run Rampant • Cats • Death (character) • Greece • Necrophilia • Psychosexual Horror • Writer as Character

Laimo, Michael.

The Demonologist. *New York: Leisure, 2005. 369p. ISBN 0843955279.*

Graphic gore galore highlights the story of a forty-two-year-old rocker who begins to suffer weird "attacks" while performing—he becomes disoriented and feels claws scratching at his brain. A widower and father, he has been forced to promote his newest hits by touring, and this is when he starts becoming disoriented and hearing voices. His doctor is of little help, but a smallish, dark-skinned man who follows him around seems to understand. **Similar titles:** *Heart-Shaped Box*, Joe Hill; *Blood Angel*, Justine Musk; The Vampire Huntress Legend, L. A. Banks; *Rosemary's Baby*, Ira Levin.

Clergy as Character • Demons • Music—Rock Music • Parenting • Religion—Satanism • Writer as Character

Lansdale, Joe R.

Mad Dog Summer and Other Stories. *Urbana, IL: Golden Gryphon Press, 2006, ©2004. 261p. ISBN 1930846428.*

(See chapter 18, "Collections and Anthologies.")

Laymon, Richard.

After Midnight. *New York: Leisure Books, 2006, ©1997. 438p. ISBN 084395180X.*

11

Alice, a twenty-six-year-old, has been abused and ill-used by men, so she has chosen a quiet and isolated life, inhabiting a garage apartment. Late one night she spots a naked stranger under the moonlight, and he sees her. Meanwhile, an unlucky young man mis-dials his ex-girlfriend's telephone number and gets caught up in Alice's drama. Events lead to Alice's unwittingly killing her would-be savior and shooting his ex, then running afoul of a rapist/torturer in the woods. **Similar titles:** *Endless Night*, Richard Laymon; *Intensity*, Dean Koontz; *The Long Last Call*, John Skipp.

12

Mistaken Identity • Rape • Serials Killers • Torture

13

Cuts. *New York: Leisure, 2008, ©1999. 301p. ISBN 0843951834.*

A teenager in Illinois goes on a killing spree, raping and mutilating women. When he is critically wounded, one of his victims takes pity on him. This graphic read contains scenes of sexual violence that are intimately detailed. **Similar titles:** *Come Out Tonight* and *In the Dark*, Richard Laymon; *Offspring*, Jack Ketchum.

14

Academia • Marriage • Rape • Serial Killers • Torture

Lee, Edward.

15

The City Infernal Series.

It's not your parents' hell anymore. Over 5,000 years, hell has evolved into a vast technocracy based on the magic and power of sorcery. It is now a metropolis—full of skyscrapers, urban sprawl, and downtown streets filled with commingling damned human souls and demons. The Mephistopolis, as it is known, is the new home of Cassie Heydon, Goth girl extraordinaire. **Similar titles:** *Eternal City*, Michael Kilpatrick and Nancy Kilpatrick; *Necropolis*, Tim Waggoner; *Daughter of Hounds* and *Murder of Angels*, Caitlin R. Kiernan.

16

17

Demons • Gothicism • Hell • Religion—Christianity • Satan (character) • Twins

City Infernal. *New York: Leisure, 2002, ©2001. 366p. ISBN 0843949880.*

Cassie Heydon, an out-of-place surviving Goth twin, is plucked from her Washington, DC, surroundings and dropped into the boonies, where she meets Fenton Blackwell, who turns out to be one of Lucifer's High Sheriffs, a satanic priest. Cassie begins to suspect that his house is a gateway to the Mephistopolis, the capital of hell, where sex, violence, and drugs prevail. In hell, Cassie is no mere Goth grrrl—she's an Etheress, and the First Saint of Hell.

18

19

Infernal Angel. *New York: Leisure, 2004, ©2003. 338p. ISBN 0843952032.*

In this sequel to *City Infernal*, Cassie, still an Etheress, looks for her twin sister, a suicide. This time she's aided by an angel, Angelese, and by Walter, a dorky student and fellow etherean, who is goggle-eyed over a blonde new resident in Lucifer's capital city, Mephistopolis.

20

But Lucifer has a time-traveling device and a clone of Jesus, and he plans to travel back to that famous cave to nip Christianity in the bud.

Angels • Replicants

Flesh Gothic. *New York: Leisure, 2005, ©2004. 404p. ISBN 0843954124.*

Reginald Hildrith, a decadent billionaire, purchases a porn production company, then holds a bloody orgy with the company's actors in his mansion where all, including himself, perish. But his wife is convinced that the fatal orgy was some sort of transformation ritual, and that Reginald is undead and hiding in another dimension. She hires psychics to search for him in the mansion, where guests are molested and sometimes killed. **Similar titles:** *The Messenger*, Edward Lee; *House of Blood*, Bryan Smith; *Tetraologist*, Edward Lee and James Wrath White.

Demons • Florida • Psychics • Psychosexual Horror

Messenger. *New York: Leisure, 2004. 337p. ISBN 0843952040.*

Dannellton, an idyllic small town on the Florida beach, boasts a low crime rate, affordable real estate, and no harsh winters. But the peace is shattered when several seemingly mild mannered residents go on bloody killing sprees. These people don't seem to be acting like their usual selves—because they're possessed by the Messenger, a minion of Satan. **Similar titles:** *The Exorcist*, William Peter Blatty; *Cell* and *Insomnia*, Stephen King; *Life Expectancy*, Dean Koontz; *Fallen* (film).

Cursed Objects • Demons • Florida • Violence, Theories of

Monstrosity. *New York: Leisure, 2003. 373p. ISBN 0843950757.*

In Florida, an archeologist discovers proof of a 10,000-year-old demon. Meanwhile, an Air Force lieutenant who was framed in a sex scandal now works as a state park security guard and finds herself embroiled in a series of mysterious disappearances and inexplicable sexual behavior from her coworkers. Then locals who are trying to steal drugs from a military research center nearby begin to vanish. **Similar titles:** *The Vanishing*, Bentley Little; *Cell* and *Insomnia*, Stephen King; *Life Expectancy*, Dean Koontz; *Fallen* (film).

Archeology • Demons • Florida • Government Officials • Ranger as Character • Violence, Theories of

Lee, Edward, and Wrath James White.

Teratrologist. *Hiram, GA: Overlook Connection Press, 2003. 116p. ISBN 1892950820.*

A young. mentally challenged woman who suffers from congenital problems is being cared for by a guardian who has problems of his own, emotionally and psychologically. So she is rescued from this predicament by a mysterious and murderous Brit who promises to take her somewhere better. As it turns out, the stranger, a multimillionaire named Farrington, is more than just depraved; he has plans to control the world by evoking an ancient goddess. **Similar titles:** *She Wakes*, Jack Ketchum; *Flesh Gothic*, Edward Lee; *Rosemary's Baby*, Ira Levin; *Demon Eyes*, L. H. Maynard and M. P. N. Sims.

Disabilities—Mental Retardation • Journalist as Character • Sado-Masochism

Little, Bentley (writing as Phillip Emmons).

Death Instinct. *New York: Signet, 2006, ©1992. 381p. ISBN 9780451219978.*

> Phoenix is full of unhappy people. There's Cathy, who cares for an ungrateful and abusive father, works a dead end job, and dates infrequently. Jimmy, a latchkey child whose father would rather drink than come home to his son, returns from school to an empty house, worried that bullies are going to jump him. And in the middle of the neighborhood stands the Lauter House, that spooky, empty dwelling like those seen in every neighborhood, where something so terrible happened in distant memory that, ten years later, it still stands vacant. **Similar titles:** *Among the Missing*, Richard Laymon; *A Terrible Beauty*, Graham Masterton; *Bed of Nails*, Michael Slade.
>
> *Arizona—Phoenix • Disabilities—Mental Retardation • Police Officer as Character • Torture*

Masterton, Graham.

A Terrible Beauty. *New York: Pocket Books, 2003. 369p. ISBN 0743462939.*

> In present-day Cork, Ireland, a farmer unearths eleven skeletons dated from the 1940s in his field. A local detective handles the case, looking for connections between this and recent grisly killings of American tourists. Masterton conjures a richly detailed world in Cork, complete with police officers speaking Gaelic into cell phones and troubled members of a minority gypsy culture. **Similar titles:** *Mulengro* and *From a Whisper to a Scream*, Charles de Lint; *Bloody Harvests*, Richard Kunzmann; *Darkroom*, Graham Masterton; *Death Instinct*, Bentley Little.
>
> *Gypsy as Character • Human Sacrifice • Ireland—Cork • Police Officer as Character*

Moorish, Robert, ed.

Thrillers Two (II, 2). *Baltimore, MD: Cemetery Dance, 2006. 229p. ISBN 1587671220.*

> (See chapter 18, "Collections and Anthologies.")

Nykanen, Mark.

The Bone Parade. *New York: Hyperion, 2004. 324p. ISBN 1401300189.*

> Ashley Stasser is world renowned for his series of bronze sculptures, each a detailed representation of a family in agonizing pain. While Stasser certainly has an eye for composition, the detail in his work does not come wholly from his imagination. Instead, he travels the country and kidnaps individual families, whom he brings back to his remote studio, where he tortures and kills his victims while making impressions of thm. **Similar titles:** *Desert Places*, Blake Crouch; *The Silence of the Lambs* and *Red Dragon*, Thomas Harris; *A Terrible Beauty*, Graham Masterton.
>
> *Artist as Character • Serial Killers • Utah*

Paine, Michael.

The Night School. *New York: Berkley, 2006. 325p. ISBN 0425209164.*

EdEnCo purchases the old George Washington High School, and disregarding local residents' warnings about how something evil haunts the property, renovates it into Washington Academy, an elite school where the wealthy can send their children. Soon after the opening, the principal finds a headless skeleton, but he walls it up and pretends that it doesn't exist. But the dead cannot be denied: the building's occupants begin killing one another, while a student-built robot demands that they find the head. **Similar titles:** *Mischief*, Douglas Clegg; *A House Divided*, Deborah LeBlanc; *The Prison*, R. Patrick Gates.

Corporate Horror • Haunted Houses • High School • Poltergeists • Secret Sin

Palahniuk, Chuck.

Haunted: A Novel of Stories. *New York: Doubleday, 2005. 404p. ISBN 9780385509480.*

Attempting to re-create the Villa Diadoti scenario that spawned Mary Shelley's *Frankenstein*, a group of aspiring authors lock themselves in an abandoned theater for three months. The results are several disturbing stories, framed by the narrative of their "retreat," where, to demonstrate their dedication to art, they are denied access to phones, electricity, and ultimately food. The resulting stories and the frame tale are gory and disturbing. **Similar titles:** *Lullaby*, Chuck Palahniuk; *Frankenstein*, Mary Shelley; *The Vampyre and Other Writings*, John Polidori.

Frame Tale • Writer as Character

Preston, Douglas, and Lincoln Child.

The Pendergast Novels.

Aloysius Pendergast was born to a wealthy Southern Creole family in New Orleans, and he graduated from Harvard and Oxford with honors, but his real talents lie in his ability to solve heinous crimes committed by serial killers. **Similar titles:** *Desert Places*, Blake Crouch; The Charlie Parker Mysteries, John Connolly; The Joe Pitt Novels, Charlie Huston; *Red Dragon*, Thomas Harris.

Federal Bureau of Investigation • Pendergast, Aloysius (character) • Serial Killers

Still Life with Crows. *New York: Warner, 2004. 592p. ISBN 0446531421.*

Mutilations, bizarre ritual murders, a young woman in jeopardy, and a town consumed by terror inform this tale of an eerie legend. FBI agent Aloysius Pendergast must use all his mental facilities to solve the ritual murders of several people in a Kansas town. The story rushes to a disturbing conclusion, the plot taking many twists and turns along the way.

Kansas

Brimstone. *New York: Warner, 2004. 752p. ISBN 044653143X.*

The body of a notorious art critic is found in his Long Island mansion. Next to the burned-beyond-recognition corpse is a cloven hoofprint. When other corpses are found in a similar state, FBI agent Aloysius Pendergast, heir apparent to Sherlock Holmes, is on the case. Critics have found Preston and

Child to be erudite, swiftly paced, and brimming with memorable characters.

Museums • New York—New York City

The Book of the Dead. *New York: Warner Books, 2006. 464p. ISBN 0446576980.*

The arrival of a package of fine dust at the Museum of Natural History makes Aloysius Pendergast wonder whether his evil genius brother Diogenes has returned. Unfortunately, Aloysius has been framed for murder and is serving time. He can't get out soon enough. In the meantime, a mysterious benefactor has funded the restoration of an ancient Egyptian tomb—leading to gory murders.

Families • Museums • New York—New York City

Schow, David J.

Havoc Swims Jaded. *Burton, MI: Subterranean Press, 2006. 301p. ISBN 1596060670.*

(See chapter 18, "Collections and Anthologies.")

Skipp, John.

The Long Last Call. *New York: Leisure, 2007. 368p. ISBN 084395843X.*

More than skin is laid bare at this rural strip club. A mysterious stranger who seems to know the psychological inner workings of the performers and audience members appears just before closing. Both the clientele and the strippers are made aware of their mutual hatred for one another, setting into motion a series of events that escalates out of control. **Similar titles:** *Live Girls,* Ray Garton; *Starr Brite Will Be with You Soon,* Joyce Carol Oates; *Cell* and *Needful Things,* Stephen King.

Addictions—Alcoholism • Demons • Psychosexual Horror • Stripper as Character • Suicide • Violence, Theories of

Slade, Michael.

Bed of Nails. *New York: Penguin-Onyx, 2003. 436p . ISBN 0451411153.*

The Ripper, a man who believes he was the notorious Whitechapel murderer once known as Jack the Ripper, is one of the prisoners in the Riverside Insane Asylum. In the darkness of his heart, he still craves the thrill of the kill, if only he could escape. Unfortunately for Riverside, he manages to do so. Royal Canadian Mountie Robert DeClercq chases a serial murderer who leaves a trail of grotesquely mutilated bodies behind. **Similar titles:** *Death Instinct,* Bentley Little; *A Terrible Beauty,* Graham Masterton; *What Rough Beast,* H. R. Knight.

Canada • Jack the Ripper (character) • Police Officer as Character • Royal Canadian Mounties • Serial Killers

Smith, Bryan.

House of Blood. *New York: Leisure, 2004. 369p. ISBN 0843954817.*

Five people arguing about a vacation that has soured during the road trip take a wrong turn off the interstate. In the middle of the woods beckons a light promising succor, but the five unwittingly enter The House of Blood, a place where the Master waits for them, wishing to play all sorts of games having to do with blood and sex. **Similar titles:** *Flesh Gothic*, Edward Lee; *Queen of Blood*, Bryan Smith; *The Long Last Call*, John Skipp; *House of 1000 Corpses* (film).

Haunted Houses • Psychosexual Horror • Tennessee

Queen of Blood. *New York: Leisure, 2008. ISBN 0843960612.*

The survivors of The House of Blood incident are still haunted by the ghost of one of their group who died there. Meanwhile, the servant of the original master of the house seeks to re-create the kingdom of suffering, as the Death Gods—otherworldly beings who require sacrifices—wait at the sacrificial altar. This fast-paced tale of murder and madness can be read in one or two sittings. **Similar titles:** *Flesh Gothic*, Edward Lee; *House of Blood*, Bryan Smith; *The Long Last Call*, John Skipp; *House of 1000 Corpses* (film).

Haunted Houses • Human Sacrifice • Parallel Universes • Revenging Revenant

Taylor, Lucy.

The Safety of Unknown Cities. *Woodstock, GA: Overlook Connection Press, 1999. 277p. ISBN 9781892950147.*

Val and Breen have a desperate need for human connection. Val attempts to achieve this connection by frequently changing sexual partners. Breen, on the other hand, achieves the same ends by burglarizing people's houses and going through their possessions; and later, through perusing the actual contents of their bodies. This graphic and disturbing novel is a winner of both a Bram Stoker and International Horror Guild Award. **Similar titles:** *Silk*, Caitlyn R. Kiernan; *In Silent Graves*, Gary A. Braunbeck; *Exquisite Corpse*, Poppy Z. Brite; *May* (film).

Families • Kleptomania • Psychosexual Horror • Torture

Tessier, Thomas.

Finishing Touches. *New York: Leisure, 2005, ©1986. 247p. ISBN 0843955597.*

A young American doctor discovers a cosmetic surgeon turned reclusive mad scientist, who tries to open his mind to the darkest of sexual and sensual desires. The young doctor becomes hooked on performance-enhancingt narcotics and, what is worse, sexual violence. His fantasy world is ripe with some of the most horrible atrocities humans can devise, and he finds himself murdering a young female stranger as part of a sex game. Then he discovers that his mentor abducts Londoners, enslaves them in his cellar, and mutilates their bodies. **Similar titles:** *The Safety of Unknown Cities*, Lucy Taylor; *Exquisite Corpse*, Poppy Z. Brite; *Zombie*, Joyce Carol Oates; *Hostel* (film).

Deformity • England—London • Europe • Physician as Character • Psychosexual Horror • Torture

Thomas, Jeffrey.

Deadstock. *Nottingham: Solaris, 2007. 414p. ISBN 1844164470.*
(See chapter 12, "Technohorror: Evil Hospitals, Military Screw-Ups, Mad Scientists, and Alien Invasions.")

Waggoner, Tim.

Darkness Wakes. *New York: Leisure, 2006. 321p. ISBN 0843957948.*
When a stereotypically hippie couple meet a mysterious man in a white suit, he offers the couple ultimate pleasure in the form of a miniature shapeless daemon that will reward its benefactors with bliss, if it is first fed. Flash forward some forty years to the life of a married, middle-class veterinarian. The woman of his fantasies is the daughter of the couple, and the drug culture of the sixties has been replaced by sex. And the mysterious creature is now the secret behind the daughter's exclusive sex club. **Similar titles:** *The Long Last Call*, John Skipp; *Flesh Gothic*, Edward Lee; *She Wakes*, Jack Ketchum.

Deformity • Demons • Eroticism • Ohio • Psychosexual Horror • Suburbia • Veterinarian as Character

Warner-Cohen, Kimberly.

Sex, Blood and Rock 'n' Roll. *Brooklyn, NY: Ig Publishing, 2006. 220p. ISBN 0977197212.*
Not for the faint of heart, the story of Cassie, a NYC bartender who lives with her musician boyfriend, delves into her rather unsavory fantasy life, perhaps triggered by childhood abuse. She falls into a Dominatrix gig and finds, after a shaky start, that she has an affinity for her new work. When a work-related incident causes her to miscarry an unplanned pregnancy, her fantasy life begins to overtake reality, with lethal results. **Similar titles:** *Starr Bright Will Be with You Soon*, Joyce Carol Oates; *The Safety of Unknown Cities*, Lucy Taylor; *Live Girls*, Ray Garton; *Dawn Song*, Michael Marano.

Gothicism • Mental Illness • New York—New York City • Sado-Masochism • Serial Killers • Stalkers

Williams, Conrad, and Jeff VanderMeer.

The Unblemished. *Northborough, MA: Earthling Publishers, 2006. 367p. ISBN 097663399X.*
(See chapter 12, "Technohorror: Evil Hospitals, Military Screw-Ups, Mad Scientists, and Alien Invasions.")

Wilson, D. Harlan, and Stanley Ashenbach.

Dr. Id-entity , or, Farewell to Plaquedemia. *Hyattsville, MD: Raw Dog Screaming Press, 2007. 199p. ISBN 1933293322.*
In a society filled with ultraviolence, Dr. Blah Blah Blah, an English professor, and his android, Dr. Identity, who teaches in his stead when the pro-

fessor doesn't feel up to the rigors of instructing "student-things," flee from the university. It seems the android has run amok and slaughtered a portion of the faculty and the student body. There are further adventures—and much more bloodshed—in store for these overnight media sensations, and stores selling action figures add fuel to the fire. **Similar titles:** *The Attraction*, Douglas Clegg; *Kornwolf*, Tristan Egolf; *The Pilo Family Circus*, Will Elliot; *Mad Dog Summer and Other Stories*, Joe R. Lansdale.

Academia • Futurism • Popular Culture • Replicants • Violence, Theories of

Film

American Psycho. *Mary Harron, dir. 2000. 101 minutes.*

Harron's film is a faithful adaptation of Bret Easton Ellis's 1991 novel by the same name and is as much a parody of the "greed is good" mentality of the eighties as it is a portrait of a serial killer. Christian Bale, Willem Dafoe, Jared Leto, and Reese Witherspoon star in this brilliant character study. **Similar titles:** *Zombie*, Joyce Carol Oates; *A Carnivore's Inquiry*, Sabina Murray.

New York—New York City • Popular Culture • Serial Killers • Torture

The Devil's Rejects. *Rob Zombie, dir. 2005. 109 minutes.*

This sequel to Zombie's 2003 *House of 1,000 Corpses* follows the demented Firefly family, now on the run from the law after their murderous endeavors have been exploited by the media. Sheriff John Quincy Wydell (played by William Forsythe) is hell-bent on bringing them in. Zombie's film is a loving and gory homage to 1970s drive-in horror classics, complete with a scene in a brothel and a shoot-out with the police. **Similar titles:** *The Attraction*, Douglas Clegg; *Offspring*, Jack Ketchum.

Families • Firefly Family (characters) • Gothicism • Police Officer as Character • Serial Killers • South, The

High Tension (Haute Tension). *Alexandre Aja, dir. 2003. 91 minutes.*

Alex, an American expatriate, returns home to her family farm after going on holiday with her friend Marie. But danger is lurking in this idyllic rural setting. Down the road waits a grungy man in a beat-up panel truck. As he observes the family from afar, he holds between his legs the severed head of a woman. And when night falls, he will pay the family a bloody call. This French film is full of twists and turns and has an unpredictable ending. **Similar titles:** *Endless Night*, Richard Laymon; *Mistress of the Dark*, Sèphera Girón.

France • Gay/Lesbian/Bisexual Characters • Kidnapping • Mental Illness • Slashers

The Hills Have Eyes. *Wes Craven, dir, 1977. 89 minutes.*

A family traveling cross-country in an RV become stranded in the Nevada desert when their vehicle breaks down. And when the sun goes down, they are terrorized by a family of violent, misshapen savages who inhabit the surrounding hills. This disturbing and original film is one of the benchmark horror flicks of the 1970s. **Similar titles:** *The Off Season* and *Offspring*, Jack Ketchum; *A Carnivore's Inquiry*, Sabina Murray.

Cannibalism • Deformity • Nevada • Rape • Torture

Hostel. *Eli Roth, dir. 2005. 94 minutes.*

Three Americans looking for hedonistic pleasures come to Amsterdam and meet a stranger on a train. The man suggests they travel farther east, to Czechoslovakia, where desperate women in this former Eastern Bloc country are happy to please wealthy Americans in any way they can. What the Americans find is a place where everything is permitted, including torture, if you have the money to pay for it. **Similar titles:** *Exquisite Corpse*, Poppy Z. Brite; *American Psycho*, Brett Easton Ellis.

Corporate Horror • Czechoslovakia • Kidnapping • Road Trips • Torture

House of 1,000 Corpses. *Rob Zombie, dir. 2003. 89 minutes.*

On a proverbial dark and stormy night, four college students on a road trip are directed by Captain Spaulding, a fried-chicken-selling, gas station clown, to the local small town attraction, a horror museum. But of course it is a big mistake to move off the beaten path, let alone take travel advice from a gas station clown—or to pick up a hitchhiker in such circumstances, no matter how attractive she is. The four end up enjoying the hospitality of the Firefly family, who have an unpleasant way of treating their guests, to say the least. **Similar titles:** *The Attraction*, Douglas Clegg; *The Off Season* and *Offspring*, Jack Ketchum.

Clowns • Firefly Family (characters) • Road Trips • Serial Killers • Torture

Saw. *James Wan, dir. 2004. 103 minutes.*

Dr. Larry Gordon, a surgeon, and Adam, a photographer, wake up in a windowless abandoned men's restroom, each chained to the wall and having no memory of how he got there. Soon Dr. Gordon discovers a tape recorder instructing him to kill Adam within the next few hours if he wishes to save his own wife and daughter, who have also been kidnapped. Saw offers a suspenseful and occasionally gory story, with many twists and turns of the plot. David Armstrong's cinematography and Kevin Greutert's film editing give the film a particularly stylish and edgy look. **Similar titles:** *The Girl Next Door*, Jack Ketchum; *After Midnight*, Richard Laymon.

Kidnapping • New York—New York City • Physician as Character • Serial Killers • Torture

June's Picks

Books: Poppy Z. Brite, *Exquisite Corpse* (Phoenix); Bret Easton Ellis, *American Psycho* (Picador Thrifty); Brian Hodge, *World of Hurt* (Earthling Publications); Graham Masterton, *A Terrible Beauty* (Pocket Books); Mark Nykanen, *The Bone Parade* (Hyperion)

Films: *American Psycho*, *The Devil's Rejects*, *The Hills Have Eyes*, *House of 1,000 Corpses*

Tony's Picks

Books: Gary A. Braunbeck, *Prodigal Blues* (Cemetery Dance Publications); Bret Easton Ellis, *American Psycho* (Picador Thrifty); Charlee Jacob, *This Symbiotic Fascination* (Leisure); Tim Waggoner, *Darkness Wakes* (Leisure)

Film: *House of 1,000 Corpses*

Chapter 16

Comic Horror:
Laughing at Our Fears

Many fans do not realize that the horror genre has always had an element of the comic in it. Freddy Krueger and the mysterious Crypt Keeper may have been the first high-profile monsters to crack jokes before disposing of victims or when introducing a tale of horror, but lines such as "she has a nice neck" were "spoken" by Max Von Schrek's vampire character when he first saw a picture of Mina in the 1922 film *Nosferatu*. Schrek's observation is nothing less than a comic threat that predates Freddy's and the Crypt Keeper's by more than fifty years. The old gypsy woman in Tod Browning's *Dracula* and the aging busybody in James Whale's *Frankenstein* are both excellent examples of minor characters used for comic relief in early Universal Studios horror films; and these works helped define the genre for decades to come. When it comes to literary horror, laughing at our fears goes back to the earliest of works. Humor in horror can be found in the understated reactions of Hrothgar's warriors to the monster Grendel in the Old English epic *Beowulf*, in the ridiculousness of the messengers' repeating "The helmet! The helmet!" in Horace Walpole's *The Castle of Otranto*, throughout Jane Austen's *Northanger Abbey*, and in the melodrama and irony of a good Poe tale.

This relationship between humor and horror should come as no surprise, for psychologically speaking, the two go hand in hand—in the reactions of both the characters in texts, as well as the reactions of the readers or viewers. Characters in these texts, especially in film, will invariably, in their hurry to escape the monster, run into posts and fall, trip over small rocks, or fall victim to their own footwear. In more recent, self-reflective horror, it is not even unusual to find an intended victim making highly ironic comments foreshadowing his or her own certain demise. As for the reader (or viewer), he or she may laugh nervously at those moments when terrifying expectations are built up—and the monster is surely about to appear—but the mysterious noise turns out to be only a cat or raccoon rummaging in a trash can. John Carpenter's film *Halloween* has many such moments, where we are set up to have Michael Myers spring out on the unsuspecting victim, only to realize that the joke is also on us, the viewers, who have been falsely alarmed by something relatively benign emerging from the left portion of the screen.

Sometimes the humor in horror is not as subtle as it is in the instances cited above, as recent films by Kevin Smith (*Dogma*), Rusty Cundieff (*Tales from the Hood*), Edgar Wright (*Shaun of the Dead*), Don Coscarelli (*Bubba Ho-Tep*), Andrew Currie (*Fido*), and Clive Sanders (*Gacy: The Crawl Space*) exemplify. As in any other genre, horror writers and directors sometimes choose parody as their method. These masters of comic horror realize how important it is that we laugh at our fears when we see them satirized. A less absurd type of humor can be found in novels such as Austen's *Northanger Abbey*, which shows that often horror is just a product of an overactive imagination; or even Kingsley Amis's *The Green Man*, which leaves the reader, in considering the possible existence of a ghost, comically suspended between the world of the supernatural and that of an alcoholic innkeeper. Obviously, the relationship between horror and comedy has not been lost on either the publication or the film industry. In film, you can experience the results in lines dripping with dramatic irony, such as when the serial killer stepfather in Joseph Ruben's film *The Stepfather* (annotated in chapter 11) tells his stepdaughter, and soon to be intended victim, "let's just bury the hatchet." It is also apparent in brilliant comic scenes such as the opening frame tale of Cundieff's *Tales from the Hood*, when three gang bangers try to put on a brave front while paying a midnight visit to a strange-looking funeral home run by a crazed mortician. Their false bravado is easily overcome when the mortician looks through a sliding window on his door, and one of the three turns to flee, running into a pole and knocking himself unconscious.

Some writers, such as Christopher Moore and Laurell K. Hamilton, have devoted their careers to writing in the comic mode. Moore is best known for his novels *Practical Demonkeeping*, about a seminary student who accidentally raises a demon and must take care of his new pet, and *Bloodsucking Fiends*, in which an encounter with a stranger in a back alley leaves a woman with something worse than an STD. Laurell K. Hamilton is best known for her Anita Blake novels, a dark fantasy paranormal romance series in which her title character, a wisecracking vampire hunter, fights and becomes romantically entangled with vampires and werewolves. Other well-known horror authors such as Dean Koontz periodically write in this mode, perhaps because they write in nearly every subgenre of horror. Two newcomers to this style of writing are Wm. Mark Simmons and Andrew Fox, who pen The Chris Csejthe and Fat White Vampire series, respectively. Over-the-top absurdity and sarcasm are the hallmarks of these series. To those horror texts that teach us that we can indeed laugh at our fears, we devote this chapter.

Note: Stories with comic elements can also be found in the collections and anthologies described in chapter 18.

Acevedo, Mario.

The Nymphos of Rocky Flats. *New York: Eos, 2007. 354p. ISBN 006143888X.*
Felix Gomez, an American soldier in Iraq who accidentally shoots a civilian, is turned into a vampire by an angry and vengeful Iraqi father. Things are going pretty badly for Felix—until a friend in the Department of Energy offers him a chance to use his supernatural talents. His mission? Investigate an outbreak of nymphomania among the female guards of a plutonium plant. Like they say, it's a dirty job, but someone has to do it. **Similar titles:** *Bottomfeeder*, B. H. Fingerman; *Live Girls*, Ray Garton; The Pine Cove Series, Christopher Moore.

New Mexico—Roswell • Psychosexual Horror • Soldier as Character • Vampire Hunters • Vampire's Point of View • War—Iraq War

Amis, Kingsley.

The Green Man. *London: Vintage, 2004, ©1969. 175p. ISBN 0099461072.*

Alcoholic innkeeper Maurice Allington sees ghosts at The Green Man Inn. Is his mind playing tricks on him, or are they real, and dangerous? A masterful and subtly humorous piece of British satire. **Similar titles:** *Northanger Abbey,* Jane Austen; *The Canterville Ghost,* Oscar Wilde; *Reassuring Tales,* T. E. D. Klein.

Addictions—Alcoholism • Haunted Houses • Revenging Revenant

Austen, Jane.

Northanger Abbey. *Oxford: Oxford University Press, 2000, ©1818. 221p. ISBN 0198337892.*

When Catherine Morland comes to Northanger Abbey, she meets all the trappings of Gothic horror, and imagines the worst. Fortunately, she has at hand her own fundamental good sense and the irresistible but unsentimental Henry Tilney. Disaster does eventually strike, in the real word, as distinct from the romantic one of her imagination. **Similar titles:** *The Green Man,* Kingsley Amis; *The Canterville Ghost,* Oscar Wilde; *The Castle of Otranto,* Horace Walpole.

England • Gothicism • Haunted Houses • Obsession

Bailey, Dale.

The Resurrection Man's Legacy and Other Stories. *Urbana, IL: Golden Gryphon Press, 2003. 332p. ISBN 1930846223.*

(See chapter 18, "Collections and Anthologies.")

Brooks, Max.

The Zombie Survival Guide: Complete Protection from the Living Dead. *New York: Three Rivers Press, 2003. 254p. ISBN 1400049628.*

Spawned from a mysterious virus called Solanum, the living dead are indeed among us. What can one do to prepare for the inevitable? The answer: read Brooks's book! Within its pages lies step-by-step information on how to prepare for and survive forthcoming epidemics, beginning with instruction on how to spot members of the undead and how to detect outbreaks. **Similar titles:** *World War Z: An Oral History of the Zombie War,* Max Brooks; *Mondo Zombie,* John Skipp (editor); *Fido* (film); *Shaun of the Dead* (film).

Apocalypse • Documentary Technique • Futurism • Zombies

Campbell, Ramsey.

Needing Ghosts. *London: Century, 1990. 80p. 9780712621595.* This is Campbell's strange dark fantasy about Simon Mottershead, a horror writer who finds himself trapped in alternate states of reality where he forgets who he is. Upon realizing that he is a writer of horror fiction and that he has a family, he returns home to find his wife and children murdered. Is Mottershead trapped in his own nightmare, or in one of his fictional works? Campbell's novella is a challenging, tongue-in-cheek text. **Similar titles:** *The Nightmare Factory*, Thomas Ligotti; *Matinee at the Flame*, Christopher Fahy; *The Yellow Sign and Other Stories: The Complete Weird Tales of Robert W. Chambers*, Robert W. Chambers.

Dreams • England • Parallel Universes • Writer as Character

Carey, Mike.

The Devil You Know. *New York: Warner, 2007. 416p. ISBN 0446580309.*

Freelance exorcist Felix Castor has bitten off more than he can chew when he agrees to purge a London museum of a ghost whose face is veiled in blood. Before the job is done, Felix will have to deal with a nasty rival exorcist, a hungry succubus, and an Eastern European pimp. Carey relates his tale in a tongue-in-cheek, hard-boiled style that is darkly humorous. **Similar titles:** The Fat White Vampire Series, Andrew Fox; The Odd Thomas Novels, Dean Koontz; *Practical Demonkeeping*, Christopher Moore.

Demons • England—London • Exorcisms • Psychosexual Horror • Shape-shifters

Clegg, Douglas.

The Attraction. *New York: Dorchester, 2006, ©2004. 151p. ISBN 9780843954111.*

A desiccated corpse billed as an Aztec mummy and displayed for all to see in a gas station is revealed to be the remains of a small child with fake fingernails glued on its hands. But when Griff suggests to his friend Ziggy that it would be funny to feed the pathetic "attraction," they end up waking The Flesh Scraper. This tale is Clegg's homage to B slasher flicks, with the requisite characters who do dumb things—such as feed a mummy. **Similar titles:** The Pine Cove Series, Christopher Moore; *From the Dust Returned* and *A Graveyard for Lunatics*, Ray Bradbury; *House of 1000 Corpses* (film); *Bubba Ho-Tep* (film).

Academia • Mummies • Popular Culture • Virginia

Davidson, Mary Janice.

Dead and Loving It. *New York: Berkley Sensation, 2006. 305p. ISBN 0425207951.*
(See chapter 18, "Collections and Anthologies.")

Egolf, Tristan.

Kornwolf. *New York: Black Cat Books, 2006. 378p. ISBN 080211816X.*

Ephraim, a mild-mannered Amish teen, transforms into a werewolf who loves satanic music, rummages through the barns and cornfields of the Pennsylvania Dutch countryside, and cannot wait until Halloween so he can make a horrifying prediction come true. Meanwhile, a reporter trying to make a name for himself "invents" stories about a local werewolf. The late Egolf writes with flair, dry wit, and sardonic humor. **Similar titles:** *Naked Brunch*, Sparkle Hayter; *Surviving Frank*, David A. Page; *The Pilo Family Circus*, Will Elliot.

Adolescence • Amish, The • Journalist as Character • Music—Metal • Music—Rock • Pennsylvania • Popular Culture • Werewolves

Elliot, Will.

The Pilo Family Circus. *Sydney, Australia: ABC Books, Australia, 2006. 312p. ISBN 9780733319815.*

When James visits the Pilo Family Circus, he gets more than he bargained for. He comes to the attention of the traveling show's troupe of clowns, who are at best masochistic, and at worst psychopathic. But in this other-worldly place that is beset by demons, the clowns aren't the worst thing that James has to worry about. **Similar titles:** *The Attraction*, Douglas Clegg; *The Devil You Know*, Mike Carey; *From the Dust Returned*, Ray Bradbury.

Carnivals • Circuses • Clowns • Demons • Mental Illness

Elrod, P. N., ed.

My Big Fat Supernatural Honeymoon. *New York: St. Martin's Griffin, 2008. 358p. ISBN 0312375042.*

(See chapter 18, "Collections and Anthologies.")

My Big Fat Supernatural Wedding. *New York: St. Martin's Griffin, 2006. 310p. ISBN 0312343604.*

(See chapter 18, "Collections and Anthologies.")

Fingerman, B. H.

Bottomfeeder. *Berkley, CA: M. Press, 2006. 268p. ISBN 9781595820976.*

Phil Merman was trapped in a dead end job when he was mugged on a subway platform by a vampire. Although he hasn't aged a day in the twenty-seven years since the attack, Phil's existence is lonely, so when he meets another vampire at a bar who makes it his mission to get him a social life, he is particularly vulnerable to being drawn in to the creature's world of orgies and harrowing adventures. **Similar titles:** The Fat White Vampire Series, Andrew Fox; *The Nymphos of Rocky Flats*, Mike Acevedo; The Love Story Series, Christopher Moore.

Movie Industry—Film Noir • New York—New York City • Psychosexual Horror • Vampire's Point of View

Fox, Andrew.

The Fat White Vampire Series.

If you think that existing on a diet of blood would be conducive to keeping a svelte figure, you're dead wrong. When cabbie turned vampire Jules Duchon drinks the blood of his victims, he also imbibes all the fat and calories they've most recently absorbed, and it's hard to find victims who exist on wheat germ and legumes in a city like New Orleans. **Similar titles:** *Headstone City*, Tom Piccirilli; *The Devil You Know*, Mike Carey; *Bottomfeeder*, B. H. Fingerman; *Habeas Corpses*, Wm. Mark Simmons.

African American Characters • Louisiana—New Orleans • Obesity • Vampire Clans • Vampire's Point of View

Fat White Vampire Blues. *New York: Ballantine, 2003. 334p. ISBN 0345463331.*

> Jules is about to get some help with his weight problem: a rival vampire runs him out of New Orleans, a city known for its great food and decadent lifestyle. Now he will have to find sustenance elsewhere. Readers familiar with John Kennedy Toole's *A Confederacy of Dunces* will enjoy this series.

> *African American Characters • Louisiana—Baton Rouge • Stripper as Character*

Bride of the Fat White Vampire. *New York: Del Rey-Ballentine, 2004. 429p. ISBN 0345464087.*

> This sequel adds even more character (in the form of some strange characters) to the series, incorporating well-known, real-world New Orleans residents, who have themselves become larger than life. Jules Duchon shape-shifts back into his human form, with one *very* important part missing. While trying to make himself whole again, he deals with feuding concerned with the renovation of a historic neighborhood (resembling the infamous public war between novelist Anne Rice and Popeye's Fried Chicken mogul Al Copeland).

> *Marriage • Shape-shifters*

Gentile, Joe, Lori Gentile, and Garrett Anderson, eds.

Kolchak: The Night Stalker Chronicles, 26 Original Tales of the Surreal, the Bizarre, and the Macabre. *Calumet City, IL: Moonstone, 2005. 329p. ISBN 1933076046.*
(See chapter 18, "Collections and Anthologies.")

Hamilton, Laurell K.

The Anita Blake, Vampire Hunter Series.

> Anita Blake is the woman vampires call the Executioner. In a future where vampires are protected by law, she is both a reanimator and a terminator, and is called on to investigate the serial killing of innocent humans and vampires alike. Hamilton's hard-boiled, quirky prose emphasizes character and action. **Similar titles:** *Sunglasses after Dark*, Nancy A. Collins; The Vampire Files Series,p. N. Elrod; The Georgina Kincaid Series, Richelle Mead.

> *Blake, Anita (character) • Eroticism • Missouri—St. Louis • Vampire Clans • Vampire Hunters • Vampire's Point of View*

Guilty Pleasures. *New York: Berkley, 2004, ©1993. 354p. ISBN 0425197549.*

> Anita's newfound vampirism problems are compounded when a powerful vampire elder named Jean-Claude takes a personal interest in her—and his advances are rebuffed.

> *Serial Killers*

The Laughing Corpse. *New York: Berkley, 2003, ©1994. 308p. ISBN 0425192008.*

> A mercenary animator's raising the dead causes problems for Anita Blake. This novel chronicles the further adventures of Hamilton's sassy and tough vampire killer, complete with the wry humor and hard-boiled edge that defines the series.

> *Zombies*

Circus of the Damned. *New York: Berkley, 2004, ©1995. ISBN 0425194272.*

Both St. Louis's master vampire and a rogue vampire who would challenge him want Anita for a servant. Meanwhile, Anita is helping the St. Louis Police investigate murders carried out by an unknown vampire pack, led by another rogue elder. Anita continues to resist the advances of Jean-Claude and becomes involved in the supernatural Circus of the Damned, where she meets the werewolf Richard.

Werewolves

Bloody Bones. *New York: Berkley, 2005, ©1996. 328p. ISBN 0425205673.*

Animator and vampire hunter Anita Blake must juggle a request to raise the dead with her need to solve a series of killings in the Branson, Missouri, area.

Missouri—Branson

The Lunatic Café. *New York: Berkley, 2005, ©1996. 344p. ISBN 0425201376.*

In this tongue-in-cheek adventure, Anita Blake must determine who or what is killing werewolves. The only problem is that this time she is personally involved in her work—she is in love with one of them.

Werewolves

The Killing Dance. *New York: Berkley, 2006, ©1997. 356p. ISBN 0425209067.*

Anita Blake is caught between warring werewolves and the master vampire Jean-Claude, and one of them has put a price on her head. Will she have to form an uneasy alliance to survive?

Werewolves

Burnt Offerings. *New York: Berkley, 2007, ©1998. 376p. ISBN 0425218848.*

Anita agrees to help track down a telekinetic pyromaniac. On the personal side, she and her sig-other, Richard, are splitting up; so Jean-Claude, her vampire master lover, asks for her help in facing down a visiting delegation of the vampire ruling council.

Precognition • Werewolves

Blue Moon. *New York: Jove, 2002, ©1998. 418p. ISBN 0515134457.*

Blake attempts to save a friend from corrupt police and werewolf clans.

Tennessee • Werewolves

Obsidian Butterfly. *New York: Jove, 2002, ©2000. 596p. ISBN 0515134503.*

Anita Blake gets a call from bounty hunter Ted Forrester, which leads her to Santa Fe to investigate serial slayings and mutilations. Not only does Anita have to deal with a centuries-old vampire with powers of magic, she must also contend with Ted's bounty hunter friends, many of whom resent her.

Bounty Hunters • New Mexico—Santa Fe • Serial Killers • Torture • Werewolves

Narcissus in Chains. *New York: Jove, 2002, ©2001. 644p. ISBN 0515133876.*

Six months after Anita Blake faced down her most powerful foe ever, she is again called upon to save the day, as a serial kidnapper targets the people she was sworn to protect. To defeat this new foe, however, Blake must join forces with the vampire Jean-Claude and Richard the werewolf.

Shape-shifters • Werewolves

Cerulean Sins. *New York: Berkley, 2003. 405p. ISBN 0425188361.*

The story begins when a sinister stranger hires Anita Blake to raise the dead, and she finds herself searching for a supernatural serial killer. Meanwhile, her personal life becomes more demanding: vampire Belle Morte demands that Jean-Claude return the vampire Asher to her. In order to save Asher, Anita must enlist the help of a werewolf.

Serial Killers • Werewolves

Incubus Dreams. *New York: Berkley, 2004. 658p. ISBN 0425198243.*

When a serial killer murders a stripper, the Regional Preternatural Crime Investigation Team seeks out Anita Blake. The evidence points to a vampire clan whose master has become a loose cannon. Even with the help of master vampire Jean-Claude, Micah the shape-shifter, and the werewolf Richard, Anita will have her hands full, especially since her ailment makes her extremely lascivious.

Serial Killers

Micah. *New York: Jove, 2006. 280p. ISBN 0515140872.*

Anita journeys to Philadelphia to reanimate a dead witness. With her is Micah, one of her six lovers, who is able to spend time alone with her for the very first time without the encumbrance of any leaders of his wereleopard pack or any of Anita's other partners. But this new intimacy might not be a good thing for their relationship.

Shape-shifters • Werewolves

Danse Macabre. *New York: Berkley, 2006. 483p. ISBN 0425207978.*

Anita discovers she's pregnant and is unsure about how she will deal with a baby while hunting vampires. To complicate matters, she does not know who got her pregnant. Because her magical powers require that she have multiple lovers, there are six possible candidates.

Pregnancy • Werewolves

The Harlequin. *New York: Berkley, 2007. 422p. ISBN 0425217248.*

The Church of the Eternal Life, desperate for help in dealing with a troop of super-secret, universally feared vampire spies, decides to make strange bedfellows with Anita and the powerful Jean-Claude. The problem is that this brings Anita to the attention of The Harlequin, a terror group that sends her a white mask as a threat.

Espionage • Werewolves

Hamilton, Laurell K., Mary Janice Davidson, Eileen Wilks, and Rebecca York.

11

Cravings. *New York: Berkley, 2004. 358p. ISBN 0515138150.*
(See chapter 18, "Collections and Anthologies.")

Harris, Charlaine.

12

<u>The Sookie Stackhouse Series</u> (aka <u>The Southern Vampire Mysteries</u>).

Vampires are a newly emerged minority who have until recently been un-fairly targeted due to superstition. It is this world in which waitress Sookie Stackhouse lives. But Sookie can handle herself. She is beautiful and intel-ligent, and can read minds. **Similar titles:** <u>The Anita Blake, Vampire Hunter Series</u>, Laurell K. Hamilton; <u>The Odd Thomas Novels</u>, Dean Koontz; <u>The Fat White Vampire Series</u>, Andrew Fox; *California Demon: The Secret Life of a Demon-Hunting Soccer Mom*, Julie Kenner.

13

Louisiana • Psychics • Stackhouse, Sookie (character) • Vampire Clans • Waitress as Character

14

Dead until Dark. *New York: Ace, 2001. 292p. ISBN 0441008534.*

Sookie's mind-reading makes dating impossible, so she just lives a quite life with her grandmother—until she meets Bill, who seems to be the perfect man. The problem is that Bill is also a vampire.

15

Families

Living Dead in Dallas. *New York: Ace, 2002. 262p. ISBN 0441009239.*

The trouble begins with a murder in Sookie's small town of Bon Temps, Louisiana, where murders are rare. A police officer too drunk to drive home leaves his car at the bar where Sookie works, only to turn up dead inside his vehicle the next day. As Sookie and her vam-pire boyfriend Bill investigate the death, they are summoned by the local vampire leader to go to Dallas, where Sookie's psychic abilities are needed to help solve a disappearing vampire problem.

16

Texas—Dallas

Club Dead. *New York: Ace, 2003. 258p. ISBN 0441010512.*

Sookie and Bill's relationship runs into a rough patch, and he has a fling with an old flame. Soon after, Bill is kidnapped, and Sookie's boss Eric enlists her help in getting him back. Still nursing the wounds from her betrayal, Sookie ventures into the supernatural scene of Jackson, Mississippi, to find him. While there, she is pro-tected by the vampire Elvis.

18

Mississippi—Jackson • Presley, Elvis (character) • Werewolves

Dead to the World. *New York: Ace, 2004. 291p. ISBN 0441011675.*

Sookie and Bill's relationship ends when he decides to go to for Peru to do some research. But his departure does not end Sookie's run-ins with supernatural creatures. Soon she finds her boss Eric naked and wandering around, suffering from a bad case of amnesia. Then

19

20

Sookie's brother disappears, and she finds herself facing a coven of extortionist witches in the Shreveport area.

Amnesia • Louisiana—Shreveport • Witchcraft • Werewolves

Dead as a Doornail. *New York: Ace, 2005, 295p. ISBN 0441012795.*

Sookie finds herself further involved in a war among supernatural creatures. Meanwhile, her own love life becomes more complicated.

Fairies • Shape-shifters • Witchcraft • Werewolves

Definitely Dead. *New York: Ace Books, 2006. 324p. ISBN 0441014003.*

Sookie travels to New Orleans to deal with the estate of her oversexed cousin who has recently died—even though she was a vampire. Along with the bewitching landlady of the apartment, Sookie discovers that her cousin made a lot of enemies, which means that she has as well.

Demons • Louisiana—New Orleans • Werewolves • Witchcraft

All Together Dead. *New York: Ace, 2006. 324p. ISBN 0441015816.*

Sophie has outgrown her career as a small town barmaid and is now the aid of Queen Sophie of Louisiana, the ruler of all the local vampires. But Hurricane Katrina ravaged Queen Sophie's domain, damaging property and killing many of her subjects. Meanwhile, Sookie begins a romance with Quinn, a were-tiger.

Shape-shifters • Weather—Hurricane Katrina • Werewolves • Witchcraf

From Dead to Worse. *New York: Ace, 2008. 359p. ISBN 0441015891.*

Quinn is missing, and the vampires and werewolves are at war with one another. Meanwhile, Sookie's perfidious vampire ex Bill returns, and Sookie discovers her family's ties to the fairy folk.

Fairies • Shape-shifters • Werewolves • Witchcraft

Hayter, Sparkle.

Naked Brunch. *New York: Three Rivers Press, 2003. 322p. ISBN 1400047439.*

Okay, so you have to howl at the moon, but is being a werewolf really that bad? Annie answers this question in a comic werewolf tale full of a great many recognizable types: the greedy Fortune 500 CEO, the scheming and vapid television anchor, the bumbling reporter . . . . All of these characters are drawn together by a series of bizarre Atlanta murders. **Similar titles:** <u>The Anita Blake, Vampire Hunter Series</u>, Laurell K. Hamilton; *The Stupidest Angel* and *A Dirty Job*, Christopher Moore; *Kornwolf*, Tristan Egolf.

Georgia—Atlanta • Journalist as Character • Werewolves

Hopkins, Brian A.

The Licking Valley Coon Hunters Club. *Alma, AR: Yard Dog Press, 2002,* ©2000. 185p. ISBN 1893687252.

After being kidnapped at an airport and taken out into the desert, private investigator Martin Zolotow is physically coerced into working for a mobster, who needs him to help save his daughter from a man who thinks he is a vampire. Zolotow must now travel to Oklahoma City to visit a vampire nightclub, if he can survive long enough to get there. A fun read—half hard-boiled detective novel, half vampire wannabe B-flick. **Similar titles:** The Anita Blake Vampire Hunter Series, Laurell K. Hamilton; *Headstone City*, Tom Piccirilli; The Vampire Files Series,p. N. Elrod.

Oklahoma—Oklahoma City • Organized Crime • Psychiatrist/Psychologist as Character

Kenner, Julie.

California Demon: The Secret Life of a Demon-Hunting Soccer Mom. *New York: Berkley Books, 2006. 342p. ISBN 042521043X.*

Kate Connor pretends to be a stay-at-home PTA mom, but she knows it's easier to fight and slay a demon than it is to raise a teenaged daughter or watch over a toddler. And her life becomes even more complicated when she discovers that a demon has infiltrated her daughter's school. This witty, down-to-earth, dialogue-driven novel perfectly combines horror and Roseanne Barr–style comedy. **Similar titles:** The Buffy the Vampire Slayer Series, various authors; The Sookie Stackhouse Series, Charlaine Harris; *Practical Demonkeeping*, Christopher Moore.

California • Demons • High School • Parapsychology • Parenting

Koontz, Dean.

The Odd Thomas Novels.

Odd Thomas is fry cook and a ghost seer living in a small California town. Oh, and he possesses the ability to see bodachs—malevolent spirits that are harbingers of imminent violence. **Similar titles:** *The Devil You Know*, Mike Carey; The Sookie Stackhouse Series, Charlaine Harris; *Gil's All Fright Diner*, Lee A. Martinez.

California • Cook as Character • Odd Thomas (character) • Precognition • Psychics

Odd Thomas. *New York: Random, 2007,* ©2003. 399p. ISBN 9780739341438.

A bodach is in close proximity to a creepy stranger whom Thomas dubs Fungus Man. During his investigations, Thomas discovers a serial killer's shrine—and a date in the near future circled on the calendar.

Presley, Elvis (character)

Forever Odd. *New York: Bantam, 2006,* ©2005. 364p. ISBN 9780553588262.

Thomas's rather odd routines, including his speaking to Elvis, must be put on hold so he can help the police figure out why his best friend is missing—and why his friend's elderly father was killed during the apparent kidnapping.

Presley, Elvis (character)

Brother Odd. *New York: Bantam, 2007, ©2006. 430p. ISBN 9780553589108.*

Odd Thomas has given up his position as a fry cook in exchange for a more contemplative life in the Abby of St. Bartholomew in the Sierra Nevada Mountains. But he can find no peace here either, and when a brother from the abbey goes missing, he is called upon to use his unusual powers.

Clergy as Character • Nevada • Road Trips

Odd Hours. *New York: Bantam, 2008. 368p. ISBN 0553807056.*

Odd Thomas, his dog Boo, and the Chairman of the Board travel to a small California coastal town, where sinister forces have gathered. But these forces will not stop Thomas from his quest to discover the meaning behind his recurring nightmare of the red tide. Thomas is drawn closer and closer to the ocean and a final confrontation with the ultimate evil—which is now ready for a showdown.

Demons • Dogs • Maritime Horror • Road Trips

Laymon, Richard.

Bite. *New York: Leisure, 1999, ©1996. 378p. ISBN 0843945508.*

When Sam's ex-girlfriend shows up at his apartment out of the blue after ten years, he is ecstatic to see her—until he finds out that she only needs him to stake a vampire stalker. This darkly comic first-person narrative explores the problems disposing of a vampire's body. **Similar titles:** *The Traveling Vampire Show*, Richard Laymon; The Vampire Files, P. N. Elrod; The Love Story Series, Christopher Moore; *Gacy: The Crawl Space* (film).

Biker as Character • California—Los Angeles • Domestic Violence • Vampire Hunters

Mack, Robert L.

Sweeney Todd: The Demon Barber of Fleet Street. *New York: Oxford University Press, 2007. 300p. ISBN 0199543445.*

(See chapter 11, "Maniacs and Sociopaths, or the Nuclear Family Explodes: Monstrous Malcontents Bury the Hatchet.")

Martin H. Greenberg, ed.

White House Horrors. *New York: BP Books, 2004, ©1996. 316p. ISBN 0743487311.*

(See chapter 18, "Collections and Anthologies.")

Martinez, A. Lee.

Gil's All Fright Diner. *New York: Tor, 2005. 268p. ISBN 0765311437.*

Guess they should have filled up when gas was only $3.00 a gallon! The Earl of Vampires and Duke of Werewolves are traveling, running on empty in more ways than one. Starving, they look for a place to eat in Rockwood, a small desert community, and there they find Gil's Diner. After helping the owner fight off zombies, they help her deal with her other problem—the health inspector. Meanwhile, Mistress Lilith seeks to destroy the world. **Similar titles:** <u>The Odd Thomas Series</u>, Dean Koontz; <u>The Sookie Stackhouse Series</u>, Charlaine Harris; *Gil's All Fright Diner*, Lee A. Martinez.

Cook as Character • Road Trips • Southwest, The • Vampire's Point of View • Waitress as Character • Werewolves • Zombies

Mead, Richelle.

The Georgina Kincaid Series.

Georgina Kincaid is a shape-shifting, centuries-old demon seductress. So it comes as no surprise that her day job as a bookstore manager in Seattle can't make this vixen happy. **Similar titles:** <u>The Anita Blake, Vampire Hunter Series</u>, Laurell K. Hamilton; *Sunglasses After Dark*, Nancy A. Collins; *Kornwolf*, Tristan Egolf.

Demons • Psychosexual Horror • Shape-shifters • Vampire Hunters • Washington—Seattle • Writer as Character

Succubus Blues. *New York: Kensington Books, 2007. 358p. ISBN 0758216416.*

> Although wild sex is no problem for Georgina, she is incapable of forming lasting bonds with men. Nevertheless, what really ticks her off is that her immortal friends, vampire and demon alike, are being exterminated.

Serial Killers

Succubus on Top. *New York: Kensington, 2008. 340p. ISBN 0758216424.*

> Georgia is falling in love with writer Seth Mortenson, but the relationship is mutually frustrating because it cannot be consummated without hastening the demise of her beloved. Meanwhile, she is busy helping a fellow incubus seduce a local right wing radio talk show host so that he may shorten her nasty and brutish life.

Radio

Moore, Christopher.

A Dirty Job. *New York: William Morrow, 2006. 387p. ISBN 0060590270.*

> When Charlie Asher, a thrift store owner, attends his wife's death in childbirth, he sees a figure invisible to everyone else in the hospital room. This heralds his introduction to his new part-time vocation—Death Merchant. In the meantime, Charlie must also deal with his lesbian sister and her partner, his Gothette shop-girl, an addle-brained ex-cop, a nostalgic police detective, and a man named Minty Green—all the while keeping his instruction manual, *The Big Book of Death*, from falling into the wrong hands.

Similar titles: *The Stupidest Angel*, Christopher Moore; *Naked Brunch*, Sparkle Hatyer; *Headstone City*, Tom Piccirilli.

California—San Francisco • Death (character) • Gay/Lesbian/Bisexual Characters • Parenting • Police Officer as Character • Reincarnation

Moore, Christopher.

The Love Story Series.

Meet Jody, a good-looking redhead turned into a vampire. Attacked in San Francisco's financial district, she wakes up under a dumpster, needing shelter and time to get used to her undead-ness. Moore's dialogue is quick and witty. **Similar titles:** *Naked Brunch*, Sparkle Hayter; The Anita Blake, Vampire Hunter Series, Laurell K. Hamilton; *Practical Demonkeeping*, Christopher Moore.

California—San Francisco • Vampire's Point of View

Bloodsucking Fiends: A Love Story. *New York: Perennial, 2004, ©1999. 300p. ISBN 0060735414.*

Jody takes up with an aspiring writer turned late-night grocery store clerk/amateur frozen turkey bowler. It's too bad that her vampire master is the jealous type and is not above framing her new love as a murderer.

Popular Culture • Serial Killers • Writer as Character

You Suck. *New York: William Morrow, 2007. 328p. ISBN 0060590297.*

Nineteen-year-old Tommy is in for more than he bargained for when Jody, his red-headed girlfriend, first turns him into a vampire, then convinces him to leave his hometown of Incontinence, Indiana, for San Francisco. Not only does blood lust make Tommy do some things that he's not proud of, now he must contend with Elijah, the ancient vampire who turned Jody behind a Safeway and left her to die, but who now wants her for himself.

Indiana

The Pine Cove Series.

Pine Cove, a quirky little California town, has seen more than its share of weirdos—and not all of them are human. This loose series introduces quirky characters and over-the-top slapstick, starring monsters. **Similar titles:** *The Attraction*, Douglas Clegg; *A Dirty Job* and *The Stupidest Angel*, Christopher Moore; *Naked Brunch*, Sparkle Hatyer; *Shaun of the Dead* (film).

California—Pine Cove

Practical Demonkeeping: A Comedy of Horrors. *New York: Perennial, 2004, ©1992. 243p. ISBN 0380816555.*

A young seminary student accidentally summons a minor demon and now is stuck as the demon's caretaker. As he travels to Pine Cove, can he figure out a way to get someone else to take the imp off his hands before all his friends and acquaintances are devoured?

Demons • Religion—Wicca • Road Trips

The Lust Lizard of Melancholy Cove. *London: Orbit, 2007, ©1999. 236p. ISBN 1841494518.*

When one of Pine Cove's residents hangs himself, the local psychiatrist, who had been handing out antidepressant prescriptions like they were going out of style, suddenly feels responsible and yanks everyone's meds. So when everyone is suffering from withdrawal, it is a truly excellent time for a leak at the local nuclear power plant to disrupt the slumbers of the giant, prehistoric lizard sleeping just off the coast.

Drugs • Prehistoric Monsters • Subterranean Monsters

The Stupidest Angel: A Heartwarming Tale of Christmas Terror. *New York: William Morrow, 2004. 275p. ISBN 0060590254.*

Pine Cove will never be your typical small, sleepy town again, since Lena Marquez killed her cheating husband on his way home from playing Santa Claus. Enter the Archangel Raziel, who should have read *Resurrecting for Dummies*. When he reanimates "Santa" to save Christmas, he also brings to life various other newly dead people, who are now attacking Pine Cove.

Angels • Holidays—Christmas • Zombies

Page, David A.

Surviving Frank. *Waterville, ME: Five Star, 2003. 293p. ISBN 0786256346.*

A famous detective named Frank T. Wolfe is assigned a new partner—only this partner's main task is to keep an eye on Frank, who seems to lose a lot of partners. The Internal Affairs spy, Ryan, soon finds out something disturbing about his target: Frank is a werewolf. But for now, Ryan has to put that aside, because the duo, investigating a murder, has uncovered a plot that could mean the governor has been targeted for assassination. **Similar titles:** *Naked Brunch*, Sparkle Hayter; *Kornwolf*, Tristan Egolf; The Anita Blake, Vampire Hunter Series, Laurell K. Hamilton.

Massachusetts—Boston • Police Officer as Character • Psychics • Werewolves

Piccirilli, Tom.

Headstone City. *New York: Bantam, 2006. 302p. ISBN 0553587218.*

If you're a member of the organized crime families in Brooklyn, you know cab driver Johnny "Dane" Danetello. Ever since a childhood carjacking turned into a horrifying accident, he's been cursed with the ability to see the dead, so he spends time between fares chatting up spirits, all of which force him to face his own haunted past: a murdered father and a fifteen-year-old girl who got the last ride of her life in Dane's cab two years earlier. The only problem is that the girl is related to a mob-connected psychic friend. **Similar titles:** *Fat White Vampire Blues*, Andrew Fox; *A Dirty Job*, Christopher Moore; *The Licking Valley Coon Hunters Club*, Brian A. Hopkins.

Cab Driver as Character • New York—Brooklyn • Organized Crime • Parapsychology • Psychics • Revenge

Simmons, Wm. Mark.

The Chris Csejthe Series.

Soon after the death of his wife and daughter, Chris must contend with a mysterious illness that seems to be claiming his life. Turns out that he is in the middle of being transformed into a vampire. This series features a witty and engaging protagonist who is prone to throw out a literary reference or two. **Similar titles:** <u>The Fat White Vampire Series</u>, Andrew Fox; <u>The Love Story Series</u>, Christopher Moore; <u>The Georgina Kincaid Series</u>, Richelle Mead.

Haim, Chris (character) • Vampire Clans • Vampire's Point of View • Werewolves

One Foot in the Grave. *Riverside, NY: Baen, 2005, ©1996. 376p. ISBN 0671877216.*

The newly transformed Chris finds himself at the center of a battle between two warring factions of vampires.

Fairies

Dead on My Feet. *Riverdale, NY: Simon & Schuster-Baen, 2003. 405p. ISBN 0743436105.*

In this tongue-in-cheek sequel, Chris gets caught up in vampire clan fights and has to rely on psychics and New Orleans' voodoo priests, all the while running into the likes of Dracula and Elizabeth Bathory, his great-great-great ancestor, who is concocting a genetically engineered virus that threatens to become epidemic. Meanwhile, his personal life seems to spiral out of control.

Academia • Epidemics • Eugenics • Louisiana—Monroe • Louisiana—New Orleans • New York—New York City

Habeas Corpses. *New York: Simon & Schuster-Baen Books, 2005. 403p. ISBN 1416509135.*

Widower Christopher Csejthe finds himself in a quandary: he has been turned by a vampire—and bitten by a werewolf. The next thing you know, he is assassinating Erzebet Bathory, the vampire master of New York. Thus, he is forced to take over the rule of the city. Rather than become an undead mayor, he absconds to Louisiana, inhabiting a creaky old house near a zombie-filled graveyard.

Louisiana • Mengele, Josef (character) • Nazism • New York—New York City • Zombies

---

Stone, Del, Jr.

 Dead Heat. *Austin, TX: Mojo Press, 1996. 186p. ISBN 1885418108.*

A loner and Harley rider becomes a zombie following a biological apocalypse, but he is different form other zombies because he can think and control the dead masses. Stone's modern classic is darkly humorous. **Similar titles:** *The Stupidest Angel*, Christopher Moore; *The Zombie Survival Guide* and *World War Z: An Oral History of the Zombie War*, Max Brooks; *Monster Island*, David Wellington; *Land of the Dead* (film); *Shaun of the Dead* (film).

Apocalypse • Biker as Character • Futurism • War—Biological Warfare • Zombies

Stross, Charles.

The Atrocity Archives. *Urbana, IL: Golden Gryphon, 2004. 273p. ISBN 0441013651.*

> (See chapter 17, "Everyday Horror: When the Mundane Becomes Monstrous.")

Thurman, Rob.

Nightlife. *New York: ROC-New American Library, 2006. 339p. ISBN 0451460758.*

> (See chapter 8, "Mythological Monsters and 'The Old Ones': Invoking the Dark Gods.")

Waggoner, Tim.

Necropolis. *Farmington Hills, MI: Gale Group-Five Star, 2004. 248p. ISBN 1410402150.*

> (See chapter 5, "Golem, Mummies, and Zombies: Wake the Dead and They'll Be Cranky.")

Wilde, Oscar.

The Canterville Ghost. *Cambridge, MA: Candlewick Press, 1997, ©1887. 126p. ISBN 0763601322.*

> In this classic tale, an American family moves into a haunted English manor and then refuses to believe in its resident ghost. The teenaged daughter begins to witness strange occurrences, but can she convince her parents of the existence of paranormal phenomena? This work is exemplary of Wilde's comic wit and flair for language. **Similar titles:** *The Green Man*, Kingsley Amis; *Northanger Abbey*, Jane Austen; *Needing Ghosts*, Ramsey Campbell; *The Canterville Ghost* (film).

Adolescence • England • Haunted Houses • Parenting

Wilson, F. Paul.

Repairman Jack Novels.

> He's not the tool man, but Repairman Jack is a fix-it man, a specialist who can be hired to right situations that might be of a questionable nature. If you're innocent and desperate, you can turn to him, even if your problems involve supernatural elements. **Similar titles:** *Nobody True*, James Her-

11

12

13

14

15

16

17

18

19

20

bert; <u>The Lawson Vampire Novels</u>, Jon F. Merz; *Surviving Frank*, David A. Page; <u>The 99 Coffins Series</u>, David Wellington.

Repairman Jack (character)

Crisscross. *New York: Tor, 2006, ©2004. 415p. ISBN 0765346060.*

A nun hires Repairman Jack to retrieve embarrassing photos that someone is using to blackmail her. He also has to infiltrate The Dormantalists, a shady cult that a young man joined before he severed all ties with his mother. Jack's jobs put those he loves in danger—this time, his pregnant girlfriend Gia and her nine-year-old daughter are threatened by the Dormantalists.

Clergy as Character • Religion—Cults

Infernal. *New York: Tor, 2006, ©2005. 421p. ISBN 0765351382.*

After their father is killed in a terrorist attack, Repairman Jack reconnects with his estranged brother, a corrupt Philadelphia judge. Jack's brother Tom wants his help looking for a Spanish ship that disappeared off the coast of Bermuda in the late sixteenth century, which contains a device that serves as a portal to another dimension.

Families • Popular Culture—Bermuda Triangle

Gateways. *New York: Tor, 2006, ©2003. 435p. ISBN 0765346052.*

Jack travels to Florida to see his estranged father, who has been in a car accident. Once there he discovers that the retirement community his father had been living in, Gateways South, was deeper in the Florida Everglades than most people would think. Furthermore, nearby lurks a Lovecraftian evil that affects the local residents.

Cthulian Monsters • Families • Florida—Everglades • Septuagenarians

Harbingers. *Colorado Springs, CO: Gauntlet Press, 2006. 361 pp. ISBN 1887368841.*

Repairman Jack, that fixer of things in the ongoing battle between the Ally and the Adversary, meets up with a group of people who claim to be doing the work of the Ally. But when it is revealed to Jack that their work includes the killing of the innocent, he sees them more as zealots and wonders if perhaps the group is instead being manipulated by otherworldly forces.

New York—Long Island

Zielinski, Stephen.

Bad Magic. *New York: Tor, 2005. 256p. ISBN 9780312878627.*

The supernatural exists around us, but similar to J. K. Rowling's Muggles, most humans either are unable to, or refuse to, see the evidence of things not seen. That's the premise here: eight quirky mages and warriors work to protect humanity from those magical creatures who plague humans, and they must do their job while maintaining the illusion that the supernatural does not exist. **Similar titles:** *Sunglasses after Dark*, Nancy A. Collins; <u>The Vampire Files Series</u>, P. N. Elrod; <u>The Georgina Kincaid Series</u>, Richelle Mead.

California—San Francisco • Vampire Hunters • Witchcraft

Film

Bubba Ho-Tep. *Don Coscarelli, dir. 2002. 92 minutes.*

Elvis (Bruce Campbell) is not dead. He is dying in obscurity in an East Texas nursing home, where he is believed to be a doddering old Elvis impersonator. But another resident (Ossie Davis), who fancies himself to be Jack Kennedy, whisked from office by his enemies that day in Dallas and dyed black, believes him. And they must work together to protect other nursing home residents from Bubba Ho-tep, a centuries-old mummy who lurks near the home—waiting to steal. **Similar titles:** *The Attraction*, Douglas Clegg; *Keepers*, Gary A. Braunbeck.

African American Characters • Aging • Kennedy, John (character) • Mummies • Nursing Homes • Presley, Elvis (character) • Texas—Nacogdoches

The Canterville Ghost. *Jules Dassin, dir. 1944. 95 minutes.*

In the seventeenth century, when Sir Simon Canterville flees a duel, his mortified father walls up his poltroonish son in the family castle, where he is doomed to exist as a ghost until a descendant can perform a brave deed. Can an American kinsman quartered in the castle with a troop of soldiers during World War II be the person who can set his soul free? Charles Laughton, Robert Young, and Margaret O' Brien star. **Similar titles:** *The Canterville Ghost*, Oscar Wilde; *Northanger Abbey*, Jane Austen.

Afterlife, The • Castles • England • Haunted Houses • Soldier as Character

Dead Alive (Braindead). *Peter Jackson, dir. 1992. 104 minutes.*

Lionel, an attractive but shy young man, would like to pursue a relationship with the beautiful Paquita; but his domineering mother does not approve, and she follows the couple to the zoo where they have their first date. While Lionel's mother sneaks and snoops around, she is attacked by a ferocious Sumarian rat monkey, whose bite turns humans into zombies. Now Lionel's undead mother, with her insatiable desire for human flesh, is an even more devouring shrew than she was while alive. **Similar titles:** *The Zombie Survival Guide* and *World War Z: An Oral History of the Zombie War*, Max Brooks.

Cannibalism • Families • New Zealand • Parenting • Zombies

Dogma. *Kevin Smith, dir. 1999. 130 minutes.*

Rufus, the thirteenth apostle, enlists the help of an abortion clinic worker to prevent two fallen angels from exploiting one of God's loopholes and getting back into heaven, thereby destroying the fabric of the universe. God is no help—she's in the hospital after being attacked by impish demons dressed as hockey players. Ben Affleck, Matt Damon, Chris Rock, George Carlin, Alan Rickman, Janeane Garofalo, Salma Hayek, and Bud Cort star, and Alanis Morissette plays God. **Similar titles:** *The Stupidest Angel*, Christopher Moore; <u>The Buffy the Vampire Slayer Series</u>, various authors.

Angels • Apocalypse • Demons God (character) • Religion—Christianity

The Evil Dead. *Sam Raimi, dir. 1981. 85 minutes.*

Five college students spending the weekend in a cabin in the woods find a copy of *The Necroconomicon* in the basement. Fortunately for them, they do not read the ancient language in which the tome is written, as reading the book aloud has the power to raise the dead. But conveniently enough, in the basement they find a taped translation of the text. Of course the five play the tape, with predictable results—the dead rise from their graves, and the group is besieged by zombies. **Similar titles:** *The Zombie Survival Guide* and *World War Z: An Oral History of the Zombie War*, Max Brooks.

Necronomicon, The • Zombies

Fido. *Andrew Currie, dir. 2006. 91 minutes.*

In the 1940s, in an alternate universe, the Allies are not engaged in fighting the Axis powers, but battle the undead after radiation from space animates the newly dead into flesh-eating zombies. ZomCom, a Haliburton-esque corporation, saves the day when its scientists invent ways to not only neutralize the zombie menace, but also tap into their potential for menial labor. Now, in a postwar boom world, middle-class couples enjoy the services of zombies who serve their meals, mow their grass, and even watch their children. **Similar titles:** *The Zombie Survival Guide* and *World War Z: An Oral History of the Zombie War*, Max Brooks.

Corporate Horror • Parallel Universes • Slavery • Suburbia • War—Cold War • War—World War II • Zombies

Gacy: The Crawl Space. *Clive Saunders, dir. 2003. 88 minutes.*

This direct-to-video dramatization of the final days of John Wayne Gacy's career as a serial killer of young boys features darkly comedic elements. While Gacy busily rapes and murders young men, his neighbors and family members constantly complain about the god-awful stench emanating from the crawl space below his house, which occasionally causes maggots to boil up into the upstairs plumbing. Nevertheless, no one seems to suspect the obvious when several young men who work for Gacy or come to his house suddenly turn up missing. **Similar titles:** *Exquisite Corpse*, Poppy Z. Brite; *American Psycho*, Bret Easton Ellis; *Serial Killers: The Methods and Madness of Monsters*, Peter Vronsky.

Clowns • Gacy, John Wayne (character) • Gay/Lesbian/Bisexual Characters • Illinois • Rape • Serial Killers • Torture

May. *Lucky McKee, dir. 2002. 93 minutes.*

May, a lonely young woman with limited social skills, makes a few attempts to connect with people her own age and fails. She then takes her mother's advice and embarks on making friends, quite literally. Fortunately for her, the sewing skills her mother taught her, combined with what she has learned about performing surgery working in a veterinary hospital, will come in handy. **Similar titles:** *The Way the Family Got Away*, Michael Kimball; *The Attraction*, Douglas Clegg.

California • Dolls • Psychosexual Horror • Spree Killers

The Mummy. *Stephen, Sommer, dir. 1999. 125 minutes.*

Librarian Evelyn Carnahan enlists the help of French Legionnaire Rick O'Connell on an archeological dig. Unfortunately for both, the dig disturbs the slumbers of Imhotep, an Egyptian priest buried alive as punishment for killing the pharaoh and sleeping with his mistress. Brendan Fraser and Rachael Weisz star. **Similar titles:** *To Wake the Dead*, Richard Laymon; *Dead Heat*, Del Stone Jr.

Archeologist as Character • Cursed Objects • Egypt • Imhotep (character) • Librarian as Character • Mummies

Re-Animator. *Stuart Gordon, dir. 1985. 86 minutes.*

Herbert West, a brilliant but insane student of Miskatonic Medical School, discovers a serum that can reanimate the dead. But the dead are not as good as new; rather, they are raving zombies. When Dr. Carl Hill finds out about West's discovery, he tries to steal it for himself, hoping it will not only make him rich and famous, but also win him the love of his boss and mentor's daughter, Megan. A battle ensues between West and Hill in this amusing loose adaptation of H. P. Lovecraft's novella by the same name. **Similar titles:** *Herbert West: Re-animator,* H. P. Lovecraft; *Frankenstein,* Mary Shelley.

Academia • Massachusetts—Arkham • Miskatonic University • Weird Science • West, Herbert (character) • Zombies

The Return of the Living Dead. *Dan O'Bannon, dir. 1985. 91 minutes.*

When an experimental drug developed by the military for the eradication of marijuana ends up reanimating corpses in the morgue of the VA hospital, the government hushes up the story by sealing the zombies into air-tight containers and shipping them off to a warehouse for safekeeping. Of course, the deadly cargo is promptly misplaced by the government; so when the containers eventually leak, all hell breaks loose, and no one is prepared to deal with the consequences. **Similar titles:** *The Zombie Survival Guide* and *World War Z: An Oral History of the Zombie War,* Max Brooks.

Funeral Industry • Kentucky—Louisville • Weird Science • Zombies

Shaun of the Dead. *Edgar Wright, dir. 2004. 99 minutes.*

Shaun, your average working stiff, wants nothing more than a cold pint with his mates after another dispiriting day managing a bunch of surly teenagers in the electronics store where he works. So when zombies first make their appearance, Shaun cannot be blamed for failing to notice, since their undeath is as mundane as his own un-life. Good thing the zombie epidemic provides a unique opportunity for him to show that he's capable of change. **Similar titles:** *The Zombie Survival Guide* and *World War Z: An Oral History of the Zombie War,* Max Brooks.

England • Suburbia • Zombies

June's Picks

Books: *Northanger Abbey,* Jane Austen (Oxford University Press); *Naked Brunch,* Sparkle Hayter (Three Rivers Press); *The Stupidest Angel: A Heartwarming Tale of Christmas Terror,* Christopher Moore (William Morrow); The Fat White Vampire Series, Andrew Fox (Ballantine); *The Canterville Ghost,* Oscar Wilde (Candlewick Press)

Films: *Bubba Ho-Tep, Dogma, Fido, Gacy: The Crawl Space, Shaun of the Dead*

Tony's Picks

Books: Tristan Egolf, *Kornwolf* (Black Cat Books); Christopher Fahy, *Matinee at the Flame* (Overlook Connection Press); Andrew Fox, *Fat White Vampire* Blues (Ballantine); Christopher Moore, *Practical Demonkeeping: A Comedy of Horrors* (Perennial); Christopher Moore, *The Stupidest Angel: A Heartwarming Tale of Christmas Terror* (William Morrow).

Films: *May*, *Shaun of the Dead*

Chapter 17

Everyday Horror: When the Mundane Becomes Monstrous

The most recent variation on the genre, everyday horror, is postmodern in its sensibilities. It transgresses boundaries and breaks the "rules" of earlier subgenres of horror, and even straddles genres. To put it another way, in more traditional works of horror, a monster violently disrupts our familiar reality. In everyday horror, our assumptions about the very nature of that reality are thrown into question. Everyday horror is the most pure example of what Freud termed the uncanny, which is "that species of the frightening that goes back to what was once well-known and had long been familiar." Freudian psychology suggests that the quarantining of the knowledge of something that is incomprehensible (and therefore unsettling) in the nether regions of the unconscious mind causes that knowledge to evolve, becoming irrational fear. Unfortunately, the knowledge does *not* stay repressed. It resurfaces—most typically in dreams, masquerading in the imagery of the nightmare. The once repressed, now newly emerged material frightens us because we do not recognize it immediately. On the surface it appears completely disassociated from our waking reality. At the same time, it bears an eerie resemblance to something that was once familiar.

In Simon Clark's *This Rage of Echoes*, for example, Mason Konrad, like everyone else, believes that he is an individual who is wholly unique in his appearance and life experience. But when Mason is followed by the Echomen, people who look exactly like him at different stages of his life, down to a scar on the back of his hand, he comes to see the fallacies in this logic. The Echomen also possess detailed knowledge of events from his life that only he could know. Through their unnerving similarity, they demonstrate to Mason that individuality and the alleged autonomy that comes with it are illusions, something he previously realized at some unconscious level.

Another example of the uncanny can be found in Jack Ketchum's *The Girl Next Door*. In a seemingly innocuous neighborhood, a mother ritualistically tortures children. However, in the context of the neighborhood, her behavior is not all that out of place—other children enjoy activities such as torturing animals. In this case, the neighborhood itself represses important knowledge, and Ketchum's fictional reality ultimately becomes uncanny—it is a place eerily similar to the neighborhoods inhabited by the novel's readers, full of people with disturbing tendencies that are hidden in plain sight.

In other words, in everyday horror, evil wears a mundane and all too familiar face, with evil surrounding us, rather than remaining confined to the periphery of existence, in places such as ancient occult texts, or the backwoods of rural America, or the mean streets of New York City. When the supernatural makes an appearance in everyday horror, it is not a strange and unbelievable force that requires a tremendous suspension of disbelief. Rather, it lies just a step ahead of our science. It is the manifestation of that which we know all too well but cannot explain or control, no matter how much we may hope to. So, for example, in Stephen King's *Cell*, mobile phones that permit people to communicate wirelessly throughout the globe (technology so sophisticated that to the average person it seems almost magical) can also be used to transmit a signal that turns all users into zombies. In some fictions, the supernatural takes the form of a parallel universe that is an extension of the one in our imaginations. In Neil Gaiman's *Coraline*, a lonely little girl with nothing to do but explore the rambling old house her parents recently moved into discovers, in a dimension inside of the walls of the family home, her "Other Mother" and "Other Father," sinister versions of her own parents. These Other parents threaten to replace the mother and father she knows and loves if Coraline cannot escape the parallel universe.

Everyday horror is not necessarily subtle. These monsters may have mundane beginnings, but events rapidly change from the just plain weird to the fantastical. For example, at the beginning of Bentley Little's novel *The Policy*, Hunt Jackson and his coworkers are harassed by an insurance salesman who encourages them to purchase policies indemnifying them against difficulties with the law, their employers' malice, and even the event of death itself. While purchasing protection against such events initially seems bizarre, it is not that huge a leap in logic in a world where one can already purchase insurance policies to protect the value of specific body parts, legal insurance, and even life insurance for children. Furthermore, there is something almost magical about the arcane legal details of an insurance policy, which seem to tell us in plain English that we are protected against certain events—while having a secret codicil that suspends coverage under certain circumstances, such as homeowner's policies that offer protection against water driven by rain, but not by flooding (so a homeowner cannot be compensated when her house is first devastated by a hurricane and then laid waste by flood waters during the same event). So after Hunt Jackson's home is damaged and his homeowner's insurance company tries to make him whole by painting all the walls black and replacing every one of his music CDs with the same Debby Boone album, he is annoyed, but not terribly surprised, because he too knows how insurance companies behave. Later in the novel, it is a just a short leap of logic that these corporations, designed to sell us protection against nearly everything, can supernaturally cause events to occur in order to prompt us to purchase even more insurance.

Horror also has mundane roots in Bret Easton Ellis's novel *Lunar Park*. Ellis himself, author of *American Psycho*, is the main character. He emerges from a haze fueled by booze and drugs a decade after being vilified for writing this splatterpunk classic and finds himself in Lunar Park, a niche of suburbia that barely needs embellishment to appear strange. In Lunar Park, parents take their two-year olds to Pilates and obsess over all facets of their diets—so the haunting of Ellis's new suburban dwelling by his late father is not a huge stretch of the imagination.

Everyday horror, then, represents a new evolutionary stage in the genre. It is dependent on the reader's familiarity with the tropes of horror, which can readily be grafted on to the bizarre complexity of modern life, onto a world that is full of rapidly mutating viruses and strange new technology and corporations that have so much data on us that their marketing departments can hack our minds to manipulate us into buying things we would have never dreamed that we "needed." In such a universe, vampires and zombies and ghosts seem to be quite at home. For readers, these texts offer nonformulaic endings, as the hero or protagonist does not always defeat the evil. In addition, the emphasis on the ordinary quality of horror lends itself to stories that use identifiable settings that do not require a radical suspension of disbelief.

Bailey, Dale, and Jack Slay Jr.

Sleeping Policemen. *Urbana, IL: Golden Gryphon Press, 2006. 208p. ISBN 193084641X.*

A carload of college boys driving back after a drunken outing in a strip club hit someone. And then things go from bad to worse: At the scene of the accident, they find a well-dressed dead man with $10,000 and a key to a bus station locker in his pocket; then they are passed by a slow-moving car at 2:00 in the morning. The driver gets their license number, tracks them, and wants to do a lot more than exchange insurance information. **Similar titles:** *Dead of Winter*, Don D' Ammassa; *Terminal*, Brian Keene; *The One Safe Place*, Ramsey Campbell.

Organized Crime • Secret Sin • South Carolina • Stalkers

Braunbeck, Gary A.

Destinations Unknown. *Baltimore, MD: Cemetery Dance, 2006. 216p. ISBN 1587670852.*

(See chapter 18, "Collections and Anthologies.")

Burton, Peter, ed.

Bend Sinister: The Gay Times Book of Disturbing Stories. *London: Gay Men's Press, 2002. 390p. ISBN 1902852427.*

(See chapter 18, "Collections and Anthologies.")

Campbell, Ramsey.

The Overnight. *New York: Tor, 2006, ©2004. 406p. ISBN 0765351536.*

When Woody takes over the management of a bookstore, the neatly arranged shelves seem to disorganize themselves overnight, and the employees are ready to come to blows with one another. Woody finally orders his staff to do an overnight inventory to put things to rights, but employees disappear into the basement one by one, leaving a shimmering trail of slime behind them. Campbell excels at fleshing out the horror of everyday work life here. **Similar titles:** *Breathe*, Christopher Fowler; *The Policy*, Bentley Little; *Darkfall*, Stephen Laws.

Bookstores • Corporate Horror • England

Cannon, Peter.

The Lovecraft Chronicles. *Poplar Bluffs, MO: Mythos Books, 2004. 179p. ISBN 0972854533.*

H. P. Lovecraft's life has become the stuff of legend. This text goes beyond a fictional biography; it is an "alternate history" that asks what if, in 1933, the prestigious New York firm of Alfred A. Knopf had actually accepted, instead of rejected, a collection of tales by Lovecraft? Would Lovecraft's life have changed? Would subsequent history have changed? **Similar titles:** *Lunar Park*, Bret Easton Ellis; *The Loved Dead and Other Revisions*, August Derleth; *Shadows Over Baker Street*, Michael Reaves and John Pelan (editors); *Tales Out of Dunwich*, Robert M. Price.

Alternative History • Alternative Literature • Cthulhian Monsters • Lovecraft, H. P. (character) • Publishing Industry

Clark, Simon.

This Rage of Echoes. *New York: Leisure, 2007. 342p. ISBN 0843954949.*

An updating of the doppelganger story à la *Invasion of the Body Snatchers*, this novel is a meditation on what it means to be human in a preprogrammed, ideological state run by corporations. The Echomen virus invades the bodies of humans of all ages, races, and sexes, making them all into copies of Mason Konrad, an all-too-ordinary young man of above average intelligence. Mason must work to eradicate them before they take over the planet. The Echomen, however, look to Mason as their reluctant god. **Similar titles:** *Death's Dominion*, Simon Clark; *The Body Snatchers*, Jack Finney; *Generation Loss*, Elizabeth Hand; *Doppelganger*, David Stahler Jr.

Doppelgangers • England • Government Officials • Replicants

D'Ammassa, Don.

Dead of Winter. *Waterville, ME: Five Star, 2007. 303p. ISBN 1594144958.*

Because her husband Sean was crazed and abusive, Laura Collier did not grieve too heavily when he died. Rather, she packed up and moved to New England to live alone in the family log cabin. But then a mysterious man begins stalking her. As the bodies start to pile up around her, Laura wonders if Sean has somehow beaten death. **Similar titles:** *Sleeping Policemen*, Dale Bailey and Jack Slay Jr.; *Blackburn*, Bradley Denton; *Terminal*, Brian Keene.

Domestic Violence • Families • Feminism • New England • Police Officer as Character • Stalkers • Wilderness

Denton, Bradley.

Blackburn: A Novel. *New York: Picador USA, 2007, ©1993. 304p. ISBN 031242695X.*

On his seventeenth birthday, Jeffrey Blackburn shoots to death a police officer who has just killed a dog, and embarks on his career as a serial killer. He devises his own moral code, which justifies his murdering of others he deems "abusive." But unlike most serial killers, Jeffery is not the product of monstrously abusive parents; instead, he comes from a fairly banal family background, punctuated by the common cruelties of childhood. **Similar titles:** Don D'Ammassa, *Dead of Winter*; *The Girl Next Door*, Jack Ketchum; The Silence of the Lambs Series, Thomas Harris.

Childhood • *Kansas* • *Serial Killers*

Dowling, Terry.

Basic Black: Tales of the Appropriate Fear. *Baltimore, MD: Cemetery Dance 2006. 314p. ISBN 188147528X.*
    (See chapter 18, "Collections and Anthologies.")

Ellis, Bret Easton.

Lunar Park. *New York: Knopf, 2005. 307p. ISBN 9780375412912.*
    The author of *American Psycho* fictionalizes himself. Making a comeback after a decade of vilification, Ellis, who moved to suburbia with his wife and child, emerges from a haze of drug and alcohol to observe strange phenomena, like parents who take their two-year-olds to Pilates classes and obsess over the minutia of their diets. But could the Ellis household be haunted by a stranger phenomenon, namely the ghost of his father, or is this too fueled by Ellis's drug- and alcohol-induced fog? **Similar titles:** *The Lovecraft Chronicles*, Peter Cannon; *American Psycho*, Bret Easton Ellis; *The Two Sams* and *American Morons*, Glen Hirshberg.

Addictions—Alcoholism • *Addictions—Drugs* • *Ellis, Bret Easton (character)* • *Haunted Houses* • *Suburbia* • *Writer as Character*

Fahy, Christopher.

Matinee at the Flame. *Hiram, GA: Overlook Connection Press, 2006. 253p. ISBN 1892950731.*
    (See chapter 18, "Collections and Anthologies.")

Fleming, Robert.

Havoc After Dark: Tales of Terror. *New York: Dafina, 2004. 241p. ISBN 0758205759.*
    (See chapter 18, "Collections and Anthologies.")

Fowler, Christopher.

Breathe: Everyone Has to Do It. *Surrey, UK: Telos. 2004. 101p. ISBN 1903889677.*
    On his first day on the job as the health officer with SymaxCorp, Ben senses there's something wrong with the building, with his colleagues, and with the entire corporate structure. His supervisor is a mean-spirited shrew. Employees are forbidden to interact with one another, and screen

savers have the power to make people black out. Then employees begin developing mysterious ailments. **Similar titles:** *Demonized*, Christopher Fowler; *The Overnight*, Ramsey Campbell; *The Town That Forgot How to Breathe*, Kenneth J. Harvey; *Darkfall*, Stephen Laws.

Corporate Horror • England • Mind Control • Popular Culture

Gaiman, Neil.

Coraline. *New York: Harper Trophy, 2002. 162p. ISBN 0380977788.*

Gaiman's preteen protagonist of the title wanders lonely through her family home, where she discovers a door to another dimension. There live her Other Mother and Other Father, who seem very nice at first. But soon it becomes apparent that Other Mother is more like Cinderella's evil stepmother, keeping Other Father locked in the cellar until she needs him again. And she will extract a terrible price from Coraline to ensure she remains with her forever. **Similar titles:** *The Tolltaker*, James Sneddon; *Fragile Things: Short Fictions and Wonders* and *Smoke and Mirrors: Short Fictions and Illusions*, Neil Gaiman; *Toybox*, Al Sarrantonio.

Childhood • England • Families • Parallel Universes

Gonzalez, J. F.

The Beloved. *New York: Leisure, 2006. 369p. ISBN 0843956941.*

Don Grant follows his cheating wife to an apartment complex to kill her and her lover, only to discover that bullets have no power against what turns out to be an incubus. Grant's story then takes a back seat to the tale of a loser named Ronnie Baker, who brings Diana, his Internet girlfriend, to Ohio to meet his father, mother, and sister. They immediately take a dislike to her because she is demanding and lazy. Little does the family know that Diana is the succubi version of the demon seen by Grant. **Similar titles:** *The Boyfriend from Hell*, Avery Corman; *Dawn Song*, Michael Marano; *Reassuring Tales*, T. E. D. Klein.

Addictions • Demons • Internet, The • Psychosexual Horror • Shape-shifters • Stalkers

Gresham, Stephen.

Haunted Ground. *New York: Pinnacle, 2003. ISBN 0786015373.*

(See chapter 14, "Psychological Horror: It's All in Your Head.")

Hand, Elizabeth.

Generation Loss: A Novel. *Northampton, MA: Small Beer Press, 2007. 265p. ISBN 1931520216.*

A photographer embedded in the New York punk movement of the 1970s would by necessity become a speed freak, or a kleptomaniacal rage-filled alcoholic; Cass Neary was no exception. In fact, that's how she made a name for herself. Her gritty photos of musicians and groupies made her successful—landing her in several art galleries and helping to procure a book deal—and leading to a rape that ends her career. But now she is thirty years older and adrift, until an old acquaintance sends her to interview a reclusive photographer and she stumbles on a murder-laden mystery. **Similar titles:** *This Rage of Echoes*, Simon Clark; *The Remains of an Altar*, Phil Rickman.

Doppelgangers • Maine • Music—Punk • Music—Rock • Photographer as Character

Harvey, Kenneth J.

The Town That Forgot How to Breathe. *New York: Picador, 2005, ©2003. 471p. ISBN 0312342225.*
> The small town of Bareneed, Newfoundland, is a fishing village in decline—cod fishing has been banned, and subsequently the local factory has closed. And then the locals begin dropping dead for no apparent reason after suddenly forgetting how to breathe. **Similar titles:** *Breathe*, Christopher Fowler; *London Revenant*, Conrad Williams; *American Morons*, Glen Hirshberg.

Canada • Maritime Horror

Hirshberg, Glen.

American Morons. *Northborough, MA: Earthling Publications. 192p. ISBN 0976633981.*
> (See chapter 18, "Collections and Anthologies.")

The Two Sams. *New York: Carroll & Graf Publishers, 2003. 210p. ISBN 0786712554.*
> (See chapter 18, "Collections and Anthologies.")

Jensen, Michael.

Firelands. *Los Angeles: Alyson Publications, 2004. 299p. ISBN 1555838405.*
> (See chapter 13, "Ecological Horror: Mother Nature Has Her Revenge.")

Keene, Brian.

Terminal. *New York: Bantam Spectra, 2005. 306p. ISBN 0553587382.*
> Tommy O'Brien's young life seems pretty bleak when at the age of twenty-five he is diagnosed with terminal cancer and given only a few months to live. Not only is he unable to afford the medicine that will make his last remaining days comfortable, but he also fears for the financial security of his family. So he robs a bank. But then the robbery goes horribly wrong: his accomplice kills everyone, and Tommy learns that there are some things worse than death. **Similar titles:** *Sleeping Policemen*, Dale Bailey and Jack Slay Jr.; *Dead of Winter*, Don D' Ammassa; *The Girl Next Door*, Jack Ketchum.

Classism • Families • Terminal Illness

Ketchum, Jack.

The Girl Next Door. *New York: Leisure, 2005, ©1989. 334p. ISBN 0843955430.*
> David is a few years younger than his first crush, sixteen-year-old Meg, the new kid on the block. Meg and her crippled sister Susan stand in stark

contrast to the other kids in the neighborhood, like ten-year-old Ralphie (nicknamed Woofer), who tortures insects and other animals. But Ralphie is par for the course for this neighborhood, which is epitomized by a single mother named Ruth (based on the real-life murderer Gertrude Baniszewski), who goes over the deep end and orchestrates the ritualistic, ongoing torture of Meg, involving children as young as eleven in her insanity. **Similar titles:** *After Midnight*, Richard Laymon; *Sleeping Policemen*, Dale Bailey and Jack Slay Jr.; *Terminal*, Brian Keene.

Adolescence • Families • High School • Mental Illness • Midwest, The • Torture • Violence, Theories of

Kimball, Michael.

The Way the Family Got Away. *New York: Four Walls, Eight Windows, 2000. 143p. ISBN 1568581556.*

Two children, a five-year-old boy and his younger sister, relate the story of a cross-country trek—with a dead sibling in the family trunk. After an infant dies of yellow fever in the small town of Mineola, Texas, the parents unearth the coffin and pack all of their belongings to head north, where the extended family resides. As the boy narrates the geographical distance traveled, enumerating the sale or trade of family possessions for gas money; his sister deals with the emotional distance by constantly comparing her doll family to her people family. **Similar titles:** *The Attraction*, Douglas Clegg; *Coraline*, Neil Gaiman; *The Hidden World*, Graham Masterton; *Tideland* (film).

Childhood • Death—Grieving • Road Trips • Texas

King, Stephen.

Cell: A Novel. *New York: Scribner, 2006. 355p. ISBN 0743292332.*

On October 1, a mysterious phenomenon occurs that wipes the minds of all cell phone users. Clayton Riddell does not own one, but he witnesses a man devouring his pet dog's ear, a blonde teenaged girl's ripping into the neck of a middle-aged bystander, and her brunette friend's senselessly bashing her head into a pole. Worried that his young son may have endangered himself by taking his cell phone to school, Clayton determines to rescue his boy. **Similar titles:** *Dead Lines*, Greg Bear; *The Vanishing* and *The Burning*, Bentley Little; *Insomnia*, Stephen King.

Cell Phones • Maine • Massachusetts—Boston • Mind Control • Parenting • Popular Culture • Violence, Theories of • Writer as Character

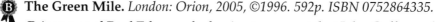 **The Green Mile.** *London: Orion, 2005, ©1996. 592p. ISBN 0752864335.*

Prison guard Paul Edgecombe begins to suspect that John Coffey, a death row inmate at Cold Mountain Penitentiary, has special powers—almost godlike powers—over living creatures. This heartbreaking tale is narrated by Edgecombe in a pseudo-journalistic format. It was originally published serially in six parts. **Similar titles:** *The Prison*, R. Patrick Gates; <u>The Blood of the Lamb Series</u>, Thomas F. Monteleone; *The Dead Zone*, Stephen King; *The Green Mile* (film).

Diary Format • Immortality • Maine • Prison Guard as Character • Prisons—Death Row • Racism

Insomnia. *London: Hodder, 2008, ©1995. 663p. ISBN 0340952792.*

After his wife's death, Ralph Roberts begins seeing things: auras around people and three small, bald-headed men in doctors' uniforms. Do these men have anything to do with the sudden violent tendencies of some of Ralph's friends? King's steadily paced and conversational writing hypnotically unsettles. **Similar titles:** <u>The Talisman Series</u>, Stephen King and Peter Straub; *Mr. X*, Peter Straub; *The Messenger*, Edward Lee; *Cell*, Stephen King.

Domestic Violence • Dreams • Insomnia • Terrorism • Violence, Theories of

🎗 **Lisey's Story.** *New York: Scribner, 2006. 513p. ISBN 9780743289412.*

Two years after the death of her husband, a Pulitzer Prize–winning author finally gets around to cleaning out his papers—when she is drawn into Boo'Ya Moon, the fantasy world her husband created. Afterward she is menaced by a stalker who demands she turn over all her husband's papers to him. **Similar titles:** *Insomnia*, *The Dark Half*, and *Rose Madder*, Stephen King; <u>The Talisman Series</u>, Stephen King and Peter Straub.

Death—Grieving • Parallel Universes • Stalkers • Writer as Character

King, Stephen, and Peter Straub.

<u>The Talisman Series.</u>

Twelve-year-old Jack Sawyer has come to the East Coast with his dying mother, B-movie actress Lily Cavanaugh. Lily just wants to die in peace and escape the machinations of her deceased husband's business partner, Morgan Sloat. Soon Jack meets Speedy Parker, who hails him as "Travelin' Jack" and introduces him to a parallel universe, the Territories. **Similar titles:** *Mr. X*, Peter Straub; *Lisey's Story*, Stephen King; *The Hidden World*, Graham Masterton.

Epic Structure • Parallel Universes • Police Officer as Character • Sawyer, Jack (character) • Shape-shifters

The Talisman. *London: Hodder, 2007, ©1984. 735p. ISBN 0340952717.*

Jack has come to believe that the Territories, a world similar to our own except that it's ruled by magic instead of science, was just a childhood fantasy. But now, as an adult, he must rediscover his fantasy world, for he must travel to the Territories and bring back the Talisman—to save his mother's life.

Actor as Character • African American Characters • California—Hollywood • Childhood • Clergy as Character • Doppelgangers • Lawyer as Character • Magic • Music—Jazz • New Hampshire • Werewolves

Black House. *New York: Random House, 2001. 624p. ISBN 0375504397.*

At the age of thirty-one, Jack has retired as a police detective after solving a particularly gruesome murder. But children are mysteriously disappearing, their dismembered bodies turning up days later. Now Jack must remember how to travel once again and venture into the Territories to catch the killer.

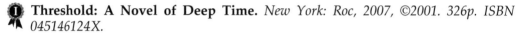

Cannibalism • Child Molesters • Disabilities—Blindness • Disc Jockey as Character •
Parenting • Septuagenarians • Serial Killers • Wisconsin

Kiernan, Caitlin R.

 Threshold: A Novel of Deep Time. *New York: Roc, 2007, ©2001. 326p. ISBN 045146124X.*

Set in Birmingham, Alabama, Kiernan's novel follows the life of Chance Matthews, a young paleontologist. The novel begins with a flashback to a drunken expedition into the waterworks tunnels set deep in the Alabama mountains. Chance and her friends, Deacon and Elsie, fueled by alcohol and pot, explore the tunnels and find that something is not quite right All three can never quite remember what exactly happened within those tunnels, only that it was evil. Now Chance, with the help of a stranger, must discover what the creatures they found there are. **Similar titles:** *The Cipher*, Kathe Koja; *Silk*, Caitlin R. Kiernan; The Odd Thomas Novels, Dean Koontz; *The Descent* (film).

Alabama—Birmingham • Gothicism • Matthews, Chance (character) • Paleontology • Subterranean Monsters

Koja, Kathe.

 The Cipher. *New York: Bantam Books, 1991. 356p. ISBN 0440207827.*

Nicholas and Nakota, two gen-x nonconformists, discover a mysterious black hole that devours and/or changes anything that ventures into it. When an adventurous Nakota tries to stick her head through, Nicholas tries to stop her, and sticks his hand in instead. After that, life is never the same, as his hand becomes a weeping sore, and he begins hearing voices. This graphic page turner won a Bram Stoker Award. **Similar titles:** *Silk* and *Threshold: A Novel of Deep Time*, Caitlin R. Kiernan; The Talisman Series, Stephen King and Peter Straub; *The Descent* (film).

Eroticism • Gothicism • Obsession • Parallel Universes

Koontz, Dean.

Life Expectancy. *New York: Bantam, 2005, ©2004. 401p. ISBN 0553588249.*

On the day Jimmy Tock is born, his grandfather lies dying in the same hospital and accurately predicts five dates when his new grandson will experience terrible events. The first day is the one on which he is born—a crazed clown goes on a shooting spree in the hospital. The next event occurs twenty years later, and then again on the day of his daughter's birth. Will the prophecies all come true? **Similar titles:** *The Messenger*, Edward Lee; *The Vanishing*, Bentley Little; *A Dirty Job*, Christopher Moore.

Clowns • Family Curse • Parenting • Precognition

Leiber, Fritz.

Our Lady of Darkness. *New York: Ace, 1984, ©1977. 183p. ISBN 0441644171.*

In this novella, a horror writer living in San Francisco finds himself becoming obsessed with a little-known occult text that chronicles paranormal activity stemming from the city itself. Will his obsession devour him, or can he be saved by a "white witch?" **Similar titles:** *The Lurker at the Threshold*, H. P. Lovecraft; *The 37th Mandala*, Mark Laidlaw; *The Divinity Student*, Michael Cisco; *The Burning*, Bentley Little.

California—San Francisco • Obsession • Parapsychology • Witchcraft

Ligotti, Thomas.

The Shadow at the Bottom of the World. *Cold Spring Harbor, NY: Cold Spring Press, 2005. 259p. ISBN 1593600585.*
(See chapter 18, "Collections and Anthologies.")

Little, Bentley.

The Burning. *New York: Signet, 2006. 391p. ISBN 0451219147.*
Between the end of the Civil War and the dawn of the twentieth century, the Chinese laborers who built the railroads in the American West were frequent targets of lynching. Now the ghosts of those murdered Asians want more than recognition of their fate—they want revenge—and they make themselves known to whites and nonwhites alike in a variety of ways. The only hope is in a small band of people who must intervene to prevent the horrors of the past from repeating themselves. **Similar titles:** *The Wind Caller*, P. D. Cacek; *Crota*, Owl Goingback; *One Rainy Night*, Richard Laymon; *Bag of Bones*, Stephen King.

Arizona • Asian American Characters • Native American Characters • Racism • Revenging Revenant • Trains • West, The • Zombies

Dispatch. *New York: Penguin, 2005. 386p. ISBN 0451216776.*
Jason Hansford never did stand out. Sandwiched between two abusive parents and a completely unsympathetic big brother, he was a true nobody—until the day he agrees to participate in a school pen pal program for extra credit. He soon discovers that writing conveys a power denied to him in other arenas of life. And Jason learns to what degree he can manipulate others by composing letters. Then a mysterious corporation recruits him to work for their firm of letter writers. **Similar titles:** *The Policy*, Bentley Little; *Matinee at the Flame*, Christopher Fahy; *Lullaby*, Chuck Palahniuk.

California • Corporate Horror • Epistolary Format • Mind Control

The Policy. *New York: Signet, 2003. 295p. ISBN 0739427393.*
When Hunt Johnson makes a claim against his renter's insurance, he discovers the devil is in the details. His policy gives him to the letter what is specified, such as replacing lost CDs with items of like monetary value. Thus, Hunt's eclectic music collection is "restored" with identical Debbie Boone CDs, while his library of videotapes and books is replaced with hardcore Nazi propaganda. And when Hunt tries to fight this vast bureaucracy, he discovers it has a power of nearly supernatural dimensions. **Similar titles:** *Dispatch*, Bentley Little; *The Overnight*, Ramsey Campbell.

Arizona • Corporate Horror • Insurance Industry

The Resort. *New York: Penguin-Signet, 2004. 400p. ISBN 0451212800.*

Located in the heart of the Arizona desert, The Reata Hotel offers cheap rates to its customers in the off season summertime. Lowell Thurman, who wants to avoid his school reunion, agrees to let his wife and three sons stay at the resort for five days of luxurious pampering. At the end of their first day at the hotel complex, all the Thurmans share the feeling that something evil permeates the place. **Similar titles:** *The Shining*, Stephen King; *Darkfall*, Stephen Laws; *The Policy*, Bentley Little.

Arizona • Corporate Horror • Hotel Industry

The Vanishing. *New York: Signet, 2007. 386p. ISBN 073948575X.*

Seven American billionaires snap, torturing and killing their loved ones before either killing themselves or vanishing. In the wake of this violence, indecipherable hieroglyphs appear scrawled in blood, and nearby plants achieve several year's growth in hours. So when reporter Brian Daniels' mother receives a letter composed solely of these hieroglyphs from his father who has been missing for the past twenty years, Brian must investigate further to discover the connection between American history and wealth generated by the California Gold Rush. **Similar titles:** *Monstrosity*, Edward Lee; *Cell*, Stephen King; *Life Expectancy*, Dean Koontz.

California • California Gold Rush • Deformity • Demons • Emmons, Phillip (character) • Journalist as Character • Social Worker as Character

Marshall, Michael.

The Straw Man Series.

(See chapter 11, "Maniacs and Sociopaths, or the Nuclear Family Explodes: Monstrous Malcontents Bury the Hatchet.")

Masterton, Graham.

Genius. *Sutton, UK: Severn House, 2003. 544p. ISBN 0727859935.*

(See chapter 12, "Technohorror: Evil Hospitals, Military Screw-Ups, Mad Scientists, and Alien Invasions.")

Monteleone, Elizabeth E., and Thomas F. Monteleone, eds.

From the Borderlands: Stories of Terror and Madness. *New York: Warner, 2004, ©2003. 428p. ISBN 0446610356.*

(See chapter 18, "Collections and Anthologies.")

Oates, Joyce Carol.

The Museum of Dr. Moses: Tales of Mystery and Suspense. *Orlando, FL: Harcourt, 2007. 229p. ISBN 0151015317.*

(See chapter 18, "Collections and Anthologies.")

Palahniuk, Chuck.

Lullaby: A Novel. *New York: Anchor Books, 2003, ©2002. 260p. ISBN 0385722192.*

When reporter Carl Streator is assigned to write a story about Sudden Infant Death Syndrome, he discovers that the victims of many of the recent cases all had books in their homes with the same poem in them. It turns out that the poem, an ancient culling song used to put to sleep those too old or too sick to survive on their own, has been mistakenly included in an anthology of lullabies—with disastrous consequences. Palahniuk is a master stylist and a deft creator of surreal worlds. **Similar titles:** *Haunted*, Chuck Palahniuk; *Dispatch*, Bentley Little.

Journalist as Character • Popular Culture—Sudden Infant Death Syndrome • Road Trips

Rickman, Phil.

The Remains of an Altar. *London: Quercus, 2006. 439p. ISBN 1905204523.*

When Merrily Watkins investigates mysterious automobile accidents that all occur on a remote road, she stumbles upon a world of raucous bar hooligans, drug traffickers, and the ghost of composer Edward Elgar, seen riding a bicycle at night. Meanwhile, her teenaged daughter gets close to being expelled from school because of her involvement with a protest group that is trying to shut down the development of a site that has an ominous reputation. **Similar titles:** *The Limits of Enchantment*, Graham Joyce; *Generation Loss*, Elizabeth Hand.

Clergy as Character • Consumerism • Revenging Revenant • Wales

Searcy, David.

 Ordinary Horror. *New York: Penguin-Viking, 2001. 230p. ISBN 0670894761.*

When gophers invade his prized rose garden, Frank Delabano, retired science teacher living alone in a tract housing neighborhood, sends away for four exotic plants that are advertised to control gophers without harming pets. However, soon all the pets and animals in the neighborhood disappear, and Delabano's neighbor begins to suspect that the plants growing next door could spell the end of the world as we know it. **Similar titles:** *Ghost Stories of Henry James*, Henry James; *Don't Dream*, Donald Wandrei; *The Day of the Triffids*, John Wyndham.

Apocalypse • Plants Run Rampant • Septuagenarians • Suburbia • Teacher as Character

Smith, Michael Marshall.

More Tomorrow. *Shrewsbury, MA: Earthling Publications. 2003. 487p. ISBN 0974420301.*

(See chapter 18, "Collections and Anthologies.")

Stahler, David Jr.

Doppelganger. *New York: HarperCollins-Eos, 2006. 258p. ISBN 0060872322.*
Parasitic shape-shifters with no identity of their own can survive only by killing someone, concealing the body, and assuming the form of the victim—for approximately three weeks—at which time they must move on to another victim. The doppelganger/narrator's first victim is a homeless alcoholic, but when Chris Parker, a young sociopath, appears, the creature takes his form and buries the body, only to find out that he must learn to function within an extremely dysfunctional family, including an alcoholic father who brutalizes his wife and preteen daughter. **Similar titles:** *This Rage of Echoes*, Simon Clark; *The Boy Who Couldn't Die*, William Sleator.

Adolescence • Doppelgangers • Families • High School

Straub, Peter, and Stephen King.

The Talisman Series.
(See King, Stephen, and Peter Straub, The Talisman Series, in this chapter.)

Stross, Charles.

The Atrocity Archives. *Urbana, IL: Golden Gryphon, 2004. 273p. ISBN 0441013651.*
James Bond, eat your heart out. MI-6 is actually an anti-occult branch of the British Secret Service, a place where people like Bob Howard, a mathematician and programmer who accidentally stumbles across powerful formulas, are sent to be kept under check. A low-level IT technician in The Laundry, a super-secret British agency, Bob gets promoted to fieldwork after he saves the day. With his palm pilot and the ability to become invisible, he is called on to fight an evil entity that feeds on matter. If only he can manage to fill out the requisite forms. **Similar titles:** *The Man from the Diogenes Club*, Kim Newman; *The Policy*, Bentley Little; The Repairman Jack Novels, F. Paul Wilson.

Corporate Horror • Cthulhuian Monsters • England • Espionage • MI-6

Tem, Steve Rasnic, and Melanie Tem.

The Man on the Ceiling. *Renton, WA: Wizards of the Coast-Discoveries, 2008. 366p. ISBN 0786948582.*
This retooling of the award-winning novella of the same name is a pseudo-autobiographical series of two surreal memoirs or vignettes. The tragic death of a child affects not only the members of the family, but the house itself, which is beset by demons. The authors expand on the original story to examine how people hold a family together despite incomprehensible tragedy. **Similar titles:** *The Two Sams* and *American Morons*, Glen Hirshberg; *Lunar Park*, Bret Easton Ellis; *The Vanishing*, Bentley Little.

Death—Grieving • Demons • Dreams • Families • Haunted Houses • Parenting

Waggoner, Tim.

Pandora Drive. *New York: Leisure Books, 2006. 370p. ISBN 0843956259.*

A young woman possesses the unique ability to make the fantasies of people around her come true—no matter how bizarre they happen to be. Unfortunately for some, her gift becomes more of a curse, because their wildest dreams have morbid, and even lethal, consequences. **Similar titles:** *Thrillers Two*, Robert Moorish (editor); *Matinee at the Flame*, Christopher Fahy.

Eroticism • Obsession • Psychosexual Horror

Warner-Cohen, Kimberly.

Sex, Blood and Rock 'n' Roll. *Brooklyn, NY: Ig Publishing, 2006. 220p. ISBN 0977197212.*

(See chapter 11, "Maniacs and Sociopaths, or the Nuclear Family Explodes: Monstrous Malcontents Bury the Hatchet.")

Wells, H. G.

The Croquet Player. *Lincoln: University of Nebraska Press, 2004, ©1937. 109p. ISBN 0803298420.*

A well-off croquet player receives disturbing news from a stranger whom he meets on a terrace. At first he refuses to believe it—that the remote English village of Cainsmarsh is the home to an evil entity that influences the island's inhabitants to fear shadows, birds, family pets, and in extreme cases, each other. At first he believes the tale is just the product of paranoia, until another stranger appears with similar information. This lesser-known Wells's novella will be a welcome addition to the libraries of fans. **Similar titles:** *War of the Worlds*, H. G. Wells; *Northanger Abbey*, Jane Austen; *Lunar Park*, Bret Easton Ellis.

Animals Run Rampant • England • Frame Tale • Mental Illness

Williams, Conrad.

London Revenant. *San Francisco: Night Shade Books, 2007, ©2004. 227p. ISBN 1597800759.*

Narcolepsy is seriously affecting Adam Buckley's perception of reality, so that it becomes increasingly surreal. He meets people at parties whom he has no recollection of later and sees shadowy figures in the London Underground who beckon him to enter tunnels that don't exist on any map. Meanwhile, someone is pushing people under the wheels of trains on the Underground. **Similar titles:** *The Town That Forgot How to Breathe*, Kenneth J. Harvey; *This Rage of Echoes*, Simon Clark; *Neverwhere*, Neil Gaiman; *Fight Club* (film).

Disabilities—Narcolepsy • England—London • Parallel Universes • Subterranean Monsters

Yarbro, Chelsea Quinn.

Apprehensions and Other Delusions. *Waterville, ME: Five Star. 2003. 344p. ISBN 0786253525.*

(See chapter 18, "Collections and Anthologies.")

Film

The Green Mile. *Frank Darabont, dir., 1999. 188 minutes.*

Film version of Stephen King's novel of the same name, in which prison guard Paul Edgecombe discovers that John Coffey, a death row inmate at Cold Mountain Penitentiary, has special powers—almost godlike powers over living creatures. Tom Hanks stars. **Similar titles:** *Bag of Bones* and *The Green Mile*, Stephen King.

African American Characters • Immortality • Louisiana • Prison Guard as Character • Prisons—Death Row

Paperhouse. *Bernard Rose, dir. 1988. 92 minutes.*

This early film by the director of *Candyman* tells the story of an adolescent named Anna, who becomes lost in the loneliness of her own world. She discovers that she can visit another one based on a house she has drawn herself, but which is mysteriously occupied by a young disabled boy. Meanwhile, across the city a dying boy whom Anna has never met gets drawn deeper into her dream; it shortly turns into a nightmare when a mysterious adult stalker begins invading it. Truly eerie, with brilliant cinematography. **Similar titles:** *Coraline*, Neil Gaiman; *The Hidden World*, Graham Masterton.

Childhood • Dreams • Parallel Universes • Parenting • Psychics • Stalkers

Signs. *M. Night Shyamalan, dir. 2002. 106 minutes.*

Graham Hess (Mel Gibson), a former minister who has lost his faith after the death of his wife in a car accident, spends his days tending to his rural Pennsylvania farm with his brother Merril (Joaquin Phoenix) and raising his children. But when Graham discovers massive and intricate crop circles in his field, his life, and the lives of everyone on Earth, change forever, as the crop circles are signs made by aliens to signal to others of their kind where to invade the planet. **Similar titles:** *The Road*, Cormac McCarthy; *Dead Sea*, Brian Keene.

Aliens • Clergy as Character • Death—Grieving • Families • Pennsylvania • Precognition

June's Picks

Books: Ramsey Campbell, *The Overnight* (Tor); Simon Clark, *This Rage of Echoes* (Leisure); Christopher Fowler, *Breathe: Everyone Has to Do It* (Telos); Neil Gaiman, *Coraline.* (Harper Trophy); Bentley Little, *The Policy* (Signet)

Films: *Paperhouse, Signs*

Tony's Picks

Books: Jack Ketchum, *The Girl Next Door* (Leisure); Michael Kimball, *The Way the Family Got Away* (Four Walls, Eight Windows); Chuck Palahniuk, *Lullaby: A Novel* (Anchor Books)

Films: *The Green Mile, Paperhouse*

11

12

13

14

15

16

17

18

19

20

Part 3

An Annotated Bibliography of
Horror Short Story Collections

Chapter 18

Collections and Anthologies

To many scholars and fans of the genre, it is common knowledge that Gothic fiction first took literary form as the full-length novel, with publications such as Horace Walpole's *The Castle of Otranto*, Anne Radcliffe's *The Mysteries of Udolpho*, and Matthew Lewis's *The Monk*, all of which appeared in England in the late 1700s. However, it can be argued that those texts are the ancestors of dark fantasy, rather than horror as we know it today. The first examples of the simultaneous use of psychological and supernatural horror with the intent to produce emotions such as fear, disquiet, and repulsion, the trait that informs modern horror, appeared in America in short story form. In the mid-nineteenth century, two American literary mainstays, Nathaniel Hawthorne and Edgar Allan Poe, made their marks in the horrific allegorical tale (which is perhaps the ancestor of the weird tale) as well as in maniacal musings of murderous madmen (the prototype of both the maniac horror novel and the true crime text).

Despite the importance of the short story to the genre, very few collections of tales by single authors take their places on the shelves of local bookstores, as these collections are usually not top sellers. Nonetheless, the short tale has proven marketable to publishers in the horror publishing business in the form of countless numbers of short story anthologies, collections of tales by diverse hands. Perhaps this is because—and the format of *Hooked on Horror* is based on this supposition—fans of the genre tend to prefer either tales that are related thematically or tales from the same horror subgenre, stories that feature the same type of monster. In this chapter we acknowledge the importance of anthologies intended for readers of particular subgenres of horror fiction. Such anthologies are not only preferable to many horror readers but are integral to the thriving of authors in the genre as well. They allow readers both to sample works by different authors with whom they may have been previously unfamiliar and to gain an increased understanding of the expanding parameters of any given subgenre. In the long run, short story anthologies encourage readers to pick up novels by up-and-coming writers.

Anthologies are also important to the vitality and marketability of the genre as a whole, because they allow writers who normally do not write horror (and who may never have considered producing a novel in the genre) a chance to dabble in the supernatural and the psychotic. Glancing through the annotations in this chapter, you will notice mainstream literary writers, such as Angela Carter, Joyce Carol Oates, Charlotte Perkins Gillman, M. Somerset Maugham, Vladimir Nabokov, Sir Alec Guinness, Eudora Welty, and James Thurber, listed as authors of horror tales. In a best-case scenario, the result of these "dabblings" could be renewed interest in horror by a writer who has much to offer the genre, as was the case with Joyce Carol Oates, who wrote only short stories in the genre until recently. Her 1997 publication of the disturbing diary of a psychopath, entitled *Zombie*, is one of the finest novel-length, first-person narratives about a maniac ever published; and it will undoubtedly help give the genre more legitimacy in the eyes of its detractors. In other cases, the results of these dabblings in a shorter fictional form could simply be the production of a fine horror text, in the form of a short story or novella. Works such as Robert Aickman's short story "Pages from a Young Girl's Journal" and Oliver Onions' novella *The Beckoning Fair One* rival any novel-length vampire, ghost, or dark erotic tale published before or since their conceptions.

The bottom line is that, for whatever reason, there is a huge market for short story anthologies; fans of the genre cannot seem to get enough of them. Horror publishers, of course, have chosen to more than meet the reader demand for these collections. The result is a list of horror anthologies on almost any subject possible, from vampires, to werewolves, to cats and dogs, to eroticism, to Lovecraftian mythologies, to horrors populated by gay and lesbian protagonists, to stories set in the White House or around particular holidays. In this chapter, we annotate as many of these anthologies as possible, concentrating on those published since 2003. We have elaborated on the annotations that appeared in the first and second editions of *Hooked on Horror*, attempting to more fully annotate and keyword those anthologies, as well as to assign more similar titles.

Anthologies in this chapter include such perpetually popular titles such as The Year's Best Fantasy and Horror Series and the Mammoth Book of Best New Horror Series. In addition, you will find Christopher Conlon's *Poe's Lighthouse*, an anthology of stories based on a fragment of "The Lighthouse," a little-known work by Edgar Allan Poe; P. N. Elrod's *My Big Fat Supernatural Wedding* and *My Big Fat Supernatural Honeymoon*, two paranormal romance anthologies; and Ellen *Datlow's Inferno: New Tales of Terror and The Supernatural*. We also include recent and notable anthologies that do not have a thematic bent but are nonetheless important because of the collector, editor, or publisher. This list includes anthologies edited by Robert Bloch, Hugh Lamb, Ellen Datlow, Charles Grant, Martin H. Greenberg, Stephen Jones, and S. T. Joshi. Our goal here is to raise awareness of the short story's place in the genre and to encourage collection development specialists in libraries that have a strong horror readership to add these thematic anthologies to their collections. You'll also find in this chapter collections of short stories by individual authors. Collections are particularly important for two reasons: they identify for readers' advisors those writers who excel in the horror genre but who write exclusively, or almost exclusively, in the short story format. After all, the horror genre was born of the short tale format, so in many ways these writers of short fiction are the keepers of tradition.

Probably the most important reason to include collections in this guide is the fact that many of these authors—namely Joseph Sheridan Le Fanu, H. P. Lovecraft, Robert Aickman, Robert Bloch, Richard Matheson, Joyce Carol Oates, Joe R. Lansdale, Thomas Ligotti, and Glen Hirshberg (arguably the best new voice in the psychological and ordinary horror subgenres)—create nothing short of masterpieces using this brief literary form. And classics such as *Carmilla*, by Le Fanu; "The Dunwich Horror" and "The Rats in the Walls," by Lovecraft; and "Duel," by Matheson have seldom been matched for their eloquence, atmosphere, and chilling effect. Horror fans have responded to these works with avid appreciation of the format.

Of course, the major appeal of the anthology or collection is the brevity of the reading experience. For those of us who lead busy lives, a twenty-page story more appropriately fits into our schedules. Then there is the concentration on similar thematic concerns. A well-conceived and edited anthology will contain stories that deal with similar concerns, or possibly even stories that show similar writing styles, but which are individuated enough so as to not create a repetitive reading experience. The anthology also allows readers to have access to the older, classic works in the genre, as well as to authors like Poe, Lovecraft, and M. R. James—benchmark authors who seldom chose to produce full-length novels.

Collections by Individual Authors

Classics

Askew, Alice, and Claude Askew.

Aylmer Vance: Ghost-Seer. *Edited by Jack Adrian. Ashcroft, BC: Ash-Tree Press, 1998. 131p. ISBN 9781899562480.*
> Among the popular husband and wife writing teams in the years before the First World War were Alice and Claude Askew. The Askews turned their hands to many different types of tales, only once applying their talents to a purely supernatural theme; the result was *Aylmer Vance: Ghost-Seer*. In these eight stories, we see Vance and his companion Dexter probing various mysteries involving vampires and unidentifiable fears. **Similar titles:** *The Captain of the "Pole-Star": Weird and Imaginative Fiction*, Arthur Conan Doyle; *The Collected Ghost Stories of E. F. Benson*, E. F. Benson; *Great Ghost Stories*, R. Chetwyn-Haynes and Stephen Jones (editors).

> *Dreams • Parapsychology • Vampire Hunters*

Benson, E. F.

The Collected Ghost Stories of E. F. Benson. *Edited by Richard Dalby. New York: Carroll & Graf, 2002, ©1992. 672p. ISBN 0786709804.*
> This is a collection of fifty macabre tales by one of the genre's early masters. Atmospheric stories include "Room in the Tower," "At Abdul Ali's Grave," "Caterpillars," "Between the Lights," "Terror by Night, "Thing in the Hall," "And the Dead Spake," "Outcast," "Mr. Tilly's Séance," and "In the Tube." Themes include troubled spirits, séances, vampires, parapsychology, and ancient gods. Also included is "The Recent 'Witch-Burning' at Clonmel," an article that describes primitive exorcism practices. **Similar titles:** *Aylmer Vance: Ghost-Seer*, Alice Askew and Claude Askew; *Ancestral Shadows*, Russell Kirk; *Great Ghost Stories*, R. Chetwynd-Haynes and Stephen Jones (editors).

> *Cursed Objects • Haunted Houses • Revenging Revenant • Witchcraft*

Blackwood, Algernon.

The Complete John Silence Stories. *Edited by S. T. Joshi. Mineola, NY: Dover, 1997. 246p. ISBN 0486299422.*

> Near the turn of the twentieth century, Blackwood, inspired by the Sherlock Holmes tales of Arthur Conan Doyle, created John Silence. The complete set of John Silence stories hadn't been in print for at least three decades. Joshi has brought together these stories in this collection, including the previously unpublished "Victim of Higher Spaces." This is a great read for horror fans who enjoy erudite prose and detective fiction. **Similar titles:** *Aylmer Vance: Ghost-Seer*, Alice Askew and Claude Askew; *Nobody True*, James Herbert; The Pendergast Novels, Douglas Preston and Lincoln Child.
>
> *Animals Run Rampant* • *Magic* • *Parapsychology* • *Religion—Ancient Egyptian*

Bloch, Robert.

Flowers from the Moon and Other Lunacies. *Edited by Robert Price. Sauk City, WI: Arkham House, 1998. 296p. ISBN 0870541722.*

> Arkham House has assembled, for the first time, a variety of Robert Bloch's early stories from *Weird Tales* and *Strange Stories* magazines. Tales range from the whimsical or darkly humorous to the straightforward. Include in this collection are "The Druidic Doom," "Fangs of Vengeance," "Death is an Elephant," "A Question of Identity," and "Death Has Five Guesses." Many of these stories are unknown and/or rarely anthologized. **Similar titles:** *White and Other Tales of Ruin*, Tim Lebbon; *I Am Legend* and *The Incredible Shrinking Man*, Richard Matheson.
>
> *Religion—Druidism* • *Revenge* • *Serial Killers*

Bradbury, Ray.

It Came from Outer Space. *Colorado Springs, CO: Gauntlet, 2004. 429p. ISBN 1887368663.*

> This oversized book contains the four screen treatments of *It Came from Outer Space*, which have never before been published. Bradbury ultimately didn't write the final version of this film, which is good news for fans, as it means that he retained the rights to his work. Also included are photos, original ads, marketing posters, reviews, and letters, as well as some never published Bradbury short stories. **Similar titles:** *The Day of the Triffids*, John Wyndham; *The Night of the Triffids*, Simon Clark; *Black Pockets and Other Dark Thoughts*, George Zebrowski.
>
> *Aliens* • *Alternative Literature* • *Horror Movie Industry*

Capes, Bernard Edward Joseph.

The Black Reaper. *Edited by Hugh Lamb. Ashcroft, BC: Ash-Tree Press, 1998, ©1989. 227p. ISBN 1899562524.*

> Until his death in 1918, Bernard Capes was a prolific, talented, and highly regarded author of short stories, reviews, articles, and more than forty novels. Among his short stories were some of the most imaginative tales of terror of his era: stories of werewolves and the Wandering Jew, of lost souls and vengeful suicides, of horrors from beyond the grave that enfold the unsuspecting. **Similar**

titles: *Tales from a Gas-Lit Graveyard*, Hugh Lamb (editor); *The Haunted Looking Glass: Ghost Stories Chosen by Edward Gorey*, Edward Gorey (editor); *The Library Window*, Margaret Oliphant.

Castles • Clergy as Character • Haunted Houses • Religion—Christianity—Catholicism • Revenging Revenant • Victorian Era • Werewolves

Chambers, Robert W.

The Yellow Sign and Other Stories: The Complete Weird Tales of Robert W. Chambers. **Call of Cthulhu Fiction series.** *Edited by S. T. Joshi. Oakland, CA Chaosium, 2000. 643p. ISBN 1568821263.*

A play titled *The King in Yellow* is so diabolical that simply having the misfortune to read its second act causes people to lose their minds. The main characters in these tales either have read the dreaded act of the play and have lost their souls, or will read it before tale's end. The collection begins with the classic "The Repairer of Reputations," perhaps the best delusional first-person story of paranoia of its time, featuring an absolute troll of a man who has been further disfigured by a hellish pet cat. Other titles include "In the Court of the Dragon," "The Mask," and the novella *The Maker of Moons* (1896). **Similar titles:** *The Nightmare Chronicles*, Douglas Clegg; *Evermore: An Anthology*, James Robert Smith and Stephen Mark Rainey (editors); *Tales of H. P. Lovecraft: Major Works*, H. P. Lovecraft.

Carcosa Mythos • Doppelgangers • Frame Tale • Futurism • Obsession • Victorian Era

Doyle, Arthur Conan.

The Captain of the "Pole-Star": Weird and Imaginative Fiction. *Ashcroft, BC: Ash-Tree Press, 2004. 460p. ISBN 1553100689.*

Although Conan Doyle is rightly acknowledged as a fine writer of detective stories, he was also an accomplished teller of weird, supernatural, and horrific tales; he wrote "The Haunted Grange of Goresthorpe" when he was only eighteen. This collection showcases thirty-seven stories of ghosts and mummies, psychic vampires and psychological terror, and horrors of the earth. **Similar titles:** *Boats of the "Glen Carrig" and Other Nautical Adventures*, William Hope Hodgson; *Apprehensions and Other Delusions*, Chelsea Quinn Yarbro; *Great Weird Tales: 14 Stories by Lovecraft, Blackwood, Machen and Others*, S. T. Joshi (editor).

Haunted Houses • Mummies • Obsession • Parapsychology • Revenging Revenant

Hodgson, William Hope.

Boats of the "Glen Carrig" and Other Nautical Adventures. *Newberg, OR: Nightshade Books, 2003. 400p. ISBN 1892389398.*

A diary found in an ancient stone house in Ireland leads to subterranean monsters. The *Mortzestus*, an unlucky ship, is haunted by "too many shadows." For stories ranging from the chilling "Ghost Pirates" to the strange and haunting the "House on the Borderland" and "The Night Land," Hodgson is recognized as one of the benchmark authors in the literature of the weird and fantastic. Included is the classic occult detective tale, "Carnacki the Ghost Finder." **Similar titles:** *The Captain of the "Pole-Star":*

Weird and Imaginative Fiction, Arthur Conan Doyle; *A Bottomless Grave and Other Victorian Tales of Terror*, Hugh Lamb (editor); *The Collected Strange Stories*, Robert Aikman.

Maritime Horror • Subterranean Monsters

Jackson, Thomas Graham.

Six Ghost Stories. *Ashcroft, BC: Ash-Tree Press, 1999, ©1919. 145p. ISBN 1899562680.*

Sir Thomas Graham Jackson (1835–1924), celebrated in his day as one of the foremost architects in England, was also a keen traveler and antiquarian, whose journeys took him throughout Britain and Europe. His wide-ranging interests were to stand him in good stead when, later in his life, he wrote several traditional ghost stories for the amusement of family and friends. **Similar titles:** *Casting the Runes* and *Ghost Stories of an Antiquary*, M. R. James; *The Mammoth Book of Modern Ghost Stories: Great Supernatural Tales of the Twentieth Century*, Peter Haining (editor).

Cursed Objects • Haunted Houses • Revenging Revenant

James, Henry.

Ghost Stories. *Hertfordshire, England: Wordsworth Editions, 2001. 344p. ISBN 1840224223.*

This collection of Henry James's supernatural tales contains an excellent introduction and very helpful endnotes, both contributed by Martin Scofield of the University of Kent at Canterbury. Wordsworth Classics collects ten of James's ghost stories, including his two most famous pieces, "The Turn of the Screw" and "The Jolly Corner." This gentle read will appeal to academic fans of the genre. **Similar titles:** *Green Tea and Other Stories* and *In a Glass Darkly*, Joseph Sheridan Le Fanu; *Ghost Stories of an Antiquary* and *Casting the Runes*, M. R. James.

Childhood • Doppelgangers • Haunted Houses • Psychosexual Horror • Victorian Era

James, M. R.

Casting the Runes, and Other Ghost Stories. *New York: Oxford University Press, 2002. 298p. ISBN 0195151178.*

James, a professor and antiquarian, set most of his stories in the contemporary (early twentieth century) ruins of England's medieval past. This fairly comprehensive collection of his work includes his marvelous tale of a vicious crank whose occult revenge is turned against him. Other stories include in this collection are "Canon Alberic's Scrap-Book," "Number 13," "Count Magnus," and "Oh, Whistle, and I'll Come to You My Lad." **Similar titles:** *Six Ghost Stories*, Thomas Jackson Graham; *Ghost Stories of an Antiquary*, M. R. James; *A Bottomless Grave and Other Victorian Tales of Terror* and *Tales from a Gas-Lit Graveyard*, Hugh Lamb (editor).

Cursed Objects • Demons • Magic • Witchcraft

Ghost Stories of an Antiquary. *New York: Dover, 1971. 152p. ISBN 0486227588.*

M. R. James's strength is his subtle way of incorporating horror into a tale, since it is what we do not see or what we think we hear that is truly frightening. This particular work is the single most influential and most sold collection of ghost stories in history and includes the classics "The Ash-Tree," "Count Magnus," and " 'Oh,

Whistle, and I'll Come to You, My Lad.' " **Similar titles:** *Six Ghost Stories*, Thomas Jackson Graham; *Casting the Runes*, M. R. James; *The Mark of the Beast and Other Horror Tales*, Rudyard Kipling.

Cursed Objects • Demons • Magic • Witchcraft

Kipling, Rudyard.

The Mark of the Beast and Other Horror Tales. *Mineola, NY: Dover Publications, 2000, ©1918. 188p. ISBN 0486414299.*

Seventeen tales by Kipling, gathered in one volume for the first time, range from comic ghost stories to tales of psychological terror and the returning dead. **Similar titles:** *Casting the Runes*, M. R. James; *Green Tea and Other Stories* and *In a Glass Darkly*, Joseph Sheridan Le Fanu; *The Strange Case of Dr. Jekyll and Mr. Hyde and Other Stories*, Robert Louis Stevenson.

Cursed Objects • England • India • Religion—Hinduism • Victorian Era

Le Fanu, Joseph Sheridan.

Green Tea and Other Ghost Stories. *Mineola, NY: Dover, 1993, ©1945. 92p. ISBN 048627795X.*

Four classic short stories by one of the nineteenth century's masters of the genre will likely appeal to more sophisticated readers, and fans of gentle reads will especially enjoy Le Fanu's subtle British voice. Works collected here include "Green Tea," "Squire Toby's Will," "The Fortunes of Sir Robert Ardagh," and "Sir Dominick's Bargain." **Similar titles:** *Ghost Stories of Henry James*, Henry James; *In a Glass Darkly*, Joseph Sheridan Le Fanu; *The Mark of the Beast and Other Stories*, Rudyard Kipling; *The Library Window*, Margaret Oliphant.

Clergy as Character • England • Families • Mental Illness • Religion—Christianity • Satan (character) • Victorian Era

In a Glass Darkly. *New York: Oxford University Press, 1999, ©1872. 347p. ISBN 0192839470.*

These fives stories were supposedly collected by Le Fanu's character Dr. Hesselius, a "metaphysical doctor" who is a sort of precursor of Bram Stoker's Abraham Van Helsing. Stories include "Green Tea," "The Familiar," "Mr. Justice Harbottle," "The Room in the Dragon Volant," and the classic vampire novella *Carmilla*. **Similar titles:** *Ghost Stories of Henry James*, Henry James; *Green Tea and Other Ghost Stories*, Joseph Sheridan Le Fanu; *The Mark of the Beast and Other Stories*, Rudyard Kipling.

Addictions • Clergy as Character • Epistolary Format • Frame Tale • Homoeroticism • Karnstein, Carmilla (character) • Obsession • Vampire Hunters • Victorian Era

Lovecraft, H. P.

The Dreams in the Witch House and Other Weird Stories. *Edited by S. T. Joshi. New York: Penguin Classics, 2004. 453p. ISBN 0142437956.*

This third in Penguin's series of Lovecraft's collected works is edited by noted Lovecraft scholar S. T. Joshi and includes "Polaris," "The Doom

That Came to Sarnath," "The Cats of Ulthar," "The Nameless City," "The Other Gods," "The Lurking Fear," "The Unnamable," "The Shunned House," "The Horror at Red Hook," "The Dreams of the Witch House," and "The Shadow Out of Time." **Similar titles:** *Tales of H. P. Lovecraft, Major Works, From the Pest Zone: Stories from New York* and *More Annotated H. P. Lovecraft*, H. P. Lovecraft; *The Loved Dead and Other Revisions*, August Derleth (editor); *The Lovecraft Chronicles*, Peter Cannon.

Cats • Cthulhian Monsters • Dreams • Haunted Houses

From the Pest Zone: Stories from New York. *Edited by S. T. Joshi and David E. Schultz. New York: Hippocampus Press 2003. 150p. ISBN 0967321581.*

This volume gathers five stories written during what Lovecraft scholars describe as his New York Exile period, between 1924 and 1926, when he sought his fortune, only to end up living what was the unhappiest period of his life. Noted Lovecraft scholars S. T. Joshi and David E. Schultz have supplied copious notes to each story, as well as a lengthy biography of the author. **Similar titles:** *Tales of H. P. Lovecraft, Major Works; Dreams in the Witch House and Other Weird Stories,* and *More Annotated H. P. Lovecraft*, H. P. Lovecraft; *The Loved Dead and Other Revisions*, August Derleth (editor); *The Lovecraft Chronicles*, Peter Cannon.

New England • New York—New York City

More Annotated H. P. Lovecraft. *New York: Dell, 1999. 312p. ISBN 0440508754.*

This illustrated volume of Lovecraft's popular stories, with annotations by Lovecraft scholar S. T. Joshi and an introduction by Peter Cannon, includes "Herbert West, Reanimator," "Pickman's Model," "The Call of Cthulhu," "The Thing on the Doorstep," and "The Horror at Red Hook." Each story is preceded by a note on its conception and publishing history. **Similar titles:** *The Loved Dead and Other Revisions*, August Derleth (editor); *Tales of H. P. Lovecraft, Major Works, From the Pest Zone: Stories from New York,* and *The Dreams in the Witch House and Other Weird Stories*, H. P. Lovecraft; *The Lovecraft Chronicles*, Peter Cannon.

Cthulhian Monsters • Miskatonic University • New England • Weird Science • West, Herbert (character) • Zombies

Tales of H. P. Lovecraft: Major Works. *Hopewell, NJ: Eccopress, 1997. 328p. ISBN 0880015489.*

Ten stories by Lovecraft, edited by Joyce Carol Oates, show why he is the master of weird tales who influenced modern-day masters of the genre, such as Stephen King and Ramsey Campbell. Oates's introduction explains how "Lovecraft initiated the fusion of the gothic tale and what would come to be defined as science fiction." Stories in this collection include "The Call of Cthluhu," "At the Mountains of Madness," and "The Music of Erich Zann." **Similar titles:** *More Annotated H. P. Lovecraft, From the Pest Zone: Stories from New York,* and *The Dreams in the Witch House and Other Weird Stories*, H. P. Lovecraft; *The Loved Dead and Other Revisions*, August Derleth (editor).

Antarctica • Cthulhian Monsters • New England

Waking Up Screaming: Haunting Tales of Terror. *New York: Ballantine, 2003. 370p. ISBN 034545829X.*

The master of the weird tale is sure to unsettle readers with tales such as "Cool Air," "The Case of Charles Dexter Ward," "The Terrible Old Man," "Herbert

West, Reanimator," "The Shadow Over Insmouth," and "The Lurking Fear." Themes include dwellings that hold evil secrets, the black arts, scientific experimentation gone awry, and ancient monsters that awaken to threaten entire towns. **Similar titles:** *The Loved Dead and Other Revisions*, August Derleth (editor); *More Annotated H. P. Lovecraft* and *Tales of H. P. Lovecraft: Major Works*, H. P. Lovecraft; *The Lovecraft Chronicles*, Peter Cannon.

Haunted Houses • Miskatonic University • New England • Weird Science • West, Herbert (character)

Lovecraft, H. P., and Harlan Ellison.

Shadows of Death: Terrifying Tales. *New York: Del Rey, 2005. 324p. ISBN 0345483332.*

A magnificent city possesses wealth beyond measure, but faces its day of reckoning. A very stubborn spirit haunts a house. A man begins a nightmarish journey. A family crypt fascinates a young boy; and an evil entity leads a man to the other side of the world. These twenty short stories chronicle the writing career of Lovecraft; the novella *The Shadow Out Of Time* is also included in the collection. **Similar titles:** *The Loved Dead and Other Revisions*, August Derleth (editor); *More Annotated H. P. Lovecraft* and *Tales of H. P. Lovecraft: Major Works*, H. P. Lovecraft; *The Lovecraft Chronicles*, Peter Cannon.

Academia • Cthulhian Monsters • Necronomicon, The • New England • Revenging Revenant • Secret Sin • Weird Science

Polidori, John [William].

The Vampyre and Other Writings. *Edited by Franklin Charles Bishop. Manchester, UK: Carcanet, 2005. 249p. ISBN 185754787X.*

John Polidori, traveling companion to Lord Byron, wrote *The Vampyre* in response to the famous contest to write a chilling tale while at Lake Geneva with Mary and Percy B. Shelley. Mary Shelley's *Frankenstein* is the best-known fruit of this contest, but the influence of Polidori's novella still persists today. In this tale, Lord Ruthven preys on men and women of good fortune, gleefully seeking their ruin. Aubrey, his traveling companion, is eventually appalled by the lord's behavior and quits his company, only to be later nursed back from death by the nobleman. Later, Ruthven appears to be fatally wounded and elicits a promise from Aubrey not to reveal his death or his evil deeds for a year and a day after his passing. Aubrey agrees, but will later have reason to regret his promise. This collection also includes some of Polidori's lesser known works, such as his poetry, an essay on the death penalty, and a medical thesis on nightmares. **Similar titles:** *Frankenstein*, Mary Shelley; *Carmilla*, Joseph Sheridan Le Fanu; *The Picture of Dorian Gray*, Oscar Wilde.

England • Greece • Lord Ruthven (character) • Secret Sin

Smith, Clark Ashton.

Collected Works.

The End of the Story. *Edited by Scott Conners and Ron Hilger. San Francisco: Night Shade, 2006. 296p. ISBN 1597800287.*

> The first of a five-volume collection of Smith's works, this volume covers his earliest years, beginning with 1929. What makes this collection unique is that the editors use correspondence and older manuscripts to reproduce what they believe to be Smith's preferred versions of his poems and prose poems. Fans of detached irony and dark humor will undoubtedly enjoy this collection. **Similar titles:** *The Adventures of Captain Volmar* and *The Door to Saturn*, Clark Ashton Smith; *The Strange Case of Dr. Jekyll and Mr. Hyde, and Other Stories*, Robert Louis Stevenson.
>
> *Futurism • Parallel Universes • Weird Science*

The Door to Saturn. *Edited by Scott Conners and Ron Hilger. San Francisco: Night Shade, 2007. 297p. ISBN 1597800295.*

> The second of a five-volume collection of Smith's works, with an introduction by Tim Powers, covers the work done in Smith's early years, up until 1933. Included are the ironic "The Testament of Athammaus," the Lovecraftian "The Return of the Sorcerer," and the fan favorite "The City of the Singing Flame." **Similar titles:** *Tales of H. P. Lovecraft: Major Works* and *More Annotated H. P. Lovecraft*, H. P. Lovecraft; *The Loved Dead and Other Revisions*, August Derleth (editor); *Red World of Polaris: The Adventures of Captain Volmar* and *The End of the Story*, Clark Ashton Smith.

Stevenson, Robert Louis.

The Strange Case of Dr. Jekyll and Mr. Hyde, and Other Stories. *New York: Barnes & Noble, 2005. 254p. ISBN 1593083505.*

> This new edition of the Stevenson classic also contains introductions from many of the top scholars and biographers of the author, as well as a chronology of contemporary historical, biographical, and cultural events that influenced Stevenson. Footnotes and endnotes will prove helpful to researchers, who will also find helpful information on imitations, parodies, poems, books, plays, paintings, operas, statuary, and films inspired by Jekyll and Hyde. **Similar titles:** *Tales from a Gas-Lit Graveyard*, Hugh Lamb (editor); *The Mark of the Beast and Other Horror Tales*, Rudyard Kipling; *Dr. Jekyll and Mr. Hyde* (film).
>
> *Cemeteries • Doppelgangers • England—London • Grave Robbing • Suicide • Victorian Era • Weird Science*

Modern Classics

Aickman, Robert.

The Collected Strange Stories. 2nd ed. *London: Tartarus Press, 2001. 2 vols. 868p. ISBN 1872621473 (v. 1); 1872621481 (v. 2).*

> These stories infuse magical realism with gothic horror. A two-volume omnibus, the collection contains the full contents of all of Aickman's short fiction collec-

tions: *We Are for the Dark: Six Ghost Stories* (1951), *Dark Entries* (1964), *Powers of Darkness* (1966), *Sub Rosa* (1968), *Cold Hand in Mine: Eight Strange Stories* (1975), *Tales of Love and Death* (1977), *Painted Devils: Strange Stories* (1979), *Intrusions: Strange Tales* (1980), *Night Voices: Strange Stories* (1985), *The Wine-Dark Sea* (1988), and *The Unsettled Dust* (1990). In addition to all the author's forty-eight stories, this edition includes essays by David Tibet and Ramsey Campbell, as well as Aickman's 1976 acceptance speech upon winning the award for Best Short Work for the vampire story "Pages from a Young Girl's Journal." **Similar titles:** *Boats of the "Glen Carrig" and Other Nautical Adventures*, William Hope Hodgson; *More Tomorrow*, Michael Marshall Smith; *Reassuring Tales*, T. E. D. Klein.

Epistolary Format • Gothicism • Maritime Horror • Marriage • Obsession • Psychosexual Horror • Terminal Illness

Bachman, Richard.

The Bachman Books: Four Early Novels. *New York: Plume, 1996. 1977. 692p. ISBN 0452277752.*
> See King, Stephen, *The Bachman Books: Four Early Novels*, in this chapter.

Howard, Robert E.

The Savage Tales of Solomon Kane. *New York: Ballantine, 2004, ©1998. 432p. ISBN 0345461509.*
> Tales of vengeful ghosts and bloodthirsty demons color this collection featuring the dark sorceries wielded by evil men and women. Standing in opposition to evil is the dour and deadly Puritan, the grim avenger known as Solomon Kane. He comes armed with a fanatic's faith and a warrior's savage heart, ready to face down the beings that inhabit this weird fantasy adventure that stretches from sixteenth-century England to remote African jungles. **Similar titles:** *Night Visions 10*, Richard Chizmar (editor); *Mojo: Conjure Stories*, Nalo Hopkinson.

Africa • Demons • Kane, Solomon (character) • Religion—African • Religion—Christianity —Puritanism • Revenging Revenant

Jackson, Shirley.

The Lottery and Other Stories. *New York: Farrar, Straus & Giroux, 2005, ©1949. 302p. ISBN 0374529531.*
> Twenty-five stories by the author of *The Haunting of Hill House* expose the elitism and racism of the self-satisfied, while making the familiar uncanny. The collection includes "The Lottery," "The Daemon Lover," "Come Dance with Me in Ireland," and "A Fine Old Firm." **Similar titles:** *The Haunting of Hill House*, Shirley Jackson; *Peaceable Kingdom*, Jack Ketchum; *The Female of the Species*, Joyce Carol Oates.

Childhood • Demons • Feminism • Marriage • Racism

11

12

13

14

15

16

17

18

19

20

King, Stephen.

Skeleton Crew. *London: Warner, 2001, ©1985. 624p. ISBN 0751504386.*

King's collection of psychological horror and campy, weird tales is reminiscent of B-movie horror flicks from the 1950s and 1960s. In the book-length story "The Mist," a supermarket becomes the last bastion of humanity as a strange acid fog menaces the planet. And in "Word Processor of the Gods," one can change reality with the stroke of a key. Also includes "The Reach," a fan favorite. **Similar titles:** *Insomnia* and *The Bachman Books*, Stephen King; *Spaces Between the Lines*, Peter Crowther; *Dispatch*, Bentley Little.

Afterlife, The • Apocalypse • Parallel Universes • Weather

King, Stephen (writing as Richard Bachman).

The Bachman Books: Four Early Novels. *New York: Plume, 1996, ©1977. 692p. ISBN 0452277752.*

This volume contains four Bachman novellas: *Rage, The Long Walk, Roadwork*, and *The Running Man*. King also includes the introduction "The Importance of Being Bachman." **Similar titles:** *Skeleton Crew*, Stephen King; *Destinations Unknown*, Gary A. Braunbeck; *Bedbugs*, Rich Hautala.

Afterlife, The • Death—Grieving • Futurism • High School • Mental Illness • Spree Killers

Klein, T. E. D.

Reassuring Tales. *Burton, MI : Subterranean Press, 2006. 167p. ISBN 1596060727.*

These ten long-awaited stories by one of the most highly regarded authors of weird fiction includes the classic tale of cosmic evil, "The Events at Poroth Farm" (novelized in *The Ceremonies*). "Curtains for Nat Crumley" tells of a man who breaks his daily routine, only to find himself transported to another reality where he is a serial killer. "Camera Shy" explains why one should never take photos of vampires. "One Size Eats All" stars a man-eating sleeping bag, while "Ladder" and "Magic Carpet" test the boundaries of reality. **Similar titles:** *Basic Black*, Terry Dowling; *20th Century Ghosts*, Joe Hill; *Matinee at the Flame*, Christopher Fahy.

Cursed Objects • Death—Grieving • God (character) • Magic • Parallel Universes • Religion—Christianity • Serial Killers

Matheson, Richard.

Bloodlines: Richard Matheson's Dracula, I Am Legend and Other Vampire Stories. *Colorado Springs, CO: Gauntlet Press, 2006. 520p. ISBN 9781887368889.*

This unusual collection is centered around Matheson's masterpiece vampire novella, *I Am Legend*, and the scripts of the two films made of the novella (*The Last Man on Earth* and *The Omega Man*). Also included are some of the author's lesser known short stories, and some of his scripts for *Dracula* (1974) and *The Night Stalker* television series. **Similar titles:** *The Incredible Shrinking Man*, Richard Matheson; *Invasion of the Body Snatchers*, Jack Finney; *Invasion of the Body Snatchers* (film).

Apocalypse • Epidemics • Futurism • Vampire Clans • Vampire Hunters

Darker Places. *Colorado Springs, CO: Gauntlet, 2004. 124p. ISBN 1887368612.*

This collection of novellas, short stories, and one script, all previously un-published, contains six early tales as well as an unproduced screenplay adaptation of John Saul's 1989 novel, *Creature*. In various plotlines, an overbearing mother becomes jealous of her little boy's new pet, but can't seem to get rid of it; a Broadway dancer ends up with a pair of haunted shoes; and a ghostly playmate slowly wins over a young girl, heart and soul. **Similar titles:** *Peaceable Kingdom*, Jack Ketchum; *The Incredible Shrinking Man* and *Bloodlines*, Richard Matheson.

Dogs • Families • Haunted Houses • Parenting • Revenging Revenant

Duel: Terror Stories. *New York: Tor. 2003. 394p. ISBN 0765306956.*

Duel gathers eighteen of Matheson's short stories that originally appeared in various magazines in the 1950s. Included are his well-known short story about road rage, "Duel," later made into a film of the same name by Stephen Spielberg; as well as offerings ranging from the weird to the hor-rifying to the humorous. In "Born of Man and Woman," a normal couple keeps chained in the basement their monstrous offspring, while a father must retrieve his daughter from another dimension in "Little Girl Lost." **Similar titles:** *White and Other Tales of Ruin*, Tim Lebbon; *I Am Legend* and *The Incredible Shrinking Man*, Richard Matheson.

Futurism • Parallel Universes • Parenting • Road Trips

I Am Legend. *New York: Tor, 2007, ©1954. 312p. ISBN 0765357151.*

This reissued collection of weird tales by Matheson includes his well-known vampire novella *I Am Legend*, a tale of a post-apocalyptic world overrun by vampires created by a virus that mutates as a result of nuclear warfare. This novella was made into a film three times: *The Last Man on Earth* (1964) starring Vincent Price, *The Omega Man* (1971) starring Charlton Heston, and *I Am Legend* (2007), starring Will Smith. **Similar titles:** *The Lottery and Other Stories*, Shirley Jackson; *The Incredible Shrinking Man* and *Duel: Tales of Terror*, Richard Matheson.

Apocalypse • California—Los Angeles • Epidemics • Futurism • Vampire Clans • Vampire Hunters • Zombies

The Incredible Shrinking Man. *New York: Tor, 2001, ©1956. ISBN 351p.* ISBN *0312856644.*

Matheson's classic novella, *The Incredible Shrinking Man*, tells the tale of a post–World War II world in which an unsuspecting man is downsized, lit-erally, when he begins to shrink, after being sprayed by a mysterious ra-dioactive mist. This story was made into an excellent but little-known film of the same name by Jack Arnold. Also included in this collection are "Duel" and "Nightmare at 20,000 Feet," which was made into an episode on *The Twilight Zone*. **Similar titles:** *I Am Legend* and *Duel: Tales of Terror*, Richard Matheson; *The Incredible Shrinking Man* (film).

Air Travel • Radiation • Road Trips

Richard Matheson's Off-Beat Uncollected Stories. *San Francisco: Subterranean Press, 2002. 240p. ISBN 1931081581.*

This mix of thirteen stories includes four previously unpublished works and a fragment of a novel. "And in Sorrow" contemplates future reproductive technologies; the condemned protagonist of "The Prisoner" races against the clock to convince his jailors that they're executing the wrong man; "Maybe You Remember Him" is a deal with the devil tale. **Similar titles:** *The Incredible Shrinking Man, I Am Legend* and *Duel: Tales of Terror*, Richard Matheson.

Futurism • Pregnancy • Prisons—Death Row • Satan (character) • Weird Science • Wish Fulfillment

Nolan, William F.

Dark Universe. *New York: Leisure, 2003. 400p. ISBN 0843951907.*

This mixture of science fiction, psychological thrillers, and horror may remind readers of the tales of H. P. Lovecraft. Titles include "The Underdweller," a post-apocalyptic vision; "Lonely Train's A 'Comin," and "Ceremony," wherein a hired killer discovers that on Halloween, even the friendliest towns can be quite dangerous. **Similar titles:** *Nightshadows* and *Nightworlds*, William F. Nolan; *Mad Dog Summer and Other Stories*, Joe R. Lansdale.

Apocalypse • Diary Format • Holidays—Halloween • Revenge • Serial Killers • Weird Science

Nightshadows: The Best New Horror Fiction by a Living Legend in Dark Fantasy. *Bonney Lake, WA: Darkwood Press, 2007. 303p. ISBN 0978907841.*

This collection of twenty-three previously uncollected stories by the International Horror Guild's 2005 Living Legend Award winner includes quite a few short horror shockers that end with a twist: A man finds his frustration with his deteriorating marriage stoked to murderous violence by a mysterious bar patron. A private detective finds himself unwittingly played by a double-crossing client. The spirit of Jack the Ripper accompanies London Bridge when it is moved to Arizona. **Similar titles:** *The God of the Razor*, Joe R. Lansdale; *Nightworlds*, William F. Nolan; *Strange Things and Stranger Places*, Ramsey Campbell.

Arizona • Jack the Ripper (character) • Revenge • Serial Killers • Werewolves

Nightworlds. *New York: Leisure, 2004. 355p. ISBN 0843951915.*

This follow-up to Nolan's collection *Dark Universe* includes "Halloween Man," "Fyodor's Law," and "He Kilt It with a Stick." All stories in this collection have been selected for inclusion by the author. **Similar titles:** *Nightshadows*, William F. Nolan; *White and Other Tales of Ruin*, Tim Lebbon; *It Came from Outer Space*, Ray Bradbury.

Futurism • Weird Science

Oates, Joyce Carol.

The Female of the Species. *New York: Harcourt, 2005. 275p. ISBN 0151011796.*

Women prove to be the deadlier of the species in this collection of stories about females who are either driven or have it in their nature to kill. Among them are a battered spouse, a child prostitute, a bored corporate wife whose sexual obsession drives her to murder, and angry salesgirls looking for revenge against a nasty customer. **Similar titles:** *The Lottery and Other Stories*, Shirley Jackson; *The God of the Razor*, Joe R. Lansdale; *Scared Stiff*, Ramsey Campbell.

Child Molesters • Domestic Violence • Families • Marriage • Prostitute as Character • Psychosexual Horror • Rape • Revenge

The Museum of Dr. Moses: Tales of Mystery and Suspense. *Orlando, FL: Harcourt, 2007. 229p. ISBN 0151015317.*

This collection of tales of the macabre deals with the horrors of day-to-day existence and real-life situations being faced by understandable character types. Included in the collection are stories about a too-friendly jogger who meets the wrong person, about the surprises that greet a couple meeting for the last time prior to their divorce, and about an aging coroner whose home hides some grotesque interests. **Similar titles:** *American Morons*, Glen Hirshberg; *More Tomorrow*, Michael Marshall Smith; *Spaces Between the Lines*, Peter Crowther.

Families • Marriage • Revenge • Secret Sin • Serial Killers

Serling, Rod.

As Timeless as Infinity: The Complete Twilight Zone Scripts of Rod Serling, Volume One. *Colorado Springs, CO: Gauntlet Press, 2004. 487p. ISBN 188736871X.*

This unusual compilation includes scripts from "The Time Element," "Where Is Everybody," "Third from the Sun," "The Purple Testament," "The Big, Tall Wish," "Eye of the Beholder," "A Most Unusual Camera," "A Most Unusual Camera" (alternate version), "The Mind and the Matter," and "The Dummy." **Similar titles:** *American Morons* and *The Two Sams*, Glen Hirshberg; *Matinee at the Flame*, Christopher Fahy; *Kolchak: The Night Stalker Chronicles, 26 Original Tales of the Surreal, the Bizarre, the Macabre*, Joe Gentile (editor).

Obsession • Twilight Zone (television show) • Wish Fulfillment

Contemporary Authors

Austin, Sherry.

Mariah of the Spirits and Other Southern Ghost Stories. *Johnson City, TN: The Overmountain Press, 2002. 181p. ISBN 1570722315.*

Thirteen ghostly tales are set chiefly in the South, including the author's native North Carolina, or New Orleans, or Atlanta, or other Southern gothic sites. Here ghosts are chiefly symbols of some human drama. Stories include "The Other Woman," "Come, Go Home with Me," "Lost Soul," and "The Dressmaker's Mannequin." Several tales concentrate thematically on slavery in the American south. **Similar titles:** *Trespassing Time: Ghost Stories from the Prairie*, Barbara J. Baldwin; *Havoc After Dark: Tales of Terror*, Robert Fleming; *Great Ghost Stories*, R. Chetwyn-Haynes and Stephen Jones (editors).

African American Characters • Families • Gothicism • Slavery • South, The

Bailey, Dale.

The Resurrection Man's Legacy and Other Stories. *Urbana, IL: Golden Gryphon Press, 2003. 332p. ISBN 1930846223.*

> Trying to deal with the death of a parent? How about working out the grieving process using a simulated person? In these weird tales, zombies rise from the grave to literally cast ballots and swing close elections; and assassins possess the ability to take over the bodies of people's loved ones so that they can get close enough to finish a job. This is the first collection of stories by Bailey, a dark fantasy and science fiction author. **Similar titles:** *As Timeless as Infinity: The Complete Twilight Zone Scripts of Rod Serling*, Rod Serling; *By Reason of Darkness*, William P. Simmons; *Apprehensions and Other Delusions*, Chelsea Quinn Yarbro; *Shivers IV*, Richard Chizmar (editor).

> *Death—Grieving • Families • Parenting • Replicants • Zombies*

Barron, Laird.

The Imago Sequence: And Other Stories. *San Francisco: Nightshade Books, 2007. 248p. ISBN 9781597800884.*

> This collection of ten stories showcases Barron's ability to write different types of fiction, ranging from the Western to the weird tale. In "Hallucenigia," "Shiva," and "Hour of the Cyclops," cosmic horrors threaten the world. The latter is a tribute to Lovecraft, in which a Pinkerton agent discovers that a series of killings are linked to a cult that is attempting to placate an ancient entity. "Bulldozer" is a period Western, while "Procession of the Black Sloth" is a tribute to Asian horror. **Similar titles:** *The Nightmare Chronicles*, Douglas Clegg; *Destinations Unknown*, Gary A. Braunbeck.

> *Aliens • Apocalypse • Cthulhian Monsters • West, The*

Braunbeck, Gary A.

Destinations Unknown. *Baltimore, MD: Cemetery Dance, 2006. 216p. ISBN 1587670852.*

> This collection includes "The Ballad of Road Mama and Daddy Bliss," where a DWI offender is given community service as a morgue employee. After finding an elderly female shut-in who has apparently committed suicide, he discovers that she was obsessed with horrifying auto accidents. But when an unknown entity kidnaps him and makes him drag race against ghouls for his very life, he realizes the disquieting, supernatural truth behind *all* highway fatalities. Also includes "Congestions" and "Merge Right." **Similar titles:** *The Bachman Books*, Stephen King; *Ghosts of Yesterday*, Jack Cady; *The Longest Single Note*, Peter Crowther; *Bedbugs*, Rick Hautala.

> *Afterlife, The • Death—Grieving • Deformity • Road Trips • Traffic Fatalities*

Brite, Poppy Z.

The Devil You Know. *Burton, MI: Subterranean Press, 2003. 198p. ISBN 1931081727.*

> In this case the devil we know is The Big Easy, as seen through the eyes of Dr. Brite and other locals. Stories paint gothic portraits of the city, including the

New Orleans Carnival (Mardi Gras), local restaurants and colorful chefs who murder for their art, area swamps haunted by mythical creatures, and the night life rock music scene. **Similar titles:** *Ghosts of Yesterday*, Jack Cady; *Scared Stiff*, Ramsey Campbell; *The Female of the Species*, Joyce Carol Oates; *The Longest Single Note*, Peter Crowther.

Cook as Character • *Louisiana—New Orleans* • *Physician as Character*

Butler, Robert Olen.

Severance. *San Francisco: Chronicle Books, 2006. 263p. ISBN 0811856143.*

In each of these sixty-two stories, a beheaded mythical or historical figure tells his or her tale in exactly 240 words, the length of utterance the author estimates would be possible before the oxygen present in a severed head runs out, making speech impossible. Narrators include a chicken, Nicole Brown Simpson, John the Baptist, Medusa, Jayne Mansfield, Robespierre, Cicero, Marie Antoinette, and Tyler Atkins, the civilian truck driver beheaded in Iraq. **Similar titles:** *The New Weird*, Ann VanderMeer and Jeff VanderMeer (editors); *Black Pockets and Other Dark Thoughts*, George Zebrowski; *Frights: Stories of Suspense and Supernatural Terror*, Kirby McCauley (editor).

Beheadings • *Popular Culture*

Cady, Jack,

Ghosts of Yesterday. *San Francisco: Night Shade Books. 2003. 239p. ISBN 1892389487.*

Jack Cady, often thought of as a "writer's writer" due to his mastery of character and technique, presents several ghost stories that display his talents. Cady's stories are not typical tales of haunting either; instead they explore the parameters of the ghost story. In "The Lady with the Blind Dog," those who fail to pursue their dreams are condemned to a bizarre penance. The humorous "Daddy Dearest" concerns a man haunted by his deceased reprobate father's ashes. And a bartender is "haunted" by a question posed by a clergyman in "Jeremiah." **Similar titles:** *20th Century Ghosts*, Joe Hill; *The Two Sams* and *American Morons*, Glen Hirshberg; *Needing Ghosts*, Ramsey Campbell.

Haunted Houses • *Revenging Revenant*

Campbell, Ramsey.

Ghosts and Grisly Things. *New York: Tor, 2001, ©1998. 300p. ISBN 0312867573.*

These twenty stories will likely appeal to readers who enjoy the classic tale of terror. Themes range from supernatural terror to psychological studies of characters forced to confront the phantoms of their minds. Stories include "Going Under," "Out of the Woods," "Through the Wall," "The Sneering," "Between the Floors," "Looking Out," "The Dead Must Die," and "Welcomeland." Also included is the novella *Ra*e*. **Similar titles:**

Scared Stiff and *Strange Things and Stranger Places*, Ramsey Campbell; *American Morons*, Glen Hirshberg; *The Museum of Dr. Moses*, Joyce Carol Oates.

Cell Phones • Journalist as Character • Obsession • Religion—Christianity • Revenging Revenants • Serial Killers

Scared Stiff: Tales of Sex and Death. *New York: Tor, 2002, ©1997. 239p. ISBN 0765300044.*

These seven stories, not typical of Campbell's usual proper British style, show that the author can excel in many subgenres, including erotic horror. Bordering on the weird tale or "strange story," tales like "The Other Woman" and "Lilith's" visit the darkest recesses of the human mind. Other stories include "Dolls," "The Seductress," "The Limits of Fantasy," and "Kill Me Hideously." Considered by many to be the finest collection of erotic horror stories published to date. **Similar titles:** *The Female of the Species*, Joyce Carol Oates; *The Devil You Know*, Poppy Z. Brite; *Ghosts and Grisly Things* and *Strange Things and Stranger Places*, Ramsey Campbell.

Cursed Objects • Eroticism • Psychosexual Horror • Religion—Christianity—Puritanism • Witchcraft

Strange Things and Stranger Places. *New York: Tor, 1993. 256p. ISBN 0312855141.*

Tor presents ten tales of dark fantasy, horror, and dystopian science fiction by Campbell, arguably the best writer in the genre. The collection is unique in that it includes his juvenilia, pieces like "Cat and Mouse" and the novella *Medusa*, as well as the more polished and experimental novella from mid-career, *Needing Ghosts*. This text also includes an introduction by Campbell, in which he gives brief background material on the stories. **Similar titles:** *Nightscape*, David Morrell; *Nightworlds*, William F. Nolan; *Ghosts and Grisly Things*, Ramsey Campbell.

Cats • Frankenstein's Monster • Haunted Houses • Obsession • Mummies • Zombies

Told by the Dead. *Harrogate, UK: PS Publishing 2003. 359p. ISBN 1902880692.*

These twenty-three tales written over thirty-five years of Campbell's career demonstrate why the author is one of the modern masters of the horror genre, particularly in short story form. An innocent choirboy finds his dreams at the mercy of a cursed chorale. A book collector accidentally channels a very dark spirit. A case of mistaken identity puts a man in prison. The stories are mostly atmospheric, creating an air of menace. Poppy Z. Brite has contributed an introduction to this collection. **Similar titles:** *Spaces in Between the Lines*, Peter Crowther; *The Devil You Know*, Poppy Z. Brite; *Ghosts and Grisly Things* and *Strange Things and Stranger Places*, Ramsey Campbell.

Cursed Objects • Mistaken Identity • Music—Choral • Revenging Revenant • Writer as Character • Zombies

Clegg, Douglas.

 The Nightmare Chronicles. *New York: Leisure, 1999. 360p. ISBN 084394580X.*

Thirteen stories, related in a unique frame tale technique, tell the story of a mysterious, brooding, young kidnapping victim—who forces his captors to listen to tales of violence and horror. Clegg crosses the line and treats various taboo subjects in this collection. **Similar titles:** *The Yellow Sign and Other Stories*, Robert W. Chambers; *The Nightmare Factory*, Thomas Ligotti; *Four Dark Nights*, Bentley Little.

Families • Frame Tale • Kidnapping • Obsession • Psychosexual Horror • Secret Sin

Wild Things: Four Tales. *Baltimore, MD: Cemetery Dance, 2006. 97p. ISBN 1587671565.*

These four novellas take as their subject matter a man who looks to nature for reassurance of his fatherly instincts, finding instead a symbol of his darkest, most hollow desires; a Vietnam POW who tricks his captors using mind control; a man who deals with his incredibly shrinking manhood; and a hunting expedition turned on its head. **Similar titles:** *The Nightmare Chronicles*, Douglas Clegg; *Four Dark Nights*, Bentley Little.

Animals Run Rampant • Birds • Dogs • Mind Control • Parenting • War—Vietnam War • Wolves

Crowther, Peter.

The Longest Single Note. *New York: Leisure, 2003. 368p. ISBN 0843950781.*

These twenty-six pieces range from a cerebral Lovecraftian tale of a young scientist who gets his arm stuck in another dimension, to a pensive, charming story of one man's realization that music is what makes life worth living, to a melancholic exploration of whether or not vampires can feel, love, and form relationships with humans. Crowther's realistic characters either find themselves in horrifying encounters with monsters or simply realizing some disquieting truth. **Similar titles:** *Spaces Between the Lines*, Peter Crowther; *Destinations Unknown*, Gary A. Braunbeck; *The Devil You Know*, Poppy Z. Brite.

Afterlife, The • Families • Kees, Weldon (character) • Parallel Universes • Vampire's Point of View • Weird Science

Spaces Between the Lines. *Burton, MI: Subterranean Press, 2007. 323p. ISBN 1596060794.*

In stories reminiscent of Rod Serling, a jukebox in an abandoned saloon forces patrons to relive moments of their lives, the last vampire in the world is discovered, a widower manages to bring his wife back from death—with ominous results, a man saves his wife by stopping time, and a chair made from the wood of Christ's cross is passed down through the ages. **Similar titles:** *The Longest Single Note*, Peter Crowther; *Told by the Dead*, Ramsey Campbell; *Skeleton Crew*, Stephen King; *The Museum of Dr. Moses*, Joyce Carol Oates.

Apocalypse • Cthulhian Monsters • Cursed Objects • Death—Grieving • Marriage • Religion—Christianity

Davidson, Mary Janice.

Dead and Loving It. *New York: Berkley Sensation, 2006. 305p. ISBN 0425207951.*

Four tales of the Wyndham werewolves describe how they find love and sexual satisfaction—in unexpected places. In "Santa Claws," lonely and unattached Alec Kilcurt, laird of Kilcurt Holding, follows his nose to a street-corner Santa, who smells of ripe peaches. Ill-tempered werewolf Janet Lupo sulks over Alec's decision to mate with a human in "Monster Love." A blind werewolf doctor in "There's No Such Thing as a Were-wolf" finds amour with a homeless young fairy, and George the Fiend and the dislocated psychic werewolf Antonia happily fall head-over-heels. **Similar titles:** *Cravings*, Laurell K. Hamilton; *My Big Fat Supernatural Wedding* and *My Big Fat Supernatural Honeymoon*, P. N. Elrod (editor); *Many Bloody Returns*, Charlaine Harris and Toni L. P. Kelner (editors).

Eroticism • Fairies • Holidays—Christmas • Werewolves

Dowling, Terry.

Basic Black: Tales of the Appropriate Fear. *Baltimore, MD: Cemetery Dance 2006. 314p. ISBN 188147528X.*

In Dowling's spin on the weird tale, the everyday and commonplace become fantastic. In "Clownettte," a stain on a hotel room wall that looks a bit like a clown turns out to be something far more sinister; and in "Cheat Light" a roll of film left in a camera reveals images of an otherworldly origin. Other tales of uncanny wonder include a gun that generates its own bullets, a train called into existence by a prank gone wrong, and ultimately the truth about the materiality of ghosts. **Similar titles:** *The Lost District and Other Stories*, Joel Lane; *The Nightmare Factory*, Thomas Ligotti; *Dark Terrors: Volume 6*, Stephen Jones and David Sutton (editors).

Clowns • Cursed Objects • Obsession • Parallel Universes • Revenging Revenant • Trains

Fahy, Christopher.

Matinee at the Flame. *Hiram, GA: Overlook Connection Press, 2006. 253p. ISBN 1892950731.*

This collection of twenty-two tales that contain modern settings and characters nonetheless fits into the category of traditional horror. An old man, hired to clean out a condemned burlesque theater, finds himself thrown before an audience that forces him to rationalize his existence. A Jewish man attending an antique auction buys a Ku Klux Klan robe that has a strange effect on his libido. Dracula shows up at a horror convention and stalks fans. A man buys an unopened pack of baseball cards and finds himself playing a game for his life. **Similar titles:** *Demonized*, Christopher Fowler; *Havoc After Dark*, Robert Fleming; *American Morons*, Glen Hirshberg.

Childhood • Cursed Objects • Dracula (character) • Magic • Racism • Septuagenarians

Fleming, Robert.

Havoc After Dark: Tales of Terror. *New York: Dafina, 2004. 241p. ISBN 0758205759.*

In these fourteen tales, characters wrestle with issues of racial identity as well as with horrifying monsters. An African American soldier comes to the realization that the atrocities of Auschwitz are all too familiar—they put him in mind of the atrocities endured by his race in America. Another African American trapped by a lynch mob is magically saved. An inner-city youth faces a grim fate in the criminal justice system. **Similar titles:** *Mariah of the Spirits*, Sherry Austin; *The Between*, Tananarive Due; *Dark Dreams*, Brandon Massey.

African American Characters • Holocaust, The • Magic • Racism • Slavery • South, The • Spree Killers

Fowler, Christopher.

Demonized. *London: Serpent's Tale, 2004, ©2003. 256p. ISBN 1852428481.*

A Jewish man who survived the Holocaust has convinced his son that the world is so unsafe for Jews that he has never been outside of the family home. A waitress has a call to serve others that compels her to wait tables at mom and pop diners all over the country. In "Hitler's Houseguest," a lovelorn journalist wrangles an invitation to the Führer's chalet in hopes of persuading a former girlfriend, now a devoted fascist, to escape with him; and a tailor seeks revenge on a sultan who takes pleasure in manipulating others. **Similar titles:** *Matinee at the Flame*, Christopher Fahy; *Fragile Things*, Neil Gaiman; *American Morons*, Glen Hirshberg; *Apprehensions and Other Delusions*, Chelsea Quinn Yarbro.

Cursed Objects • Hitler, Adolph (character) • Nazism • Obsession • Religion—Judaism • Waitress as Character

Gaiman, Neil.

Fragile Things: Short Fictions and Wonders. *New York: William Morrow, 2006. 400p. ISBN 0060515228.*

In this eclectic collection of twenty-three short stories and eight poems, you'll find tales about an old woman who dines on a pet and two teenage boys who crash an alien-infested house party. Meanwhile, a man partially consumed by a cannibal recalls how he made the acquaintance of the person who dined on his flesh, and a mysterious large, black bird convinces a writer to try horror. **Similar titles:** *Demonized*, Christopher Fowler; *Smoke and Mirrors*, Neil Gaiman; *Reassuring Tales*, T. E. D. Klein.

Adolescence • Aliens • Cannibalism • Writer as Character

Smoke and Mirrors: Short Fictions and Illusions. *New York: Avon, 2005, ©1998. 365p. ISBN 0380789027.*

This collection of thirty prepublished short stories and narrative poems, from various stages of Gaiman's life, also includes an introduction by the author. Gaiman visits themes such as sex, death, dreams, and the apocalypse, and explains how the Holy Grail ended up at an antique shop, purchased by a very unreasonable customer. The collection also contains adult versions of Snow White, Santa Claus, and "The Three Billy Goats Gruff." **Similar titles:** *Fragile Things*, Neil Gaiman; *Reassuring Tales*, T. E. D. Klein; *Demonized*, Christopher Fowler.

Alternative Literature • Apocalypse • Arthurian Legend • Cursed Objects • God (character) • Holidays—Christmas • Popular Culture—Fairy Tales • Satan (character) • Vampire's Point of View

Gavin, Richard.

Omens. *Poplar Bluff, MO: Mythos Books, 2007. 132p. ISBN 0978991125.*

These stories read like nightmares with twisted logic. "In the Shadow of the Nodding God" tells the story of a blue-collar worker whose collages, made from objects bought at a mysterious shop, come to life. "The Pale Lover" features a seductive succubus and a magical erotic bookstore. In

"The Bellman's Way," a family that has recently moved to a rural neighborhood finds out that there is a local creature that demands tribute. **Similar titles:** *Sleep Disorders*, Jack Ketchum and Edward Lee; *The Nightmare Factory*, Thomas Ligotti; *The Nightmare Chronicles*, Douglas Clegg.

Cursed Objects • Dreams • Magic • Shape-shifters

Hautala, Rick.

Bedbugs. *New York: Dorchester, 2003, ©1999. 390p. ISBN 0843950749.*

These twenty-six stories show Hautala's ability to create regional scenes and recognizable characters from his Maine upbringing. The plotlines are simple and easy to follow, but the author also has a penchant for surprising twists where the unlucky and the deserving meet horrifying ends. Stories include "Voodoo Queen," "Colt .24," "A Little Bit of Divine Justice," "Bird in the House," and "Rubies and Pearls." **Similar titles:** *The Bachman Books*, Stephen King; *Ghosts of Yesterday*, Jack Cady; *The Longest Single Note*, Peter Crowther.

Afterlife, The • Carnivals • Deformity • Satan (Character) • Secret Sin

Hill, Joe.

20th Century Ghosts. *New York: William Morrow, 2007. 316p. ISBN 0061147974.*

The characters in Joe Hill's collection include the ghost of a theater, an idiot-savant child who builds a cardboard fort with doors into other dimensions, a kidnapped child locked in a subterranean cell with an antique phone that receives calls from the dead, and an eight-foot locust. *20th Century Ghosts* also received the British Fantasy Award, and the concluding work in the collection, *Voluntary Committal*, won the 2006 World Fantasy Award for Best Novella. **Similar titles:** *American Morons*, Glen Hirshberg; *Ghosts of Yesterday*, Jack Cady; *Reassuring Tales*, T. E. D. Klein.

Childhood • Cursed Objects • Disabilities—Savant Syndrome • Mental Illness • Parallel Universes

Hirshberg, Glen.

American Morons. *Northborough, MA: Earthling Publications, 2006. 192p. ISBN 0976633981.*

Seven atmospheric and sometimes surreal stories explore the sinister lurking behind the everyday. In the title story, a young couple's car breaks down while they are traveling in Italy; and they realize that they cannot take for granted that those who might wish to harm them will be punished for doing so. In "Safety Clowns," the reader learns the surprising truth about the contents of ice cream trucks. And in Hirschberg's ghost story, "The Muldoon," two children sneak into forbidden places in their home. **Similar titles:** *Demonized*, Christopher Fowler; *20th Century Ghosts*, Joe Hill; *The Two Sams*, Glen Hirshberg; *The Museum of Dr. Moses*, Joyce Carol Oates.

California—Los Angeles • Carnivals • Clowns • Haunted Houses • Religion—Judaism • Subterranean Monsters • Suburbia • Terminal Illness

The Two Sams. *New York: Carroll & Graf Publishers, 2003. 210p. ISBN 0786712554.*

This collection includes five stories. "Struwwelpeter" introduces Peter Andersz, an angst-ridden teen whose best friend, Andrew, returns to the location of a ghostly occurrence on the same night that Peter's violent tendencies reach a murderous head. "Shipwreck Beach" tells the story of a guilty young man who faces his past on the deck of a mysterious ship. "Mr. Dark's Carnival" depicts a professor's journey through a haunted house that brims with mythology and spectral figures. In "Dancing Men," a boy visits his dying grandfather and experiences a rite of passage through which he learns the family's connection to the Holocaust. And finally, "The Two Sams" shows a man's struggle to cope with the loss of two unborn children and the relationship he develops with their nightly presence. **Similar titles:** *Demonized*, Christopher Fowler; *20th Century Ghosts*, Joe Hill; *The Museum of Dr. Moses*, Joyce Carol Oates.

Death—Grieving • Families • Haunted Houses • Holocaust, The • Maritime Horror • Secret Sin

Ketchum, Jack.

Peaceable Kingdom. *New York: Leisure, 2003. 415p. ISBN 0843952164.*

This collection begins with Ketchum's powerful story "Rifle," about a mother who must make a painful decision when she finally realizes her child's true nature. Other equally disturbing stories mainly focus on plots involving eerie juxtapositions of lives or strange family relationships rather than supernatural agency. **Similar titles:** *The Lottery and Other Stories*, Shirley Jackson; *Sleep Disorders*, Jack Ketchum and Edward Lee; *Darker Places*, Richard Matheson.

Body Modification—Tattoos • Cursed Objects • Doppelgangers • Marriage • Parenting • Writer as Character

Ketchum, Jack, and Edward Lee.

Sleep Disorders. *Colorado Springs, CO: Gauntlet, 2003. 149p. ISBN 1887368698.*

This collection of five collaborative stories by the authors includes a tale about a nymphomaniac young woman who spurns wimpy suitors and pays for it. In other stories, an alluring female zombie turns tables on a group of drooling barflies, a man has a secret dream existence, and magically endowed masks bring out the subconscious impulses of an intimate couple. Ketchum provides an insightful afterword. **Similar titles:** *Omens*, Richard Gavin; *Peaceable Kingdom*, Jack Ketchum; *The Nightmare Factory*, Thomas Ligotti.

Cursed Objects • Doppelgangers • Dreams • Psychosexual Horror • Zombies

Kiernan, Caitlin R.

Alabaster. *Burton, MI: Subterranean Press, 2006. 182p. ISBN 1596060603.*

Dancy Flammarion, who is half-human, half-faerie, treks through rural Georgia in these five stories, speaking to angels and hunting demons. As one of many human avatars fighting against demonic forces in earthly battles, Dancy is taken captive and held in a decaying mansion full of grotesque phenomena, all the while attempting to defeat an ancient evil that has infested an abandoned church. Kiernan imbues the tales with disquieting gothic imagery. **Similar titles:** *Murder of Angels, Daughter of Hounds,* and *Threshold,* Caitlin R. Kiernan;

Demons • Georgia • Gothicism

Kirk, Russell.

Ancestral Shadows: An Anthology of Ghostly Tales. *Grand Rapids, MI: W.B. Eerdmans, 2004. 406p. ISBN 080283938X.*

Political conservative and American historian Russell Kirk (1918–1994) also wrote fiction that reflected his beliefs; and nineteen of his ghost stories are collected in this volume. Kirk, a Catholic, was a believer in good, evil, and redemption, so not surprisingly, the wraiths of his stories are the agents of God's judgment. **Similar titles:** *The Mammoth Book of Modern Ghost Stories: Great Supernatural Tales of the Twentieth Century,* Peter Haining (editor); *The Collected Spook Stories of E. F. Benson,* E. F. Benson.

Demons • Religion—Christianity—Catholicism • Revenging Revenant

Lane, Joel.

The Lost District and Other Stories. *San Francisco: Night Shade, 2006. 190p. ISBN 1597800392.*

Lane's collection of stories set in the bleak, post-Thatcher Midlands feature necrophiliacs, a cast of teens, drug addicts, cruising gays, and office workers so insensitive that they snack at the local cemetery. Lane's tales are very dark, with just a touch of the fantastic. **Similar titles:** *Basic Black,* Terry Dowling; *By Reason of Darkness,* William P. Simmons; *The Man from the Diogenes Club,* Kim Newman.

England—The Midlands • Necrophilia

Lansdale, Joe R.

Bumper Crop. *Urbana, IL: Golden Gryphon Press, 2004. 275p. ISBN 193084624X.*

Ever hear of a deity that inspires serial killers? A set of possessed false teeth? You'll find them here, in twenty-six over-the-top stories written by Joe R. Lansdale between 1982 and 2003. This volume contains "God of the Razor," "Chompers," "On a Dark October," "Bar Talk," "The Companion" and "Bestsellers Guaranteed." Lansdale has also written a short introduction for each of the tales in this volume. **Similar titles:** *God of the Razor* and *Mad Dog Summer and Other Stories,* Joe R. Lansdale; *Peaceable Kingdom,* Jack Ketchum; *Bubba Ho-tep* (film).

Cursed Objects • Serial Killers • Texas

God of the Razor. *Burton, MI: Subterranean Press, 2007. 295p. ISBN 9781596061156.*

This collection is centered around Lansdale's 1987 novel, *The Nightrunners*, in which Monty and Becky Jones go on a retreat to Galveston to put their marriage back together after Becky's savage gang rape. However, when Becky's assailants follow the couple to finish what they started, the God of All Things Sharp makes his bloody appearance. **Similar titles:** *Peaceable Kingdom*, Jack Ketchum; *Sleep Disorders*, Jack Ketchum and Edward Lee; *Madman Stan and Other Stories*, Richard Laymon.

Marriage • Rape • Revenge • Texas—Galveston

Mad Dog Summer and Other Stories. *Urbana, IL: Golden Gryphon Press, 2006, ©2004. 261p. ISBN 1930846428.*

Imagine *The Wild, Wild West* combined with *Transformers*, where a wormhole allows time travel, resulting in the creation of a creature that is part reincarnation of Priapus and part vampire. Lansdale also fictionalizes the 1900 hurricane that wiped out Galveston, Texas. These stories contain plenty of violence, gore, sex, and depravity. **Similar titles:** *Bumper Crop* and *The God of the Razor*, Joe R. Lansdale; *Peaceable Kingdom*, Jack Ketchum; *Sleep Disorders*, Jack Ketchum and Edward Lee.

Psychosexual Horror • Texas • Torture • Weather • Wells, H. G. (character)

The Shadows Kith and Kin. *Burton, MI: Subterranean, 2007. 283p. ISBN 1596060816.*

Enter the mind of a mass murderer who cloaks the truth of the business he's about in eerily self-deceiving metaphors. Read about a redneck's antic efforts to capture and race a legendary wild white mule. Meet Lansdale's preacher/gunfighter as he pits his skills against a nightmarish walking corpse animated by a live hornet's nest or battles a prehistoric monster. **Similar titles:** *Bumper Crop* and *The God of the Razor*, Joe R. Lansdale; *Peaceable Kingdom*, Jack Ketchum; *Sleep Disorders*, Jack Ketchum and Edward Lee; *Bubba Ho-Tep* (film).

Clergy as Character • Spree Killers • West, The • Whitman, Charles (character) • Zombies

Laymon, Richard.

Madman Stan and Other Stories. *Baltimore, MD: Cemetery Dance Publications, 2004. 315p. ISBN 158767078X.*

This collection of twenty stories offers a mixture of works that appeared in anthologies such as the <u>Night Visions</u> series, as well as work that was not published during the writer's lifetime. Included are an introduction by Stanley Wiater and an afterword by Leisure Horror editor Don D'Auria. **Similar titles:** *Come Out Tonight* and <u>The Beast House Chronicles</u>, Richard Laymon; *Horrorween*, Al Sarrantonio; *The Restless Dead*, Deborah Noyes.

Adolescence • Cats • Popular Culture—Babysitting • Serial Killers

Lebbon, Tim.

Fears Unnamed. *New York: Leisure, 2004. 337p. ISBN 0843952008.*

Fears Unnamed collects four of Lebbon's novellas. An archeologist discovers an underground city of the dead in Africa. A seemingly-endless snowstorm traps six vacationers in a cabin. The cost of escaping death is higher than the sole survivor of a plane crash wishes to pay; and a strange disease has turned much of the human and animal population into zombies. **Similar titles:** *White and Other Tales of Ruin,* Tim Lebbon; *Four Dark Nights,* Bentley Little; *Night Visions 10,* Richard Chizmar (editor).

Africa • Archeology • Weather • Zombies

White and Other Tales of Ruin. *San Francisco: Night Shade Books 2003. 342p. ISBN 1892389347.*

This collection blends science fiction and horror, and several of the works feature dystopian futures. In *White,* the title novella, humans lost in a blizzard are picked off by a band of snow phantoms. "From Bad Flesh" describes the travels of a man afflicted with tumors, searching for someone to cure him, while in "The Origin of Truth," a family dreads the coming of a nanotech virus. **Similar titles:** *Fears Unnamed,* Tim Lebbon; *Duel: Tales of Terror,* Richard Matheson; *Monsters in Our Midst,* Robert Bloch (editor).

Epidemics • Futurism • Terminal Illness • Weather

Ligotti, Thomas.

The Nightmare Factory. *New York: Carroll & Graf, 1996. 551p. ISBN 0786703024.*

This selection of works from four Ligotti collections (*Songs of a Dead Dreamer, Grimscribe, Noctuary,* and *Teatro Grotesco and Other Tales*) includes a foreword by the author and demonstrates why Ligotti is one of the contemporary masters of the weird tale. Also includes "The Consolation of Horror," an essay in which the writer reflects on what sort of reader enjoys horror stories. **Similar titles:** *Basic Black,* Terry Dowling; *Omens,* Richard Gavin; *The Nightmare Chronicles,* Douglas Clegg.

Dreams • Obsession

The Shadow at the Bottom of the World. *Cold Spring Harbor, NY: Cold Spring Press, 2005. 259p. ISBN 1593600585.*

A small town is suddenly bathed in surreal darkness. An antiquarian uncovers a set of ancient, arcane artifacts composed of a malevolent force. This collection gathers many of the tales originally published in *The Nightmare Factory.* **Similar titles:** *Basic Black,* Terry Dowling; *Omens,* Richard Gavin; *The Nightmare Chronicles,* Douglas Clegg; *American Morons,* Glen Hirshberg.

Antiquarianism • Dreams • Obsession • Parallel Universes

Lumley, Brian.

Brian Lumley's Freaks. *Burton, MI: Subterranean Press, 2004. 82p. ISBN 1596060042.*

The freaks that populate the five stories in this slim collection all defy easy categorization. While some are generated by nuclear radiation, others are mere genetic aberrations. But similar to the deformed and differently-abled circus performers that populate Tod Browning's 1932 film *Freaks*, the real monsters are the "normal" people who come in far more innocuous packages. **Similar titles:** *In Silent Graves*, Gary A. Braunbeck; *The Pilo Family Circus*, Will Elliot; *The Funhouse*, Dean Koontz; *Freaks* (film); *Blood Moon* (film).

Circuses • Deformity • Radiation

Harry Keogh: Necroscope and Other Weird Heroes! *New York: Tor. 2005, ©2003. 319p. ISBN 0765310600.*

This collection of short stories chronicles the early years of Harry Keogh, the vampire hunter who can speak with the dead. It also recounts the adventures of other characters from the Necroscope series, such as David Hero, Titus Crow, and Eldin the Wanderer. **Similar titles:** The Lawson Vampire Novels, Jon F. Merz; The Vampire Earth Series, E. E. Knight.

Keogh, Harry (character) • Vampire Hunters

The House of Cthulhu. *New York: Tor, 2005. c. 1984. 254p. ISBN 0765310732.*

Set in 1967, after a volcanic eruption that revealed a long hidden cache of documents, the stories in this collection, based on the works of noted 1960s fictional scholar Thelred Gustau, chronicle the discovery of ancient secret tomes concerning the lost continent Theem'hdra. One of its scholars, the White Wizard Teh Atht, documents battles with sorcerers like Mylarkhrion the most terrible, who was instrumental in summoning Cthulhu, the old god of doom. **Similar titles:** *The Loved Dead and Other Revisions*, August Derleth (editor); *More Annotated H. P. Lovecraft* and *Tales of H. P. Lovecraft: Major Works*, H. P. Lovecraft.

Academia • Alternative Literature • Cthulhian Monsters • Frame Tale • Magic

The Taint and Other Novellas: Best Mythos Tales, Volume One. *Burton, MI: Subterranean Press, 2007. 279p ISBN 1596061251.*

This collection of seven of Lumley's Cthulhu Mythos tales includes the favorite, "The Horror at Oakdeene," set in an insane asylum; the inventive "Born of the Winds," which marries Cthulhian mythology with the native American Wendigo and Ithaqua myths; and "The Taint," set in Innsmouth, familiar to many Lovecraft fans. Other tales of these ancient, malevolent gods that lure humans into hellish servitude include "Fairground Horror," "Rising with Surtsey," "Lord of the Worms," and "House of the Temple." **Similar titles:** *Dark Wisdom: New Tales of the Old Ones*, Gary Myers and Robert M. Price (editors); *The Loved Dead and Other Revisions*, August Derleth (editor); *Tales Out of Dunwich*, Robert M. Price.

Cthulhian Monsters • Cursed Objects • Dreams • New England • Psychics • Religion—Native American

Morrell, David.

Nightscape. *London: Subterranean Press, 2004. 238p. ISBN 159606000X.*

This collection of Morrell's shorter work showcases his ability to write both horror and science fiction. In "Resurrection," a son works to find a cure so that he can reanimate his cryogenically suspended father; a father labors to bring to justice the serial killer who murdered his daughter in

"Nothing Will Hurt You." A small town doctor contends with the 1918 influenza pandemic in "If I Should Die Before I Wake," and a Santa Fe police officer is obsessed with someone repeatedly leaving shoes along the highway o in "Rio Grande Gothic." **Similar titles:** *Black Pockets and Other Dark Thoughts*, George Zebrowski; *Monsters in Our Midst*, Robert Bloch (editor); *Strange Things and Stranger Places*, Ramsey Campbell.

Epidemics • Futurism—Cryogenics • Obsession • Parenting • Serial Killers • Weird Science

Newman, Kim.

The Man from the Diogenes Club. *Austin, TX: MonkeyBrain, 2006. 389p. ISBN 1932265171.*

Newman elaborates on the Diogenes Club from his <u>Anno Dracula</u> series of novels in this collection of short stories about characters ranging from a group of vampire hunters to paranormal investigators who explore all manner of supernatural phenomena. In the psychedelic seventies, Richard Jepson and his stunningly beautiful fellow agent Vanessa investigate ghostly manifestations in the United Kingdom. **Similar titles:** <u>The Anno Dracula Series</u>, Kim Newman; *The Lost District and Other Stories*, Joel Lane; *The Many Faces of Van Helsing*, Jeanne Cavelos (editor).

Diogenes Club • England • Parapsychology • Vampire Hunters

Partridge, Norman.

Mr. Fox and Other Feral Tales: A Collection, a Recollection, a Writer's Handbook. *Burton, MI: Subterranean Press, 2005, ©1992. 391p. ISBN 1596060328.*

This reissue of the Partridge collection includes the originally published seven stories, plus eleven juvenilia items and an excerpt from an unpublished novel. Plot twists and dark comedy abound in these stories, which include "Mr. Fox," "The Baddest Son of a Bitch in the House," "Save the Last Dance for Me," "Cosmos," "Stackalee," and others. This edition also includes author's notes and advice for writers. **Similar titles:** *God of the Razor*, Joe R. Lansdale; *The Man on the Ceiling*, Melanie Tem and Steve Rasnic Tem; *Spaces Between the Lines*, Peter Crowther.

Serial Killers • Writer as Character • Zombies

Prill, David.

Dating Secrets of the Dead. *Burton, MI: Subterranean Press. 2003. 139p. ISBN 1931081603.*

Prill riffs on traditional horror themes in his usual offbeat way in this collection. In the title piece, two zombie teens in love ponder the usual potential obstacles to their union in addition to the difficulty of expressing one's amour when encased in a decaying body. In "Carnyvore," the members of a traveling carnival exact their revenge in Grand Guignol fashion on the inhabitants of a town whose bureaucracy has banned them from visiting. **Similar titles:** *Havoc Swims Jaded*, David J. Schow; *The Restless Dead*, Deborah Noyes (editor).

Adolescence • Carnivals • Revenge • Zombies

Sarrantino, Al.

Horrorween. *New York: Leisure, 2006. 324p. ISBN 0843956399.*

This collection contains two previously published (in slightly different form) stories, "Hornets" and "The Pumpkin Boy," as well as the 2002 novella *Orangefield.* Part I, "Something's Coming," deals with a case of writer's block from hell, while Part II, "False Leads," tells the story of a mechanized boy with a pumpkin for a head. *Horrorween* ends with the three-part novella that was once *Orangefield,* including the introduction of Annabeth Turner (from *Hallows Eve*) in her incarnation as "The Wizard." **Similar titles:** *Madman Stan and Other Stories,* Richard Laymon; *The Restless Dead,* Deborah Noyes (editor); *Toybox,* Al Sarrantonio.

Animals Run Rampant • Dreams • Magic • Psychics • Replicants • Wasps • Writer as Character

Toybox. *New York: Leisure Books, 2003, ©1999. 255p. ISBN 0843951745.*

Stories in this collection of adult horror fiction have as their protagonists either preteens or teenagers. "Pumpkin Head" introduces readers to a preteen girl who is picked on as the new student in class, during a Halloween party. "The Man with Legs" tells of a brother-sister pair who visit a mysterious stranger. "Under My Bed" is a weird doppelganger tale. "The Spook Man," a fan favorite, chronicles the adventure of four brave children who visit the boogeyman. "The Corn Dolly" is a well-written tale reminiscent of Rod Serling. **Similar titles:** *Madman Stan and Other Stories,* Richard Laymon; *The Restless Dead,* Deborah Noyes (editor); *Horrorween,* Al Sarrantonio.

Childhood • Deformity • Doppelgangers • Families • Holidays—Halloween • Religion— Paganism • Revenge

Schow, David J.

Havoc Swims Jaded. *Burton, MI: Subterranean Press, 2006. 301p. ISBN 1596060670.*

Schow frequently plays with the conventions of the horror genre itself. In some tales in this collection, he contrasts commercially produced monsters with real and very terrifying monsters; in others, he reveals that the true monster is in the mirror. Other stories manipulate the conventions of narrative. In "Expanding Your Capabilities Using Frame/Shift™ Mode" and "Plot Twist," characters wander away from the plot established by the writer into a trajectory that they find more interesting. **Similar titles:** *Dating Secrets of the Dead,* David Prill; *The Dark* and *Inferno,* Ellen Datlow (editor).

Carnivals • Cursed Objects • Popular Culture • Sartre, Jean Paul (character) • Writer as Character • Zombies

11

12

13

14

15

16

17

18

19

20

Simmons, William P.

By Reason of Darkness. *Canton, OH: House of Dominion, 2003. 282p. ISBN 1930997450.*
Simmons's short stories are mainly set in the fictional town of Harper's Mill, a sort of supernatural Spoon River where the despair of the individual inhabitants coalesces into a force that transforms reality. In "Following the Stones," a grieving man is unable to leave the cemetery that contains his loved ones; in "The Right Size," an itinerant undertaker chooses his clients by how well they fit the burial suit he has to offer. **Similar titles:** *The Lost District and Other Stories*, Joel Lane; *Grave Intent*, Deborah LeBlanc; <u>The Grimm Funeral Home Series</u>, R. Patrick Gates.

Death—Grieving • Funeral Industry

Smith, Michael Marshall.

 More Tomorrow. *Shrewsbury, MA: Earthling Publications. 2003. 487p. ISBN 0974420301.*
Smith explores the horrors of everyday life in this collection, which includes four previously unpublished tales. In "Being Right," a man in an unhappy marriage transforms his relationship through divine intervention when he finds a volume that permits him to summon an angel who proves him correct in any domestic dispute. A town is populated by Lovecraftian monsters in "To See the Sea," while God operates a junk shop in "When God Lived in a Kentish Town." **Similar titles:** *The Museum of Dr. Moses*, Joyce Carol Oates; *Destinations Unknown*, Gary A. Braunbeck; *The Collected Strange Stories*, Robert Aickman.

Angels • Cthulhian Monsters • God (character) • Maritime Horror • Marriage

Suzuki, Koji.

Dark Water. *New York: Vertical Press, 2004. 279p. ISBN 1932234101.*
This collection of short stories by the author of *Ring* (the Japanese novel on which the 2002 film *The Ring* was based) includes the story "Floating Water," also made into a film in Japan and the basis of the American film *Dark Water* (2005), starring Jennifer Connelly. **Similar titles:** *Straight to Darkness: Lairs of the Hidden Gods*, Ken Asamatsu (editor); *Ring*, Koji Suzuki; *The Ring* (film); *Dark Water* (film).

Haunted Houses • Japan • Revenging Revenant

Yarbro, Chelsea Quinn.

Apprehensions and Other Delusions. *Waterville, ME: Five Star. 2003. 344p. ISBN 0786253525.*
This collection of thirteen weird previously published tales does not feature Yarbro's most famous creation, Count Saint-Germain. Instead, the author transforms the mundane world, imbuing it with horror and wonder. In "Traditional Values," everyone must change sexes as a crucial stage in his or her lifetime. An empowered teen is able to escape his unhappy home by drinking the blood of small animals in "Renfield's Syndrome." And a priest grapples with a cursed piano in "Fugues." **Similar titles:** *The Captain of the "Pole-Star": Weird and Imaginative*

Fiction, Arthur Conan Doyle; *The Resurrection Man's Legacy and Other Stories*, Dale Bailey; *Demonized*, Christopher Fowler.

Clergy as Character • Cursed Objects • Vampires

11

The Saint-Germain Chronicles. *New York: Pocket Books, 1983. 206p. ISBN 0671459031.*

This collection of short stories ranges chronologically from 1889 to 1981. "Renewal" chronicles the vampiric creation of James Emmerson Tree. "Cabin 33" shows Saint-Germain's handling of a fellow vampire who is quite villainous and naïve. **Similar titles:** <u>The Saint-Germain Chronicles</u>, Chelsea Quinn Yarbro; *Repentant*, Brian Thomsen and Martin H. Greenberg (editors).

Saint-Germain, Count Ragoczy de (character) • Vampire's Point of View

12

13

Zebrowski, George.

Black Pockets and Other Dark Thoughts. *Urbana, IL: Golden Gryphon, 2006. 275p. ISBN 1930846401.*

Rare horror tales by the well-known science fiction author are collected here for the first time, in three different sections—personal, political, and metaphysical fears. A woman has all too realistic dreams. A young man has the ability to channel other people's fears. A lonely man discovers love in an alternate world. A man trapped in a time vacuum has to suffer and struggle before being able to resume his previous life. **Similar titles:** *Nightworlds*, David Morrell; *Monsters in Our Midst*, Robert Bloch (editor); *The New Weird*, Ann VanderMeer and Jeff VanderMeer.

Doppelgangers • Dreams • Parallel Universes • Religion—Christianity • Revenge

14

15

16

Edited Anthologies Featuring Multiple Authors

Anthologies Featuring Similar Monsters

17

Allen, Angela C., ed.

Dark Thirst. *New York: Pocket Books, 2004. 304p. ISBN 0743496663.*

This anthology of sensual vampire stories by and about African Americans includes contributions by Omar Tyree, Linda Addison, Donna Hill, Kevin S. Brockenbrough, and Allen herself. **Similar titles:** *Havoc After Dark*, Robert Fleming; *The My Soul to Keep Series*, Tananarive Due; *Dark Dreams*, Brandon Massey (editor); *Blade* (film); *Blacula* (film).

African American Characters • Eroticism • Vampire's Point of View

18

19

Baldwin, Barbara J., Jerri Garreston, Linda Maul, and Sheri L. McGathy.

Trespassing Time: Ghost Stories from the Prairie. *Manhattan, KS: Ravenstone Press, 2005. 239p. ISBN 0965971260.*

20

These ghost stories by four Kansas authors are set on the American prairie. Some tales capture the loneliness and danger of the nineteenth-century frontier and feature haunted homesteads. In one story, an elderly man wishes to glimpse an ancient Native civilization that is only open to our world one night each half century; in yet another, aviation and hydroelectric power transform the rural landscape in ghostly fashion. **Similar titles:** *Mariah of the Spirits and Other Southern Ghost Stories*, Sherry Austin; *Matinee at the Flame*, Christopher Fahy; *More Tomorrow*, Michael Marshall Smith.

Haunted Houses • Kansas • Midwest, The • Native American Characters • Wilderness

Cavelos, Jeanne, ed.

The Many Faces of Van Helsing. *New York: Penguin-Ace, 2004. 382p. ISBN 0441011705.*

He has been called fanatical, vengeful, genius, mad, and heroic. He has been portrayed on screen by some of the finest actors in history. He is the man known simply as Van Helsing. This unusual collection explores Bram Stoker's character, reinventing the man who fights all evil. Some tales speculate about his formative years, when he had his first supernatural encounter. **Similar titles:** *The Journal of Professor Abraham Van Helsing*, Allen C. Kupfer; *Van Helsing*, Kevin Ryan; *The Man from the Diogenes Club*, Kim Newman.

Dracula (character) • Vampire Hunters • Van Helsing, Abraham (character)

Chetwynd-Haynes, R., and Stephen Jones, eds.

Great Ghost Stories. *Carroll & Graf, 2004. 327p. ISBN 0786713631.*

This anthology collects twenty-five stories from the <u>Fontana Book of Great Ghost Stories</u> series, edited by Chetwynd-Hayes from 1972 to 1984. Contributors are a mixture of old and new names, including Amelia B. Edwards, Ambrose Bierce, Sir Walter Scott, J. Sheridan Le Fanu, F. Marion Crawford, Daniel Defoe, E. Nesbit, Stephen King, Steve Rasnic Tem, Ramsey Campbell, Tina Rath, Washington Irving, Guy de Maupassant, Brian Lumley, and R. Chetwynd-Hayes. **Similar titles:** *The Collected Ghost Stories of E. F. Benson*, E. F. Benson; *H. P. Lovecraft's Book of the Supernatural: 20 Classics of the Macabre, Chosen by the Author Himself*, Stephen Jones (editor).

Haunted Houses • Revenging Revenant

Datlow, Ellen, ed.

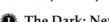 **The Dark: New Ghost Stories.** *New York: Tor, 2003. 378p. ISBN 0765304449.*

This collection of ghost tales includes Tanith Lee's pseudo-sleuth tale "The Ghost of the Clock," Terry Dowling's psychological drama "One Thing About the Night," Mike O'Driscoll's wonderfully eerie "The Silence of the Falling Stars," and Gahan Wilson's gory "The Dead Ghost." This anthology will be well received by fans of the gothic, the atmospheric, and the eerie. **Similar titles:** *Havoc Swims Jaded*, David J. Schow; *Horror: The Best of the Year*, John Betancourt (editor); *Inferno*, Ellen Datlow (editor).

Cursed Objects • Gothicism • Obsession

Ford, Michael Thomas, ed.

Midnight Thirsts: Erotic Tales of the Vampire. *New York: Kensington, 2004. 325p. ISBN 0758206631.*

This volume brings together four of Kensington's most popular authors of gay fiction, in four erotic novellas featuring men whose kisses are more than deadly. It includes *The Nightwatchers* by Greg Herren, *Carnival* by Michael Thomas Ford, *The Vampire Stone* by Timothy Ridge, and *Vampires, Inc.* by Sean Wolfe. **Similar titles:** *Bend Sinister: The Gay Times Book of Disturbing Stories* and *Death Comes Easy: The Gay Times Book of Murder Stories*, Peter Burton (editor); *Shadows of the Night: Queer Tales of the Uncanny and Unusual*, Greg Herren (editor).

Carnivals • Cursed Objects • Eroticism • Gay/Lesbian/Bisexual Characters • Vampire's Point of View

Gorey, Edward, ed. and illus.

The Haunted Looking Glass: Ghost Stories Chosen by Edward Gorey. *New York: New York Review of Books, 2001, ©1959. 251p. ISBN 0940322684.*

Edward Gorey collected these twelve tales, with his preference being the "classics" by many of the genre's masters. Selected authors include M. R. James, L. P. Hartley, Charles Dickens, Wilkie Collins, Bram Stoker, and Algernon Blackwood. Gorey's anthology is excellent for fans of traditional horror and gentle reads. **Similar titles:** Joshi, *Great Weird Tales: 14 Stories by Lovecraft, Blackwood, Machen and Others*, S. T. Joshi (editor); *The Complete John Silence Stories* and *Incredible Adventures*, Algernon Blackwood.

Cursed Objects • Demons • Haunted Houses • Revenging Revenant • Victorian Era

Haining, Peter, ed.

The Mammoth Book of Modern Ghost Stories: Great Supernatural Tales of the Twentieth Century. *New York: Carroll & Graf, 2007. 582p. ISBN 0786719605.*

This is perhaps the most inventive line-up of contributors ever in a horror anthology. Some of the authors in this collection are unexpected visitors to the genre, most notably W. Somerset Maugham, Vladimir Nabokov, Sir Alec Guinness, Eudora Welty, and James Thurber. Traditional horror classics include M. R. James's "Oh Whistle, and I'll Come to You, My Lad," Arthur Machen's "Phantom Ranks: Supernatural at War. Bowmen," Algernon Blackwood's "Vengeance Is Mine," and Elizabeth Bowen 's "Pink May." **Similar titles:** *Six Ghost Stories*, Thomas Graham Jackson; *Ancestral Shadows*, Russell Kirk; *The Haunted Looking Glass*, Edward Gorey (editor).

Cursed Objects • Haunted Houses • Multimedia—Videotape • Obsession • Revenging Revenant • Wilderness

Hamilton, Laurell K., Mary Janice Davidson, Eileen Wilks, and Rebecca York.

Cravings. *New York: Berkley, 2004. 358p. ISBN 0515138150.*

Four novellas are collected here. In Hamilton's *Beyond the Ardeur*, a wedding draws virtually all the characters from Anita Blake's past back into her life. York, in *Burning Moon*, chronicles the tryst between a blind tarot reader and a werewolf. Wilks's *Originally Human* follows a succubus suffering from amnesia, while Davidson writes of a vampire's romance with her classmates in *Dead Girls Don't Dance*. **Similar titles:** <u>The Anita Blake, Vampire Hunter Series</u>, Laurell K. Hamilton; *Dead and Loving It*, Mary Janice Davidson; *My Big Fat Supernatural Wedding* and *My Big Fat Supernatural Honeymoon*, P. N. Elrod (editor).

Amnesia • Blake, Anita (character) • Eroticism • High School • Psychics • Revenge • Vampire Hunters • Vampire's Point of View • Werewolves

Harris, Charlaine, and Toni L. P. Kelner, eds.

Many Bloody Returns. *New York: Ace, 2007. 355p. ISBN 0441015220.*

Thirteen new vampire stories feature those by Harris and Kelner, along with others who have earned their credentials as creators of the undead. Some tales mix pathos and comedy, and star Jack Fleming, Sookie Stackhouse, or Henry Fitzroy, three fan favorites. Christopher Golden pens a poignant coming-of-age story, while Kelley Armstrong tackles the question of when vampires celebrate their birthdays. **Similar titles:** *The Mammoth Book of Vampires*, Stephen Jones (editor); *Dead and Loving It*, Mary Janice Davidson; *My Big Fat Supernatural Wedding* and *My Big Fat Supernatural Honeymoon*, P. N. Elrod (editor).

Fitzroy, Henry (character) • Fleming, Jack (character) • Holidays—Birthdays • Kidnapping • Precognition • Psychics • Serial Killers • Stackhouse, Sookie (character) • Vampire's Point of View

Jones, Stephen, ed.

The Mammoth Book of Vampires. *New York: Carroll & Graf, 2004, ©1992. 621p. ISBN 0786713720.*

This collection of stories by thirty-six luminaries of the horror, fantasy, and science fiction genres includes contributions by Clive Barker, Brian Lumley, Brian Stableford, Ramsey Campbell, Nancy Kilpatrick, Robert Bloch, Christopher Fowler, Hugh B. Cave, David J. Schow, R. Chetwynd-Hayes, Karl Edward Wagner, Basil Copper, Dennis Etchison, Chelsea Quinn Yarbro, Melanie Tem, Manly Wade Wellman, Tanith Lee, Graham Masterton, F. Paul Wilson, Nancy Holder, Neil Gaiman, Steve Rasnic Tem, Harlan Ellison, and Kim Newman. **Similar titles:** *Many Bloody Returns*, Charlaine Harris and Toni L. P. Kelner (editors); *Dark Thirst*, Angela C. Allen; *The Many Faces of Van Helsing*, Jeanne C. Cavelos (editor); *Midnight Thirsts: Erotic Tales of the Vampire*, Michael Thomas Ford (editor).

Vampire Hunters • Vampire's Point of View

Skipp, John, ed.

(B) (mark) **Mondo Zombie.** *Baltimore, MD: Cemetery Dance, 2006. 497p. ISBN 1587670402.*

The undead break the rules of being a zombie as often as they adhere to them in this collection. Contributors include Lucy Taylor, Richard Laymon, Caitlin Kiernan, Jack Ketchum, Yvonne Navarro, Richard Bloch, John Skipp, Steve Rasnic Tem and Melanie Tem, Robert Devereaux, Nancy Kilpatrick, Lisa Morton, Brian Hodge, and Douglas E. Winter. **Similar titles:** *The Zombie Survival Guide: Complete Protection from the Living Dead*, Max Brooks; *The Boy Who Couldn't Die*, William Sleator; *Herbert West: Re-Animator*, H. P. Lovecraft.

Zombies • Zombie's Point of View

Thomsen, Brian, and Martin H. Greenberg, eds.

Repentant. *New York: Daw, 2003. 313p. ISBN 0756401631.*

Divided into four sections, this entertaining, thirteen-story collection covers werewolves and witches, the dead, the undead, and the demonic. A police chief investigates a werewolf sighting by his daughter. A woman who has been dead three years is forced to reexamine her policy of destruction. A writer working on a book discovers a Hollywood legend at the hotel. **Similar titles:** *Apprehensions and Other Delusions*, Chelsea Quinn Yarbro; *100 Hair-Raising Little Horror Stories*, Martin H. Greenberg and Al Sarrantonio (editors).

Demons • Revenging Revenant • Saint-Germain, Count Ragoczy de (character) • Vampire's Point of View • Zombies

Anthologies That Pay Homage to Specific Authors

Asamatsu, Ken, ed.

Straight to Darkness: Lairs of the Hidden Gods. *Fukuoka, Japan: Kurodahan Press, 2006, ©2002. 344p. ISBN 490207513X.*

This well-received collection of original stories and articles inspired by H. P. Lovecraft was published in Japan as a two-volume set under the name *Hishinkai*. The list of contributing authors is a who's who of Japanese horror fiction, featuring some of the finest writers in Japan today, including Tanaka Hirofumi, Sano Shiro, Tomono Sho, and Shimotsuki Aoi. **Similar titles:** *Ring* and *Dark Water*, Koji Suzuki; *The Loved Dead and Other Revisions*, August Derleth (editor); *Tales out of Dunwich*, Robert M. Price (editor); *The Ring* (film); *Dark Water* (film).

Cthulhian Monsters • Japan • New England • Religion—Christianity

Bloch, Robert, ed.

The Horror Writers Association Presents Robert Bloch's Psychos. *New York: Pocket, 1998. 373p. ISBN 0671885987.*

Diverse horror writers pay homage to Bloch, the master and one of the modern fathers of the subgenre of maniac fiction with his 1959 novel

Psycho. Contributors include Stephen King, Charles Grant, Ed Gorman, Richard Matheson, Yvonne Navarro, Billie Sue Mosiman, Del Stone Jr., and Jane Yolen. **Similar titles:** *Monsters in Our Midst*, Robert Bloch (editor); *Death Comes Easy: The Gay Times Book of Murder Stories*, Peter Burton (editor); *The Horror Writers Association Presents the Museum of Horrors*, Dennis Etchison (editor).

Jack the Ripper (Character) • *Serial Killers* • *Vigilantism*

Monsters in Our Midst. *New York: Tor, 2000, ©1993. 303p. ISBN 0312869436.*

A garbage disposal becomes a weapon of revenge. A homemade gasoline additive leads to mysterious deaths. A neurotic actress starts to feel underappreciated. Bloch has pieced together an original anthology of seventeen horror stories and penned the introduction himself. This unique anthology includes such favorites as Ray Bradbury, Ramsey Campbell, Richard Christian Matheson, Chet Williamson, Charles L. Grant, Billie Sue Mosiman, S. P. Somtow, and Steve Rasnic Tem. **Similar titles:** *White and Other Tales of Ruin*, Tim Lebbon; *Nightworlds*, David Morrell; *Black Pockets and other Dark Thoughts*, George Zebrowski; *The Horror Writers Association Presents Robert Bloch's Psychos*, Robert Bloch (editor).

Actor as Character • *Families* • *Revenge* • *Serial Killers*

Conlon, Christopher, ed.

Poe's Lighthouse. *Baltimore, MD: Cemetery Dance, 2006. 326p. ISBN 158767128X.*

The basis of this unusually themed anthology is Edgar Allan Poe's "The Lighthouse," a story fragment found among his papers consisting of three diary entries of a lighthouse keeper who is new to his post. Editor Conlon invited twenty-three horror writers to write their own narratives based on this fragment. Contributors include Chelsea Quinn Yarbro, Gary A. Braunbeck, and John Shirley. **Similar titles:** *Severance*, Robert Olen Butler; *Evermore: An Anthology*, James Robert Smith and Stephen Mark Rainey (editors); *Taverns of the Dead*, Kealan Patrick Burke (editor).

Alternative Literature • *Lighthouses* • *Poe, Edgar Allan (character)*

Derleth, August, ed.

The Loved Dead and Other Revisions. *New York: Carroll & Graf, 1997, ©1970. 243p. ISBN 0786704454.*

August Derleth, Lovecraft's protégé, serves up fourteen tales of cosmic horror by diverse hands who have each worked with Lovecraft on his or her tale. Most of the stories include Lovecraft's Cthulhu Mythos, incorporating it into modern urban horror, haunted house tales, and science fiction stories about alternative dimensions or realities. Authors include Adolphe de Castro, Zealia Bishop, Hazel Heald, Sonia H. Greene, C. M. Eddy Jr., Henry S. Whitehead, Duane W. Rimel, and R. H. Barlow. **Similar titles:** *More Annotated H. P. Lovecraft* and *The Dreams in the Witch House and Other Weird Stories*, H. P. Lovecraft; *The Taint and Other Novellas: Best Mythos Tales, Volume One*, Brian Lumley; *The Lovecraft Chronicles*, Peter Cannon.

Cthulhian Monsters • *Haunted Houses* • *New England* • *Parallel Universes* • *Weird Science*

Etchison, Dennis, ed.

The Horror Writers Association Presents the Museum of Horrors. *New York: Leisure, 2001. 374p. ISBN 0843949287.*

This mass market anthology contains some high-quality and truly satisfying work by such horror luminaries as Joyce Carol Oates, Peter Straub, Ramsey Campbell, and the late Charles Grant and Richard Laymon. It also contains a startling range in the type of stories selected. **Similar titles:** *Horror: The Best of the Year*, John Betancourt (editor); *The Horror Writers Association Presents Robert Bloch's Psychos*, Robert Bloch (editor); *Inferno*, Ellen Datlow (editor).

Cats • Haunted Houses • Obsession • Serial Killers

Jones, Stephen, ed.

H. P. Lovecraft's Book of the Supernatural: 20 Classics of the Macabre, Chosen by the Author Himself. *New York: Pegasus Books, 2006. 488p. ISBN 1933648015.*

In his 1927 essay "Supernatural and Horror in Literature," H. P. Lovecraft examines the evolution of the genre and gives examples of writers he considers to be the finest in the field. Jones has collected these stories in this unusual anthology, which includes works by Washington Irving, Robert Louis Stevenson, Guy de Maupassant, Edgar Allan Poe, Ambrose Bierce, Henry James, F. Marion Crawford, Mary E. Wilkins-Freeman, Charlotte Perkins Gilman, Rudyard Kipling, Bram Stoker, Sir Arthur Conan Doyle, William Hope Hodgson and Arthur Machen. **Similar titles:** *Tales of H. P. Lovecraft: Major Works*, H. P. Lovecraft; *Great Weird Tales: 14 Stories by Lovecraft, Blackwood, Machen and Others*, S. T. Joshi (editor); *Great Ghost Stories*, R. Chetwynd-Haynesn and Stephen Jones (editors).

Cursed Objects • Haunted Houses • Obsession • Revenging Revenant

Myers, Gary, and Robert M. Price, eds.

Dark Wisdom: New Tales of the Old Ones. *Poplar Bluff, MO: Mythos Books, 2007. 121p. ISBN 0978991133.*

The twelve stories here include tales involving the online auction of a black magic text, evil optical illusions and puzzles, a fast-food chain that serves some suspicious fare, a Cthulhian version of the creature from the Black Lagoon, a young pregnant girl escaping from the clutches of a bizarre cult, a weird chance encounter at a Goth night club, and various tales of cursed artifacts. **Similar titles:** *The Taint and Other Novellas: Best Mythos Tales, Volume One*, Brian Lumley; *The Lovecraft Chronicles*, Peter Cannon; *More Annotated H. P. Lovecraft*, H. P. Lovecraft..

Cthulhian Monsters • Cursed Objects • Horror Movie Industry • Necronomicon, The • Obsession • Pregnancy

Pelan, John, and Benjamin Adams, eds.

The Children of Cthulhu. *New York: Ballantine: 2003, ©2002. 469p. ISBN 0345449266.*

This anthology represents the newest generation of Mythos writers: Mark Chadbourn, Paul Finch, Alan Foster Dean, Michael Reaves, James S. Dorr, and Brian Hodges. **Similar titles:** *The Loved Dead and Other Revisions*, August Derleth (editor); *The Taint and Other Novellas: Best Mythos Tales, Volume One*, Brian Lumley; *Tales Out of Dunwich*, Robert M. Price (editor); *The Lovecraft Chronicles*, Peter Cannon.

Cthulhian Monsters • Necronomicon, The • New England

Price, Robert M., ed.

Tales Out of Dunwich. *New York: Hippocampus Press, 2005. 302p. ISBN 0974878995.*

This collection of reprinted stories, plus one new tale ("Dunwich Dreams, Dunwich Screams," by Eddie Bertin) features an introduction by the venerable Price. Tales include Harper Williams's novella *The Thing in the Woods*, which features a lycanthrope rather than one of the typical Lovecraftian monsters. Stanley C. Sargent's "Black Brat of Dunwich" retells "The Dunwich Horror." **Similar titles:** *The Taint and Other Novellas: Best Mythos Tales, Volume One*, Brian Lumley; *The Children of Cthulhu*, John Pelan and Benjamin Adams (editors); *The Loved Dead and Other Revisions*, August Derleth (editor).

Alternative Literature • Cthulhian Monsters • Necronomicon, The • New England • Rhode Island

Reaves, Michael, and John Pelan, eds.

Shadows Over Baker Street. *New York: Ballantine-Del Ray, 2003. 464p. ISBN 0345455282.*

This unusual anthology collects eighteen original tales in which Sherlock Holmes and other Doyle characters confront the horror created by H. P. Lovecraft in his pulp stories. Contributors include Neil Gaiman, Brian Stableford, Poppy Z. Brite, Tim Lebbon, Caitlin R. Kiernan, John Pelan, Michael Reaves, and David Niall Wilson. **Similar titles:** *The Many Faces of Van Helsing*, Jeanne Cavalos (editor); *100 Malicious Little Mysteries*, Martin H. Greenberg (editor); *The Lovecraft Chronicles*, Peter Cannon.

Alternative Literature • England—London • Holmes, Sherlock (character) • Lovecraft, H. P. (the works of) • Popular Culture—Baker Street • Watson, Dr. John H. (character)

Smith, James Robert, and Stephen Mark Rainey, eds.

Evermore: An Anthology. *Sauk City, WI: Arkham House, 2006. 237p. ISBN 0870541854.*

The sixteen stories in this anthology include twelve original pieces, all of which attempt to reinterpret or modernize Poe's tales and poems. "The White Cat" interprets the prose poem "Eureka," marrying the events in the poem to possible occurrences during the final days of Poe's life. Charlee Jacob's "Night Writing," set in an insane asylum, also takes a look at Poe's final days. **Similar titles:** *Poe's*

Lighthouse, Christopher Conlon (editor); *The Black Reaper*, Bernard Edward Joseph Capes; *The Loved Dead and Other Revisions*, August Derleth (editor).

Alternative Literature • Cats • Mental Illness • Parallel Universes • Poe, Edgar Allan (character)

11

Anthologies Based on a Concept

Anderson, M. W., and Brett Alexander Savory, eds.

12

The Last Pentacle of the Sun: Writings in Support of the West Memphis 3. *Vancouver, BC: Arsenal Pulp Press, 2005, ©2004. 288p. ISBN 1551521628.*

This unusual anthology of fiction and nonfiction about murders and miscarriages of justice was generated in support of the West Memphis 3, three teen Goths convicted of murdering three boys on shaky evidence. Profits from this volume are donated to a fund for their defense. Contributors include Peter Straub, Caitlin R. Kiernan, Poppy Z. Brite, Clive Barker, John Pelan, Michael Marano, David Niall Wilson, Brian Hodge, Gary A. Braunbeck, Bentley Little, Stephen Dedman, Elizabeth Massie, and Scott Nicholson. Illustrated by Clive Barker. **Similar titles:** *Death Comes Easy: The Gay Times Book of Murder Stories*, Peter Burton (editor); *13 Horrors: A Devil's @Key = Dozen Stories Celebrating 13 Years of the World Horror Convention*, Brian A. Hopkins (editor).

Government Officials • Revenge • Serial Killers

13

14

15

Briggs, Patricia, Karen Chance, Eileen Wilks, and Sunny.

On the Prowl. *New York: Berkley, 2007. 341p. ISBN 0425216594.*

A collection of paranormal romances by four authors, these tales from today's hottest authors feature a female werewolf who comes into her own, a lord who crosses paths with a fiery mage, a mixed-blood Child of the Moon who faces an uncertain future, and a woman whose sixth sense proves to be a dangerous talent. Stories include "Alpha and Omega" by Briggs, "Inhuman" by Wilks, "Buying Trouble" by Chance, and "Mona Lisa Betwining" by Sunny. **Similar titles:** *My Big Fat Supernatural Wedding* and *My Big Fat Supernatural Honeymoon*, P. N. Elrod (editor); *Hot Blooded*, Christine Feehan (editor); *Night's Edge*, Maggie Shayne (editor).

Eroticism • Magic • Precognition • Werewolves

16

17

18

Burke, Kealan Patrick, ed.

Night Visions 12. *Burton, MI: Subterranean, 2006. 271p. ISBN 9781596060708.*

The latest installment of this anthology series, which always showcases the work of three well-known authors in the genre, includes work by Simon Clark, P. D. Cacek, and Mark Morris. Clark's contributions include a retelling of *Frankenstein*. Morris's stories include an autistic protagonist, while Cacek's work includes a novella about a psychiatrist and his patient with multiple personality disorder. **Similar titles:** *Taverns of the Dead*, Kealan Patrick Burke (editor); *Shivers IV* and *Night Visions 10*, Richard Chizmar (editor); *Thrillers Two*, Robert Moorish (editor).

Alternative Literature • Frankenstein, Victor (character) • Mental Illness • Psychiatrist as Character

19

20

Taverns of the Dead. *Baltimore, MD: Cemetery Dance Publications, 2005. 423p. ISBN 1587670828.*

An Irish pub, tainted by the political hatreds of its patrons, literally turns musicians into murderers. A wanderer who makes his way into a local watering hole misinterprets the customs of the locals and suffers a dismal fate. A tavern becomes a convenient locale for the dead to lecture the living about the proper way to remember them. This collection is a virtual who's who of horror writers, including F. Paul Wilson, P. D. Cacek, Ramsey Campbell, Jack Cady, Melanie Tem, Neil Gaiman, Thomas Ligotti, Norman Partridge, Gary A. Braunbeck, Peter Crowther, Steve Rasnic Tem, Yvonne Navarro, Charles L. Grant, and Peter Straub. **Similar titles:** *Night Visions 12*, Kealan Patrick Burke (editor); *By Reason of Darkness*, William P. Simmons (editor); *White House Horrors*, Martin H. Greenberg (editor).

Addictions—Alcoholism • Haunted Houses • Music • Spree Killers

Burton, Peter, ed.

Bend Sinister: The Gay Times Book of Disturbing Stories. *London: Gay Men's Press, 2002. 390p. ISBN 1902852427.*

A gay senior citizen is accosted by two young, gorgeous hunks who happen to be vampires. A man attempts to exorcise the pain of being abandoned by his lover by opting for anonymous sex in a cemetery. A serial killer picks up, tortures, kills, and dismembers young men. These stories, some more unsettling than others, treat such themes as serial murder, split personalities, lost love, and ghosts, to name but a few. **Similar titles:** *Death Comes Easy: The Gay Times Book of Murder Stories*, Peter Burton (editor); *Midnight Thirsts: Erotic Tales of the Vampire*, Michael Thomas Ford (editor); *Shadows of the Night: Queer Tales of the Uncanny and Unusual*, Greg Herren (editor).

Cemeteries • Gay/Lesbian/Bisexual Characters • Mental Illness • Serial Killers

Death Comes Easy: The Gay Times Book of Murder Stories. *London: Gay Men's Press, 2003. 459p. ISBN 190285246X.*

This anthology of stories by polished master writers explores the human fascination with homicide. As the name suggests, the protagonists in all of these stories are gay. From the Roman Empire to the Far East and from a dangerously repressed priest to strangers on a plane, these stories by Perry Brass, Hugh Fleetwood, Patrick Gale, Drew Gummerson, Francis King, Josh Lanyon, Felice Picano, Steven Saylor, and Michael Wilcox know no boundaries in their pursuit of violent killers and bloody endings. **Similar titles:** *Bend Sinister: The Gay Times Book of Disturbing Stories*, Peter Burton (editor); *The Horror Writers Association Presents Robert Bloch's Psychos*, Robert Bloch (editor); *Shadows of the Night: Queer Tales of the Uncanny and Unusual*, Greg Herren (editor).

Clergy as Character • Gay/Lesbian/Bisexual Characters • Revenge • Serial Killers

Chizmar, Richard, ed.

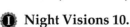 **Night Visions 10.** *Burton, MI: Subterranean Press, 2001. 293p. ISBN 1931081069.*

Nearly twenty years ago, the legendary <u>Night Visions</u> series was conceived by Dark Harvest Press as a showcase for the outstanding short fiction being produced by the best of the established authors and the most talented of the new writers in the fields of horror and dark fantasy. *Night Visions 10* returns with original novellas by Jack Ketchum (*The Passenger*) and John Shirley (*Her Hunger*), and five new stories from David B. Silva. **Similar titles:** *The Savage Tales of Solomon Kane*, Robert E. Howard; *Fears Unnamed*, Tim Lebbon; *As Timeless as Infinity: The Complete Twilight Zone Scripts of Rod Serling*, Rod Serling; *Night Visions 12*, Kealan Patrick Burke (editor).

Childhood • Demons • Kidnapping • Lawyer as Character • Obsession • Psychosexual Horror • Shape-shifters • Torture

Shivers IV. *Baltimore, MD: Cemetery Dance, 2006. 314p. ISBN 1587671298.*

The stories in this fourth collection in Cemetery Dance's Shivers series are reminiscent of the television show, *The Twilight Zone*, in the preponderance of "weird tales," a type of fiction in which the supernatural is more suggested than firmly established as part of the fictional reality. Contributors include Randy Chandler, T. M. Wright, Tim Lebbon, Ray Garton, and Stephen Mark Rainey. **Similar titles:** *As Timeless as Infinity: The Complete Twilight Zone Scripts of Rod Serling*, Rod Serling; *Night Visions 12*, Richard Chizmar (editor); *The Resurrection Man's Legacy and Other Stories*, Dale Bailey.

The Twilight Zone (television show)

Elrod, P. N., ed.

My Big Fat Supernatural Honeymoon. *New York: St. Martin's Griffin, 2008. 358p. ISBN 0312375042.*

A sequel to *My Big Fat Supernatural Wedding*, this lighthearted anthology of honeymoon-themed supernatural romance stories introduces psychic detectives in Chicago, as well as Elrod's ever-popular vampire private eye Jack Fleming, who hunts for a vanished bridegroom. Then there is the stalking and inevitable fighting between a newlywed werewolf couple, and a newly married undead pirate who must face an ancient Roman pirate. **Similar titles:** *On the Prowl*, Patricia Briggs (editor); *My Big Fat Supernatural Wedding*, P. N. Elrod (editor); *Dead and Loving It*, Mary Janice Davidson; *Many Bloody Returns*.

Eroticism • Fleming, Jack (character) • Maritime Horror • Marriage • Pirates • Vampire's Point of View • Werewolves

My Big Fat Supernatural Wedding. *New York: St. Martin's Griffin, 2006. 310p. ISBN 0312343604.*

Talented writers of supernatural fiction, such as Elrod herself and Esther M. Friesner, as well as contemporary luminaries Sherrilyn Kenyon and Charlaine Harris, create stories that follow the travails of the modern, psychic descendants of the feuding Hatfields and McCoys. They build on many popular romance themes, such as pirates, a mousy but ultimately spirited heiress, and a scheming rogue, and present a wedding where the wedding singer is an Elvis impersonator—or is he? **Similar titles:** *My Big Fat Supernatural Honeymoon*, P. N. Elrod (editor); *On the Prowl*, Patricia Briggs (editor); *Dead and Loving It*, Mary Janice Davidson.

Eroticism • Families • Pirates • Presley, Elvis (character) • Vampire's Point of View • Weddings • Werewolves

Feehan, Christine, Maggie Shane, Emma Holly, and Angela Knight.

Hot Blooded. *New York: Jove, 2004. 392p. ISBN 0515136964.*

An immortal shape-shifter, a werewolf romance, highly erotic kinky love between a vampire and a baker, and a world of Magi—witches and vampires out to save human beings from destruction—inform these tales. Each of these stories plays up the erotic and romantic angles of the plotlines, but fans will find much horror to enjoy here as well. **Similar titles:** *On the Prowl*, Patricia Briggs (editor); *My Big Fat Supernatural Wedding* and *My Big Fat Supernatural Honeymoon*, P. N., Elrod (editor).

Arthurian Legend • Eroticism • Magic • Vampire Hunters • Vampire's Point of View • Werewolves

Gelb, Jeff, and Michael Garrett, eds.

Hotter Blood. *New York: Kensington-Pinnacle, 2004, ©1991. 352p. ISBN 0786016442.*

Masters of horror are here to entertain with grisly whimsy and the grotesque. This volume contains twenty-four new stories of nocturnal submission, degenerate vices, and erotic nightmares. A geek wreaks a hideous revenge, while a devil's deal is gruesomely updated when a rock star sells his soul for success. **Similar titles:** *Hot Blooded*, Christine Feehan (editor); *Cravings*, Laurell K. Hamilton (editor); *Dead and Loving It*, Mary Janice Davidson; *Creepin'*, Monica Jackson (editor).

Eroticism • Psychosexual Horror

Gentile, Joe, Lori Gentile, and Garrett Anderson, eds.

Kolchak: The Night Stalker Chronicles, 26 Original Tales of the Surreal, the Bizarre, the Macabre. *Calumet City, IL: Moonstone, 2005. 329p. ISBN 1933076046.*

Carl Kolchak, played by the late Darren McGavin, is an icon of horror television. A nose-to-the-grindstone reporter who got his story at any cost, he now appears in twenty-six original, illustrated short stories by authors like P. N. Elrod and Richard Valley. "Interview with a Vampire" has Kolchak meeting Barnabas Collins. Diversity is the strength of this anthology. **Similar titles:** *As Timeless as Infinity: The Complete Twilight Zone Scripts of Rod Serling, Volume One*, Rod Serling; *Bloodlines: Richard Matheson's Dracula, I Am Legend and Other Vampire Stories*, Richard Matheson.

Alternative Literature • Collins, Barnabas (character) • Journalist as Character • Kolchak, Carl (character) • Parapsychology • Television Industry

Greenberg, Martin H., ed.

My Favorite Horror Story. *New York: BP Books, 2004, ©2000. 384p. ISBN 0886779146.*

Today's top horror authors tell who they read in introductions to these fifteen memorable stories, each personally selected by these famous writers. Tales include "Sweets to the Sweet" by Robert Bloch, "Father-thing" by Philip K. Dick, "Distributor" by Richard Matheson, "Warning to the Curious" by M. R. James, "Opening the Door" by Arthur Machen, "Colour Out of Space" by H. P. Lovecraft, and other classics. **Similar titles:** *Monsters in Our Midst* and *Robert Bloch's Psychos*, Robert Bloch (editor); *Horror Writers Association Presents the Museum of Horrors*, Dennis Etchison (editor).

Carnivals • Cthulhian Monsters • Cursed Objects • Demons • Dreams

White House Horrors. *New York: BP Books, 2004, ©1996. 316p. ISBN 0743487311.*

In this unusual collection of sixteen stories about the presidency and the White House, plotlines include a possessed writing machine, a black magic attempt at a political coup, an encounter with a centuries-old ghost, and a president obsessed with his exit from the Oval Office. Includes stories by Billie Sue Mosiman, Brian Hodge, Barbara Collins, and Edward Lee, among others. **Similar titles:** *Taverns of the Dead*, Kealan Patrick Burke (editor); *Haunted Holidays*, Martin H. Greenberg and Russell Davis (editors); *Strangers in Strange Lands*, Stephen Jones (editor).

Government Officials • Politician as Character • United States Presidents • Washington, DC

Greenberg, Martin H., Isaac Asimov, and Joseph D. Olander, eds.

100 Malicious Little Mysteries. *New York: Sterling, 2004, ©1981. 432p. ISBN 1402711018.*

One hundred baffling mysteries, by authors such as Isaac Asimov, Michael Gilbert, Wdward Wellen, Edward D. Hack, Bill Pronzini, Lawrence Treat, and Francis Nevins Jr. cover themes ranging from aggravating neighbors to class reunions and revenge killings. Fans of dark mysteries with unexpected twists, puzzles, moments of epiphany, and above all maliciousness will find this collection difficult to put down. **Similar titles:** *The Complete John Silence Stories*, Algernon Blackwood; *Aylmer Vance: Ghost-Seer*, Alice Askew and Claude Askew; *Shadows Over Baker Street*, Michael Reaves and John Pelan (editors).

Organized Crime • Police Officer as Character • Serial Killers • Stalkers

Greenberg, Martin H., and Al Sarrantonio, eds.

100 Hair-Raising Little Horror Stories. *New York: Sterling, 2003, ©1993. 496p. ISBN 1402709757.*

Master editor Martin H. Greenberg and horror author Al Sarrantonio showcase the best of the best in this anthology, which includes short works by Edgar Allan Poe and H. P. Lovecraft, Fritz Leiber, Nathaniel Hawthorne, Stephen Crane, Charles Dickens, Robert Barr, and Washington Irving. **Similar titles:** The Mammoth Book of Best New Horror Series, Stephen Jones (editor); The Year's Best Fantasy and Horror Series, Ellen Datlow (editor); *Dark Terrors, Volume Six*, Stephen Jones and David Sutton (editors).

Haunted Houses • Obsession • Serial Killers • Zombies

Greenberg, Martin H., and Russell Davis, eds.

Haunted Holidays. *New York: DAW, 2004. 310p. ISBN 0756402239.*

This holiday-themed anthology of thirteen stories proves that Halloween is not the only scary time of year. Contributors include David Niall Wilson, Peter Crowther, Esther Friesner, David Bischoff, Nancy Holder, and Brian A. Hopkins. **Similar titles:** *Dark Arts*, John Pelan (editor); *White*

House Horrors, Martin H. Greenberg (editor); *Taverns of the Dead*, Kealan Patrick Burke (editor).

Holidays—Christmas • Holidays—Thanksgiving

Herren, Greg, ed.

Shadows of the Night: Queer Tales of the Uncanny and Unusual. *Binghamton, NY: Harrington Park Press, 2004. 208p. ISBN 156023394X.*

This groundbreaking anthology of the dark side of gay and lesbian fiction offers stories of murder and mayhem that savor every lurid detail. A gay travel writer finds he has a one-way ticket to horror, a murdered lesbian plots bloody revenge from the grave, a young man is terrified of Jewish vampires, and much more. **Similar titles:** *Bend Sinister: The Gay Times Book of Disturbing Stories* and *Death Comes Easy: The Gay Times Book of Murder Stories*, Peter Burton (editor); *Midnight Thirsts: Erotic Tales of the Vampire*, Michael Thomas Ford (editor).

Gay/Lesbian/Bisexual Characters • Revenging Revenant • Serial Killers • Writer as Character

Hopkinson, Nalo, ed.

Mojo: Conjure Stories. *New York: Warner Aspect, 2003. 307p. ISBN 0446679291.*

Contrary to popular opinion, the word "mojo" did not originate in the American South among practitioners of voodoo, but was instead brought to this country by African slaves. A "mojo" is a small cloth bag containing powerful magic. Hopkinson has collected nineteen original stories about African gods, magic, and spirituality in this unusual anthology, set everywhere from Africa to Oakland. Contributors include Tananarive Due, Barbara Hambly, Gerard Houraner, and Neil Gaiman. **Similar titles:** *Dark Thirst*, Angela C. Allen (editor); *Whispers in the Dark* and *Dark Dreams: A Collection of Horror and Suspense by Black Writers*, Brandon Massey (editor).

African American Characters • Magic • Religion—African • Religion—Voodoo • Witchcraft

Jackson, Monica, ed.

Creepin'. *Washington, DC: Kimani, 2007. 392p. ISBN 0373830602.*

Each of the five novellas in this collection focuses on the deception and betrayal that women sometimes face from loved ones—and how they cope with it. L. A. Banks writes of a woman whose ex simply won't behave, so one of her friends hires a werewolf to help her. Donna Hill tells of a woman who becomes obsessed with sexual gratification—to the point that it takes over her life. Monica Jackson pens a tale in which a woman loses her fiancé to a vampire. J. M. Jeffries contributes a voodoo revenge story, and Janice Sims presents a supernatural love triangle. **Similar titles:** *The Female of the Species*, Joyce Carol Oates; *Scared Stiff*, Ramsey Campbell; *Hotter Blood*, Jeff Gelb and Michael Garrett (editors); *Night's Edge*, Maggie Shayne (editors).

Eroticism • Louisiana—New Orleans • Marriage • Obsession • Religion—Christianity • Religion —Voodoo • Revenge • Werewolves

Summer Chills: Strangers in Strange Lands. *New York: Carroll & Graf, 2007. 476p. ISBN 0786719869.*

This collection of twenty-one horror stories about journeys to twenty-one locales includes two benchmark authors. Brian Lumley's "The Sun, the Sea and the Silent Scream" is about a tropical vacation gone awry, while Ramsey Campbell's "Seeing the World" describes the outcome of a very boring vacation slide show. Contributors include Karl Edward Wagner, Robert Silverberg, Nancy Holder, Harlan Ellison, Dennis Etchison, Tanith Lee, Christopher Fowler, Clive Barker, Michael Marshall Smith, and Graham Masterton. **Similar titles:** *Dark Arts*, John Pelan (editor); *Taverns of the Dead*, Kealan Patrick Burke (editor); *Haunted Holidays*, Martin H. Greenberg and Russell Davis (editors).

Africa • Asia • Europe • Mexico • Road Trips • South America

Joshi, S. T., ed.

Great Weird Tales: 14 Stories by Lovecraft, Blackwood, Machen and Others. *Mineola, NY: Dover Publications, 1999. 239p. ISBN 0486404366.*

Noted literary critic Joshi puts together a collection of various weird tales published during the golden age of science fiction and horror, roughly between 1880 and 1940. In addition to the masters noted in the title, this anthology includes works by William Hope Hodgson, Ambrose Bierce, Fitz-James O'Brien, Ralph Adams Cram, Fiona Macleod, W.C. Morrow, F. Marion Crawford, Lord Dunsany, R. H. Barlow, and Fitz-James O'Brien. **Similar titles:** *H. P. Lovecraft's Book of the Supernatural: 20 Classics of the Macabre, Chosen by the Author Himself*, Stephen Jones (editor); *Boats of the "Glen Carrig" and Other Nautical Adventures*, William Hope Hodgson; *The Dreams in the Witch House and Other Weird Stories, More Annotated H. P. Lovecraft*, H. P. Lovecraft.

Dreams • Serial Killers • Weird Science

Lamb, Hugh, ed.

A Bottomless Grave and Other Victorian Tales of Terror. *Mineola, NY: Dover Publications, 2001, ©1977. 224p. ISBN 0486415902.*

Lamb has unearthed twenty-one little-known tales by well-known American and British authors and put them together in a single collection, with commentary at the beginning of each tale that provides important historical information. Contributors include benchmarks authors Ambrose Bierce, Joseph Sheridan Le Fanu, Frank Norris, and Guy de Maupassant. **Similar titles:** *Boats of the "Glen Carrig" and Other Nautical Adventures*, William Hope Hodgson; *Tales from a Gas-Lit Graveyard*, Hugh Lamb (editor); *Casting the Runes* and *Ghost Stories of an Antiquary*, M. R. James.

England—London • Maritime Horror • Parapsychology • Revenge • Suicide • Victorian Era

Tales from a Gas-Lit Graveyard. *Mineola, NY: Dover Thrift Editions, 2004, ©1979. 224p. ISBN 048643429X.*

Assembled by an authority on vintage thrillers, these seventeen Victorian stories of the macabre include works from around the world by celebrated authors such as Ambrose Bierce, Robert Barr, R Murray Gilchrist, Mrs. H. H. Riddell, Richard Marsh, and Guy Boothby. Discerning lovers of horror and suspense will take particular pleasure in the rarity of these tales, none of which has been reprinted since its original publication. **Similar titles:** *The Strange Case of Dr. Jekyll and Mr. Hyde and Other Stories*, Robert Louis Stevenson; *Casting the Runes* and *Ghost Stories of an Antiquary*, M. R. James; *A Bottom-less Grave and Other Victorian Tales of Terror*, Hugh Lamb (editor).

England • Haunted Houses • New England • Victorian Era

Little, Bentley, ed.

Four Dark Nights. *New York: Dorchester, 2003, ©2002. 326p. ISBN 0843951532.*

The events in each of these four novellas occur in the space of one terrifying evening—in one neighborhood. Little's *The Circle* presents three interrelated events. In Douglas Clegg's *The Words* two alienated teens are led into the "world of nowhere." A supernatural experience allows a woman some closure with her deceased father in Christopher Golden's *Pyre*. And a former faith healer attempts to rescue his son from the underworld in Tom Piccirilli's *Jonah Rose*. **Similar titles:** *Fears Unnamed*, Tim Lebbon; *The Nightmare Chronicles*, Douglas Clegg; *By Reason of Darkness*, William P. Simmons.

Childhood • Death—Grieving • Frame Tale • Psychosexual Horror • Suburbia

Massey, Brandon, ed.

Dark Dreams: A Collection of Horror and Suspense by Black Writers. *New York: Kensington, 2004. 307p. ISBN 0758207530.*

Stories by up and coming writers and seasoned black authors touch on themes such as racism, voodoo and slavery, as well as universal human themes. Contributors include Robert Fleming, Tananarive Due, and the editor himself. **Similar titles:** *Havoc After Dark*, Robert Fleming; *Dark Thirst*, Angela C. Allen; *Mojo: Conjure Stories*, Nalo Hopkinson (editor); *Whispers in the Night*, Brandon Massey.

African American Characters • Racism • Religion—Voodoo • Slavery

Voices from the Other Side. *New York: Kensington, 2006. 336p. ISBN 0758212321.*

This second collection by up and coming and seasoned black authors treats themes as diverse as unemployment, werewolves, and mental institutions. Contributors include Tananarive Due, L. A. Banks, and the editor himself. **Similar titles:** *Havoc After Dark*, Robert Fleming; *Dark Thirst*, Angela C. Allen; *Mojo: Conjure Stories*, Nalo Hopkinson (editor); *Whispers in the Night*, Brandon Massey.

African American Characters • Racism • Religion—Voodoo • Slavery

Whispers in the Night. *New York: Dafina, 2007. 313p. ISBN 0758217412.*

Robert Fleming, Tananarive Due, and Randy Walker all contribute stories to this anthology. The stories range from drug use, to slavery reparations, to possession, to zombies, to spirituality, to spousal abuse. **Similar titles:** *Dark Dreams*, Brandon

Massey (editor); *Dark Thirst*, Angela C. Allen; *Mojo: Conjure Stories*, Nalo Hopkinson (editor).

African American Characters • *Slavery* • *Zombies*

Moorish, Robert, ed.

Thrillers Two (II, 2). *Baltimore, MD: Cemetery Dance, 2006. 229 pp. ISBN 1587671220.*

Gemma Files, Tim Waggoner, R. Patrick Gates, and Caitlin R. Kiernan make up the stellar collection of authors here. Files's *Pen Umbra* is an engrossing tale of an artist/scholar who is advised to make some extra money by volunteering to be a part of a mysterious parapsychological study. Waggoner's stories stretch the boundaries of the genre, with teens engaging in sadomasochism and beetle-like aliens falling out of the sky in a rain of blood. **Similar titles:** *Dark Terrors, Volume Six*, Stephen Jones and David Sutton (editors); *Borderlands 5*, Elizabeth E. Monteleone and Thomas F. Monteleone (editors); *Night Visions 10*, Richard Chizmar (editor).

Aliens • *Obsession* • *Parapsychology* • *Psychics* • *Psychosexual Horror* • *Weird Science*

Noyes, Deborah, ed.

The Restless Dead: Ten Original Stories of the Supernatural. *Cambridge, MA: Candlewick Press, 2007. 253p. ISBN 0763629065.*

The dead won't stay that way in these ten original tales. A teen rashly buries the only copies of his poems with his deceased girlfriend, sets out to retrieve them, and digs up the wrong grave. A narrator tells of the time before penicillin, when infections easily carried away their victims. Though this anthology is marketed to teens, adults will also enjoy these stories by luminaries of both YA fiction and horror literature. **Similar titles:** *Dating Secrets of the Dead*, David Prill; *Toybox*, Al Sarrantonio; The Corbin Family Novels, James A. Moore.

Cursed Objects • *Revenging Revenant* • *Secret Sin* • *Writer as Character* • *Zombies*

Pelan, John, ed.

Dark Arts. *Forest Hill, MD: Cemetery Dance, 2006. 293p. ISBN 1587671247.*

In this cleverly themed anthology, artists of various stripes create the horrific, including a performance artist who infects himself with deadly diseases to remind his audience of their mortality; a painter of crime scenes who works from reality; and a musician who can free the spirits of the dead with his playing. **Similar titles:** *Dark Delicacies*, Del Howison and Jeff Gelb (editors); *Haunted Holidays*, Martin H. Greenberg and Russell Davis (editors); *Summer Chills: Strangers in Strange Lands*, Stephen Jones (editor).

Afterlife, The • *Artist as Character* • *Deformity* • *Music* • *Revenging Revenant*

Shayne, Maggie, Barbara Hambly, and Charlaine Harris.

Night's Edge. *Don Mills, ON: HQN, 2004. 377p. ISBN 0373770103.*

Here are three novellas by three well-known paranormal romance authors: *Her Best Enemy*, by Maggie Shayne; *Someone Else's Shadow*, by Barbara Hambly, and *Dancers in the Dark*, by Charlaine Harris. Shayne's ghost story follows a skeptical journalist who debunks local psychics—until she is made a believer by a haunted house. Hambly writes about a woman who must rely on the kindness of a mysterious stranger. Harris pens a vampire tale of a dancer who cannot deal with her past. **Similar titles:** *Creepin'*, Monica Jackson (editor); *Hotter Blood*, Jeff Gelb and Michael Garrett (editors); *On the Prowl*, Patricia Briggs (editor).

Dancer as Character • Haunted Houses • Journalist as Character • Parapsychology • Psychics • Stalkers

Silver, Steven H., and Martin H. Greenberg, eds.

Horrible Beginnings. *New York: Daw, 2003. 316p. ISBN 0756401232.*

This collection of seventeen horror debuts, introduced by the authors, includes a 1934 tale by Robert Bloch, Ramsey Campbell's "The Church in High Street," and Neil Gaiman's "The Case of the Four and Twenty Blackbirds." Scholars and fans alike will enjoy the comparisons between the juvenilia of benchmark authors. Other authors included are Henry Kuttner, Tanith Lee, Edward Bryant, and P. N. Elrod. **Similar titles:** *My Favorite Horror Story*, Martin H. Greenberg (editor); *Monsters in Our Midst* and *Robert Bloch's Psychos*, Robert Bloch (editor); *Horror Writers Association Presents the Museum of Horrors*, Dennis Etchison (editor).

Dracula (character) • Haunted Houses • Vampire's Point of View

VanderMeer, Ann, and Jeff VanderMeer, eds.

The New Weird. *San Francisco: Tachyon Publications, 2008. 414p. ISBN 1892391554.*

In this groundbreaking collection, examples of a new crossover subgenre of horror, science fiction, and fantasy dubbed "the new weird" by various online communities, are collected. Contributors include Jeff VanderMeer, Clive Barker, and China Miâville. Also included is a transcript of the month-long chat room discussion between various authors and fans in which "the new weird" was defined, as well as several scholarly essays on the subgenre. **Similar titles:** *Black Pockets and Other Dark Thoughts*, George Zebrowski; *Frights: Stories of Suspense and Supernatural Terror*, Kirby McCauley (editor); *King Rat*, China Miâville.

Academia • Internet, The • Parallel Universes • Zombies

Best Of . . . Anthologies

Betancourt, John, ed.

Horror: The Best of the Year. *Rockville, MD: Prime Books, 2006. 319p. ISBN 0809556480.*

These seventeen stories feature a haunting tale that captures the desolation and desperation of downtown Manhattan in the immediate aftermath of 9/11, a surreal absinthe dream about an encounter with an otherworldly race, and a story about a teenager who instantaneously loses her personality. Authors include Joe

R. Lansdale, Jack Cady, Joe Hill, Caitlin R. Kiernan, Clive Barker, Ramsey Campbell, Michael Marshall Smith, and David Niall Wilson. **Similar titles:** *Inferno* and *The Dark*, Ellen Datlow (editor); *The Horror Writers Association Presents the Museum of Horrors*, Dennis Etchinson (editor).

Cthulhian Monsters • Haunted Houses • Mental Illness • New York—New York City • Obsession • Popular Culture—Mining Disasters • Terrorism

Datlow, Ellen, ed.

Inferno: New Tales of Terror and the Supernatural. *New York: Tor, 2007. 381p. ISBN 0765315580.*

This collection of writings by horror luminaries exemplifies the breadth and sophistication of the genre, running the gamut from the subtle to the grotesque. Stories cover such plotlines as a biker's last ride with his old girlfriend, a disturbing childhood incident, an apiary, a tale of Hollywood in the 1960s, and a parent's living out his worst nightmare. Contributors include Joyce Carol Oates, Terry Dowling, Conrad Williams, P. D. Cacek, Lucius Shepard, and Stephen Gallagher. **Similar titles:** *Horror: The Best of the Year*, John Betancourt (editor); *The Dark: New Ghost Stories*, Ellen Datlow (editor); <u>The Year's Best Fantasy and Horror Series</u>, Ellen Datlow (editor).

Bees • Biker as Character • Cats • Childhood • Manson, Charles (character) • Parenting

Datlow, Ellen, et al., eds.

Ⓑ **The Year's Best Fantasy and Horror.** *Annual. New York: St. Martin's Press.*
These large tomes (most volumes fall within the 500–600 page range) are impressive collections of fantasy and horror short stories and poetry written by both luminaries in the field and up and coming authors. Each collection is more than just a who's who of horror and fantasy writers, however. Datlow and her co-editors, who have changed over the years, excel in their ability to select high quality works that transcend the parameters of genre fiction. Also useful are the editors' comprehensive year-end summations of the genres and long lists of honorable mentions, which are valuable resources for collection development. The seventeenth annual collection is the recipient of a Bram Stoker Award.

Magic

Etchison, Dennis, Ramsey Campbell, and Jack Dann, eds.

Gathering the Bones. *New York: Tor, 2003. 447p. ISBN 0765301792.*
Etchison, Campbell, and Dann have drawn about equally from their countries of residence (the United States, the United Kingdom, and Australia) in putting together this collection of thirty-four stories by a mix of well-known authors and newcomers. Contributors include Terry Dowling, Robert Devereaux, Kim Newman, Lisa Tuttle, Thomas Tessier, Gahan Wilson, Ray Bradbury, Michael Marshall Smith, Steve Rasnic Tem, Peter Crowther, Tim Waggoner, Melanie Tem, and Graham Joyce. **Similar titles:** *The Horror Writers Association Presents the Museum of Horrors*, Dennis

Etchison (editor); *Horror: The Best of the Year*, John Betancourt (editor); *The Horror Writers Association Presents Robert Bloch's Psychos*, Robert Bloch (editor).

Popular Culture—The Land of Oz • Secret Sin • Vampires

Hopkins, Brian A., ed.

13 Horrors: A Devil's Dozen Stories Celebrating 13 Years of the World Horror Convention. *Kansas City: KaCSFFS Press, 2003. 255p. ISBN 0935128042.*

> Various award-winning authors in the horror genre contributed to this collection, including the likes of Chelsea Quinn Yarbro, Ramsey Campbell, Michael Bishop, and Graham Masterton. Hopkins also includes a foreword by Joe R. Lansdale. **Similar titles:** *The Last Pentacle of the Sun*; M. W. Anderson and Brett Alexander Savory (editors); *The Horror Writers Association Presents Robert Bloch's Psychos*, Robert Bloch (editor); *The Horror Writers Association Presents the Museum of Horrors*, Dennis Etchison (editor).

> *Central America • Dreams • Holidays—Christmas • Religion—Mayan • Revenge*

Howison, Del, and Jeff Gelb, eds.

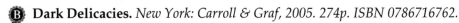 **Dark Delicacies.** *New York: Carroll & Graf, 2005. 274p. ISBN 0786716762.*

> This collection includes new stories by many luminaries of horror. Ray Bradbury pens a tale of the dead returning to the living to wax poetic on death and loss, Clive Barker contributes a story about a mad scientist's encounter with a zombie, and Gahan Wilson writes about an artist whose grim subjects bear more than a passing resemblance to reality. Other contributors include Ramsey Campbell, Lisa Morton, Whitley Streiber, and John Farris. **Similar titles:** *Dark Delicacies II*, Del Howison and Jeff Gelb (editors); <u>The Mammoth Book of Best New Horror Series</u>, Stephen Jones (editor); *Dark Arts*, John Pelan (editor).

> *Artist as Character • Weird Science • Zombies*

Dark Delicacies II: Fear, More Original Tales of Terror and the Macabre by the World's Greatest Horror Writers. *New York: Carroll & Graf, 2007. 269p. ISBN 0786719516.*

> A second collection of new stories by horror luminaries includes Barbara Hambly, Joe R. Lansdale, Peter Atkins, Tananarive Due, Max Brooks, Ray Garton, John Farris, Greg Kihn, Glen Hirschberg, and Caitlin R. Kiernan. Jeff Gelb is the editor of the <u>Hot Blood Series</u>, while Del Howison is the proprietor of the Dark Delicacies horror bookstore in Los Angeles. **Similar titles:** *Dark Delicacies*, Del Howison and Jeff Gelb (editors); <u>The Mammoth Book of Best New Horror Series</u>, Stephen Jones (editor); *Dark Terrors: Volume 6*, Stephen Jones and David Sutton (editors).

> *Dogs • Weird Science*

Jones, Stephen, ed.

The Mammoth Book of Best New Horror 14. *New York: Carroll & Graf, 2003. 590p. ISBN 0786712376.*

> This annual anthology includes contributions by Neil Gaiman, China Miâville, David J. Schow, Nicholas Royle, Stephen Gallagher, Brian Hodge, Glen Hirshberg, Ramsey Campbell, Jay Russell, Basil Copper, Kelly Link, Kim

Newman, Caitlin R. Kierman, Graham Joyce, and Jeff VanderMeer. **Similar titles:** The Year's Best Horror and Fantasy Series, Ellen Datlow (editor); *Dark Terrors: Volume 6*, Stephen Jones and David Sutton (editors); *The Mammoth Book of Modern Ghost Stories: Great Supernatural Tales of the Twentieth Century*, Peter Haining (editor).

Haunted Houses • Obsession • Revenge • Revenging Revenant • Serial Killers

The Mammoth Book of Best New Horror 15. *New York: Carroll & Graf, 2004. 624p. ISBN 0786714263.*

This annual anthology includes contributions by Ramsey Campbell, Marc Laidlaw, Dale Bailey, Christopher Fowler, Michael Marshall Smith, John Farris, Steve Rasnic Tem, Gemma Files, Caitlin R. Kiernan, Joyce Carol Oates, Glen Hirshberg, Neil Gaiman, Simon Clark, and Tim Lebbon. **Similar titles:** The Year's Best Horror and Fantasy Series, Ellen Datlow (editor); *Dark Terrors: Volume 6*, Stephen Jones and David Sutton (editors); *The Mammoth Book of Modern Ghost Stories: Great Supernatural Tales of the Twentieth Century*, Peter Haining (editor).

Haunted Houses • Obsession • Revenge • Revenging Revenant • Serial Killers

The Mammoth Book of Best New Horror 16. *New York: Carroll & Graf, 2005. 610p. ISBN 0786716002.*

This annual anthology includes contributions by Neil Gaiman, Ramsey Campbell, Brian Keene, Tina Rath, Christa Faust, Stephen Gallagher, Tanith Lee, Michael Marshall Smith, Tim Lebbon, Glen Hirshberg, Poppy Z. Brite, Jay Russell, Kelly Link, Kim Newman, Dale Bailey, and Lisa Tuttle. **Similar titles:** The Year's Best Horror and Fantasy Series, Ellen Datlow (editor); *Dark Terrors: Volume 6*, Stephen Jones and David Sutton (editors); *The Mammoth Book of Modern Ghost Stories: Great Supernatural Tales of the Twentieth Century*, Peter Haining (editor).

Haunted Houses • Obsession • Revenge • Revenging Revenant • Serial Killers

The Mammoth Book of Best New Horror 17. *New York: Carroll & Graf, 2006. 562p. ISBN 0786718331.*

This annual anthology includes contributions by Ramsey Campbell, Peter Atkins, China Miéville, Elizabeth Massie, Brian Hodge, Gahan Wilson, Glen Hirshberg, Caitlin R. Kiernan, David Morrell, Clive Barker, and Brian Lumley. **Similar titles:** The Year's Best Horror and Fantasy Series, Ellen Datlow (editor); *Dark Terrors: Volume 6*, Stephen Jones and David Sutton (editors); *The Mammoth Book of Modern Ghost Stories: Great Supernatural Tales of the Twentieth Century*, Peter Haining (editor).

Haunted Houses • Obsession • Revenge • Revenging Revenant • Serial Killers

Jones, Stephen, and David Sutton, eds.

Dark Terrors: Volume 6. *London: Orion, 2004, ©2002. 499p. ISBN 0575074078.*

The world's biggest and best anthology series of original horror and dark fantasy returns with a bumper collection of thirty-six new short stories and novellas from the hottest names and most talented newcomers: Trey R. Barker, Stephen Baxter, John Burke, Ramsey Campbell, Basil Copper,

Les Daniels, Graham Masterton, Tim Lebbon, and Christopher Fowler. Hardcore fans will rate this anthology highly. **Similar titles:** *Dark Delicacies* and *Dark Delicacies II*, Del Howison and Jeff Gelb (editors); <u>The Mammoth Book of Best New Horror Series</u>, Stephen Jones (editor); <u>The Year's Best Fantasy and Horror Series</u>, *Borderlands 5* and *From the Borderlands*, Elizabeth Monteleone and Thomas F. Monteleone (editors).

Museums • Parallel Universes • Precognition • Time Travel

McCauley, Kirby, ed.

Frights: Stories of Suspense and Supernatural Terror. *New York: Ibooks, 2003,* ©*1976. 287p. ISBN 0743458559.*

These seventeen stories of dark fantasy and fear contain editorial and chronological notes by the editor, as well as an introduction by Fritz Leiber. Stories included are "There's a Long, Long Trail A-Winding," by Russell Kirk; "Whisperer," by Brian Lumley; "Armaja Das," by Joe Haldeman; "Kitten," by Poul Anderson and Karen Anderson; "Dead Call," by William F. Nolan; "Companion," by Ramsey Campbell; "It Only Comes out at Night," by Dennis Etchison; and "Compulsory Games," by Robert Aickman; among others. **Similar titles:** *The New Weird*, Ann VanderMeer and Jeff VanderMeer (editors); *The Resurrection Man's Legacy and Other Stories*, Dale Bailey.

Demons • Mental Illness • Obsession • Stalkers

Monteleone, Elizabeth E., and Thomas F. Monteleone, eds.

(B) Borderlands 5: An Anthology of Imaginative Fiction. *Grantham, NH: Borderlands Press, 2003. 281p. ISBN 1880325373.*

The <u>Borderlands</u> anthologies are known to push the borders of the genre, and this anthology is no exception. Contributors include Gary A. Braunbeck, Barry Hoffman, John Farris, Brian Freeman, Dominick Cancilla, Whitley Streiber, Bentley Little, David J. Schow, Tom Piccirilli, and Stephen King. **Similar titles:** *Dark Terrors: Volume 6*, Stephen Jones and David Sutton (editors); *From the Borderlands*, Elizabeth E. Monteleone and Thomas F. Monteleone (editors); *Night Visions 10*, Richard Chizmar (editor).

Families • Obsession • Parallel Universes • Parenting • Secret Sin

From the Borderlands: Stories of Terror and Madness. *New York: Warner, 2004,* ©*2003. 428p. ISBN 0446610356.*

These tales of psychological horror make readers rethink their views on exercise, priests, faces, occupations, fairy tales, and their high school years, realizing the horrors behind each. The editors do a good job of mixing well-known writers with new authors, including stories such as Lon Prater's "Head Music," about a man's relationship to a monster from the sea, and John McIlveen's "Infliction," in which a man is forced to see the sins of his past. **Similar titles:** *Matinee at the Flame*, Christopher Fahy; *Borderlands 5*, Elizabeth E. Monteleone and Thomas F. Monteleone (editors); *Night Visions 10*, Richard Chizmar (editor).

Families • Obsession • Parallel Universes • Parenting • Secret Sin

Pelan, John, ed.

Alone on the Darkside: Echoes from Shadows of Horror. *New York: Roc, 2006. 353p. ISBN 0451461053.*

> This multithemed anthology includes stories by Gerard Houarner, Brian Hodge, Glen Hirshberg, and Lucy Taylor. **Similar titles:** <u>The Mammoth Book of Best New Horror Series</u>, Stephen Jones (editor); <u>The Year's Best Fantasy and Horror Series</u>, Ellen Datlow (editor); *Dark Terrors, Volume Six*, Stephen Jones and David Sutton (editor).
>
> *Haunted Houses • Obsession • Revenge • Revenging Revenant • Serial Killers*

A Walk on the Darkside: Visions of Horror. *Roc, 2004. 391p. ISBN 0451459938.*

> This is a blend of work by newer authors and better known writers in the genre. Included are works by Michael Laimo, Tim Lebbon, Jeffrey Thomas, Mehitobel Wilson, Brian Keene, Tom Piccirilli, Caitlin R. Kiernan, Brian Hodge, Brian Hopkins, Steve Rasnic Tem, and the editor himself. **Similar titles:** <u>The Mammoth Book of Best New Horror Series</u>, Stephen Jones (editor); <u>The Year's Best Fantasy and Horror Series</u>, Ellen Datlow (editor); *Dark Terrors, Volume Six*, Stephen Jones and David Sutton (editors).
>
> *Haunted Houses • Obsession • Revenge • Revenging Revenant • Serial Killers*

June's Picks

> Robert Bloch (editor), *The Horror Writers Association Presents Robert Bloch's Psychos* (Pocket); Poppy Z. Brite, *The Devil You Know* (Subterranean Press); Ellen Datlow (editor), *Inferno: New Tales of Terror and the Supernatural* (Tor); Christopher Fowler, *Demonized* (Serpent's Tale); Jack Ketchum, *Peaceable Kingdom* (Leisure); Richard Matheson, *I Am Legend* (Tor), *The Incredible Shrinking Man* (Tor)

Tony's Picks

> Robert Aickman, *The Collected Strange Stories* (Tartarus Press); Robert W. Chambers, *The Yellow Sign and Other Stories* (Chaosium); Peter Crowther, *The Longest Single Note* (Leisure); Glen Hirshberg, *American Morons* (Earthling Publications); Al Sarrantonio, *Toybox* (Leisure Books); Michael Marshall Smith, *More Tomorrow* (Earthling Publications)

Part 4

Further Reading in the Genre

Chapter 19

Reference

Although there are a limited number of reference works in the horror genre, those that exist are important to readers because they make available important information that sheds light on many a horror writer and his or her literary oeuvre, and because they often offer other information of interest to horror fans. These reference works remind horror fans and scholars that the monsters populating the works of Ramsey Campbell, Stephen King, Dean Koontz, Bentley Little, H. P. Lovecraft, Kim Newman, Joyce Carol Oates, Edgar Allan Poe, Phil Rickman, Bram Stoker, Peter Straub, and countless other writers of the grotesque and the horrific are often descendants of folklore and fairy tale creatures that once were invoked by adults to teach young and old alike tough lessons about the dangers of the world and about giving in to base human desires.

In this chapter readers will find lists and brief descriptions of encyclopedias, dictionaries, and bibliographies that deal with the horror genre, including representative titles such as Mike Ashley's *Who's Who in Horror and Fantasy Fiction*, which, although dated, makes accessible biographical and bibliographical information on some benchmark writers in the genre. Ashley's groundbreaking bio-bibliography and other older titles may no longer be in print, but they are readily available through other means, such as ILL and World Wide Web services that find out-of-print texts, and librarians will find that acquiring them is well worth the trouble. Also included is Neil Barron's *Horror Literature*, perhaps the single most important reference work that deals with the speculative genres of science fiction, horror, and fantasy as a whole. Other works, lesser known but just as important to horror fans, such as Thomas C. Clarke's *Occult Bibliography*, Peter Haining's *A Dictionary of Ghost Lore and Terror: A History of Horror Illustrations*, Jack Sullivan's *The Penguin Encyclopedia of Horror*, and Everett F. Bleiler's *Supernatural Fiction Writers*, are also found in this chapter. For the purpose of creating a practical categorization for these works, the chapter is subdivided into four sections, on reading guides to the horror genre, reference books about horror, history and criticism of the genre, and periodicals and organizations that deal with horror.

Readers' Guides to the Horror Genre

Barron, Neil.

Fantasy and Horror: A Critical and Historical Guide to Literature, Illustration, Film, TV, Radio, and the Internet. *Lanham, MD: Scarecrow Press, 1999. 832p. ISBN 0810835967.*

> This guide directs readers and viewers to the historically important works of the fantastic imagination, as well as to the scholarship that helps us understand their nature and appeal. Arranged chronologically, narrative introductions provide historical and analytical perspectives on the period or subjects covered, while annotated bibliographies describe and evaluate the books and other materials judged most significant for literary or historical reasons. More than 2,300 works of fiction and poetry are discussed, each cross-referenced to other works with similar or contrasting themes.

Horror Literature: A Reader's Guide. <u>Garland Reference Library of the Humanities 1220.l</u>. *New York; London: Garland, 1990. 596p. ISBN 0824043472.*

> Barron pens this bibliography and critical introduction to the horror genre, which is a good basic source, though now somewhat dated.

Barron, Neil, et al., eds.

What Fantastic Fiction Do I Read Next? A Reader's Guide to Recent Fantastic Fiction, Horror & Science Fiction. *Farmington Hills, MI: Gale, 1999. 1954p. ISBN 0787644765.*

> Barron et al. briefly annotate some 5,000 books in the fantasy, horror, and science fiction genres. Approximately one-fourth of Barron's selective bibliography is dedicated to horror.

Herald, Diana.

Genreflecting: A Guide to Popular Reading Interests. 6th ed. *Edited by Wayne Wiegand. Westport, CT: Libraries Unlimited, 2006. 559p. ISBN 1519582245.*

> Covering more than 5,000 titles in such popular genres as crime, adventure, romance, Western, science fiction, fantasy, and horror, Herald's indispensable reference defines each, describes its characteristics and subgenres, and groups authors and books according to type or subject. Readers will find everything they need to know about traditional genre literature, and they will learn about some of the latest subgenres to emerge.

Databases

NoveList. *CD-ROM/Online. 1994– .*

> *NoveList* helps librarians, students, and teachers find fiction based on books they have read or topics in which they are interested. Utilizing the EBSCOhost search engine, it features expanded searching, such as Boolean, Natural Language, and full-text of reviews. Readers can search for books by title or author or by simply describing a book that would be interesting to read. *NoveList* now offers the ability

to search for books based on readability (Lexlie) scores. It provides access to more than 100,000 searchable fiction titles and more than 36,000 individual subject headings based on Hennepin County Public Library's renowned cataloging system.

Readers' Advisor Online. *Libraries Unlimited/Greenwood Publishing Group. 2006– .*

> The *Readers' Advisor Online* is based on Libraries Unlimited's print Genreflecting series. Multiple points of access and selective coverage by genre experts make this an extremely efficient tool for finding related titles. It also features a free blog. Designed to make life easier for readers' advisors, the Readers Advisor Online Blog (www.readersadvisoronline. com/blog) includes Cindy Orr's weekly "RA Rundown," "Most Wanted Mash-up," and "Under the Radar," as well as regular columns by RA experts Diana Tixier Herald, Sarah Statz Cords, and others.

What Do I Read Next? *CD-ROM/Online. Gale Research, 1996– .*

> This online database contains brief descriptions of more than 63,000 adult, young adult, and children's titles. Gale gives libraries and their users 96,000 titles, more than 52,000 plot summaries, 533 award titles, several recommended reading lists, and biographical information. To be included in *What Do I Read Next?*, a book must be an award winner, be a best seller, or have appeared on a recommending reading list. Genres include inspirational, mystery, romance, science fiction, fantasy, horror, Western, and historical novels; general fiction; classic fiction; and nonfiction. The user-friendly software includes custom, in-depth search options by title, author, subject, genre, locale, and more.

Reference Books on the Horror Genre

Bush, Laurence C.

Asian Horror Encyclopedia: Asian Horror Culture in Literature, Manga, and Folklore. *San Jose, CA: Writers Club Press, 2001. 226p. ISBN 0595201814.*

> Bush, a long-time reviewer of horror texts, collects information dealing with supernatural horror literature in Japan and China.

Clute, John.

The Darkening Garden: A Short Lexicon of Horror. *Cauheegan, WI: Payseur and Schmidt, 2006. 162p. ISBN 0978911407.*

> This illustrated, dictionary-style series of essays on terms such as *aftermath, visitation, revel, infection, sighting,* and *thickening*—words that the author claims are integral to viewing horror—also contains an interview with Clute and a pack of thirty postcards bearing the artwork from the book. The book references *The Encyclopedia of Fantasy* by Clute and John Grant.

Clute, John, and John Grant.

The Encyclopedia of Fantasy. *New York: St. Martin's Press, 1997. 1,079p. ISBN 0312198698.*

>A benchmark work in the genre, Clute and Grant's illustrated encyclopedia contains over 1,000 pages of entries on science fiction, horror, and fantasy.

Jones, Stephen, ed.

Clive Barker's A-Z of Horror. *New York: HarperPrism, 1997. 256p. ISBN 0061052779.*

>One of the masters of horror, Clive Barker takes readers on an encyclopedic tour of the genre. This book is based on a BBC television series that inspired the <u>Arts and Entertainment</u> series.

Ⓑ Jones, Stephen, and Kim Newman, eds.

Horror: 100 Best Books. *New York Carroll & Graf, 1998. 224p. ISBN 0881844179.*

>This is a reissue of a Bram Stoker Award–winning survey of horror scholarship.

Horror: Another 100 Best Books. *New York: Carroll & Graf, 2005. 456p. ISBN 0786715774.*

>Popular genre authors such as Poppy Z. Brite, Tananarive Due, Ellen Datlow, and S. T. Joshi identify their favorite texts in the genre, with an emphasis on the fluidity of horror's boundaries. This is a continuation of Jones's and Newman's *Horror: The Best 100 Books* (Carroll & Graf, 1998).

Joshi, S. T., ed.

Icons of Horror and the Supernatural: An Encyclopedia of Our Worst Nightmares. *2 vols. Westport, CT: Greenwood, 2007. 407p. ISBN 0313337810 (v.*

>1); 389p. ISBN 0313337829 (v.

>2). Scholars and casual fans alike will appreciate these variously penned, extended essays on twenty-four horror icons, from the alien, to the ghost, to the haunted house, to the zombie, to the doppelganger, and many others. Each essay examines the history of its subject and traces its evolution in various formats, including literature, film, comics, and science.

Supernatural Literature of the World: An Encyclopedia. *Westport, CT: Greenwood Press, 2005. 443p. ISBN 0313327750 (v. 1); 436p. ISBN 0313327769 (v. 2); 544p. ISBN 0313327777 (v.*

>3). An indispensable resource, this three-volume set contains entries of varying length with information about writers, monster types, themes, and trends in the horror genre.

Mulvey-Roberts, Marie, ed.

The Handbook to Gothic Literature. *Washington Square, NY: New York University Press, 1998. 294p. ISBN 0814756093.*

>Mulvey-Roberts writes an academic, encyclopedic treatment of gothic literature, from Brontë to Melville.

Quigley, Christine.

The Corpse: A History. *Jefferson, NC: McFarland Publishing. 2005. 358p. ISBN 0786401702.*

11

This book attempts to do for the corpse what Mary Roach did for the human cadaver in *Stiff: The Curious Life of Human Cadavers* (2003). Quigley takes on topics as diverse as the representation of corpses in art and photography, the embalming of the corpse, the treatment of organ donors, the use of autopsies, and even occurrences of cannibalism.

12

Reference Works Dealing with Horror Subgenres

Maniacs

13

Evans, Stewart P., and Keith Skinner, eds.

The Ultimate Jack the Ripper Companion: An Illustrated Encyclopedia. *New York: Carroll & Graf, 2001. 758p. ISBN 078670926X.*

14

The next best thing to squatting amid Scotland Yard's dusty files yourself, this collection of police and autopsy reports, witness statements, letters, newspaper stories, and sometimes gory photos presents the primary sources, including thirty-two plates of illustrations, without interpretation.

15

Newton, Michael.

The Encyclopedia of Serial Killers. *New York: Facts on File, 2006, ©1999. 515p. ISBN 0816061955.*

16

Newton's encyclopedia is a fairly comprehensive reference source about hundreds of nineteenth- and twentieth-century serial killers. It includes appendixes of solo killers, team killers, and unsolved serial killer homicides.

17

Vampires

Bunson, Matthew.

The Vampire Encyclopedia. *New York: Gramercy Books, 2000, ©1993. 303p. ISBN 0517162067.*

18

This is an excellent, illustrated source of vampire lore and beliefs.

Melton, J. Gordon.

19

The Vampire Book: The Encyclopedia of the Undead. 2nd ed. *Detroit: Visible Ink Press, 1998. 919p. ISBN 157859071X.*

Gordon produces this artistic encyclopedia of literary and historical vampires, including notes on history, folklore, and societies.

20

The Vampire Gallery: A Who's Who of the Undead. *Detroit: Visible Ink Press, 1998. 500p. ISBN 1578590531.*

> Melton covers the spectrum of vampirism, from terminology, to geography, to organizations, to literary characters.

Reference Works about Horror Authors

General Author Reference

Ashley, Mike.

Who's Who in Horror and Fantasy Fiction. *New York: Taplinger, 1978, ©1977. 240p. ISBN 080088275X.*

> Ashley collects an impressive, alphabetical list of important horror writers, with a brief biography and bibliography of each.

Bloom, Clive, ed.

Gothic Horror: A Guide for Students and Readers. *Basingstroke, UK: Palgrave Macmillan, 2007. 311p. ISBN 9780230001770.*

> Bloom has assembled an essential guide to gothic criticism, covering everything from *Frankenstein* and *Dracula* to <u>The Silence of the Lambs Trilogy</u> and *Alien Invasion*.

Gothic Horror: A Reader's Guide from Poe to King and the Beyond. *New York: St. Martin's Press, 1998. 301p. ISBN 0312212380.*

> This guide contains excerpts of writings by psychologists and well-known horror critics, who comment on the genre.

Etchison, Dennis, ed.

The St. James Guide to Horror, Ghost and Gothic Writers. *Detroit: St. James-Gale, 1998. 746p. ISBN 1558622063.*

> Etchison collects bio-bibliographic information on ghost stories, gothic literature, and horror.

Wiater, Stanley.

 **Dark Thoughts on Writing: Advice and Commentary from Fifty Masters of Fear and Suspense.** *Grass Valley, CA: Underwood Books, 1997. 206p. ISBN 188742430X.*

> Based on interviews with fifty horror writers, Wiater presents a text that examines why writers of horror enjoy the genre, where they get their ideas, and how they deal with censorship.

Reference Works on Individual Authors

Robert Aickman

Crawford, Gary William.

Robert Aickman: An Introduction. *Baton Rouge, LA: Gothic Press, 2003. 76p. ISBN 0913045101.*

> This brief text is a condensed biographical, critical, and bibliographical examination of Robert Aickman that draws on firsthand research conducted over the past twenty years. The author works from information gained by contacting Aickman's closest colleagues and creates a portrait of a complex and enigmatic figure. Most of Crawford's book, however, is critical in nature.

M. R. James

Joshi, S. T., and Rosemary Pardoe, eds.

Warnings to the Curious: A Sheaf of Criticism on M. R. James. *New York: Hippocampus Press, 2007. 338p. ISBN 0977173488.*

> Dedicated to the ghost stories of M. R. James, this volume of scholarly criticism, written in highly accessible language, looks at biography, influences, thematic concerns, and interpretations of the tales. The essays include an excerpt from H. P. Lovecraft.

Dean Koontz

Greenberg, Martin, ed.

The Dean Koontz Companion. *New York: Berkley Books, 1994. 312p. ISBN 0425141357.*

> This first-ever look at Koontz and his career includes an exclusive interview, his first published short story, a complete annotated guide to his work, and more.

H. P. Lovecraft

Joshi, S. T., ed.

Sixty Years of Arkham House: A History and Bibliography. *Sauk City, WI: Arkham House, 1999. 218p. ISBN 0870541765.*

> Joshi's bibliography continues August Derleth's *Thirty Years of Arkham House* (1970), by cataloging Arkham House's publications. Joshi also includes brief notes and indexes of authors and titles.

Lovecraft, H. P.

Collected Essays. *5 vols. S. T. Joshi, ed. New York: Hippocampus Press, 2004–2006. 440p. ISBN 0972164421 (v. 1); 350p. ISBN 0972164499 (v. 2); 357p. ISBN 0974878979 (v. 3); 300p. ISBN 097615921X (v. 4); 382p. ISBN 0976159228 (v. 5).*

This impressive collection of Lovecraft's essays includes five sections: "Amateur Journalism"; "Literary Criticism"; "Science, Travel, and Philosophy"; "Autobiography"; and "Miscellany." All volumes are wonderfully annotated by noted Lovecraft scholar Joshi.

Edgar Allan Poe

Smith, Don G.

The Poe Cinema: A Critical Filmography of Theatrical Releases Based on the Works of Edgar Allan Poe. *Jefferson, NC: McFarland Publishing, 2003, ©1999. 315p. ISBN 078641703X.*

> Smith collects these lists of credits, casts, story summaries, and production and marketing techniques for films based on the works of Edgar Allan Poe made from 1908 to 1992. The text includes films from various countries, and each entry contains a brief critique section.

Sova, Dawn B.

Edgar Allan Poe, A to Z: The Essential Reference to His Life and Work. *New York: Facts on File, 2001. 310p. ISBN 0816038503.*

> Sova collects information on Poe's life and literary works and categorizes them as encyclopedia entries. She also includes a Poe timeline, a chronology of his works, and a listing of Poe research collections.

Mary Shelley

Wilt, Judith, ed.

Making Humans: Complete Texts with Introduction, Historical Contexts, Critical Essays. *Boston: Houghton Mifflin, 2003. 359p. ISBN 0618084894.*

> This critical edition of Mary Shelley's *Frankenstein* and H. G. Wells's *The Island of Dr. Moreau* provides a rare opportunity to explore commonalities of both texts, such as natural sciences in the nineteenth century.

Clark Ashton Smith

Smith, Clark Ashton.

Selected Letters of Clark Ashton Smith. *Edited by David E. Schultz and Scott Connors. Sauk City, WI: Arkham House, 2003. xxvii, 417p. ISBN 087054182X.*

> Smith's letters are revelatory and engaging, and this text is particularly useful because only small scraps of his correspondence have so far appeared. Included are letters to the California poet George Sterling, as well as later correspondence with August Derleth and Donald Wandrei.

Peter Straub

Collings, Michael R.

Hauntings: The Official Peter Straub Bibliography. *Woodstock, GA: Overlook Connection Press, 1999. 193p. ISBN 1892950154.*

> This is the first volume documenting and collecting Peter Straub's work for the last thirty years. It includes an interview with Straub.

Straub, Peter.

Sides. *Baltimore, MD: Cemetery Dance Publications, 2007. 310p. ISBN 1587671654.*

> This is Straub's first collection of nonfiction, including twenty years of introductions, afterwords, and essays, as well as a series of short editorials by the author's alter ego, fictional literary critic Putney Tyson Ridge. Also included is "The Fantasy of Everyday Life," Straub's speech at the 1998 International Conference of the Fantastic in the Arts (ICFA).

Bram Stoker

Joslin, Lyndon W.

Count Dracula Goes to the Movies: Stoker's Novel Adapted, 1922–1995. 2nd ed. *Jefferson, NC: McFarland Publishing, 2006, ©1999. 272p. ISBN 0786426012.*

> Joslin pens this complete guide to eleven films based on Stoker's classic tale of horror. This expanded edition includes complete cast and credit information for the Universal and Hammer studios films, as well as information for the "Shadow Stoker" films, or ones that are indebted to Stoker's *Dracula,* although they do not actually cite his novel as their source.

Horror Film and Television Reference and Resources

Atkins, Rick.

Let's Scare 'Em: Grand Interviews and a Filmography of Horrific Proportions, 1930–1961. *Jefferson, NC: McFarland Publishing, 1997. 250p. ISBN 078640373X.*

> Atkins documents and illustrates the suspension of disbelief and audience manipulation employed over these three decades of horror, fantasy, and monster movies. He includes photographs, interviews, and a filmography of 251 of the best-known (and some not-so-well-known) releases.

Brunas, Michael, John Brunas, and Tom Weaver.

Universal Horrors: The Studio's Classic Films, 1931–1946. 2nd ed. *Jefferson, NC: McFarland Publishing, 2007, ©1990. 608p. ISBN 97807864297.*

> Brunas's work is the definitive study of the eighty-five horror films produced by Universal Studios between 1931 and 1946. It is generously illustrated and includes complete cast lists, credits, storylines, behind-the-scenes information, production history, commentary from the cast and crew, and in-depth critical analysis.

Dendle, Peter.

The Zombie Movie Encyclopedia. *Jefferson, NC: McFarland Publishing, 2001. 249p. ISBN 0786408596.*

> Dendle's publication is an exhaustive overview of over 200 zombie movies from sixteen countries, spanning approximately sixty-five years..

Fischer, Dennis.

Horror Film Directors, 1931–1990. *Jefferson, NC: McFarland Publishing, 1991. 877p. ISBN 0899506097.*

> Fischer offers a lengthy and exhaustive study of the major direction of horror films in the past six decades. Each entry includes a complete filmography, including television work, a career summary, critical assessment, and behind-the-scenes production information.

Flynn, John L.

Cinematic Vampires: The Living Dead on Film and Television, from *The Devil's Castle* **(1896) to** *Bram Stoker's Dracula* **(1992).** *Jefferson, NC: McFarland Publishing, 1992. 320p. ISBN 0899506593.*

> Flynn pens a complete look at 372 vampire films, including alternate titles and original titles of non-English films.

Grams, Martin, and Patrik Wikstrom.

The *Alfred Hitchcock Presents* **Companion.** *Arlington, VA: OTR Publishing, 2001. 660p. ISBN 0970331010.*

> The bulk of this text serves as a guide to the Hitchcock television series, discussing everything from spoofs and comic books to movies, followed by a list of Hitchcock collectibles: board games, sheet music, LP albums, soap, and videos. The book also contains an episode guide to the television series *Alfred Hitchcock Presents* and *The Alfred Hitchcock Hour.*

Grams, Martin, Jr.

The *I Love a Mystery* Companion. *Churchville, MD: OTR Publishing, 2003. 391p. ISBN 0970331053.*

> This is wonderful entertainment even for those readers who have no earthly idea what the radio program was about; for those who fondly remember *I Love a Mystery*, this book is pure gold. Grams features quotes and stories from cast and crew, including some recognizable names like Tony Randall.

Holston, Kim R., and Tom Winchester.

Science Fiction, Fantasy and Horror Film Sequels, Series and Remakes: An Illustrated Filmography, with Plot Synopses and Critical Commentary. *Jefferson, NC: McFarland Publishing, 1997. 601p. ISBN 0786401559.*

> Holston and Winchester analyze more than 400 horror, science fiction, and fantasy films in this comprehensive reference to the genre's sequels, series, and remakes.

Kinnard, Roy.

Horror in Silent Films: A Filmography, 1896–1929. *Jefferson, NC: McFarland Publishing, 1999. 278p. ISBN 0786400366.*

> This filmography includes all silent films that were horrific in nature or contained one or more of the stock movie elements. Annotations include release date, running time, cast, and credits, and in the case of foreign films, the original title and country of origin.

Mayo, Mike.

VideoHound's Horror Show: 999 Hair-Raising, Hellish, and Humorous Movies. *Detroit: Gale-Visible Ink, 1998. 524p. ISBN 1578590477.*

> Mayo's lengthy tome is a large catalog of horror and suspense films, with a brief annotation of each.

Ostow, Micol, and Steven Brezenoff.

The Quotable Slayer. *New York: Simon Pulse, 2003. 202p. ISBN 0743410173.*
> Fans of the series' wordplay will love this collection of the funniest and most memorable quotes in the genre, divided into sections devoted to The Quotable Slayer, The Quotable Watcher, The Quotable Scoobies, Quotable Other People, Quotable Music, and The Quotable Finale.

Senn, Bryan, and John Johnson.

Fantastic Cinema Subject Guide: A Topical Index to 2,500 Horror, Science Fiction, and Fantasy Films. *Jefferson, NC: McFarland Publishing, 2007, ©1992. 682p. ISBN 9780786437665.*
> Senn and Johnson annotate over 2,500 genre films, providing year of release, distribution company, country of origin, producer, screenwriter, cinematographer, cast credits, plot synopsis, and critical commentary.

Silver, Alain, and James Ursini.

Roger Corman: Metaphysics on a Shoestring. *Los Angeles: Silman-James Press, 2006. 323p. ISBN 1879505428.*

> The authors argue that Corman may be one of the most influential filmmakers of all time, having directed and produced more than 200 films, and having helped jumpstart the directorial careers of award winners Francis Ford Coppola and Jonathan Demme. This filmography is filled with solid research, insightful film criticism and interpretation, and revealing interview answers.

Topping, Keith.

A Vault of Horror: A Book of 80 Great British Horror Movies from 1956–1974. *Tolworth, Surrey, UK: Telos, 2004. 427p. ISBN 1903889588.*

> This collection of thoughts and little-known facts about eighty horror movies includes well-known titles such as *Dracula, Village of the Damned, The Haunting,* and *The Wicker Man,* as well as little-known gems, like *Quartermass and the Pit, Dr. Phibes Rides Again,* and *Captain Kronos: Vampire Hunter.* The typical entry contains the following information: movie title, time, format (color versus black and white, for example), producer, writer, director, a full cast listing, the tagline, a plot summary, thematic concerns, trivia (such as sinister animals, ephemera, "outrageous methods of dispatch," etc.), alternate versions, quotes, and reviews.

Zicree, Mark Scott.

The *Twilight Zone* Companion. 2nd ed. *Beverly Hills, CA: Silman-James, 1992, ©1982. 466p. ISBN 1879505096.*

> This homage to one of the greats will sit well with the millions of fans whose imaginations were broadened by years of exposure to the "what if" scenarios of Serling, Charles Beaumont, and Richard Matheson. Zicree spent five years researching and writing to produce the definitive book on the series. It is difficult to imagine watching a *Twilight Zone* episode without this guide.

Writing Guides

Castle, Mort.

On Writing Horror: A Handbook. *Cincinnati, OH: Writer's Digest Books, 2007, ©1997. 260p. ISBN 1582974209.*

> A published writer himself, Castle creates a "how-to" book on writing horror, including examples of tales and interviews with writers. This edition has been expanded.

Nolan, William F.

How to Write Horror Fiction. *Cincinnati, OH: Writer's Digest Books, 1991. 143p. ISBN 0898794420.*

> Nolan discusses writing horror, from the idea stage to the production process.

Williamson, J. N., ed.

How to Write Tales of Horror, Fantasy and Science Fiction. *Cincinnati, OH: Writer's Digest Books, 1991, ©1987. 242p. ISBN 0898794838.*
> Williamson reprints excerpts from essays on writing by Robert Bloch, Ray Bradbury, Dean Koontz, Charles Grant, Robert McCammon, Ramsey Campbell, Richard Christian Matheson, Douglas Winter, and himself.

History and Criticism

Certainly one of the most noticeable trends in the horror genre has been its gradual acceptance into the university curriculum, which indicates that more and more readers are beginning to realize how important the genre is as a cultural barometer. More professors and instructors of literature, gender studies, and sociology are beginning to understand how Stephen King's *Carrie* chronicles male fears of female sexuality in the 1970s, or how Bret Easton Ellis's *American Psycho* parodies the "greed is good" mindset of the 1980s. Even literary scholars find themselves becoming interested in the evolution of particular thematic concerns in horror. For example, one could trace the evolving manifestations of the zombie through texts such as the film *White Zombie*, H. P. Lovecraft's *Herbert West, Re-Animator*, Richard Matheson's *I Am Legend*, George Romero's <u>Night of the Living Dead Series</u>, up to Max Brooks's *World War Z* and David Wellington's <u>Monster Nation Trilogy</u> and the film *28 Days Later*. This trajectory reveals the anxieties of Western civilization, particularly American society, contemporary to each writer or director.

Moreover, university students flock to the horror classes of these professors as quickly as they are offered. At Louisiana State University back in the 1990s, when we team taught courses in horror fiction and vampire fiction, classes would fill up in two hours or less (which is record time), and we often ended up with standing room only. The trend continues; when June offers her zombie literature course each Christmas break during the winter session, honors students are quick to register, as they particularly enjoy the chance to seriously study works they had previously read or watched for pleasure. The reserve reading materials for these classes always consisted of works concerned with the history of the genre and with critical interpretation of its most historically famous texts. These secondary sources are included in this edition of *Hooked on Horror* for the same reason that we included them in our course descriptions: they help readers better understand and appreciate horror. In general, the works in this chapter reflect the differing interests we noted among the critics of the genre. Various studies examine the nature of horror itself, or why it appeals to the human emotions, as do Stephen King's *Danse Macabre*, James Twitchell's *Dreadful Pleasures*, William Patrick Day's *In the Circle of Fear and Desire*, and Terry Heller's *The Delights of Terror: An Aesthetics of the Tale of Terror*. Other texts seem more concerned with what horror fiction has to say about the societies in which we live, or in which our ancestors lived. Studies such as David Punter's *The Literature of Terror*, Nina Auerbach's *Woman and the Demon* and *Our Vampires, Ourselves*, Carol J. Clover's *Men, Women and Chainsaws*, Teresa

Goddu's *Gothic America*, and Kelly Hurley's *The Gothic Body* speak to us of our cultural fears and desires.

However, to view horror scholars as merely social or historical critics would be a great oversimplification. Many writers who are, for want of a better term, aficionados of horror literature, publish simply to share their love of the genre and to impart their individual insights concerning its value as an excellent storytelling device. Jack Sullivan's *Elegant Nightmares*, S. T. Joshi's *The Weird Tale*, and Tony Magistrale's and Michael Morrison's *A Dark Night's Dreaming* are excellent examples of texts that not only analyze what horror literature has to say, but show an appreciation for how horror literature delights its fans in saying it.

History and Criticism about the Genre in General

Aguirre, Manuel.

The Closed Space: Horror Literature and Western Symbolism. *Manchester, UK: Manchester University Press, 1990. 234p. ISBN 0719032075.*
> Aguirre is known for his psychological/sociological theories of horror and horror symbolism, as seen in this monograph.

Andriano, Joseph.

Our Ladies of Darkness: Feminine Daemonology in Male Gothic Fiction. *University Park: Pennsylvania State University Press, 1993. 182p. ISBN 0271008709.*
> Andriano presents psychological theories on Otherness and the feminine in gothic/horror fiction.

Botting, Fred.

The Gothic. *New York: Routledge, 1996. 201p. ISBN 0415132290.*
> Botting explains the fundamental premise of gothic literature and defines its parameters.

Day, William Patrick.

In the Circles of Fear and Desire: A Study of Gothic Fantasy. *Chicago: University of Chicago Press, 1985. 201p. ISBN 0226138909.*
> In this benchmark work, Day analyzes the attraction/repulsion reaction to horror.

Halberstam, Judith.

Skin Shows: Gothic Horror and the Technology of Monsters. *Durham, NC: Duke University Press, 1995. 215p. ISBN 082231651X.*
> Halberstam presents a comprehensive view of the gothic revival in England, chronicling the roles of monsters in British film and literature.

Heller, Terry.

The Delights of Terror: An Aesthetics of the Tale of Terror. *Urbana, IL: University of Chicago Press, 1987. 218p. ISBN 025201412X.*

11

>In this excellent study, Heller analyzes the appeal of horror to the reader or viewer.

Jancovich, Mark.

12

Horror. *London: Bansford, 1992. 128p. ISBN 0713468203.*

>Jancovich produces a brief but informative beginner's guide to the study of horror.

13

Horror: The Film Reader. *London: Routledge, 2002. 188p. ISBN 0415235618.*

>This comprehensive resource for students of horror film explores central issues and critical debates in horror film, ranging from *The Cabinet of Dr. Caligari* to *The Blair Witch Project.*

14

Rational Fears: American Horror in the 1950s. *Manchester, UK: Manchester University Press, 1996. 324p. ISBN 0719036232.*

>Jancovich's study of American horror cinema in the 1950s links it to novels and comics.

15

Jones, Darryl.

HORROR: A Thematic History in Fiction and Film. *London. Arnold Publishing-Oxford University Press, 2002. 220p. ISBN 0340762527.*

16

>If you love horror and are serious about wanting to gain a better understanding of the genre, consider this highly entertaining, scholarly thematic history that declares *The Texas Chain Saw Massacre* to be the greatest of all modern horror movies.

Joshi, S. T.

17

The Modern Weird Tale. *Jefferson City, NC: McFarland, 2001. 278p. ISBN 078640986X.*

>Joshi presents this critical study of many of the leading writers of horror and supernatural fiction since World War II.

18

Kendrick, Walter M.

The Thrill of Fear: 250 Years of Scary Entertainment. *New York: Grove-Weidenfield, 1991. 292p. ISBN 0802111629.*

19

>Kendrick pens this popular study of English and American horror tales and films.

20

King, Stephen.

Stephen King's Danse Macabre. *New York: Berkley Books, 2001, ©1981. 400p. ISBN 042518160X.*

> King discusses many books and movies that were not exactly on Main Street USA's radar, but were successful to some degree. In addition, he posits his personal theory of the psychology of horror, as well as its origins, arguing that all modern horror stories stem from three writers of supernatural literature—Bram Stoker, Mary Shelley, and Robert Louis Stevenson.

Leonard, Elisabeth Anne, ed.

Into Darkness Peering: Race and Color in the Fantastic. *Westport, CT: Greenwood, 1997. 198p. ISBN 0313300429.*

> Leonard collects essays about race in horror, science fiction, and fantasy.

Lovecraft, H. P.

The Annotated Supernatural Horror in Literature. *Edited by S. T. Joshi. New York: Hippocampus Press, 2000. 182p. ISBN 0967321506.*

> Joshi edits the definitive edition of H. P. Lovecraft's extended essay tracing horror fiction from its earliest (biblical) manifestations to the modern masters of the 1930s. Lovecraft's discussions of specific works are fairly extensive, and Joshi's notes make this an indispensable tool for any scholar of the genre.

Magistrale, Tony, and Michael A. Morrison.

A Dark Night's Dreaming: Contemporary American Horror Fiction. *Columbia: University of South Carolina Press, 1996. 141p. ISBN 1570030707.*

> This is part of the <u>Understanding Contemporary American Literature</u> series dealing with history and criticism in the genre.

Prince, Stephen, ed.

The Horror Film. *New Brunswick, NJ: Rutgers University Press, 2004. 272p. ISBN 0813533627.*

> This collection of essays by noted horror scholars explores various themes in the genre.

Punter, David, and Glennis Byron.

The Gothic. *Malden, MA: Blackwell Publishing, 2004. 315p. ISBN 0631220623.*

> Punter and Byron's study of the gothic provides a comprehensive overview of the genre for students and scholars alike.

Skal, David J.

The Monster Show: A Cultural History of Horror. *New York: Norton, 1993. 432p. ISBN 0393034194.*

> Skal studies horror film and fiction, from the early Universal Studios horror flicks to Stephen King and beyond.

Sullivan, Jack.

Elegant Nightmares: The English Ghost Story from Le Fanu to Blackwood. *Athens, OH: Ohio University Press, 1978. 155p. ISBN 0821403745.*

> Sullivan takes a general look at horror in this nice, basic text for the uninitiated fan interested in horror criticism.

Tropp, Martin.

Images of Fear: How Horror Stories Helped Shape Modern Culture (1818–1918). *Jefferson, NC: McFarland Publishing, 1990. 235p. ISBN 0899505139.*

> Tropp examines how before the actual horror of World War I, many of the fears we still face came from the pages of popular fiction, such as *Frankenstein* and *Dr. Jekyll and Mr. Hyde.*

Twitchell, James. B.

Dreadful Pleasures: An Anatomy of Modern Horror. *Oxford: Oxford University Press, 1988, ©1985. 353p. ISBN 0195050673.*

> Twitchell analyzes the appeal of horror fiction and film.

Criticism of Horror Classics

Auerbach, Nina.

Woman and the Demon: The Life of a Victorian Myth. *Cambridge, MA: Harvard University Press, 1982. 255p. ISBN 0674954068.*

> Auerbach studies the relationship between women and monsters in Victorian gothic/horror fiction.

Bayer-Berenbaum, Linda.

The Gothic Imagination: Expansion in Gothic Literature and Art. *London: Associated University Press, 1982. 155p. ISBN 0838630685.*

> In this classic, Bayer-Berenbaum writes about the psychology behind gothic literature and about writer motivation.

Briggs, Julia.

Night Visitors: The Rise of the English Ghost Story. *London: Faber, 1977. 238p. ISBN 0571111130.*

> Brigg's emphasis is on the traditional ghost tale à la M. R. James, with an argument that the subgenre is dead.

DeLamotte, Eugenia C.

Perils of the Night: A Feminist Study of Nineteenth-Century Gothic. *Oxford: Oxford University Press, 1990. 352p. ISBN 0195056930.*

> DeLamotte presents a feminist study of Victorian gothicism.

Punter, David.

The Literature of Terror: A History of Gothic Fiction from 1765 to the Present Day. *New York: Longman, 1996, ©1980. 234p. ISBN 0582237149.*

> This is one of the benchmark studies of horror fiction; it elaborates on English and American horror.

Horror Themes/Motifs and Subgenres

Ghosts

Kovacs, Lee.

The Haunted Screen: Ghosts in Literature and Film. *Jefferson, NC: McFarland Publishing, 2005, ©1999. 183p. ISBN 0786426055.*

> The literature-based ghost films of the 1930s and 1940s provide the underpinnings for many of the gentle supernatural films of the 1990s. The following are examined in this monograph: *Wuthering Heights, The Ghost and Mrs. Muir, Portrait of Jennie, Letter from an Unknown Woman, The Uninvited, Liliom, Our Town, Ghost,* and *Truly, Madly, Deeply.*

Golem (Mummies)

Cowie, Susan D., and Tom Johnson.

The Mummy in Fact, Fiction and Film. *Jefferson, NC: McFarland Publishing, 2007, ©2001. 202p. ISBN 9780786431144.*

> This text compares the religious, social, and scientific aspects of mummies to how they are portrayed in fiction and movies.

Maniacs

Coville, Gary, and Patrick Lucanio.

Jack the Ripper: His Life and Crimes in Popular Entertainment. *Jefferson, NC: McFarland Publishing, 2008, ©1999. 193p. ISBN 0786440457.*

> Coville and Lucanio survey the literary, filmic, television, and radio treatments of Jack the Ripper and his crimes.

Gordon, R. Michael.

Alias Jack the Ripper: Beyond the Usual Whitechapel Suspects. *Jefferson, NC: McFarland Publishing, 2001. 353p. ISBN 0786408987.*

> Gordon takes a comprehensive look at the crimes and the case evidence, with a discussion of the life of the man Gordon believes was the actual killer.

Larson, Erik.

The Devil in the White City: Murder, Magic and Madness at the Fair That Changed America. *New York: Crown, 2004. 447p. ISBN 0609608444.*

> Larson's work of nonfiction juxtaposes the opening of the 1893 World's Fair in Chicago with serial murderer H. H. Holmes.

Vampires

Auerbach, Nina.

Our Vampires, Ourselves. *Chicago: University of Chicago Press, 1995. 231p. ISBN 0226032019.*

> Auerbach notes the cultural significance of vampirism, from Dracula to Lestat.

Barber, Paul.

Vampires, Burial and Death: Folklore and Reality. *New Haven, CT: Yale University Press, 1988. 236p. ISBN 0300041268.*

> Barber writes an ethnographic/folkloric examination of mainly Eastern European vampire mythology. This monograph is a favorite among vampire fans.

Gordon, Joan, and Veronica Hollinger, eds.

Blood Read: The Vampire as Metaphor in Contemporary Culture. *Philadelphia: University of Pennsylvania Press, 1997. 264p. ISBN 0812234197.*

> Readable essays on post-1970s vampires cover fiction and film.

Heldreth, Leonard G. and Mary Pharr

The Blood Is the Life: Vampires in Literature. *Bowling Green, OH: Bowling Green State University Popular Press, 1999. 275p. ISBN 0879728035.*

> Heldreth and Pharr collect nineteen essays concerned with literary vampires, from Polidori's "The Vampyre" to Nancy A. Collins's <u>Sonja Blue Series</u>.

McNally, Raymond T., and Radu Florescu.

In Search of Dracula: The History of Dracula and Vampires. *Boston: Houghton, Mifflin, 1994, ©1973. 297p. ISBN 0395657830.*

> This is one of the first books to examine the history and folklore of fifteenth-century Romanian berserker Vlad Tepes, thought to be the historical basis for Dracula by some scholars, and the source of folklore about vampires in general. It includes a filmography, an appendix of folk stories about Tepes, a bibliography of vampire fiction and nonfiction sources about Tepes and vampires, and a travel guide to Dracula-related places in Romania and the United Kingdom.

Witches

Summers, Montague

The History of Witchcraft and Demonology. *New York: Citadel Press, 1994, ©1926. 353p. ISBN 0806514523.*

> This reissue of one of the most important analyses of the development, spread, persecution, and survival of witchcraft was written by a Catholic priest. The author is considered one of the leading scholars of witchcraft, vampirism, and satanism. Extremely important historically, the text is fairly well-written in reasoned, erudite language.

Criticism of Horror Authors

Clive Barker

Hoppenstand, Gary.

Clive Barker's Short Stories: Imagination as Metaphor in The Books of Blood and Other Works. *Jefferson, NC: McFarland Publishing, 1994. 223p. ISBN 0899509843.*

> Hoppenstand pens a detailed study of significant themes in Barker's writing, placing him in the British gothic tradition of Marlowe, Saki, and others.

Ramsey Campbell

Joshi, S. T.

Ramsey Campbell and Modern Horror Fiction. *Liverpool, UK: Liverpool University Press, 2001. 180p. ISBN 0853237654.*

> One of the premier scholars in the genre traces the career of arguably the best writer in horror today, Ramsey Campbell, from his early Lovecraftian stories to his novels of modern psychological horror.

Stephen King

Bloom, Harold, ed.

Stephen King. *New York: Chelsea House, 2007, ©1998. 228p. ISBN 0791093174.*

> Bloom collects essays on the history and criticism of horror, with emphasis on placing the fiction of Stephen King.

Russell, Sharon A.

Stephen King: A Critical Companion. *Westport, CT: Greenwood Press, 1996. 171p. ISBN 0313294178.*

> Russell discusses the history and criticism of American horror, with an emphasis on King.

Spignesi, Stephen J.

Lost Work of Stephen King: A Guide to Unpublished Manuscripts, Story Fragments, Alternate Versions and Oddities. *New York: Citadel, 2002, ©1998. 361p. ISBN 0806523905.*

Spignesi guides readers through King's unpublished works.

Underwood, Tim, and Chuck Miller, eds.

Fear Itself: The Early Works of Stephen King. *San Francisco: Underwood Miller, 1993. 239p. ISBN 0887331742.*

Underwood and Miller examine King's early novels. This critical work includes an introduction by author Peter Straub and an afterword by filmmaker George Romero.

Dean Koontz

Kotker, Joan G.

Dean Koontz: A Critical Companion. *Westport, CT: Greenwood, 1996. 184p. ISBN 031329528X.*

Kotker discusses American horror, with emphasis on Koontz.

Ramsland, Katherine.

Dean Koontz: A Writer's Biography. *New York: HarperPrism, 1997. 508p. ISBN 006105271X.*

Ramsland pens this illustrated biography of one of America's most famous horror writers.

Richard Laymon

Laymon, Richard.

A Writer's Tale. *Apache Junction, AZ: Deadline Press, 1998. 348p. ISBN 0963136771.*

This autobiographical chronicle takes readers behind the scenes in the life of a dedicated artist, one who, despite often sizeable odds, persisted to become one of the best-selling horror writers in England and around the world.

Joseph Sheridan Le Fanu

Walton, James.

Vision and Vacancy: The Fictions of J. S. Le Fanu. *Dublin: University College Dublin Press, 2007. 229p. ISBN 1904558798.*

Walton examines the lesser known tales of Le Fanu, as well as the often studied ones, concentrating on the author's use of visual stimuli in his short stories and novellas.

H. P. Lovecraft

Joshi, S. T.

The Annotated H. P. Lovecraft. *New York: Dell, 1997. 360p. ISBN 0440506603.*
> Joshi, an acclaimed Lovecraft scholar and coeditor of *Necrofile: The Review of Horror Fiction*, annotates the works of Lovecraft.

Schweitzer, Darrell.

Discovering H. P. Lovecraft. *Holicong, PA: Wildside Press, 2001, ©1987. 163p. ISBN 1587154706.*
> Schweitzer collects essays on the fiction of H. P. Lovecraft.

Edgar Allan Poe

Carlson, Eric W., ed.

A Companion to Poe Studies. *Westport, CT: Greenwood, 1996. 604p. ISBN 0313265062.*
> Carlson's lengthy study of Poe's detective and horror fiction also includes bibliographical references.

Kennedy, J. Gerald, and Liliane Weissberg, eds.

Romancing the Shadow: Poe and Race. *Oxford: Oxford University Press, 2001. 292p. ISBN 0195137108.*
> Collection of essays about Poe and race.

Anne Rice

Hoppenstand, Gary, and Ray B. Browne, eds.

The Gothic World of Anne Rice. *Bowling Green, OH: Popular Press, 1996. 261p. ISBN 0879727071.*
> The editors have gathered fifteen essays on Anne Rice's novels, including an essay by Katherine Ramsland, one of Rice's biographers.

Keller, James R., ed.

Anne Rice and Sexual Politics: The Early Novels. *Jefferson, NC: McFarland Publishing, 2000. 175p. ISBN 0786408464.*
> Keller collects diverse essays about Rice's *Interview with the Vampire, The Feast of All Saints, Cry to Heaven*, the <u>Sleeping Beauty Series</u>, *Exit to Eden*, and the <u>Mayfair Witch Series</u>.

Ramsland, Katherine.

The Anne Rice Reader. *New York: Ballantine, 1997. 359p. ISBN 0345402677.*
> Ramsland writes this popular criticism and interpretation of American's top vampire fiction writer.

11

Smith, Jennifer.

Anne Rice: A Critical Companion. *Westport, CT: Greenwood, 1996. 193p. ISBN 031329612X.*
> Smith writes criticism and interpretation of Rice, with emphasis on her use of witchcraft, mummies, women, and vampires.

12

13

Robert Louis Stevenson

Nollen, Scott Allen.

Robert Louis Stevenson: Life, Literature and the Silver Screen. *Jefferson, NC: McFarland Publishing, 1994. 468p. ISBN 0899507883.*
> Nollen examines the film adaptations of Stevenson's work.

14

Bram Stoker

15

Belford, Barbara.

Bram Stoker: A Biography of the Author of Dracula. *Cambridge, MA: Da Capo Press, 2002, ©1996. 381p. ISBN 0306810980.*
> Belford collects biographical information about and criticism on Bram Stoker, with emphasis on his theatrical ties.

16

Glover, David.

Vampires, Mummies and Liberals: Bram Stoker and the Politics of Popular Fiction. *Durham, NC: Duke University Press, 1996. 212p. ISBN 0822318032.*
> Glover analyzes what vampires, mummies, and eroticism reflected about the popular culture of nineteenth- and twentieth-century England.

17

18

Hughes, William.

Beyond *Dracula*: Bram Stoker's Fiction and Its Cultural Context. *New York: St. Martin's Press, 2000. 216p. ISBN 0312231369.*
> Hughes uses cultural and sociological theories to analyze Bram Stoker's fiction other than *Dracula*, with emphasis on his treatment of race, religion, and society.

19

Leatherdale, Clive,, ed.

Bram Stoker's *Dracula* Unearthed. *Westcliff-on-Sea, Essex, UK: Desert Island Books, 1998. 512p. ISBN 1874287120.*

20

Particularly interesting about Leatherdale's edition of this classic novel are the co-pious notes that accompany virtually every page of text. A *Dracula* scholar him-self, Leatherdale makes the work more interesting by informing the reader of how certain details and scenes changed between drafts, and to what effect; how partic-ular passages are often interpreted; what areas specific place-names refer to, and whether these areas are real or fictional; what information is known about various ethnic groups and their religious beliefs (which are important in this text); and sometimes how he himself teaches specific scenes.

Miller, Elizabeth, and Clive Leatherdale.

Dracula: Sense and Nonsense. *Westcliff-on-Sea, Essex, UK: Desert Island Books, 2000. 256p. ISBN 1874287244.*

Was Vlad the Impaler the inspiration for Bram Stoker's *Dracula*? Did Stoker write about Transylvania from firsthand experience? Must Count Dracula stay out of the sunlight? Miller exposes popular misconceptions about Stoker and his novel.

Criticism Dealing with Horror Film

Clover, Carol J.

Men, Women and Chainsaws: Gender and the Modern Horror Film. *Princeton, NJ: Princeton University Press, 1997, ©1992. 260p. ISBN 0691006202.*

This is Clover's critically acclaimed and highly popular study of women's roles in horror films, from *Psycho* to *The Silence of the Lambs*.

Freeland, Cynthia A.

The Naked and the Undead: Evil and the Appeal of Horror. *Boulder, CO: Westview, 2000. 320p. ISBN 0813367026.*

Freeland offers a cognitive and feminist study of how horror films work, and why they appeal to their audiences. Illustrated with scenes from the films, 1930 to the present.

Gallardo, Ximena C., and C. Jason Smith.

Alien Woman: The Making of Lt. Ellen Ripley. *New York: Continuum, 2004. 241p. ISBN 0826415695.*

This well-researched but highly accessible book examines Lieutenant Ellen Ripley, Sigourney Weaver's futuristic heroine of four *Alien* films, as a product of the ongoing construction of sex and gender in the four films. According to Gallardo and Smith, Ripley stands alone as the enduring, self-reliant female pro-tagonist of science fiction film.

Grant, Barry Keith, and Christopher Sharrett, eds.

Planks of Reason: Essays on the Horror Film. *Rev. ed. Oxford, England: Scarecrow Press, 2004, ©1984. 416p. ISBN 0810850133.*

This scholarly classic is still a relevant and informative work for anyone interested in a broad academic treatment of the horror genre. The book is divided into two parts: first one deals with definitions of horror film and the approaches to studying it, and the second analyzes individual films and subgenres.

Jancovich, Mark.

Rational Fears: American Horror in the 1950s. *Manchester, UK: Manchester University Press, 1996. 324p. ISBN 0719036232.*

Jancovich's study of American horror cinema in the 1950s links it to novels and comics.

Jensen, Paul M.

The Men Who Made the Monsters. <u>*Twayne's Popular Film Series*</u>. *New York: Twayne, 1996. 401p. ISBN 0805793380.*

Jensen collects biographical and critical notes on horror producers and directors in the United States and Britain.

Muir, John Kenneth.

Terror Television: American Series, 1970–1999. *Jefferson, NC: McFarland Publishing, 2008, ©2001. 675p. ISBN 0786438843.*

Muir documents the genre, from the dawn of modern horror television through more than thirty programs, including those of the 1998–1999 season. Includes complete histories, critical reception, episode guides, cast, crew and guest star information, as well as series reviews.

Paul, William.

Laughing Screaming: Modern Hollywood Horror and Comedy. *New York: Columbia University Press, 1994. 510p. ISBN 0231084641.*

Paul examines the roles of comedy, sensationalism, sex, and violence in horror film.

Presnell, Don, and Marty McGee.

A Critical History of Television's *The Twilight Zone,* **1959–1964.** *Jefferson, NC: McFarland Publishing, 2008, ©1998. 282p. ISBN 078643886X.*

Presnell and McGee compile a complete history of the show, including incisive analysis of all 156 episodes. Also included are biographical profiles of writers and contributors.

Rockoff, Adam.

Going to Pieces: The Rise and Fall of the Slasher Film, 1978–1986. *Jefferson, NC: McFarland, 2002. 223p. ISBN 0786412275.*

Rockoff chronicles the modern slasher film, which he argues began with John Carpenter's 1978 film *Halloween* rather than Tobe Hooper's *Texas Chainsaw Massacre.* He is particularly interested in how the genre flourished, in spite of opposition from vocal parents' groups who chased out of the theater releases such as *Silent Night, Deadly Night.*

Skal, David J.

Dark Carnival: The Secret World of Tod Browning—Hollywood's Master of the Macabre. *New York: Doubleday, 1995. 359p. ISBN 0385474067.*
Skal chronicles the life and filmmaking career of filmmaker Browning.

Periodicals (Including E-Zines) and Horror Organizations

Periodicals

Recent trends in horror account for the variety of journals, fan magazines, and electronic magazines that can be found at the local newsstand or on the World Wide Web. The trend toward incorporating horror into the literary canon in colleges and universities across the nation has led to a surge in popularity of scholarly studies of horror, as seen in *The Journal of the International Association for the Fantastic in the Arts*, as well as *Dissections* (http://www.simegen.com/writers/dissections/) and *Dead Reckonings: A Review Magazine for the Horror Field*. Of course, fan-oriented magazines that exist to entertain the hard-core horror fans, such as *Fangoria* and *Cemetery Dance*, continue to thrive. The popularity of the Internet has also left its mark on horror periodicals, as there are now more e-zines and small press magazines with Web sites, making it possible for amateur and rookie writers of dark fiction to publish. Hopefully this opening of the doors for publication will ultimately help publishers and fans alike discover new voices in horror, some of which may produce quality fiction. To make publishing even more interesting for the writer and reader, some e-zines allow for interactive storytelling, whereby writers can add to stories in progress or even sell their characters (if their characters are marketable) to be used by other writers or for future tales. In short, horror periodicals, like periodicals in all fields, range from the sublime to the ridiculous, from the strictly informational to the graphically erotic. Web sites in this chapter were verified on May 26, 2008.

> **Aberrations** publishes a broad range of fiction in the sister genres of science fiction, adult horror, and dark fantasy, from the pulp style of storytelling of the 1930s and 1940s to the more experimental and literary fiction of today. It promises a "wild literary ride going where most fiction does not go." *Aberrations* is published monthly by Experiences Unlimited of Walnut Creek, California. ISSN 1058-2509.

> **Cemetery Dance,** the genre's most revered popular magazine, was in its eighteenth year of publication in 2008. This quarterly, edited by Richard T. Chizmar out of Baltimore, Maryland, has won the World Fantasy Award. *Cemetery Dance* features regular columnists and has published works by King, Barker, Rice, Straub, Campbell, Simmons, Bloch, Ellison, and Matheson, as well as by hundreds of others. It includes both original fiction and reviews of film and books. *Cemetery Dance* can be found at http://www.cemeterydance.com/page/CDP/CTGY/MAGS. ISSN 1047-7675.

Champagne Horror, a print journal published by Champagne Productions out of Canada, began in 1990 and is published annually. *Champagne Horror* includes horror fiction, poetry, and art. ISSN 0847-1711.

Crypt of Cthulhu, a pulp thriller and theological journal that publishes general critical articles on the fiction of H. P. Lovecraft and his literary disciples, regularly includes fiction and poetry by fans and major writers. It is published irregularly by Cryptic Publications of Mount Olive, North Carolina. ISSN 1077-8179.

Dead of Night, an annual refereed serial containing horror fiction, fantasy, mystery, and science fiction, is published by Dead of Night Publications in Longmeadow, Massachusetts. ISSN 1049-0892.

Dead Reckonings is a biannual review of horror fiction edited by Jack Haranga and S. T. Joshi. The first issue was published in the spring of 2007 by Hippocampus Press of New York. ISSN 1935-6110.

Dissections: The Journal of Contemporary Horror, an electronic peer-reviewed journal that commenced publication in 2006, is published biannually and edited by Gina Whisker and Michelle Bernard. It can be found at http://www.simegen.com/writers/dissections/. ISSN not supplied.

Fangoria, one of the all-time most popular horror magazines, is also one of the oldest. Published ten times a year out of New York City by Starlog Group, this visually appealing fan magazine covers horror in film, television, comics, literature, videos, and games. ISSN 0164-2111.

Haunts publishes tales of unexpected horror and the supernatural triannually. It is published by Nightshade Publications of Providence, Rhode Island. ISSN 1043-3503.

Hellnotes, formerly titled *Horror Show*, is "your weekly insider's guide to the horror field" and is edited by horror writer David B. Silva. It includes nonfiction, interviews, best-seller lists, publicity trends, and other horror-related information, and is self-published. It can be found at http://www.hellnotes.com/. ISSN not supplied.

The Journal of the Fantastic in the Arts is published quarterly by The International Association for the Fantastic in the Arts (see horror-related organizations in this chapter). This organization includes academics, scholars, researchers, writers, and fans of science fiction, fantasy, and horror. The journal is produced by Florida Atlantic University. *JFA* includes some original work by big name writers such as Dan Simmons, but is composed mainly of articles and studies in horror, science fiction, and fantasy. The journal also occasionally publishes guest speeches delivered at the annual International Conference of the Fantastic in the Arts. ISSN 0897-0521.

11

12

13

14

15

16

17

18

19

20

Lovecraft Studies is a scholarly journal issued biannually by Necronomicon Press of West Warwick, Rhode Island, and edited by noted Lovecraft scholar S. T. Joshi. As the name implies, it is concerned with the works of H. P. Lovecraft. ISSN 0899-8361.

Necrofile: The Review of Horror Fiction, although now defunct, offers back issues. This quarterly is indispensable for librarians in horror collection development, as the journal published the most comprehensive listing of all new horror titles in the United States and Britain up until the year 2000. Most of the content of this small journal (produced by Necronomicon Press of West Warwick, Rhode Island, and edited by horror experts Stefan Dziemianowicz, S. T. Joshi, and Michael A. Morrison) was made up of authoritative, extended book reviews of both current fiction and newly released older fiction. Back issues can be purchased from www.necropress.com. ISSN 1077-8187.

Necropsy: The Review of Horror Fiction, located at http://www.lsu.edu/necrofile, is a now defunct e-zine that continued *Necrofile: The Review of Horror Fiction*. Back issues are still housed at Louisiana State University. It featured extended reviews of novels, collections of short fiction, poetry, graphic novels, and films in the genre. It is unaffiliated with any publisher, and its staff consisted primarily of academics and librarians. The editors were June Pulliam and Tony Fonseca, two former *Necrofile* reviewers. It can be found at http://www.lsu.edu/necrofile. ISSN not supplied.

Red Scream, a glossy magazine for fans of the horror genre, commenced publication in 2005. Published five times a year, it includes original fiction and art that leans toward splatterpunk; interviews with writers, actors, and directors; and columns. ISSN 1932-8915.

Terminal Fright, published by Charles McKee Books, provides a forum for writers in the genre. This is a quarterly magazine of traditional horror fiction. ISSN 1080-6873.

Horror-Related Organizations

In this section are the sources that are the most difficult to find: human beings (and groups of human beings) who are experts in the genre. Horror fans often join societies and attend conventions, such as The World Horror Convention, The International Association for the Fantastic in the Arts Convention, The Popular Culture Association's Conference, and NECON (The Northeast Writer's Conference). These conventions are excellent places to hear readings of early drafts of both primary and secondary works in the genre, to meet writers and critics, and to exchange ideas and e-mail addresses with other readers and fans.

Note: The URLs for these organizations were verified on May 26, 2008.

The British Fantasy Society (http://www.britishfantasysociety.org/) promotes the enjoyment of fantasy, science fiction, and horror in all its forms, and hosts Fantasy Con (a conference for fantasy, science fiction, and horror) annually. Members receive a newsletter six times per year (Prism UK) and a free copy of *Dark Horizons*. Members also receive a preferential rate at Fantasy Con. The current president is Ramsey Campbell. Its mailing address is 5 Greenbank, Barnt Green, Birmingham, B45 8DH England.

The **Edgar Allan Poe Society of Baltimore** (http://www.eapoe.org/) was officially established following a commemorative celebration of Poe's birthday on January 18, 1923. It offers information about Poe including, but not limited to, general topics, his works, his life, his home, his death, and his burial site. Prospective members should visit the society's Web site.

The **Horror Writers Association** (http://www.horror.org/) brings together writers and others with a professional interest in horror. Members receive a newsletter, e-mail bulletins, and access to private online services. Its current president is Deborah LeBlanc. This organization votes on and awards the most prestigious honor in the genre, the Bram Stoker Awards for fiction and nonfiction. Interested parties can contact the HWA via e-mail (hwa@horror.org) or mail at Horror Writers' Association, 244 5th Avenue, Suite 2767, New York, NY 10001.

The **International Association for the Fantastic in the Arts** (www.iafa.org), an organization of scholars and fans of horror, science fiction, and fantasy, meets annually at their conference in Orlando, Florida. Readers seeking further information should contact Stacey Haynes at esmeraldus@earthlink.net.

The **Popular Culture Association** (http://www.pcaaca.org/) is dedicated to the study of popular culture in all forms, including horror. Phil Simpson is the current chair for the horror section of PCA. For further information about PCA, readers should contact Lynn Bartholome at Monroe Community College, English and Philosophy Department, 1000 E. Henrietta Road, Rochester, NY 14623 (E-mail: lbartholome@monroecc.edu). Prospective members should visit the PCA's Web site for membership information.

The **Transylvanian Society of Dracula, Canadian Chapter** (http://www.ucs.mun.ca/~emiller/trans_soc_dracula.html) is a nonprofit cultural/historical organization that serves as a clearing house of information pertaining to the serious study of Dracula and related topics. Its members include historians, folklorists, literary critics, researchers, students, and film enthusiasts. Its current president is Dr. Elizabeth Miller (emiller@mun.ca), who can be contacted by prospective members via e-mail.

The **UK Chapter of the Horror Writers Association** (http://www.horror.org/uk/) is a subset of the American-based Horror Writers Association. Membership in the HWA allows membership in the UK chapter as well, and one does not have to live in the United Kingdom to join the UK chapter. The organization offers a monthly newsletter and various publications.

Chapter 20

Major Awards

This chapter lists and briefly describes the major awards given annually for the genre of horror fiction, from the prestigious Bram Stoker Awards for best horror to the smaller but just as meaningful International Horror Guild Awards. For awards prior to 2003, consult the previous two editions of *Hooked on Horror* or the Web sites of : The Horror Writers Association (http://www.horror.org/stokers.htm) and the International Horror Guild (http://www.horroraward.org/).

The Bram Stoker Awards, Winners, and Nominees

The Horror Writers Association (HWA) gives the Bram Stoker Awards for Superior Achievement in fiction annually. The winners are determined by vote of the active members of HWA, and the awards themselves are presented at HWA's Annual Meeting and Awards Banquet.

Winners are denoted in boldface. The other items listed are nominees.

2007

When we went to press with *Hooked on Horror III*, the entire ballot for the 2007 Bram Stoker Award was not available.

Novels

Langan, Sarah, *The Missing*

First Novels

Hill, Joe, *Heart-Shaped Box*

Fiction Collection (Tie)

Arnzen, Michael A., *Proverbs for Monsters*

Straub, Peter, *5 Stories*

Anthology

Braunbeck, Gary A., and Hank Schwaeble, eds., *Five Strokes tzzo Midnight*

Nonfiction

Maberry, Jonathan, and David F. Kramer, eds., THE CRYPTOPEDIA: A Dictionary of the Weird, Strange & Downright Bizarre

Lifetime Achievement

John Carpenter, Robert Weinberg

Richard Laymon President's Award

Mark Worthen, Stephen Dorato, Christopher Fulbright

2006

Novel

Braunbeck, Gary A., Prodigal Blues

King, Stephen, Lisey's Story

Maberry, Jonathan, Ghost Road Blues

Piccirilli, Tom, Headstone City

Strand, Jeff, Pressure

First Novel

Kenyon, Nate, Bloodstone

Langan, Sarah, The Keeper

Maberry, Jonathan, Ghost Road Blues

Sokoloff, Alexandra, The Harrowing

Fiction Collection

Braunbeck, Gary, Destinations Unknown

Dowling, Terry, Basic Black: Tales of Appropriate Fear

Ford, Jeffrey, The Empire of Ice Cream

Hawkes, Angeline, The Commandments

Hirshberg, Glen, American Morons

Anthology

Lansdale, Joe, ed., Retro Pulp Tales (Tie)

Pelan, John, ed., Alone on the Darkside

Sizemore, Jason, and Gill Ainsworth, eds., Aegri Somnia: The Apex Featured Writer Anthology

Skipp, John, ed., Mondo Zombie (Tie)

Nonfiction

Largo, Michael, *Final Exits: The Illustrated Encyclopedia of How We Die* **(Tie)**

Morris, Mark, ed., *Cinema Macabre*

Paffenroth, Kim, *Gospel of the Living Dead: George Romero's Visions of ell on Earth* **(Tie)**

Wood, Rocky, *Stephen King: Uncollected, Unpublished*

Lifetime Achievement

No lifetime achievement award for 2006

2005

Novel

Braunbeck, Gary, *Keepers*

Jacob, Charlee, *Dread in the Beast* **(Tie)**

Morrell, David, *Creepers* **by (Tie)**

Piccirilli, Tom, *November Mourns*

First Novel

Burke, Kealan Patrick, *The Hides*

Clark, Alan M., and Jeremy Robert Johnson, *Siren Promised*

Ochse, Weston, *Scarecrow Gods*

Fiction Collection

Hill, Joe, *20th Century Ghosts*

Link, Kelly, *Magic for Beginners*

Miâville, China, *Looking for Jake*

Palahniuk, Chuck, *Haunted*

Anthology

Holder, Nancy, and Nancy Kilpatrick, eds., *Outsiders*

Howison, Del and Jeff Gelb, eds., *Dark Delicacies: Original Tales of Terror and the Macabre*

Jones, Stephen, ed., *Weird Shadows Over Innsmouth*

Sevin, Julie, and R. J. Sevin, eds., *Corpse Blossoms*

Nonfiction

Jones, Stephen, and Kim Newman, *Horror: Another 100 Best Books*

McCarty, Michael, *More Giants of the Genre*

Rhoades, Loren, *Morbid Curiosity # 9*

Weller, Sam, *The Bradbury Chronicles*

Wilcox, Rhonda, *Why Buffy Matters: The Art of Buffy the Vampire Slayer*

Lifetime Achievement Award

Peter Straub

Richard Laymon President's Award

Lisa Morton

2004

Novel

Cacek, P. D., *The Wind Caller*

King, Stephen, *The Dark Tower VII: The Dark Tower*

Laimo, Michael, *Deep in the Darkness*

Straub, Peter, *In the Night Room*

First Novel

Everson, John, *Covenant* **(Tie)**

Kidman, James, *Black Fire*

Mamatas, Nick, *Move Under Ground*

Thomas, Lee, *Stained* **(Tie)**

Fiction Collection

Arnzen, Michael, *100 Jolts: Shockingly Short Stories*

Clegg, Douglas, *The Machinery of Night*

Fowler, Christopher, *Demonized*

Lebbon, Tim, *Fears Unnamed*

Monteleone, Thomas F., *Fearful Symmetries*

Anthology

Burke, Kealan Patrick, ed., *Quietly Now*

Cavelos, Jeanne, ed., *The Many Faces of Van Helsing*

Chizmar, Richard, ed., *Shivers III*

Datlow, Ellen, Kelly Link, and Gavin Grant, eds., ***The Year's Best Fantasy and Horror, 17th Annual***

Roden, Christopher , ed., *Acquainted with the Night*

Nonfiction

Conley, Ralan, *Ralan's SpecFic & Humor Webstravaganza*

McCabe, Joseph, *Hanging Out with the Dream King*

Monteleone, Thomas F., *The Complete Idiot's Guide to Writing a Novel*

Rohrig, Judi, ed., ***Hellnotes***

Vincent, Bev, *The Road to the Dark Tower*

Lifetime Achievement Award

Michael Moorcock

2003

Novel

King, Stephen, *The Dark Tower V: Wolves of the Calla*

Moore, James A., *Serenity Falls*

O'Nan, Stewart, *The Night Country*

Piccirilli, Tom, *A Choir of Ill Children*

Straub, Peter, ***Lost Boy, Lost Girl***

First Novel

Gagliani, William D., *Wolf's Trap*

Keene, Brian, ***The Rising***

Thomas, Jeffrey, *Monstrocity*

Vandermeer, Jeff, *Veniss Underground*

Fiction Collection

Braunbeck, Gary A., *Graveyard People: The Collected Cedar Hill Stories Vol. 1*

Campbell, Ramsey, *Told by the Dead*

Hand, Elizabeth, *Bibliomancy*

Ketchum, Jack, ***Peaceable Kingdom***

Taylor, Karen, *Fangs and Angel Wings*

Anthology

Congreve, Bill , ed., *Southern Blood: New Australian Tales of the Supernatural*

Dann, Jack, Ramsey Campbell, and Dennis Etchison, eds., *Gathering The Bones*

Datlow, Ellen , ed., *The Dark*

Datlow, Ellen, and Terri Windling, eds., *The Year's Best Fantasy & Horror: 16th Annual Collection*

Monteleone, Elizabeth, and Thomas F. Monteleone, eds., *Borderlands 5*

Nonfiction

Braunbeck, Gary A., *Fear in a Handful of Dust*

Conley, Ralan , ed., *Ralan.com*

Millidge, Gary Spencer, and Smoky Man, eds., *Alan Moore: Portrait of an Extraordinary Gentleman*

Monteleone, Thomas, F., *The Mothers and Fathers Italian Association*

Rohrig, Judi , ed., *Hellnotes*

Lifetime Achievement Award

Martin H. Greenberg

Anne Rice

The International Horror Guild Awards

The International Horror Critics Guild was created in 1995 as a way to recognize the achievements of those who toil in the horror field. Before that date only the Bram Stoker Award, which is presented by the Horror Writers Association, was considered a mark of distinction, but voting on it is limited to HWA members. The International Horror Guild Award represents a large, unaffiliated group of writers who are recognized for excellence by their peers. Note that when we went to press with this edition of *Hooked on Horror*, IHG award winners for 2007 were not available.

Best Novel

2006—*The Unblemished*, Conrad Williams

2005—*Lunar Park*, Bret Easton Ellis

2004—*The Overnight*, Ramsey Campbell

2003—*Lost Boy, Lost Girl*, Peter Straub

Best First Novel

2004—*The Ghost Writer*, John Harwood

2003—*Jinn*, Matthew B. J. Delaney

Best Collection

2006—*Basic Black*, Terry Dowling (tie)

2006—*American Morons*, Glen Hirshberg (tieE)

2005—*20th Century Ghosts*, Joe Hill

2004—*The Wavering Knife*, Brain Evenson

2003—*The Two Sams*, Glen Hirshberg (tie)

2003—*More Tomorrow and Other Stories*, Michael Marshall Smith (tie)

Best Anthology

2006—*Lords of the Razor*, William Sheehan and Bill Schafer

2005—No award given   in 2005

2004—*Acquainted with the Night*, Barbara Roden and Christopher Roden

2003—*The Dark: New Ghost Stories*, Ellen Datlow

Best Publication (Award Given for Best Periodicals Devoted to Horror)

2006—*Subterranean*

2005—*Postscripts*

2004—*The Third Alternative*

2003—*All Hallows: The Journal of the Ghost Story Society*

Living Legend Award

2006—Ramsey Campbell

2005—Chelsea Quinn Yarbro

2004—Gahan Wilson

2003—Stephen King

2003—Everett F. Bleiler

2003—Jack Cady (award presented posthumously)

Appendix: Stretching the Boundaries—Cross-Genre Horror Fiction

Many readers come to the horror genre from other genre fiction. For example, readers who love thrillers will find Dean Koontz and Steve Alten much to their liking, and the current spate of vampire romance novels has inspired some fans of romance to pick up Anne Rice's or Chelsea Quinn Yarbro's vampire series. Of course it can work the other way around as well, with Stephen King fans moving into fantasy or thrillers, or Neil Gaiman fans making the transition to graphic novels.

In this appendix we list those horror works that "cross over" into other genres, such as action-adventure, classic fiction, detective fiction, fantasy, gentle reads, romance, science fiction, thrillers, Westerns, and young adult.

Action Adventure

The following titles contain high levels of action and adventure, which will appeal to readers of those genres as well as to horror fans who enjoy a fast-paced, action-oriented read.

Alten, Steve. *The Loch*, <u>The Meg Series</u>.

Armstrong, Kelley. <u>The Women of the Otherworld Series</u>.

Banks, L. A. <u>The Vampire Huntress Legend</u>.

Crouch, Blake. <u>The Andrew Thomas Novels</u>.

D'Ammassa, Don. *Dead of Winter*.

Farris, John. *You Don't Scare Me*.

Hamilton, Laurell K. <u>The Anita Blake, Vampire Hunter Series</u>.

Hinton, S. E. *Hawkes Harbor*.

Howard, Robert E. *The Savage Tales of Solomon Kane*.

Kenner, Julie. *California Demon: The Secret Life of a Demon-Hunting Soccer Mom*.

Masterton, Graham. *Genius*.

McGrew, Chandler. *The Darkening*.

Nicholson, Scott. *They Hunger*.

Piñol, Albert Sánchez. *Cold Skin*.

Racina, Thom. *Deadly Games.*

Saberhagen, Fred. *A Coldness in the Blood.*

Smith, Clark Ashton. *Red World of Polaris: The Adventures of Captain Volmar.*

Strieber, Whitley, Roland Emerick, and Jeffrey Nachmanoff. *The Day After Tomorrow.*

Wellington, David. <u>The 99 Coffins Series</u>.

Wilson, F. Paul. *Midnight Mass.*

Classics

The following titles are considered classics in the genre, and they will appeal most to readers who enjoy classic and canonical literature.

Aickman, Robert. *The Collected Strange Stories.*

Amis, Kingsley. *The Green Man.*

Askew, Alice and Claude Askew. *Aylmer Vance: Ghost-Seer.*

Austen, Jane. *Northanger Abbey.*

Benson, E. F. *The Collected Ghost Stories of E. F. Benson.*

Blackwood, Algernon. *The Complete John Silence Stories, Incredible Adventures.*

Blatty, William Peter. *The Exorcist.*

Bloch, Robert. *American Gothic; Psycho.*

Bradbury, Ray. *It Came from Outer Space.*

Brontë, Emily. *Wuthering Heights.*

Brown, Charles Brockden. *Edgar Huntly, or, Memoirs of a Sleep-Walker, with Related Texts; Wieland, or the Transformation.*

Capes, Bernard Edward Joseph. *The Black Reaper.*

Chambers, Robert W. *The Yellow Sign and Other Stories: The Complete Weird Tales of Robert W. Chambers.*

Cheiro. *A Study of Destiny.*

Davis, Grubb. *The Night of the Hunter.*

De la Mare, Walter. *The Return.*

DeVito, Joe, Brad Strickland, and Delos Wheeler Lovelace. *Merian C. Cooper's King Kong.*

Doyle, Arthur Conan. *The Captain of the "Pole-Star": Weird and Imaginative Fiction.*

Du Maurier, Daphne. *Rebecca.*

Gorey, Edward, ed. *The Haunted Looking Glass: Ghost Stories Chosen by Edward Gorey.*

Greenberg, Martin H., and Al Sarrantonio, eds. *100 Hair-Raising Little Horror Stories.*

Haining, Peter, ed. *The Mammoth Book of Modern Ghost Stories: Great Supernatural Tales of the Twentieth Century.*

Hawthorne, Nathaniel. *The House of Seven Gables.*

Hodgson, William Hope. *Boats of the "Glen Carrig" and Other Nautical Adventures; The House on the Borderland.*

Jackson, Shirley. *The Haunting of Hill House; The Lottery and Other Stories.*

Jackson, Thomas Graham. *Six Ghost Stories.*

James, Henry. *Ghost Stories.*

James, M. R. *Casting the Runes, and Other Ghost Stories; Ghost Stories of an Antiquary.*

Jones, Stephen, ed. *H. P. Lovecraft's Book of the Supernatural: 20 Classics of the Macabre, Chosen by the Author Himself.*

Joshi, S. T., ed. *Great Weird Tales: 14 Stories by Lovecraft, Blackwood, Machen and Others.*

Kipling, Rudyard. *The Mark of the Beast and Other Horror Tales.*

Lamb, Hugh, ed. *A Bottomless Grave and Other Victorian Tales of Terror; Tales from a Gas-Lit Graveyard.*

Leatherdale, Clive, ed. *Bram Stoker's Dracula Unearthed.*

Le Fanu, Joseph Sheridan. *Green Tea and Other Ghost Stories; In a Glass Darkly; Uncle Silas: A Tale of Bartram-Haugh.*

Leiber, Fritz. *Our Ladies of Darkness.*

LeRoux, Gaston. *The Phantom of the Opera.*

Levin, Ira. *Rosemary's Baby; The Stepford Wives.*

Lewis, M[atthew] G. *The Monk: A Romance.*

Lovecraft, H[oward] P[hillip]. *At the Mountains of Madness; The Case of Charles Dexter Ward; The Dreams in the Witch House and Other Weird Stories; From the Pest Zone: Stories from New York; The Lurker at the Threshold; More Annotated H. P. Lovecraft; The Shadow Out of Time; Tales of H. P. Lovecraft: Major Works; Waking Up Screaming: Haunting Tales of Terror.*

Marsh, Richard. *The Beetle.*

Matheson, Richard. *Bloodlines: Richard Matheson's Dracula, I Am Legend, and Other Vampire Stories; Come Fygures, Come Shadowes; Darker Places; Duel: Terror Stories; Earthbound; Hell House; I Am Legend; The Incredible Shrinking Man Richard Matheson's Off-Beat Uncollected Stories; Stir of Echoes.*

Maturin, Charles Robert. *Melmoth the Wanderer.*

Oliphant, Margaret. *The Library Window.*

Onions, Oliver. *The Beckoning Fair One.*

Polidori, John. *The Vampire and Other Tales of the Macabre.*

Reeve, Clara. *The Old English Barron.*

Shelley, Mary. *Frankenstein.*

Smith, Clark Ashton. *The Door to Saturn; The End of the Story; Red World of Polaris: The Adventures of Captain Volmar.*

Stevenson, Robert Louis. *The Body Snatchers and Other Tales; The Strange Case of Dr. Jekyll and Mr. Hyde; The Strange Case of Dr. Jekyll and Mr. Hyde and Other Stories.*

Stoker, Bram. *Dracula; The Jewel of Seven Stars.*

Wallace, Edgar, and Merian C. Cooper. *King Kong.*

Walpole, Horace. *The Castle of Otranto: A Gothic Story; The Mysterious Mother: A Tragedy.*

Wells, H. G. *The Croquet Player; The Invisible Man; The War of the Worlds.*

Wilde, Oscar. *The Canterville Ghost; The Picture of Dorian Gray.*

Wyndham, John. *The Day of the Triffids.*

Detective Fiction

The following titles feature detectives, police officers in criminal investigations, private investigators, and plot lines that emphasize the discovery of a crime. These often appeal to readers of detective fiction, as well as to horror fans who enjoy a good mystery being solved.

The Angel Investigations Series.

Ballard, J. G. *Kingdom Come.*

Blackwood, Algernon. *The Complete John Silence Stories.*

Bonner, Hilary. *When the Dead Cry Out.*

Boyne, John. *Crippen.*

Carey, Mike. *The Devil You Know.*

Cave, Hugh B. *The Restless Dead.*

Christopher, Shane. The Kinsella/Rodriguez Novels.

Connolly, John. The Charlie Parker Mysteries.

Delaney, Matthew B. J. *Jinn.*

De Lint, Charles. *Mulengro: A Romany Tale.*

De Lint, Charles (as Samuel M. Key). *From a Whisper to a Scream.*

Elrod, P. N. <u>The Vampire Files.</u>

Evenson, Brian. *The Open Curtain.*

Fowler, Christopher. *Full Dark House.*

Fox, Andrew. <u>The Fat White Vampire Blues Series.</u>

Gagliani, W. D. *Wolf's Trap.*

Gallagher, Diana G., and Constance M. Burge. *Something Wiccan This Way Comes: An Original Novel.*

Gallagher, Stephen. *Valley of Lights.*

Greenberg, Martin H., Isaac Asimov, and Joseph D. Olander, eds. *100 Malicious Little Mysteries.*

Hamilton, Laurell K. <u>The Anita Blake, Vampire Hunter Series.</u>

Hand, Elizabeth. *Generation Loss: A Novel.*

Harper, Andrew. *Red Angel; Night Cage.*

Harris, Thomas. <u>The Silence of the Lambs Series.</u>

Herbert, James. *Nobody True.*

Hodgson, William Hope. *Boats of the "Glen Carrig" and Other Nautical Adventures.*

Hopkins, Brian A. *The Licking Valley Coon Hunters Club.*

Huston, Charlie. <u>The Joe Pitt Novels.</u>

Kiernan, Caitlin R. *Daughter of Hounds, Low Red Moon.*

King, Stephen. *From a Buick 8: A Novel.*

Kingsbury, Evan. *Fire and Flesh.*

Koontz, Dean. *Darkfall.*

Kostova, Elizabeth. *The Historian: A Novel.*

Kunzmann, Richard. *Bloody Harvests.*

Lansdale, Joe R. *Lost Echoes.*

Ligotti, Thomas. *The Shadow at the Bottom of the World.*

Little, Bentley (writing as Phillip Emmons). *Death Instinct.*

Lorrah, Jean. *Blood Will Tell.*

Lumley, Brain. *The House of Cthulhu.*

Manguel, Alberto. *Stevenson under the Palm Trees.*

Mariotte, Jeff. The Angel Series.

Masterton, Graham. *The Devil in Gray; The Doorkeepers; A Terrible Beauty.*

Merz, Jon F., The Lawson Vampire Novels.

Michaels, Barbara, and Elizabeth Peters. *Prince of Darkness.*

Moss, Tara. *Fetish.*

Newman, Kim. *The Man from the Diogenes Club.*

Nolan, William F. *Nightshadows: The Best New Horror Fiction by a Living Legend in Dark Fantasy.*

Oates, Joyce Carol (writing as Rosamund Smith). *Starr Bright Will Be with You Soon.*

Page, David A. *Surviving Frank.*

Pearl, Matthew. *The Dante Club.*

Piccirilli, Tom. *The Midnight Road.*

Preston, Douglas, and Lincoln Child. The Pendergast Novels.

Priest, Cherie. The Eden Moore Trilogy.

Pronzini, Bill. *Masques: A Novel of Terror.*

Randisi, Robert J. *Cold Blooded; Curtains of Blood.*

Reaves, Michael, and John Pelan, eds. *Shadows Over Baker Street.*

Rhodes, Evie. *Criss Cross.*

Rhodes, Jewel Parker. *Voodoo Season: A Marie Laveau Mystery.*

Rickman, Phil. *The Remains of an Altar.*

Sarrantonio, Al. *Halloweenland.*

Shepard, Lucius. *The Golden.*

Sigler, Scott. *Infected: A Novel.*

Slade, Michael. *Bed of Nails.*

Straub, Peter. *Koko.*

Stein, Jeanne C. The Anna Strong Chronicles.

Tessier, Thomas. *Wicked Things.*

Thomas, Jeffrey. *Deadstock.*

Waggoner, Tim. *Necropolis.*

Wellington, David. The 99 Coffins Series.

Whitfield, Kit. *Benighted.*

Woodworth, Stephen. The Violet Series.

Fantasy

The following titles have elements of fantasy. Some titles include some of the standard fantastical creatures such as nymphs and elves, while others are better described as either dark fantasy or paranormal romance or verge on magical realism.

Aickman, Robert. *The Collected Strange Stories.*

Armstrong, Kelley. <u>The Women of the Otherworld Series</u>.

Asamatsu, Ken, ed. *Straight to Darkness: Lairs of the Hidden Gods.*

Bailey, Dale. *The Resurrection Man's Legacy and Other Stories.*

Barker, Clive. *Galilee.*

Benson, Amber. *Witchery: A Ghosts of Albion Novel.*

Benson, Amber, and Christopher Golden. *Ghosts of Albion: Accursed.*

Bishop, K. J., *The Etched City.*

Bradbury, Ray. *From the Dust Returned.*

Braunbeck, Gary A. *In Silent Graves*

Bray, Libba. <u>The Gemma Doyle Trilogy</u>.

Briggs, Patricia, Karen Chance, Eileen Wilks, and Sunny. *On the Prowl.*

Campbell, Ramsey. *The Hungry Moon; Needing Ghosts; Strange Things and Stranger Places.*

Clark, Francis. *Waking Brigid.*

Clark, Simon. *The Night of the Triffids*

Clegg, Douglas. <u>The Vampyricon Trilogy</u>.

Connolly, John. *The Book of Lost Things.*

Corman, Avery. *The Boyfriend From Hell.*

Crowther, Peter. *The Longest Single Note.*

Dowling, Terry. *Basic Black: Tales of the Appropriate Fear.*

Gardner, T. L. <u>The Demon Hunter Series</u>.

Gaiman, Neil. *American Gods; Coraline; Fragile Things: Short Fictions and Wonders; Neverwhere: A Novel.*

Golden, Christopher. *The Boys are Back in Town; The Ferryman; The Myth Hunters; Wildwood Road.*

Golden, Christopher, and James A. Moore. *Bloodstained Oz.*

Hamilton, Laurell K. <u>The Anita Blake, Vampire Hunter Series</u>.

Hand, Elizabeth. *Mortal Love.*

Harrison, M. John. *The Course of the Heart*.

Hearn, Julie. *The Minister's Daughter*.

Hendee, Barb, and J. C. Hendee. <u>The Noble Dead Series</u>.

Hill, Joe. *20th Century Ghosts*.

Hodgson, William Hope. *Boats of the "Glen Carrig" and Other Nautical Adventures*.

Howison, Del, and Jeff Gelb, eds. *Dark Delicacies; Dark Delicacies II: Fear; More Original Tales of Terror and the Macabre by the World's Greatest Horror Writers*.

Huff, Tanya. <u>The Smoke Trilogy</u>.

Jackson, Liam. *Offspring*.

Kiernan, Caitlin R. *Alabaster; Daughter of Hounds; Murder of Angels*.

King, Stephen. *From a Buick 8: A Novel; Lisey's Story*.

King, Stephen, and Peter Straub. *Black House*.

Klein, T. E. D. *Reassuring Tales*.

Knight, Brian. *Feral*, <u>The Vampire Earth Series</u>.

Koontz, Dean. *Lightning*.

Lane, Joel. *The Lost District and Other Stories*.

Lee, Edward. <u>The City Infernal Series</u>.

Mamatas, Nick. *Move Under Ground*.

Matheson, Richard. *Richard Matheson's Off-Beat Uncollected Stories*.

Masterton, Graham. *The Doorkeepers; The Hidden World*.

McCauley, Kirby, ed. *Frights: Stories of Suspense and Supernatural Terror*.

McCoy, Robert Wayne. *The King of Ice Cream*.

Miâville, China. *King Rat*.

Morrell, David. *Nightscape*.

Nolan, William F. *Nightshadows: The Best New Horror Fiction by a Living Legend in Dark Fantasy; Nightworlds*.

Pinborough, Sarah. *The Hidden*.

Rainey, Stephen Mark. *The Lebo Coven*.

Sarrantonio, Al. *Hallows Eve*.

Sedia, Ekaterina. *The Secret History of Moscow*.

Shirley, John. *Demons*.

Smith, Bryan. *Deathbringer*.

Sneddon, James. *The Tolltaker.*

Spector, Craig. *Under-ground.*

Straub, Peter. *Mr. X.; In the Night Room.*

Thorne, Tamara, <u>The Sorority Trilogy</u>.

Thurman, Rob. *Nightlife.*

VanderMeer, Ann, and Jeff VanderMeer. *The New Weird.*

Waggoner, Tim. *Necropolis.*

Williams, Conrad. *Use Once, Then Destroy.*

Wilson, D. Harlan, and Stanley Ashenbach. *Dr. Id-entity, or, Farewell to Plaquedemia.*

Zebrowski, George. *Black Pockets and Other Dark Thoughts.*

Historical Fiction

The following titles make use of historical events or characters in their plots, some more faithfully than others.

Austin, Sherry. *Mariah of the Spirits and Other Southern Ghost Stories.*

Banks, L. A. *The Cursed: A Vampire Huntress Legend.*

Barker, Clive. *Galilee.*

Benson, Amber. *Witchery: A Ghosts of Albion Novel.*

Benson, Amber, and Christopher Golden. *Ghosts of Albion: Accursed.*

Berliner, Janet, and George Guthridge. <u>The Madagascar Manifesto</u>.

Betancourt, John. *Horror: The Best of the Year.*

Bleys, Olivier. *The Ghost in the Eiffel Tower.*

Bloch, Robert. *American Gothic.*

Boyne, John. *Crippen.*

Butler, Robert Olen. *Severance.*

Clark, Francis. *Waking Brigid.*

Clegg, Douglas. <u>The Vampyricon Trilogy</u>.

Cutter, Leah R. *The Caves of Buda.*

Cox, Michael. *The Meaning of Night: A Confession.*

DeCandido, Keith R. A. *Blackout.*

Due, Tananarive. *Joplin's Ghost.*

Elrod, P. N. <u>The Jonathan Barrett Series</u>; <u>The Vampire Files</u>.

Fleming, Robert. *Havoc After Dark: Tales of Terror*.

Franklin, Tom. *Smonk, or Widow Town: Being the Scabrous Adventures of E. O. Smonk & the Whore of Evangeline in Clarke County, Alabama, Early in the Last Century*.

Greenberg, Martin H., ed. *White House Horrors*.

Hand, Elizabeth. *Mortal Love*.

Jensen, Michael. *Firelands*.

Ketchum, Jack. *The Crossings*.

Kostova, Elizabeth. *The Historian: A Novel*.

Manguel, Alberto. *Stevenson under the Palm Trees*.

Newman, Kim. <u>The Anno Dracula Series</u>.

O'Brien, Edna. *In the Forest*.

O'Nan, Stewart. *A Prayer for the Dying*.

Pearl, Matthew. *The Dante Club*.

Reese, James. <u>The Book of Shadows Trilogy</u>.

Rice, Anne. *Blood and Gold: The Story of Marius*; <u>The New Tales of the Vampire Series</u>; *The Servant of the Bones*; <u>The Vampire Chronicles</u>; <u>The Mayfair Witch Series</u>.

Rook, Sebastian. <u>The Vampire Plague Series</u>.

Sedia, Ekaterina. *The Secret History of Moscow*.

Simmons, Dan. *The Terror*.

Wellington, David. *99 Coffins: A Historical Vampire Tale*.

Welsh, T. K. *Resurrection Men*.

Yarbro, Chelsea Quinn. <u>The Saint-Germain Series</u>.

Mainstream and Contemporary Literary Fiction

Readers who do not usually enjoy what is commonly referred to as genre fiction will appreciate these titles, which include many of the elements of horror, without slavishly adhering to its conventions.

Due, Tananarive. *The Between*.

Haining, Peter, ed. *The Mammoth Book of Modern Ghost Stories: Great Supernatural Tales of the Twentieth Century*.

Hirshberg, Glen. *The Two Sams; American Morons*.

Jensen, Michael. *Firelands.*

Oates, Joyce Carol. *The Museum of Dr. Moses: Tales of Mystery and Suspense.*

Palahniuk, Chuck. *Haunted: A Novel of Stories.*

Siddons, Anne Rivers. *The House Next Door.*

Sullivan, Thomas. *Second Soul.*

Romance

The following titles are paranormal romance and contain love stories or romantic heroes and heroines. They will appeal to readers of romance fiction, particularly fans of bodice rippers, as well as to horror fans who enjoy a love story with supernatural elements.

Armstrong, Kelley. <u>The Women of the Otherworld Series</u>.

Austen, Jane. *Northanger Abbey.*

Briggs, Patricia, Karen Chance, Eileen Wilks, and Sunny. *On the Prowl.*

Brontë, Emily. *Wuthering Heights.*

Davidson, Mary Janice. *Dead and Loving It.*

Du Maurier, Daphne. *Rebecca.*

Elrod, P. N. <u>The Jonathan Barrett, Gentleman Vampire Series</u>; <u>The Vampire Files</u>; *My Big Fat Supernatural Wedding; My Big Fat Supernatural Honeymoon.*

Feehan, Christine, Maggie Shane, Emma Holly, and Angela Knight. *Hot Blooded.*

Hamilton, Laurell K., Mary Janice Davidson, Eileen Wilks, and Rebecca York. *Cravings.*

Hart, Raven. <u>The Savannah Vampire Series</u>.

Hamilton, Laurell K. <u>The Anita Blake, Vampire Hunter Series</u>.

Jackson, Monica, ed. *Creepin'.*

Lorrah, Jean. *Blood Will Tell.*

Michaels, Barbara, and Elizabeth Peters. *Prince of Darkness.*

Rice, Anne. <u>The Mayfair Witch Series</u>.

Shayne, Maggie. <u>The Twilight Hunger Series</u>.

Shayne, Maggie, Barbara Hambly, and Charlaine Harris. *Night's Edge.*

Science Fiction

The books listed under this heading will appeal to fans of science fiction because they are about the horrific side of space travel, aliens, science, or technology.

Ballard, J. G. *Kingdom Come.*

Bloch, Robert, ed. *Monsters in Our Midst.*

Bradbury, Ray. *It Came From Outer Space.*

Campbell, Ramsey. *Strange Things and Stranger Places.*

Clark, Simon. *The Night of the Triffids.*

Crowther, Peter. *The Longest Single Note.*

Derleth, August, ed. *The Loved Dead and Other Revisions.*

Freedman, Dave. *Natural Selection.*

Hideaki, Sena, and Tyran Grillo. *Parasite Eve.*

Howison, Del, and Jeff Gelb, eds. *Dark Delicacies; Dark Delicacies II: Fear; More Original Tales of Terror and the Macabre by the World's Greatest Horror Writers.*

King, Stephen. *Cell: A Novel.*

Knight, E. E. The Vampire Earth Series.

Lansdale, Joe R. *Mad Dog Summer and Other Stories.*

Lebbon, Tim. *White and Other Tales of Ruin.*

Matheson, Richard. *Bloodlines: Richard Matheson's Dracula, I Am Legend and Other Vampire Stories; Duel: Terror Stories; I Am Legend; The Incredible Shrinking Man; Richard Matheson's Off-Beat: Uncollected Stories.*

Morrell, David. *Nightscape.*

Nolan, William F. *Dark Universe; Nightshadows: The Best New Horror Fiction by a Living Legend in Dark Fantasy; Nightworlds.*

Powers, Tim. *Three Days to Never.*

Schatzing, Frank. *The Swarm.*

Smith, Clark Ashton. *The Door to Saturn; The End of the Story; Red World of Polaris: The Adventures of Captain Volmar.*

Stone, Del, Jr. *Black Tide.*

Strieber, Whitley, Roland Emerick, and Jeffrey Nachmanoff. *The Day After Tomorrow.*

VanderMeer, Ann, and Jeff VanderMeer. *The New Weird.*

Williams, Conrad, and Jeff VanderMeer. *The Unblemished.*

Wilson, D. Harlan, and Stanley Ashenbach. *Dr. Id-entity, or, Farewell to Plaquedemia.*

Wyndham, John. *The Day of the Triffids.*

Zebrowski, George. *Black Pockets and Other Dark Thoughts.*

Thriller

The following titles will appeal to fans of thrillers, works filled with suspense and a lot of twists and turns of the plot. Not surprisingly, many of the selections in this list are novels about fiendishly clever maniacs and those who are on their trail.

Alten, Steve. <u>The Meg Series</u>.

Bailey, Dale, and Jack Slay, Jr. *Sleeping Policemen.*

Campbell, Ramsey. *The Doll Who Ate His Mother; The Nameless; The One Safe Place.*

Connolly, John. <u>The Charlie Parker Mysteries</u>.

Crouch, Blake. <u>The Andrew Thomas Novels</u>.

D'Ammassa, Don. *Dead of Winter.*

Earley, Pete. *The Apocalypse Stone.*

Evenson, Brian. *The Open Curtain.*

Harris, Thomas. *Black Sunday;* <u>The Silence of the Lambs Series</u>.

Johnson, Adam. *Parasites Like Us.*

Koontz, Dean. *The Bad Place; The Face of Fear; The Funhouse: A Novel; Intensity; The Servants of Twilight; Shattered; The Vision; The Voice of the Night; Whispers.*

Laymon, Richard. *Among the Missing; Blood Games; Darkness, Tell Us.*

Lebbon, Tim. *Face.*

Little, Bentley (writing as Phillip Emmons). *Death Instinct.*

Masello, Robert. *Bestiary.*

Masterton, Graham. *A Terrible Beauty.*

Matheson, Richard. *Hunted Past Reason.*

Matthews, A. J. *Follow.*

McCammon, Robert R. *Mine.*

Moorish, Robert, ed. *Thrillers Two (II, 2).*

Newman, James, *Midnight Rain.*

Nykanen, Mark. *The Bone Parade.*

Piccirill, Tom. *The Dead Letters*.

Prescott, Michael. *In Dark Places*.

Priest, Cherie. The Eden Moore Trilogy.

Sarrantonio, Al. *Halloweenland*

Schatzing, Frank. *The Swarm*.

Slade, Michael. *Bed of Nails*.

Western

The following titles feature Western settings and cowboys or Western pioneers, and they will appeal to readers of Westerns as well as to horror fans who enjoy stories set in the old West.

Franklin, Tom. *Smonk, or Widow Town: Being the Scabrous Adventures of E. O. Smonk & the Whore of Evangeline in Clarke County, Alabama, Early in the Last Century.*

Ketchum, Jack. *The Crossings*.

Young Adult

These titles will appeal to young adult readers, as they all have adolescent protagonists who are wrestling with issues such as authority, identity, and sexuality. Some of these titles are even issued by young adult imprints as books for teen readers. Nevertheless, they have been included in *Hooked on Horror* because they will appeal to adults, too.

Andrews, V. C. *Secrets in the Attic*.

The Angel Investigations Series.

Berman, Steve. *Vintage: A Ghost Story*.

Bradbury, Ray. *Farewell Summer*.

Bray, Libba. The Gemma Doyle Trilogy.

The Buffy the Vampire Slayer Series.

The Charmed Series.

Ciencin, Scott. *Mortal Fear*.

Clegg, Douglas. *Mischief*.

Cole, Stephen. The Wereling Trilogy.

Collins, Nancy A. The Final Destination Series.

Gaiman, Neil. *Coraline; Neverwhere: A Novel*.

Greenberg, Martin H., and Russell Davis. *Haunted Holidays*.

Hearn, Julie. *The Minister's Daughter*.

Hinton, S. E. *Hawkes Harbor*.

Hoffman, Nina Kiriki. *A Stir of Bones*.

Hubbard, Susan. *The Society of S*.

Izzo, Anthony. *Cruel Winter*.

Keene, Brian. *Ghoul*.

King, Stephen. *Christine; Cycle of the Werewolf; The Girl Who Loved Tom Gordon*.

Klause, Annette Curtis. *Blood and Chocolate*.

Lackey, Mercedes. *Burning Water: A Diana Tregarde Investigation*.

Laymon, Richard. The Beast House Chronicles; *Come Out Tonight; Madman Stan and Other Stories; Once Upon a Halloween; The Traveling Vampire Show*.

Mariotte, Jeff. The Angel Series.

Massie, Elizabeth. *Sineater*.

Moore, James A. *Dark Carnival; Possessions; Rabid Growth; Newbies*.

Mosiman, Billie Sue, The Red Moon Series.

Noyes, Deborah, ed. *The Restless Dead: Ten Original Stories of the Supernatural*.

Passarella, J. G. The Wendy Ward Series.

Rees, Celia. The Witch Child Series.

Sarrantino, Al. *Horrorween, Toybox*.

Saul, John. *Black Creek Crossing; In the Dark of the Night*.

Sleator, William. *The Boy Who Couldn't Die*.

Smith, Michael Marshall. *The Servants*.

Stahler, David Jr. *Doppelganger*.

Straub, Peter. *Shadowland*.

Van Belkom, Edo, ed. *Wolf Pack*.

Welsh, T. K. *Resurrection Men*.

Westerfield, Scott. *Peeps*.

The Wicked Willow Series.

Author/Title Index

Subject/Keyword Index

About the Authors

ANTHONY J. FONSECA, Head of Serials/Electronics Resources Librarian at Nicholls State University in Louisiana, has contributed articles to *Icons of Horror and the Supernatural, Dissections: The Journal of Contemporary Horror, Louisiana Libraries,* and *The Dictionary of Literary Biography: Asian American Writers.*

JUNE MICHELE PULLIAM is Instructor of English and Women's and Gender Studies, Louisiana State University, Baton Rouge, where she also teaches a class on horror fiction.

Together, they are authors of the award-winning *Hooked on Horror* (Libraries Unlimited, 1999) and *Hooked on Horror II* (Libraries Unlimited, 2003), as well as *Read On . . . Horror Fiction* (Libraries Unlimited, 2006). In addition, they are the former co-editors of the online quarterly journal *Necropsy: The Review of Horror Fiction* (http://www. lsu.edu/necrofile). Both also currently review for *Dead Reckonings: A Review of Horror Literature.*